Detroit Tigers 1984: What a Start! What a Finish!

Mark Pattison and
David Raglin, editors

Detroit Tigers 1984
Editors: Mark Pattison and Dave Raglin
Design and Production: James J. Murray

Published by:
The Society for American Baseball Research, Inc.
4455 E. Camelback Road, Ste. D-140
Phoenix, AZ 85018

Phone: (800) 969-7227 or (602) 343-6455
Web: www.sabr.org
Facebook: Society for American Baseball Research
Twitter: @SABR

Copyright © 2012 Society for American Baseball Research, Inc.
All rights reserved.
Reproduction in whole or part without permission is prohibited.

ISBN 978-1-933599-44-1
(Ebook ISBN 978-1-933599-45-8)

DETROIT TIGERS 1984: WHAT A START! WHAT A FINISH!

CONTENTS

What a Start!

Foreword, by Paul Carey	v
Introduction, by Mark Pattison	vi
Acknowledgments	vii
How Kirk Gibson Became a Tiger, by Richard L. Shook	1
Building the Team, by Gary Gillette	2
The Hernandez-Bergman Trade, by Richard L. Shook	7
Detroit in 1984, by Jeanne M. Mallett	8
The 35-5 Start Chart	12

The 1984 Season in Review

April, by Brian Borawski	13
May, by Brian Borawski	16
June, by Brian Borawski	19
July, by Brian Borawski	24
August, by Brian Borawski	27
September, by Brian Borawski	31

The Players

Glenn Abbott, by Clifford Corn	35
Rod Allen, by Rick Vosik	38
Doug Bair, by David MacGregor	40
Doug Baker, by Richard Newhouse	42
Juan Berenguer, by Jason Lenard	45
Dave Bergman, by Jerry Nechal	49
Tom Brookens, by Larry Hilliard and Pat Kilroy	54
Marty Castillo, by John McMurray	58
Scott Earl, by Kent and Chuck Ailsworth with Carl Shinkle	60
Darrell Evans, by David L. Fleitz	65
Barbaro Garbey, by Doug Hill	69
Kirk Gibson, by Bill Bishop	73
Johnny Grubb, by Mike McClary	79
Willie Hernandez, by Gary Gillette	82
Larry Herndon, by Glen Vasey	90
Howard Johnson, by David Raglin	94
Ruppert Jones, by Adam J. Ulrey	99
Rusty Kuntz, by Mike McClary	103
Mike Laga, by David Laurila	106
Chet Lemon, by Mike McClary	109
Aurelio Lopez, by Gary Gillette	113
Dwight Lowry, by Brian Borawski	120
Roger Mason, by Nick Edson	122
Sid Monge, by Tracy J.R. Collins	124
Jack Morris, by Stew Thornley	129
Randy O'Neal, by Charles Faber and Paul Geisler	133
Lance Parrish, by Mike Lassman	135
Dan Petry, by Don Peterson	140
Dave Rozema, by Chip Greene	142
Bill Scherrer, by Jeffrey Shand-Lubbers	147
Nelson Simmons, by Malcolm Allen	151
Alan Trammell, by John Milner	154
Lou Whitaker, by John Milner	159
Milt Wilcox, by Maxwell Kates	164

DETROIT TIGERS 1984: WHAT A START! WHAT A FINISH!

Carl Willis, by Mike McClary — 168

The Brass

Tom Monaghan, by Gary Gillette — 172

Bill Lajoie, by Richard L. Shook — 180

Sparky Anderson, by Cindy Thomson — 183

Gates Brown, by Dave Gagnon — 187

Billy Consolo, by Joanne Hulbert — 191

Roger Craig, Richard L. Shook — 196

Alex Grammas, by Maxwell Kates — 199

Dick Tracewski, by Peter M. Levine — 203

The Broadcasters

Paul Carey, by Matt Bohn — 206

Bill Freehan, by Trey Strecker — 209

Ernie Harwell, by Matt Bohn — 212

Al Kaline, by Nick Waddell — 217

George Kell, by Matt Bohn — 221

Larry Osterman, by Matt Bohn — 226

What a Finish!

The 1984 Postseason Game by Game, by Brian Borawski — 229

The 1984 Tigers and the Hall of Fame, by Alan Reifman — 232

Tiger Stadium, by Dan Scott — 236

Contributors — 239

What a Start!

Foreword
by Paul Carey

IN THE SPRING of 1984, I was beginning my 12th season as Ernie Harwell's partner in the Tigers' radio booth and hoped the Tigers would have another season in which they would contend, having finished second to the Orioles in '83, six games back in the American League East. It had become a custom in spring training in Lakeland, Florida, for Patrick Zier, longtime sportswriter for the Lakeland Ledger, to ask members of the media their predictions for the coming season. Since I tended to be pessimistic, I picked the Tigers to finish third in the Eastern Division. Zier's column was printed the Sunday we broke camp and played the Mets in St. Petersburg to close out the exhibition season. Before the game, I ventured into the Tigers' clubhouse. Big mistake. Kirk Gibson and Lance Parrish were reading the paper and jumped all over me for not picking them to win. And, boy, did they ever win!

It was almost benumbing as the Tigers built their record to 35 and 5, winning 17 straight on the road, including Jack Morris' no-hitter in the fourth game of the season. It was ironic that the road-game streak ended with three straight losses in Seattle, one of the weaker teams in the league.

But the Tigers were never really threatened the rest of the way in their wire-to-wire season, playing slightly over .500 ball—well, it was really 69-53, .565 ball, but after that magnificent start all else seems to pale in comparison—to finish 15 games ahead of Toronto in the AL East.

Many point to a trade made during spring training which brought Willie Hernandez and Dave Bergman on board, dealing John Wockenfuss and Glenn Wilson to the Phillies, as the key to the season. Perhaps it was, because Willie's screwball befuddled the American League hitters so much that he won the Cy Young and the MVP awards and Bergie made big contributions. But I think the stage was set for this 1984 championship season back in the mid-'70s when the Tigers made some excellent draft choices and they began to show up in 1977. Look at 'em: Lance Parrish, Lou Whitaker, Alan Trammell, Dave Rozema, and Jack Morris. And two years later, Dan Petry, Kirk Gibson, and Tom Brookens arrived. Those eight formed the nucleus of that 1984 title team. That's what gave such wonderful satisfaction to front-office people like Jim Campbell, Bill Lajoie, Rick Ferrell, and Hoot Evers and to all those in baseball who believe that winning starts at home.

Obviously, there are significant memories of that season for me. It began early when Morris threw his no-hitter in Chicago. Jack may not have been the easiest guy to get along with, though Ernie and I never had any problem with him, but that afternoon he did something special for us. We had no hookup in the dugout, so Jack went through the crowd to an elevator, took some stairs, and came to us in our little booth in old Comiskey Park to be interviewed.

Another similar incident came at the very end of the season, after the fifth game of the World Series. Our radio station, WJR, had contracted with Alan Trammell to be interviewed from the dugout by Ernie and me after each game of the Series. After each game, Alan was pressured by members of the media for his comments, but he steadfastly went to the end of the dugout and did his interview with us. When the Tigers won Game Five and the championship and Tram was named MVP, the pressure from network television and national media was crushing, but Alan told them to wait, he had a job to do, and he did his interview with us. That showed the character of Alan Trammell and was a reflection of that '84 team.

The contributions that made the year so remarkable came from so many. Chet Lemon's play in center field and his spectacular catch that saved a game in Anaheim ... Darrell Evans hitting a three-run homer in his first Tigers game on April 3, Opening Day, in Minnesota, and then hitting another three-run homer in his Tiger Stadium debut for the home opener on April 10, and giving the team a veteran presence in the clubhouse ... Milt Wilcox winning 17 and winning both of his postseason starts ... workhorse Aurelio Lopez with 14 saves and 10 relief victories and always ready. There were many others, from Howard Johnson to Marty Castillo to Barbaro Garbey and Larry Herndon. From Johnny Grubb to Rusty Kuntz and Ruppert Jones.

One very special moment for me was the 10th inning of a game at Tiger Stadium with Toronto on June 4. Game tied 3-3 in the bottom of the 10th. The Tigers had two men on with two out, and Dave Bergman faced Roy Lee Jackson. I always did the play-by-play of the 10th and 11th innings, so I had the privilege of describing Bergie fouling off pitch after pitch and then, on the 13th pitch, hitting a blast into the seats in right.

A very personal note. My wife of 23 years, Patti, became ill late in the season and before Game Three of the World Series, I learned that she had a terminal brain tumor and a craniotomy was scheduled for Tuesday, the day Game Six was to be played. That Friday of Game Three, I told the radio station that I would not work Games Six or Seven, but Kirk Gibson's two home runs in Game Five on Sunday made those games unnecessary. Patti died the following March. Because of her illness, much of the ALCS and the Series was kind of a haze to me.

I would be remiss if I didn't express my admiration for the late white-haired skipper, George "Sparky" Anderson. For 12 seasons, I had to interview Sparky before every Tiger game and got to know him quite well. There were some highs and lows in Sparky's tenure with Detroit, but 1984 gave him a chance to prove that his titles in Cincinnati were no fluke. Sparky could play the media like a concert violinist and he did some fiddling with me, too, but that was OK because I had immense respect for the man. He may slaughter the English language, but he was one of the smartest men I've ever met.

I was privileged to be a part of the 25th reunion of the '84 Tigers at a dinner and a luncheon. As a testament to that team's closeness, 19 players, three coaches, a trainer, equipment manager, traveling secretary, and Sparky showed up for a marvelous two days of remembrances and friendship.

Here's to the 1984 Tigers and the best season a broadcaster could ever experience.

Paul Carey spent 19 years (1973-91) in the Detroit Tigers' broadcast booth alongside Ernie Harwell. Nicknamed "The Voice of God" because of his deep and resonant vocal timbre, Carey broadcast the middle innings on Tigers radiocasts.

Introduction
by Mark Pattison

ONE OF THE contributors to this book told me in 2008 that the 1984 Tigers felt they never got the respect or the love that the 1968 team did, and that they could never understand why they couldn't get the kind of accolades their predecessors did.

Both teams won the World Series. One could argue that the 1968 team had to overcome more adversity, what with playing in a city that had been badly scarred by rioting the year before—not to mention all those thrilling late-inning Detroit comebacks on the field. The 1984 team, by contrast, led the American League East wire to wire, from game 1 through game 162. They had an almost ridiculously easy time of dispensing with their foes as they amassed that amazing 35-5 start, which has yet to be matched, let alone bettered.

Both clubs had their larger-than-life personalities—tales you'll read in this book.

But what may set the two clubs apart the most is simple demographics.

For many in the baby-boom generation, 1968 was the first brush with greatness we had experienced with a Detroit sports team. Only the oldest members of the baby-boom generation had any memories of the Detroit Lions winning a National Football League championship (that last championship, by the way, came in 1957, and in the half-century since, they've won all of one playoff game). The Detroit Red Wings hadn't won a Stanley Cup championship since 1955. Basketball's Detroit Pistons, transplanted from Fort Wayne, Indiana, a decade earlier, were pretty much a doormat in the National Basketball Association. So, despite Detroit's being then one of just a handful of cities at the time having teams in all four major professional team sports, the law of averages wasn't working in the Motor City's favor. Detroit fans were hungry for a championship, and the 1968 Tigers got that for them. The boomer generation could idolize the stars whose images flickered on television screens and smiled at them from baseball cards—and idolize them they did.

But the 1984 team is every bit as important to the boomer crowd. Rather than our pretending that we were Al Kaline or Denny McLain or Willie Horton or Norm Cash—players two or three times older than us in 1968—the 1984 Tigers, in essence, were us. No longer did we need to pretend we were Kaline, Jim Northrup, Mickey Stanley, or a host of other Tigers by making sound effects when we were throwing a ball or swinging a bat to give our efforts some hoped-for sense of authenticity. No, these 1984 Tigers wore their hair long, like us. They chafed at the square music being pumped out of the antiquated speakers at Tiger Stadium, like us. They saw the movie *The Natural*, which was released that year, and inevitably drew comparisons between Roy Hobbs and his fictional New York Knights and the magic the Tigers were working that season, just as we did. The phrase "the boys of summer," which came from Roger Kahn's book of the same name, had already become an American catchphrase for more than a dozen years by the time of the Tigers' championship run. But those Tigers were our own boys of summer.

And it's not as if those 1984 Tigers have been treated as pariahs in the community compared to their 1968 brethren. Consider:

- Xochimilco Restaurant in the Mexicantown section of southwest Detroit still has what it calls the "Willie Hernandez table" and the "Aurelio Lopez table."

- Lance Parrish had two separate three-year stints as a Tigers coach, bookending a brief run as a Tigers TV broadcast analyst.

- Kirk Gibson followed in Parrish's footsteps, first as a TV analyst and then as a Tigers coach for three seasons.

- Jack Morris got his broadcast-booth start in Detroit as well, doing over-the-air TV games for a year until the Tigers let the contract lapse, turning over virtually its entire schedule to cable TV.

- Dan Petry tried his hand at broadcasting, too, and has wound up doing corporate sales for the Detroit Lions.

- Lou Whitaker financed his wife Crystal's clothing boutique, which was popular for a while until the vagaries of the Detroit economy prompted its closing.

DETROIT TIGERS 1984: WHAT A START! WHAT A FINISH!

- Dave Bergman parlayed his nine seasons with Detroit into a highly successful post-baseball career as a financial adviser.

- Tom Brookens, after more than a decade away from the game, has steadily risen through the managerial ranks in the Tigers' farm system, having taken two of Detroit's minor-league affiliates to the playoffs before landing back in the Motor City as the Tigers' first-base, outfield and baserunning coach.

- Milt Wilcox chose to settle in the Detroit area to raise purebred dogs.

- Alan Trammell coached for Detroit after his retirement as an active player, and later managed the Tigers from 2003 through 2005—three painful seasons, painful primarily because the front office had stripped the roster of most of its talent, and much of the talent that remained was injured at inopportune times.

- Dave Rozema may be forever enshrined as the team's resident goofball for the eight seasons he wore the Old English D, but that doesn't stop him from accepting the Tigers' invitation to throw batting practice in a fantasy-camp atmosphere at Comerica Park.

- Even Barbaro Garbey, not exactly a household name when people think of the 1984 Tigers, capitalized on the team's reflected glory to work as a hitting instructor in the Detroit system for a few years in the early 2000s.

I can remember when, working at a weekly newspaper in suburban Detroit, it was my turn to go out with a photographer to ask one of those "man in the street" questions. Given the difficult economic climate in Detroit and Michigan at the time, most of the questions seemed to do with the economy, politics, or some combination of the two. In any event, the respondents grumbled their way through the answers—if, indeed, they had any opinion at all.

This feature needs a lighter tone, I thought. We went to a gas station and asked folks filling up their cars, "How 'bout those Tigers?" Their answers may have been as uninformed as what they were spouting off on about the economy and such, but nobody refused to talk. While I was at the gas station, I distinctly remember hearing a song parody made popular by one of the FM rock stations' morning shows, "Every Pitch You Take," a send-up of the Police's "Every Breath You Take," with the morning show's sidekick impersonating the voices of "George Swell" and "Al Foulline."

I can also remember following through on a couple of other nascent traditions that took on greater importance now that the Tigers were involved. One tradition involved going to Savina's Place, an unheralded (compared with Buddy's and Shield's) pizza place on East Davison Street in Detroit. My friend Pat Wagner and I would watch a postseason game on the 19-inch (if that) TV mounted high on a side wall of the bar, have a beer, eat a pizza, and crack wise. In 1984, though, this idea was hardly our own. By this time, Savina's had purchased one of those big-screen projection TVs with a bigger but fuzzier picture. We stayed in the room with the big-screen TV for a brief while, but once we saw there was a table open in view of the old 19-incher, we took up our customary positions in plenty of time to see the Tigers push across the lone run in the 1-0 Game Three AL Championship Series clincher.

Another tradition was to visit the house of my friend and high-school classmate George Eichorn if there was a big sports event on TV. The first such event was the Detroit Lions-San Francisco 49ers NFL playoff game in which Eddie Murray's field goal try on the last play of the game went wide. Ah, but this time it was Game Five of the World Series, with Detroit up three games to one over San Diego (a church musicians' group I had helped found in Detroit had scheduled a daylong workshop during Game Four; what could we have been thinking?). We saw Detroit put a satisfying exclamation point to its wire-to-wire season in its 8-4 thumping of the Padres. And, as was popular during the Howard Cosell era on Monday Night Football, we turned down the sound on the TV and turned on the radio to hear the postgame bedlam from the Tigers' clubhouse. It was then and only then that I ever had any inkling that Detroit radio play-by-play man Paul Carey had called the games while helping his wife, Patti, struggle with the cancer that soon claimed her life.

That World Series win was, for me, close to half a lifetime away. Detroit played in the Series in 2006 ad 2012, and made a valiant run for the AL East title in 1987 but got hustled out of the playoffs by the Minnesota Twins. I have since enjoyed a fistful of championships by the Red Wings and the Pistons (the Lions, well, that's for somebody else's book). I'm so very glad I could celebrate the Tigers' victory then, and I'm appreciative that I can place it in the context of my life and that of so many others today. This book is for all who can remember those golden days of 1984—and for those who long for the season when they can revel in their own way, cementing custom into tradition with unrestrained joy as the mortar.

Acknowledgments

FIRST OFF, WE give our deepest thanks to all of the writers and editors who participated in this project. We owe an extra debt of gratitude to several of the writers who pinch-hit when some of the original biographers found themselves unable to make good on their commitments.

Our team of proofreaders and fact-checkers hung tough throughout the course of this book. We could not have produced this book—and certainly could not have produced it as well—without their unfailing efforts. We believe that with our system of utilizing three proofreaders and two fact-checkers on each essay, this work is as free from error as possible. However, since ours were the last eyes to gaze upon the unpublished version of this book in its finished form, any errors are ours and ours alone.

Thanks also to Myra Kreiman, who stepped in during the final stages of preparation for this book to serve as photo editor. Her experience in detecting and selecting photos and in negotiating favorable rates for their usage is a skill many of us wish we had.

Not only are there a few dozen contributors to this book, but the entire effort was produced under the aegis of the BioProject Committee of the Society for American Baseball Research. The committee, under its founding chairman, Mark Armour, endeavors to have a suitable biography written of every person who ever played in a major league game, and has accepted biographies of other pivotal figures in the game—and even ballparks. Our thanks also go to SABR executive director Marc Appleman and his predecessor, John Zajc, for their forthrightness in addressing issues surrounding the development of the manuscript.

Maybe the biggest thanks of all go to our spouses: Barb Mantegani (Dave's wife) and Judith McCullough (Mark's wife). Their love and support, truth be told, are even more inspiring than is the story of the 1984 Tigers. Special thanks go to Cyntia "Go Tigers Go!" Pattison, Mark's daughter, who, upon waking from her nap one Father's Day, learned well which team to claim as her own.

Bios for Gates Brown, Bill Freehan, Ernie Harwell, Al Kaline, George Kell, Larry Osterman, and Dick Tracewski were originally published by Maple Street Press LLC in *Sock It to 'Em, Tigers: The Incredible Story of the 1968 Detroit Tigers*, edited by Mark Pattison and David Raglin, © 2008, Society for American Baseball Research.

The bio for Jack Morris was originally published by Nodin Press in *Minnesotans in Baseball*, edited by Stew Thornley, © 2009, Society for American Baseball Research.

How Kirk Gibson Became a Tiger
by Richard L. Shook

THE FIRST TIME Bill Lajoie saw Kirk Gibson play baseball he wasn't impressed.

"He was crude," said Lajoie, who first eyeballed Gibson's baseball skills when Gibson was at Waterford Kettering (Michigan) high school. The Tigers' scouting director was looking at Gibson's summer team—to watch a third baseman by the name of Mike Grace, not Gibson.

"His speed was his best point," Lajoie recalled. "After that I kind of forgot about him. He was not a prospect at that point. He didn't have any experience."

Gibson was more of a highly regarded football wide receiver than a baseball player. Even in today's game, a 6-foot-4, 215-pound receiver who thinks running through walls is more fun than speeding around them is a prized commodity on the gridiron.

He went to Michigan State University and became an All-American receiver. By his junior year it was widely anticipated that he would become a first-round National Football League draft choice.

To give himself some leverage for the 1979 NFL draft, Gibson accepted a standing invitation to join the MSU baseball team in the spring of his junior season.

The Spartans played their spring schedule in Texas that year, and the games were routinely watched by representatives from the Major League Scouting Bureau. One day Lajoie grabbed a report from the bureau and did a double-take at how Gibson was graded out on the traditional baseball 20-80 scale.

"The Scouting Bureau turned him in as an 80 runner with 80 power," Lajoie said. "So now we slowly start picking our spots and watching this guy. Everything is cool. We're playing it low key."

Gibson, though, was not playing it low key. He was like the guy trying to kill ants with a hand grenade. He was on his way to a .390 batting average in 48 collegiate games with 52 runs scored and a school-record 16 home runs. He was playing like a guy who wanted to get noticed.

Nobody outside the baseball world was taking Gibson's baseball efforts seriously at that time. Even Gibson was downplaying his baseball skills, which some felt was a deliberate attempt on his part to scare off every major-league team but the Detroit Tigers.

Every few days there would be a paragraph in the Detroit papers about some Gibson exploit in a Michigan State game. But most of the stories carried a tone of wondering why a bona-fide football star would be risking his NFL career by wearing a pair of baseball spikes. He just wasn't taken seriously.

The attitude for a large part of the baseball world was not how high on their draft board he was rated, but whether to draft him at all. That wasn't the case in Detroit.

Tigers general manager Jim Campbell set up a secret workout for Gibson at Tiger Stadium. I got wind of the session and sauntered over to watch, maybe a write a story for my employer, United Press International.

Gibson showed up and coach Dick Tracewski set up to throw batting practice to this blond, left-handed slugger.

Gibson roped one line drive after another into the Tiger Stadium outfield, each one with topspin like a Sandy Koufax curve. Granted, the outfield grass was dry, but from ground level I could see fountains of dirt spray four to five feet into the air with each line drive.

Yes, it was only BP, but he sure looked like the real deal.

"So now I talked to Kirk after the workout," Lajoie said. "I ask him, 'So, Kirk, are you going to be a football player or a baseball player?' He tells me, 'I will play baseball, but only for the Detroit Tigers.'

"So I told him, 'That's easy enough for you to take care of.'"

Lajoie was always coy in public about Detroit's interest in Gibson. The future Tiger, for his part, continued to downplay baseball because he still had his senior season of football for Michigan State in the fall. And if he wanted to play for Detroit, it was in his interest to dissuade the 11 teams drafting in front of the Tigers from looking seriously at him.

Detroit had the 12th pick in the June draft in 1978, while the other two teams supposedly most interested in Gibson were Seattle, which drafted sixth, and the New York Yankees, who picked 18th.

Gibson called the Mariners and Yankees and told them bluntly that if they drafted him, he would not sign and would play football instead.

"Meantime," Lajoie said, "the Toronto Blue Jays were holding a tryout six blocks from my house (in Livonia). They had 40 players—and you were only supposed to have five at a time. I stopped by on my way home and Pat Gillick was there.

"I told him, 'The two guys you want to see (Gibson and Bruce Fields) are down at Tiger Stadium working out right now. Good-bye.'"

Draft day rolled around, and the Tigers' executives gathered in one of the offices in Tiger Stadium, along with a certain UPI representative who was allowed to watch and report on the proceedings.

Campbell, a big man anyway, was visibly nervous as the teams began drafting. He'd take out his handkerchief and wipe the sweat from his bald head every few minutes.

Atlanta took third baseman Bob Horner first, and Toronto followed with center fielder Lloyd Moseby. The New York Mets opted for third baseman Hubie Brooks, and Oakland selected right-handed pitcher Mike Morgan. San Diego took right-hander Andy Hawkins, who would later face Gibson in the 1984 World Series.

After San Diego, the teams to pick before Detroit were, in order, Seattle, San Francisco, Milwaukee, Montreal, Cleveland, and Houston (none of their picks made it to the major leagues). After each organization picked, Campbell would either let go with a "whew" or take that hanky out for another head circuit.

Campbell let out a big sigh of relief when the Astros chose pitcher Rod Boxberger. (Boxberger made it as far as Double A). After a suitable pause, Lajoie announced, "The Detroit

DETROIT TIGERS 1984: WHAT A START! WHAT A FINISH!

Tigers select outfielder Kirk Harold Gibson of Michigan State University," and applause rippled through the room.

(Incidentally, in the second round, the Baltimore Orioles made a nepotism selection, a third baseman by the name of Cal Ripken Jr.)

"Somewhere along the line," Lajoie recalled, "I got a pretty good idea of what it was going to take to sign him."

It didn't take long. Maybe about the time it took Gibson to leg out a triple.

Detroit signed him to a minor league contract that Lajoie with a bonus that remembered as being "$150-$160,000, with incentives that made it worth about $185,000." Gibson's autobiography, *Bottom of the Ninth*, put it at $200,000, while *Baseball America* said it was more than $200,000—although it didn't say how much more.

Now came another tricky part.

Right after Detroit signed Gibson to a minor league contract, it put him on its major league roster.

"That was to hide the bonus," Lajoie said.

Under the rules in place at that time, minor-league contracts were the business of the player, the club, and his agent.

But major league contracts had to be divulged to the Players Association. And Gibson would have had to be paid a higher salary had he signed a major league contract.

Gibson began his pro career in 1978 with high-Class A Lakeland of the Florida State League, leaving early when football camp began at Michigan State.

Instead of being a first-round NFL draft choice, he lasted until the seventh round, when football's St. Louis Cardinals took a flier on a flier.

He opened 1979 with Evansville, Detroit's Triple-A affiliate at the time, so the five one-year contracts the football team sent him only served as bragging material.

"He's walking around the locker room," Lajoie said, "waving these contracts around until finally one of the guys said, 'Well, why the heck don't you leave?' That shut him up right there."

Detroit brought up Gibson for 12 late-season games in 1979. He was on his way to World Series fame and glory.

References

Shook, Richard L. Eyewitness observations in 1979.
Shook, Richard L. Interview with Bill Lajoie.

Building the Team
by Gary Gillette

IN THE GLORIOUS summer of 1984, Detroit led the American League East Division from wire to wire. The old ballpark at the corner of Michigan and Trumbull, just west of downtown Detroit, rocked to near-capacity crowds night after night. A true cross-section of Detroit society rubbed elbows at Tiger Stadium while rooting for their heroes. After their unbelievable 35-5 start to the season, the Bengals cruised to an easy AL East title.

The confident Tigers then annihilated the Kansas City Royals in the American League Championship Series before humbling the overmatched San Diego Padres in the World Series. In September, Sparky Anderson became the first manager to win 100 games with two clubs; in October, he became the first to win a World Series in each league.

The Tigers were clearly the class of the national pastime in 1984. They had it all: pitching, defense, and a powerful lineup. In fact, Detroit looked so good that many were predicting a dynasty had begun. Exactly how did they get to be so powerful? And who deserves the credit for building the championship club?

The Roar About To Be Heard 'Round the Baseball World

After finishing second to eventual World Series champion Baltimore in the AL East in 1983, the Tigers were at No. 2 on the charts—with a bullet. New owner Tom Monaghan was generating headlines, soaking up the limelight, and living a dream. After all, if you couldn't play on a championship team in the World Series, what could be better than owning the team itself?

The '84 Tigers had roots that went way back to the 1960s. In fact, two of the team's coaches in 1984, Dick Tracewski and Gates Brown, had played for the '68 champions. Club president Jim Campbell had been general manager in 1968, earning Executive of the Year honors from *The Sporting News*.

Though the Tigers had lost the 1967 pennant on the last day of the season while the ashes were still smoldering from the devastating Detroit riot that summer, the 1968 Tigers won the pennant going away. Detroit's heroes then beat Bob Gibson's favored Cardinals in seven games to win the Tigers' first World Series title since 1945. Given universal credit for helping heal the racially polarized city, the 1968 Tigers attained the status of demigods in Michigan—and the 16 years that had passed had not changed their lofty status one iota.

The core of the 1968 team held on for several years to win the American League East title in 1972, then finally collapsed of exhaustion during the 1973 pennant race. The rest of the 1970s were largely forgettable, except for Mark Fidrych's incandescent 1976 season. But as Fidrych was grooming the mound, the Tigers' brain trust was planting the seeds that would yield a bountiful harvest in 1984.

The first attempt to rebuild the Tigers failed in the mid-1970s under the stewardship of veteran manager Ralph Houk.

DETROIT TIGERS 1984: WHAT A START! WHAT A FINISH!

Nevertheless, by the end of the decade, the Detroit organization was chock full of young players about to make their mark. When hired during the 1979 season, new manager Sparky Anderson boldly predicted that his team would win the World Series within five years. Anderson fulfilled that prediction by molding a team whose talent was largely already in the Tigers' system when the prematurely white-haired quote machine arrived.

Anderson's young Tiger cubs played no better in 1979 (fifth place, .528) and 1980 (fourth, .519) than they had in 1978 before he arrived (fifth, .531). In the strike-riven year of 1981, the Tigers jumped to a .550 winning percentage, "contending" in the second half of the bifurcated divisional race while finishing third in the meaningless overall standings. A year later, the Detroiters backslid to fourth place, barely over .500 (.512).

Finally, in 1983, the team jelled, winning 92 games and posting a .568 won-lost percentage. Six of the club's nine regular position players started for Detroit in '83 (albeit not all at the same positions). The Tigers' rotation was identical from 1983 to 1984, and its bullpen featured two key contributors to the World Series championship. Only a few changes were needed to catapult the club to excellence—including the much-sought-after but still underappreciated Willie Hernandez.

Dawn of a New Era

After his up-and-coming charges finished second in the AL East to the 1983 World Series champion Orioles, Anderson and his boys faced the 1984 season with a confidence bordering on cockiness. That was a portentous echo of 1968, when the veteran Tigers who had missed so narrowly a year earlier, assumed they would win it all. In 2008, Jim Northrup recalled, "[W]e were going to win it in '68, and nothing was going to stop us because we knew how good we were." Anderson's 1984 team was even more confident—if such a thing could be possible.

It was obvious to outsiders, too: Baseball writer and Chicago native Stuart Shea remembers seeing "the [Jack] Morris no-hitter on NBC in early '84 and…thinking that the Tigers were carrying themselves like a championship team even then and that the White Sox, coming off a division championship, were not."

With Morris as the staff ace, Dan Petry as the No. 2 starter, Lance Parrish at catcher, Lou Whitaker at second, Alan Trammell at shortstop, Chet Lemon in center field, and Kirk Gibson in right, Detroit had the kind of strength up the middle that baseball teams throughout history have dreamed of.

More importantly, it was the kind of up-the-middle talent that most champions are built around. With seven past or future All-Stars in the lineup—one who may yet end up in the Hall of Fame (Morris), and two others who deserve to make the Hall (Trammell and Whitaker)—the Tigers truly should have been on the threshold of greatness. Those key players, plus offseason acquisition Hernandez, were all in their mid- to late 20s, most in the prime of their careers.

Detroit was both lucky and good that year: While the trade of mediocre outfielder Glenn Wilson for Hernandez was clearly shrewd, no one dreamed that the southpaw set-up pitcher with the baffling screwball would win both the 1984 American League MVP and Cy Young Awards. Few now remember that Detroit streaked to a record 35-5 start and an insurmountable lead before Hernandez became the closer.

Extraordinary Continuity in the Front Office

John Fetzer sold the Tigers to Tom Monaghan after the 1983 season for $53 million—then a record amount for any sports franchise. The hefty price reflected the copious amount of talent the team possessed, the club's almost unparalleled (in terms of modern baseball) stability, its favorable lease arrangement with the city of Detroit for historic Tiger Stadium—plus nouveau-riche billionaire Monaghan's willingness to spend whatever it took to realize his dream.

Fetzer had become sole owner of the Tigers in November 1961; he had been a part owner for five years before that. Campbell had been with the Tigers' organization since 1949, becoming a vice president a decade later at the age of 35. After the 1962 season, the no-nonsense executive became general manager, passing the baton to Bill Lajoie 21 years later, in October 1983. Lajoie, Campbell's understudy, had been with the club since November 1968, when he was hired as a scout. He moved into the front office two years later, becoming director of player procurement in 1975 and vice president/baseball in 1978. In building their World Series team, both Campbell and Lajoie specialized in acquiring underrated veterans for mediocre prospects and overvalued young pitchers, many of the latter being left-handers.

The dedication to Fetzer's 1997 biography shows how incredibly tight-knit the Detroit brain trust was. Fetzer wrote, "This book is dedicated to Jim Campbell, who showed me the strength of honesty…to Bo Schembechler, who taught me the meaning of courage…and particularly to Sparky Anderson, for friendship that knows no bounds." (While University of Michigan football coach Schembechler was not then formally affiliated with the Tigers, he would later be named club president by Monaghan.)

In his biography, Fetzer called Campbell his "most loyal employee." The sale of the club was described thusly: "John Fetzer hand-picked Tom Monaghan to purchase the Tigers and continue its history in the pure tradition of baseball." To complete the picture of a loyal, happy family, Anderson was tagged as Fetzer's "favorite manager."

Detroit's elite status in Major League Baseball was demonstrated by the team's robust support as well as by the price Monaghan paid for the club. The Tigers drew above the American League average in attendance in all but six years from 1934 through 1983—and in only two of those subpar seasons did attendance fall as much as 10 percent below league average. TV ratings in Detroit were good even when the Tigers didn't have a winning team, and when Detroit was in contention, ratings were absolutely huge. Prior to the 1990s, the Motor City was a baseball town right down to its Motown soul.

DETROIT TIGERS 1984: WHAT A START! WHAT A FINISH!

When the Tigers won pennants in 1934, 1935, and 1945, they drew more than twice as many fans as the typical American League team. In 1940 Detroit drew 80 percent higher than the league norm. In 1968 Detroit's attendance was almost twice the league average, despite the deleterious effects of the bloody 1967 riot that had ripped the city apart. By 1972, though, the fans had come back as Detroit attendance was 218 percent of that of the garden-variety American League club while the team was winning its first East Division title.

So the stage was set by the time the ball was dropped on New Year's Eve 1983. An experienced yet still young club was in place for 1984, with a stable front office, a wealthy new owner, and an adoring fan base.

Where the 1984 Tigers Came From and When They Arrived in Motown

The final pieces of the championship puzzle were added in the 1983-84 offseason. The Hernandez coup was engineered to acquire a left-handed pitcher—preferably a reliever, although starting pitchers were also under consideration—not to acquire a closer to replace Aurelio Lopez.

When rehashing the 1983 season, the Detroit brain trust had concluded that it needed to add at least one reliable left-handed pitcher to its mound corps. True, the up-and-coming Tigers had improved by nine games over 1982 and had finished second in the tough American League East, only six games behind the eventual 1983 World Series champion Orioles. But the Tigers hadn't gotten any closer than 4½ games to the Orioles in the last month of the season, even though Baltimore's lineup was really an over-the-hill gang enjoying its last hurrah. Detroit's substantially younger lineup, meanwhile, had plenty of major-league experience and, thus, was no longer able to use its relative youth as an excuse for not winning.

Only four lefties had appeared on the hill for the Tigers in '83, making only six starts and hurling only 7 percent of the staff's innings. Three of those southpaws were dispatched in the 1983-84 offseason; the fourth, Howard Bailey, would wind down his pro career in the Tigers' minor-league system in '84.

The official team photo of the 1984 Detroit Tigers. It would be one of the few times that season when Tiger Stadium would be empty with the "Bless You Boys" in uniform. Top row from left: Lance Parrish, Willie Hernandez, Dwight Lowry, John Grubb, Glenn Abbott, Rod Allen, Barbaro Garbey, Chet Lemon, Lou Whitaker, Larry Herndon, trainer Pio DiSalvo, Dr. Clarence Livingood. Middle row from left: trainer Bill Behm, Kirk Gibson, Juan Berenguer, Rusty Kuntz, Darrell Evans, Dave Bergman, Marty Castillo, Milt Wilcox, Dave Rozema, Dan Petry, Jack Morris, equipment manager Jim Schmakel, traveling secretary Bill Brown. Front row from left: Doug Bair, Aurelio Lopez, Howard Johnson, coach Billy Consolo, coach Alex Grammas, coach Roger Craig, manager Sparky Anderson, coach Gates Brown, coach Dick Tracewski, Alan Trammell, Tom Brookens. Seated from left: batboys Dom Nieto, David Cowart, Dave Ruczko. (National Baseball Hall of Fame Library, Cooperstown, New York)

DETROIT TIGERS 1984: WHAT A START! WHAT A FINISH!

After shopping around without success for most of the offseason, GM Bill Lajoie made the storied deal with Philadelphia that finally brought a lefty to Detroit. The Tigers, unlike the Phillies or the Cubs before them, astutely and accurately appreciated that Hernandez could be more than a late-inning situational lefty. They also understood that he could in fact close out games if needed. That said, there was more than a little luck involved—the "residue of design" that Branch Rickey honored with his famous aphorism.

Perhaps the most succinct summary was provided by Roger Craig in a 2008 interview. When asked, "What did you expect from Willie Hernandez when Detroit traded for him in spring training before the start of the '84 season?" Craig was straightforward.

"I didn't really know him that well. We had good reports from our scouts on him, and we needed a left-handed pitcher. I'll tell you that this guy had ice water in his veins. He had a good screwball, and then he learned to throw a cutter in on the hands of right-handed batters."

They Played the Game

The Tigers used 35 players to beat the world in 1984, including 14 pitchers, one less than the average number of players and pitchers employed by major-league clubs that year. The 25 players manager Sparky Anderson took north from Lakeland, Florida, in April were:

Starting pitchers: Jack Morris, Dan Petry, Milt Wilcox, Juan Berenguer, Dave Rozema.

Relief pitchers: Aurelio Lopez, Willie Hernandez, Doug Bair, Glenn Abbott.

Catchers: Lance Parrish, Dwight Lowry, Marty Castillo.

Infielders: Dave Bergman, Darrell Evans, Lou Whitaker, Alan Trammell, Howard Johnson, Barbaro Garbey, Tom Brookens.

Outfielders: Larry Herndon, Chet Lemon, Kirk Gibson, John Grubb, Rusty Kuntz, Rod Allen.

A positive side effect of having a relatively young team was that the Tigers placed only two players on the disabled list all year in 1984. Alan Trammell was disabled for three weeks in July with a sore throwing shoulder, and Tom Brookens was disabled for 16 days late in the year due to a hamstring pull. The typical major-league club used the DL nine times in '84, losing 402 days during the season to disabling injuries. Only up-and-coming Toronto lost fewer days than Detroit to the M*A*S*H list.

The Steel Backbone

The core of Detroit's championship club was homegrown, drafted by the Tigers from 1974 through 1978. On the mound, ace Jack Morris became part of the Tigers' future in June 1976 when Detroit selected him in the fifth round out of Brigham Young University. Dan Petry, the No. 2 starter, was selected a round earlier that same year. Up the middle were durable catcher Lance Parrish and the magnificent keystone combination of Lou Whitaker and Alan Trammell. Whitaker led off for the Tigers in 1984, with his double-play partner batting in the two hole. Strongman Parrish hit cleanup.

Parrish was drafted in the first round in 1974, with scrawny Whitaker coming in the fifth round in 1975 and the slender Trammell being selected in the second round a year later. All three made their major-league debuts in early September 1977; the trio would anchor the team up the middle at "The Corner" until the end of the 1986 season, when Parrish left.

Kirk Gibson was a surprise pick by Detroit at 12th overall in the first round in the June 1978 draft. No one except the Tigers thought the All-American football player at Michigan State University would pass up a career on the gridiron for the diamond. Gibson started the '84 season batting fifth against right-handers and eighth against lefties. By mid-May his stock had risen so much that he was the No. 3 hitter in the potent Detroit lineup.

The Rest of the Rotation and Regulars

While the remaining starters didn't all come through the Detroit system like Morris and Petry, all showed the keen judgment of the Tigers' brain trust. Rookie Howard Johnson was drafted in January 1979 in the secondary phase. Popular veteran Larry Herndon came to Detroit after the 1981 season via another favorable trade engineered by Campbell, who sent two young southpaws to the Giants. Stalwart flyhawk Chet Lemon—upon whom Detroit's pitching staff depended to run down long drives in Tiger Stadium's cavernous center field—was acquired from the White Sox straight-up for greatly overrated "slugger" Steve Kemp after the 1981 season. No. 5 starter Dave Rozema was drafted in the fourth round of the January 1974 secondary draft out of a community college. No. 4 starter Juan Berenguer had been cast off by the Toronto Blue Jays in the spring of 1982 after he had gone 2-13 in 1981, but Detroit quickly signed the wild young pitcher and ultimately turned the imposing right-hander into a reliable big-league starter. No. 3 starter Milt Wilcox had flopped around the majors for a half-dozen years without much success, including a stint under Sparky Anderson in Cincinnati, before being purchased by the Tigers from the Chicago Cubs in 1976.

The Bench and Bullpen

All of Detroit's important relief pitchers in 1984 were acquired via trade. "Señor Smoke," Aurelio Lopez, was the longest-tenured relief pitcher on the club, having been acquired by trade from the Cardinals in December 1978. Doug Bair, the No. 2 righty, also came to Motown from St. Louis; he was picked up in midseason 1983 in return for lefty Dave Rucker—another young lefty whose trade value was much greater than his potential. Swingman Glenn Abbott, who reached the end of the line in '84, was sold by the Seattle Mariners to Detroit in August 1983 for $100,000.

DETROIT TIGERS 1984: WHAT A START! WHAT A FINISH!

The platoon players and spare parts came to Detroit via various routes. Barbaro Garbey was signed as an amateur free agent in 1980. Tom Brookens was drafted in January 1975; Marty Castillo was a fifth-round pick in the June 1978 draft; Dwight Lowry was drafted by the Tigers in the 11th round in June 1980. John Grubb was picked up via a trade with Texas for reliever Dave Tobik before the '83 season. (Tobik was yet another product of Detroit's amazingly productive 1975 drafts.) Finally, overachieving Rusty Kuntz was acquired from the Twins for yet another pitcher without much of a future after the 1983 season in one of Bill Lajoie's first deals as a new GM.

Last-Minute Reinforcements

The trade for Hernandez also netted Dave Bergman, valued mostly for his glove at first base. Bergman was also coming off his best year offensively (.286 batting average, .394 on-base average, .457 slugging average with the Giants). With an all-right-handed starting staff, it was critical to have good defense on the right side of the infield, and Bergman—who had excellent range, a strong arm, and soft hands—filled that gap nicely alongside Whitaker. Bergman's left-handed swing also was a plus. Though not expected to start, Bergman actually played more at first base in 1984 than anyone else, partly due to Darrell Evans' disappointing first season in Detroit.

Veteran National League slugger Evans was the first big-name, big-bucks free agent signed by the fiscally conservative Tigers. With Monaghan's money, though, the staid Tigers quickly stepped out of character and inked him to a three-year contract to provide more left-handed power. Evans was coming off the second-best year with the bat of his 15-year career, and his fly-ball swing was seemingly tailored to Tiger Stadium's right-field porch. That proved to be true, but it took a year longer than expected for Evans to find the range, as his 16 homers in 1984 were less than half of the 34-plus he averaged from 1985 to '87 in the Detroit lineup.

Outfielder Ruppert Jones was another last-minute addition. Sent to Triple-A Evansville after being signed as a free agent on April 10, the 29-year-old Jones showed he had some sock left in his hickory after an off-year in San Diego in 1983. Recalled in early June when left fielder Larry Herndon failed to get going even two months into the season, Jones smacked a three-run homer in his second game in Detroit to break open a tie game and was a solid platoon contributor thereafter. Like so many other moves made by the Tigers that year, Jones' signing was a combination of shrewd judgment and luck. Jones left Detroit as a free agent after '84, and was finished as a big-leaguer three years later at the age of 32.

Additions

Ten players were added to the Detroit roster at one point or another during the season. Only Ruppert Jones played an important role; his acquisition is discussed with the regular players above. The remaining players who appeared for the Tigers in 1984 were infielders Mike Laga, Doug Baker, and Scott Earl, outfielder Nelson Simmons, and pitchers Bill Scherrer, Sid Monge, Carl Willis, Randy O'Neal, and Roger Mason.

Of the nine others in the "also-played" group, all but two were products of the Tigers' organization. Laga (first round of January draft, 1980, community college), Baker (ninth round, 1982 June draft, college), Earl (14th round, 1981 June, college), Simmons (second round, 1981 June, high school), O'Neal (first round, 1981 June secondary draft, college), Mason (undrafted amateur free agent, signed out of college in 1980), and Willis (23rd round, 1983, college) were all developed by Detroit.

Ten-year major-league veteran reliever Monge was purchased from the San Diego Padres in mid-June to add a second left-hander to the bullpen. Willis was traded to Cincinnati for Scherrer within two months of his Detroit debut. Scherrer was drafted by the Reds out of high school in January 1977, then traded to Detroit in August for player-to-be-named-later Willis and cash when Monge was deemed not to be the solution in the second-lefty relief role.

Summary and Analysis

In 1990, the bible of baseball's minor leagues, *Baseball America*, pondered whether the 1975 draft was "the weakest pool ever." Evidence of just how astute Detroit's scouting and player-development staff was can be found by looking at the talent the Tigers managed to find in those thin pools in January and June: Lou Whitaker, Tom Brookens, Dave Rozema, and Dave Tobik. To reinforce that theme, the bumper crop of players—Alan Trammell, Jack Morris, Dan Petry, and Steve Kemp—drafted by Detroit in 1976 is widely acknowledged as one of the best annual drafts ever made by any team.

The heart of a World Series-winning club was born and bred in Detroit's productive farm system of the mid- to late 1970s. Six key players—Morris, Petry, Parrish, Whitaker, Trammell, and Gibson—were in the organization by 1978, and half of the 1984 team's 14 regulars (defined as the nine position starters plus top four starting pitchers and the closer) were in the fold before 1979. To be sure, four regulars and three other important contributors were added to the club from 1982 to 1984, but most of them could have been replaced by others of similar talents. True, Most Valuable Player and Cy Young Award winner Hernandez couldn't have been easily replaced but—given the extent of their dominance in 1984—the Tigers still would have won the pennant without their dominant closer.

Despite their achievements, however, the 1984 Tigers were not exceptional in terms of short-term or long-term continuity (measured in how many games or innings pitched the pennant winners from the 1980s got from players on their roster a year earlier or five years earlier). And that is the only flaw in the strategic plan of the Detroit management, where tremendous stability begat tremendous advantages overall—but also diminished the sense of urgency.

The provenance of the majority of the other important players who were not drafted and developed by Detroit was mostly via the sharp-eyed trade where general managers Campbell or Lajoie grabbed a valuable or undervalued player in return for superfluous major-league players or overvalued prospects. Detroit's beloved 1984 team took a long time to jell, but the end result was an unqualified success.

The Hernandez-Bergman Trade
by Richard L. Shook

SPARKY ANDERSON called his shot. "You get that guy," Anderson told Tigers general manager-in-waiting Bill Lajoie in the fall of 1983, "and we'll win it next year."

"That guy" was Willie Hernandez, and the legendary Hall of Fame manager was spot-on in his assessment that the addition of the workhorse left-handed reliever to the Detroit Tigers would translate into a championship for the rapidly improving American League team.

The deal between Detroit and Philadelphia wasn't finalized until March 24, 1984, but there's no question that the acquisition of Hernandez, who went on to win both the Most Valuable Player and Cy Young awards in 1984, was the key to the Tigers' AL title and World Series win that year.

But it might never have happened had Anderson not been doing color commentary on radio during the 1983 postseason, which gave him an opportunity to see players he might not otherwise have witnessed.

Philadelphia won the National League East Division title and defeated the Los Angeles Dodgers three games to one in the best-of-five NL playoff. The Phillies then lost to Baltimore, four games to one, in the World Series.

Detroit had finished six games behind Baltimore that season, a year Lajoie felt the Tigers could—maybe should—have won.

Because of Anderson's persona and the prominence he achieved during the 1970s with the Cincinnati Reds, he was recruited by radio networks to provide insights into the playoffs in years when Detroit was not involved, which at that time was every year. Who wouldn't want the outrageous, colorful No. 11? "Anderson-isms" were as much fun to unravel as they were to listen to.

Lajoie journeyed to the postseason to watch the games and see about possible business.

Going to the playoffs and World Series isn't obligatory; some executives deem it a nuisance. You can't announce news during the World Series (takes away from baseball's showcase attraction), not everybody is there, and many teams like to get their in-house meetings out of the way as part of laying groundwork for offseason maneuvering.

"Sparky had done a couple of broadcasts," Lajoie said. "We both see Willie Hernandez. And Willie just throws the beans out of the ball.

"Sparky said, 'Bill, you get that guy and we'll win it next year.' He said that right there on the spot."

Hernandez featured a screwball that bored back in on left-handed hitters and away from right-handers. It isn't seen much anymore because it's pretty tough on the elbow. But it worked for Hernandez.

He had gone 4-6 with 10 saves for the Cubs in 1982, working 75 innings in 75 games with a 3.00 ERA.

Philadelphia pried him from the Cubs on May 22, 1983, essentially for Dick Ruthven and Bill Johnson, believing he could help set up closer Al Holland, who had 25 saves and a 2.26 ERA that season. Hernandez went 9-4 in 1983 with eight saves and a 3.28 ERA for both the Cubs and Phils, pitching 74 games but with a workload that went up to $115^{1/3}$ innings with 93 strikeouts and 109 hits allowed.

Anderson, like most managers, was a "what-have-you-done-for-me-lately?" guy. Because their jobs are on the line every day, managers tend to lose patience with players who don't perform.

Aurelio Lopez had been a Tigers bullpen mainstay since he joined the club in 1979 but was starting to show wear and tear, though he rebounded in 1983. However, Lopez jumped the team on August 2, which may have been a red flag for his manager.

"He got ticked off because Sparky didn't use him in a save role or something," Lajoie said. "I wasn't officially the GM at that time but I was making all the deals and transactions. But Jim [Campbell, the official GM] wouldn't let me get a reliever. I felt if we had gotten somebody, we would have won that year, too.

"So now the next spring comes. Sparky, he's pretty much on me about this all the time. So I call the Phillies. They need an outfielder and they ask about Glenn Wilson. We played an exhibition game and Glenn hit the ball over the fence all the time in batting practice so they got real interested.

"Next time we go over there to play them and I set it up so Glenn goes on the trip and does his thing again. So now they're really hot for him.

"However, we need a first baseman who's a defensive guy and a left-handed hitter. So I told them we needed a [Dave] Bergman type of guy. They said they could get Bergman [from San Francisco] but they needed [John] Wockenfuss. It just so happened that San Francisco liked one of Philadelphia's outfielders so they were able to get Bergman.

DETROIT TIGERS 1984: WHAT A START! WHAT A FINISH!

"So we made the deal."

The Phillies outfielder, by the way, was Alejandro Sanchez, who joined the Tigers in 1985. But on one day—March 24, 1984—Bergman moved from San Francisco to Philadelphia to Detroit (or would that be from Phoenix to Clearwater to Lakeland?), bringing Hernandez with him on the last leg of the whirlwind journey.

There was a little more to it, though.

Lajoie knew the Philadelphia brain trust typically hung out at a certain restaurant for the dinner hours. He figured that rather than call when they were hungry, maybe a little edgy from the long day, he'd wait until they'd finished eating and were feeling better about things.

He made the call after dinner and they made the deal.

"Willie came over and the rest is what it is," Lajoie said. "He was always ready to pitch in Chicago and they used him a lot. They used him a lot in Philadelphia, too.

"But I'll always remember Sparky saying, 'You get that guy and we'll win.' That's pretty good."

References

Shook, Richard L. Telephone interview with Bill Lajoie, July 3, 2008.

Detroit in 1984
by Jeanne M. Mallett

BY JANUARY 1984 almost 16 years had passed since the fabled 1968 Detroit Tigers' World Series championship, an event that many saw then as reuniting a city that had been torn apart by the 1967 riot. By 1984, however, it was clear that Detroit had been reunited for only a fleeting moment in 1968. The problems that plagued the city before 1967, most notably racial division and overwhelming dependence of the local economy on the automobile industry, continued to bedevil Detroit throughout the 1970s and into the 1980s.

But as 1984 dawned there was a sense of cautious optimism that some things were beginning to change. To paraphrase the memorable presidential campaign slogan of that year, it seemed for most of the year to be "morning again in Detroit." This time the Detroit Tigers' championship run, beginning with its incredible 35-5 start, only added to a general feeling that Detroit was on the upswing again. But the violent end to the celebration after the Tigers won the World Series reminded Detroiters once again of how much they still had to overcome. In the end 1984 was, as Detroit's mayor at the time, Coleman Young, put it, a "contradictory year."

New Year's Day 1984 began quietly. Detroiters awoke to a cloudy Sunday with temperatures in the 20s but no snow. Sports fans were still absorbing the pain of the Detroit Lions' New Year's Eve last-minute defeat by the San Francisco 49ers in the NFC playoffs, as the usually reliable Eddie Murray missed a 43-yard field goal attempt with just seconds to go. Still, the fact that the Lions were in the playoffs at all was a good sign, just as the Tigers' second-place finish in the American League East in 1983 augured well for their future. It had been many years since either team—or, for that matter, Detroit's other major sports franchises, the NBA's Pistons and the NHL's Red Wings—had been truly competitive.

All Detroiters had to be somewhat cheered as well that New Year's Eve revelry had resulted in no deaths, although 11 were wounded by the gunfire that traditionally marked New Year's Eve celebrations. The Detroit tradition was to ring in the new year by taking to the streets to fire guns randomly into the air. Three people had been killed the year before. Along with the Devil's Night fires before Halloween, this tradition added to Detroit's reputation nationally as a violent town. But in 1984 Detroiters got by New Year's Eve and New Year's Day without a violent death of any sort. The first murder did not occur until January 2, a small victory in the city that had been known as Murder City since the early 1970s. Still, there had been 622 murders in 1983—down from the high of 801 in 1974, but up from 548 in 1982.

Detroiters also finally had some good news on the business front. Convention attendance hit a record high. More than 836,000 people attended 590 conventions in the metropolitan Detroit area, a 24 percent increase over the year before. This continued a steady increase of convention business that started when the Renaissance Center opened in 1977. This massive complex of hotel, businesses, and office space, popularly known as the RenCen, had been a calculated gamble by the city government and civic leaders, primarily the Ford family, to rescue the dying Detroit downtown. Now it finally seemed to be paying off.

The convention business news and predictions of a good year for the auto industry were both better news than Detroiters had endured just one year before. Then, on top of a fourth straight year of depressed auto sales, the iconic J.L. Hudson Company closed its flagship store on Woodward Avenue, driving a huge nail into the coffin of downtown Detroit. Detroit had already suffered important losses to business and its esteem since 1968. Motown Records had decamped to Los Angeles in 1972. WXYZ-TV and -AM, seminal stations in the Motor City, had left for suburban Southfield with their sister station, album-rock powerhouse WRIF-FM. That flight could be seen as one of many businesses headed for the suburbs. But Hudson's departure was particularly galling. Hudson's was synonymous with Detroit, just as Macy's is with New York City and Marshall Field was with Chicago. The Hudson's

DETROIT TIGERS 1984: WHAT A START! WHAT A FINISH!

building was mammoth and the store where Detroiters bought everything. Hudson's sponsored Detroit's own Thanksgiving Day Parade, which for years rivaled Macy's. Detroiters knew their city was shrinking in population and that those who remained were blacker and poorer. Detroit had suffered more white flight than any other major American city. In 1974 the city's population was still more than 50 percent white; by 1984 it was almost two-thirds black. The oil embargo of the 1970s began to topple the domestic auto industry, upon which so many Detroiters depended for their livelihood. Detroiters could see the shells of many buildings and homes left untouched since the 1967 riot. The city had been on the brink of bankruptcy in 1981. But the closing of Hudson's was still a shock. It seemed to many the final death rattle of a once-great American city. To wake up in January 1984 and find that they had not only not expired but had some signs of hope seemed like a miracle to many Detroiters.

January 1984 also marked the completion of a decade in office for Detroit's first black mayor, Coleman Young. A former auto worker, labor organizer, and state legislator, among other jobs, Young had lived in Detroit since he was 5 years old. He had lived through the city's glory days and its decline. When he first took office in 1974, the scars of 1967 were still fresh; white flight from the city was continuing at an alarming pace, and the remaining population suffered with 20 percent unemployment and high crime rates. Throughout his first 10 years, Young had to deal with the worst kinds of urban ills. Alternately confrontational and conciliatory, he doggedly worked with civic leaders and pleaded his case to the state and federal government to bring new development and business to the city. At the same time he tried to address the causes of the 1967 riot, most notably by increasing through affirmative action black representation at all levels in the previously white-dominated police force.

By 1984 Young, too, was cautiously optimistic that his administration's master plan, called "Moving Detroit Forward," was making progress. A new General Motors assembly plant was being built in Poletown, a neighborhood on the Detroit-Hamtramck border; work had begun on an automated elevated train, later known as the People Mover, to circle downtown; not only the RenCen but Joe Louis Arena, new luxury apartments, and business development planned by Stroh Brewery and others were providing new life to a new downtown center along the Detroit River. Ford Motor Company reported record profits in 1983. Detroit had already been showcased by being the site of the 1980 Republican National Convention and hosting the 1982 Super Bowl. And native Detroiter Tom Selleck was starring in a highly popular TV series, *Magnum, P.I.*, episodes of which made positive references to Detroit and on which Selleck was often shown wearing a Detroit Tigers cap. The uptick in the economy, relatively lower violent-crime statistics, and the return to respectability of both the Lions and the Tigers all signaled to Detroiters that, after a long, scary night, morning might just be coming again for the city. Detroit even had a new song that received a good deal of national play in 1984. "Hello Detroit,"

recorded by Sammy Davis Jr. for Motown Records, was a promotional song with a difference. Ultimately optimistic, it did not gloss over hard times. The opening lyrics were "You're a fighter, you're a lover. You're strong and you recover from whatever gets you down." The song reflected how many Detroiters thought of themselves. Tough, down but not out, and coming back.

Detroiters, like the rest of the country, started the new year with a new telephone company. As a result of a landmark antitrust decision, AT&T, known as Ma Bell to friend and foe alike, was broken into seven regional phone companies, or "baby Bells." Michigan Bell advertisements in the Sunday papers assured customers that service would continue as always. On television the big three broadcast networks, ABC, CBS, and NBC, still dominated programming and viewers. In addition to *Magnum, P.I.*, Detroiters were watching *The A-Team, Cheers, Hill Street Blues, Dallas,* and *The Dukes of Hazzard*. The big three in pop music scored with memorable albums: Michael Jackson (*Thriller*), Prince (*Purple Rain*), and Bruce Springsteen (*Born in the U.S.A.*). Detroiters could buy a subcompact Chevrolet Chevette for around $5,700, or less with their GM employee discounts, or a Ford F-150 truck for around $6,800. Gasoline was averaging $1.77 a gallon as prices continued their downward trend following the 1979 energy crisis. In-state tuition for a year at the University of Michigan was $2,166; at Michigan State the figure was $1,867, and at hometown Wayne State University, in-state students paid $1,760. It was also a presidential election year. Incumbent President Ronald Reagan was a lock for the Republican nomination. But the Democratic primary season started with several interesting candidates, including the first significant run by a black candidate, the Rev. Jesse Jackson.

In 1984, as in other years, once winter started it lingered into spring in Detroit. A late-February blizzard socked the city hard, shutting schools and bringing traffic to a halt. Even as the Tigers finally opened their home season on April 10, ice was still clogging the St. Clair River. But signs of a good spring were already popping up like crocuses through the snow. All three major auto companies reported record first-quarter profits. And the Tigers, after a so-so 11-17 spring training record, came home already 5-0, including a Jack Morris no-hitter among the victories.

The Tigers won their home opener before a sellout crowd of 51,238, and won many more games on their way to a 35-5 start that made believers out of the most cynical of Detroiters. WDIV-TV, which carried the over-the-air Tigers telecasts, began an ongoing feature showing Detroiters from all walks of life saying "Bless You Boys," a phrase that soon found its way on to T-shirts, buttons, and other memorabilia. And there followed Tiger bread, Tiger cheese, Tiger placemats, and even a wine cooler named Tiger Fever as Detroiters became more exuberant about the team. Magazines featuring the Tigers on their covers regularly sold out in a couple of days. As *Detroit News* writer Tom Gage later wrote in *The Sporting News* 1985 Baseball Yearbook, the enthusiasm was widespread. The president of Detroit's Chamber of Commerce, Frank Smith,

DETROIT TIGERS 1984: WHAT A START! WHAT A FINISH!

expressed the hope that the Tigers' winning would help instill a new sense of pride by Detroiters in their city, not a vain hope since Detroiters have always had a big stake in their sports teams, especially the Tigers. Gage interviewed hospital personnel at Pontiac's St. Joseph Mercy Hospital, who reported a new spirit among patients, even the critically ill. One surgical ward nurse told him: "My call lights never go off when the game is on. They don't need the pain shot and they don't notice the discomfort during the games. Some of them can't tell you what day it is or what they ate for dinner last night. But they can tell you what the score was and who was pitching and who hit the home runs."

The late spring turned to a brilliant summer. The Tigers continued to win, although not at the pace of those first few weeks. And other things continued to go Detroit's way. The economy continued to rebound. People were feeling good about themselves and the city. So when in July WJR, the city's pre-eminent radio station and the radio home of the Tigers, suddenly announced that it would move its operation out of the landmark Fisher Building to suburban Troy, there was shock but no longer resignation. Intensive negotiation with city leaders and pressure on the Federal Communications Commission to deny the request led WJR executives to back down. By December, WJR announced that it would relocate within Detroit's city limits, keeping its "golden tower of the Fisher Building" location and expanding to the RenCen. As the song said, Detroit was getting stronger and beginning to recover. By the end of the summer WDIV-TV even had President Reagan saying, "Bless You Boys."

Detroiters rode the good feeling of the summer into the fall as the Tigers clinched their division, then the league playoffs to go into the World Series against the San Diego Padres, a series Detroiters confidently predicted would end quickly with a championship. The Tigers did not disappoint their fans, defeating the Padres in five games. And then suddenly, just as the Tigers and Detroit reached that championship moment and the celebration started, the magic of 1984 ended for Detroit. Around 8 p.m., as the happy crowd of 51,901 exited the stadium, some with sod from the field and parts of seats as souvenirs, they melded into a crowd outside that had grown through the late afternoon and evening to more than 100,000. It took only minutes before the first act of serious vandalism occurred as some fans attacked a police car, overturned it, and then torched it. By the time a heavy rain came around midnight to help overwhelmed police disperse the rowdy crowd, one man was dead, more than 100 were injured, and three women had reported rapes. Police arrested 34 people for charges ranging from assault and robbery to disorderly conduct. Newspapers across the country the next day featured the violent aftermath over the World Series victory itself, printing photos of burning cars along with headlines like "Motown Madness" and "World Series Rampage." Although other cities had had destructive championship celebrations in the past and would in the future, only Detroit's night of wanton revelry has endured in the public mind. Even in 2008, Tonight Show host Jay Leno used the past disorder and violence—as if it typified Detroit then and now—as fodder for his monologue.

Local leaders and columnists worried that all the hard work and slow recovery of Detroit had been destroyed. As Halloween came with Devil's Night fires so soon after the World Series disorders, Detroit's national reputation took another blow. Yet these incidents were actually less typical of Detroit in 1984 than they would have been in prior years. A renewed war on crime in 1984, including more precinct patrols and greater school security, allowed Police Chief William Hart to say that, outside of the World Series and Devil's Night incidents, Detroit "had one of the quietest summers in the last decade."

As the year ended, statistics showed that homicides, assaults, and rapes had all dropped significantly. Other year-end statistics showed a solid year of recovery for Detroit businesses, most notably the auto industry, upon which so much else depended. Detroiters still had reason to hope for the future. *The Detroit News* began 1985 with a 15-part series, "Metro Detroit: A Look Ahead," that detailed the problems and proposed solutions. Detroiters seemed ready to get to work improving their city. There was perhaps no better indicator that things could still change for the better than the year-end news that Chrysler would begin hiring 1,700 people for the second shift of its new high-tech Sterling Heights plant in early January 1985. Chrysler had survived bankruptcy only five years earlier with the help of $1.5 billion in federal loan guarantees. By 1984 it had record earnings for two straight years. In a tough town built on the auto industry, this was as good a sign as any that Detroit itself could endure and maybe even prosper in years to come.

Not many years since have been as good to Detroit as 1984. But some of the projects started then and the plans made have come to fruition and Detroit has continued to fight through difficulties.

References

Publications

Brooks, Tim, and Earle Marsh. *The Complete Directory to Prime Time Network and Cable TV Shows 1946-Present* (Sixth Edition). New York: Ballantine Books. 1995.

Detroit Free Press. *The Roar of '84*. Detroit: Detroit Free Press. 1984.

Articles

Alpert, Bruce. "Young sees good, bad in '84." *Detroit News*, December 23, 1984. 1A.

Chargot, Patricia. "One killed, others hurt amid revelry." *Detroit Free Press*, October 15, 1984. 1A.

DETROIT TIGERS 1984: WHAT A START! WHAT A FINISH!

Flanagan, Brian. "Homicide, rape down; auto theft up." *Detroit Free Press*, December 28, 1984. 1A.

Gage, Tom. "Detroit, City of Champions." *The Sporting News 1985 Baseball Yearbook*, 1985. 15.

Gilchrist, Brenda J. "Convention attendance in Detroit sets record." *Detroit Free Press*, January 4, 1984. 1A.

Goldberg, Susan, Joe Swickard, and Patricia Chargot. "Rowdy revelry attracts attention." *Detroit Free Press*, October 16, 1984. 13A.

Graff, Gary. "A trio of male superstars dominates the rock scene." *Detroit Free Press*, December 28, 1984. 1C.

Kresnak, Jack. "11 wounded as gunshots mar revelry." *Detroit Free Press*, January 2, 1984. 1A.

Kresnak, Jack. "1984 saw new war on crime in Detroit." *Detroit Free Press*, January 6, 1985. 1A.

McClure, Sandy. "City Has First Slaying of '84." *Detroit Free Press*, January 3, 1984. 3A.

McFarlin, Jim. "Radio '84: Proof truth is stranger than fiction." *Detroit News*, December 31, 1984. 1C.

McGill, Andrew R. "Metro Detroit: A Look Ahead, Part 1: An Overview: Our future is optimistic, but not without changes." *Detroit News*, January 6, 1985. 1A.

McGill, Andrew R. "Metro Detroit: A Look Ahead, Part 3: Black & White: Race: A troublesome road toward a new era of trust." *Detroit News*, January 8, 1985. 1A.

McGill, Andrew R. "Metro Detroit: A Look Ahead, Part 5: Crime & Image: A tale of 3 forces: Crime, urban neglect, media." *Detroit News*, January 10, 1985. 1A

McGill, Andrew R. "Metro Detroit: A Look Ahead, Part 11: New Education: Public schools hurt by hidden recession." *Detroit News*, January 16, 1985. 1A.

Olmstead, Larry. "Aftermath of a win: Violence downtown." *Detroit Free Press*, October 16, 1984. 1A.

Rohan, Barry. "Chrysler Will Hire 1,700 in January." *Detroit Free Press*, December 27, 1984. 1A.

Shellum, Bernie, Linda Brenners-Stulberg, Betsey Haniph, Luther Jackson, and Alan Lenhoff. "1984: A year of recovery." *Detroit Free Press*, December 30, 1984. 1F.

Web Sites

http://www.census.gov

http://www.eia.doe.gov

http://www.sammydavisjunior.com

Other Sources

The Tonight Show with Jay Leno, National Broadcasting Company, June 5, 2008, and July 24, 2008.

The Tigers' 35-5 Start Chart

Gm#	Game Date	Opponent	Result	Record	GA	Tigers W/L/S
1	Tuesday, April 3	at Minnesota	W, 8-1	1-0	Tied	Morris
2	Thursday, April 5	at Minnesota	W, 7-3	2-0	Tied	Petry
3	Friday, April 6	at Chicago	W, 3-2	3-0	Tied	Wilcox, Hernandez
4	Saturday, April 7	at Chicago	W, 4-0	4-0	+0.5	Morris
5	Sunday, April 8	at Chicago	W, 7-3	5-0	+1.5	Lopez
6	Tuesday, April 10	vs. Texas	W, 5-1	6-0	+2.5	Petry
7	Thursday, April 12	vs. Texas	W, 9-4	7-0	+3.0	Morris
8	Friday, April 13	at Boston	W, 13-9	8-0	+3.0	Bair
9	Wednesday, April 18	vs. Kansas City	W, 4-3 (10)	9-0	+2.5	Hernandez
10	Thursday, April 19	vs. Kansas City	L, 2-5	9-1	+1.5	Petry
11	Friday, April 20	vs. Chicago	W, 3-2	10-1	+2.5	Lopez
12	Saturday, April 21	vs. Chicago	W, 4-1	11-1	+3.5	Rozema, Bair
13	Sunday, April 22	vs. Chicago	W, 9-1	12-1	+4.5	Berenguer
14	Tuesday, April 24	vs. Minnesota	W, 6-5	13-1	+5.5	Morris
15	Tuesday, April 24	vs. Minnesota	W, 4-3	14-1	+5.5	Abbott, Lopez
16	Wednesday, April 25	at Texas	W, 9-4	15-1	+5.5	Wilcox, Hernandez
17	Thursday, April 26	at Texas	W, 7-5	16-1	+6.0	Bair, Lopez
18	Friday, April 27	vs. Cleveland	L, 4-8 (19)	16-2	+5.0	Abbott
19	Saturday, April 28	vs. Cleveland	W, 6-2	17-2	+5.5	Morris
20	Sunday, April 29	vs. Cleveland	W, 6-1	18-2	+6.0	Petry
21	Tuesday, May 1	vs. Boston	W, 11-2	19-2	+6.5	Wilcox
22	Wednesday, May 2	vs. Boston	L, 4-5	19-3	+5.5	Berenguer
23	Thursday, May 3	vs. Boston	L, 0-1	19-4	+5.0	Morris
24	Friday, May 4	at Cleveland	W, 9-2	20-4	+5.0	Petry, Hernandez
25	Saturday, May 5	at Cleveland	W, 6-5	21-4	+5.0	Abbott, Lopez
26	Sunday, May 6	at Cleveland	W, 6-5 (12)	22-4	+5.0	Lopez
27	Monday, May 7	at Kansas City	W, 10-3	23-4	+5.5	Berenguer, Bair
28	Tuesday, May 8	at Kansas City	W, 5-2	24-4	+6.0	Morris
29	Wednesday, May 9	at Kansas City	W, 3-1	25-4	+7.5	Petry, Lopez
30	Friday, May 11	vs. California	W, 8-2	26-4	+7.5	Wilcox, Hernandez
31	Saturday, May 12	vs. California	L, 2-4	26-5	+7.5	Berenguer
32	Monday, May 14	vs. Seattle	W, 7-5	27-5	+8.0	Lopez
33	Tuesday, May 15	vs. Seattle	W, 6-4	28-5	+8.0	Morris, Hernandez
34	Wednesday, May 16	vs. Seattle	W, 10-1	29-5	+8.0	Wilcox
35	Friday, May 18	vs. Oakland	W, 8-4 (6)	30-5	+7.5	Petry
36	Saturday, May 19	vs. Oakland	W, 5-4	31-5	+7.5	Morris, Lopez
37	Sunday, May 20	vs. Oakland	W, 4-3	32-5	+8.5	Wilcox, Hernandez
38	Tuesday, May 22	at California	W, 3-1	33-5	+8.0	Berenguer, Lopez
39	Wednesday, May 23	at California	W, 4-2	34-5	+8.0	Petry, Hernandez
40	Thursday, May 24	at California	W, 5-1	35-5	+8.5	Morris

April 1984
by Brian Borawski

April 3, 1984
Tigers 8, Twins 1 (1-0)

Jack Morris was about as impressive as a pitcher could be in an Opening Day appearance, pitching seven innings while giving up only one run on five hits—all while striking out eight. The Tigers drew first blood in the third with an RBI double by Howard Johnson and an Alan Trammell single. After scoring these two runs, the Tigers never looked back, as the only dent the Twins made was in the bottom half of the inning, when they put one on the board. In what would become a trend all season, Aurelio Lopez pitched a perfect eighth inning and Willie Hernandez pitched a perfect ninth. It wouldn't always be those same innings, but those two guys were the anchor of a great pen, and you'll be seeing their names pop up quite often in these accounts.

April 5, 1984
Tigers 7, Twins 3 (2-0)

Dan Petry gave up the lead early in this one (two runs in the second), but the Tigers bounced back by scoring one in the third and three in the fourth. Petry calmed, and ended up going seven. Hernandez then did the job by pitching perfect eighth and ninth innings. Trammell and Kirk Gibson led the way on offense. Both hit home runs (Gibby's was a three-run shot to put the Tigers up for good in the fourth), and Tram went 4-for-5.

April 6, 1984
Tigers 3, White Sox 2 (3-0)

The Tigers drew first blood as they scored three runs before the White Sox even batted. Dave Bergman came up with a big two-out, two-run single to give the Tigers that three-run lead. All those runs grew in importance as they got only three more hits the rest of the way. Milt Wilcox pitched seven quality innings, giving up only four hits and one run. He walked four, and one of those, Harold Baines, was the only player to score on him. And then the Tigers got a minor scare in eighth. Pitching in his third consecutive game, Willie Hernandez gave up one run in the eighth, but slammed the door shut in the ninth, giving the Tigers their third straight win and earning his first save of the season.

April 7, 1984
Tigers 4, White Sox 0 (4-0)

For the second game in a row, the Tigers had just five hits, but that was more than enough in this one, as Jack Morris went the distance and threw the Tigers' first no-hitter since Jim Bunning did it in 1958. Morris actually walked the bases loaded in the fourth inning, but got Greg Luzinski to hit into a 1-2-3 double play, then whiffed Ron Kittle to get out of the jam. I distinctly remember this game. It was on a Saturday, which was the day we usually went to evening Mass. The game wasn't finished when we left, so I made everyone listen to the game on the radio on the drive over there, and I even waited until the game was done before getting out of the car. I was glued to the radio.

April 8, 1984
Tigers 7, White Sox 3 (5-0)

Dave Rozema pitched four decent innings, but had to leave the game in the fifth before recording an out when his arm tightened up. He left with a three-run lead. Señor Smoke, Aurelio Lopez, slammed the door, giving up only one run (a Harold Baines homer), one hit, and striking out four in four strong innings. The Tigers got to Tom Seaver early as well, scoring five runs in the first five innings. Kirk Gibson hit his second homer of the season. Alan Trammell stole his fourth base. Barbaro Garbey doubled twice and drove in three runs. This game went 3 hours and 17 minutes. Back then, that was a pretty long game. And one odd quirk about the 1984 season is the Tigers played in four home openers. They opened the Metrodome, Comiskey, Fenway, and, of course, Tiger Stadium. They rained on everyone's parade that year.

April 10, 1984
Tigers 5, Rangers 1 (6-0)

Dan Petry went the distance in the home opener, yielding a run and two hits in the first inning, and then giving up only two hits the rest of the way, all while striking out seven. Once again, the Tigers only had five hits, but they made them all count. Darrell Evans hit a three-run homer on his very first swing at Tiger Stadium in the first inning. Dave Stewart didn't even make it out of the first inning (five walks, two hits, and four runs in two-thirds of an inning). And with the win, the Tigers tied their franchise record for best start ever. One interesting thing about the Tigers' 1984 season is that Jack Morris and Willie Hernandez got quite a bit of the credit for carrying this team, but it was Dan Petry and Milt Wilcox who helped Morris anchor a great rotation. In fact, in some respects Dan Petry had an even better year than Morris. He didn't have the no-hitter, but his ERA was better (3.24 vs. 3.60) and so was his WHIP—walks plus hits per inning pitched—1.273 vs. 1.282. Both had just about the same number of strikeouts (144 for Petry and 148 for Morris). This doesn't diminish Morris' role, because he was the leader, but Petry had an outstanding year in his own right.

April 12, 1984
Tigers 9, Rangers 4 (7-0)

Alan Trammell, Chet Lemon, and Lou Whitaker all homered as the Tigers trounced the Rangers. Through five innings, Texas was hanging in there, but the Tigers scored four in the sixth to put the game out of reach. Jack Morris was his usual self, going seven innings while giving up seven hits and one walk. The only two runs he gave up were unearned. And with that win, the Tigers broke the franchise record for most consecutive wins to start the season. They also already had a three-game lead in their division. The only question for Tiger fans was how long they could keep it up.

DETROIT TIGERS 1984: WHAT A START! WHAT A FINISH!

April 13, 1984
Tigers 13, Red Sox 9 (8-0)

Neither Milt Wilcox nor Boston starter Bruce Hurst made it past the first inning in this slugfest. The Tigers started things off by scoring eight runs in the top half of the first inning. Thirteen Tigers—including Dave Bergman pinch-hitting for Barbaro Garbey—batted in the inning. Oddly, Lance Parrish was responsible for all three outs, striking out in his first at-bat, then grounding into a double play to end the inning. Boston responded with five runs of its own in the bottom half of the first, chasing Wilcox. Doug Bair, another key member of the Tigers' bullpen, followed and pitched 4.1 innings, giving up only three hits and one walk, striking out five. Seven Tigers had at least two hits apiece in this Friday the 13th game, and the Tigers improved to 8-0. In an unusual stretch of the season, the Tigers then had four consecutive days off because of wet weather—rain and even snow.

April 18, 1984
Tigers 4, Royals 3, 10 innings (9-0)

After a four-day break because of rain, the Tigers started right where they left off, beating the Royals 4-3 for their franchise-best ninth straight victory to start the season. Jack Morris got off to a great start, but he gave up a 3-0 lead in the eighth inning, surrendering a three-run homer to Jorge Orta. Morris pitched nine innings, but yielded to Willie Hernandez in extra innings. Hernandez got the win by pitching a perfect 10th. With two out and Alan Trammell on third, Larry Herndon hit a grounder to Frank White, the Royals' eight-time Gold Glove-winning second baseman. White bobbled the ball, allowing Tram to score the winning run.

April 19, 1984
Royals 5, Tigers 2 (9-1)

Despite what everyone in Detroit might have thought at the time, the Tigers couldn't win them all, and—16 days after their season opened, they finally dropped their first game to the Royals. A great pitching performance by rookie pitcher Bret Saberhagen, who earned his first career victory, was basically all the Royals needed as the Tigers could manage only seven hits and two runs. The Tigers took the lead early, as Lance Parrish drove in Lou Whitaker on a groundout in the first inning. The Royals got two in the third, one in the sixth, and then two insurance runs in the eighth. Kirk Gibson hit a solo shot in the ninth, but it was too little, too late, as the Tigers finally put a notch in their loss column.

April 20, 1984
Tigers 3, White Sox 2 (10-1)

This time, the Tigers got 11 hits, but they had a hard time making them count as they also left 11 men on base in this nail-biter. The Tigers never had the lead in this one until the game ended, and Milt Wilcox, despite not getting the win, threw a great game to keep the Tigers in this one, going eight innings and giving up eight hits, three walks, and only two runs. The Tigers were down 2-1 going into the seventh when Larry Herndon drove in Barbaro Garbey on a single. Then in the ninth, with the score tied 2-2, Lou Whitaker drew a leadoff walk. Alan Trammell bunted him over to second. Dave Bergman grounded out, but moved Whitaker over to third, and Lance Parrish drove in Whitaker on a two-out single to end the contest. A great game, and the fans were beginning to appreciate what the Tigers were doing, as 33,554 turned out, the most since opening day.

April 21, 1984
Tigers 4, White Sox 1 (11-1)

It's not often that a player scores three of the team's four runs in a game, but that's what Lou Whitaker did in this one. Sweet Lou led off the Tigers' half of the first with a homer. In the third he drew a walk, and eventually came across on a Darrell Evans groundout. And then in the seventh, he singled and scored on Alan Trammell's single, Tram being out at second after six Chisox handled the ball on the play. Whitaker knew how to get on base. Over his career, he walked about 100 more times than he struck out (1,197 to 1,099), and was an excellent two-strike hitter. He wasn't the prototypical leadoff man because he didn't steal a lot of bases, but he worked the count well and managed to put together some nice seasons in the middle 1980s. Dave Rozema really shut down the White Sox. He went six innings and allowed just two hits and two walks while striking out seven. Doug Bair came in to finish the game and get a three-inning save. And with that, the Tigers tied the mark for the best start of the season by an American League team. They stood at 11-1, and were already out to a 3.5-game lead in the AL East.

April 22, 1984
Tigers 9, White Sox 1 (12-1)

A Kirk Gibson two-run homer in the first inning was all the Tigers needed, but they got a lot more. They scored nine runs on 18 hits. Five Tigers had multihit games, including a 4-for-4 outing by Chet Lemon. Six Tigers scored, and five Tigers drove in a run, indicative of a good all-around team effort. Juan Berenguer was exceptional in his first start of the season. He pitched seven shutout innings, struck out seven, and gave up only two hits and a walk. He had a no-hitter going into the fifth, but gave up a single to Kalamazoo native Mike Squires. Mike also made his first—and only—pitching appearance here, getting the final out in the eighth inning.

April 24, 1984, first game
Tigers 6, Twins 5 (13-1)

Jack Morris had his worst outing of the season so far, but managed to walk away with his fourth straight victory. He went the distance, giving up five runs on seven hits and five walks. But as was typical of this magical season, it was just enough as the Tigers won in dramatic fashion. The Tigers entered the bottom of the ninth down 5-3. Kirk Gibson led off the inning with a triple. John Grubb reached base on a fielder's choice and left the game for pinch-runner Rusty Kuntz. Dave Bergman then drove in Gibson with an RBI

DETROIT TIGERS 1984: WHAT A START! WHAT A FINISH!

single, cutting the lead to one run. Then, the wheels really came off the Twins' wagon as relief pitcher Ron Davis, in his second inning of work, put one in the dirt, allowing the tying run to score on a wild pitch, with Bergman moving to second. Howard Johnson popped out to third and with one out, Chet Lemon was given an intentional pass. Lance Parrish lined out to second base. With two outs, and runners on first and second, Lou Whitaker singled and drove in Bergman to win the game.

April 24, 1984, second game
Tigers 4, Twins 3 (14-1)

In the nightcap, Lance Parrish hit a three-run homer in the fifth inning and Aurelio Lopez shut the Twins down in the final three innings. Starter Dan Petry was forced to leave the game after facing one batter in the fourth. Glenn Abbott took over in the fourth and gave up two runs in the top half of the fifth, but Parrish answered in the bottom half of the inning with his three-run belt. Aurelio Lopez got the three-inning save with shutout pitching, giving up only one hit and two walks while striking out three.

April 25, 1984
Tigers 9, Rangers 4 (15-1)

Dave Stewart hadn't made it out of the first inning in the Tigers' home opener, and he didn't pitch well in this one as the Tigers nicked him thrice in the first six innings, then unloaded on him in the seventh. By the end of the game, the Tigers had scored nine runs on 13 hits. John Grubb, Howard Johnson, and Lance Parrish hit homers. In fact, Parrish's was his second three-run shot in as many games. Milt Wilcox went six innings, and Willie Hernandez finished by pitching the final three innings as he picked up his second save of the season.

April 26, 1984
Tigers 7, Rangers 5 (16-1)

Neither starter was effective in this one. Future Tiger Frank Tanana gave up six runs in less than four innings, and Dave Rozema was marginally better as he gave up five runs in 4.1 frames. Once the starters were pulled—Tanana in the fourth and Rozema in the fifth—things really calmed down. The only scoring the rest of the way was a single run the Tigers collected in the seventh. Doug Bair pitched two shutout innings to notch his second relief win of the year, and Aurelio Lopez threw 2.2 perfect innings for his second save. Lou Whitaker, Alan Trammell, Larry Herndon, and Chet Lemon all had multihit games, and Lance Parrish homered in his third consecutive game, boosting his season total to five. With the win, the Tigers improved to 16-1 and had a six-game lead in the AL East. Everyone points to their 35-5 start—which is, simply put, an incredible start—but only after you go back and see what they actually did throughout those first couple of months can you appreciate what this team accomplished.

April 27, 1984
Indians 8, Tigers 4, 19 innings (16-2)

It took 5:44 for this game to run its course, but the Tigers' seven-game winning streak came to an end as they burned the midnight oil in a 19-inning affair. After the Indians batted in the top half of the second inning, the score was even at 3-3. Seven innings later, the game still stood at 3-3. Both the Indians and the Tigers scored a run in the 10th, and then it wasn't until the Indians scored four unearned runs in the 19th inning that this one was, well, put to bed. Another standout performance by Aurelio Lopez, as he threw 4.2 shutout innings to follow up his 2.2 perfect innings the day before. He kept the Tigers in the game, but Glenn Abbott, who had shut the Indians down for four innings, committed two errors in the 19th that helped the Indians score four runs to give the Tribe the lead for good. In all, the Tigers committed four errors, leading to six Indians runs in the game. In the 19th, the Tigers made errors on three consecutive plays. The Tigers only had one extra-base hit, a double by Lou Whitaker, despite having 66 official at-bats. And possibly the oddest line of the night was Andre Thornton, the Indians' DH, who went 0 for 9.

April 28, 1984
Tigers 6, Indians 2 (17-2)

In his book on the 1984 season, *Bless You Boys,* Sparky Anderson mentions that he sent Jack Morris home in the 13th inning of the previous night's game, and that move may have made the difference in this one, as he shut down a tired Indians team. He gave up only three hits and three walks in nine innings, and the three runs the Tigers scored in the first two innings were all they needed in this one. Chet Lemon and Lou Whitaker hit homers. Alan Trammell knocked in two with a double and stole his seventh base of the season. Detroit was also efficient in this one, garnering ten 10 and two walks, while stranding only four baserunners.

April 29, 1984
Tigers 6, Indians 1 (18-2)

Dan Petry had a no-hitter broken up in the eighth inning by a two-out George Vukovich double to lead the Tigers to their 18th victory of the season. When it was all over, Petry had pitched eight innings, giving up only the one hit and two walks with seven strikeouts. The Indians got another hit, and their only run, off Willie Hernandez. Kirk Gibson went 3-for-4 with three RBIs. Alan Trammell was put into the game in the seventh inning and doubled in his only at-bat. The base hit extended his hitting streak to 17 games. The last game he didn't get a hit was the third game of the season. And with April 30 being an exhibition game at Cincinnati against the Reds, the Tigers finished the month of April 18-2, a franchise record for the best April by a Tigers team.

May 1984
by Brian Borawski

May 1, 1984
Tigers 11, Red Sox 2 (19-2)

When all was said and done, the Tigers had racked up 11 runs on 16 hits. Rusty Kuntz, Barbaro Garbey, and Chet Lemon all had three hits—including two home runs by Chet Lemon—and Alan Trammell extended his hitting streak to 18 games with a double and single. Eight Tigers scored runs, and probably the oddest line was that only three players had RBIs. Kuntz had three, and Lemon and Garbey each had four. Milt Wilcox had a fine game as well, as he pitched eight innings and gave up only seven hits and two runs (one earned) as he advanced to 3-0. With the win, the Tigers sat on a 19-2 record, giving them a .905 winning percentage. This was the last time they'd be above the .900 mark, but it just shows how impressive this run was. At this point, they were 16-3 away from their fabulous 35-5 run. And while 16-3 is very impressive, the fact that they started 19-2 to get there is equally impressive.

May 2, 1984
Red Sox 5, Tigers 4 (19-3)

The Tigers' shortest winning streak of the season came to an end although they definitely made a game of this one. Down 5-0, the Tigers scored four unanswered runs, including two in the ninth inning, to make the Red Sox sweat. Unfortunately, Kirk Gibson was stranded at second base after Darrell Evans grounded out and John Grubb struck out to end the game. Juan Berenguer had a tough time, giving up five runs in six innings, and while Doug Bair and Willie Hernandez combined to throw three scoreless innings, it was too little, too late. Kirk Gibson led the way at the plate as he went 4-for-5 with a double, a triple, two runs, and an RBI.

May 3, 1984
Red Sox 1, Tigers 0 (19-4)

A few firsts in this one. This was the first time the Tigers were shut out. It was also their first two-game losing streak. And finally, it was Jack Morris' first loss, despite the fact that he threw a heck of game. His only real blemish was an eighth-inning solo homer by Dwight Evans, but that was all the Red Sox needed. For the second game in a row, the Tigers outhit the Red Sox but walked away with a loss. The Tigers threatened in the ninth, so once again, they didn't go down without a fight. Lance Parrish singled with one out and Larry Herndon walked. But Chet Lemon flied out and Kirk Gibson struck out to end the game.

May 4, 1984
Tigers 9, Indians 2 (20-4)

Dan Petry got all the support he needed in this one. The scoreboard doesn't indicate it, but he really struggled. He lasted only five innings and gave up six hits and six walks. In the fourth, he walked three batters but got out of the inning unscathed. Willie Hernandez, on the other hand, was simply incredible as he slammed the door on any chance of an Indians comeback. He pitched four shutout innings, gave up only two hits, and struck out three while earning his third save of the season. Lou Whitaker was the hitting star in this one, as he went 4-for-5 and scored two runs. Larry Herndon went 3-for-5. Lance Parrish drove in two on a pair of sacrifice flies.

May 5, 1984
Tigers 6, Indians 5 (21-4)

Even the good teams have bad overall games in which one player rises above the rest and carries everyone on his back. And that's exactly what Chet Lemon did in this one. He got the Tigers off to a good start with a two-run single in the first inning. Then he scored runs in the fourth and the sixth innings (the sixth-inning run tied the game). Finally, in the eighth, he hit a solo homer to give the Tigers an insurance run that they'd end up needing. In all, he went 4-for-4, scored three runs, and drove in three. He had four of the Tigers' 10 hits, and either scored or drove in five of the Tigers' six tallies. Sparky Anderson's "fourth starter by committee" pulled together another win, as Glenn Abbott pitched $5^{1/3}$ decent innings to garner his second win of the season. Aurelio Lopez got the two-inning save.

May 6, 1984
Tigers 6, Indians 5, 12 innings (22-4)

The Tigers looked as though they were going to drop this one, but a four-run eighth, which included three hits and three walks, tied the game after the Tigers were down 5-1. Then an RBI single by Lou Whitaker in the 12th put it away. Milt Wilcox struggled in his five innings (although he did strike out five), but the bullpen combined for seven shutout innings (only four hits) to let the Tigers back into the game as they scored in the sixth, seventh, and eighth innings to come back after being down 5-0.

May 7, 1984
Tigers 10, Royals 3 (23-4)

Chet Lemon had another great game, going 2-for-3 with three RBIs, and Alan Trammell went 3-for-5 with two runs. At this point, according to the Sparky Anderson memoir Bless You Boys, Lemon had 27 RBIs in 27 games, and Tram was hitting .373. Juan Berenguer pitched into the seventh inning, and Doug Bair nailed the door shut the rest of the way. Another day, another win.

May 8, 1984
Tigers 5, Royals 2 (24-4)

For most of the early 1980s, when you thought of closers, you thought of Dan Quisenberry. With his submarine pitching style, Quisenberry led the league in saves in five of six seasons from 1980 through 1985. He wasn't a big strikeout guy, but he rarely walked batters, and had a career 1.175 WHIP. He was also a more durable closer than today's models; during

DETROIT TIGERS 1984: WHAT A START! WHAT A FINISH!

his prime years (with the exception of strike-shortened 1981) he never pitched fewer than 128 innings. And 1984 was one of those league-leading years for Quisenberry, but for the first time in his career, he made the biggest mistake possible. With the Tigers down 2-1, he inherited the bases loaded from starter Bud Black, and Alan Trammell cashed in as he sent the ball over the left-field fence for his third homer and the Tigers' first grand slam of the season. It was the first grand slam Quisenberry had ever surrendered. Give credit to Jack Morris as well. He pitched another complete game, giving up only seven hits and two runs while striking out five.

May 9, 1984
Tigers 3, Royals 1 (25-4)

This one was all about pitching. Dan Petry threw 6²/₃ strong innings before walking two batters in the seventh. Sparky Anderson then handed the ball to Aurelio Lopez, and Señor Smoke did the job. He got out of the jam in the seventh, and walked only one batter in 2¹/₃ innings to shut down the Royals the rest of the way. En route, he struck out four and collected his fourth save of the season. A big part of winning championships is catching magic in a bottle. If you look at most of the "surprise" championship teams, you have players having career years. Lopez was having one of those years, and was an integral part of the Tigers' championship run. He set a career high in innings pitched with 137²/₃, won 10 games, and saved 14. And this was in a season in which another reliever on the same team won the MVP and the Cy Young Award. Lopez basically gave Sparky a closer-quality pitcher on the right to partner with Hernandez on the left. With the win, the Tigers tied the 1955 Dodgers' mark for the best start in history.

May 11, 1984
Tigers 8, Angels 2 (26-4)

The Tigers were the toast of the town as they broke the record for the best start ever by a team. This one wasn't much of a contest, as the Tigers went up 2-0 in the second frame and never looked back. Six Tigers had multihit games, and Dave Bergman drove in three runs. Milt Wilcox pitched six shutout innings to improve to 4-0, and Willie Hernandez, although shaky, finished the game off. Pushing through the turnstiles were 44,187 fans who came out to see the Tigers break the record set by the 1955 Dodgers, and the Tigers didn't let them down.

May 12, 1984
Angels 4, Tigers 2 (26-5)

It took a 250-game winner to do it, but the Detroit Tigers finally lost their fifth game of the season. Tommy John went the distance, giving up only eight hits and two runs. Chet Lemon and Lou Whitaker both had two hits, but only twice did the Tigers garner more than one hit in a single inning. Sparky Anderson was ejected for arguing an interference call in the ninth inning. But the fans at this point were really getting into the team, as another 38,516 of them came out to see the boys.

May 13, 1984
Angels vs. Tigers
Rained out.

May 14, 1984
Tigers 7, Mariners 5 (27-5)

It didn't take long for the Tigers to get back to their winning ways. They struggled in this one, but two runs in the bottom of the eighth finished off the Mariners. Alan Trammell followed up two hitless games with a 3-for-5 outing, which included his fourth homer of the year. Rusty Kuntz doubled, scored the go-ahead run on Dave Bergman's triple, and went 3-for-4 with three runs. The pitching wasn't so great. Dan Petry struggled through five innings plus three batters in the sixth but held the Mariners to three runs. Doug Bair, who had been rock-solid and had a 1.17 ERA in six relief appearances going into the game, gave up two runs in only two innings of work. Aurelio Lopez shut down the Mariners in the final two innings to notch his fourth win.

May 15, 1984
Tigers 6, Mariners 4 (28-5)

When your starter walks five and your team makes three errors, you don't usually expect to win. The Tigers almost blew a 6-1 lead in this one, but held on with some good relief pitching by Willie Hernandez. Jack Morris notched his seventh win, but he walked five and gave up four runs (three earned). Hernandez came into the game in the eighth, and was awesome. He struck out five of the six batters he faced and earned his fifth save. The Tigers showed some patience as they needed only five hits to get their six runs, thanks to 12 walks. Kirk Gibson drove in two without getting a hit (two sacrifice flies), and Howard Johnson had a two-run single.

May 16, 1984
Tigers 10, Mariners 1 (29-5)

The Mariners never had a chance in this one as five Tigers runs in the first put it out of reach. Eight Tigers drove in runs, and John Grubb hit his third homer of the season. Milt Wilcox improved to 5-0, pitching six innings of four-hit ball. Doug Bair, Willie Hernandez, and Aurelio Lopez each pitched a shutout inning to finish the game.

May 18, 1984
Tigers 8, Athletics 4 (30-5)

This game barely got past the fifth inning, but it had the makings of a high-scoring affair. The Tigers scored five runs in the first and scored in four of the five innings in which they batted. Lance Parrish and Kirk Gibson each drove in two runs, and Barbaro Garbey and Darrell Evans hit home runs. Dan Petry went the (truncated) distance to get his sixth win. He struggled, giving up seven hits and four runs. But the bats were there for him. A crowd of 41,136 came out to see the home team win its 30th of the season.

DETROIT TIGERS 1984: WHAT A START! WHAT A FINISH!

May 19, 1984
Tigers 5, Athletics 4 (31-5)

Jack Morris pitched into the eighth inning and improved to 8-1 as the Tigers rattled off their fifth straight win and their 12th win in their last 13 games. Morris had a tough time finding the plate as he walked six, but also struck out six. He got an assist from Aurelio Lopez, who picked up the save despite giving up a solo homer in the ninth inning. Lou Whitaker homered and drove in a pair of runs, and Darrell Evans went 3-for-4 with two RBIs.

May 20, 1984
Tigers 4, Athletics 3 (32-5)

Milt Wilcox improved to a perfect 6-0 as the Tigers finished up a sweep over the Athletics in a front of a home crowd. Wilcox surrendered two runs in his six innings of work while Willie Hernandez impressed with three innings of near-perfect pitching. He did yield a run on a solo shot, but it was the lone hit he gave up. Dwight Lowry hit his first career home run, and Johnny Grubb singled, drew a walk, scored, and drove in a run each.

May 22, 1984
Tigers 3, Angels 1 (33-5)

It's amazing how the great teams get exactly what they need to win. A few games ago, the Tigers needed a five-run first inning to beat Oakland. Good starts garnered them a sweep, despite some late-inning comeback attempts. And things didn't change here. If your offense scores only three runs, you're not likely to win the game. But Juan Berenguer and Aurelio Lopez combined for a five-hitter to give the Tigers their 33rd win of the season. Berenguer struck out nine batters in six innings to get his third win of the season. He walked three and gave up three hits, but only one Angel, Rod Carew on a solo shot, crossed the plate. Lopez shut out the Angels the rest of the way to lead the Tigers to victory. In Anaheim, 41,253 fans came out to see the Angels play the Tigers—on a Tuesday, no less. And with the win, the Tigers won their 15th straight on the road, one shy of the American League record.

May 23, 1984
Tigers 4, Angels 2 (34-5)

Lance Parrish hit a two-run home run in the seventh inning to lead the Tigers to their AL record-tying 16th consecutive road victory. Only the 1912 Washington Senators had won as many road games in a row as the 1984 Detroit Tigers. Dan Petry threw a gem of a game to pick up his seventh win. He walked two and gave up five hits, but the only real damage was the two-run shot he gave up to Doug DeCinces in the fourth inning. Willie Hernandez pitched two perfect innings and struck out the side in the ninth to pick up his seventh save.

May 24, 1984
Tigers 5, Angels 1 (35-5)

Jack Morris is one of those players who ends up in history-making situations. He was a part of it in 1984 as he won the game that crowned the Tigers' 35-5 start. Morris was shaky at the outset, giving up two hits and one unearned run in the first. He then gave up only two hits the rest of the way while ending up with 10 strikeouts. Alan Trammell's two-run homer in the fourth led to a four-run inning that put the Tigers up for good. Lance Parrish added a solo home run in the sixth. With the win, the Tigers improved to 35-5, the best start ever over the course of the first quarter of the season (and the best 40-game stretch ever). They broke an American League record with their 17th consecutive road victory, and also tied the 1916 New York Giants' major-league record for consecutive road wins. It was truly a memorable day, and the 35-5 start went down as possibly the single greatest accomplishment in franchise history.

May 25, 1984
Mariners 7, Tigers 3 (35-6)

It all had to end eventually. But to be sitting near the end of May, and to have just six losses, is quite an accomplishment in itself. The major-league consecutive road victory streak record remained intact, and has yet to be broken. Milt Wilcox never got on track in this one. He gave up three runs in the first two innings, and then gave up three more in the fifth inning. He drew his first loss of the season. The pen pitched well, but the Tigers couldn't put the runs on the board to come back. The only real hitting highlights were Alan Trammell's sixth home run and a double, and Darrell Evans putting up a two-hit, two-walk game.

May 26, 1984
Mariners 9, Tigers 5 (35-7)

This one was over early. Starter Juan Berenguer, who suffered from inconsistency throughout the season, managed to get only one out before getting pulled. In all, he gave up four runs. Three of the four Tigers relievers gave up runs in what could only be called a blowout. The Tigers fought back with three in the top half of the ninth, but they couldn't pull off the nearly impossible. Kirk Gibson hit his sixth home run, and Rusty Kuntz hit his second.

May 27, 1984
Mariners 6, Tigers 1 (35-8)

For the first time this season, the Tigers had a three-game losing streak. The lone run came on a solo homer by Chet Lemon, and while the Tigers picked up ten hits in the contest, the one run was all they got. Dan Petry dropped to 7-2 in a tough outing in which he gave up four runs and nine hits in just four innings. Aurelio Lopez didn't help out the cause, either. He gave up a pair of solo homers in his four innings pitched. This had to be one of the oddest series of the year. After coming off the high of the 35-5 start, the Tigers were swept in Seattle. And in all three games, Seattle beat Detroit pretty handily—mystifying in part because Seattle had gotten off to a sub-.500 (20-24) start at the time Detroit rolled up a 35-5 mark. Attendance was unusual for this weekend series. The Friday and Sunday games drew 15,722 and 12,755 for

DETROIT TIGERS 1984: WHAT A START! WHAT A FINISH!

the bookend games of the series, but 41,342 for the Saturday contest. Maybe they were giving something away in Seattle.

May 28, 1984
Tigers 6, Athletics 2 (36-8)

A four-run first sealed this one pretty early as Jack Morris didn't give the A's much to work with. He improved to 10-1, went the distance, and gave up only seven hits while striking out eight. On top of that, just one of the two runs he gave up was earned. Morris was definitely the Tigers' ace. This term gets thrown around a lot, but the standard definition should be a great pitcher who can stop a losing streak, someone who goes out and, no matter how badly the team is doing, gets a win. And that's exactly what Morris did here. He had his troubles later in the year (10-1 was his pinnacle of '84, as he went 9-10 the rest of the way), but the Tigers needed a win here to stop the three-game skid. Around this point the "30-win" talk began to heat up. Lance Parrish hit his eighth homer of the season. Alan Trammell went 3-for-4.

May 29, 1984
Athletics 8, Tigers 5 (36-9)

Oakland pummeled Milt Wilcox, who dropped to 6-2. He exited during the fourth inning with the score 6-1, with the A's scoring twice more (just one charged to Milt) before the carnage ended. Chet Lemon hit his ninth homer, and only one other Tiger, Barbaro Garbey, had an extra-base hit. Oakland's closer, Bill Caudill, earned his 10th save of the season. Oakland was a sub-.500 team, but using the benchmark save statistic for closers, you could make the argument that Caudill was more effective than either Willie Hernandez or Aurelio Lopez, both of whom had a lower save total. In fact, Caudill ended the season with 36 saves, four more than Cy Young Award and MVP-winning Willie Hernandez. Interestingly enough, two relievers finished in the top three of the MVP balloting in 1984. Hernandez, of course, won it, but Dan Quisenberry came in third. They also finished first and second in the Cy Young. Accordingly, 1984 was the only season relievers finished at the top of the ballots for either award.

May 30, 1984
Tigers 2, Athletics 1 (37-9)

Big players come up in big ways, and two big players came up big in this one. Juan Berenguer was cruising along, having given up just two hits through four innings. Then the wheels came off the wagon. An error and three walks—including a bases-loaded walk after Berenguer had issued an intentional pass to load the bases—allowed Oakland to score the game's first run in the fifth. Then with two outs and the bases still loaded, Captain Hook was true to form and brought in his horse, Willie Hernandez, from the pen. Hernandez got Mike Davis to ground out to end the inning and stop the damage. The Tigers answered immediately in the sixth. Barbaro Garbey tripled to lead off the inning. And then, with one out and Garbey at third, future Tiger Tony Phillips made an error that allowed Garbey to score and tie the game. Hernandez shut down the A's through the eighth, and in the top half of the ninth, with one out, Kirk Gibson homered to give the Tigers the lead for good. Aurelio Lopez finished the game to earn his seventh save.

June 1984
by Brian Borawski

June 1, 1984
Tigers 14, Orioles 2 (38-9)

At the beginning of June, the Tigers held a 5½-game lead over second-place Toronto, which was 32-15 (the second-best record in the majors) and were 10½ games ahead of the Baltimore Orioles, who sat at a respectable 28-21. Had the O's been in any other division, they would have been in first place (in the American League West by three games). They tapered off later in the year, but were in the midst of a five-game winning streak as they went off to Detroit to face the Tigers. In front of 47,252 fans, Dan Petry pitched six shutout innings, giving up only three hits. More importantly, he'd been handed a 13-run lead as the Tigers scored the most runs in a game so far in that season. They would match the 14 runs on August 20, but not surpass it. Alan Trammell, Chet Lemon, and Lance Parrish all hit homers with at least one man on base. The Tigers had a six-run lead after two innings, a nine-run lead after three, and a 12-run lead after four. Petry improved to 8-2, and Doug Bair earned his third save of the season. The save was of the three-garbage-innings variety. No offense to Bair, though, who continued to give the Tigers quality innings whenever they needed them.

June 2, 1984
Orioles 5, Tigers 0 (38-10)

Jack Morris never quite got on track, as he gave up at least one run in each of the first three innings. Nobody scored after that, but it was enough for Storm Davis, who pitched a complete-game three-hit shutout against the Tigers. Toronto won its game to sit only 4½ games back, with the Jays' first series against Detroit only two days away.

June 3, 1984
Orioles 2, Tigers 1 (38-11)

Another poor performance all the way around by the Tigers as Mike Flanagan pitched a complete-game seven-

DETROIT TIGERS 1984: WHAT A START! WHAT A FINISH!

hitter. The only ding against him was a solo shot by Tom Brookens, his first homer of the season. Milt Wilcox struggled, but kept Detroit in the game. He walked six in 5 2/3 innings. Dave Rozema finished the game by pitching 3 1/3 innings of one-hit ball. Tomorrow, the Tigers had their first season series against the Blue Jays, who were now 4½ games back of Detroit. The Tigers were mired in a slump that would have been considered impossible, as they lost six of nine after starting the season 35-5.

June 4, 1984
Tigers 6, Blue Jays 3 (10 innings) (39-11)

A couple of big blasts by some unlikely players gave the Tigers a much-needed win against the hard-charging Blue Jays. Starter Juan Berenguer pitched a decent but not great game, giving up three runs through 6 2/3 frames. Willie Hernandez was the pitching star, however. Even though he was brought in with a three-run deficit, unheard of for a closer in a game a score of years later, he got the Tigers out of a jam in the critical seventh inning. He ended up pitching three shutout innings to help the Tigers earn the win. The seventh inning was critical because in the bottom half, the Tigers came back. Third baseman Howard Johnson tied the game with a three-run homer. The game was tied at the end of nine, and in the bottom of the 10th, the Tigers struck again. Dave Bergman, the Tigers' role player and backup first baseman, came to bat with runners on first and second and two outs. He worked the count full against Roy Lee Jackson, then, according to Sparky Anderson, fouled off seven straight pitches. On the 13th pitch, Bergman hit what was probably the most memorable homer of his career into the upper deck in right field. In his book *Bless You Boys*, Sparky called it the greatest at-bat he had seen in his life. Great relief pitching and timely hitting. The Tigers widened their lead to 5½ games over the Jays, but they still had three more games to play in this series.

June 5, 1984
Blue Jays 8, Tigers 4 (39-12)

A six-run fourth inning and four home runs by the Blue Jays did the Tigers in. Starter Glenn Abbott couldn't make it through four innings, and the ever-reliable Doug Bair was hit hard as well. Detroit managed eight hits and eight walks, but only four men crossed the plate. Tom Brookens (double) and Larry Herndon (triple) had the only extra-base hits, and Kirk Gibson went 2-for-4.

June 6, 1984
Blue Jays 6, Tigers 3 (39-13)

The Tigers' losing ways continued, as they had now dropped eight of 12 since their torrid start. Dan Petry was shelled, giving up 10 hits in four innings, and the Jays had five runs on the board before the Tigers got one. Aurelio Lopez pitched four strong innings of relief to keep the Tigers in it, but like the day before, they couldn't get it done with men on base as they left 10 runners stranded. Venezuelan native Luis Leal improved to 6-0 for the Jays, impressive for a man who had only 51 career wins. Lou Whitaker went 3-for-5, and Howard Johnson was 2-for-3. At this stage of the season, the Tigers' lead now stood at 3½ games. We all know how this story ends, but at this point, there was some genuine concern. Fortunately for the Tigers, they'd go on a run, and this was the closest the Jays ever got.

June 7, 1984
Tigers 5, Blue Jays 3 (40-13)

When in doubt, put the ball in Jack Morris' hands. Nine innings, seven hits, and one walk was the final line as he improved to 11-2. The big blast of the night was by Ruppert Jones, who had made his Detroit debut the night before. Injury problems and a few rough seasons saw Jones on the chopping block at San Diego, and the Tigers signed him in April and sent him to Triple-A Evansville. He was brought up the night before, and in his June 6 debut he made a favorable impression on the Detroit faithful with a double, a walk, and a run scored. In the bottom of the sixth inning of this game, with the score tied, Jones continued his good work, taking starter Jim Clancy deep for a three-run shot to give the Tigers what they needed to win it. (During the season, Jones became known for his batter's box routine, which came to be called the Ruppert Jones Lumber Trance. He'd hold the bat up near his eyes and just stand there staring at the bat.) With the win, the Tigers left Detroit with a split of the series against the Jays, so they walked away with the same lead they walked in with. Three of the four games drew 35,000-plus to Tiger Stadium, which was pretty good for a weekday series. Now the Tigers had to go to Baltimore to face a team that had beat them twice the week before.

June 8, 1984
Tigers 3, Orioles 2 (41-13)

The Tigers beat the Orioles in front of 50,361 fans at Memorial Stadium. In a tight affair, Milt Wilcox threw six solid innings to win his seventh game, and the bullpen was stellar. The Tigers' pitchers gave up only six hits and three walks. Once Wilcox was taken out, Doug Bair threw a perfect seventh, and Willie Hernandez finished things by pitching two strong innings to earn his eighth save. The Tigers stranded 10 baserunners again, but this time it didn't cost them a win. Down 2-1, the Tigers scored two runs in the top half of the seventh on a double by Howard Johnson, an error by Orioles outfielder Jim Dwyer, and a sacrifice fly by Alan Trammell.

June 9, 1984
Orioles 4, Tigers 0 (41-14)

For the second time in a week, Mike Flanagan was too much for the Tigers as he pitched nine shutout innings, walking none, and giving up only six singles and a double. Aurelio Lopez was rocked. He gave up three hits and a walk while getting only one out. He was relieved by Carl Willis, who made his major-league debut and pitched 2 1/3 shutout innings. Starter Juan Berenguer was erratic, allowing four walks but striking out six in 5 1/3 innings. Barbaro Garbey went

DETROIT TIGERS 1984: WHAT A START! WHAT A FINISH!

2-for-4, and Chet Lemon had the Tigers' only extra base hit of the game, a ninth-inning double.

June 10, 1984, Game 1
Tigers 10, Orioles 4 (42-14)

This doubleheader seemed liked a big win at the time, but in retrospect it marked the point at which the Tigers continued to widen the distance between themselves and Toronto. They'd come to Baltimore with a 4½-game lead and left with a seven-game lead. Toronto pulled a little closer in the next week, and cut the Tigers' lead to six games in early July, but the 35-5 start gave the Tigers too strong a base to start with. Another tough outing by Glenn Abbott. He didn't make it through the third, giving up seven hits and three runs in 2⅔ innings. At the end of the fourth, the game was still tied, but then the Tigers' bats took over. Lou Whitaker, Alan Trammell, and Kirk Gibson, the Tigers 1-2-3 hitters, were a combined 8-for-13. Whitaker went 3-for-4 and scored five runs. Trammell was 2-for-4 with a double and triple, had four RBIs, and scored twice. Kirk Gibson went 3-for-5 and chalked up four RBIs. Four Orioles errors led to five unearned runs. Doug Bair hurled 3⅓ innings of one-hit ball to pick up his third win, and Willie Hernandez pitched three innings to chalk up his ninth save.

June 10, 1984, Game 2
Tigers 8, Orioles 0 (43-14)

In the nightcap of this twin bill, Detroit kept on piling up runs—3-0 through five innings, 4-0 through seven, then three runs in the eighth to leave no doubt. Dan Petry bounced back from his bad start on June 6 to throw a three-hitter. Alan Trammell, Kirk Gibson, and Howard Johnson each had three hits, and HoJo hit his fourth homer of the year. The turnstiles recorded 51,764 fans attending the doubleheader.

June 11, 1984
Tigers 5, Blue Jays 4 (44-14)

With the score tied at 3-3, Lou Whitaker hit a two-run homer in the fourth inning to put the Tigers up by a pair. It seemed like a modest lead, but it turned out to be the difference, although not without some nail-biting by Tigers fans. With two outs in the bottom of seventh, Willie Hernandez came in with that two-run lead and runners on first and third. Willie allowed the runner at third to score and cut Detroit's lead to one run, but he got the final seven Blue Jays out (three by strikeouts) to earn his 10th save of the year. With the win, the Tigers extended their lead to eight games.

June 12, 1984
Blue Jays 12, Tigers 3 (44-15)

Jack Morris was clobbered, and the bullpen followed suit with some equally bad pitching. This was the most runs the Tigers gave up in a game all season (matched in the lid-lifter of an August 7 doubleheader, but not surpassed). Three innings, eight hits, and six runs was the final line for Morris—by far his worst outing of the season. Sid Monge, picked up by Detroit on June 10, pitched four innings and gave up three runs, two of them earned. Even the reliable Aurelio Lopez gave up three runs in an eighth inning that by then didn't mean too much. Detroit hitting stars included Lou Whitaker, who was 3-for-4 with two RBIs. John Grubb went 2-for-4, and Howard Johnson was 2-for-3 and scored twice. Chet Lemon was the only other player to get a hit.

June 13, 1984
Blue Jays 7, Tigers 3 (44-16)

The Tigers ran into a brick wall in Dave Stieb and never really had a chance in this one. Stieb pitched seven shutout innings, giving up only three hits. It wasn't until the eighth inning, against relievers Jimmy Key and Dennis Lamp (and with some shoddy Toronto fielding), that the Tigers managed to get on the board with three runs, two of them unearned. Milt Wilcox threw five mediocre innings, and Doug Bair was lit up for three runs in his two innings of relief. No real hitting stars in this one, since the Tigers managed to get only seven hits, and nobody had more than one. The Tigers had a chance to really extend their lead, but by dropping the last two games, they gave Toronto some help. Six games was a nice cushion, but hardly insurmountable this early in the season.

June 15, 1984
Tigers 3, Brewers 2 (45-16)

The Tigers scored two runs in the top of the eighth inning to take the lead for good in this tight pitching matchup. John Grubb reached base on Rick Manning's error on a sacrifice fly and drove in the tying run, while Larry Herndon had an infield single with the bases loaded to drive in what proved to be the winning run. Lance Parrish hit his 10th home run while going 2-for-3, and Herndon also contributed two hits. Dan Petry pitched another fine game, throwing seven innings of seven-hit ball. Willie Hernandez nailed the door shut with two shutout innings to earn his 11th save.

June 16, 1984
Tigers 6, Brewers 0 (46-16)

Juan Berenguer was impressive, throwing what turned out to be his only complete-game shutout of the season. He pitched a five-hitter and never gave up more than one hit in any inning. Darrell Evans had the hot bat, hitting a three-run homer in the sixth, and adding another RBI with a sacrifice fly. Dave Bergman went 3-for-4, and Ruppert Jones had two hits, one of them his second home run of the season. The Blue Jays had also won their last two since the Detroit series, and remained six games back, close enough to cause concern.

June 17, 1984
Tigers 7, Brewers 4 (47-16)

Dave Rozema improved to 3-0 with a solid five innings of four-hit ball. Aurelio Lopez inherited a five-run lead, and although he wasn't stellar, picked up his eighth save by going four innings to finish the game. The Tigers did the bulk of their damage in the fifth when they scored five runs. Tom Brookens

DETROIT TIGERS 1984: WHAT A START! WHAT A FINISH!

had a two-run triple, and Barbaro Garbey stole home. Chet Lemon led the hit parade, going 3-for-5 and driving in two runs. The Tigers headed home with three straight wins to face a struggling Yankees team, and still maintained a six-game lead over Toronto. The AL East was a two-team race at this point as Baltimore had tapered off to 11½ games back (but still with a better record than the AL West-leading California Angels).

June 18, 1984
Yankees 2, Tigers 1 (47-17)

A crowd of 40,315 came out to see knuckleballer and eventual 300-game winner Phil Niekro shut down the Tigers to break their three-game winning streak. Despite pitching for the sub-.500 "Bronx Bummers," Niekro improved to 10-3 by throwing 8⅔ innings of three-hit ball. The only Tiger who crossed the plate was Kirk Gibson (he got two of the three hits), who hit a first-inning solo homer. Niekro's career was impressive. From 1977 through 1979, he threw no fewer than 330 innings in each season, something that would be unheard of today. He also led the league in hits allowed and runs given up. The Hall of Fame pitcher never won a Cy Young Award, but finished in the top six in the voting six times. In 1967, he led the league with a 1.87 ERA, throwing 207 innings in 46 games (20 starts, 26 relief appearances). He's 16th all-time in wins with 318, fourth in games started at 716, and fourth in innings pitched with 5,404⅓. The three players ahead of him in innings pitched all threw before 1928. And this day, he got the best of the Tigers. Milt Wilcox threw seven quality innings of seven-hit ball, but it wasn't enough.

June 19, 1984
Tigers 7, Yankees 6 (48-17)

This was another classic example of the bullpen bailing out the Tigers. With starter Carl Willis getting hit hard, Doug Bair came into the game in the fifth inning with Dave Winfield on base with one out, walked Oscar Gamble, and then retired the next two batters to limit the damage the Yanks had done against Willis (a two-run homer by Don Mattingly). Bair threw two more shutout innings before making way for Aurelio Lopez. Señor Smoke threw a hitless eighth, but started the ninth by giving up a walk, followed by a fly out, and another walk. Hernandez relieved with two on and one out. The first batter facing him reached base on an error, scoring one. The next batter grounded out, scoring another run, before Hernandez got the final out. Larry Herndon drove in the tying run with the bases loaded in the bottom of the eighth, and Rusty Kuntz followed it up with a two-run single to give the Tigers the lead for good. Lance Parrish and the Yanks' Don Mattingly both hit their 11th homers of the season. The Blue Jays finally lost, allowing the Tigers to extend their lead to 6½ games. Another 41,192 fans came out to Michigan and Trumbull to see the Tigers.

June 20, 1984
Tigers 9, Yankees 6, 13 innings (49-17)

The Tigers won a back-and-forth affair when Howard Johnson hit a three-run homer in the bottom of the 13th inning. The Yankees had a 2-0 lead and a 4-2 advantage before the Tigers picked up a run in the third and another in the sixth to tie it. Then they took turns scoring one run each until the game ended in regulation with the score tied 6-6. Willie Hernandez pitched four strong innings of relief, and Doug Bair improved to 4-0 by pitching two innings of one-hit ball. Alan Trammell, Lance Parrish, and Chet Lemon (4-for-5) all homered to go along with HoJo's extra-inning blast.

June 21, 1984
Brewers 4, Tigers 3 (49-18)

Don Sutton held the Tigers hitless for the first 4⅓ innings as he and two relievers combined for a four-hitter. The Tigers made a run in the seventh by scoring three runs, two coming from Larry Herndon's first home run of the year. From that point on, Rollie Fingers pitched 2⅓ innings of one-hit ball to shut down the Tigers. Other than Herndon's two-run blast, there wasn't much to note in this one other than Chet Lemon's doubling home the first run and being on base for Herndon's homer. Juan Berenguer pitched decently but not well enough for the win, while Sid Monge and Aurelio Lopez combined for 3⅔ shutout innings to give the Tigers a chance for a comeback that was not to be.

June 22, 1984
Tigers 7, Brewers 3 (50-18)

Well, it wasn't exactly a "full" house, but 48,497 fans showed up at Tiger Stadium to see the Tigers win their 50th game of the season. Five runs in the first inning and a solid if unspectacular six innings by Dave Rozema, who improved to 4-0, got the Tigers off to a nice start, and Willie Hernandez struck out five in 2⅓ innings of one-hit ball to earn his 13th save of the season. Kirk Gibson and Larry Herndon drove in two and Tom Brookens was 2-for-2.

June 23, 1984
Tigers 5, Brewers 1 (51-18)

The Tigers got off to a quick start, scoring all five of their runs by the end of the third inning. Kirk Gibson hit his ninth home run and Howard Johnson hit his sixth (another three-run blast). Milt Wilcox pitched a gem, going eight innings and giving up only four hits. The Brewers didn't score off him until the eighth inning, when Jim Gantner drove in Ed Romero with a sacrifice fly. Doug Bair pitched a perfect ninth to complete the combined four-hitter. At this point, despite their recent rough stretch, the Tigers were still on pace to win close to 120 games. And they were still drawing close to 40,000 per game.

June 24, 1984
Tigers 7, Brewers 1 (52-18)

Jack Morris had missed a couple of starts with a sore elbow, and the rest must have done him some good, as he bounced back nicely. He allowed just one hit over six innings to improve to 12-3, and Aurelio Lopez pitched the final three to earn his ninth save. In all, the Brewers only had three hits.

DETROIT TIGERS 1984: WHAT A START! WHAT A FINISH!

Lance Parrish went 3-for-4 and hit his 13th homer of the year, and Ruppert Jones, lumber trance and all, hit his third, a three-run poke in the sixth. With the win, the Tigers expanded their lead to 8½ games heading into a road series with the Yankees. It was a nice cushion that slowly grew over time as the Blue Jays themselves hit a rough patch.

June 25, 1984
Yankees 7, Tigers 3 (52-19)

This game was a tight pitching affair until the seventh inning. With the score tied 1-1 at that point, the Tigers scored two to take a 3-1 lead on Barbaro Garbey's second homer of the year. Then, in the bottom half of the inning, the Yankees took the lead with three runs. They added three more in the bottom of the eighth. Dave Winfield had a terrific game, going 5-for-5 and driving in four runs. Willie Hernandez had a rough outing, one of the few times he was hit hard during the 1984 campaign. Dave Winfield, the runner Hernandez inherited in the seventh inning, scored on a Tom Brookens error. Hernandez then gave up three runs in the eighth on two hits and three walks. Doug Bair took the loss to drop to 4-1.

June 26, 1984
Tigers 9, Yankees 7, 10 innings (53-19)

This was an exciting, if not exactly a back-and-forth affair. The Tigers started things off with four runs on five hits in the second inning, with the help of two wild pitches and a walk by Shane Rawley. The Yankees bounced back with three runs in the third, one in the fifth, two in the sixth, and one in the seventh to take a 7-4 lead. Then the 1984 magic happened once again. In the top half of the eighth, with two outs, the Tigers scored three runs to tie it up on singles by Alan Trammell and Darrell Evans. And in the top of the 10th, Lance Parrish hit a two-run homer to seal the deal. Willie Hernandez really bounced back in this game. After a poor performance the night before, he pitched $2^{2/3}$ innings to improve to 3-0 for the season. With the win, the Tigers had finally put a double-digit lead between themselves and the Blue Jays. Not even halfway into the season, they stood 10 games ahead of the nearest competitor in their division.

June 27, 1984
Yankees 5, Tigers 4 (53-20)

You definitely can't win them all, and this is one that the Tigers let get away. With a two-run lead, rookie Carl Willis gave up three runs in the bottom of the eighth inning (although two of them were allowed by Doug Bair, who inherited the runners) as the Tigers dropped the series. The Tigers had only five hits. Barbaro Garbey drove in two runs and scored one, and Chet Lemon drove in a run and scored as well. Tom Brookens had Detroit's other RBI.

June 29, 1984, Game 1
Twins 5, Tigers 3 (53-21)

Jack Morris was roughed up, surrendering 10 hits in $5^{2/3}$ innings. Doug Bair pitched $3^{1/3}$ innings of two-hit ball to give the Tigers a chance to come back, but it was too much to overcome as they hit the ball (11 hits), but couldn't get men across the plate. Lou Whitaker went 3-for-5, and Lance Parrish had a two-run double.

June 29, 1984, Game 2
Tigers 7, Twins 5 (54-21)

Another win for the bullpen. It's amazing how game in and game out, the relief corps allowed this team to get back into games. Milt Wilcox gave up five runs in five-plus innings, allowing the Twins to take a one-run lead. But the usual combo of Aurelio Lopez and Willie Hernandez slammed the door—after Lopez allowed an inherited runner score in the sixth—to let the Tigers come back to win this one. Lopez went $2^{1/3}$ innings, and Hernandez went $1^{2/3}$ himself to improve to 4-0. Kirk Gibson had a big day, hitting two homers and driving in four runs. Ruppert Jones and Chet Lemon hit solo shots.

June 30, 1984
Tigers 4, Twins 3 (55-21)

Dan Petry pitched $8^{1/3}$ strong innings, giving up three runs on seven hits while striking out 10, but it almost wasn't enough. Down 3-2, the Tigers tied the game in the seventh on a sacrifice fly by Ruppert Jones, and then scored the go-ahead run in the bottom of the eighth on a wild pitch by the Twins' Ron Davis. Willie Hernandez picked up his 14th save by getting the final two batters. Dave Bergman hit his second homer of the season, while Chet Lemon picked up two hits and scored a run.

July 1984
by Brian Borawski

July 1, 1984
Twins 9, Tigers 0 (55-22)

A very tough day for the home team, as the Tigers were beaten in just about every way imaginable. Frank Viola pitched a four-hit shutout, and Juan Berenguer was pounded in his five innings of work. Probably the oddest thing about this game was that backup outfielder Rusty Kuntz, who ended his career in 1985 with a .236 batting average in 441 at-bats, was in the leadoff spot, probably giving Lou Whitaker a night off against the lefty Viola. The Tigers had three four-game losing streaks during the 1984 campaign, and this was the beginning of the first one.

July 2, 1984
White Sox 7, Tigers 1 (55-23)

Two bruising losses in a row. Once again, neither the pitching nor the offense was there. The Tigers managed only one run on five hits, and starter Dave Rozema was sent to the showers after only four innings of work. Alan Trammell had two hits as the designated hitter. Sparky Anderson mentions in Bless You Boys that Tram's arm was bothering him at the time, so he played him at DH during this series. Doug Baker, who played bits and pieces of seven seasons for the Tigers and Twins, made his major-league debut in place of Trammell at shortstop.

July 3, 1984
White Sox 9, Tigers 5 (55-24)

This one was pretty ugly. Jack Morris gave up eight runs on nine hits in $4^{1}/_{3}$ innings after the Tigers scored three runs in the first on a three-run homer by Lance Parrish. Hall of Famer Tom Seaver got the win for the White Sox. Near the end of a Hall of Fame career, Tom Seaver went 15-11 in 1984, and won 16 games the following year. In 1986, he pitched for the AL pennant-winning Red Sox, but missed the postseason. Ruppert Jones and Howard Johnson also had home runs, and Kirk Gibson went 2-for-3.

July 4, 1984
White Sox 8, Tigers 2 (55-25)

The Tigers were no doubt happy to get out of Chicago. Three games. Three drubbings. Richard Dotson pitched eight innings of three-hit ball to shut down the Tigers. The Tigers opened the ninth inning with a home run and a double, but fell way short of a comeback. Milt Wilcox walked seven and gave up five hits and six runs, all in the sixth inning. Darrell Evans and John Grubb hit homers for Detroit to account for their two runs. Forty games after starting 35-5, the Tigers still stood at 30 games over .500. After a 40-game stretch of .500 ball, they stood seven games ahead of Toronto, losing 1½ games from where they were after the first 40 games.

July 5, 1984
Tigers 7, Rangers 4 (56-25)

Down 4-1 in the ninth, the Tigers scored six runs on five hits to pull it out. Even more amazing was that they scored all six runs with two outs. Lou Whitaker had a two-run single. Then Alan Trammell got a one-run single. The big blow was by the Tigers' Mr. Clutch, Kirk Gibson. He finished off the Rangers with a three-run blast. Knuckleballer Charlie Hough went the distance and took the loss. Dan Petry was hit hard, but the bullpen once again shut down the opponents to allow the Tigers a chance to come back. Doug Bair pitched $1^{1}/_{3}$ innings of no-hit ball. Aurelio Lopez yielded just one hit in his $1^{2}/_{3}$ innings to improve to 7-0, and Willie Hernandez got the final out of the game to earn his 15th save. The win put the Tigers at 56-25 at the halfway point of the season, on pace to win 112.

July 6, 1984
Rangers 5, Tigers 3 (56-26)

Juan Berenguer lasted only $2^{2}/_{3}$ innings, giving up five hits, two walks, and three runs. The Tigers' only runs came in the eighth inning on a three-run blast by Darrell Evans. Future Tigers manager Larry Parrish hit his 13th homer of the season for the Rangers, going 3-for-4. Berenguer dropped to 4-7. Aurelio Lopez followed Sid Monge's scoreless inning with a yeoman $4^{1}/_{3}$ innings of relief. The only other Tigers notable was Chet Lemon, who was 2-for-4.

July 7, 1984
Tigers 5, Rangers 2 (57-26)

A nice win. At this stage of the season, Dave Rozema was basically a fifth starter/long reliever. In this slot, you wouldn't have expected too much from him, but he threw a fine game, pitching six innings and giving up only one earned run. Willie Hernandez pitched the final three innings, surrendering only one hit and striking out five, to earn his 16th save of the season. Lance Parrish hit his 16th homer and scored twice. Ruppert Jones was 3-for-4, scoring once and driving in a run.

July 8, 1984
Rangers 9, Tigers 7 (57-27)

Doug Bair got his only start of the season, and got waxed. Jack Morris had been picked to pitch in the All-Star Game, so Sparky Anderson had to give him this Sunday off. Bair lasted only $2^{2}/_{3}$ innings, and by the end of the third, the Tigers found themselves down 7-0. An inning later, it was 8-2. The Tigers made a comeback, scoring four in the sixth and one in the seventh, but it wasn't enough. Chet Lemon was 2-for-5 with three RBIs, and Howard Johnson hit his eighth homer of the year and drove in three runs. It was the ninth win of the season for Detroit native—and future Tiger—Frank Tanana. After starting 35-5, the Tigers went into the All Star break still exactly 30 games above .500, meaning they had played .500 ball for games 41 through 74. They held a seven-game lead, but it still didn't seem enough.

DETROIT TIGERS 1984: WHAT A START! WHAT A FINISH!

July 10, 1984
National League 3, American League 1

The National League scored a run in each of the first two innings, and that's all they needed. Montreal catcher Gary Carter hit a home run off Dave Stieb in the second inning, and ended up the game's Most Valuable Player. Jack Morris blanked the National Leaguers in the third and fourth innings, allowing two hits and one walk while fanning two. Other Tigers notables included the following:

Lou Whitaker, 2-for-3
Chet Lemon, 1-for-2
Lance Parrish, 0-for-2
Willie Hernandez, 1 inning, 1 strikeout, gave up a solo homer to Dale Murphy

July 12, 1984
Twins 4, Tigers 2 (57-28)

Another tough loss, as a relatively strong pitching performance by Dan Petry was wasted. Petry went $7^{1/3}$ innings, giving up nine hits and four runs (three earned). The Twins' Frank Viola was better: eight innings, five hits, one run, and five strikeouts. This was Viola's breakout season.

July 13, 1984
Tigers 5, Twins 3, 11 innings (58-28)

Jack Morris and the usual suspects in the bullpen, Aurelio Lopez and Willie Hernandez, kept the Tigers in this one long enough for the bats to get going and win the game for them. Morris pitched one of his better games in a while, going $7^{1/3}$ innings, walking none, and giving up eight hits and three runs (one earned). The game was saved by Kirk Gibson, who threw Tim Teufel out at the plate with two out in the bottom of the ninth. Then in the top half of the 11th, Tom Brookens smacked a two-out triple and Lou Whitaker hit a two-run inside-the-park homer to put the Tigers up for good. Willie Hernandez improved to 5-0, and Aurelio Lopez earned his 10th save.

July 14, 1984
Tigers 6, Twins 5, 12 innings (59-28)

Chalk up another win for the bullpen. Starter Milt Wilcox pitched $5^{2/3}$ mediocre innings before leaving the game with the Tigers down 4-3. Doug Bair pitched $3^{1/3}$ perfect innings, and Willie Hernandez allowed one hit in three innings of work to earn his second win in as many games. With the Tigers down by a run in the ninth, Dave Bergman, pinch-hitting for Doug Baker, whacked a solo homer to send the game into extra innings. Then an RBI single by Chet Lemon and a sacrifice fly by Dave Bergman in the 12th put the game away. Tim Teufel homered with the bases empty off Hernandez in the bottom of the 12th, but it wasn't enough.

July 15, 1984
Tigers 6, Twins 2 (60-28)

Dave Rozema pitched $5^{1/3}$ strong innings and Aurelio Lopez pitched $3^{2/3}$ innings of one-hit ball to notch his 11th save of the season. Each pitcher had five strikeouts. Rozema had some nice years for the Tigers, but never reached his full potential. In 1977, he was the Tigers Rookie of the Year and The Sporting News' American League Rookie Pitcher of the Year after going 15-7 with a 3.09 ERA. That he struck out only 92 batters in $218^{1/3}$ innings hinted that this first season might have been an anomaly. He finished eighth in the Cy Young Award voting that year, but he never reached double digits in wins again. By 1984, Rozey was near the end of his career. He did have a fine season, as all the Tigers seemed to that year, playing the role of spot starter and long reliever for the Tigers, pitching 101 innings and winning seven while losing six with an ERA of 3.74. In this game, Lou Whitaker went 4-for-5 and Darrell Evans had three RBIs and a home run. Chet Lemon, Dave Bergman and Howard Johnson each had two hits.

July 16, 1984
Tigers 7, White Sox 1 (61-28)

Glenn Abbott pitched his best game of the season, throwing a five-hit complete game. Abbott was used as a fourth or fifth starter in certain situations, making eight starts in his 13 appearances. After a rough stretch, the Tigers ended up releasing him on August 14, 1984, ending his major-league career. Kirk Gibson was the hitting star, driving in three runs on a home run and a triple, and scoring two himself. Chet Lemon had two hits, and Lou Whitaker, Darrell Evans, Dave Bergman, and Ruppert Jones also drove in runs.

July 17, 1984
Tigers 3, White Sox 2 (62-28)

The Tigers scored three runs in the first inning on a sacrifice fly by Kirk Gibson and a two-run homer by Darrell Evans. Eight innings later, they were still sitting on the three-run lead, but it was just enough to walk away with a win. Dan Petry pitched another fine game. He went $7^{2/3}$ innings, and gave up five hits and one walk while striking out five to improve to 12-4. Willie Hernandez finished things up by throwing $1^{1/3}$ perfect innings, striking out three of the four batters he faced, to earn his 17th save.

July 18, 1984
White Sox 10, Tigers 6 (62-29)

It's not too often that your ace gets shelled to stop a nice winning streak, but that's what happened as Jack Morris gave up 10 hits and seven runs in four innings of work. Morris had last won a start on June 24, nearly a month earlier. Larry Herndon drove in three runs on a triple, and Lance Parrish hit his 18th homer of the season.

July 19, 1984
Tigers 9, Rangers 2 (63-29)

A three-run second inning put the Tigers up for good as they racked up nine runs on 13 hits, chasing starter (and future four-time 20-game winner) Dave Stewart in the fifth inning. Lou Whitaker was 3-for-5, Ruppert Jones went a perfect 4-for-4, and Lance Parrish and Kirk Gibson each hit home runs. Milt Wilcox threw a nice game, giving up only two runs in $7^{1/3}$

DETROIT TIGERS 1984: WHAT A START! WHAT A FINISH!

innings. The usual suspects, Willie Hernandez and Aurelio Lopez, finished the game.

July 20, 1984
Tigers 3, Rangers 1 (64-29)

Dave Rozema pitched eight solid innings, yielding six hits and one run to give the Tigers the win. Willie Hernandez garnered his 18th save with a perfect ninth inning. Future Tiger Frank Tanana pitched nearly as well, but he gave up a two-run homer to Barbaro Garbey in the third inning and a solo shot to Chet Lemon in the fourth. He went the distance, but took his ninth loss of the season. Lemon ended up with three of the eight Tiger hits.

July 21, 1984
Tigers 7, Rangers 6 (65-29)

Bullpen, bullpen, bullpen. Tigers starter Glenn Abbott was shelled in the third inning, giving up five runs and getting chased out of the game, but Sid Monge, who had been used only sporadically until now, pitched four innings of three-hit ball to let the Tigers come back. The Tigers got five runs in the bottom of the fifth to finish off the Rangers. Ruppert Jones had an RBI single, Chet Lemon a two-run double, and Howard Johnson a two-run single. Willie Hernandez pitched the eighth and ninth, giving up one hit and earning his 19th save.

July 22, 1984
Tigers 2, Rangers 0 (66-29)

Dave Bergman led off the Tigers' half of the first inning with a solo homer. It was all the Tigers needed. He also scored the Tigers' other run on a wild pitch. Dan Petry was simply outstanding. He pitched 8$^{2/3}$ innings, gave up only four hits and one walk, and struck out eight. Willie Hernandez got the final out of the game—on just one pitch—to earn his 20th save of the season. The sweep put the Tigers 37 games above .500, their best mark of the season thus far. They were near the end of the run in which they'd win 11 of 12, to increase their lead over the Blue Jays to nine games.

July 23, 1984
Tigers 4, Indians 1 (67-29)

The Indians gave Jack Morris a rough time, walking five times and getting five hits in six innings. But Morris kept everyone from crossing the plate. The Indians didn't score until the bottom of the ninth on a solo home run by Andre Thornton off Doug Bair. In back-to-bat at-bats in the first inning, Kirk Gibson hit his 15th homer and drove in two runs, and Lance Parrish belted his 20th home run, to lead the Tigers' offense.

July 24, 1984
Tigers 9, Indians 5 (68-29)

Milt Wilcox threw a nice game to win his 10th of the season, going 6$^{2/3}$ innings, giving up six hits, a walk, and four runs, all unearned. He left Willie Hernandez with a nice lead, and the future Cy Young and MVP winner finished things off. Lou Whitaker went 3-for-5 with three runs, and Kirk Gibson, Larry Herndon, and Lance Parrish each had two RBIs. Whitaker, Gibson, and Dave Bergman all homered. Doug Baker, Alan Trammell's fill-in while Tram was on the 15-day disabled list, was 4-for-5 and scored two runs batting ninth. The Tigers held an 11½-game lead over the Blue Jays, who had hit a rough patch. By now, the pennant race seemed little more than a formality even though there were two months left before the playoffs.

July 25, 1984
Indians 4, Tigers 1 (68-30)

Of course the Tigers couldn't win them all. Dave Rozema pitched a solid 6$^{1/3}$ innings, but Cleveland rookie Roy Smith shut down the Tigers. The only real damage was a solo home run by Darrell Evans in the second inning. Even with the loss, Toronto continued to struggle, so the Tigers remained 11½ games up. The final game of the series was rained out.

July 27, 1984, Game 1
Tigers 9, Red Sox 1 (69-30)

Another masterful outing by Dan Petry led the way for the Tigers. Dan went the distance on a six-hitter, with Rich Gedman's homer in the ninth inning spoiling the shutout. Chet Lemon hit his 14th home run, and Lance Parrish his 21st. The Tigers collected nine hits, one each by nine batters.

July 27, 1984, Game 2
Red Sox 4, Tigers 0 (69-31)

Bob Ojeda turned the tables on the Tigers as he surpassed Dan Petry's work in the first game. Ojeda pitched a three-hitter, striking out five. Glenn Abbott last only 3$^{1/3}$ innings, giving up 10 hits and four runs. The bullpen shut the Red Sox down, but the Tigers couldn't figure out Ojeda. Juan Berenguer, Sid Monge, Doug Bair, and Aurelio Lopez pitched shutout ball (2$^{2/3}$ innings by Berenguer). A 70-30 start would have been nice, but the Tigers fell just short. Another loss by the Blue Jays put the Tigers up by a season-high 12 games, though, so the team had to be feeling good about itself.

July 28, 1984
Red Sox 3, Tigers 2 (69-32)

The 70th win of the season kept eluding Detroit, as Jack Morris pitched his best game in a while but still came away with the loss. Morris threw seven innings, giving up eight hits and three runs (two earned) while striking out seven. But three Boston pitchers—starter John Henry Johnson and relievers Bob Stanley and Mark Clear—held the Tigers to two runs, while striking out ten. Lou Whitaker, Chet Lemon, and Kirk Gibson each had two hits. Whitaker hit his eighth homer of the year.

July 29, 1984
Tigers 3, Red Sox 0 (70-32)

Milt Wilcox threw a gem as he pitched eight shutout innings, giving up only three hits and walking none. Willie Hernandez earned his 21st save by tossing a perfect ninth.

DETROIT TIGERS 1984: WHAT A START! WHAT A FINISH!

The Tigers managed only four hits against Dennis "Oil Can" Boyd, but they made them count. Boyd struck out ten Tigers, and the only extra-base hit in the game was a triple by Ruppert Jones. Doug Baker and Lance Parrish had Detroit's two RBIs.

July 31, 1984, Game 1
Tigers 5, Indians 1 (71-32)

Juan Berenguer set the stage with 6 1/3 innings of four-hit ball. Doug Bair finished the game, retiring all five batters he faced while allowing the Tribe's only run to score on a Tony Bernazard groundout. Once again, a fine showing by the bullpen, and this time the usual Lopez-Hernandez tandem wasn't needed. The Tigers scored all five of their runs in the second inning. After singles by John Grubb and Howard Johnson and a walk to Dave Bergman loaded the bases, Doug Baker cleared them with a triple. Lou Whitaker's sacrifice fly scored Baker, and Ruppert Jones followed with a solo home run. Kirk Gibson had two hits.

July 31, 1984, Game 2
Indians 6, Tigers 4 (71-33)

Dave Rozema was rocked and left the game in the third inning. Despite an amazing pitching performance by Aurelio Lopez, the Tigers couldn't overcome a 6-1 deficit accumulated by the middle of the third inning. Lopez, ordinarily the Tigers' set-up man, started pitching in the third and finished the game, hurling 6 2/3 innings of shutout relief. He gave up four hits and one walk and struck out five. No triumphant comeback occurred in this one, although the Tigers tried. Larry Herndon went 2-for-3 with an RBI. Barbaro Garbey was 3-for-4 but didn't figure in the scoring (no RBIs, no runs scored). Other RBIs were by Lou Whitaker, Lance Parrish, and Howard Johnson. Having Bair, Lopez, and Hernandez—three quality arms—in the bullpen gave Sparky Anderson a ton of flexibility.

August 1984
by Brian Borawski

August 1, 1984
Indians 4, Tigers 2 (71-34)

A good pitching performance by Dan Petry went to waste, Peaches allowed three runs (two earned) on six hits, with one walk and five strikeouts, in 7 1/3 innings, but Cleveland's Steve Farr was better over 6 1/3 innings. Reliever Ernie Camacho finished things off, tossing one-hit shutout ball for 2 2/3 innings to pick up his 13th save. The Tigers managed only three hits, one of which was a two-run homer by Dave Bergman, his sixth. Tom Brookens made two errors at shortstop; one of them, dropping a foul fly by George Vukovich, gave life to the Tribe batter, who smacked a homer later that at-bat.

August 2, 1984
Tigers 2, Indians 1 (72-34)

Jack Morris bounced back nicely after a bad stretch of outings by throwing eight solid innings. He gave up seven hits, walked none and struck out one. The only damage against him was a solo homer by Andre Thornton. Bert Blyleven threw a nice game as well, but a two-run homer in the fifth by Lou Whitaker was all the Tigers needed.

August 3, 1984
Royals 9, Tigers 6 (72-35)

Milt Wilcox was cruising until the Royals hit him hard in the fourth. Before he could get anyone out in that inning the Royals were up 8-2, Wilcox was yanked and Aurelio Lopez was in the game. Lopez threw six innings of relief, but it wasn't enough. Lou Whitaker went 4-for-5, and Alan Trammell and Tom Brookens hit home runs.

August 4, 1984
Royals 9, Tigers 5 (72-36)

Glenn Abbott was hit hard again, giving up eight hits and four runs in 5 1/3 innings. Doug Bair and Sid Monge also were rocked, as the Royals scored nine runs for the second time in as many nights. Kirk Gibson was 3-for-5 and Ruppert Jones had three RBIs. Neither starter got a decision. Rookie Mark Gubicza pitched only 4 1/3 innings for the Royals. He'd eventually go on to have a nice career with the team, winning 20 games in 1988. They survived, but their lead over the Blue Jays once again dropped into single digits.

August 5, 1984, Game 1
Royals 5, Tigers 4 (72-37)

Playing one doubleheader can give a manager headaches. In fact, teams no longer played scheduled doubleheaders as they had in the past. But because of rainouts, the Tigers were forced to play not one, not two, but three consecutive doubleheaders, beginning today. They kicked things off with their third straight loss. Willie Hernandez gave up two runs in the ninth inning, his third inning of work, and suffered his first loss of the season. Dave Rozema had thrown six solid innings in which he gave up three runs on 10 hits and one walk with two strikeouts. Larry Herndon doubled twice and drove in a pair of runs while Alan Trammell was 1-for-3 with two walks, a run and an RBI.

August 5, 1984, Game 2
Royals 4, Tigers 0 (72-38)

The nightcap of the Tigers' Sunday doubleheader with the Royals didn't go any better. The Tigers were held to just

DETROIT TIGERS 1984: WHAT A START! WHAT A FINISH!

six hits in the shutout loss, their fourth straight defeat. Alan Trammell had two of the Tigers' hits, a double and single, and reached base a third time when he drew a free pass. No other Tiger reached base more than once, and the other four hits were all singles. Juan Berenguer pitched his second complete game of the season but fell to 5-8, giving up four runs on eight hits and two walks with eight strikeouts. All four runs came in the first inning, and the eight strikeouts were his second highest mark so far in the season.

August 6, 1984, Game 1
Tigers 9, Red Sox 7 (73-38)

Dan Petry didn't have his best stuff and gave up six runs (four earned) and 11 hits in only 4⅔ innings, but Bob Ojeda was just as bad, as the Tigers also scored six on the Red Sox starter. Aurelio Lopez pitched 2⅔ innings to improve to 8-0, and Willie Hernandez picked up his 23rd save. Chet Lemon and Lance Parrish knocked in three runs each and hit homers. Tom Brookens added a solo home run and scored two runs.

August 6, 1984, Game 2
Red Sox 10, Tigers 2 (73-39)

A drubbing, plain and simple. Carl Willis got one batter out before being pulled, and Doug Bair didn't fare much better. By the end of the fourth inning, the Tigers were down 9-1. Rookie starter Roger Clemens threw eight strong innings, holding the Tigers to six hits while striking out nine. Tom Brookens had the only multihit game, going 2-for-4, and Howard Johnson hit a solo home run.

August 7, 1984, Game 1
Red Sox 12, Tigers 7 (73-40)

Jack Morris was pounded. Coming off the best start he'd had in a while, Morris gave up six hits, two walks, and nine runs—including grand slams by Bill Buckner and Tony Armas—in 1⅓ innings, forcing Sparky Anderson to go to the bullpen early. The 12 runs coughed up equaled the most the Tigers gave up in one game in '84 (the other time was June 12). Bruce Hurst was hardly stellar, but when you're given a seven-run lead after two innings, there's not much you can do to lose the game. Alan Trammell and Howard Johnson each hit home run No. 10 and Lance Parrish added his 23rd. Kirk Gibson went 3-for-4.

August 7, 1984, Game 2
Tigers 7, Red Sox 5, 11 innings (74-40)

Milt Wilcox cruised through the first six innings, then gave up four runs in the seventh to give the Red Sox a 5-4 lead. Foreshadowing Boston's 1986 World Series debacle, Dave Bergman scored in the ninth on an error by first baseman Bill Buckner that sent the game into extra innings. In the top of the 11th Lance Parrish hit a two-run homer to give the Tigers the lead. Aurelio Lopez and Willie Hernandez combined for 4⅓ perfect innings while striking out seven. Parrish had two homers and three RBIs. Kirk Gibson and Larry Herndon also hit home runs.

August 8, 1984
Red Sox 8, Tigers 0 (74-41)

An error by Howard Johnson, playing shortstop in this contest, led to five unearned first-inning runs, and starter Glenn Abbott couldn't get out of the inning. Probably the strangest thing about the inning was that Abbott struck out Wade Boggs. Dennis "Oil Can" Boyd threw a complete-game seven-hitter. John Grubb (2-for-3) was the only Tiger to figure him out.

August 10, 1984
Tigers 5, Royals 4 (75-41)

It sounds like a broken record, but the usual suspects in the bullpen did it again. Dan Petry pitched 6⅔ innings, but left with the game tied 4-4. Aurelio Lopez and Willie Hernandez were nearly flawless the rest of the way, allowing Ruppert Jones to put the Tigers ahead with a solo home run in the eighth inning. Lopez improved to 10-0 and Hernandez saved his 25th game. The contributions Lopez and Hernandez made throughout the 1984 season were incredible. They threw a combined 278 innings, were a combined 19-4, and saved 46 games, all while striking out 206 batters and serving up two incredibly low numbers: a 1.054 WHIP (walks plus hits per inning pitched) and a 2.43 ERA. Those numbers were by far better than any of the starters achieved and shows why Hernandez got the support he did for the Cy Young Award.

Lance Parrish didn't hit for average in 1984, but he hit for power. His booming blasts led Mel Allen on "This Week in Baseball" to dub Parrish "The Big Wheel" of the Motor City's offense. (National Baseball Hall of Fame Library, Cooperstown, New York

DETROIT TIGERS 1984: WHAT A START! WHAT A FINISH!

August 11, 1984
Tigers 9, Royals 5 (76-41)

It wasn't his best outing of the year, but Jack Morris fell just one batter short of going the distance as he gave up five runs on 11 hits—three runs and five hits coming in the ninth inning. His 9-2 lead had become 9-5 and two runners were on base when Lopez entered the game to strike out the final batter and earn his 12th save. Larry Herndon, Lance Parrish, and Kirk Gibson all hit home runs, and Alan Trammell had four hits.

August 12, 1984
Tigers 8, Royals 4 (77-41)

A four-run first inning put the Tigers up for good. Milt Wilcox held the Royals scoreless through the first six innings. The Royals tagged Milt for three runs in the seventh, but the tandem of Aurelio Lopez and Willie Hernandez finished the game to give the Tigers the weekend series sweep. Ruppert Jones smacked a two-run homer, his ninth in an abbreviated season, and Alan Trammell was 2-for-5 with two RBIs.

August 14, 1984, Game 1
Angels 6, Tigers 4 (77-42)

The Tigers lost the first of two in a see-saw affair. The Angels took the lead three times, only to see the Tigers tie it up, but in the top of the ninth the Angels took the lead for good. A Doug DeCinces two-run single off Willie Hernandez was the winning blow, as Hernandez lost his second game of the season. Juan Berenguer pitched reasonably well, but for one of the few times this season, the Aurelio Lopez-Willie Hernandez combo didn't come through. Lopez gave up a run in his sole inning and Willie gave up his two while pitching two innings. Lou Whitaker, Alan Trammell, Howard Johnson, and Lance Parrish all hit home runs, and all but Johnson had two hits.

August 14, 1984, Game 2
Angels 12, Tigers 1 (77-43)

The 12 runs by California matched the Tigers' season worst for runs given up in a game—once on June 12 and again just a week prior, on August 7. Dave Rozema didn't get far in this outing. A seven-run third inning put the Angels up for good. Doug Bair was also shelled, and it seemed as if the Tigers' pitching had no chance. And there were no notables on offense. The Tigers spread out seven singles, and Darrell Evans drove in the only run. With the two losses, the Tigers' lead over Toronto had dwindled to 7½ games. What looked like a runaway race was tightening up quickly.

August 15, 1984
Tigers 8, Angels 3 (78-43)

At this stage of the season, with Jack Morris' struggles, Dan Petry had become the ace, seeming to come up with a win to put a stop to any kind of substantial losing streak. He pitched eight solid innings, giving up eight hits and three runs. The Angels had the lead once, going up 2-1 in the fourth, but the Tigers bounced back with two runs in the bottom half of the inning to take the lead for good. Willie Hernandez pitched a perfect ninth to finish off the Halos. Tom Brookens was 3-for-3 with two RBIs and Barbaro Garbey also went 3-for-3. Dave Bergman drove in three runs, and Kirk Gibson scored three times. It was a solid all-around performance by the team.

August 16, 1984
Tigers 8, Angels 7, 12 innings (79-43)

Some back-and-forth, wild and crazy games can be called roller-coasters. If that's the case, then this one was Millennium Force. The Tigers took a 5-0 lead after two innings, essentially giving Jack Morris some easy sailing. And he didn't take advantage of it. Two innings later Morris was gone and the Tigers were down 7-5, as once again, he struggled to get batters out. With the Tigers down 7-5 in the eighth, Alan Trammell drove in two with a single to tie the game. In the bottom of the 12th inning, Barbaro Garbey hit an RBI double to win the game. A sweet come-from-behind win. But give a huge dose of credit to the bullpen. Doug Bair, Aurelio Lopez, and Willie Hernandez combined for 8$\frac{1}{3}$ innings of three-hit shutout baseball as the Tigers salvaged a 2-2 split of the series.

August 17, 1984
Tigers 6, Mariners 2 (80-43)

The Tigers last opened a series against Seattle on May 25, the day after their heralded 35-5 start. The Mariners had gone on to hand the Tigers losses six, seven, and eight in a three-game sweep, and the Tigers got their revenge in this one. By the end of the third, the Tigers were up 4-0, and that was all they needed. Milt Wilcox pitched a nice game for his 13th win, giving up one run on seven hits in eight innings. Alan Trammell, Ruppert Jones, and Kirk Gibson all had two hits in this one as six different Tigers scored runs off starter (and future Tiger) Mike Moore. In *Bless You Boys*, Sparky Anderson mentions that this was the game in which the Tigers broke the attendance record set in 1968. For only the second time, they pulled in 2 million fans. They'd end up drawing 2,704,794, the Tiger Stadium record and a franchise mark that lasted until 2007. They'd draw 2 million three more times during the 1980s (1985, '87 and '88) and then wouldn't draw that many again until 1999, the final season at Tiger Stadium. Comerica Park's opening season brought 2 million fans to the ballpark, but it took Detroit's World Series season of 2006 to reach those heights again. In fact, the Tigers topped 3 million in 2007, 2008, and 2012.

August 18, 1984
Tigers 4, Mariners 3 (81-43)

This Tigers' current winning streak was the beginning of the end of any chance the Blue Jays had to catch up to them. With this win, the Tigers extended their lead to 11 games, with only a month and a half left in the season. Juan Berenguer had probably his best start of the season, throwing 8$\frac{1}{3}$ innings and giving up three hits and two earned runs (three total) while striking out 12. Two of the three runs came in the top of the ninth, when Willie Hernandez allowed inherited baserunners

DETROIT TIGERS 1984: WHAT A START! WHAT A FINISH!

to score on a pinch-single by Steve Henderson, but still earned his 26th save. The Tigers were held to five hits, but one was a three-run homer by Kirk Gibson. The home run was his 20th of the season, making this the first of five consecutive seasons in which he'd hit 20 homers and steal 20 bases.

August 19, 1984
Mariners 4, Tigers 1 (81-44)

Rookie starter Mark Langston shut down the Tigers, giving up four hits and one run in 8 1/3 innings and striking out 11. Langston led the league in strikeouts in his rookie campaign, and went on to do it again in 1986 and 1987. A fine game by Dan Petry was wasted, as he dropped to 15-6 while going the distance and giving up 10 hits while striking out 11 as well. Just to show how badly the offense was clicking, the Tigers' only run came when Langston walked Marty Castillo with the bases loaded.

August 20, 1984
Tigers 14, A's 1 (82-44)

Not even with the way Jack Morris had been pitching could he have blown this one. The Tigers scored 14 runs, tying their high-water mark of the season (set June 1), on 20 hits. Larry Herndon, Doug Baker, and Darrell Evans had three hits each, Kirk Gibson scored three times, and Chet Lemon drove in three runs. Lance Parrish, Chet Lemon, and Evans all homered. By the end of third, the Tigers had a 6-1 lead. With five in the fifth, they went into double figures. Morris won his 16th by pitching seven innings of three-hit ball, and Dave Rozema pitched two scoreless innings of relief.

August 21, 1984
Tigers 12, A's 6 (83-44)

For the second straight game, the Tigers' bats allowed the pitchers a virtual night off. Aurelio Lopez and Willie Hernandez each gave up two runs in an inning of work, but four runs in the first inning three in the third, and four in the sixth pretty much sealed this game early. Milt Wilcox pitched six solid innings, striking out seven and pushing his record to 14-7. Lance Parrish, Larry Herndon, and Darrell Evans hit home runs. Parrish's belt was a grand slam in the first inning, and Evans was 4-for-5, scoring three times and driving in three runs.

August 22, 1984
Tigers 11, A's 4 (84-44)

For the third straight game, the Tigers scored in double figures against the Oakland pitching staff. Barbaro Garbey, Alan Trammell, Marty Castillo, and Doug Baker each had two hits, and the Tigers scored all 11 runs without a homer. Detroit stole. Juan Berenguer pitched seven quality innings, giving up five hits and one run. With the win, the Tigers extended their lead to 12 1/2 games with 34 left. The only question on Tigers fans' minds was who their likely playoff opponent from the AL West would be. The Minnesota Twins held a 5 1/2-game lead over the Angels and Royals at this stage of the season.

August 24, 1984
Angels 5, Tigers 3 (84-45)

Dan Petry gave up four runs in the first inning, and that was the difference in the game. After the first he calmed down and finished the game, but home runs by Chet Lemon and Marty Castillo weren't enough for the Tigers to get the lead. Angels starter Mike Witt threw a nice game, going eight innings and giving up eight hits and three runs while striking out six. Kirk Gibson had a 3-for-3 day with a walk and one run scored.

August 25, 1984
Tigers 5, Angels 1 (85-45)

It was certainly nice to see Jack Morris put together back-to-back quality outings. In his 17th win of the season, Morris pitched eight innings and gave up nine hits and one run. Willie Hernandez pitched a perfect ninth to finish off the game. The big blow was a three-run homer by Ruppert Jones in the sixth inning. Darrell Evans hit a solo shot, and Lou Whitaker went 3-for-5.

August 26, 1984
Tigers 12, Angels 6 (86-45)

Kirk Gibson had a monster day, getting three hits, scoring four runs, and driving himself in twice on a pair of solo homers. Marty Castillo had three hits as s well, also scoring three times and homering with the bases empty. And Chet Lemon had the blow that set the stage for the win, a grand slam in top of the third. Milt Wilcox cruised to his 15th win, going six innings, striking out five, and surrendering five hits and three unearned runs. Doug Bair struggled, but by the time the Angels scored their first run, the Tigers had 11. Aurelio Lopez closed the game, retiring the final four batters in order.

August 28, 1984
Tigers 5, Mariners 4 (87-45)

Another great comeback win for the Tigers. With the game tied 1-1 in the bottom of the seventh and Juan Berenguer pitching, Seattle loaded the bases on a Howard Johnson error with two outs. The Mariners went on to score three unearned runs before newly acquired left-hander Bill Scherrer came in to get the final out. It didn't take long for the Tigers to bounce back. In the top of the eighth, Ruppert Jones led off with a double And Dave Bergman singled to put runners at first and third. Lou Whitaker drove in a run on a sacrifice fly, then Alan Trammell hit a two-run, two-out homer to tie the game. In the top of the ninth, Darrell Evans got a one-out single. Rusty Kuntz ran for Evans and moved to second on a wild pitch by reliever Mike Stanton. John Grubb struck out, and with two outs, Dave Geisel was brought in to face Ruppert Jones, who promptly drove in Kuntz with a double to give the Tigers the lead. Willie Hernandez pitched the eighth and ninth, giving up only one hit to improve to 8-2. The day before, Bill Lajoie pulled the trigger and got Sparky Anderson another left-handed arm in the pen. For cash and a player to be named (Carl Willis), the Tigers acquired Scherrer from the Cincinnati

DETROIT TIGERS 1984: WHAT A START! WHAT A FINISH!

Reds. He gave the Tigers a much-needed relief option, and ended up throwing 19 innings with an ultra-low 1.89 ERA.

August 29, 1984
Mariners 5, Tigers 1 (87-46)

A week and a half before, rookie starter Mark Langston shut down the Tigers with a four-hit, 11-strikeout performance over 8 1/3 innings. This time he did himself one better, pitching a two-hit complete game and striking out 12 Tigers. Dan Petry was the opposing pitcher the last time the Tigers faced Langston, and a nice outing was wasted. This time he didn't fare as well, but it really didn't matter because Langston was on his game. Petry was gone by the end of the fifth inning and suffered his eighth loss of the season. At one point the Tigers actually had the lead in this game. In the top of the second, Rusty Kuntz drove in Lance Parrish with a single for the Tigers' lone run.

August 30, 1984
Mariners 2, Tigers 1 (87-47)

Starters Jack Morris and Jim Beattie both took shutouts into the eighth inning. In the bottom of the inning the wheels came off for Morris as the Mariners scored their two runs without a hit. Spike Owen led off with a walk. Second baseman Jack Perconte laid down a bunt, and according to Retrosheet, Morris dove for the pop-up, missed it, and threw the ball into right field while sitting down. To make matters worse, Kirk Gibson picked up the ball and threw it into the Mariners' dugout trying to get Perconte at third base. Morris pitched a great game. He went the distance, gave up only four hits, and struck out eight. The Tigers tried to answer in the ninth. Barbaro Garbey and Larry Herndon walked and Howard Johnson singled to load the bases, but the Tigers got just one run, on a walk to Alan Trammell. Kirk Gibson grounded to second to end the game.

August 31, 1984
A's 7, Tigers 6, 13 innings (87-48)

Milt Wilcox struggled as he walked five batters and gave up four hits in 3 2/3 innings. By the time he left the game the A's were up 5-4. The Tigers tied it in the fifth on a homer by Alan Trammell. With the score tied 5-5 each team scored a run in the ninth to put the game into extra innings. In the bottom of the 13th, Athletics right fielder Mike Davis scored with two out on a Dave Rozema wild pitch to win the game. Once again, the usual combo of Aurelio Lopez and Willie Hernandez kept the Tigers in this one and at least gave them a chance to win. Combining for 8 1/3 innings, they gave up only three hits and one run, while striking out eight. The loss once again dropped the Tigers into a single-digit lead over the Blue Jays. With 27 games left, they were 9 1/2 games ahead of Toronto.

September 1984
by Brian Borawski

September 1, 1984
A's 7, Tigers 5 (87-49)

This one was over pretty quickly, as Juan Berenguer couldn't escape Oakland's hitting and his own less-than-stellar pitching. By the end of the first inning, he was gone, with the Tigers down 6-0. Berenguer gave up three hits and issued three walks in two-thirds of an inning, with a stolen base, sacrifice fly, and a Lance Parrish passed ball thrown in. Doug Bair and Bill Scherrer pitched 7 1/3 great innings of relief, holding Oakland to one more run, but the Tigers couldn't eliminate the deficit. Lou Whitaker and Rusty Kuntz each drove in two runs, and Barbaro Garbey scored twice. Chuck Rainey, relieving starter (and Saginaw native) Curt Young, did his best Willie Hernandez impersonation, and held the Tigers scoreless in 3 1/3 innings of relief. Toronto won, so the lead now stood at 8 1/2 games. A nice cushion, but after losing four straight, Sparky Anderson and the boys hardly felt secure.

September 2, 1984
Tigers 6, A's 3 (88-49)

Dan Petry gave up 11 hits in 5 1/3 innings, but let only three A's cross the plate as the Tigers topped Oakland. Detroit put four runs on the board in the third inning and that was enough to win the game. Aurelio Lopez pitched 1 2/3 innings of one-hit ball, stranding the two runners he inherited from Petry in the sixth, and Willie Hernandez threw two perfect innings to earn his 27th save. Lance Parrish drove in two runs, and Barbaro Garbey hit his fifth homer of the season.

September 3, 1984
Orioles 7, Tigers 4 (88-50)

Jack Morris hit some bumps in the road, giving up nine hits and four walks, and throwing a wild pitch in the first seven innings, before hitting a deep pothole in the eighth as he loaded the bases. Aurelio Lopez, coming into the game with two out, coughed up a grand slam to Mike Young. Darrell Evans hit his 14th homer, while Alan Trammell, Howard Johnson, and John Grubb each collected two hits.

September 4, 1984
Orioles 4, Tigers 1 (88-51)

Captain Hook was true to form as Dave Rozema gave up back-to-back singles, a sacrifice fly to Cal Ripken Jr., and a third single before Sparky Anderson pulled the plug in the first inning. Bill Scherrer came in to stop the damage, as he got the final two batters out. But after he walked leadoff batter

DETROIT TIGERS 1984: WHAT A START! WHAT A FINISH!

Wayne Gross in the second, Sparky went to rookie Roger Mason, making his major-league debut. Mason pitched the rest of the way, giving up five hits and striking out six. One of those hits was a two-run circuit clout by Rick Dempsey. Alan Trammell and Howard Johnson each had two hits. Rookie Nelson Simmons, also making his major-league debut, drove in the only run for Detroit. With the loss, the Tigers' lead was cut to 7½ games. With a series against the Jays coming up, things were looking pretty dicey, and the fans had to be a little worried.

September 5, 1984
Tigers 1, Orioles 0 (89-51)

In the bottom of the first inning, Alan Trammell scored on an error by Cal Ripken Jr. That was the game's only scoring. Orioles starter Mike Flanagan pitched a fine game, going the distance and giving up six hits and the one unearned run. Juan Berenguer was just a little bit better, as he pitched 7⅓ innings of two-hit shutout ball. Willie Hernandez came in to finish the game, earning his 28th save in the process. The Jays lost, so the Tigers increased their lead to 8½ games. With a day off before facing the Blue Jays in a three-game series, the Tigers' magic number stood at 15.

September 7, 1984
Tigers 7, Blue Jays 4, 10 innings (90-51)

Up 4-0, future Tiger Doyle Alexander of the Blue Jays was cruising along until the top half of the eighth inning. Dave Bergman doubled to lead things off. John Grubb grounded out to short. Lou Whitaker drew a walk and Alan Trammell flied out to right. Then Kirk Gibson hit a three-run blast to cut the lead to one. Lance Parrish drew a walk. Jimmy Key relieved Alexander, and pinch-hitter Barbaro Garbey singled. Key was relieved by Roy Lee Jackson. Larry Herndon, also in a pinch-hitting role, walked to load the bases. Then Chet Lemon drew a bases-loaded walk to tie the game, 4-4. Willie Hernandez came in and neither team scored until the tenth, when Dave Bergman—shades of June 4—hit a three-run homer off Blue Jays reliever Ron Musselman. Hernandez walked one in the bottom half of the 10th, but that was all Toronto could do as he earned his ninth win. With the victory, the Tigers' magic number was 13. They controlled their own destiny; they just had to fulfill it.

September 8, 1984
Tigers 10, Blue Jays 4 (91-51)

This game was cruising along, tied 2-2 going into the seventh, when the Tigers got two runs in the seventh and exploded for six in the eighth. Jack Morris left the game with the bases empty and one out in the fifth with the score tied at 2-all. Bill Scherrer took over and pitched an inning and two-thirds. Aurelio Lopez finished the game, going three innings and giving up two meaningless runs in the bottom of the ninth while earning his 13th save. Alan Trammell went 3-for-5 with three RBIs, John Grubb hit two solo homers and scored three times, and Darrell Evans had a solo four-bagger. The win cut the Tigers' magic number to 11.

September 9, 1984
Tigers 7, Blue Jays 2 (92-51)

Another late-inning surge pushed the Tigers past the Blue Jays. With Detroit up 3-2, Kirk Gibson hit a three-run homer in the top of the seventh to give the Tigers a nice cushion. John Grubb added a bases-empty homer. Milt Wilcox gave Detroit six solid innings before letting the bullpen close out the game; Bill Scherrer and Willie Hernandez combined for three no-hit innings. The Tigers had been struggling before coming into Toronto, but they really came through when it counted. With a magic number of nine, they had a realistic chance of clinching the division by the following weekend.

September 10, 1984
Orioles 3, Tigers 1 (92-52)

For the second time in a week, Mike Flanagan shut down the Detroit bats. Kirk Gibson hit his 26th homer and had two of the Tigers' five hits, and was the only Tiger to cross the plate. A good outing by Juan Berenguer went to waste, as he pitched seven decent innings, and not even three Detroit double plays could bail him out. The Blue Jays matched the Tigers by losing, so the magic number was now eight. The Tigers could split half of their remaining 18 games and it wouldn't matter if the Jays won every one of theirs. It was that close to being over.

September 11, 1984
Tigers 9, Orioles 2 (93-52)

This game was scoreless through four innings before the Tigers exploded for five runs in the fifth. Larry Herndon had a big day, going 3-for-3 and driving in three runs. Kirk Gibson was 3-for-5 and Darrell Evans was 4-for-4 and hit his 16th homer of the season. Dan Petry worked 6⅔ innings, giving up five hits and two runs while fanning six. Doug Bair and Willie Hernandez finished the game, allowing just one baserunner between them. Toronto was also victorious, but the Tigers' magic number was cut to seven.

September 12, 1984
Orioles 3, Tigers 1 (93-53)

Orioles starter Dennis Martinez shut down the Tigers, as he gave up only six hits and one run while going the distance. Chet Lemon scored the Tigers' only run on a wild pitch. Roger Mason made his first career start, going four innings and giving up three runs. Randy O'Neal made his major-league debut in relief of Mason, pitching three solid innings of one-hit ball. The Blue Jays won again, so the Tigers' magic number remained at seven.

September 14, 1984
Blue Jays 7, Tigers 2 (93-54)

Jack Morris limped through another rough outing and fell to 17-11. It was Morris' third loss in a row, and in this one, he gave up five runs on seven hits and three walks in six innings.

DETROIT TIGERS 1984: WHAT A START! WHAT A FINISH!

Three of the seven hits left the park, and Bill Scherer didn't fare much better out of the pen. He gave up a pair of runs in his one inning of relief. Lou Whitaker was Detroit's hitting star, playing a role in both of the Tigers' runs. He finished 2-for-4 with one run scored and one RBI. The Jays had lost the night before while the Tigers were idle, so the magic number was down to six, where it remained after the Detroit loss this day.

September 15, 1984
Tigers 2, Blue Jays 1 (94-54)

What a performance by Milt Wilcox to pick up his 17th and final win of the season: seven innings, one hit, one walk, and eight strikeouts. The only blemish was a solo home run in the top of the second by George Bell. Willie Hernandez finished the game by pitching the eighth and ninth innings to earn his 29th save of the season. Ruppert Jones was the batting hero. With the game tied in the fourth, he hit a solo homer to put the Tigers up for good. With the win, the Tigers cut their magic number to four.

September 16, 1984
Tigers 8, Blue Jays 3 (95-54)

This one was over quickly as the Tigers struck for seven runs in the first three innings. Six Tigers drove in runs, and seven scored. Marty Castillo, Tom Brookens, and Larry Herndon all hit homers. Four Detroit pitchers combined to hold the Jays to six hits and three runs (two earned). Juan Berenguer pitched five good innings to earn his ninth win. The Tigers took the series and essentially won the division with two nice performances against their closest rivals. They drew more than 135,000 fans for the three-game series, as Tigers fans everywhere were celebrating. And, if you're counting, the Tigers' triumph over the Jays cut the magic number to just two.

September 17, 1984
Tigers 7, Brewers 3 (96-54)

The Tigers easily handled the Brewers, but had to wait at least another day to celebrate, as the Blue Jays beat the Red Sox. The Tigers' magic number was now down to one. Roger Mason pitched six quality innings. The rookie gave up six hits and two runs, striking out four. Lance Parrish hit his 30th home run; he ended the season with 33. Lou Whitaker's 11th homer was a grand slam off Jack Lazorko.

September 18, 1984
Tigers 3, Brewers 0 (97-54)

It was time to celebrate as the Tigers won their first division title since 1972. Randy O'Neal and Willie Hernandez combined for a six-hit shutout, Lance Parrish drove in two runs, Alan Trammell had two doubles and scored a run, and Tom Brookens put the dot on the exclamation point with a solo homer to close the scoring. The Royals held a razor-thin margin over the Twins and the Angels in the AL West, so the Tigers' opponent in the first round still wasn't clear.

September 19, 1984
Tigers 4, Brewers 2 (98-54)

Although the rest of the regular season was largely meaningless, the Tigers had a few more things to play for. One hundred wins was within their reach. Only four times previously had the Tigers won 100 games: 1915, 1934, 1961, and 1968. Only the '34 and '68 teams won pennants. They also had a shot at the 1968 team-record 103 wins. Jack Morris took them one step closer to both of those marks with a typical Morris performance—nine hits in six innings including a Roy Howell solo homer—but it was more than enough to pick up his 18th win of the season. It was nice to see how well he pitched down the stretch of what for him was an up-and-down season. After scoreless relief innings from Bill Scherrer and Dave Rozema, Willie Hernandez pitched a shutout ninth inning to earn his 31st save. Sparky Anderson was also trying out some of the kids. Nelson Simmons made the most of his start in right field by going 3-for-4. Howard Johnson scored twice as part of a 2-for-4 game.

September 21, 1984
Yankees 5, Tigers 3 (98-55)

The Tigers got off to a hot start, scoring three runs on an Alan Trammell homer and a Ruppert Jones double. All three runs came off starter John Montefusco, but that's all they got in the game as they collected just three more hits the rest of the way. Milt Wilcox gave up three in the third and two more (one unearned) in the sixth. He gave up only five hits, but walked five en route to the loss.

September 22, 1984
Tigers 6, Yankees 0 (99-55)

After Jack Morris' no-hitter, Dan Petry had probably the best starting performances for the 1984 Tigers. And he saved some of his best stuff for last, as he went the distance, gave up only four hits, and struck out nine. He won his 18th of the season in what was his next-to-last start of the regular season. Chet Lemon drove the biggest nail into the coffin by hitting a three-run blast in the bottom of the eighth inning. Lou Whitaker and Alan Trammell each had two hits.

September 23, 1984
Tigers 4, Yankees 1 (100-55)

It seemed fitting that both Jack Morris and Willie Hernandez would be key in the Tigers' 100th victory. Morris pitched six shutout innings of two-hit ball before handing the ball to Bill Scherrer. After Scherrer pitched a perfect seventh inning, Willie Hernandez finished the game, pitching the eighth and ninth. He gave up an unearned run in the eighth but earned his 32nd and final save of the season. Marty Castillo was 2-for-3 with a solo shot and two RBIs. Kirk Gibson added a solo homer, his 27th of the season. And for the first time since 1968, the Tigers won 100 games. Tiger Stadium rocked with 39,198 fans who made it out to see the Tigers get it done once again.

DETROIT TIGERS 1984: WHAT A START! WHAT A FINISH!

September 24, 1984
Tigers 7, Brewers 3 (101-55)

Juan Berenguer joined Jack Morris, Milt Wilcox, Dan Petry, and Aurelio Lopez as pitchers on the Tigers' staff who won 10 or more in 1984. He pitched five solid innings, giving up only five hits and one run, before yielding to the bullpen. And Dave Rozema, Doug Bair, Bill Scherrer, and Lopez each pitched an inning of relief, with only Bair allowing runners to cross the plate on a two-run seventh-inning home run by Robin Yount. Chet Lemon smacked his 20th homer of the season, and Lou Whitaker hit his 12th. Dave Bergman was 3-for-5 with a run, Ruppert Jones was 2-for-3 with an RBI, Nelson Simmons went 2-for-4 with a run scored, and Doug Baker was 2-for-4, with a run scored and an RBI.

September 25, 1984
Tigers 9, Brewers 1 (102-55)

Four runs in the first inning put this game away quickly as Howard Johnson hit a grand slam, his 12th homer of the season. Lance Parrish hit a solo homer in the third, and the Tigers coasted to their 102nd win of the season. Sparky Anderson went with the rookies on the mound, and Randy O'Neal improved to 2-0 by pitching five shutout innings, giving up only two hits and striking out three. Sid Monge, Bill Scherrer, Aurelio Lopez, and Willie Hernandez pitched an inning apiece, the Brewers tagging Lopez for a run in the eighth. The Brewers got only six hits. And now the Tigers stood one short of the record 103 wins set by the 1968 team. With five games left, the record was within reach.

September 26, 1984
Brewers 7, Tigers 5 (102-56)

The Tigers would have to wait for another game to have a shot at tying the 1968 team's 103 wins, and for one of the few times this season, it was the bullpen that was to blame. Milt Wilcox cruised through the first five innings, giving up only one run on four hits. Roger Mason gave up two runs in the sixth to narrow the Detroit lead to 4-3. Then with the Tigers up 5-3 in the bottom of the eighth, Aurelio Lopez gave up four runs on three hits (including a two-run double by former Tiger Ben Oglivie) and two walks. After 68 games and 135 1/3 innings pitched, Lopez finally lost a game. Chet Lemon's three hits were a home run short of the cycle. Rookie Nelson Simmons added two RBIs in going 3-for-5. Dwight Lowry went 2-for-3 with two RBIs and a run scored.

September 27, 1984
Yankees 2, Tigers 1 (102-57)

The duo of Willie Hernandez and Aurelio Lopez lost four games all season. Two were in the final week of the season—consecutive games at that. Good from the standpoint of how dominating they were for so long, but not good from the standpoint of Sparky Anderson's being worried about his best arms going out on him. Lance Parrish had given the Tigers a 1-0 lead in the fourth inning on his 32nd home run, off starter Bob Shirley. Jack Morris had one his best starts in a long time—possibly his best start of the season outside of the no-hitter. He pitched seven innings of two-hit ball. Six walks came back to haunt him, though, as the Yankees' Bobby Meacham walked in the sixth, and was eventually driven in by Dave Winfield to tie the game at 1-1. In the bottom of the eighth, Meacham scored again on a single by Don Baylor off Hernandez. Darrell Evans had a chance to put the Tigers ahead in the ninth inning, but he flied out with runners on first and second with two outs. The Tigers had to split the series to exceed the 1968 team's 103 victories, and they got off to a tough start. Now they had to win two of three.

September 28, 1984
Tigers 4, Yankees 2, 12 innings (103-57)

The Tigers tied the team record with their 103rd win of the season. They scored their first run with no outs in the first when leadoff batter Rusty Kuntz doubled and Barbaro Garbey singled. Dave Winfield drove in the tying run in the sixth with a double off Dan Petry. Petry pitched six solid innings before giving way to the bullpen after the sixth. The Tigers regained the lead in the seventh on an RBI single by Lance Parrish, but in the bottom of the eighth, the Yankees tied it up again on a sacrifice fly by Bobby Meacham. Doug Bair did the job in this game by pitching four shutout innings, giving up no hits and two walks, and the Tigers tagged reliever Joe Cowley in the 12th inning on a two-run blast by Lou Whitaker. Bair pitched a scoreless 12th inning to pick up his fifth win. The Tigers ended the game with 16 hits, left 17 men on base. The Tigers had two more chances to set a franchise win record, and they had to do it on the road.

September 29, 1984
Tigers 11, Yankees 3 (104-57)

With a strong offensive performance, and with only one game left in the season, the Tigers won their 104th game, setting the franchise record for victories. The game was close until the sixth, when the Tigers scored five runs in the sixth inning to break open a 1-1 tie. They added five more in the ninth to seal the win. Juan Berenguer pitched a gritty game to improve to 11-10. He went six innings, giving up only one run on two hits, but six walks were a concern. He got out of bases-loaded jams in the second and the third innings to come away with a winning record for the season. Roger Mason finished the game, going three innings and earning his first career save. Larry Herndon, Lance Parrish, and Dwight Lowry hit home runs and Howard Johnson hit a three-run double. Herndon went 3-for-5 with two RBIs and three runs scored. Parrish was 2-for-4, and his two-run homer was his 33rd. Rusty Kuntz had two hits and a walk, with one RBI and one run scored. It was a historic day for the franchise, and fitting for what most people felt was the Tigers' greatest season ever.

September 30, 1984
Yankees 9, Tigers 2 (104-58)

Sparky Anderson rested most of his starters and gave his bullpen a final tune-up game before the playoff run. Starter

Randy O'Neal was tagged for seven runs and didn't escape the fourth inning. The Yankees scored in three of the four innings in which he pitched. Doug Baker and Barbaro Garbey drove in the Tigers' runs. The bright spot of the game for the Tigers was the shutout pitching of Aurelio Lopez, Bill Scherrer, and Willie Hernandez from the sixth through the eighth. With the loss, the Detroit Tigers' regular season ended. They'd be playing in the postseason for the first time since 1972, when they lost to the Oakland A's in the AL Championship Series.

The Players
Glenn Abbott
by Clifford Corn

GLENN ABBOTT is filled with stories and memories and good feelings about his days in the major leagues.

The former American League pitcher is forthright, open, and honest as he conjures up a past filled with recollections of warm summer days in big-league cities around the country. And although he played his last big-league game in August 1984—when the Detroit Tigers cut him after a terrible stretch following the All-Star break—he continues to make his presence felt in the game he loves by coaching up-and-coming young arms in the Pacific Coast League.

Abbott's tale is a long and interesting one: a leap from being a member of the World Series-winning Oakland A's of the 1970s to the expansion Seattle Mariners to the impressive Tigers teams of 1983 and '84.

William Glenn Abbott was born on February 16, 1951, in Little Rock, Arkansas.

"When I was a kid, everybody played baseball," he told an interviewer in 2008. "I always loved it. When I was 14 or 15, we'd ride bicycles over to the baseball fields and would play a little workup or something and then help prepare the field. It's just what kids did then.

"The Cardinals were big in Little Rock. I can remember when Dick Allen came to Little Rock; he was the first black to play there. I remember Ferguson Jenkins and guys like that who played there.... I've always loved it and played the game. This is not a job to me. I really enjoy what I do. It's my 39th season, and I love it. I like working with the young kids."

In his early days with the sport, Abbott played the infield and caught as well as pitched.

That changed when he entered high school. "I realized that I had the chance to go on beyond high-school ball," he said "I realized that I had some ability and didn't want to take a chance of breaking a finger or something like that."

Abbott played baseball and basketball in high school and had planned to continue with both sports in college. But he was drafted out of high school in the eighth round by the Oakland A's in June 1969, and signed immediately. He was 18 years old. For a couple of years during the offseason, he attended State College of Arkansas, now called the University of Central Arkansas. He made the big leagues when he was 22 years old.

Starting in the Rookie-classification Northwestern League, Abbott quickly worked his way through minor-league ball and made his debut with Oakland on July 29, 1973, when he started against the Texas Rangers. He was taken out in the fourth inning with Oakland leading, 4-2, and Texas runners on second and third (the A's eventually won, 7-4).

Though Abbott's major-league pitching record was just 62-83, he had his moments.

September 28, 1975, the last game of the season, was a good example. Abbott was the second of four pitchers who combined to throw a no-hitter against the California Angels. Abbott pitched one inning and retired the side in order.

Abbott said the A's were preparing for the playoff series against the Boston Red Sox, and the manager, Alvin Dark, already had decided that Vida Blue would start but pitch no more than five innings. Abbott was slated to pitch the sixth, Paul Lindblad would throw the seventh inning, and Rollie Fingers would wrap things up in the eighth and ninth, regardless of the score.

"When I went out to take the mound in the sixth inning, the home crowd was booing—people were booing," Abbott said. "But they weren't booing me. They were booing because Vida Blue came out of the game and he was pitching a no-hitter. I said to myself, 'Lord, please don't let me give up a hit.'" And he didn't.

Abbott pitched for Oakland for four seasons and compiled a 13-16 record.

His years with the A's brought a lot of smiles. "I was on a team where you hear all the stuff about how wild they were, with all the fights and stuff. But the players were all-for-one when they were at the ballpark and on the field. They expected to win. In my first year we won the league championship." Oakland went on to win the World Series as well.

His next stop in an 11-year major league career was with the Seattle Mariners, when he became the 24th pick in the 1976 expansion draft.

Abbott viewed the change from winning a title in Oakland to moving to an expansion team in Seattle as a positive experience as well.

DETROIT TIGERS 1984: WHAT A START! WHAT A FINISH!

"I went from a team that expected to win to a team that didn't have a lot of confidence," he said. "They thought they could win but weren't sure. It was a big adjustment. In expansion, you always have a bunch of Triple-A players who never had a chance to play in the majors. It's a big step to make. If you can play Double-A ball, you can pretty much play Triple-A ball. But they don't understand the jump to the majors. It's like daylight and dark. A lot of guys can't comprehend that."

Abbott's promise was realized in the 1977 campaign, the first of the Mariners' existence. He compiled a 12-13 record with a 4.45 ERA, fanning 100 batters. He was the longest-serving of the original Mariners players—his last game for Seattle was on August 21, 1983. In all, his record with the Mariners was 44-62 with an ERA that ranged from 3.94 to 5.27.

Abbott missed the 1982 season because of floating bone chips in his elbow. His arm problems were compounded by a serious bout of viral meningitis. He lost 30 pounds, as well as some vision and hearing, and still had repercussions from the illness into June 1983. He was finally able to pitch again in midsummer of 1983.

Abbott was purchased by the Tigers on August 23, 1983, for $100,000, and stayed with Detroit for parts of two seasons.

"Detroit is a good baseball town, and I wanted an opportunity to go to a winning ball club," he said during an interview at PGE Park in Portland, Oregon, his baseball home in 2008, where he was the pitching coach for the Portland Beavers, the San Diego Padres' Triple-A affiliate. "You really appreciate a chance like that. It's huge to get that opportunity."

He was released by the Detroit organization on August 14, 1984, during the height of the championship run to the World Series. Abbott immediately started a coaching career that topped his pitching career for longevity.

Standing 6-foot-6, Abbott had a playing weight of around 200 pounds, and added a few pounds after his coaching career started. To an interviewer, his native Arkansas showed up in his easy drawl: the word "four" became a two-syllable word when it left Abbott's mouth.

In talking about the differences between the two leagues, Abbott made a definitive observation about his playing days: "National League umps were far more consistent back then," he said, though he wouldn't comment on the current umpiring situation in the major leagues.

"I wish I could have played in National League as a pitcher," he said. "I like the game a lot better. There's more things going on, more decisions to be made, pitcher having to hit, et cetera. It's also a better league to pitch in. The designated hitter means that teams like Boston and New York have no weaknesses in the lineup."

The right-hander's feelings about his time with the Tigers?

"I knew I had a chance to go to a contending ball club, and you don't realize how important that is until later. I was very fortunate," he said.

He made his Tigers debut on August 27, pitching seven innings against Toronto and leaving with the scored tied, 2-2.

His best game for the Tigers that season was a 5-0 shutout of the Cleveland Indians on September 14. His mark with the Tigers in '83 was 2-1 with a 1.93 ERA in seven starts.

"The Tigers made a run in '83 and came up a game or two short [actually six games behind Baltimore]. I pitched well for them then, with Sparky [Anderson, the manager] and Roger Craig as the pitching coach. And in '84, that team started 35-5 and set a record. We set the [American League] record in Anaheim for the most consecutive games won on the road and got a standing ovation.

"But I was in the bullpen and wasn't getting a chance to pitch much because the starters were so good. It made it really difficult; it's difficult to perform at a high level if you don't get the chance to play. But Jack Morris and Dan Petry and those guys were just dealing."

Abbott took the second loss of the '84 season when the Tigers were 16-1 but recalled few details of the 19-inning game in his interview, despite the fact that he committed two errors that contributed to the loss.

"Two errors? That's bad. Maybe that's why I can't remember," he said.

During Detroit's wire-to-wire American League East championship run in 1984, Abbott pitched in 13 games, eight of them starts, with a 3-4 record and a 5.93 ERA before he was cut. His best game that season was a complete-game victory over the Chicago White Sox on July 16, in which he gave up only five hits and one walk.]

Abbott had fond recollections of his teammates from that charmed 1984 season, even though it was a truncated one for him.

Of Sparky Anderson, he said: "He didn't talk to you much. He would say hi, but that's the way managers were then. I had no problems with Sparky at all. He was a pretty positive guy. He had some good players on the team. It was amazing; those guys came to play. They never even complained about playing charity games against Cincinnati on an off day."

Roger Craig, the Tigers' pitching coach during Abbott's tenure in Detroit, "was one of the most positive people I've ever been around. He was always telling you how good you were. You have to be positive with the guys, and Roger was always that way."

Jack Morris, the Tigers' acknowledged ace throughout the 1980s, according to Abbott, "had tremendous confidence. He was probably the best pitcher of that decade—or one of the best, I'll say that. He was just getting better and better at the time. Jack was a winning-type pitcher. He threw a no-hitter in April in one of the first televised games [of the season] in Chicago. I remember a fan was yelling after every inning, 'Hey Morris, you got a no-hitter going'—trying to get him off stride. And about the eighth inning, Jack said back to him, 'Damn right. Stay right there 'cause you're gonna see one.' He was a quality pitcher."

Dan Petry, considered the number two man in Detroit's rotation for most of the 1980s, "didn't say a lot," Abbott said, "but he was very consistent. You knew what you were going to get every time you went out there."

DETROIT TIGERS 1984: WHAT A START! WHAT A FINISH!

Abbott also had good words for two relievers who not only saved his bacon on more than one occasion in 1984, but that of other Tigers hurlers during the championship season. Guillermo Hernandez, the 1984 AL Cy Young Award winner and Most Valuable Player, "couldn't do anything wrong," he recalled. Aurelio "Señor Smoke" Lopez, who notched a 10-1 record and 14 saves in the midst of Hernandez' spectacular season, "also was very consistent." Abbott said.

Alan Trammell, Detroit's shortstop and the World Series MVP in 1984, "was just as solid as they come. He was a ballplayer. He could handle the bat so well. He was underrated at that time. Howard Johnson was coming along at that time, too, playing third base. They were all very professional, and they expected to win. There was a lot of confidence—a good atmosphere to be in.

"Darrell Evans did a good job. It was the end of his career, but he was very consistent and made a tremendous impact on the club. Whittaker and Trammell and Lance Parrish and Kirk Gibson and Dave Rozema—it makes a difference when your players come up together. You've got to have talent, but you need chemistry, too, and it all fell together with the Tigers."

Abbott said he got a ring and a share of the World Series money that year, even though he left the ballclub in August.

"It might have been a three-quarter share; I can't remember. It just makes you feel good that your teammates appreciate you," he said.

His time in the majors flew by, but the memories lingered.

"I had never seen a no-hitter in professional games, and in the first three years I was in the league, I saw one every year, including being involved in the one against the Angels when I was with Oakland. [It was actually four.] The Angels at that time were a bad ballclub, but Vida Blue was on that day. It was just five innings, but he walked through them.

"I had a chance to play with guys like Catfish Hunter. They made a big impression on me. They were very professional about the way they approached the game."

One of his greatest thrills was pitching in Yankee Stadium for the first time. "It was really an experience to go see those monuments for the first time. If you love baseball, that is really something. That's why I hate to see Yankee Stadium moving. It's one thing that bothers me. There's so much history. If you think of the people who played there, Yankee Stadium is like hallowed ground. You hate to see that happen, but I understand it when teams have to go to larger parks.

"The dugouts in Tiger Stadium were so small that everybody couldn't sit down when you came off the field. It was like a bunker in the bullpen."

As for Detroit's fans: "The Tigers have great fans. Everywhere you go you'd hear people talking about the Tigers. Every night they had big crowds. It was really a unique experience. It was really a cool deal there. I really enjoyed that—very much."

Abbott came to the Binghamton (New York) Mets, the New York Mets' AA-level entry in the Eastern League, as pitching coach after serving the Savannah Sand Gnats in the same capacity in 2011. Abbott's Sand Gnats staff led the South Atlantic League in 2011 with a 3.26 ERA. They also combined for the most saves (50) and lowest WHIP (1.223).

Prior to his time with the Mets, Abbott was a pitching coach for five years in the San Diego Padres' system, spent four seasons in the Texas Rangers organization, and logged 13 years at various levels with the Oakland Athletics. The Arkansas native began his coaching career with the Little Falls Mets in 1985, the year after the Tigers cut him loose, working with his old friend Mel Stottlemyre; this began a five-year tenure with the Mets' organization before heading to Oakland.

After getting drafted by the Athletics in the eighth round in 1969, Abbott spent 11 seasons in the major leagues as a starting pitcher for the A's (1973-76), Seattle Mariners (1977-83), and Detroit Tigers (1983-84). In 248 career games, the right-hander made 206 starts, went 62-83, amassed a 4.39 ERA, struck out 484 batters, and hurled five shutouts.

As a member of the Athletics in 1975, Abbott was part of the first four-pitcher no-hitter in MLB history. On Sept. 28, he combined with Vida Blue, Paul Linblad and Rollie Fingers to baffle the Angels on the final day of the regular season.

Abbott was married in 1973. He and his wife, Patti, live in Arkansas in the offseason, and wherever he is working during the season. The eldest of their three children. Todd, pitched in the Oakland minor-league system from 1995 through 1998 and became a high-school teacher and baseball coach in Bentonville, Arkansas. Their second son, Jeff, also became a teacher, in Bolivar, Missouri. Daughter Amy, the youngest child, is married with two children and lives in North Little Rock.

Even though Glenn Abbott hasn't thrown a pitch in the major leagues since 1984, he has never stopped being a positive influence on the game he loves.

References

Web Sites

www.baseball-reference.com

www.wikipedia.org

Other Sources

Corn, Clifford. Interview with Glenn Abbott, April 21, 2008.

Rod Allen
by Rick Vosik

"WHO WOULDA thunk it? A kid from Santa Monica getting drafted in the sixth round! What an honor!" exclaimed Rod Allen.

On the other hand, who would have thought that this journeyman ballplayer, who played a total of 31 major-league ballgames, would become a big-time color analyst on television?

If Roderick Bernet Allen's baseball career had not extended beyond the 15 games he played for the 1984 world champion Detroit Tigers—he was awarded a World Series ring and full winner's money share by the team—that would have been impressive enough. But there's more, much more, to Allen's three decades in and around the game.

Allen, born on October 4, 1959, grew up in Santa Monica, California, and was drafted at the age of 17 in 1977 out of Santa Monica High School by the Chicago White Sox. In two weeks, he was on the way to Sarasota, Florida, for Rookie-level ball in the Gulf Coast League, young and scared until he got to know some of his teammates—and hit .307 for the short season. "You were pretty much on your own. It was a real eye opener. You grew up pretty quickly," said Allen in a 2007 interview.

In 1978, Allen played outfield on a tremendous Appleton team in the Low-A Midwest League, a club that won 81 games, a league one-season record. Against the stronger competition, Allen batted .243, and was promoted in 1979 to Double-A Knoxville of the Southern League, where he hit .267 with 6 home runs. In 1980, he batted .355 in a short stint at Double-A Glens Falls of the Eastern League, and batted .260 at Triple-A Iowa in the American Association. In 1981, the White Sox kept Allen in Triple A, this time at Edmonton of the Pacific Coast League, where he hit .294, with 11 home runs and 52 RBIs. Then, after five seasons working his way up the White Sox organizational ladder, on December 11, 1981, he was dealt with Todd Cruz and Jim Essian to the Seattle Mariners for Tom Paciorek. Seattle sent him right back to the PCL at Salt Lake City, where he hit .323 with 15 homers and 75 RBIs in 1982.

Along the way, Allen played winter ball—in Puerto Rico, in Mexico, in the Dominican Republic. "Baseball was how I had to feed myself," he told his interviewer in 2007.

In 1983, Allen played 81 games at Salt Lake City, hitting .324 with 12 home runs and 69 RBIs, and made it to the majors for 11 games, playing in the outfield and as a designated hitter for Seattle (2-for-12, one run scored). He became a free agent that winter, and signed with the Detroit Tigers. "I didn't know much about the Tigers," said Allen.

As Allen told it, "I was performing well" in minor-league spring training. "Word made its way to Sparky [Anderson, Detroit's manager] that there was this kid tearing the cover off the ball." He was asked to come over to the major league camp. "Once I got there, [Tigers coach] Billy Consolo read off the starting lineup. I was in the lineup!"

Allen expressed the belief that his spring-training performance led directly to a vital piece of the puzzle for the '84 Tigers. Allen made the Tigers out of spring training; he maintains that "Glenn Wilson was considered to be a stud, but because of my hot start, they were willing to trade him."

In fact, that trade was instrumental in the Tigers' 1984 success, since it brought them that year's American League Most Valuable Player and Cy Young winner. Wilson was traded, along with John Wockenfuss, to the Philadelphia Phillies for reliever Willie Hernandez and first baseman Dave Bergman. Hernandez, of course, went on to win the MVP and Cy Young Award that year, while Bergman was an important contributor to the team as well. So, Allen believed, his spring performance contributed meaningfully to the acquisition of key players for the Tigers' successful '84 World Series run.

Allen was with Detroit when the regular season began. He made his Tigers debut on April 5, 1984, when he started at designated hitter, going 1-for-3 (singling off Frank Viola in the fourth inning) and scoring a pair of runs as Detroit beat the Twins 7-3 in Minnesota. "I was there for the 35-5 start; I played in Jack Morris' no-hitter," he said. Allen was the starting DH in that game, in which Morris no-hit the White Sox that April 7 at Comiskey Park, the fourth game of the season. He struck out twice and grounded out before being lifted for a pinch-hitter. "But that season was one of pain, too," Allen said; he was sent down to Triple-A Evansville after playing 15 games. His last game with the Tigers was on May 27, when he pinch-hit and singled off Paul Mirabella in the ninth inning of a 6-1 loss to the Mariners in Seattle. For his abbreviated big-league stay, Allen compiled a .296 average in 27 at-bats, with six runs scored, three RBIs, two walks, and a stolen base. Still, Allen took home a ring, plus a bonus. The Tigers "were nice enough to give me a share" of the World Series money.

On April 9, 1985, Allen was traded to the Baltimore Orioles for Luis Rosado. After a season with the Orioles' Triple-A team at Rochester, he was granted free agency on October 15, but was re-signed by Baltimore on January 8, 1986. Then he was released by Baltimore on April 3. He played some summer ball in the Mexican League, but that did not work out. "I was a newlywed, and my wife stayed behind initially in Salt Lake City," said Allen. Once his wife arrived in Mexico, they quickly decided to move back to Salt Lake City. Not long afterward, Allen received a call from Cleveland, signed with the Indians May 20, and found himself in Double-A ball in Waterbury, Connecticut, in 1986, but moved up quickly to Triple A with the Indians' Maine Guides team in the International League. The next year, the Indians moved their Triple-A team to Buffalo of the American Association and there Allen hit .302 with 17 home runs and 92 RBIs. In 1988, the Indians moved their Triple-A team again, to Colorado Springs of the Pacific Coast League, and there Allen hit .324 with personal highs of 23 home runs and 100 RBIs.

DETROIT TIGERS 1984: WHAT A START! WHAT A FINISH!

Allen's time in the Indians' organization included a five-game stint in the majors for Cleveland in 1988, He debuted for the Indians on September 10, when he pinch hit and flied out in the ninth inning of a 6-0 loss to the Red Sox in Boston. His last game for Cleveland—and his last major-league appearance—was on October 2 in Cleveland's season finale, as they beat the Red Sox 6-5 at Municipal Stadium in Cleveland. Allen entered the game as a pinch-hitter in the fifth inning, hitting a double off Bruce Hurst and eventually scoring a run. He stayed in the game as DH, and had one more at-bat, this time facing Tom Bolton and flying out to end the sixth inning in his last major league at-bat. Allen was released by the Tribe on November 28.

With Allen's blessing, his contract was sold to the Hiroshima Carp in Japan. "I was finally able to make some money—I made good money in Japan," he told his interviewer. However, the opportunity was not without its challenges. "My wife was pregnant with our first child together. I left her behind once again. I made more money than I ever made in my life. But it was a tough adjustment. Americans had to learn to check their ego at the airport. After three years with the same teammates, they still referred to me as 'gaijin' [foreigner] rather than use my name." Still, Allen had success in Japan, spending three years there. He hit four home runs in four consecutive at-bats, setting a record, and hit two home runs for the Carp in the 1991 Japan Series.

Allen came back to the States, just as Cecil Fielder had done after his stint in Japan. Allen tried out with the Mariners in 1992, but did not make the team.

Between seasons, Allen had given private baseball lessons to young players. This led him to a decision to stay in the game as a coach. John Boles Jr., then the vice president of player development for the Marlins, told Allen he could play in Triple A for years or he could pursue coaching. Allen became a hitting instructor for Florida, and managed in the instructional league. Allen was with the Marlins organization from 1992 to 1995.

Allen's family had moved to Arizona, and when the Arizona Diamondbacks were awarded a National League franchise, Allen expressed interest in joining the organization. He went to spring training as a hitting instructor, but as the team neared its first game, he took a fateful tour of the stadium's construction site with the Diamondbacks' director of broadcasting, Thom Brennaman.

Brennaman walked with Allen around the hole in the ground that was to become Bank One Ballpark (later named Chase Field). They talked baseball the whole time, and then Brennaman shocked Allen by asking him to consider becoming an on-air analyst. "Very few guys that are in my position, as a career minor leaguer, are doing major-league broadcasts. I'd never thought about it. But Brennaman did," Allen said.

Brennaman arranged for Allen to work some Arizona Fall League games, and Allen did some on-air work with the Giants' Triple-A club in Tucson as well. Allen also spent time with legendary broadcaster Joe Garagiola, whose son, Joe Jr., was the Diamondbacks' general manager.

Allen spent five seasons with the Diamondbacks as an analyst for radio and television. He also worked as an analyst for the Fox network's Saturday regional baseball telecasts and the 1997 National League Division Series between the Atlanta Braves and Houston Astros. He worked the Diamondbacks' radio broadcasts for their 2001 postseason run: the Division Series victory over the St. Louis Cardinals, the Championship Series win over the Atlanta Braves, and the World Series victory over the New York Yankees.

Allen got his second World Series ring with the Diamondbacks. But he saw a dark cloud on the horizon. "I knew when Mark Grace was done playing, he was going to get my job. So I called [Tigers president Dave] Dombrowski." (Dombrowski had been his boss with the Marlins.) Soon, Allen was headed to Detroit, and in 2003 he made his debut as color analyst for the Tigers' FSN Detroit broadcasts, teaming with play-by-play announcer Mario Impemba.

When Allen arrived, the Tigers were struggling, to say the least. But it wasn't the cold weather or the abysmal team that was the most difficult part of the transition. "The toughest was from a family point of view. I had a son in high school. Not only was the team horrific [a 43-119 season], but it was a tough adjustment as a man with a family," Allen recalled. But he stuck it out; 2012 was his tenth year with the Tigers.

Allen quickly became beloved by the Detroit faithful for his perceptive opinions and colorful, often humorous commentary. He famously picked the Tigers to win the American League Central crown in 2006 after watching Justin Verlander and Joel Zumaya in spring training. The Twins squeaked by to win that title by one game, but the Tigers, claimants of the wild card, went to the World Series.

Allen developed a unique parlance, calling a fastball "cheese"; former Tigers outfielder Craig Monroe "Baby Boy"; Impemba "Padnuh." "Country strong" hitters "elevated" pitches. Great pitches could be "nasty" or "filthy," while Detroit starter Jeremy Bonderman's slider earned the nickname "Mr. Snappy" from Allen. A broken bat "died a hero," and an inside pitch "got in his [the batter's] kitchen."

As of 2008, Allen had won two Michigan Emmys for his work. He provided studio and on-location analysis for the Fox network's postgame coverage during the Tigers World Series run in 2006. And he served as analyst for a Fox Saturday Game of the Week regional telecast on July 22, 2006, when the Tigers lost 9-5 to the Oakland Athletics.

Rod married Adrian in 1985, and they had four children: sons Rod Jr. and Andrew, and daughters Rachel and Rhonda. Rod Jr. was a freshman All-American while at Arizona State, then played minor-league ball in the Yankees and White Sox organizations. Andrew was picked in the 2007 draft by the Diamondbacks in the 43rd round, but he chose not to sign and instead played for the University of Arizona.

Three decades in baseball. Playing in the Japan Series. Two World Series rings. A high-profile broadcasting job. All for this kid from Santa Monica who had just 51 at-bats in the majors. Who woulda thunk it?

DETROIT TIGERS 1984: WHAT A START! WHAT A FINISH!

References

Articles

Block, Joe. "Major voice learned in minors." Available from callofthegame.com. Accessed October 27. 2007.

Kirby, Tim. "Announcer Allen Gets Second Emmy." Available from http://mlb.mlb.com/news/article.jsp?ymd=20070619&content_id=2036320&vkey=news_det&fext=.jsp&c_id=det. Accessed July 11, 2008.

Parker, Rob. "Allen has the gift of foresight." *Detroit News*, April 4, 2007.

Web Sites

http://detroit.tigers.mlb.com/team/broadcasters.jsp?c_id=det

http://www.baseball-reference.com/

http://www.thebaseballcube.com

Other Sources

Vosik, Rick. Interview with Rod Allen, December 26, 2007.

Doug Bair
by David MacGregor

THERE IS NO definitive record of precisely when Charles Douglas Bair began playing baseball, but it's not beyond the realm of possibility that he was working on his two-seam fastball before he could walk. Simply put, Doug Bair is a baseball man. He always has been, and it's a good bet that he always will be. Born in Defiance, Ohio, on August 22, 1949, to Charles E. and Roberta (Merritte) Bair, Doug was one of four children. His father worked at the Continental Can Company for 46 years, and with that kind of job security, the family stayed put. Bair went to Defiance High School and then enrolled at Bowling Green State University.

It was there that Bair established himself as one of the best college pitchers in the country. He pitched a no-hitter against Miami (Ohio) on April 24, 1970, and was named to the second team All-Mid-American Conference. In 1971, Bair's 120 strikeouts set a conference record, and he was named to the first team All-MAC. On June 8, he was drafted by the Pittsburgh Pirates in the second round of the free agent draft, and signed with the Pirates later that month. Being drafted by Pittsburgh proved to be a double-edged sword. On the one hand, it was nice being part of an organization that would go on to win the World Series in 1971, but on the other hand it was harder to ascend to the big-league roster.

And so began Bair's odyssey through the minor leagues. He was first sent to the Salem Rebels, the Pirates' Class A affiliate in the Carolina League, and before the season was over he had progressed to the Double-A Waterbury Pirates in the Eastern League. In 1972, he was back at Salem (with the Rebels now known as the Pirates) and, after compiling a 15-7 record with a 2.85 earned-run average, he was promoted to the Pirates' top farm club, the Charleston Charlies of the Triple-A International League, where he was 0-1. Bair spent the next four seasons, through 1976, at Charleston. In his first full season there, 1973, the Charlies won the league's South Division championship, but lost to Pawtucket in the playoff finals. While in Charleston, Bair played alongside former and future big leaguers Dave Parker, Kent Tekulve, and Tony La Russa. Bair met Charleston native Connie Lea Taylor and married her on October 22, 1977. One oddity of Bair's minor-league career was that he was exclusively a starter through 1975, and then exclusively a reliever from 1976 on—a trend that continued in the majors until one 1983 start in Detroit.

Bair finally made his big-league debut for the Pirates on September 13, 1976. Brought up at the end of the season, he pitched 6⅓ innings in four games, giving up four hits and four runs. In his big-league bow, he pitched two perfect innings, the eighth and ninth frames of a 5-0 loss to the New York Mets. Then, just before the 1977 season opener, he was traded. In what is considered by some as one of the more lopsided trades in major-league history, Bair, Mitchell Page, Tony Armas, Rick Langford, Doc Medich, and Dave Giusti were sent to the Oakland A's for Chris Batton, Tommy Helms, and Phil Garner. (The Pirates won a World Series in 1979 with Garner in the lineup.) Bair pitched four games in April for Oakland, but before the month was out was dispatched to its Triple-A affiliate, the San Jose Missions in the Pacific Coast League. Bair was recalled in midseason to bolster the A's relief corps. He did a serviceable job, posting a 3.46 ERA with eight saves in 45 games including his April stint, but was traded once again during spring training in 1978.

This time, Bair was sent to the Cincinnati Reds in exchange for Dave Revering and cash. It turned out to be an excellent deal for the Reds, for 1978 turned out to be Bair's *annus mirabilis*. Under the eye of manager Sparky Anderson, he relieved in 70 games, accounting for 28 saves and posting a sterling 1.97 ERA, along with seven wins. Despite Bair's efforts, Cincinnati failed to make the playoffs. But in 1979 Bair got his first taste of postseason action, against his old team, the

DETROIT TIGERS 1984: WHAT A START! WHAT A FINISH!

Pirates, after the Reds won the West Division title, with Bair contributing an 11-7 record, all in relief, and 16 saves. But the Reds were swept in three games in the National League Championship Series, with Bair taking the loss in Game Two by giving up the winning run in the tenth inning.

After pitching for a third season for the Reds in 1980, going 3-6 with six saves, Bair could be forgiven if he thought he might not be such a travelin' man. But as the 1981 season wound down, Bair found himself on the move once again, this time being traded to the St. Louis Cardinals on September 10 for Joe Edelen and Neil Fiala. Both the Cardinals and the Reds were excellent teams that year, with the Reds finishing with the best record in the West Division and the Cardinals compiling the best record in the East. However, neither the Reds nor the Cardinals qualified for postseason play because this was the strike-shortened 1981 season, and Major League Baseball resorted to a split-season format to determine which teams made the playoffs. So it was that Bair (4-2 overall), Edelen, and Fiala came to share the dubious distinction of playing for the teams with the two best records in the National League but not making the playoffs.

That changed for Bair in 1982, as the Cardinals again compiled the best record in the NL East. In the NL Championship Series, the Cardinals swept the Atlanta Braves in three games. Bair's only appearance came in Game Two as he relieved starter John Stuper before giving way to Bruce Sutter, who collected the win as the Cardinals came from behind. In the World Series, the Cardinals faced the Milwaukee Brewers in a seesaw battle that went the limit, with the Cardinals finally triumphing, 6-3, in Game Seven at Busch Stadium. Bair pitched two scoreless innings in Game Two and walked the only batter he faced in Game Three. In Game Four, Bair took the loss, giving up a walk and a single to the only two batters he faced as the Brewers won the game with a six-run seventh inning. Manager Whitey Herzog kept Bair on the bench for the remainder of the Series.

Halfway through the 1983 season, Bair found himself back in the American League, as the Cardinals traded him to the Tigers for a player to be named later, pitcher Dave Rucker. Bair may have had reason to complain about the manner in which he kept getting bounced from team to team, but he certainly couldn't complain about the quality of the teams he was sent to. After being drafted by the 1971 Pirates, he played on the Reds of the late 1970s, the Cardinals of the early 1980s, and finally the Tigers of the mid-1980s. For the '83 season, he was 1-1 with one save in 26 games for the Cards, but an impressive 7-3 with four saves in 27 appearances for Detroit.

Reunited with manager Sparky Anderson, Bair found himself once again on a powerhouse team, this time a club that rocketed off to a 35-5 start to begin the 1984 season—a good thing since, as a free agent, he had chosen to re-sign with Detroit for 1984. Throughout the year, much was made of the relative youth of the Tigers, and in his diary from that year, *Bless You Boys*, Anderson repeatedly refers to his players as "our kids." At the age of 34, Bair was one of the veterans on the club, and he held the distinction of being the only player on the team who could slip on a World Series ring for special occasions. Milt Wilcox, Dave Bergman, and Willie Hernandez were the only other Tigers players to make it to the 1984 playoffs who had seen postseason action, but none of them had played on a World Series winner as Bair had.

For his part, Anderson was delighted to have Bair on his squad, saying on April 13, "Doug is throwing just like when I first got him at Cincinnati back in 1978. His confidence is back and he has a better slider. He will be very important in long relief to help us get to Lopez and Hernandez later in the game." In his own diary of the 1984 season, *Inside Pitch*, pitching coach Roger Craig echoed this sentiment, calling Bair "the unsung hero of my staff" and adding, "I have the best relief staff of any club with Hernandez, Lopez, Bair, and Rozema." The statistics bear out Bair's effectiveness early in the season. After Detroit's first 70 games, Bair was 4-0 with three saves and a 3.14 ERA.

After a fine half-season, however, Bair's performance fell off. To rest his starters, Anderson gave Bair, with a 2.63 ERA at the time, his only start of the season on July 8, the day before the All-Star break. Bair responded by giving up six runs in $2^{2/3}$ innings, and never quite recaptured his early-season form. As Craig lamented in August, "He has fallen into a bad habit of failing to use the fastball—his best pitch—to put away batters. Doug often gets ahead in the count and then tries to finesse batters instead of going after them aggressively." Anderson echoed this sentiment, saying, "Doug Bair is having a tough time." Bair pulled a muscle in his right side in September and missed nine days, but came back and got the victory against the Yankees in New York, the Tigers' 103rd win of the season, which tied the club record for victories in a season.

Bair did not appear in the American League Championship Series, in which the Tigers handily swept the Kansas City Royals in three games. He pitched in only one game of the World Series, Game Two in San Diego. With starter Dan Petry unable to hold the 3-0 lead he was staked to in the first inning, Bair was one of several relievers brought in to hold the Padres at bay. With San Diego ahead 5-3 in the seventh inning, Bair relieved Bill Scherrer with one out and Kurt Bevacqua on first. Bair struck out the only batter he faced, Carmelo Martinez, and Bevacqua was thrown out trying to steal second to end the inning. San Diego wore down the rest of the bullpen in that game, and the Tigers suffered their only loss in the World Series.

Despite picking up his second World Series ring, Bair was soon on the move again. Released by the Tigers on August 22, 1985, Bair was picked up by one of his old teams, the Cardinals, but pitched just two innings for them the rest of the year. Granted free agency after the season, Bair began the 1986 season pitching for the Tacoma Tigers, the Triple-A affiliate of another of his old teams, Oakland, and eventually worked his way back to the big league club, where he was 2-3 with four saves. This became the pattern in his career over the next few years.

Bair began 1987 pitching for the Triple-A Maine Guides of the International League before being called up by the Philadelphia Phillies. In 1988 he started in Triple A with the

Syracuse Chiefs before being called up to the Toronto Blue Jays. In 1989 he began again with the Chiefs before being sold to yet another of his old teams, the Pirates, for whom he pitched from mid-June to the end of the campaign (2-3, one save) and again at the start of the 1990 season before being demoted to the Triple-A Buffalo Bisons. Bair was called up to the Pirates in mid-August for what turned out to be his last stint in the major leagues. Having begun his major-league pitching career with the Pirates, he had come full circle to end it with them as well, appearing in his last major-league game on October 3, 1990, the last day of the regular season. But this didn't mean Doug Bair was done pitching. In 1991 he pitched for Triple-A clubs in the Tigers and Blue Jays organizations, and in 1992 he started six games for the Edmonton Trappers of the Pacific Coast League, the Triple-A affiliate of the California Angels. Those six starts were more than he had compiled in his 15-year major-league career. And was Doug Bair, now 42 years old, finally done pitching? Well, no.

After a childhood, college career, and adulthood spent throwing a ball, Bair was in no mood to stop now. There was still the Men's Senior Baseball League (otherwise known as the Roy Hobbs League) in Ohio. Anyone who has played professionally has to wait a year before joining the league, but once he was eligible, Bair signed up to play in the replica of Crosley Field that was built in Blue Ash, Ohio. Later, Bair returned to organized baseball as a pitching coach. In 2006 he was the pitching coach for the Billings Mustangs, the Rookie-level minor league affiliate of the Cincinnati Reds. In 2007 and 2008 he was with the Dayton Dragons, the Reds' low-A affiliate in the Midwest League. Let go by the Dragons after the 2008 season, as of 2012 Bair was semi-retired and living in Southern Ohio, where he still offers his advice to young pitchers learning their craft.

At 6 feet tall and listed at weighing between 170 and 180 pounds, Bair was never an especially intimidating presence on the mound, but he was a hard-throwing right-hander whose best pitch was his fastball. When given a choice, he favored the uniform number 40. He played on some of the best teams of his era and for some of the game's most legendary managers as well (Whitey Herzog, Sparky Anderson, and Tony La Russa). Despite his 15 seasons in the major leagues (and 14 seasons in the minor leagues) and two World Series titles, it's unlikely Bair will ever receive a call from Cooperstown. His stellar 1978 season aside, Bair was essentially a journeyman middle reliever who twice was on the right team at the right time. Still, his résumé lists two halls of fame: He was inducted into the Bowling Green State University Hall of Fame in 1978 and the Northeast Indiana Baseball Association Hall of Fame in 2008. As Sparky Anderson enthused, "There'll never be another bullpen like that of the Tigers of 1984. Never. There couldn't be." Doug Bair was an integral part of that bullpen. And many others.

References

Books

Anderson, Sparky. *Bless You Boys*. Chicago: Contemporary Books. 1984.

Craig, Roger, with Vern Plagenhoef. *Inside Pitch: Roger Craig's '84 Tiger Diary*. Grand Rapids, Mich.: Wm. B. Eerdmans Publishing Co. 1984.

Doug Baker
by Richard Newhouse

DOUG BAKER HAD many things working against him when the time was right to become a Detroit Tiger. First, at 5-feet-9 and 165 pounds, he was small—even by baseball standards in the mid-1980s. Second, the majors had begun making the transition from the Mark Belanger or Eddie Brinkman-style good-glove, no-hit shortstops of days gone by. Finally, and perhaps most important, is that Baker had a major impediment blocking his path to regular work in the majors— Alan Trammell, the Tigers' regular shortstop for the past half-dozen years and destined to play the role for a decade longer.

Douglas Lee Baker was born in Fullerton, California, on April 3, 1961, to an athletic family; the Bakers produced two sons who would eventually reach the pinnacle of their sport. Doug's older brother, Dave, had the proverbial cup of coffee as a 24-year-old third baseman with the Toronto Blue Jays in September 1982.

Doug graduated from Granada Hills (California) High School in 1978 as a fellow alumnus of football great John Elway. Granada Hills High also produced Ryan Braun and Gary Matthews Jr., baseball stars of a later generation.

After graduating, Baker entered Los Angeles Valley Junior College, attending for three years before transferring to a larger school more suitable for his talents on the diamond, Arizona State University. "You have to remember that I was so good when I was a kid that I red-shirted my first year at Los Angeles Valley. A JC redshirt. How many kids today are going to be happy with that ... hearing the coach say, 'We'd love for you to come to our school, but by the way, you're not good enough to play yet.' I was just happy to be playing baseball," Baker told writer David Rawnsley of the Web site perfectgame.com. While still attending LA Valley, Baker developed his talent to the extent that he caught the eye of a scout for the Oakland Athletics, who drafted him at the age of 19 in the January phase of the 1981 amateur draft. Doug elected to continue college and play baseball for Jim Brock at Arizona State that fall rather than sign a professional contract.

DETROIT TIGERS 1984: WHAT A START! WHAT A FINISH!

In the spring of 1982, the pros came calling again and Baker was selected by the Tigers in the ninth round of the amateur draft. This time he chose to sign. Baker was assigned to the Tigers' Double-A affiliate in Birmingham, Alabama (Southern League), bypassing the rookie league and Class A. But he struggled, hitting just .225 and committing 14 errors in just 70 games at shortstop.

It was apparent that Baker would need some additional seasoning at the Double-A level, so he returned to Birmingham in the spring of 1983. He adjusted enough to the pitching to nudge his average to .241, while showing some plate discipline with only 51 strikeouts and 65 walks—giving him a respectable .352 on-base percentage in a league-leading 146 contests, split between shortstop and the outfield. His performance that summer earned Baker a spot on the Southern League All-Star squad.

Baker's improvement at the plate and his fine glove work prompted Tigers management to add him to the list of nonroster invitees to their 1984 major-league camp in Lakeland, Florida. His performance that spring caught the eye of manager Sparky Anderson, but with All-Star Trammell at short and handyman Tom Brookens backing him up, the Tigers had no immediate need for a kid less than two years removed from college. Baker, however, moved another rung up the organizational ladder when he was assigned that spring to the Tigers' Triple-A affiliate in Evansville, Indiana (American Association). He thrived as the Triplets' shortstop, hitting .259 and showing some pop with eight home runs in only 243 at-bats. He continued to draw walks with his on-base percentage rising to .377. His defense earned him Baseball America's recognition as the best defender at shortstop in the American Association, with the best arm of any infielder in the league.

On July 2, 1984, barely two years after signing his first professional contract, Doug Baker received the call. With Alan Trammell experiencing arm soreness, Anderson, remembering "the kid with the good glove" from spring training, called Baker up from Evansville. He was immediately inserted into the lineup, batting ninth against the White Sox and lefty Floyd Bannister.

Baker spelled Trammell off and on until July 12, when Trammell's arm trouble finally put him on the disabled list. On July 13, in his seventh game and 14th at-bat, Baker picked up his first major-league hit—a sixth-inning single leading off against the Twins' John Butcher in Minnesota.

A week and a half later, Doug stroked four singles in a 9-5 victory at Cleveland.

After clearing the bases with a triple in the first game of a home doubleheader against the Indians on July 31, Baker, hitting just .157, was sent back to Evansville. "Baker is a good kid who will be a good player, but we need that right-handed hitting because right now, ours stinks," Anderson wrote in his memoir, *Bless You Boys: Diary of the Detroit Tigers' 1984 Season*.

"I'm not jumping up and down about it," Baker said of his demotion. "Nobody likes to be sent back down, but I expected it sooner or later. The last thing I wanted to do was come up and get in the way of what's going on up here. If I helped a little, I'm going back pleased."

Baker's return to Evansville was short-lived as Trammell's arm troubles lingered. He returned to the Tigers and started at short on August 11. Three days later, Anderson inserted him into the lineup for both ends of the Tigers' sixth doubleheader in 19 days. Then, on August 20, he contributed three hits as part of a 20-hit attack as the Tigers overwhelmed Oakland 14-1. This was during a stretch when Baker was filling in at second base for Lou Whitaker, himself ailing with a sore back, with five games in five days, the last four of them starts. Despite his spurts of offensive prowess, Baker ended the season hitting just .185 for the American League East champion Tigers.

Anderson named Baker as a reserve infielder for the American League Championship Series against Kansas City. Baker came in for Trammell at shortstop in the ninth inning of the Tigers' 8-1 victory in Game One. That was his only postseason appearance as he was left off the World Series roster. Baker, however, stayed with the team throughout its postseason trek to a world championship.

"It's exactly what you think it would be. There's nothing better. You're on top of the world," Baker told writer Rawnsley about his experience as a role player on a World Series winner, just 28 months after signing his first professional contract.

After arthroscopic surgery on his left knee performed immediately after the World Series, Baker came to spring training physically renewed in 1985 and with the confidence that he had a role as a backup infielder. But in one of the more head-shaking moments in Tigers history, Anderson had the airport-bound bus stop at Tigertown and made Baker get off. Baker found himself optioned to the Nashville Sounds, the Tigers' new American Association affiliate.

Serving as the primary shortstop for the Sounds for the balance of the summer of 1985, Baker hit just .218 in 107 games. Called up with rosters expanding in September, Doug appeared in 12 games, going 5-for-25 in the waning weeks for the Tigers, spelling Trammell in the late innings and in occasional starts. Coupled with his 0-for-2 performance in three games for Detroit earlier in the season, Baker matched his .185 batting average of 1984.

Baker began 1986 with the Tigers, again used sparingly—appearing in just three games in two weeks—before being optioned to Nashville, where he again served as the Sounds' regular shortstop and improved his batting average to .274. He was pulled from the bushes with roster expansion in September. He got to start five straight games at shortstop, September 25-30. But he hit just .125 with one of his three hits a double.

A veteran of 71 games with the Tigers in three seasons of secondary duty, Baker came to spring training in 1987 assuming again that as in the prior two seasons, he would accompany the team as it headed north. Manager Sparky Anderson instead elected to save the roster spot, filling the backup shortstop role with Brookens, who had been the primary third baseman before the arrival of Darnell Coles in 1986.

DETROIT TIGERS 1984: WHAT A START! WHAT A FINISH!

Again the Tigers' Triple-A shortstop, but this time in Toledo, Baker batted .247 in 117 games for the Mud Hens. Baker was summoned to Detroit in September and appeared defensively in eight games, going hitless in one at-bat.

Doug Baker's opportunities as a backup to Alan Trammell had diminished a great deal after he logged 43 games in 1984, with just 15 games in 1985, then 13 in 1986, and only eight in September 1987. The reduced role for Baker as a backup infielder for the Tigers ended abruptly. Around the time the full squad was scheduled to join the pitchers and catchers at spring training camp in Lakeland in February 1988, Baker found himself wearing new colors as he was dealt by Detroit to the Minnesota Twins for minor leaguer Julius McDougal.

Joining a new organization carried with it hope of greater opportunity for Baker. Yet incumbent Twins shortstop Greg Gagne proved to be as immovable as Trammell had been. When camp broke, Baker was assigned to Triple-A Portland of the Pacific Coast League, where he hit .245 for the 1988 season with a career-high 17 steals. As in each of the prior four seasons, Baker returned to the American League as a September call-up, appearing in 11 games for Minnesota and going 0-for-7 at the plate.

The following spring, he was again dispatched to Triple-A, but this time he was at Portland for just a month before the Twins called him east to back up Gagne. Returned to Portland just two weeks later, Baker resumed his shortstop duties for the Beavers. Early in July, he found himself back in Minnesota, but this time he contributed offensively, smacking four hits in his first six official at-bats, bunching in a walk, a sacrifice, and a sacrifice fly. He now stood at 6-for-11 for the season, combined with the 2-for-5 performance earlier in the season, and was poised to finally break into the lineup—which he did, starting nine games in next 12 days. He cooled off to a .310 average by the end of July, and by the middle of August, after a few more starts, was returned to Portland still sporting a healthy .293 batting average. Baker remained stellar in the field for Portland though hitting just .237. He appeared in 13 more games for the Twins in September, coming just a hit shy of .300, finishing the year at .295 (23-for-78)—easily his best stint hitting at the big-league level.

His reward for the success of the 1989 season was a trip north with the Twins in the spring of 1990. However, this round-trip lasted just three games and one at-bat—his final swing in the big leagues—resulting in a fly out to left field off Dennis Eckersley in the top of the eighth inning of a 5-3 Twins loss in Oakland on April 10, 1990. Back at Portland, the 29-year-old Baker took on a utility role—playing several games at second, third, and the outfield, and even twice at first base—while patrolling the familiar shortstop post in 43 contests with only four errors. However, a .216 average kept him off the September big-league squad for the first time in seven seasons.

The Twins granted Baker free agency in October 1990. He signed a minor-league contract with the Houston Astros and joined the Triple-A Tucson Toros for the 1991 season. Again playing in mostly a utility role, Baker slumped to .183 in 73 games for the eventual Pacific Coast League champion Toros, his worst mark ever as a regular. With the prospects of returning to the major leagues becoming increasingly dim for an aging minor-league infielder whose skills—at least with the bat—were apparently diminishing, Baker retired after the 1990 season.

Reminiscing to David Rawnsley about his career, Baker talked about playing for Sparky Anderson and the Twins' Tom Kelly: "For a player like me, Kelly was by far the best manager I could have. You've often heard about how a manager 'gets the most out of his players,' well, that was Kelly. He cared about the 25th player on the team (usually me) as much as the stars and made sure that you felt you were contributing. If you got some at-bats one day and had a hit or two, he'd make sure that you were out there again the next day just to get your confidence up.

"Sparky, on the other hand, knew who his studs were and with guys like Alan Trammell, Lou Whitaker, Lance Parrish, Kirk Gibson, and Jack Morris, the Tigers obviously had some good ones. He took care of them and the bench guys knew our role was to take care of them, too. Whitaker (a left-handed hitter) tended to have a sore back or flu-like symptoms only when we were facing some nasty left-handed pitcher, so I'd be out there not having seen a live pitch in two weeks and trying to hit off Ron Guidry or Mark Langston or Frank Viola. So hitting .185 (his batting average in 1984) doesn't seem so bad in retrospect."

Baker also described the famous double-play combination he occasionally subbed for: "Playing behind Trammell and Whitaker was a treat because they were such talented players, and very different personalities. Trammell is from Southern California and was one of the best teammates I ever had. Super guy who was nice to a fault with everyone.

"Whitaker was an immensely talented player who could do just about anything he wanted on the field. He'd go on these streaks with no explanation where he'd say, 'I'm going to pull the ball in the air for a few days,' or 'I'm going to hit line drives over the shortstop for a few days' and just do it. Heck, I couldn't do that in BP. But he was a very different personality, that's for sure."

After retiring as a player, Baker served as a minor-league coach for a season before moving on to serve as a scout for the Atlanta Braves for three years and then for the Cleveland Indians organization for eight years.

Doug returned to his roots in Southern California, joining Perfect Game USA, touted on its web site as the "World's Largest Scouting Report Service" in 2003, assuming the duties of West Coast scouting supervisor shortly thereafter.

In 2009 Baker was assisting in other player development programs either as a guest instructor or on paid staff, in either capacity with such organizations as MVP Baseball, the ABD Academy, and the Katy Sting Academy.

Working at developing young talent in the game he loves, Baker encourages them to "play like it's fun to play. I know it's trite but they still call this a 'game' and that's what it should be. I know I grew up like every kid with a glove and cleats thinking that I wanted to be a big leaguer. I was very lucky. But when I went on the field I was just thinking how great it was that I was playing baseball with my friends."

References

Publications

Anderson, Sparky. *Bless You Boys: Diary of the Detroit Tigers' 1984 Season*. Chicago: Contemporary Books, Inc. 1984.

Paladino, Larry. *1985 Detroit Tigers Official Yearbook*. Detroit: Detroit Tigers. 1985.

Paladino, Larry. *1987 Detroit Tigers Official Yearbook*. Detroit: Detroit Tigers. 1987.

Articles

Gage, Tom. "Tigers Alter Roster During Twin Bill." *The Sporting News*, August 13, 1984.

Rawnsley, David. "PG Supervisor and former Big Leaguer Doug Baker." www.perfectgame.org. 2005.

Web Sites

www.baseball-reference.com

www.retrosheet.com

www.thebaseballcube.com

Acknowledgements

Emily Newhouse

Harrison Newhouse

David Rawnsley

Jeff Samoray

Juan Berenguer
by Jason Lenard

JUAN BERENGUER combined a high-90s fastball and a menacing appearance to become the first Panamanian-born pitcher to win a World Series ring, starting 27 games for the Detroit Tigers in their 1984 championship season. And he did it again three years later, earning the monikers "Señor Smoke" and "El Gasolino" for the 1987 Twins.

Berenguer was born on November 30, 1954, in Aguadulce, Panama, one of nine children born to Francisco and Bienvenda Berenguer. He played in youth leagues as a third baseman until the age of 16. Noting his rocket arm, Berenguer's brother Jose convinced his younger sibling that he could be a successful pitcher. Jose's advice was a turning point in the blossoming career of the younger Berenguer, and led to 15 years in the big leagues.

In 1972, at the age of 18, Berenguer, a right-hander, made the Panamanian National Team, traveling to various locations with his fellow countrymen. While playing a game in Cuba, Berenguer met Tony Oliva and Luis Tiant, Cuban-born players who had made the jump to America and the major leagues. Oliva was then starring with the Minnesota Twins and Tiant with the Boston Red Sox. "They told me to work hard, and that they would soon see me in America," Berenguer said in an interview in 2009. "I never thought I had a chance to come to America."

That advice and encouragement from two of the game's most influential Latinos motivated Berenguer, and three years later, in 1975, a New York Mets scout, former major leaguer Nino Escalera, spotted him in a game in Panama. He saw enough to know that Juan had a major-league arm, and he showed up at the Berenguers' front door at 6 o'clock the following morning, taking Berenguer's mother by surprise. Reluctant to wake Juan, she tried to send Escalera away, explaining that Juan was still asleep. Luckily for Juan, brother Jose intervened, woke his kid brother and ushered in Escalera, contract in hand. By 6:45 p.m., Berenguer's name was on the contract, and he was bound for spring training in St. Petersburg, Florida.

At that camp, Berenguer met Mets pitchers Tom Seaver, already a 146-game winner, and Jerry Koosman, among other players. For a boy making his first trip to America, those names were as foreign as the language. However, the two were gracious veterans, and they told Berenguer to keep working hard.

Berenguer spent the 1975 through 1978 seasons working his way up to the high minors—5-4 and a 2.94 ERA in 1975 with Wausau (Wisconsin) in the Class A Midwest League, 10-13 and 3.61 in 1976 with Lynchburg (Virginia) in the Class A Carolina League, and 9-8 and 3.43 in 1977 with Jackson (Mississippi) in the Double-A Texas League. He reached a peak in 1978 with Tidewater in the Triple-A International League, winning the league's Pitcher of the Year Award with a record of 10-7, a 3.67 ERA, eight complete games, and three shutouts. His reward was a call-up to the parent club and making his first big-league start, at the age of 23, on August 17 in front of 9,003 fans at Shea Stadium. The opponent that evening was the San Diego Padres, and Berenguer had to pitch against the legendary Gaylord Perry, then well on his way to 300 victories. The Mets, by comparison, were well on their way to a last-place finish in the National League's Eastern Division.

"My leg was shaking," Berenguer recalled. "I was very nervous to go against one of the best players in baseball. But Nino [Escalera] told me to go in and pitch hard."

The top of the first inning was rocky as he walked the first two batters, which led to a run for the Padres. Berenguer settled down until the third inning, when San Diego plated four runs, two of them on a home run by Tucker Ashford. Berenguer finished the third, but was removed for a pinch-hitter in the bottom of the inning. The line for his first big league start: 3 IP, 4 H, 5 ER, 4 BB, 2K.

After four more appearances, including two additional starts, Berenguer ended his first major-league season with an 0-2 record, an ERA of 8.31, and the knowledge that he needed another pitch to complement his fastball.

Winter ball in Venezuela was the next stop, with the goal of finding the elusive breaking ball. "I had a good fastball," said Berenguer. "But I needed to find another pitch. The changeup wasn't it. Every time I used a changeup, someone took me deep. They could see it coming."

Winter ball and two more stints in Triple-A, although helpful, failed to produce the secondary pitch Berenguer desired, and he made only sporadic late-season appearances for the Mets in 1979 and 1980. He spent the bulk of 1979 on loan to the Tacoma Tugs, Cleveland's affiliate in the Pacific Coast League, going 8-8 with a 4.88 ERA. It was in that season that Berenguer earned his first big-league win, pitching $7^{1}/_{3}$ innings, allowing two earned runs and registering four strikeouts in a Mets victory over the St. Louis Cardinals at Busch Stadium on September 28. Preserving the win for Berenguer was 23-year-old rookie Jeff Reardon, who earned his first save for a player who would be his World Series teammate eight years later, in 1987. The 1980 season found Berenguer at Triple-A Tidewater, where he posted a 9-15 mark with an improved 3.84 ERA.

Late in spring training of 1981, buried on the Mets' depth chart, Berenguer got word from manager Joe Torre that his Mets days were over, and that he was headed to Kansas City for a fresh start. "Joe told me that I was going someplace where I could pitch in the big leagues," Berenguer said.

Berenguer was dealt for Marvell Wynne and John Skinner, neither of whom ever played for the Mets. Former minor-league pitching instructor Bill Connors had taken the first of his several major-league pitching coach positions with the Royals a year earlier. And he wanted Juan.

For the first time, Berenguer opened a season with the big club, making his first appearance on April 20. After seven more appearances, including three starts, giving him an 0-4 record and an 8.69 ERA, Berenguer's 1981 season came to a halt on June 12 as the Major League Baseball Players Association voted to strike in the name of free agency. On August 8, the eve of resumption of play, Berenguer was sold to Toronto to join a young Blue Jays squad that had gone 16-42 before the strike.

As luck would have it, the Royals ended up in the playoffs because of the unique split-season rules necessitated by the strike that year, and Berenguer missed a chance at postseason baseball. However, the trade gave Berenguer an opportunity to throw big innings; he started 11 games for the Blue Jays in the second half of the split season. The highlight of his Toronto tenure was his first American League victory, coming against the Tigers, the club that signed him as a free agent eight months later.

Playing in front of a crowd of 10,526 at Tiger Stadium on August 11, 1981, Berenguer entered the game in the second inning. The Blue Jays were up, 6-3. They had scored six runs in the top of the first against Dan Schatzeder, but the Jays' Paul Mirabella gave up three in the bottom of the inning. With two on and two out in the second, Berenguer replaced Mirabella, fanned Alan Trammell for his only strikeout of the game, and pitched into the seventh before surrendering the ball to Roy Lee Jackson, who preserved his second career win.

Berenguer won just one more game that season and finished the season with a 2-13 record (0-4 for the Royals, 2-9 for the Blue Jays), with a 5.26 ERA. His career record was now 3-17.

Another year, 1982, brought another spring training disappointment for Berenguer as the Jays released him, less than two weeks before teams headed north.

But in a moment that marks one of the turning points of his career, Berenguer got the call from Detroit and signed as a free agent on April 4. He was to play for Sparky Anderson, a manager about whom he knew two things: Anderson won two World Series as manager of the Cincinnati Reds in 1975 and '76, and had a reputation for impatience with pitchers.

"Sparky had a reputation as Mr. Hook," Berenguer recollected. "You know, walk one guy and you're gone. I thought, 'We're going to have trouble. I need to work on my control.'"

Twenty-five players headed north as the Tigers broke camp to begin the season in Kansas City, but Berenguer wasn't one of them. Instead, Anderson told him to stay behind in Lakeland, then report to Evansville to play for the Triplets, the Tigers' Triple-A affiliate. Starting 24 games for the Triplets that season, Berenguer logged 11 wins against 10 losses, with an ERA of 4.61.

As had become a familiar routine during his time as a Met, Berenguer was a late-season call-up in 1982, making his Tigers debut at the corner of Michigan and Trumbull in a starting role on September 2. His line was another parallel to his days in New York; he walked five California Angels and departed after three innings—but this time he gave up only three earned runs. Nine days later the story was the same, this time out of the bullpen, as Berenguer struck out five Boston Red Sox but walked four, giving him nine walks in $6^{2}/_{3}$ innings.

After another offseason of hard work, Berenguer left Florida with the Tigers in 1983 to begin the season that changed his life as a major leaguer.

DETROIT TIGERS 1984: WHAT A START! WHAT A FINISH!

"Sparky and Roger Craig saved my career," Berenguer said. Craig, the Tigers' pitching coach, "taught me to throw the split-finger, and I learned it in about a week." That season, Berenguer finished on the plus side of .500 for the first time, going 9-5 with a 3.14 ERA in 157$^{2}/_{3}$ innings. He appeared in 37 games and made 19 starts.

Berenguer got permission from Anderson to play winter ball to perfect the split-finger pitch. Berenguer knew winter ball would also help him satisfy one of Anderson's other requirements: weight.

"Sparky would send the players a sheet in December that said what weight to report at," Berenguer recalled. "I had to keep in shape."

Berenguer entered the spring of 1984 as he had every other in his career, with the mindset that someone was going to try to take his job. This year, someone almost did, with Berenguer's wildness nearly costing him a spot in the starting rotation.

After almost three weeks of sitting in the bullpen, with Anderson using Jack Morris, Dan Petry, Milt Wilcox, and Dave Rozema en route to an AL East-leading 11-1 record, Berenguer started on April 22 against the Chicago White Sox at Tiger Stadium. The game-time temperature was frigid, punctuated with periods of sleet, but not cold enough to chill Berenguer's heater as he pitched a game that was in stark contrast to the majority of his previous big-league appearances. He dominated the White Sox hitters for seven scoreless innings of two-hit ball while striking out seven. But the best number of the afternoon was in the BB stat line, as Berenguer issued only one free pass.

His next start, five days later against the visiting Cleveland Indians, proved that his first outing was no fluke. Berenguer went 7$^{2}/_{3}$ innings, struck out six and allowed one earned run, but got no decision in an extra-inning affair.

One of the season's most spectacular moments came on May 12, Berenguer's fifth start, when Detroit hosted the California Angels in front of more than 38,000 fans. Led by aging veterans Tommy John and Reggie Jackson, the Angels came into the contest one game above .500 to play the red-hot, 26-4 Tigers. After being hit by a pitch in the first inning and striking out in the third, Jackson came to the plate in the fifth inning with a man on first and the Angels trailing 2-0. Berenguer ran the count to 3-2 before Jackson, according to Berenguer, uttered, "Come to papa" from the batter's box, knowing a fastball was likely from the right-hander. He got it, and—aided by a 20 mph wind—cleared the right-field roof for his 485th home run, a mammoth blast reminiscent of the shot he hit in the 1971 All-Star Game.

The Angels grabbed the lead in the seventh, and Tommy John scattered eight hits in a 4-2 complete-game victory, a line that took a back seat to the Berenguer-Jackson encounter midway through the game.

Berenguer alternated wins and losses for most of the season, with the losses somewhat more frequent, and his record stood at 8-10 in mid-September before a three-game winning streak allowed him to finish above .500 at 11-10 with a respectable ERA of 3.48.

Heading into the American League Championship Series against the Royals, Berenguer knew he was on the outside of the pitching rotation looking in, both as a starter and a reliever. Before the opening game, pitching coach Craig explained to Berenguer his postseason role. "Roger told me before the playoffs, 'This is the situation. I am going to push my starters into the eighth. You are my innings 4 through 6 guy. Anything later than the sixth and it'll be [Doug] Bair, [Aurelio] Lopez, and [Willie] Hernandez.'"

Typically, Berenguer accepted his role with ease. "I knew the rule," he said. "I am a team player. I wanted to win."

The postseason for the Tigers lasted a scant eight games, with the starters doing the job Craig had envisioned. In the Championship Series, Detroit relievers got only seven innings of work. Jack Morris pitched seven strong innings in Game One, with Hernandez hurling the final two; Dan Petry went seven innings in Game Two, but Hernandez blew the save and the win went to Lopez in extra innings; and Wilcox pitched eight innings in Game Three, with Hernandez saving it.

The World Series featured two complete-game victories by Morris in Games One and Four, and two subpar performances by Petry in Games Two (4$^{1}/_{3}$ innings) and Five (3$^{2}/_{3}$ innings). Lopez, Hernandez, Bair, and Bill Scherrer did Detroit's relief duty in the Series. Berenguer, despite 27 starts and 168$^{1}/_{3}$ innings for the Tigers during the season, never left the bullpen in the postseason.

According to Berenguer, that inactivity was made easier by the support system he had on the team, mainly Hernandez, Lopez, and utility player Barbaro Garbey. That support, he said, enabled him to succeed during his time in Detroit.

"I talked to everyone on the team," Berenguer said. "Lopez and Willie would say, 'You start, then give the ball to me.' I put that in my head. I knew I didn't have to go nine innings. I would get to six or seven and let those guys come in.

"I felt like I found a home in Detroit. The crowd made you feel comfortable and everyone supported you. They made you feel good, and I wanted to pitch well for them."

Berenguer pitched one more season in Detroit, a disappointing season in which his starts declined to 13, his record dipped to 5-6, and his ERA rose to 5.59. On the day after the '85 season ended, Berenguer left the home he thought he had found and headed west to join the San Francisco Giants. Berenguer, backup catcher Bob Melvin and pitcher Scott Medvin were sent to San Francisco in exchange for catcher Matt Nokes and pitchers Eric King and Dave LaPoint. There, Berenguer would join the man who had tutored him in the art of the split-finger fastball, Roger Craig, the team's manager.

By the time he joined the Giants, Berenguer had accepted his role as a reliever. However, San Francisco already had a crowded bullpen. As a result, Berenguer joined the Giants starting rotation, at least at the outset of the 1986 season, alongside players like Mike Krukow and Vida Blue.

Berenguer made his first start at Candlestick Park on April 30 in front of just 5,147 attendees, and didn't last through the third inning. After two more lackluster starts, Berenguer and his 6.00 ERA were sent back to the bullpen. By June 12, his

DETROIT TIGERS 1984: WHAT A START! WHAT A FINISH!

ERA was down to 2.93, and almost a week later, with other relievers injured, Berenguer got the chance to close. Between June 18 and June 22, Berenguer saved three games and won one before returning to middle relief.

With an overstocked bullpen in July, Giants general manager Al Rosen met with Berenguer and asked where he might want to be traded. Rosen asked him to pick one team. Around the same time, his old acquaintance Tony Oliva, then a batting coach for Minnesota, told Berenguer that the Twins were trying to acquire him. So Berenguer told Rosen that he wanted to be traded to Minnesota—a request Rosen declined because, according to Berenguer, "he didn't want anyone from Minnesota." So Berenguer stayed with the Giants.

Berenguer finished the 1986 season with a 2.70 ERA in 73 1/3 innings of work, a solid year that landed him a spot on his second World Series winner.

He was released by the Giants on December 19, 1986, and signed on the following January 9 with the Twins to be their closer. He finally landed the elusive job at the back end of the bullpen that he was looking for. And it lasted less than a month. On February 3, the Twins traded four players to the Expos to obtain the Terminator, Jeff Reardon, who had 76 saves over the previous two seasons.

Oliva calmed Berenguer's fears, informing him that, with only two bona fide starters, Bert Blyleven and Frank Viola, a relief pitcher on the Twins would be in high demand during the 1987 season. Oliva's prediction proved correct, and the result for Juan was 112 innings of work in six starts and 41 relief appearances with a 3.94 ERA. He posted the best strikeout-to-walk ratio of his career, striking out 110 and walking only 47, and finished the season with an 8-1 record. He became known as Señor Smoke.

The Twins finished 85-77 for the year, winning the American League West by two games over the Royals, and were headed to the postseason for the first time since the Harmon Killebrew-led 1970 team.

The only team between the Twins and the pennant was the 98-win Detroit Tigers, winner of the East by two games over the Blue Jays and the owner of the best record in baseball. The Tigers won the division in dramatic fashion, winning the last four games of the season at home against Toronto—which came into the series with the division lead.

On paper and in the standings, the Tigers held the advantage. But after an 8-5 victory by the Twins in Game One at the Metrodome, the regular-season records were quickly forgotten. Berenguer finally broke his postseason pitching drought in Game Two, pitching what could be called the best 1 2/3 innings of his 15-year career.

Bert Blyleven started. Leading 6-2 in the eighth inning, he gave up a solo home run to the Tigers' Lou Whitaker. Enter Señor Smoke; Twins manager Tom Kelly's plan was that he would get the final two outs of the inning before turning the ball over to Reardon.

Berenguer promptly struck out Kirk Gibson on three pitches, the final one swinging, and got Alan Trammell to ground into a force play at second. Kelly saw something in Berenguer that made him change his plan, and with the Twins holding a three-run lead, he left Berenguer in for the ninth.

Matt Nokes, one of the players the Tigers got for Berenguer, led off the inning. Berenguer struck him out swinging. Next was Chet Lemon, a player Berenguer admired during his time in Detroit for his spectacular defense. Strikeout swinging. The final batter of the game was Pat Sheridan. Another strikeout swinging.

With the nation watching on television and his family in attendance, Berenguer was fired up, pumping his fist after each strikeout in a display of emotion that did not sit well with his former Tigers manager.

"Don't ever try to embarrass my players," said a peeved Anderson after the game. "Whatever this is, with the glove coming up and the hand coming down, don't wake the sleeping dog."

Berenguer saw it differently. "I was not trying to embarrass anyone," he said in 2009. "I played with those guys, and respect them all."

Berenguer pitched a hitless inning in Minnesota's Game Three win, 2 2/3 hitless innings in the Twins' Game Four victory, and two-thirds of an inning in the deciding Game Five victory --- his no-hit, no-run string broken up by a home run by Chet Lemon. The Twins were going to their first World Series in 22 years to face the St. Louis Cardinals.

Berenguer struggled early in the Series, allowing two earned runs in an inning of work in Game Two, and taking the loss after allowing three earned runs in one-third of an inning in Game Three.

After the loss, Berenguer received a tip that he had heard before: He was relying too much on his fastball. In his next appearance, in Game Six, he served a steady dose of sliders and forkballs in three innings of scoreless work as the Twins evened the Series at three victories each. They defeated the Cardinals in Game Seven for Berenguer's second World Series title in four seasons.

The reliever's popularity soared after the World Series thanks to "Berenguer Boogie," a music video that featured Juan dancing to the beat in a trench coat and briefcase. It achieved new life in the 21st century thanks to several Internet video sites.

Berenguer pitched in Minnesota through 1990, with a record of 33-13 in his four years of work as a Twin. After testing free agency, Berenguer signed with the Atlanta Braves, and as had happened with the Twins four years earlier, made another run at a title.

The Braves, 65-97 in 1990, went from worst to first in 1991, with Berenguer, at the age of 36, playing a key role early in the season. He had 17 saves, more than in his previous 13 years combined, when an injury derailed his season. While home wrestling with his children on an off-day, Berenguer broke his pitching arm and missed out on much of the Braves' run to the National League West title, followed by the pennant and subsequent loss to Berenguer's former team, the Twins, in Game Seven of the World Series. The winning pitcher for the Twins in that game? Ex-Tigers teammate Jack Morris.

In 1992, Berenguer returned to pitch for Atlanta, going 3-1 with a 5.13 ERA, but was dealt near the interleague trade deadline to the Royals in exchange for another former teammate, Mark Davis. With a 1-4 record and a 5.64 ERA with the Royals, Berenguer's major-league career came to an end. He hung on until 1997, spending 1993 and 1994 in the Mexican League, part of 1994 with Minneapolis in the independent North Central League, and 1995 through 1997 with Minneapolis and Southern Minny in the independent Prairie League. As ERAs ranging from 0.82 (with Minneapolis in 1995, albeit with a 2-3 mark) to 6.14 (with Saltillo in 1993, with a not-surprising 1-5 record) indicate, his work was inconsistent. The end came in 1997 with an 8-3 slate and 3.09 ERA. At 41, Berenguer retired.

During his 15-year career, the man known by the nicknames Pancho Villa (referring to his facial hair) and the Panama Express registered 67 career wins, the record for a Panamanian-born player until 2008 when Mariano Rivera posted win number 68 with the New York Yankees. Berenguer registered 975 career strikeouts, 32 saves and a 3.90 ERA in 490 games, with 1,205 1/3 innings pitched—and two rings.

Berenguer returned to Minnesota, the site of his greatest baseball success, and worked in marketing for a television station. He was married for the second time in 2004. His sons from his first marriage followed in his athletic footsteps: Chris as a defenseman for the Hamline University hockey team in St. Paul, and Andrew following in his dad's footsteps on the diamond at Mesabi Range Technical College in Virginia, Minnesota.

References

Publications

Zaret, Eli. '84—*The Last of the Great Tigers*. South Boardman, Mich.: Crofton Creek Press, 2004.

Articles

Anderson, Dave. "A Tale of Two Bullpens." *New York Times*, October 9, 1987.

Durso, Joseph. "Offseason for Baseball Isn't What It Used to Be." *New York Times*, January 11, 1988.

Goessling, Ben. "Former Twin Enjoys Chaotic, Happy Retirement as Salesman and Father." *Minneapolis Star-Tribune*, March 22, 2006.

Web Sites

atlanta.braves.mlb.com

www.baseball-reference.com

www.panama-guide.com

www.retrosheet.org

www.thebaseballcube.com/pitching/1982/10517.shtm

www.wikipedia.org

Other Sources

Lenard, Jason. Juan Berenguer interview. January 14, 2009.

Dave Bergman
by Jerry Nechal

DAVE BERGMAN played nine seasons in a Tigers uniform, but when his name is mentioned in Detroit, a single at-bat is etched in the minds of most fans. Dave's 13-pitch battle with Roy Lee Jackson with two outs in the tenth inning of a pivotal game against the Toronto Blue Jays, on June 4, 1984, has become part of local sports folklore. Coach Dick Tracewski called that at-bat, which ended in a game-winning walk-off three-run homer, "the best at-bat I've ever seen." For Bergman, his mental and physical battle on that night with Jackson exemplifies what allowed him to have a 17-year career in the major leagues as a utility role player. He made himself successful by maximizing his skills both physically and mentally. Bergman's high-school baseball coach characterized him as an overachiever. From hidden-ball tricks to extra batting practice, he constantly strove to do what he needed to improve his game and to contribute to his team. In 1984, Bergman told the *Oneonta* (New York) *Daily Star*, "I think the mental part of the game is the biggest difference in my game. I'm not as talented as some of these guys so I have to make up for what I lack in ability by using my head."

To survive as long as he did in the major leagues as a utility player is a testament to Bergman and his approach to the game. During his 14 full seasons in the majors, he averaged only 189 at-bats per year. He was a career .258 hitter who never had more than seven home runs or 44 runs batted in in a single season. But Bergman accepted his fate as a part-timer early in his major-league career. At each stop along the way, like an apprentice aspiring for a journeyman's card, he learned what he could from some of the best managers in the game. Bergman prepared himself for whatever the team needed from him, whether it was as a pinch-hitter or a late-inning defensive replacement. In discussing Bergman in 1991, Sparky Anderson said, "He knows his role and that's why he stayed in the big leagues a long time. If he thought it was another role, it might have been a short career." At the end of Bergman's career, Anderson praised his preparedness: "In all the years I've managed Dave, there's never been one time—not one game—that he didn't come to the park ready to play."

David Bruce Bergman was born to Donald Bergman, an electrician, and Gloria Bergman in Evanston, Illinois, on June 6, 1953, the second oldest of five children. Growing up in the near north suburbs of Chicago, Bergman was a Cubs fan in the era of Ernie Banks, Billy Williams, and Ron Santo.

He attended Maine South High School in Park Ridge, Illinois, where in addition to baseball he played football, basketball, and soccer. George Verber, Dave's high-school baseball coach, in 2007 remembered that Bergman's "biggest asset was that he was a tremendously hard worker." Verber added, "He was the first one to practice and the last one to leave. In all the years I coached I never had anyone work harder than Dave." Bergman wasn't even considered the best player on his high-school team. That honor belonged to Joe Zdeb, who later played for the Kansas City Royals. The big-league scouts came to see Zdeb play, but were subsequently impressed by Bergman. In 2007 Bergman recalled, "I had no idea I was being scouted and was totally surprised when I was drafted in the 12th round by the Cubs in 1971. My whole life changed for me in 24 hours."

Bergman turned down his hometown Cubs and elected to attend Illinois State University. Recalling those events in 2001, Bergman said, "It was a tough decision not to sign! I truly felt a college degree was more important." He went on to play three years for the Illinois State Redbirds with a career .365 average while becoming the school's first Division I All-American. Bergman was also a batting champion, with a .341 average while playing for Chatham in the Cape Cod League for college players in the summer of 1973.

In June 1974, after his junior year, Bergman was drafted by the New York Yankees in the second round, and turned pro. He adapted well to pro ball playing for Oneonta, where he was the batting champion at .348 and the New York-Penn League Player of the Year. Based upon this impressive debut, in 1975 the Yankees moved him up to Double-A West Haven, but after six weeks he was hitting only .180. In a *New York Daily News* interview, Bergman said his manager, Pete Ward, told him, "I don't care if you hit .150, you're going to be in there every day. I know you can hit." Bergman responded to this vote of confidence by finishing the season at .311. Once again he was the league batting champion and Player of the Year.

On August 26, 1975, Bergman was called up to the Yankees as a replacement for Alex Johnson in the outfield. After being told only the previous night of his promotion, Dave rushed to New York. Not taking the time to eat, the excited rookie played in that evening's game on an empty stomach. On a wet field in Shea Stadium (the Yankees' home field while Yankee Stadium was being reconstructed), he slipped and fell in the second inning fielding a line-drive single by Billy Williams. At the plate he was 0-for-2, including a strikeout in his first big-league at-bat. After the game Bergman told the *New York Times*, "I can't believe I'm here. When something happens that you've wanted to do ever since you were a kid, it takes a while to set in." It also took a while for him to get his first major-league hit. It did not happen in 1975 as he went 0-for-17. In 2008 he recalled, "I just couldn't buy a hit. I tried bunting a couple of times. There is no doubt in my mind that on two of those bunts I was absolutely safe. One of the umpires said, 'You're not going to get your first hit on a bunt base hit,' and I said [to myself], 'Okay, welcome to the big leagues.'"

After batting .300 in winter ball, Bergman looked forward to spring training in 1976, but soon faced another obstacle to making the Yankees' roster: his manager, Billy Martin. In 2008 he remembered Martin telling him, "I don't even know why you are here. You are the worst player I have ever seen in a major-league uniform." Bergman's fortunes seemed to turn with Martin after participating in a bench-clearing brawl. "He was pulling me off the pile and I turned around to nail him and that's when I started playing, after that." Bergman received a lot of playing time because of injuries to the starters. "I was the most valuable player in spring training. I thought I had made the team and that I was going to start in the outfield." To his surprise, he was sent to Triple-A Syracuse instead.

In spite of his disappointment at not making the parent club, Bergman enjoyed a successful summer. He hit .295 with 65 RBIs and the Syracuse Chiefs, under the guidance of manager Bobby Cox, won the postseason Governor's Cup, the championship trophy of the International League. Also during that summer, Bergman married Cathryn Link, whom he had met in college.

His future with the Yankees appeared promising. The team protected him in the November 1976 expansion draft and signed him to a two-year contract. But the following spring, unable to land a roster spot on the talented and eventual world championship 1977 team, he was again sent to Syracuse.

In June Bergman's career took an abrupt turn when he became "the player to be named later" in a trade with Houston in which the Yankees received Cliff Johnson. Bergman was unable to clear waivers and was the center of a controversy over where he should finish the season. He was officially still the property of the Yankees, but unofficially committed to Houston. The Astros wanted him to report to their farm club in Charleston, West Virginia, but he wanted to remain in Syracuse. His wish was granted, and he remained at Syracuse, finishing the year with a .312 average, 16 home runs, and 29 stolen bases. Still coveted by the Yankees, Dave was a

DETROIT TIGERS 1984: WHAT A START! WHAT A FINISH!

September call-up. He remembered, "Billy Martin told me, 'You are not going anywhere.' There was a rumor that Cliff Johnson was damaged goods." On September 25 in Toronto, Bergman got his first major-league hit, a single off Mike Willis in the ninth inning of a 15-0 Yankees victory after replacing Johnson at first in the seventh inning. The hit broke his 0-for-18 streak dating back to 1975.

For the 1978 season Bergman became a Houston Astro. Commissioner Bowie Kuhn denied a request by the Yankees that the trade be nullified. Bergman told *The Sporting News*, "I am glad to be with Houston.…I think I'll get a chance here." It was at Houston that Bergman realized that his destiny in the majors was to be a utility player and not a regular. Bill Virdon, the Astros' manager, told him, "You have the potential to play in the big leagues for 15 years if you will channel all of your energies on the job description that I think is going to be with you for a long period of time." Taking this advice to heart, Bergman indicated that he decided to focus his energies on being "the best utility player I can possibly be. I am going to work twice as hard to make sure my skill set is very solid at first base and the outfield." That, he said, was "when my career started taking off."

In 1978 Dave got off to a slow start with the Astros, hitting .143 while playing sparingly at the All-Star break. After the All-Star Game, over a span of 26 games, he was inserted into the starting lineup, almost always as a left fielder against right-handed pitching. Bergman responded well, hitting .313 with 16 walks. He finished the season at .231 with only 186 plate appearances in 104 games. In 1978 he also completed the coursework for his business degree and graduated from Illinois State.

At the end of spring training in 1979 Bergman, who had a remaining option, was sent down to Charleston. "I was very disappointed," he said. "I still felt at that time I could compete at the major league level." Jim Beauchamp, the Charleston manager, was supportive of Bergman. "He was determined to work with me and get me back to the big leagues.… It seemed like the harder I worked, the worse I got. I had developed a hitch in my swing from trying to hit the ball to left field in Houston." Beauchamp brought in a hitting instructor to work with Bergman in the second half of the season and got his batting average up to .280 by the end of the International League season. Houston was in the middle of a pennant race when he rejoined the team that September. Bergman did his part in the stretch drive, going 6-for-15, but the Astros finished a game and a half behind the Reds. On September 26, he hit his first major-league home run, a pinch-hit shot off Phil Niekro, who notched the win and evened his record at 20-20. Phil's brother Joe took the loss for the Astros, putting him at 20-11.

The following spring Bergman made the Houston roster and at the age of 26 he was in the big leagues to stay for the next 13 seasons. The 1980 season was a memorable one for the Astros franchise. Houston battled for first place all season long. With only three games to play in the last series of the season, against Los Angeles, Houston held a three-game lead over the Dodgers, so needed only to win one game to clinch the National League West Division. They lost all three by one run, but prevailed 7-1 over the Dodgers in a one-game playoff. Bergman appeared in 90 games, often as a late-inning defensive replacement, with only 78 at-bats and a .256 average. He did make his contribution when called upon, including going 10-for-23 (.435) in August and September.

Many consider the playoff series between Houston and Philadelphia to be the best ever. It went the full five games, with the last four going into extra innings. In Game Two, Bergman's two-run triple off Kevin Saucier highlighted a four-run 10th-inning that sealed the victory for the Astros. He told the Syracuse Herald, "I'm Dave Bergman, so I figured [Saucier] was going to challenge me. He came in with a fastball and I came through this time." Ultimately the Phils won in the series, winning Game Five, 8-7.

After starting the 1981 campaign with Houston, on April 20 Bergman was traded to San Francisco. "I was very disappointed because we were starting to put together what we thought was going to be a very solid team for a long period of time. They felt they needed to make some changes," he recalled. Frank Robinson was the new manager of the Giants. Bergman said Robinson "taught me more about baseball than anybody I ever played for. He shared with me the little things about the game that I am not so sure that everybody has had the opportunity to learn at the major-league level. He created a monster in me. At that point in time I really, really became a student of the game."

In his three seasons at San Francisco Bergman averaged 135 at-bats and 84 games, playing mostly at first base with some time in the outfield as well as pinch-hitting. His batting average improved each year, with his best year being 1983, when he finished at .286. He started slowly that year but warmed up at the plate when he began to play more regularly in August after an injury to Champ Summers. He hit .392 in August and September. On August 30 Bergman had two home runs and five RBIs in a 13-2 win over Montreal. Frank Robinson told *The Sporting News*, "Bergie is our secret weapon. He's done a fine job without complaining about his situation. He's a professional and he's had a great attitude on this club." He also had great success as a pinch-hitter in 1983, ranking third in the National League with a .355 average.

Despite his success in 1983, on March 24, 1984, Bergman was traded by the Giants to Philadelphia for Alejandro Sanchez, an outfielder. The Phillies immediately sent Bergman and relief pitcher Willie Hernandez to Detroit for catcher-outfielder John Wockenfuss and outfielder Glenn Wilson.

Bergman told the *Detroit Free Press*, "The trade to the Tigers didn't please me at first. I thought I had done a good job with San Francisco last year, and then all of a sudden I'm being traded for a minor leaguer."

Bergman's mood changed quickly. Upon his arrival with the team, his former Giants teammate Darrell Evans told him, "You are going to be pleasantly surprised. This is going to be a real good team." After honing his skills for parts of eight seasons in the majors with three clubs, Bergman was ready to apply all he had learned to help his new team. For the Tigers,

DETROIT TIGERS 1984: WHAT A START! WHAT A FINISH!

1984 was a magical season, and for Bergman it was one of the best in his career. The Tigers roared off to a record start, going 35-5. Bergman found himself playing more regularly. Manager Sparky Anderson inserted him in the starting lineup on Opening Day. He appeared in 31 of those first 40 games, getting his batting average up to .286 through the first 39 of those contests and making some key contributions. On April 6, his first-inning two-run, two-out single gave the Tigers a three-run lead in what was ultimately a 3-2 win over the Chicago White Sox. On April 24 Bergman had an RBI single and scored the winning run as the Tigers rallied from two runs down in the bottom of the ninth against the Minnesota Twins. On May 11, he had two hits and drove in three runs in an 8-2 victory over California. Against Seattle on May 14, his pinch-hit triple in the eighth inning knocked in the winning run. The triple extended his six-game hitting streak, in which he had gone 11-for-22.

Throughout the season Anderson inserted Bergman in the lineup late in games for defensive purposes at first base. In this role he became an important figure in the late innings of Jack Morris' no-hitter on April 7. In the seventh inning he snared over his left shoulder the hardest-hit ball of the day, a line drive off the bat of Tom Paciorek. Many have speculated that the right-handed Barbaro Garbey, whom Bergman replaced at first base that inning, would have been unable to make the play. In the eighth inning, Dave went to his knees to knock down Jerry Hairston's hard-hit line drive, tossing the ball to Morris covering first to preserve the no-hitter.

The circumstances around Bergman's memorable June 4 home run contributed to the drama. Detroit's eight-game lead had shrunk to 4½ as second-place Toronto arrived in town. The Tigers had lost six of their last nine while the Blue Jays had won 10 of their last 12. The Tigers overcame a 3-0 deficit to tie the game in the seventh inning. Facing Roy Lee Jackson in the 10th with two out and two runners on base, Dave worked the count to 3-2. He then fouled off seven pitches in a row. Of that at-bat years later, Bergman told writer George Cantor: "There comes a time in every season when a hitter puts all his mechanics together. That night was it for me." The eighth pitch was a slider six inches off the ground that Bergman hit into the upper deck in right field for a 6-3 victory. "I don't have to tell you that it was the biggest thrill of my career," he said.

The Tigers went on to finish in first place by 15 games. They swept Kansas City in the best-of-five American League Championship Series and beat San Diego in five games in the World Series. Bergman appeared in 120 games and hit .273 with career highs of 44 RBIs and seven home runs. He went 1-for-1 in the ALCS but 0-for-5 in the World Series. In 2000 Bergman reflected back on that year: "That was just a collective team effort. We went to the ballpark every day knowing that we were going to win.... We had everyone pulling the cart in the same direction."

Fortunes changed in 1985. The Tigers finished in third place, 15 games back behind division-winning Toronto. Bergman suffered a torn elbow muscle in spring training. He returned after arthroscopic elbow surgery, playing in only 69 games and hitting just .179.

There was speculation in spring training in 1986 that Bergman was expendable. The Tigers had three left-handed-hitting first basemen on their roster. Nevertheless, Bergman survived the final cuts and in the second game of the season, on April 9, beat Boston with a pinch-single in the bottom of the 10th inning. He finished the year at .231, appearing in 65 games, while Detroit again finished third. One highlight for the season took place on June 17 when Bergman tagged out Alan Wiggins in the third inning of a 6-3 win at Baltimore using the hidden-ball trick.

Again early in 1987 there were rumors that Bergman would be released. Dave told the *Detroit Free Press*, "I've been going through this for ten years. I've never had it easy." Bergman responded to the challenge, hitting .370 in April with three home runs, six RBIs and seven walks with a .486 on-base percentage. The season was a thrilling one. The Tigers battled Toronto for first place at the end of the season with the two teams facing each other seven times in the final 11 days. Detroit prevailed, winning 1-0 in the last game of the season to clinch the AL East title. The Tigers lost the best-of-seven ALCS to Minnesota four games to one. Bergman appeared in 91 games that season, batting .273 with six homers. He said, "That was a team that really overachieved. It was a different type of atmosphere. I think we all knew that we weren't as good as years past. Everybody strapped it on every day and gave it everything they had. It was a fun, fun team." (One of Bergman's teammates that season was Jim Walewander, also a graduate of Bergman's high school, Maine South.)

The 1988 season was another exciting one for the aging Tigers. They battled for first place all season. On August 21 they held a four-game lead before experiencing injuries to key players. The team faded and finished second, just a game behind Boston. Bergman hit .323 through August, when he suffered a groin injury. After returning in September Dave batted only .203, but finished at a career-high .294. In 116 games that year with 289 plate appearances he hit in all nine spots in the batting order.

In 1989 the Tigers' performance dropped off dramatically, with the team losing 103 games. But for Bergman, it was an opportunity to play more regularly than at any other time in his career. He appeared in 137 games with career highs in at-bats (385) and hits (103), and a .268 average. He again appeared in all nine spots of the batting order. There were two other memorable moments. On August 5 Bergman caught Ozzie Guillen napping with the hidden-ball trick in the seventh inning of a 7-6 Tigers loss to the White Sox. "I tagged him so hard I think that I stunned him a little bit, that he just laid there." On August 10 his single with one out in the ninth broke up a bid for a no-hitter by the Texas Rangers' Nolan Ryan. In 2001 Bergman remembered, "In the late innings, I thought he was getting tired. I looked for a breaking ball and got it!"

At the end of the season the Tigers re-signed Bergman for another two years. On a losing team there was value in having a veteran who remained positive and came to the ballpark every day ready to play. Bergman told the *Detroit Free Press*, "Win or lose, I'm the same. I keep my mouth shut and play hard." With Cecil Fielder now playing first base and hitting home runs, Bergman's playing time in 1990 dropped off. He played in 100 games with 205 at-bats while hitting .278.

In his last two seasons, 1991 and 1992, Bergman played sparingly and hit .237 and .232, respectively. After the 1992 season he debated whether to return for another year. The Tigers indicated they did not have a place for him on the team. There were possible opportunities with Minnesota and Atlanta. Dave consulted with Sparky Anderson on his options. Bergman said Anderson told him, "David, you want to walk away from the game rather than the game throwing you away." In January 1993, at the age of 39, Bergman announced his retirement.

Looking back at his career in 2000, Bergman said, "I was lucky, very lucky to play as long as I did…. I worked very hard at my trade. Everyone I played for, I think would say something like, 'He was probably one of the hardest workers on our club and was always ready to play.' That's how I want to be remembered." Regarding his nine years playing for Sparky Anderson, Dave described him as "a great manager, he taught me how to be a man, and was a great role model."

While with the Tigers, Bergman made the Detroit area his permanent home. In 1989 he began work as a financial adviser for Sigma Investment Counselors. He helped the firm expand from a managed portfolio of $22 million to more than $500 million 19 years later. Dave was also very active in the Grosse Pointe Baseball Organization, sponsoring four teams. He was elected to the Illinois State University Hall of Fame. Approaching the 25-year reunion of the 1984 Tigers, he resided in Grosse Pointe, Michigan, and was the father of three grown children, Troy, born in 1979; Bria, born in 1982; and Erika, born in 1985—a year after some of her dad's greatest accomplishment in a uniform.

References

Publications

Cantor, George. *Wire To Wire*. Chicago: Triumph Books. 2004. 79-80.

Detroit Tigers 1986 Yearbook. Detroit: Detroit Tigers. 1986.

Articles

Brodsky, Marty. "Bergman Just Doing His Job for Tigers," *Oneonta Daily Star*, August 12, 1991. 12.

Brown, Clifton. "Bergman Not Ready To Give Up," *Detroit Free Press*, April 18, 1987. 1C.

Chass, Murray. "Yankees Rookie on Cloud 9," *The New York Times*, August 28, 1975. 27.

Forman, Ross. "Bergman's Autograph Collection Includes DiMaggio, Brett, Ryan." *Sports Collectors Digest*, February 4, 2000, 106.

Gage, Tom, "Bergman is Tigers' Mr. Cool in Clutch." *The Sporting News*, June 18, 1984. 15.

Guidi, Gene, "Survivor Bergman, 36, Will Return." *Detroit Free Press*, September 9, 1989. 1C.

Guidi, Gene. "Bergman Accepts Role." *Detroit Free Press*, September 6, 1984. 1D.

Guidi, Gene. "Bergman Seeks Return As Tiger Next Season." *Detroit Free Press*, September 29, 1992. 4C.

Pepe, Phil. "Johnson Out, Bergman In As Yanks Look to Future." *New York Daily News*, August 27, 1975. C22.

Peters, Nick. "Bench Production A Rare Bright Spot." *The Sporting News*, September 12, 1983. 24.

Richmond, Milton. "Houston's 'A.A' Popular…Astros Anonymous." *Syracuse Herald-Journal*, October 9, 1990.

Shattuck, Harry. "Ex-Yank Bergman Welcomes Change With Astros." *The Sporting News*, February 18, 1978. 62.

Tingley, Ken. "Bergman Reaches Prime," *Oneonta Daily Star*, August 8, 1984.

Web Sites

www.astrodaily.com/players/interviews/Bergman_Dave.html

www.baseball-reference.com

www.retrosheet.org

Other Sources

Nechal, Jerry, Interview with Dave Bergman, May 22, 2008.

Nechal, Jerry, Interview with George Verber, December 29, 2007.

Tom Brookens
by Larry Hilliard and Pat Kilroy

NUMBERS DON'T define Tom Brookens, but one has to start somewhere. Third base was his primary home for 10 major-league seasons with the Detroit Tigers, starting on July 10, 1979, through the 1988 season, followed by one-year stints with the New York Yankees and Cleveland Indians. His last major-league game was on September 30, 1990. Brookens played 1,206 games for the Tigers, 113 of them in the memorable 1984 season that garnered a World Series championship. During his Detroit career he played in 978 games at third base. In 1984 he backed up Alan Trammell at shortstop for 28 games, and Lou Whitaker at second base 26 times. In 1985, he even caught five innings for the Tigers and eventually played every position for Detroit except left field and pitcher.

Many refer to Brookens as a fan favorite. One Brookens admirer posted on the baseballfever.com Web site: "The man may not have had the best bat or glove, but you had to love his desire and hustle, the spectacles, and of course, that 'stache." Brookens, during a 2008 interview, disclosed a belated scoop of sorts. His photo from the 1980 Detroit Tigers Yearbook shows him clean-shaven. How can this be? Blame manager Sparky Anderson: "That was Sparky's rule, when I first got to Detroit in 1979. Originally Sparky had a rule—no mustaches allowed—and then in 1980 he really let loose. I had a mustache (in the minors) the day I was called up, and shaved the day I got to Tiger Stadium." Most times since 1980, though, Brookens' face has borne his trademark whiskers.

As to his nicknames, Brookens said, "They used to call me Brooky. …They didn't want to call me Brooks because I was certainly no Brooks [Robinson], that's for sure." Tigers radio broadcaster Ernie Harwell, combining Brookens' hitting prowess and birthplace—and mixing in a little musical history—conferred upon him the sobriquet "The Pennsylvania Poker."

Born Thomas Dale Brookens on August 10, 1953, in Chambersburg, Pennsylvania, he quickly made Fayetteville, a town outside Chambersburg, his home. Brookens married Krista Schoenfelt on New Year's Eve in 1976. "I knew her in high school and she's still puttin' up with me." Their union produced three daughters.

"In my hometown, Fayetteville, baseball was the thing for kids to do in the summertime. Baseball, it was always baseball," he said. "My dad was never a professional player but he was a sandlot player, a dairy farmer. I grew up on a farm and my mom worked at the elementary school as a cook." Baseball was a family affair for the Brookenses. Tom's identical twin brother, Tim, though drafted by Texas, played in Detroit's minor-league system. Ike Brookens, a cousin, pitched in the Detroit organization in the early 1970s and got into three games with the Tigers in 1975.

Attracting attention at Mansfield (Pennsylvania) State College (now Mansfield University), Brookens was the Tigers' first-round pick—fourth overall—in the January 1975, draft. "That's a little misleading, because everybody says you were a first-round pick, but I was taken in the January supplemental draft," Brookens said in typical modest fashion. "There might have only been 10 guys drafted in that whole draft, I don't know." Actually, future Tigers teammates Dave Rozema (fourth round) and Dave Tobik (first round, second pick overall) were picked in that draft; so too was Tigers teammate Ed Putman, the first-round (third overall) pick of the Chicago Cubs. Rozema was a key clubhouse figure on the 1984 team, with a carefree attitude the near polar opposite of Brookens' grind-it-out persona. Tobik, after parts of five years in a Detroit uniform, was an opposing pitcher in one of Brookens' best days as a major leaguer; Tom went 4-for-4 against the Texas Rangers on May 22, 1983, with an eighth-inning home run off Tobik.

But before the majors, Brookens toiled for 4½ seasons in the Detroit farm system. He started in that summer of 1975 in Montgomery, Alabama, appearing in 100 games for the Double-A Rebels, and stayed in Montgomery in 1976 for 137 more games, showing speed on the basepaths, making improvements across the board—batting, runs, RBIs, doubles, triples, homers, walks, and steals—and demonstrating his ability to play any infield position. That earned Brookens a promotion for 1977 to the Triple-A Evansville Triplets, where he showed he belonged, batting a solid .289 in 118 games, scoring 70 runs, and knocking in 52, while stealing 18 bases against better trained pitchers.

Brookens' path to Detroit was blocked by Tigers third baseman Aurelio Rodriguez, who held down the position capably for the Tigers with his steady glove and rocket arm. Meanwhile, blocking Brookens at the keystone positions were shortstop Alan Trammell and second baseman Lou Whitaker, both promoted in 1977, forming a major-league tandem with the parent club on Opening Day in 1978. Brookens had a shortened campaign in 1978. "I had a sore arm that year and it cut down on some of my playing time," Brookens said. "I was playing in Venezuela in winter ball and was in a car accident. I wasn't seriously injured but I dislocated my throwing shoulder in that car accident, and then when I came back to spring training (in '79) I never had a sore arm after that. So it was a little blessing in disguise."

Seventy-seven games into the 1979 season, Brookens was hitting .306, with 14 home runs and 46 RBIs, for manager Jim Leyland's Evansville Triplets. It was this level of performance that paved the way for his promotion to Detroit on July 10, 1979.

Aurelio Rodriguez's backup, Phil Mankowski, had played with Brookens in Montgomery, but broke a finger and had to be put on the disabled list. That gave Brookens an opening with the Tigers, in large part because of Leyland's recommendation. The rest of the Detroit brass wanted to go outside the organization and get Jim Morrison of the Philadelphia Phillies—Morrison finally got to Detroit in a mid-1987 trade—but Leyland suggested they give Brookens a shot because of the year he was having at Evansville.

DETROIT TIGERS 1984: WHAT A START! WHAT A FINISH!

"When I played for [Leyland] at Evansville, I wasn't the only one who thought [his] next stop would be managing the Tigers." Brookens said. "I've always appreciated [his recommending me]. But frankly, I thought it wouldn't be long before I was playing for him and we'd both be in Detroit. Then the Sparky [Anderson hiring] happened, and Jim kind of got lost in the shuffle." Leyland finally got his chance, being hired for 2006 and taking the Tigers to the World Series his first year at the helm.

Leyland wasn't the only one lost in the shuffle. "I played for Les [Moss in the minors] for four seasons, and I really liked Les Moss as a person and as a manager," Brookens said. Moss was promoted to manage the parent club for 1979, but was shown the door after 53 games and a 27-26 record to make way for eventual Hall of Fame skipper Anderson. In any case, Tom noted, the situation was out of the players' control: "I guess we don't think about it as much as the normal fan does. We just follow orders."

Brookens' first major-league game—and base hit—occurred on the night of his call-up, July 10, at Tiger Stadium. His debut single came off Minnesota's Geoff Zahn to left field in the second inning; then Brookens was the subject of a pickoff attempt but advanced to second on Zahn's errant throw. Moments later Brookens was caught trying to steal third. Nevertheless, the Tigers won, 6-5. Brookens had a better baserunning experience five days later against the Chicago White Sox, on July 15 at Comiskey Park. In the second inning he hit an RBI single scoring Lance Parrish, stole second, advanced to third on a throwing error by catcher Milt May, and finally stole home with Trammell at the plate.

The San Diego Padres purchased Rodriguez's contract after the 1979 season, and the Tigers traded Mankowski to the New York Mets along with outfielder Jerry Morales for third baseman Richie Hebner.

In 1980, his first season as a regular, and most frequently batting in the eighth spot, the 26-year-old Brookens hit a career-high .275 with 25 doubles, nine triples and 10 home runs. He drove in 66 runs. His range was very good at third, as it was most of his career, but he made 29 errors. Brookens' best game came on August 20, 1980. He started a triple play and went 5-for-5 on the road against the Milwaukee Brewers in an 8-6 Detroit win.

Brookens earned the respect of most fans but some—including those in the Detroit brass—never accepted his solid glove and light bat as good enough.

Though the young Tigers team was built around Trammell, Whitaker, and Parrish, Brookens became the closest thing to a regular third baseman that the Tigers had during the 1980s. Still, that didn't stop Sparky Anderson from trying to find more offense from the hot corner. Among the third basemen Sparky looked to replace Brookens with were Glenn Wilson (in a 1984 spring-training game that made Wilson even more determined to bolt from Detroit), Barbaro Garbey, Howard Johnson, Marty Castillo, Darrell Evans, Darnell Coles, Chris Pittaro, Lou Whitaker (spring 1985, with Anderson-anointed wunderkind Pittaro at second), Enos Cabell, Wayne Krenchicki, Jim Morrison, Ray Knight, and Luis Salazar.

Brookens had a great 4-for-5 day against the Yankees in New York on April 12, 1983, in a 13-2 whipping. On September 22 the Tigers, keyed by two Brookens hits, sent a late season "wait till next year" message to the eventual 1983 world champion Orioles with 5-4 win.

"We didn't have anything special in spring training, we were just plugging along," Brookens said of the 1984 Grapefruit League season. "I don't even know if we had a .500 record in spring training. [It was 11-17.] But then we come out 35-5 and that's when we realized we got the team right here…and things have a way when you're going good it just keeps going good, and when you're struggling, you stay struggling. But we knew we had a good team in '83."

Brookens' most memorable season was with that 1984 Tigers team with its 35-5 start. His personal start wasn't nearly as good as the team's. He started the season 0-for-12 in the first seven games he played, all Detroit wins. He got a couple of hits on April 13 at Boston in a 13-9 win, but didn't get another at-bat until April 18 when he got two more hits to double his season total. But the die had been cast; Sparky would use switch-hitting Howard Johnson for 108 games at third, and Brookens would also share time at the position with Marty Castillo, Barbaro Garbey, and Darrell Evans. Though not a full-time starter, Brookens appeared in 68 games at third and proved an indispensible utility man for Detroit, appearing in 28 games at shortstop and 26 at second base.

If one game during the Tigers' incredible start typified Brookens' team-oriented contributions, it was against the Indians on May 6. Playing in Cleveland's Municipal Stadium, the Tigers came from four runs down to tie the score in the top of the eighth. Brookens came in as a defensive replacement and was asked to lay down two sacrifice bunts, the second of which put the eventual winning run in scoring position. The Tigers won the game, 6-5, raising their record to 22-4.

As a future manager, Brookens understood the dilemma of needing a certain amount of offensive production out of each position. "I think the reason I fought every year to hold my job was that I was not a great offensive player," he said. "If I would have been a player that put up 20 home runs and drove in 70, 80, 90 runs, I don't think Sparky would have been looking for a new third baseman all the time. But I was not that type of offensive player and that's why I think they continued to search for someone that could give a little more offense on a consistent basis."

Brookens hit a key two-run triple on June 17, 1984, keying a sweep of the Brewers at home. Five days later he once again victimized Milwaukee. This time he went 2-for-2 with an RBI in the Tigers' 7-3 win. Brookens opened August with one of his few bad games, making two errors at shortstop and wasting a good effort by Dan Petry in a 4-2 loss to Cleveland. However, Brookens shook off the miscues almost immediately. Two days later he hit a home run against the Kansas City Royals in a loss. On August 6 in the opening tilt of a doubleheader at Boston, Brookens started off with a solo shot and scored two

DETROIT TIGERS 1984: WHAT A START! WHAT A FINISH!

runs in a tight 9-7 Tigers victory. In the second game he got two hits and scored a run off a rookie named Roger Clemens in a 4-2 Tigers loss. (Brookens hit a career .375 off Clemens.) On August 15 Brookens came through for Petry, going 3-for-3 plus a sacrifice bunt with two RBIs in an 8-3 home win against the Angels.

As they had at the beginning of the season, the Tigers got off to a quick start on September 16. Brookens was one of four Tigers who hit homers in a 8-3 victory over the second-place Toronto Blue Jays. "That series was the clinching blow that won it for us," Brookens said. Detroit had vanquished its closest foes and had come just shy of taking the American League East title in their presence.

But he wasn't done contributing yet. In the seventh inning of the division-clinching win, against the Brewers on September 18, Brookens hit a solo homer for Detroit's final run in the 3-0 win. After the Tigers clinched the division, Brookens started only two more games that season, both in the final weekend. Physical woes kept him from starting, but not from getting a spot on the postseason roster. Brookens played in the first two games of the 1984 American League Championship Series against Kansas City and in Games One, Two, and Four of the 1984 World Series.

Brookens' best friend on that 1984 team was probably Alan Trammell. "Probably him and Jack Morris, those two guys, more than the other guys some. Dave Bergman is a good friend." As for the season's catalyst reliever Willie Hernandez, "He seemed to make it all come together when he came in and gave us a stopper. I don't know what the real missing ingredient was. Darrell Evans came over at that time, too, and became the first baseman. He gave us a veteran player and was kind of a team leader," Brookens recalled. He and his Tigers teammates continued to keep in touch over the years with the Tigers' fantasy camp in Lakeland, Florida. The highlight of 1984 "was just being on that club, we didn't have a single 20-game winner, we didn't have anybody that drove in 100 runs, and those are earmarks for superstars. That tells you it must've been a team effort for us to win. Even guys who were part-time players won games for us."

Brookens had another big day against a Hall of Fame pitcher in 1985, when Don Sutton started but didn't stay long, as Brookens went 4-for-5 with an RBI single on May 17 at Oakland in a 10-2 Tigers victory over the A's. This great day at the plate is also memorable in another respect: In the Tigers' half of the ninth inning, a Brookens-batted ball hit the umpire and stayed in his coat. On the same date in 1987, Brookens put the hurt on another Hall of Fame pitcher, taking Cleveland's Steve Carlton deep for a home run.

Brookens again whacked a Carlton pitch over the left-field wall in the first inning of a game on August 18, 1987, when Carlton's hanging-on tour of the majors was sputtering to a stop and the Tigers were neck-and-neck with Toronto for the American League East flag. On September 23 Brookens keyed a must-win game at Boston with two doubles. The Tigers finally shook off the Blue Jays, sweeping them on the last weekend of the season in Tiger Stadium, but ran up against the eventual world-champion Minnesota Twins in a very loud Metrodome.

"We were disappointed that we ended up getting beat by Minnesota, but they had a nice ballclub too and ended up winning the World Series," Brookens said. He remembered the Metrodome as "something else, I'm playing third base and hollering at Jack Morris on the mound, and he can't hear me. That place gets rockin', and usually not in your favor." In all, Brookens was hitless in 13 postseason at-bats.

In his final year with the Tigers, 1988, Brookens batted in six Tigers runs on June 14, going 4-for-4 with a double and a second-inning grand slam off the Orioles' Dickie Noles, who had been a Tigers teammate at the tail end of the '87 season.

In spring training 1989, Chris "Tin Man" Brown came to Detroit with Keith Moreland from San Diego for pitcher Walt Terrell and was handed the starting third-base job. Before spring training was over, Brookens was dealt to the Yankees; Brown was such a bust that the Tigers released him in mid-May. "Sparky called me in to the office and told me I'd been traded to the Yankees for Charlie Hudson," he remembered. "[I] spent that season with the Yankees, was released by them at the end of the year. Cleveland signed me to a one-year deal in 1990, and then I retired at the end of that year." By the time he hung up his spikes, Brookens had played in 1,336 games—all but 130 for Detroit—and hit .246 with 175 doubles, 40 triples, and 71 home runs.

Tom lost his mother to cancer in 1982. "That was a tough go…but my dad is still alive and living in Pennsylvania," he said in a 2008 interview. Fellow Pennsylvanian Don Wert, the 1968 Tigers' third baseman, is a mutual acquaintance, as is John Hiller, a teammate of Brookens in 1979 and 1980. Hiller and Wert are fellow Tigers fantasy camp coaches who reunite with Brookens over the years. "They (the 1968 team) had a great team and so did we. Who was better?" Brookens asked aloud. "Let the fans decide that one."

Brookens was an accomplished darts player as a young man growing up in Pennsylvania, and in his offseasons and retirement years he liked to use guns and a bow to hunt turkey and deer. He also played golf in the warm weather, especially with many of his former teammates while in Lakeland for the Tigers' fantasy camp.

Brookens was out of the game after his retirement following the 1990 season and was committed to staying close to home while his young daughters grew to college age during the 1990s, but he held out some hope that he could return to the game, and the Tigers called in 2005, hiring him to manage the Oneonta Tigers, their short-season A-ball affiliate in the New York-Penn League. The club earned a playoff spot in 2005. After 2006 the Tigers rewarded Brookens with a promotion to the Class A West Michigan Whitecaps in 2007; the club won the Midwest League title in that year. In 2008 he became manager of his third minor-league team in four years, the Erie SeaWolves of the Double-A Eastern League, landing one playoff appearance in his two seasons there.

DETROIT TIGERS 1984: WHAT A START! WHAT A FINISH!

"You manage a little bit different as you make some more pitcher moves because you go with a little bit more with match-ups here [in Double-A] where in the lower classifications you'll just run a pitcher out there and you're going to pitch this inning no matter what happens and show me what you can do," Brookens said, explaining his managerial style. "Here you may get another guy up to come in in a right-lefty matchup, that type of situation, because you're really preparing them — a little bit more now — for what they're going to encounter if they go to Triple-A, or even to Detroit."

Brookens' performance in the Tigers' minor-league system helped him land a position on manager Jim Leyland's staff as first base, outfield, and baserunning coach for the 2010 season.

References

Publications

Falls, Joe. *Detroit Tigers: An Illustrated History*. New York: Prentice-Hall, 1989.

Middlesworth, Hal, ed. *Detroit Tigers 1980 Yearbook*. Detroit: Detroit Tigers. 1980.

Pattison, Mark, and David Raglin. *Detroit Tigers Lists and More: Runs, Hits and Eras*. Detroit: Wayne State University Press. 2002.

Articles

Borawski, Brian, "Kenny Rogers, Livan Hernandez and Tom Brookens." November 16, 2007, available online at http://www.tigerblog.net/kenny-rogers-livan-hernandez-and-tom-brookens/

Cassidy, Mike "Erie Sweeps Doubleheader Over Bowie." April 5, 2008, available online at http://www.tigersminors.com/category/erie-seawolves-april-2008/

Web Sites

Dave's Blog, 1984 Tigers Tribute Site: Paying Tribute to the Greatest Tiger Team of My Generation http://www.1984tigers.com/

- posted November 15, 2004 "The Great Debate - 1975 Reds vs. 1984 Tigers - Howard Johnson" by Brian @ 9:09 pm Filed under Debate, Howard Johnson
- June 1 "Tigers Sweep Brewers, Remain Six Games Up"
- June 22 "Tigers Upend Brewers in Front of Full House"
- August 1 "Tigers Start August Off on Rough Note"
- August 15 "Petry Pitches Tigers to Victory"
- September 16 "Tigers Pound Jays, Magic Number Now Two"

http://www.baseball-fever.com/showthread.php?referrerid=8503&t=66079

http://en.thinkexist.com/quotes/tom_brookens/2.html

http://www.thebaseballpage.com/players/brookto01.php

http://www.thebaseballcube.com/

- statistics/1984/11.shtml
- box/1983/DET198309220.shtml

http://www.retrosheet.org/boxesetc/1979/B07150CHA1979.htm

http://www.retrosheet.org/boxesetc/1983/B04120NYA1983.htm http://www.retrosheet.org/boxesetc/1984/B05060CLE1984.htm

http://www.retrosheet.org/boxesetc/1985/B05170OAK1985.htm

http://www.retrosheet.org/boxesetc/1987/B09230BOS1987.htm

1987 ALCS Game Two—www.retrosheet.org/boxesetc/1987/B10080MIN1987.htm

Other Sources

Hilliard, Larry, and Pat Kilroy. Interview with Tom Brookens, April 5, 2008, in Bowie, Maryland.

Leonardi, Ron. Interview with Tom Brookens, September 1, 2008, in Erie, Pennsylvania

http://www.erietube.com/kickapps/_Interview-with-Tom-Brookens/audio/190495/3766.html

Acknowledgments

Thanks to the Mayo Smith Society and of course to Tom Brookens for granting us the interview.

Marty Castillo
by John McMurray

ALTHOUGH MARTY Castillo appeared in only 70 games for the 1984 Detroit Tigers, he is best remembered for his clutch postseason production. Not only did Castillo knock in the winning run to clinch the pennant in the third game of the American League Championship Series, but he also put the Tigers ahead to stay in Game Three of the World Series with a home run. After that homer, *Sports Illustrated* put his accomplishment in context, saying: "Gionfriddo, Larsen, Drabowsky, Weis, Doyle, Bevacqua.... To the list of unlikely Series heroes, add the name Marty Castillo."

The 1984 season was Castillo's best in the major leagues. He set personal highs in almost every major offensive category—modest as they were—while serving as a valuable defensive substitute at both catcher (36 games) and third base (33 games). Those offensive numbers included a .234 batting average, 33 hits—11 of them for extra bases—and 17 RBIs. On August 26, 1984, Castillo went 3-for-4 and scored three runs in a victory over the Los Angeles Angels. On September 23, he went 2-for-3 with a home run and 2 RBIs to help the Tigers win their 100th game of the season, a 4-1 victory over the New York Yankees.

Still, devoted fans of the team may recall Castillo more for his outgoing nature and for his reputation as a practical joker than for what he did on the field. (His reputation as a prankster goes back to his childhood, when, at the age of four, he accidentally set his family's house on fire and burned the place down.)

In Game Three of the 1984 Championship Series against the Kansas City Royals, Castillo drove in Chet Lemon when he grounded into a force out at second base in the second inning. The Royals tried to turn a double play that would have negated Lemon's run but Castillo, hardly a speedster, beat the relay to first. Castillo's RBI turned out to be the only run the Tigers scored off Kansas City Royals starter Charlie Leibrandt, who lost 1-0 despite pitching a complete game. Castillo also went 2-for-4 in Game One, with another RBI to his credit.

Castillo continued with his timely offense in the World Series. In Game Three, with the Tigers and the San Diego Padres at one win apiece, Castillo came to bat against Padres starter Tim Lollar in the second inning with Lemon on base and the game scoreless. He drove a 1-2 pitch into the left-field seats at Tiger Stadium to give his team a lead in the game that it did not relinquish. Writing about the game, *Detroit News* sportswriter Tom Gage wrote, "[Castillo is] Sparky Anderson's version of the Mickey Stanley move of 1968 [when manager Mayo Smith moved the outfielder to shortstop for the World Series], maybe not as daring, but so far as successful." Howard Johnson had played the lion's share of innings at third base in 1984, but manager Anderson lost confidence in him near season's end. Tom Brookens, who always seemed to be battling to hold onto his job at the hot corner, may have been too injured to play regularly, making just two brief appearances in the American League Championship Series and three in the World Series. Darrell Evans and rookie Barbaro Garbey, who had also played third for Detroit in '84, actually had put in more time at first base and were being relied on by Anderson, along with Dave Bergman, in a first base/designated hitter/pinch hitter rotation. That left Castillo, and he responded.

The day after Game Three, Thomas Boswell of the *Washington Post* wrote, "The night's recipient of the Kurt Bevacqua Award is: Marty Castillo of the Tigers. There are probably people related to Castillo that don't know he's playing in the Series these days. That didn't keep the No. 9 batter, whose usual position is 'bench,' from hitting a game-winning, two-run homer."

Castillo modestly pointed out that he did not celebrate as effusively as Bevacqua did when he homered to beat the Tigers in Game Two. "Marty Castillo isn't Kurt Bevacqua," Castillo said. "Bevacqua has been around. He's established. I could just see myself doing that and (Goose) Gossage knocking me upside the head the next time I came to the plate. It's not my personality to do something like that."

Anderson said Castillo "hit the ball a lot harder than Bevacqua did. He nailed it." Yet Castillo was more modest in summing up the biggest moment of his career: "[Lollar] just happened to throw a fastball and hit my bat where I was swinging it. He made a mistake pitch, and I'm supposed to hit mistakes. It's as simple as that."

In Game Five, Castillo walked in the eighth inning and was on base when Kirk Gibson hit the iconic three-run homer that sealed the game, and the Series, for Detroit. For the World Series, Castillo batted .333 (3-for-9) with a .455 on-base percentage and a .667 slugging percentage, with two runs scored, a pair of walks, and two RBIs from his own memorable home run.

Martin Horace Castillo was born on January 16, 1957, in Long Beach, California. He was drafted by the Minnesota Twins in 1975 and by the California Angels in 1977 but chose to attend Chapman College (now University) in Orange, California. Selected by the Tigers in the fifth round of the amateur draft in 1978, he signed with the team and spent 1978 through 1983 making his way through the Tigers' farm system. He started with Class A Lakeland, spent part of a season at Double-A Montgomery, and was at Triple-A Evansville for five seasons, with two short spells with the Tigers.

Castillo appeared with Detroit for six games in 1981—he made his major-league debut on August 19 against the Minnesota Twins, starting at third base. He appeared in one game in 1982, then stuck with the team in 1983. But with Tom Brookens as the team's regular third baseman—more often than not, anyway—Castillo quickly assumed a role as a backup, taking occasional turns at third base and catcher.

Castillo hit his first major-league home run on June 28, 1983, against Milwaukee's Jim Slaton, and it put the Tigers ahead 5-4 in the top of the ninth inning in a game Detroit held on to win. The victory put the Tigers into a three-way tie for first place in the American League East. "It's the best feeling of my whole life," said Castillo, who had been called up from Evansville only eight days before.

Yet Castillo was mostly valued for his defense. In May 1984, Gene Guidi of the *Detroit Free Press* commented that "[Castillo's] versatility puts [Anderson] at ease just about anywhere on the field. He's the perfect insurance policy. Most games, Castillo sits in the Tigers dugout and roots for pals like Tom Brookens or Howard Johnson to come up with a big hit or defensive gem. He knows that he'll play only if a teammate is hurt or needs a day off.

"My wife (Julie) and I were discussing my situation the other day and I told her that I love Brookie and HoJo (Howard Johnson) and can't pull for them not to do well just so I get a chance to play more," Castillo said. "When they're out there, I hope they hit a home run or make a diving stop.... And I take a lot of pride in being ready in case they need me."

Castillo worked with former Tigers catcher Bill Freehan to improve his own skills behind the plate. Early in the 1984 season, Castillo conceded that he could get rusty when he did not catch for a while, which may explain his five errors at the position during that season. Still, Anderson endorsed Castillo wholeheartedly: "He can play first, third and catch, and that makes him very valuable," Sparky said. "Guys like Castillo will always help good teams. Maybe he wouldn't be able to help a bad team that couldn't use him right, but good teams always have a player or two like Marty."

Popular with his teammates, Castillo was praised for his skills in playing "toss" with them in pregame warmups. *Detroit News* writer Gary Santaniello called him "the Tigers' funkmaster of the sidelines," and first baseman Mike Laga claimed that "Marty's got it all: knuckle-curve, forkball, knuckler. His fastball's a little straight, though." Still, teammate Nelson Simmons was impressed with Castillo's ability, saying: "Some pitchers can't throw that good."

Castillo even appeared in a Detroit-area commercial for Little Caesars Pizza, expressing mock outrage that he was not included among the star players who were pictured on commemorative glasses offered by the chain. According to *Sports Illustrated*: "[Castillo] is an outgoing practical joker, one of the more popular Tigers. He's so nice that Tom Monaghan, owner of the club and Domino's Pizza, doesn't object to Castillo's endorsing Little Caesars Pizza. When asked if the [World Series] home run might open the door to more commercial opportunities, Castillo said, 'I'm not going to worry about it. But my new phone number is…'"

Castillo played in five seasons with the Tigers and had to struggle to make the team every year. When he heard about the large bonuses that teammates had in their contracts, he cracked: "I've got an attendance clause in my contract, too. It kicks in when the team draws two billion people." The right-handed-throwing, right-handed-hitting Castillo played in 201 games for the Tigers over the five seasons, never more than 70 in a season, batting .190 with 8 home runs and 32 RBIs. It may be to some a dubious distinction, but Castillo made the cut in Al Pepper's book *Mendoza's Heroes: Fifty Batters Below .200*, which chronicled the career exploits of—in Pepper's estimation—the 50 best position players whose career batting average fell below the mythical "Mendoza line," named after Pittsburgh, Seattle, and Texas infielder Mario Mendoza, who had five sub-.200 seasons at the plate, including four in a five-year span.

In a 2001 article in the *Detroit News*, Castillo was asked about his toughest moment in the big leagues. He replied, "It happened in Kansas City. The players threw grasshoppers all over me." But tougher times were in store. After being released by Detroit on January 16, 1986, on his 29th birthday, Castillo had hoped to get another chance in major-league baseball. At the time of his release, he was playing winter ball for the Escogido Leones in the Dominican Republic. The day before, Castillo had filed for salary arbitration and was upset at the Tigers' offer of only a modest salary increase, leading him to request his release.

"Actually, it's not the money," said Castillo. "What I really want is the chance to get more than one at-bat in a five-week period." Castillo had been on the All-Star team in the Dominican Republic, where he was an exceedingly popular player. "Maybe I'll retire. Maybe I'll open a shack down here and sell conch shells," he cracked. Within hours of Castillo's release, the Tigers traded for Dave Engle from the Minnesota Twins to take Castillo's spot on the roster as the team's backup catcher. It turned out to be a bust, as Engle caught only three games in a season when regular catcher Lance Parrish was hampered with back miseries. Dwight Lowry, Mike Heath, and Matt Nokes each caught more games than Engle, while Castillo landed a job with the Minnesota Twins' top farm club in Toledo for his last season in professional baseball. Castillo didn't get behind the plate at all for the Mud Hens, instead playing third base and the outfield.

After leaving baseball, Castillo kept a low profile. A 2006 *Detroit Free Press* article reported that he owned a place called the Upper Deck in Cape Coral, Florida, which was run by his wife, Shelly LaPaglia; they had a son together named A.J. But even that wispy trail vanishes. *The Detroit News* and the *Detroit Free Press* were unable to locate him when they published retrospectives about the team, and the Tigers themselves were not able to provide any information about his whereabouts. His missing-in-action status spawned at least one likely tall story about his activities—that Castillo was in Malaysia managing a local baseball team called the Tioman Tsunamis on Tioman Island, a small volcanic island in the South China Sea with a predominantly Muslim population. The legend was first posted on Wikipedia, and others were citing the online reference service as the source for the story, but Wikipedia's editors retracted the assertion from Castillo's biography on the site when no independent verification could be found.

DETROIT TIGERS 1984: WHAT A START! WHAT A FINISH!

References

Publications

Detroit News. *The Magic Season*. Indianapolis: News Books International, 1984.

Articles

Boswell, Thomas, "Two-Run Homer Wins for Tigers," *Washington Post*, October 13, 1984, F1.

Bragg, Brian, "Tigers Win on Castillo HR," *Detroit Free Press*, July 29, 1983.

Guidi, Gene, "Ability, Wit Make Castillo Popular," *Detroit Free Press*, May 13, 1984, 1D.

Macnow, Glen, "Castillo Has Lots of Fans But No Job," *Detroit Free Press*, January 20, 1986, 1D.

Santaniello, Gary, "Castillo Crowned King of the Toss," *Detroit News*, May 29, 1985, 1D.

Vincent, Charlie, "Utility Man Proves Useful at Plate," *Detroit Free Press*, October 13, 1984, 1D.

Wulf, Steve. "Detroit Jumped All Over 'Em: The Tigers Leaped to the Fore in Every Game as They Bounded Past the Padres to Win the 81st World Series," *Sports Illustrated*, October 22, 1984. (Available online at http://sportsillustrated.cnn.com/baseball/mlb/features/1997/wsarchive/1984.html).

Web Sites

http://en.wikipedia.org/wiki/Marty_Castillo

www.baseball-reference.com.

www.retrosheet.org.

Scott Earl
by Kent and Chuck Ailsworth with Carl Shinkle

FROM SEPTEMBER 10 through September 30, 1984, Scott Earl appeared in 14 games for the Detroit Tigers. In those games, he played in some of the now-gone classic ballparks of the American League: parks like Yankee Stadium in New York, County Stadium in Milwaukee, and Memorial Stadium in Baltimore, for and against Hall of Fame managers, witnessed the batting championship, and played against future Hall of Famers Robin Yount, Don Sutton, Dave Winfield, Eddie Murray, and Cal Ripken Jr. He was also part of a team about to win its first World Series in nearly a generation.

In Earl's debut, on September 10, the visiting Detroit Tigers were losing to the defending world champions from 1983, the Baltimore Orioles. Baltimore finished the season as one of only two teams with a winning record against the Tigers (the other was the Boston Red Sox). On the mound for the Orioles was former Cy Young Award winner Mike Flanagan. Up to that point, all three of Flanagan's starts against Detroit that season had been complete games in which he allowed a total of three earned runs. In 1984 Flanagan was one of two pitchers to win three games against Detroit, with his only loss coming in a 1-0 game.

During this game, Flanagan was cruising into the eighth inning, leading 2-1 and having allowed just four hits. Other than Kirk Gibson's solo home run in the fourth inning, the Tigers were looking pretty harmless. After Marty Castillo flied out to lead off the eighth, Rusty Kuntz came in to pinch-hit. The ever-optimistic Sparky Anderson had already promised a rookie, fresh from Evansville, a pinch-running major-league debut if Kuntz could get on. Rusty came through, doing what no other Tiger had yet accomplished in the game: he drew a walk. Scott Earl, wearing No. 24 on his uniform, officially became a major-leaguer as he ran for Kuntz.

Baltimore's first baseman was future Hall of Famer Eddie Murray, who was well on his way to winning his third consecutive Gold Glove award. Earl recalled of his debut 25 years later: "Sparky said if Rusty got on I was going to pinch-run and the steal sign would be if [coach] Roger Craig put his arm over the top of the bench seats. Eddie Murray was playing first and wouldn't shut up. So I told him I was kind of busy and couldn't talk." Whatever Craig might have done with his arm, Earl remained stranded on first as Barbaro Garbey and Alan Trammell made outs peacefully to end the inning. Earl stayed in the game at second base and had a great view of one of Murray's 504 career home runs in the bottom of the eighth inning as Flanagan's Orioles went on to win 3-1. The game ended before Scott got a chance to bat.

William Scott Earl was born on September 18, 1960, in Seymour, Indiana, a small town about 65 miles south of Indianapolis, to Bill and Doris Earl. He was one of three children; there were two daughters, Sherri and Sandy. Earl went to college about 150 miles away at Eastern Kentucky University in Richmond, where he played varsity baseball. He set the Colonels' record for most consecutive games hit safely, at 27.

Earl, who went by the first name of Scott to differentiate himself from his same-named father, was playing for Danville

DETROIT TIGERS 1984: WHAT A START! WHAT A FINISH!

in the Central Illinois Collegiate League in 1981 when the Detroit Tigers selected him in the 14th round (353rd pick) of the June amateur draft. Earl recalled in 2009, "My father called me late one night after a game to inform me the Tigers drafted me. I was both relieved and nervous knowing I was to talk to the Tigers the next day about a contract. [My] friends and family were all excited and proud."

Earl started playing in the Detroit organization in 1981 on the lowest rung of the Organized Baseball ladder. He began with the Bristol (Virginia) Tigers in the Rookie-level Appalachian League. Scott said, "I started the first game over two other second basemen. I think it was in Johnson City and I went 1-for-3." In 52 games that season, he had 47 hits, including three home runs. He batted .260 and stole 13 bases without being caught.

In 1982 Earl moved up to the Tigers' Lakeland affiliate in the Class A Florida State League. In 136 games he had 133 hits with 12 home runs, and batted .287. He made the all-star team, leading the league's second basemen in total chances (742), putouts (292), and double plays (96), and he showcased his speed with 34 steals.

Earl moved up to Double-A ball in 1983, playing for Birmingham in the Southern League. In 144 games he had 138 hits, including ten triples, ten home runs, and a .261 batting average. He led Birmingham with 36 steals, was named to the Southern League's All-Star team, and was rated the league's best defensive second baseman by *Baseball America*.

In 1984 Earl climbed to the top of the minor-league ladder with his promotion to Triple-A Evansville of the American Association. He played in 153 games for the Triplets and batted .251 with 134 hits, eight triples, and 11 home runs. He tied for the league lead with 77 walks. His fielding once more won raves as he led the league's second basemen in games (137), putouts (277), assists (423), total chances (721), and double plays (105). He was named to the American Association and Topps/National Association Triple-A Team. After consulting with the league's managers, Baseball America named him the fastest baserunner in the American Association.

Earl's 1984 numbers, along with his range and slick fielding, drew attention in Detroit. At the time of his debut, Kirk Gibson was leading Detroit with 26 stolen bases, and the Tigers as a team swiped 106 bases by season's end. No doubt Earl's 41 steals had a lot to do with his breaking in as a pinch-runner.

After his big-league debut, Earl made three additional appearances in the field as a late-inning replacement for Tigers second baseman Lou Whitaker, but got no at-bats. At Tiger Stadium on his 24th birthday, September 18, the Tigers clinched the American League East title for the first time since 1972, defeating the Milwaukee Brewers. Earl remembered in 2009: "There was a lot of celebrating in the clubhouse and plans to party afterwards. Sparky told me I was starting the next day so I went home" early. On September 19, Earl finally got his first start. He led off for the Tigers, and his first at-bat, in the first inning, resulted in a fly out to right field. He batted again in the second and connected for a triple off the Brewers' Tom Candiotti, driving in Doug Baker for the Tigers' third run. "After the triple. Alex Grammas got the ball for me and Rusty Kuntz wrote the info on it," Earl recalled. Jack Morris and a lineup of Tigers rookies and backups beat the Brewers, 4-2.

A week later, in Milwaukee, Earl tried his hand at larceny against the Brewers with his first stolen-base attempt. Gold Glove winner Cecil Cooper was playing first base, Hall of Fame pitcher Don Sutton was on the mound, and six-time Gold Glove winner Jim Sundberg was behind the plate. Sundberg was the only American League catcher in 1984 to throw out at least half of those trying to steal on him. The undaunted Tiger rookie pilfered second and scored on a single by Nelson Simmons.

The Tigers clinching the division was the highlight of Earl's 1984 season. Other memorable moments for him included "seeing [Cal] Ripken playing in my first major-league game and being a part of [Don] Mattingly winning the batting title over [Dave] Winfield." In Mattingly's final at-bat of the season, he hit a ball far to Earl's left, between first and second base. Scott got to the ball, but it took a bad hop over his glove and was ruled a hit. Earl recalled that Mattingly "later said he didn't think I would get near it." Winfield, batting next in the Yankees order, could no longer catch Mattingly for the title and hit into a force out in his final at-bat. Mattingly took the AL batting title, .343, to Winfield's .340. Had Earl's play been ruled an error and a still-hopeful Winfield had followed up with a hit, the results would have been different, with Winfield winning the title, .3422 to 3416.

Earl's top two personal triumphs in baseball were the triple off Candiotti, and his performance in another Tigers-Yankees game. On September 29, the Tigers were looking for win number 104 to pass the 1968 Tigers for the team's most wins in a season. Pitching for the Yankees was former Cy Young Award winner Ron Guidry. Earl had two hits that day as the team set the record with its 11-3 triumph.

Earl started at second base for eight of his 14 Tigers games. He had four hits (three singles and the triple) in 35 at-bats. He scored three runs, stole one base, and drove in one run. In the field, Scott had a .959 fielding average and was involved in nine double plays, three with Trammell. After the World Series, he became one of only 35 who could claim they played for the 1984 world champions. Having joined the team after September 1, Earl was not eligible for the postseason roster.

Tigers reliever Bill Scherrer, who joined the club in August 1984, accidentally discovered that there were three different types of World Series rings given by the Tigers. According to Scherrer, once this discovery was made, everybody on the team got their rings appraised. The low-end rings were worth about $80 to $250, and the high-end rings about $3,000. Scherrer found out frontline players received the top rings, followed by "scouts and people like that," with partial-playoff-share players getting the low-end rings. Even so, Scherrer said his ring would never be sold. It also meant a lot to Scherrer when he heard that Jack Morris no longer always wore his ring once he found out about the three grades. (Years later,

DETROIT TIGERS 1984: WHAT A START! WHAT A FINISH!

as a scout with Cincinnati in 1990, Scherrer got his high-end World Series ring.)

Yet there was an even lower rung on the ladder; Earl never got a World Series ring from the Tigers. Asked about it, he said, "I never understood why we all didn't get rings. I had someone tell me that he researched the ten previous [to 1984] World Series champs and the ten following World Series champs and (all) those organizations gave every player rings who played on either their 25- or 40-man roster as long as they actually were on the team at some point. ... I heard the grounds crew guy in Lakeland even got a ring. ... Oh, well, it goes that way sometimes." (He did not put in a bid on Doug Baker's ring, which was put up for auction on eBay in 2010.) About the same time as the ring fiasco was taking place, baseball card manufacturer Donruss produced a 1985 card (#491) of a "promising young second baseman" by the name of Scottie Earl.

As a middle infielder, Earl's path was blocked on the Tigers by Whitaker at second and Alan Trammell at shortstop. Both players were All-Stars and Gold Glove winners. Earl remembered, "It was enjoyable watching them play, but it was frustrating seeing probably ten or twelve second basemen in the league I could beat out." His 1984 Triple-A statistics compared with the American League numbers of the 62 players who appeared at second base in the American League that season would have placed him eighth in hits, fifth in homers and RBIs, and second in steals.

So making the 1985 Tigers as an infielder would be no easy task with Whitaker and Trammell guaranteed starting jobs. In addition, a very capable Tom Brookens could fill in for them. Also, a surprise was in store for Earl and the Tigers that spring. The 1985 *Sports Illustrated* annual scouting report summed it up best:

"Howard Johnson went to the Mets for pitcher Walt Terrell, but [Sparky] Anderson has seen fit to replace him with rookie [Chris] Pittaro, who is replacing Whitaker, who returns to second to replace Pittaro, who was replacing Whitaker in the first place.

"'As the Infield Turns,' in the words of [Lance] Parrish, began when Anderson fell in love with Pittaro, a second baseman who hit .284 at Class AA Birmingham last year. The manager decided that because Whitaker would eventually be his third baseman, it was the ideal time switch, a move, he said, that was 'etched in stone.' But when Whitaker had second thoughts about playing third, the experiment ended after five days. 'From now on, all my moves will be etched in Jell-O,' says Anderson."

Sparky was known for predicting greatness from unproven talent. Long before poor Pittaro, Kirk Gibson— no slouch himself—was going to be Sparky's next Mickey Mantle, and, years later, Torey Lovullo would have to carry a similar burden. Scott said in 2009, "I thought I would make the [1985] team until Sparky went nuts over Chris Pittaro." The gifted Hall of Fame manager, like Earl, also played second base and after just one season in the big leagues, neither ever got a second chance. Yet, as numerous other Reds and Tigers declared before him, Earl had to agree, "I enjoyed playing for Sparky."

In 1985, Pittaro lasted just 28 games at third base before Brookens took over. The Tigers then picked up 10-year veteran Doug Flynn from the Montreal Expos as Whitaker's backup. Flynn, who had been a starting second baseman the previous seven seasons, usually got to watch Whitaker, who played in 152 of the 162 scheduled games.

Scott Earl spent all of 1985 with the Tigers' new Triple-A affiliate in Nashville. He batted .236, hit seven home runs, drove in 44 runs while scoring 55, and stole 23 bases. He led American Association second basemen in games played with 118 and putouts (263). Former 1984 Tigers Doug Baker, Dave Bergman, Rusty Kuntz, Mike Laga, Dwight Lowry, Sid Monge, Randy O'Neal, and Nelson Simmons were teammates of Earl in Nashville at one time or another that season—as was Pittaro.

In 1986, Earl again played for Nashville. He appeared in 128 games and batted .239, with 97 hits, eight home runs, 41 RBI, and 30 stolen bases. He saw time at various infield positions and also played in the outfield.

In 1986, for the first time in his career, Earl also pitched an inning of professional baseball. Reminiscing about his relief stint, he said, "Now my pitching appearance I could talk all day about. I had been pestering my manager all year long to let me pitch just one inning. Finally, we were on the end of a long road trip, Omaha, Des Moines, Denver, and finally Oklahoma City. Our relievers were spent, we were getting hammered by Oklahoma City, so Leon Roberts, our manager, asked me if I wanted to pitch the bottom of the eighth inning. So I went to the bullpen all excited. I had nasty stuff, breaking ball was sharp, for a person that had never pitched before, even in high school. [I] had a little change going, and my fastball was smoking hot, probably around 78 miles per hour. So my time had come, I went to the mound in front of about 20,000 fans.

"Brian Harper was the catcher. He came to the mound and said, 'What pitch is working for you?' I said my breaking ball was on fire. He said 'Let's start this guy off with one he will never expect, a first-pitch breaking ball from a shortstop that has never pitched before.' So Jeff Kunkel steps to the plate, Brian put down the three sign, I wind up, threw him my nastiest breaker and he promptly hits it about 500 feet over the left-field wall. Next batter, Manny Mota's son [Jose], I had him 0-2. He later said he was scared to death I was going to strike him out. I walked him. Next batter, Jim Maler. I looked at my left fielder and, no kidding; he was standing about two feet from the foul line on the warning track. Maler hit a rocket right to him. Tim Tolman didn't have to take a step. The ball was hit so hard it didn't get four feet off the ground. So I walk the next batter and the next gets a base hit. It was hit so hard I thought it was going to kill our second baseman,

DETROIT TIGERS 1984: WHAT A START! WHAT A FINISH!

Pedro Chavez. By now my legs are Jell-O. Tommy Dunbar came to the plate and promptly hits one about 550 feet over the left-field wall. He hit it over a waterbed sign and the deal was if an 89ers player did that he won a free waterbed. I never let Tommy forget he owed me. The last out was an absolute rocket to Doug Baker at short. So that is my pitching career. I never did ask to pitch again." In all, he gave up four runs, for a career earned-run average of 36.00.

In 1987, the Tigers won another Eastern Division title. However, Earl spent the entire season in Toledo. The International League Toledo Mud Hens had replaced Nashville as the Tigers' top farm team. Earl's playing time decreased as he shared starting duties with younger players like Jim Walewander. Scott still played in 89 games, batted .246, had four home runs and 33 RBIs and swiped 12 bases.

In 1988 Earl was back in Nashville, but by now it was a Cincinnati Reds affiliate. He played in 113 games and hit .239. In 1989 he split time between Toledo again and Columbus, the Yankees' International League affiliate. Between the two, Earl played in 89 games and had a .231 batting average with three home runs.

Of the Tigers-to-Reds-to-Tigers-to-Yankees shuttle, Earl said: "The Reds were trying to trade for me for years, according to them when I got there, but the Tigers wouldn't 'give me up.' So when I became a six-year minor-league free agent they called me and invited me to big-league spring training. With one week to go in spring training, I had already been sent down to Triple-A, the manager pulled me out of a game in the fourth inning telling me I was flying out the next day with the big-league team. A spot opened up because Buddy Bell was going on the disabled list. I flew to Cincinnati excited that I made the team. I had a great spring training with them. We played two exhibition games with Whitey Herzog's St. Louis Cardinals. Monday morning was Opening Day in Cincinnati, and I got a phone call from the traveling secretary saying Buddy Bell was refusing to go on the disabled list, leaving us with 26 men on the roster, and I had to go back down to Triple-A. The next year, I was released in spring training by the Reds and went home to Indy. A couple of weeks later, the Tigers called and wanted to re-sign me because Lou Whitaker hurt his knee dancing at a wedding reception. They called up Torey Lovullo and they wanted me to fill his spot in Toledo. Figures. I played behind Lou for six years and he never got hurt, I leave for 1½ years and he hurts himself dancing. Anyway, I got traded to the Yankees and Bucky Dent's Columbus Clippers later that year. My whole career, I always put it on the Yankees for some reason, always played my best against them. [I] finished out my career with them."

Before the 1990 season, Earl recalled, "I was called by the Toronto Blue Jays, but they said I had no shot at making the team or even going to the major-league camp. I was living with my wife-to-be in Indy and I had just had enough of Triple-A, so I said no and shut it down." Scott's professional baseball career was over. He had played in 1,029 minor-league games, the last 697 of them at the Triple-A level. His minor-league totals included 3,352 at-bats, 844 hits, 58 home runs, and a .252 batting average. Earl played the majority of his minor-league career at second base, appearing in 786 games at second, 128 at short, 56 at third, 49 in the outfield, and one game each at first base and on the mound. His speed helped account for 210 stolen bases and 528 runs scored.

After his baseball career ended, Earl and his wife had two daughters, Jordan and Jesse. He stayed in Indianapolis and took a job as a sales representative for Westfield Steel. In remembering his playing days in a 2008 e-mail exchange, Earl said, "Baseball was a very important part of my life growing up. As with any sport, it teaches competitiveness, teamwork, discipline, and dedication—all important things one needs in life in general." He added, "Baseball has changed for me from being a professional player to a fan of the sport in general. I appreciate the game because it played a significant part of molding me to the person I am today." He has some fond memories from his time as a Detroit Tiger. "I liked Darrell Evans, Larry Herndon, Billy Consolo, Alan Trammell, and the clubhouse guy, Jim Schmakel. ... I still keep in touch with six or seven minor- and major-league friends on a regular basis." And in case anyone was curious, Earl declared: "Favorite team? Of course, the Detroit Tigers."

References

Publications

Beckett, Dr. James, *Baseball Card Alphabetical Checklist #11*. Dallas: Beckett Media LP. 2005.

Campbell, Dave, Denny Mathews, Brooks Robinson, and Duke Snider. *The Scouting Report: 1985*. New York: Harper & Row, Publishers. 1985.

Craig, Roger, with Vern Plaegenhoef. *Inside Pitch*. Grand Rapids, Mich.: William B. Eerdmans. 1984

Detroit Free Press. *The Roar of '84*. Detroit: Detroit Free Press. 1984.

Detroit Tigers. *World Champion Detroit Tigers*. Detroit: Detroit Tigers.1985.

Detroit Tigers. *1986: The Year of The Detroit Tigers*. Detroit: Detroit Tigers. 1986.

Detroit Tigers. *1987 Detroit Tigers Press, TV & Radio Guide*. Detroit: Detroit Tigers. 1987.

Detroit Tigers. *1988 Detroit Tigers Press, TV & Radio Guide*. Detroit: Detroit Tigers. 1988.

Detroit Tigers. *The Press Guide! 1989*. Detroit: Detroit Tigers. 1989

DETROIT TIGERS 1984: WHAT A START! WHAT A FINISH!

Detroit Tigers. *1990 Press Guide*. Detroit: Detroit Tigers. 1990.

Gillette, Gary, and Pete Palmer. *The ESPN Baseball Encyclopedia, 4th ed*. New York: Sterling. 2007.

Hollander, Zander. *1985 The Complete Handbook of Baseball, 15th ed*. New York: American Library. 1985.

Major League Baseball. *World Series 1984 Media Guide & Scorebook*. New York: Major League Baseball. 1984.

Neft, David S., Richard M. Cohen, and Michael L. Neft. *The Sports Encyclopedia: Baseball 2007, 27th ed*. New York: St. Martin's Press. 2007.

Paladino, Larry, ed. *Detroit Tigers 1984 Yearbook*. Detroit: Gaylord Printing Co. 1984.

Paladino, Larry, ed. *Detroit Tigers 1985 Yearbook*. Warren, Michigan: Paladino Publications. 1985.

Pattison, Mark, and David Raglin, eds. *Sock It to 'Em Tigers: The Incredible Story of the 1968 Detroit Tigers*. Hanover, Mass.: Maple Street Press. 2008.

Pietrusza, David, Matthew Silverman, and Michael Gershman. *Baseball: The Biographical Encyclopedia*. Kingston, New York: Total Sports Publishing. 2000.

Smith, Fred T. *Tiger S.T.A.T.S.* Ann Arbor, Michigan: Momentum Books. 1991.

Thorn, John, Pete Palmer, and Michael Gershman. *Total Baseball, 7th ed*. Kingston, New York: Total Sports Publishing. 2000.

Zaret, Eli, *'84: Last of the Great Tigers*. South Boardman, Michigan: Crofton Creek Press. 2004.

Articles

"A Whole New Lineup." *Sports Illustrated*, April 15, 1985.

Downey, Mike. "The Word According to Sparky." *Inside Sports*, April 1985.

MacLean, Norman. "AL Previews." *Baseball Preview, Volume 7*, 1985.

Snyder, Bob. "Minor Leagues." *Street & Smith's Baseball Yearbook*, 1985.

Tully, Mike. "Don Mattingly: Yankee With a Sweet Swing." *Major League Baseball Yearbook '85*. 1985.

Web Sites

www.baseball-almanac.com

www.baseball-reference.com

www.retrosheet.org

www.thebaseballcube.com

Other Sources

Earl, Scott. E-mail to Kent Ailsworth, October 2009.

Earl, Scott. E-mail to Carl Shinkle, August 2008.

Acknowledgements

Annalisa Ailsworth.

Tom Lyons.

Ray Schmekel.

Darrell Evans
by David L. Fleitz

IN PART BECAUSE Darrell Evans retired after the 1989 season with a career batting average of only .248, baseball statistician Bill James has called him "the most underrated player in baseball history, absolutely number one on the list," due to his power, his ability to draw walks, and his outstanding on-base percentage. He was a good-fielding, hard-hitting third baseman in the National League for 15 seasons before the Detroit Tigers signed him as a free agent before their World Series-championship campaign in 1984. Evans, who played mostly at first base for Detroit, suffered through one of the worst seasons of his 21-year career in 1984, but found his hitting stroke in 1985 and gave the Tigers three more years of solid production.

Darrell Wayne Evans, of Welsh, Spanish, and Mexican descent, was born on May 26, 1947, in Pasadena, California, to a baseball-oriented family. His father, Richard, a sheet-metal worker at an aircraft factory, had played semipro ball, and his mother, Eleanor, had starred on a women's professional softball team, the Pasadena Ramblers. One of Darrell's aunts had played pro softball with his mother, while a grandfather and an uncle had performed in the minor leagues. Darrell, who grew up a Dodgers fan and attended as many as 40 games a year at the Los Angeles Coliseum and Dodger Stadium, knew at a young age that he wanted to become a major leaguer. "I got my first baseball uniform when I was 4 or 5 years old," he said in an interview on MLB.com in 2008. "It's what I always wanted to be."

A left-handed batter and a right-handed thrower, Darrell excelled in baseball and basketball at John Muir High School despite his poor eyesight, which he corrected with glasses and, later, contact lenses. He then attended Pasadena Junior College, where he led the baseball and basketball teams to national titles. A power-hitting third baseman, he was one of the most sought-after players in the college ranks, and was drafted five times (once by the Tigers in 1966) before signing with the Kansas City Athletics in June 1967. He performed well in the Athletics' minor-league system until he suffered torn ligaments in his right shoulder, which hindered his hitting and made it difficult for him to throw a ball across the infield. His future looked bleak, and the team (which moved to Oakland in 1968) decided to groom Sal Bando as its third baseman of the future. The Athletics left Evans unprotected in the Rule 5 draft, and on December 2, 1968, the Atlanta Braves claimed him from Oakland.

Evans, who stood 6-feet-2 and weighed about 200 pounds, played in 12 games for the Braves in 1969, but veteran Clete Boyer was established at third base. Evans spent most of the next two seasons with Atlanta's Richmond farm team. Military reserve duty interrupted his progress, but his fine performance at Richmond in 1970 and 1971 convinced the Braves that Evans was ready for the major leagues. He became the team's starting third baseman midway through the 1971 season, after a dispute between Boyer and general manager Paul Richards resulted in Boyer's release in June.

Eddie Mathews, the All-Star third baseman of the Braves during the 1950s and '60s, was a coach with Atlanta when Evans joined the team for good in 1971. "I was just like you when I first came up," Mathews told the 24-year-old Evans. "I couldn't catch the ball and I couldn't throw either." Mathews spent untold hours helping Evans improve his fielding skills. As Evans commented, "Eddie would hit hard liners and grounders to me at third then, as I got better, he would gradually move up the line and hit them even harder." Evans eventually became a good third baseman, and his hitting improved with experience. By 1972, when his mentor Mathews became manager of the club, Darrell was solidly entrenched in the Atlanta starting lineup.

After hitting 19 homers in 1972, his first full season in the majors, Evans enjoyed a power spike in 1973. He hit 41 home runs, scored 114 runs, and drove in 104 while batting a career-high .281 and playing in the All-Star Game for the first time. Teammates Dave Johnson (43 home runs) and Hank Aaron (40) joined Evans in the 40-homer club, making the Braves the first team in history with three 40-homer men in the same season. One of Evans' biggest thrills in baseball came on April 8, 1974, when he reached first base on an error in the fourth inning and then scored when Hank Aaron belted his 715th career homer, breaking Babe Ruth's long-standing record.

During the early part of his career, Evans' nickname was Howdy, because of a perceived resemblance to the television character Howdy Doody. When the Braves, at owner Ted Turner's direction, used nicknames instead of last names on the backs of the players' uniform shirts in 1976, Evans wore "Howdy" above his number. Later, his nickname became UFO, because Evans spoke often about seeing an unidentified flying object with his wife, LaDonna, in 1982. The experience made him a believer in the supernatural and the extraterrestrial. "I believe there is something out there," he once told a reporter for *USA Today*. "If there are aliens, they've been out there longer than we have. They've evolved beyond war. They've got through it and they want to come and show us how. I hope it happens."

Though his batting average fell to .240 in 1974, Evans led the National League in walks for the second season in a row and scored 99 runs. His fielding improved, and though his home-run output fell from 41 in 1973 to 25 in 1974 and 22 the following year, he was one of the bright spots for an Atlanta team that sank to the bottom of the National League West. However, Evans' time in Atlanta was coming to an end. He was moved to first base because the Braves acquired hot prospect Jerry Royster from the Dodgers. Always a slow starter—his career .232 batting average for April is his lowest of any month—he began the 1976 season in a horrid slump. Though he drew at least one walk in each of his first 15 games, his average dipped below the .200 mark and stayed there.

"It was the one time in my career when I really doubted myself," Evans said. "I couldn't seem to do anything right. I

DETROIT TIGERS 1984: WHAT A START! WHAT A FINISH!

couldn't see the ball very well and I wasn't being patient at the plate. Then I'd take a pitch and it would be right down the middle." In early June, with the Braves mired in fifth place and Evans' average at .173, the club traded him and infielder Marty Perez to the San Francisco Giants for first baseman Willie Montanez and three others.

Evans welcomed the move, as it returned him to his home state of California. He went hitless in his first 11 at-bats in a San Francisco uniform before belting a home run off New York Mets ace Tom Seaver. In his first home game as a Giant, Evans regained his power stroke against the San Diego Padres. "I had been doing poorly in Atlanta," Evans said, "but on my first day at Candlestick, it was a doubleheader and I hit home runs in both games to win both games. There was a pretty good-sized crowd and it was a great feeling to make a good first impression and to show the Giants they didn't make a mistake."

Evans spent the next eight years in San Francisco. The Giants used him mostly at first base in 1976, then shuffled him around the field in 1977, with Evans seeing action at third, first, and the outfield. Late in the 1977 season, veteran slugger Willie McCovey suggested to manager Joe Altobelli that Bill Madlock be moved from third base to second base and Evans be moved to third base full time. Altobelli agreed, and Evans played only at third in 1978, 1979, and 1980.

The 1978 season was the best one the Giants had during Evans' tenure. The team played at a .500 pace through April and in early May, then won 12 of 13 to move into first place. Evans shone during the streak, hitting .381 with a .491 on-base percentage. On May 19 he went 3-for-3 with two home runs as the Giants won their eighth straight game. The Giants finished the month with a 20-6 mark. On June 11, in the middle of a seven-game winning streak, Evans went 3-for-5 with a home run, two RBIs, and three runs to help San Francisco beat the Mets 7-5.

The Giants remained in first place, with the exception of one day, until August 11. However, they went 20-22 the rest of the way to finish in third place, six games out, with an 89-73 record. Evans hit only .206 down the stretch but clubbed 10 home runs during that time as the Giants finished their best season since 1971.

Evans was eligible for free agency after the 1978 season, and he was unhappy that the Giants did not offer him what he and his agent, Jerry Kapstein, considered a fair deal during the season. In the early days of free agency, players could sign with only a limited number of teams, the teams determined in a draft. Evans was chosen by ten teams, short of the maximum 13, in addition to the Giants. Those teams were Oakland, San Diego, California, Cleveland, Minnesota, Milwaukee, the New York Mets, Baltimore, Los Angeles, and Montreal.

The Angels and the Padres each talked to Evans, but he elected to re-sign with the Giants when they increased their offer to $1.435 million over five years, very close to his reported demand of five years and $1.5 million. After signing, Evans said, "It's nice to feel wanted. … Last season was enjoyable and we're going to get better." However, that was not to be the case, as the Giants won only 71 and 75 games over the next two seasons. It was not Evans' fault; he had typical Darrell Evans seasons each year: hitting 17 and 20 home runs with .356 and .359 on-base averages for those two seasons. When veteran first baseman Willie McCovey retired at midseason in 1980, Darrell was named to replace the future Hall of Famer as captain of the team.

The 1982 season was the Giants' second best during Evans' time there, but it was full of turmoil for the 35-year-old veteran. Despite statistics that were not much different than a typical Evans season (.241 average but with five home runs and a .351 on-base percentage), manager Frank Robinson announced on June 4 that Tom O'Malley would be the regular third baseman. Evans reacted strongly: "It's hard to understand the move—and I don't. It's not like I'm being replaced by a phenom who will hit 40 home runs." Trades with the White Sox and Oakland fell through, causing Evans to retort, "I don't understand why they would not trade one obscure player for two obscure players." Part of the move was out of desperation as the Giants were 22-30 at the time, 8½ games out of first place.

Evans saw some action at first base in June while Reggie Smith recovered from injuries and even had eight starts at shortstop in late July and early August before regaining the regular third-base job. Maybe not so coincidentally, San Francisco got hot in early August; the Giants were 50-55 on August 2 before winning 37 of their final 57 games to finish 87-75.

The 1983 season, the final year of Evans' five-year pact, was his best in San Francisco. With free agency approaching

Darrell Evans was Detroit's first big-ticket free-agent signing. While his 1984 numbers seemed not to justify his contract, he brought leadership intangibles to the club; Evans was the first Braves captain after Hank Aaron, and the first Giants captain after Willie McCovey. (National Baseball Hall of Fame Library, Cooperstown, New York)

DETROIT TIGERS 1984: WHAT A START! WHAT A FINISH!

again, Darrell moved back to first base and made the All-Star team for the second time, hitting 30 home runs with 82 runs batted in. He also showed his versatility, appearing in nine games at shortstop for the injury-riddled team. Despite his advancing age, this solid performance made the 36-year-old veteran one of the most coveted players in baseball at season's end.

Many observers were surprised when the Detroit Tigers pursued Evans that fall. The Tigers had not signed a single high-priced player since the era of free agency began several years before, preferring to develop players through the farm system rather than lavish large contracts on veteran stars. However, Detroit had finished second to Baltimore in the American League East in 1983, and management believed that one more powerful left-handed hitter might move the Tigers past the defending champion Orioles. Detroit's incumbent first baseman, Enos Cabell, also a free agent, had signed with Houston, and the Tigers looked to Evans as an upgrade at that position. After his All-Star campaign for the Giants in 1983, Evans was a hot commodity, and the bidding for his services turned into a two-team contest between the Tigers and the New York Yankees.

On December 17, 1983, the Tigers signed Evans to a three-year contract worth $2.25 million. The Yankees had offered more money, but the Tigers were a better team, and Evans was intrigued by the possibility of playing in a World Series for the first time in his career. "I want a World Series ring on my finger," he said. "I've played 15 years, but have never gone to spring training thinking I was on a team with a shot to win it all. Now I am." He said Tigers manager Sparky Anderson had a crucial role in his decision to play for Detroit. Seventeen teams had selected Evans in the free-agent draft, but Anderson was the only manager who phoned him at home and urged him to sign. "That basically sealed my decision," he told the *San Francisco Examiner*. "Sparky was the only manager who bothered to talk to me during the entire decision-making process, and he was totally honest with what he had to say." After Evans signed, he received another call at home from sportscaster Howard Cosell. Said Evans to the *Los Angeles Times* in 2008, "Cosell called to say he couldn't believe that I would choose Detroit over New York."

Evans got off to a hot start with his new team. On April 3, 1984, in his first game as a Tiger, he belted a three-run homer off Minnesota's Keith Comstock in an 8-1 Detroit win. In the home opener at Tiger Stadium on April 10, he smacked a long home run into the right-field upper deck—already designated by one banner-waver as "Evansville"—off Texas pitcher Dave Stewart in his first time at bat. To ease his adjustment to a new league, Anderson played him mostly against right-handed pitchers during the first two months of the season. On May 25, Evans' batting average stood at .308, and it appeared that the team's investment in the power-hitting first baseman had paid off.

However, Evans quickly fell into a prolonged slump at the plate. Though the division-leading Tigers were winning games at a record pace, Evans' bat went strangely silent. He hit only one home run in June, putting together a number of 0-for-3 and 0-for-4 days as his average fell with each passing week. "I've been getting myself out," Evans told *The Sporting News* in early July. "Here I'm supposedly known as a patient hitter, and I'm chasing pitches all the time. It has to stop." The death of his father, Richard, in July may have had an effect on Evans, as did his lack of a permanent fielding assignment. He saw action in Detroit at both first and third base, with designated hitter and pinch-hitting duties added in. Pressing at the plate, Evans saw his average fall to the .230 level, where it remained for the rest of the campaign.

Evans enjoyed a few highlights in 1984. On August 20 and 21, he went 7-for-8 with two homers, scoring five runs and driving in four in two wins against Oakland. On September 11 he belted four hits, including a home run and a double, as the Tigers defeated Baltimore, 9-2. Still, such heroics were few and far between for Evans, who ended his first American League season with a .232 average and 16 home runs, only six of which came at Tiger Stadium. Despite his hitting troubles, Anderson wanted the experienced Evans in the starting lineup during the postseason, and Darrell played two games at first base and one at third as the Tigers swept the Kansas City Royals in the American League Championship Series.

Though he won his first and only World Series ring with the Tigers that year, the five-game victory over the San Diego Padres was bittersweet for Evans, who managed only one single in 15 times at bat during the Series for an .067 average. However, he was determined to look on the bright side. The 1984 season, he told the *Kansas City Times* a year later, "was by far my best year in baseball. It had to be. How many times do you play for a world champion? But in all honesty, I wasn't happy with my numbers. I expected to do better than that."

Evans started the 1985 season slowly amid rumors that the Tigers, disappointed with his lack of production, would soon trade him to the Yankees. On May 14, he was batting only .167 when the club brought up Mike Laga from its Nashville farm team and put him on first base, moving Evans to the designated-hitter slot. The move caused something to click with Evans, who belted homers in each of the next four games and went on an 11-for-17 tear at the plate. On June 2 Laga was returned to the minors, and Evans reclaimed first base. His yearlong hitting slump had ended as mysteriously as it had begun. Though the Tigers failed to repeat as champions, the 38-year-old Evans led the American League in home runs with 40, becoming the oldest player in the American League ever to hit 40 in a season. He also became the first player to hit 40 or more homers in each league, having hit 41 for the Braves 12 years before. At season's end Evans was presented with the Tiger of the Year award by the Detroit baseball writers.

Evans put together another fine season in 1986, with 29 home runs and 85 runs batted in, and he became a free agent again after his three-year contract expired that fall. With ownership collusion in full swing, Evans drew no interest from any team except Detroit, which offered him a one-year contract for $525,000, a 33 percent pay cut from the year before. With no other options available, he accepted the offer and returned to Detroit for the 1987 season. At 40, Evans was baseball's oldest everyday player. "I'm not old," he told a *New York Times* reporter. "I was just born before a lot of other people." He proved that his career was not over, hitting 34 home runs with 99 runs batted in for the division champion Tigers.

Age finally caught up with Evans in 1988, when he batted only .208 while sharing the starting first-base job with Dave Bergman and Ray Knight. On September 20 he hit the 400th home run of his career, off Cleveland's John Farrell, but Evans' tenure with the Tigers was drawing to a close. Released by Detroit at season's end, he returned to Atlanta for one final campaign, his 21st in the major leagues. He retired after the 1989 season with a .248 career batting average and 414 home runs, a total that at the time placed him 21st on baseball's all-time list. His total of 1,605 walks was the eighth highest of all time at the time.

Evans coached for the New York Yankees in 1990 and worked as a minor-league instructor for the Tigers and the Boston Red Sox. He managed the Tyler WildCatters of the independent Texas-Louisiana League in 1997, the Wilmington Blue Rocks (Kansas City high A, Carolina League) in 1998, the Huntsville Stars (Milwaukee Double-A, Southern League) in 1999, and the Aberdeen Arsenal of the independent Atlantic League in 2000. In 2005 Evans became the first manager of the Long Beach Armada in the independent Golden Baseball League in Southern California, winning a division title in 2007. In 2008 he remained in the Golden Baseball League as a hitting coach for the Orange County Flyers, managed by Hall of Fame catcher Gary Carter. Evans managed the Victoria Seals in the same league in 2009 before being fired for looking for another managerial job while still being paid by the Seals. Another Golden Baseball League club, the St. George Roadrunners, hired him as manager for the 2010 season. At that time, Evans and his wife, LaDonna, lived in Long Beach, California. They had four grown children.

References

Publications

Conan, Neil, *Play by Play: Life in the Last Chance League*. New York: Three Rivers Press. 2003.

James, Bill. *The New Bill James Historical Baseball Abstract*. New York: The Free Press. 2000.

Porter, David L., ed. *Biographical Dictionary of American Sports: Baseball, revised and expanded edition*. New York: Greenwood Press. 2000.

Articles

Anderson, Dave. "The Second Black Manager?" *New York Times*, April 18, 1978.

Associated Press. "Former Big-Leaguer Darrell Evans Thriving Among Huntsville Stars." *Tuscaloosa News*, July 11, 1999.

"Evans' Career Begins to Take Off After Witnessing Flying Objects," *USA Today*, April 12, 1984.

Fish, Mike. "Evans Is Heating Up With Age." *Kansas City Times*, August 30, 1985.

Gage, Tom. "At 38, Evans Having His Finest Season." *The Sporting News*, September 23, 1985.

Lapointe, Joe. "Evans a Big Hit in Detroit." *The New York Times*, September 30, 1987.

Minshew, Wayne. "Evans Soars Like Rocket to Stardom." *The Sporting News*, September 8, 1973.

Moore, Terence. "Evans Finds Contentment in Detroit." *San Francisco Examiner*, April 19, 1984.

Peters, Nick. "Giants Are Jolly Over Darrell's Decision to Stay." *The Sporting News*, December 30, 1978.

Peters, Nick. "Evans Frustrated as Deals Collapsed." *The Sporting News*, June 28, 1982.

Spander, Art. "Giant Hands-Off Policy Turned Evans' Bat to 'On.'" *The Sporting News*, July 24, 1976.

Stewart, Larry. "He Passed On Pitch From Cosell." *Los Angeles Times*, February 11, 2008.

Web Sites

"Chop Talk: Evans Going to Bat for Earth," on http://www.atlanta-braves.mlb.com/news.

Darrell Evans page at http://www.baseball-reference.com/bullpen. Accessed June 1, 2008.

Darrell Evans page at http://www.thebaseballpage.com.

http://www.detroit-tigers-baseball-history.com.

http://www.goldenbaseball.com/longbeach/subcontent.aspx?SecID=785.

http://www.retrosheet.com.

http://www.smoaky.com/news/View.php?ArticleID=89.

Barbaro Garbey
By Doug Hill

TO THE CASUAL baseball fan Barbaro Garbey was not unlike thousands of other former major leaguers. That is, he came, he played, and—almost before you'd gotten a chance to get to know him—he was gone.

A 2007 study by a University of Colorado research team pegs the average big-league career at 5.6 years. By that measure, Garbey was decidedly atypical, lasting parts of just three seasons (1984-85 with Detroit and 1988 with Texas) before vanishing into the relative obscurity of the minors and the Mexican League. His story, however, is far from typical.

Even to ardent supporters of the Tigers of the mid-1980s Garbey is today nothing more than a footnote in history. Some might remember him as the early-season platoon partner to Dave Bergman at first base, while others might recollect how he and Johnny Grubb were sharing designated-hitter duties by season's end. Some, with terrific memories, might remember how his second-inning infield single off Kansas City Royals starter Charlie Leibrandt in Game Three of the American League Championship Series helped push across the lone run (scored by Chet Lemon after reaching on a fielder's choice that forced Garbey at second) that clinched the American League pennant for the Tigers.

But mostly Garbey was a complementary player on a team full of larger-than-life personalities with names like Trammell and Whitaker, Parrish and Gibson, and Morris and Petry.

To get a truer sense of what Garbey meant to baseball, one needs to travel 90 miles southwest of Key West, Florida, to Havana, Cuba. That is where the Barbaro Garbey story must start and where almost a quarter-century after his disappearance from the major leagues, he was still revered by many.

"Everyone knows who he is in Cuba," Chicago White Sox pitcher Jose Contreras told *USA Today* in 2005. "Everyone knows he's the first one."

Indeed, it was on a May night in 1980 that Garbey climbed aboard a cramped fishing boat with about 200 other Cuban refugees as part of the Mariel boatlift—or "freedom flotilla"—that eventually saw an estimated 125,000 Cubans seek a new life in the United States through an agreement between Cuban President Fidel Castro, the U.S. government, and Cuban-Americans.

Garbey's decision to board that vessel made him the first member of the Cuban national baseball team to leave for the United States since Castro closed the borders to his nation's athletes in 1961.

Barbaro Garbey, the youngest of nine children, was born on December 4, 1956, in Santiago de Cuba to Aristides and Noelia Garbey. It is from his birth date—the feast of St. Barbara on the Catholic Church's liturgical calendar and a significant celebration in Cuba—that his name originates. Garbey said many born on December 4 have either the name Barbaro or Barbara.

Garbey came by his athletic prowess naturally; two of his siblings were world-class athletes. Older brother Rolando fought as a light-middleweight in the 1967 Pan American Games and won a gold medal in boxing. Rolando won a silver in the 1968 Mexico City Olympics and added a bronze at the 1976 Montreal Games. He coached the Cuban boxers at the 2004 Athens Olympics. Garbey's sister Marcia placed fourth in the 1972 Munich Olympics as a long jumper.

Like many young children the world over, Garbey began playing baseball as a little leaguer in Santiago de Cuba. His family moved to Havana when he was 8 years old and it was only a matter of time before government officials learned of Garbey's natural ability to hit a baseball and invited him to attend Escuela de Iniciación Deportiva Escolar—Sport Initiation School—in Havana. Garbey entered the school when he was 11 and further honed his skills—playing baseball nearly every day—before eventually making it to the Cuban National Series (the country's elite league) and playing for Havana Industriales, the Cuban equivalent of the New York Yankees.

Garbey played in the National Series from 1974 to 1978 and compiled solid career statistics, finishing with a .290 batting average while slugging at a .399 clip. Just 17 years old when he made his debut, Garbey totaled 78 extra-base hits—including 19 home runs—during his 309-game career. He led the National Series in RBIs with 40 during his final season. Twice named to the Cuban national team (1976 and 1977), Garbey won the world amateur titles as the Cubans' designated hitter in 1976.

Garbey's name vanished from the rosters and record books for the 1979 season, however, when he was apparently implicated in a gambling scheme. He remained silent on the topic until May 22, 1983, when he revealed to the *Miami Herald* that he had been involved in run-shaving to keep scores close as many as seven times.

"I know I did right when I do what I do in Cuba, because I had to," he told the *Herald*. "A lot of people say it was wrong. I still say it was right. I was making 95 pesos a month (the equivalent of $860 a year). I can do nothing in Cuba with 95 pesos. I believe no one in the world can live on 95 pesos. With the prices in Cuba, you can't afford it."

Though Garbey never directly said as much, his ban from the Cuban National Series led to his decision to board that fishing boat in Mariel Harbor in early June 1980.

"I did not defect from the national Cuban team," he said. "I came on the Freedom Flotilla"—the Mariel boatlift—"in 1980. I mean, that was the time where Castro say, 'Anybody who wants to go to the United States, they can go' and I was one of the ones who jumped in the boat. It was not like I defected from the team. I just left Cuba to play here or try to get the chance, to give the chance to play over here professional ball."

Still, Garbey told *The Sporting News* in 1983, it was not easy for him to get out of Cuba.

"The first time I tell 'em I want to come here, they say, 'No! The people leaving are people we don't like.'… The second time I go to the immigration office, they say, 'No! What I tell you before?' So I go a third time and tell 'em I don't want to stay there, I want to go to the United States. They say okay and they let me on this big boat."

Shortly after arriving in Key West, Garbey was shipped off to one of many U.S. holding centers for Cuban refugees. His was in the Army base at Indiantown Gap, Pennsylvania, where Tigers scout Orlando Peña—himself a Cuban and a pitcher for 14 years in the major leagues—found him playing pepper in a pair of rolled-up blue jeans and a T-shirt and looking anything but a world-class baseball player.

"A guy said, 'That's Garbey' and I said, 'Really? He doesn't look like a ballplayer,'" Peña recalled.

Eventually Peña asked Garbey if he wanted to play baseball and if he could hit. Garbey's response: "Get me out of here and feed me well and you'll see how well I can hit."

Peña offered the penniless refugee $2,500 to sign a contract with the Tigers and that's exactly what he did on June 6, 1980. The only problem was that Garbey couldn't be released from the Pennsylvania holding camp to Peña; only to a relative. Garbey's cousin Merta, an old childhood playmate from their days in Cuba, was in New York City and had told friends in the Cuban section of Miami to keep an eye out in the paper (the *Miami Herald* was publishing the names of arrivals) for Garbey's name. Merta received a copy of the paper with Barbaro's name, recognized it, and drove to Indiantown Gap to take Barbaro to her home.

Shortly after arriving in New York, Garbey received a plane ticket to Tampa from the Tigers and was assigned to Lakeland of the Single-A Florida State League, where he showed Peña how well he could hit. Garbey finished his first season of U.S. professional baseball with a .364 batting average in 88 at-bats.

The next year Garbey was assigned to the Double-A Birmingham Barons of the Southern League and batted .286. His season was interrupted by a shattered cheekbone that cost him a week in the hospital. He also earned a brief July call-up to the Triple-A Evansville Triplets during which he went 1-for-12 and—so distraught over his play—was brought to tears following one game. After playing in just four games, he was sent back to Birmingham to finish the season. He stayed there for all of 1982 as well.

"We didn't want to risk breaking his confidence," then-Triplets' manager Jim Leyland said.

Garbey thrived back in Birmingham in 1982, earning all-star honors while batting .298 with 32 doubles, 17 homers, and 99 RBIs—a season, Garbey said, that started with a 0-for-16 slump but didn't include any tears.

Garbey was assigned to Triple-A Evansville for the 1983 season and had a terrific year on the field but tumultuous one off. He finished the campaign with a .321 average and belted 14 homers in 377 at-bats.

Off the field was another matter altogether, and it began with the *Miami Herald* story in which he admitted to taking part in the Cuban game-fixing scandal. The article, which ran on May 22, 1983, came when Garbey was hitting .308 for Evansville and after he had been placed on the Tigers' 40-man roster before the season. The story, written by *Herald* writer Peter Richmond, was wide-ranging and delved not only into Garbey's role with run-shaving, but also his continuing homesickness for his wife, Maria, and daughters, Dyjami and Dunia, and how off days were the worst because he had nothing to do but think of the family he was forced to leave behind in Cuba.

"I want to give my little girls some good life," he said. "In Cuba, the way I was I cannot give my little girls that life. I can't give it. So I sacrifice things. I sacrifice a couple of years. And if I don't make the big leagues, I'll take some different way to get my family here."

A week after the article appeared, John H. Johnson, president of the National Association, the minor leagues' governing body—with the blessing of baseball commissioner Bowie Kuhn—placed Garbey on probation, which meant he could continue to play for Evansville but wouldn't be eligible for a Detroit call-up until the incident could be more thoroughly investigated.

Just a month later, Garbey's world nearly collapsed around him. Evansville hosted Louisville on June 28, and in the ninth inning, Triplets manager Gordie MacKenzie moved Garbey from left field to third base. With a runner on second, the batter laid down a bunt and pitcher Dave Rucker sprang off the mound and sailed one high and wide of Garbey at third. The crowd groaned in disgust as the runner scored, but one fan was relentless, asking Garbey how much he was paid to drop that one, how badly his wife and children must be starving to not catch it, and whether he was trying to throw another game to get his picture into *Sports Illustrated*. After the game, Garbey—carrying a fungo bat—went to the parking lot to question the man; words were exchanged, and Garbey hit the man across the right shoulder with the bat.

John Johnson acted swiftly, suspending Garbey for 30 days.

"I think for a long time that as soon as I hit him, that was it, my career was ruined," Garbey said at the time. "I would have to go back to Miami and find a job. No more baseball." Charges by the fan against Garbey were later thrown out and Garbey was cleared of wrongdoing.

Already emotionally fragile because of his homesickness, the revelation of the game-fixing scandal, and now without the escape playing baseball offered, Garbey's life began slipping away. His sleeping and eating patterns were erratic and his behavior became a big concern—so much so that Triplets general manager Chuck Murphy got Garbey in touch with a local psychiatrist who prescribed some medication for his sleeping and urged him to become more socially active.

"The doctor helped me," Garbey said. "For a long time I just wanted to be alone. I didn't want to see anybody. I needed time."

Garbey played well upon his return to the lineup in late July, but his probationary period due to the game-fixing wouldn't allow for him to be recalled by the Tigers with other September call-ups.

A career outfielder and designated hitter to this point, Garbey, as the Tigers desired, was working at both corner infield positions during the latter stages of the 1983 season.

DETROIT TIGERS 1984: WHAT A START! WHAT A FINISH!

He also played there in the Instructional League (where he batted a league-high .347) and in the Dominican League (where he hit .333). The idea was to have him fill either position at the big-league level in 1984. Then, during the offseason, the Tigers signed free-agent corner infielder Darrell Evans and then traded John Wockenfuss and Glenn Wilson for first baseman Dave Bergman and pitcher Willie Hernandez late in spring training. Suddenly Garbey was a man without a position on a very good team.

Still, Garbey had an impressive spring training in 1984 and manager Sparky Anderson—who had three years earlier called him "the next Roberto Clemente"—chose to bring the versatile Garbey north with the parent club. Anderson's decision paid off as Garbey was instrumental in Detroit's memorable 35-5 start. In fact, after 21 games (in which the Tigers were 19-2) Garbey was batting a torrid .463 with 15 RBIs in only 45 plate appearances.

When Garbey made his major-league debut on Opening Day in Minnesota after being inserted as a pinch-hitter in the eighth inning for Bergman—he grounded out to second—he became the first Cuban-born and -trained player to debut in the majors since Tony Perez 20 years before.

"I was a little nervous," Garbey recalled, "because I could not believe I was in the big leagues. I had waited for that moment for such a long time, been through so much. I could not believe it."

Garbey made his first start on April 7, when he manned first base for the first six innings of Jack Morris' no-hitter against the White Sox. Garbey's first big-league hit came the next day at Chicago's Comiskey Park when he pinch-hit for Bergman and drove a Juan Agosto offering into right field for a two-run double. During his sensational first month, Garbey earned the reputation as a clutch-hitting run-producer. The first 13 times he batted with runners in scoring position, he delivered nine hits.

Garbey maintained his hot start through May and was still hitting .330 on June 1. His May highlights included a four-RBI performance against the Boston Red Sox on May 1, his first big-league pinch-hit the next night, against Red Sox closer Bob Stanley, and his first big-league home run on April 25 in a 6-5 win at Cleveland.

He finished the 1984 regular season with 110 games played and a .287 batting average. Of the Tigers with at least 300 at-bats, just Alan Trammell and Lou Whitaker finished with higher batting averages—.314 and .289, respectively. Garbey also proved quite a versatile player, logging some time at first, second, and third base, as well as all three outfield positions and designated hitter.

Garbey went 3-for-9 in the American League Championship Series against Kansas City. The World Series wasn't as kind, and he went 0-for-12 against the San Diego Padres in four games as designated hitter.

Despite a disappointing Series personally, Garbey was understandably thrilled with the outcome: "This moment I've never known in baseball," he said. "We were champions in Cuba in 1974, but it didn't mean too much. I was happy, but it wasn't like this. This means you are part of one of the best baseball teams in the world."

The following season wasn't as great for Garbey or his teammates. The Tigers finished 84-77 and in third place in the AL East, 15 games behind first-place Toronto. Garbey appeared in 86 games and batted .257. He played sparingly in September after the late-season call-ups. He hit the last of his 11 home runs as a Tiger on September 14, off Baltimore's Mike Flanagan, collected his final hit on September 28 against Boston, when he pinch-hit successfully for catcher Bob Melvin, and appeared in his final game as a Tiger on October 4, when he again pinch-hit for Melvin.

Though a disappointing year professionally, 1985 did have a significant personal moment for Garbey. On Monday, August 19, he was married to Kimberly Grutza of Farmington, Michigan, in an 11 a.m. ceremony attended by manager Sparky Anderson, hitting coach Vada Pinson, and teammate Nelson Simmons. (Garbey has since remained mum on the family he left behind in Cuba.) The 19th was originally scheduled as an off day, but due to the brief in-season players' strike earlier that summer, Detroit had an evening makeup game in Kansas City before heading west to Oakland. The *Detroit Free Press* reported that Garbey narrowly made the 3:45 p.m. team charter to Kansas City and then sat out the game, which featured the Royals' right-handed ace Bret Saberhagen.

After the season, Garbey made the demand of being played every day or being traded; and on November 13, the Tigers traded him to Oakland for speedy outfielder Dave Collins. Once in Oakland, Garbey found little opportunity to play with sluggers Dave Kingman and Dusty Baker holding down the designated-hitter spot, Bruce Bochte at first base, and a solid outfield corps of Mike Davis, Dwayne Murphy, and the young, Cuban-born Jose Canseco. Consequently, Garbey was released on March 21, 1986, just before the start of the season, and didn't latch on with another major-league team.

He spent the next season in the Mexican League, playing for the Two Laredo Owls. Garbey found trouble again during the offseason when he was arrested in the early morning of November 21, 1986, after being pulled over for speeding on Miami's Biscayne Boulevard. As he got out of the car, he attempted to toss a folded dollar bill under his Buick sedan. North Miami police said the bill contained cocaine. Arresting officer Frank Irvine, himself a former Chicago Cubs minor leaguer, said Garbey told him: "Can you cut me a break? I'm a professional baseball player and this will ruin my career." The officer declined and Garbey spent a few hours in the Dade County Jail before posting $5,000 bail. The charges were later dismissed when he entered a pretrial intervention program.

Garbey found work in 1987 with the Campeche Pirates of the Mexican League and, hoping to rehabilitate his reputation, played for Mazatlan in the Winter League, where he batted .309 and was impressive enough to be offered a free-agent contract by the Texas Rangers; he signed December 13, 1987.

Garbey began the 1987 season at Triple-A Oklahoma City and was recalled to the Rangers twice. He got into his first action with the Rangers on June 17, playing less than three weeks—through July 5—before he was sent down. He was brought back and played with Texas from August 21 to season's end. Garbey appeared in 30 games, including a dozen pinch-hitting appearances, during the 1988 season and batted just .194. He played in his final major-league game on October 2, when he pinch-hit for DH Geno Petralli and flied out to right field against the Seattle Mariners' Bill Wilkinson.

Garbey bounced around between the minors and the Mexican League each of the next six seasons. He played with Montreal's Double-A Jacksonville team during 1989 and was signed by the Los Angeles Dodgers to a minor-league contract for 1990, but was optioned to the Mexico City Tigers before the year began. He earned a brief call-up to Triple-A Albuquerque but never made it back to the big leagues. In 1991 he played with the Mexico City Tigers, and won another championship as a Tiger—Mexico City's version—in 1992. His final year of professional baseball was the 1994 season with the Yucatan Lions.

Once out of baseball, Garbey found his way to Put One in the Upper Deck, an indoor batting cage in Northville, Michigan, a Detroit suburb, where he eventually became the general manager. There, he got a break that led him into the ranks of professional coaching. Former Tiger and Detroit native Willie Horton was bringing his grandson to Put One in the Upper Deck, liked the way Garbey worked with the hitters, and recommended him to the Tigers' front office.

"I wasn't giving any thought to [professional coaching]," Garbey said. "The opportunity came and I took it."

In 2002 Garbey was assigned to work as hitting coach for the Oneonta Tigers, Detroit's farm team in the short-season A-ball New York-Penn League. He spent 2003 with the low-A West Michigan Whitecaps, the Tigers' Midwest League affiliate, before being let go by the organization after the season.

Back in the Detroit area, Garbey went to work at Total Baseball, an indoor baseball academy in suburban Wixom. He latched on with the Chicago Cubs' organization for the 2006 season, working as a hitting coach for the Single-A Peoria Chiefs (Midwest League). He spent the 2007 and 2008 seasons with the Double-A Tennessee Smokies in Kodak, north of Gatlinburg and Great Smoky Mountain National Park. He was back in Peoria for 2009.

Garbey and his wife, Kimberly, settled in Livonia, a Detroit suburb, with their three children, Isabel, Barbaro Jr., and Gabriela.

References

Publications

Anderson, Sparky. *Bless You Boys: Diary of the Detroit Tigers' 1984 Season*. Chicago: Contemporary Books, Inc. 1984.

Articles

Associated Press. "Garbey Draws Suspension for Alleged Attack on Fan." *Miami Herald*. July 3, 1983. 1C.

Bragg, Brian. "Kuhn Orders Game-Fixing Inquiry; Garbey Put Under Probe." *Detroit Free Press*. May 26, 1983.

Bragg, Brian. "Tigers Might Want to Promote Him; Union Protests Freeze on Garbey." *Detroit Free Press*. June 30, 1983.

Gage, Tom. "Garbey Tough Clutch Hitter." *The Sporting News*. May 14, 1984. 23.

George, Tommy. "Barbaro Garbey Learned to Rely on Himself." *Detroit Free Press*. October 15, 1984.

Guidi, Gene. "Average Hits .387: Garbey's Swinging Sweetly." *Detroit Free Press*. May 12, 1984.

Kram, Mark. "Barbaro TV, Cigarets, Baseball Fill the Lonely Void for Troubled Garbey." *Detroit Free Press*. August 7, 1983.

Lapointe, Joe. "A Cuban With Clout." *New York Times*. May 7, 1984.

McGraw, Bill. "Garbey Seems a Cinch for the Tigers." *Detroit Free Press* February 22, 1984.

Ortiz, Jorge L. "New Chance for Garbey: Cuban-Born Player Surfaces with Rangers." *Miami Herald*. June 23, 1988. 2D.

Ramos, Reinaldo. "Mariel Ex-Major Leaguer Busted." *Miami Herald*.. November 26, 1986. 1B.

Richmond, Peter. "Barbaro Garbey Finally Takes Off His Mask." *Miami Herald*.. October 7, 1884. 2C.

Richmond, Peter. "Cuban Star Fixed Games to Support His Family Refugee From Mariel Still May Reach Majors." *Miami Herald*.. May 22, 1983. 1A.

Richmond, Peter. "Cuba's Baseball Stars, Young and Old ... For Garbey, Culture, Shock, Controversy May Cease in Detroit." *Miami Herald*.. March 19, 1984. 1D.

Richmond, Peter. "Tigers Put Hot-Hitting Garbey to Good Use." *Miami Herald*.d. April 20, 1984. 7E.

Staff reports. "Garbey Walks Down Aisle, Then Flees to Kansas City." *Detroit Free Press*. August 20, 1985.

Swanson, Pete. "Two Dreams Drive Triplets' Garbey." *The Sporting News*. May 23, 1983. 52.

Weir, Tom. "Garbey's Brother, Sister Enjoy Olympic Success." *USA Today*. July 6, 2005.

Weir, Tom. "Cuban Ballplayers Remember Garbey." *USA Today*. July 6, 2005.

Wilstach, Nancy. "Cuban Refugee Hurdling Barriers." *The Sporting News*. July 18, 1981. 41.

Web Sites

http://en.wikipedia.org/wiki/Industriales

www.baseballreference.com

www.pbs.org/stealinghome/league/alltime.html

www.retrosheet.org

www.sciencedaily.com/releases/2007/07/070709131254.htm

Other Sources

Hill, Doug. Telephone interview with Barbaro Garbey. July 2, 2008.

Kit Krieger for Cuban National Series statistics, www.cubaballtours.com.

Pattison, Mark. Interview with Barbaro Garbey. March 10, 2003.

Kirk Gibson
by Bill Bishop

IMMORTALIZED BY two dramatic World Series home runs, one in 1984 for the Detroit Tigers and another in 1988 for the Los Angeles Dodgers, Kirk Gibson was noted for his competitiveness and clutch hitting. Plagued by injuries, he never lived up to the hype created by his manager, Sparky Anderson, when he referred to Gibson as "the next Mickey Mantle." However, Gibson did combine blinding speed with power capable of producing tape-measure home runs. He played baseball as if he were in a football game. As a hometown boy, Gibby (as he was known) had a strange relationship with Detroit Tigers fans. They either loved his fiery spirit and drive to win, or hated him for his arrogance, rude demeanor, and gruffness toward autograph seekers. But in the end they respected him and selected him in 1999 for the all-time Tigers outfield alongside legendary players Ty Cobb and Al Kaline.

Kirk Harold Gibson was born on May 28, 1957, in Pontiac, Michigan. He was the youngest of Bob and Barbara Gibson's three children. His father was an auditor for the state of Michigan and later became a math teacher at Kettering High School in suburban Waterford, where Kirk went to school. Barbara taught theater and speech at nearby Clarkston High School. Kirk admitted to being a mama's boy growing up. Her calm, reassuring presence was a stark contrast to his father's pressure to excel. His two sisters, Jocelyn and Christina, helped spoil him. As Kirk remembered it, "My parents never made me work. When I grew up, all we did was screw around with motorcycles and water-skiing. I had it pretty easy. My dad pushed me hard in athletics. He built me a home plate and mound in the backyard and a hoop over the garage, and he made me practice." His father made him do drills and practice constantly, and Kirk appreciated the discipline and mental toughness it instilled when he became older. At the time, however, he began to almost hate athletics because of his father's constant pressure. Kirk noted that his parents were always very supportive and never missed any of his games, and he proudly cited them as his role models and heroes. During high school, he spent the summers playing American Legion baseball—winning a state championship in 1975. In a foreshadowing of things to come, Gibson hit a game-winning home run to put his team into the championship round.

Gibson played football, baseball, and basketball as well as running track at Waterford Kettering High, but football was his true love. He had several outstanding games and as a senior was named All Oakland County in the fall of 1974. He was lightly recruited, so when Michigan State University offered him a football scholarship, he jumped at it.

In 1975, Kirk was determined to be a starter as a freshman at Michigan State. He tried to outwork, outhustle, and outplay everyone else on the team. For him, everything was a competition. He learned he was going to be starting at flanker and quickly called his parents with the news. The first game, against Ohio State, was an eye-opener as the Spartans fell 21-0. Gibson soon realized that the learning process never stopped and was more determined than ever to succeed. The following week he scored his first touchdown, helping MSU end Miami of Ohio's 25-game winning streak. The Spartans finished 7-4 with Kirk catching four touchdown passes, including an 82-yard bomb in their season-ending victory over Iowa.

Gibson had his eyes set on a Rose Bowl berth, but his dreams were shattered when the Spartans were placed on three years' probation in January 1976. The remainder of his football career was spent with no televised games and no hope for a bowl game. Additionally, the coach, Denny Stolz, was fired and Darryl Rogers took over the reins as football coach. Initially, Rogers thought about making Kirk an outside

DETROIT TIGERS 1984: WHAT A START! WHAT A FINISH!

linebacker but decided his speed was needed on the offensive side of the ball. The team finished 4-6-1 in 1976, but Gibson had 39 receptions for 748 yards, leading all Big Ten receivers. The team responded to Rogers' innovative offense and improved to 7-3-1 in 1977.

After his junior season, Gibson was approached by Michigan State baseball coach Danny Litwhiler about playing baseball. Gibson's father had always wanted him to play baseball as well as football, and Rogers gave his blessing, telling Kirk it might give him some leverage in the NFL draft. To Gibson's surprise, he thoroughly enjoyed playing baseball, and he attracted a lot of scouts with his power and speed. In his one year of college baseball, he batted .390, hit 16 home runs, batted in 52 runs, and stole 21 bases in 48 games. He established school records for homers and RBIs, and was selected to the All-American team in baseball. Gibson was approached by several major-league scouts and was touted as a possible first-round selection for the amateur draft. The Detroit Tigers invited him to come to Tiger Stadium for some batting practice. Gibson put on a tremendous display of power, convincing Tigers assistant general manager Bill Lajoie that Gibson was his No. 1 choice for the coming baseball draft. The Tigers had the 12th selection, and Gibson wanted to play for his hometown team. When teams with earlier picks than the Tigers inquired about his future plans, he made it clear that he would return to Michigan State for his final football season. Apparently the question marks loomed large enough that the Tigers were able to select Gibson with the No. 12 pick on June 6, 1978. His decision to play professional baseball surprised a lot of people. But for Gibson it came down to money and long-term goals. Baseball had free agency—which football at the time did not. The players had longer careers, and the benefits obtained through the players' union were much better in baseball. A week after the draft, Gibson signed a six-year deal for $200,000 and reported to Class-A Lakeland in Florida. The contract contained a clause allowing him to return to Michigan State and play football, beginning approximately August 14, 1978.

Gibson's first professional baseball manager was Jim Leyland. Leyland met him at the Miami airport and immediately set Gibson straight about who was in charge and what was expected of a raw rookie. Kirk responded as he always did; he took it as a challenge and worked hard on all facets of his game. And he developed a professional respect for Leyland and his approach to the game. Gibson played in 54 games with Lakeland, hitting .240 with eight home runs and 40 RBIs. He also struck out 54 times in 175 at-bats.

Gibson returned to East Lansing for his final football season. The team ended up co-champion of the Big Ten, setting a scoring record that lasted for 16 years. The team's final record of 8-3 included a huge upset of Michigan, the co-champion. But the Spartans were still under suspension and could not play in the Rose Bowl. Kirk was named All-American as a flanker in football—and as an outfielder in baseball. He had set several Spartans career football records, including 24 touchdown catches, 112 receptions, and 2,347 receiving yards. He also had two touchdowns rushing. Despite his baseball contract, the National Football League's St. Louis Cardinals drafted him in the seventh round in 1979.

During spring training in 1979, Gibson was invited to the major-league spring training camp. His display of power and speed attracted a lot of attention, and Kirk felt he had a good shot at making the major-league roster. He was devastated when he was assigned to Triple-A Evansville. He suffered a knee injury in his very first exhibition game with the minor-league team when he collided with another outfielder. He had arthroscopic surgery, and reported to Evansville after a month's rehabilitation. There, Leyland, now Evansville's manager, was waiting for him. Gibson's numbers weren't overwhelming—a .245 batting average, 9 home runs, and 20 stolen bases—but he heated up toward season's end and helped the Triplets win their division and the playoff championship, hitting .429 with three stolen bases in the American Association playoffs. The day after the Triplets' last game, Leyland told Gibson he was to report to the Tigers.

Gibson sat on the bench for the Tigers for three days before seeing any action. Finally he persuaded manager Sparky Anderson to put him in as a pinch-hitter. It was a September 8 home game against the New York Yankees, and Gibson faced Goose Gossage. The score was 5-4 Yanks with the tying run on first base and two outs. Gibson managed to foul off the first two pitches before Goose blew a third strike by him to end the game. In Gibson's first start, in right field on September 19, he got his first hit—a single off Baltimore's Dennis Martinez—as part of a 2-for-4 day with a run scored. Less than a week after that, on September 25, Gibson hit his first major-league home run, off the Orioles' Steve Stone. His brief time with the Tigers (.237 in 38 at-bats) was enough to persuade Anderson to put Gibson on the parent club in 1980.

Gibson began 1980 as the starting center fielder and was featured on the cover of *Sports Illustrated* as the "Rip Roaring Rookie." The Tigers had a solid core of young players growing up together under Anderson's tutelage. Gibson had a triple and home run in the season opener, an April 10 night game in Kansas City. Pinch-hitting for Rick Peters in the bottom of the ninth inning in the nightcap of a June 16 doubleheader at Tiger Stadium against Milwaukee, Gibson felt a pop in his wrist swinging at a changeup. Alan Trammell had to finish the at-bat. Gibson woke up the next day in severe pain. The team doctors could not find a problem, so the wrist was put in a cast to rest it. The injury resulted in a truncated season in which Gibson hit .263 with nine home runs. In August, he visited the Mayo Clinic, where doctors found the problem: an abnormal development in his arm bones. They shortened his ulna bone and inserted a steel plate. Gibson was told that he would need eight months of rehabilitation. There were no guarantees that the wrist would hold up or that Gibson would ever play baseball again. The irony was that the wrist injury would not have affected his playing football.

During spring training in 1981, Gibson tested the wrist gradually, waiting until nearly the end of camp to go all-out. His eagerness for the beginning of the new season was dimmed

DETROIT TIGERS 1984: WHAT A START! WHAT A FINISH!

when Anderson inserted him into right field on Opening Day, April 9 against Toronto. Right field in Tiger Stadium was the sun field and was made even more difficult by the overhang of the second deck. Gibson had a tough first game, with a fly ball bouncing off his head after he lost it in the sun, and later he was charged with an error when he lost another ball in the overhang, to give the Blue Jays a 2-1 lead (Detroit ultimately won, 6-2), and the fans in the sold-out stadium booed Gibson loudly. Gibson may have reinjured his wrist on May 12 and did not return to the starting lineup for the rest of the month (he pinch-ran twice). Back in the lineup on June 1, he started until June 11, the last game before the players' strike. Gibson finished the strike-split season on a tear, raising his batting average to .328 (9 home runs, 40 RBIs) from a paltry .235 when play resumed on August 10. The Tigers were in the playoff hunt until the final series of the season, when they lost to the Milwaukee Brewers. Anderson made the team watch the Brewers celebrate and told them to "think about that in the offseason." Despite his early-season travails, Gibson was honored as Tiger of the Year by the Detroit baseball writers.

Everyone, including Gibson, thought 1982 was going to be his year. But once again the injury jinx struck. He appeared in 69 games, missing time with injuries to his knee, calf, and wrist, as well as being mysteriously sidelined by what turned out to be an intestinal parasite. The year began with Gibson mired in an 8-for-50 slump in the first two weeks. He had a run-in with Anderson over being pulled in the seventh inning of a game for defensive purposes. Later in the season, Gibson was in the middle of a brawl with the Minnesota Twins in which his good friend Dave Rozema suffered a season-ending knee injury trying to karate-kick a Twins player. Gibson's season ended in a pinch-running role on July 8 with a .278 average and 8 home runs, after he reinjured his wrist.

The 1983 season, during which Gibson turned 26—an age at which observers expect continued improvement from promising players—proved to be his hardest. Anderson decided Gibson was too arrogant and egotistical and needed to improve his professionalism on and off the field. Talking to Tigers beat writers the previous autumn, Anderson had spoken about players needing to be polite and sign autographs, to appreciate the fans, and to be grateful for their position in life. Few doubted that his words were meant for Kirk Gibson. Sparky's lessons began at the end of spring training when he announced that Chet Lemon would be the starting center fielder. On Opening Day, Sparky told Gibson that he would be platooned, batting only against right-handers. Additionally, Gibson would be primarily used as a designated hitter. Kirk was so angry he shut the door and backed Sparky into a corner. But Anderson held his ground, and after Gibson finished his rant, Anderson asked if he was done and told him to "open the door and get your ass outta here."

Gibson had a streaky year. He started out in a slump, batting just .164 into mid-May. He had missed ten games when he had a bone chip removed from his knee. He then hit .319 for the next month and on June 14 crashed a 523-foot home run over the right-field roof at Tiger Stadium. In the same game his speed led him to try for an inside-the-park home run. In a strange play at the plate, the runner in front of him, Lou Whitaker, was tagged out by the Red Sox catcher, Rich Gedman. Gibson, a mere 20 feet behind Whitaker, crashed into the umpire, Larry Barnett. While signaling the out on Whitaker, Barnett apparently stepped in front of Gibson, who managed to knock the ball loose from catcher Gedman and was ruled safe. Peter Gammons wrote in a *Sporting News* article headlined "Most Exciting Player? Gibson": "He also is as much fun to watch as any player in this league, whether hitting 523-foot home runs, racing out of control around the bases, or just plain running. Unlike some of the supposedly exciting base-running types, he is worth the price of admission every time he goes into motion." The game brought Gibson's average to .236, and he reached .253 by June 20. But then he seemed to lose his stroke, and his batting average skidded to .227 by season's end, albeit with 15 home runs. He was mercilessly booed by the fans, and Anderson dropped him lower and lower in the batting order. By the end of the year, the manager's message had gotten through. The world and the Tigers did not revolve around Kirk Gibson. Gibson had his detractors in the media as well. He could be arrogant and unpleasant; one writer described him as hostile and menacing. Years later, Gibson reflected on his struggles: "I lost my focus. I wasn't a good player. I had poor work habits."

Up to then, Gibson had usually spent his offseason hunting and fishing. He preferred the company of his hunting dogs to people. But after all the troubles with his manager, the media, and the fans in 1983, Gibson realized he had hit bottom and needed help. He contacted his agent, Doug Baldwin, who told Kirk he should try a place in Seattle called the Pacific Institute. He spent four days with an instructor named Frank Batenetti, who turned his life around. Gibson managed to overcome the negative mindset from the 1983 season and learned to imprint a positive image in his mind. He embarked on a strenuous workout program, much as he did before beginning his college football career.

The change in Gibson in spring training of 1984 was immediately apparent. He was clean-shaven and had cut his hair. He looked trimmer and sported a positive attitude. Gibson had refused to spend the winter playing ball and learning how to play first base. In 1983, he had told reporters that he wanted Anderson to "keep me out of right. I hate it out there." But now, with his new attitude, he accepted playing that position. The Tigers decided he needed tutelage in right field and brought in Hall of Famer Al Kaline to work with him. Kaline and Gibson worked tirelessly on positioning and throwing. Gibson got additional support from pitching coach Roger Craig, who spent many hours hitting grounders and fly balls to Gibson and helping him reaffirm the positive attitude he learned from the Pacific Institute. Craig also went to bat on Gibson's behalf with Anderson. He helped convince Sparky that Gibson should play every day. The Tigers expressed their faith in Gibson by trading promising young outfielder Glenn Wilson to the Philadelphia Phillies as part of a package that brought reliever Willie Hernandez to the Tigers.

DETROIT TIGERS 1984: WHAT A START! WHAT A FINISH!

The Tigers got off to a great start, going 35-5, and Gibson contributed several key hits. His regained confidence at the plate and in the field ensured that his name would be on the lineup card daily. He played in 149 games, becoming the team's first "20-20" man, smashing 27 home runs and stealing 29 bases, to go with a .282 average and 91 RBIs. He set a team record with 17 game-winning RBIs. Craig noted the growth of Gibson as a leader in the clubhouse and called him a born winner who thrives on pressure. The Tigers won their division easily, finishing 15 games ahead of their closest competitor, the Toronto Blue Jays. Their opponent in the American League Championship Series was the Kansas City Royals. The Tigers cruised in Game One, winning 8-1. Gibson's big contribution came on a defensive play he made on a line drive by George Brett with the bases loaded and two out in the third inning, and the Tigers clinging to a 2-0 lead. Detroit won Game Two 5-3 in 11 innings, with Gibson contributing a double and a home run, scoring twice and driving in two runs. The Tigers completed the sweep in Game Three, winning 1-0 behind the pitching of Milt Wilcox and Willie Hernandez. Gibson was named the MVP of the series.

The Tigers' World Series opponent was the San Diego Padres, who had come back from two games down to beat the Chicago Cubs, three games to two. The Tigers won the opening game, 3-2, with Jack Morris pitching a complete game. Gibson was hitless but contributed a key play in the seventh inning when his throw helped cut down Kurt Bevacqua trying to stretch a leadoff double into a triple, keeping the bases empty and preserving Detroit's one-run margin. He went 2-for-4 in Game Two with a stolen base, but Detroit's early 3-0 lead did not hold up as the Padres rallied to win, 5-3. But Gibson was saving his best for last.

The Tigers won Game Three, 5-2, and Game Four, 4-2. Game Five was played at Tiger Stadium on a gray Sunday afternoon. Gibson slugged a two-run home run in the first inning to get the Tigers' offense started. But the Padres showed signs of life when they rallied to tie the game, 3-3. Gibson led off the fifth inning with an infield single. He moved to second on a long fly ball and two third on two walks. With one out, pinch-hitter Rusty Kuntz hit a popup to shallow right field caught by the second baseman, Alan Wiggins. Gibson took everyone by surprise by tagging up and scoring on the play, giving the Tigers the lead. When Gibson came to bat in the eighth inning, he had runners on second and third with one out, with the Tigers again clinging to a one-run lead, 5-4. On the mound was his old nemesis, Goose Gossage. When Padres manager Dick Williams went to the mound, Sparky Anderson flashed four fingers at Gibson. He was indicating he thought the Padres would walk Gibson to set up a possible double play. But Gossage was convincing his manager that he could handle Gibson, as he had in the past. Gibson yelled to Sparky, "Ten bucks they pitch to me and I crank it." The first pitch was a fastball off the plate. Gibson was sitting on the next fastball and launched it deep into the right-field bleachers for a three-run homer, and everyone knew the ballgame was over. The most famous image from the World Series was Gibson leaping, arms above his head in triumph, after he circled the bases. The Padres went out meekly in the ninth inning, and the Tigers were World Series champions.

The Tigers were the toast of the town, feted and celebrated throughout the offseason. Most pundits picked them to repeat in 1985. Gibson sought to keep his personal fire burning, posting an "I'm Ornery" sign over his locker in spring training. He went on to have perhaps his finest season as a Tiger, playing in 154 games, scoring 96 runs, knocking in 97 runs, stealing 30 bases, and hitting 37 doubles and 29 home runs, while finishing with a .287 batting average. But despite other noteworthy individual seasons, particularly by Whitaker, Lance Parrish, and Darrell Evans, the Tigers finished third in the AL East, 15 games in back of the Blue Jays.

Several events occurred after the 1985 season that significantly affected Gibson's future. He married JoAnn Sklarski in December as part of a double wedding ceremony with teammate and best friend Dave Rozema, who married JoAnn's sister Sandy. Gibson's carefree bachelor days were over, and he would be focused on his family when considering future baseball prospects. Gibson was a free agent after the end of the 1985 season, and with the season he had, he was expecting a lot of suitors from the other teams. Surprisingly, teams that seemed interested earlier suddenly backed out of negotiations. This was later found by an arbitrator to be collusion on the part of the major-league teams. At the time, however, Gibson felt that he had little choice but to accept the Tigers' offer. He called them from his honeymoon in New Zealand with one minute remaining before the deadline. The three-year, $4.1 million contract made Gibson the highest-paid Tiger.

Gibson got off to a hot start in 1986, hitting two home runs in a 4-for-4 day with five RBIs on Opening Day, April 7, as the Tigers beat the Red Sox, 6-5. On April 22, Gibson was hitting a robust .359 when the injury jinx struck again. Returning to first base on a pickoff play, he severely twisted his ankle and foot. He missed 33 games. The Tigers went from a game out of first to nine back. Despite playing in only 119 games in 1986, Gibson still managed to hit 28 home runs, drive in 86 runs, and steal 34 bases. He also set a major-league record by collecting game-winning hits in four consecutive games.

The 1987 season started ominously for Gibson when he tore a rib muscle during batting practice and began the season on the disabled list. When he finally returned to action on May 5, the Tigers were 9-15, and were 11 games out of first place. They went 89-49 the rest of the way in an exciting pennant race that came down to the final three-game series against the Toronto Blue Jays. A week earlier, the Tigers had seemed hopelessly out of contention after dropping three in a row to the Jays. But they came back to win the fourth game with Gibson blasting a game-tying home run in the ninth inning off closer Tom Henke, and knocked in the winning run in the 13th inning as the Tigers kept their slim hopes alive. Going

DETROIT TIGERS 1984: WHAT A START! WHAT A FINISH!

into the final series in Detroit, the Tigers needed a sweep to win the pennant outright—and they got it. The Tigers went into the AL playoffs a big favorite over the Twins, but lost in five games. Gibson had another fine season despite the early injury, hitting batting .277, with 79 RBIs, 95 runs scored, 24 home runs, and 26 stolen bases. During the offseason, he set an altitude flying record for a Cessna 206, reaching a height of 25,200 feet. (During Gibson's second term of service with the Tigers, he often flew a small plane from his home in upstate Lapeer to Detroit City Airport, then drove to Tiger Stadium for the game.)

Once again Gibson was on the verge of free agency. The Tigers tried to trade him to the Los Angeles Dodgers for Pedro Guerrero, but the deal fell through when the Dodgers learned Gibson was going to be declared a "second look" free agent due to an arbitrator's collusion ruling against the owners. He continued to negotiate with the Tigers, but ended up signing a three-year, $4.5 million contract with the Dodgers. Gibson was stung when the Tigers new owner, Tom Monaghan, called him "a disgrace to the Tiger uniform with his half-beard, half-stubble." Monaghan continued bashing Gibson on the radio, declaring that the Tigers would be better off without him.

Gibson quickly established his presence in the Dodgers' clubhouse in 1988 spring training. His teammates played a prank on him that led to his storming off the field and demanding a team meeting to set things straight. He made it clear he was there to win a championship and he would do whatever it took to do so. Gibson led the Dodgers in home runs, runs scored, doubles, slugging percentage, and on-base percentage as the Dodgers won the National League West by seven games over the Cincinnati Reds. The championship series with the New York Mets went the full seven games. Gibson contributed a game-winning homer in the top of the 12th inning of Game Four that tied the series. The following day he hit a three-run homer in the fifth inning that put the Dodgers up 6-0 in a 7-4 victory. But Gibson injured his left knee stealing second base in the ninth inning after having been intentionally walked. He played in Game Six after receiving a cortisone shot, but the Mets won, forcing a deciding seventh game on October 12. Gibson got the Dodgers out to an early lead with a sacrifice fly in the first inning. In the second, Los Angeles scored five more runs to put the Mets in a deep hole. Gibson was again walked intentionally and injured his right knee sliding hard into second base. He tried to gut it out, but finally came out of the game in the fourth inning. The Dodgers went on to win the game easily, 6-0.

The World Series against the Oakland A's was scheduled to begin three days later, on Saturday, October 15. The Dodgers' medical team worked feverishly trying to get Gibson ready to play, but to no avail. When the Game One introductions took place, he was in the clubhouse with ice on both legs. The A's rode a Jose Canseco grand slam to a 4-3 lead going into the ninth inning. Oakland's star closer, Dennis Eckersley, easily retired the first two batters. When the inning started, Gibson had hobbled over to a batting tee and begun taking practice cuts. He told the clubhouse attendant to get the manager, Tommy Lasorda. Gibson told the manager he could pinch-hit. In the meantime, with two outs, Mike Davis, pinch-hitting for Alfredo Griffin, worked Eckersley for a walk. As Gibson climbed up the dugout steps onto the field, the Dodger Stadium crowd went crazy. Eckersley quickly got ahead of Gibson, 0-2 as he barely fouled off the first two pitches. Gibson managed to work the count full and stepped out of the box. The Dodgers' advance scout, Mike Didier, had told Gibson that if he ever faced Eckersley with a full count, Eckersley was certain to throw a backdoor slider. And that's the pitch Gibson drove into the right-field bleachers for the game-winning home run. He limped around the bases with his arm held high celebrating the shocking turn of events. (Broadcaster Jack Buck, famous for his "I can't believe what I just saw" call of the homer, also mistakenly said the Tigers had won the ballgame.) The Dodgers had seized momentum from Oakland and went on to win the Series in five games. It was Gibson's only appearance in the 1988 World Series.

Gibson had a thoroughly enjoyable offseason. He was named the National League Most Valuable Player for 1988. (Gibson was the first, and through 2008 the only MVP winner to never appear in an All-Star game. He had been selected twice, in 1985 and 1988, but declined to attend.) Gibson even got an apologetic phone call from Tom Monaghan. The call included an invitation to lunch with his former owner, which Gibson declined. But when spring 1989 rolled around, Kirk's hamstring problems continued to plague him. He played in only 71 games, finishing his season in Pittsburgh on July 22 before deciding to undergo exploratory surgery. Doctors found that the hamstring had been torn, and after they cleaned it up, Gibson began a long rehab. He missed almost a full year, returning to play against Cincinnati in Los Angeles on June 2, 1990. Those two partial seasons were disappointing ones for the Dodgers, despite Gibson's 26 steals in 89 games in 1990, and Los Angeles made no effort to re-sign him after the 1990 season. He wanted to return to the American League and agreed to a two-year contract with the Kansas City Royals. Gibson got off to a good start in 1991, hitting six home runs in April. But manager John Wathan was fired after 37 games and replaced by Hal McRae. Gibson and McRae had had a run-in back in Gibson's rookie year, and Gibson believed McRae still held a grudge. Indeed, McRae told Gibson in spring training the following year that he had no chance of winning a starting job. On March 10, 1992, Gibson was traded to the Pittsburgh Pirates for pitcher Neal Heaton. The good news for Gibson was that he was reuniting with his first manager, Jim Leyland. But Gibson could never get untracked, and after hitting just .196 in 16 games with the Pirates, he was given his unconditional release on May 5. Gibson, 35 years old, returned home to Michigan and spent the summer with his family.

DETROIT TIGERS 1984: WHAT A START! WHAT A FINISH!

By now, the Tigers had a new owner, Mike Ilitch, who had always loved the way Gibson played the game, and wanted to bring him back. Gibson signed a one-year deal for $500,000 for the 1993 season. He had a good season, contributing 13 home runs and 62 RBIs to a team that improved by 10 games in the win column. The 1994 season was shortened by the strike, and the Tigers sagged to last place in the AL East, but just one game behind fourth-place Boston and two behind third-place Toronto. Despite the Tigers' disappointing performance, Gibson hit .276, hammered 23 home runs, and drove in 72 runs in the short, 115-game season, and was named Tiger of the Year by the Detroit sportswriters.

Gibson and the Tigers reached a last-minute agreement for the 1995 season. But, now 38, he found himself lacking the fire and drive that typified his playing career. When the Tigers conceded that their season was over by trading two of their top pitchers, starter David Wells to Cincinnati on July 31 and closer Mike Henneman to Houston ten days later, Gibson decided it was time to retire. He played his final game on August 10, 1995. In 1,635 major-league games over 17 seasons, he batted .268 with 255 home runs, 284 stolen bases, 985 runs scored, and 870 runs batted in.

After his baseball career ended, Gibson ran an investment firm. He enjoyed spending time with his wife, JoAnn, and his four children, Kevin, Kirk, Cameron, and Colleen. For a brief time he served as a color analyst for Tigers games on Fox Sports Net Detroit, and as a co-host of a popular sports talk radio show. But the lure of the game was too much, and Gibson returned to the Tigers as a bench coach beside his friend and onetime teammate Alan Trammell from 2003 through 2005. After Trammell was fired, Gibson interviewed for a couple of managerial posts and finally caught on as a bench coach for the Arizona Diamondbacks—then managed by another onetime Tigers teammate, Bob Melvin—in 2007, remaining with the team after Melvin was fired early in the 2009 season. But after Melvin's successor, A.J. Hinch, was fired, Gibson was given the manager's position July 2, 2010.

Gibson was an enigmatic baseball player. His early promise was never fulfilled, and he was considered a below-average outfielder with a weak throwing arm. But he will always be remembered for the intangibles he brought to his teams. Sparky Anderson once wrote of Gibson, "I've never seen a player change his direction so completely. His personality, his drive, his dedication are unsurpassed. He knew how to make things happen. Gibby gets the highest rating as a player from me."

References

Publications

Anderson, Sparky. *Bless You Boys: Diary of the 1984 Detroit Tigers' Season*. Chicago: Contemporary Books, 1984.

Cantor, George. *Wire to Wire: Inside the 1984 Detroit Tigers Championship Season*. Chicago: Triumph Books, 2004.

Craig, Roger. *Inside Pitch: Roger Craig's '84 Tigers Journal*. Grand Rapids, Mich.: William B. Eerdmans Publishing Co., 1984.

Stanton, Tom. *The Detroit Tigers Reader*. Ann Arbor, Mich.: University of Michigan Press, 2005.

Zaret, Eli. *'84: The Last of the Great Tigers: Untold Stories From an Amazing Season*. South Boardman, Mich.: Crofton Creek Press, 2004.

Articles

Fimrite, Ron. "The Tigers Roar to the Pennant." *Sports Illustrated*, October 15, 1984:

Fimrite, Ron. "The Happy Hunter." *Sports Illustrated*, December 10, 1984.

Gage, Tom. "Tigers All Set for Gibson Payoff." *The Sporting News*, December 8, 1979: 52.

Gage, Tom. "Old Injury Hex Confronts Gibson." *The Sporting News*, February 28, 1983: 35.

Gage, Tom. "Lemon and Gibson to Duel in Center." *The Sporting News*, March 14, 1983: 28.

Gage, Tom. "Sparky Wants Lemon for CF." *The Sporting News*, April 11, 1983: 36.

Gage, Tom. "Right Is All Wrong for Injured Gibson." *The Sporting News*, April 25, 1983: 25.

Gage, Tom. "A Titanic Shot By Kirk Gibson." *The Sporting News*, June 27, 1983: 20.

Gage, Tom. "Sparky Fidgets as Kirk Flounders." *The Sporting News*, August 8, 1983: 12.

Gage, Tom. "Sparky Hasn't Given Up on Gibson." *The Sporting News*, February 6, 1984: 43.

Gage, Tom. "Signing Gibson May Be a Problem." *The Sporting News*, December 10, 1984: 52.

Gage, Tom. "Gibson Won't Gamble." *The Sporting News*, January 20, 1986: 43.

Gammons, Peter. "Most Exciting Player? Gibson." *The Sporting News*, June 27, 1983: 27.

Hawkins, Jim. "Instant-Star Gibson Falls Into Tigers' Net." *The Sporting News*, July 1, 1978: 15, 40.

Hawkins, Jim. "Bengals Glance the Other Way as Gibson Runs Pass Patterns." *The Sporting News*, December 2, 1978: 56.

Kurkjian, Tim. "Go-Go Gibby." *Sports Illustrated*, May 17, 1993.

Young, Dick. "Showboating by Ump Causes Foul-Up." *The Sporting News*, June 27, 1983: 4.

Web Sites

www.baseballlibrary.com

www.espn.com

www.retrosheet.com

www.thebaseballcube.com

www.thebaseballpage.com

www.wikipedia.com

Johnny Grubb
by Mike McClary

THE 1984 DETROIT Tigers were a team filled with larger-than-life personalities, from a media-savvy manager in Sparky Anderson to a confident and boisterous leader in Kirk Gibson. And while some of the bigger names on the Tigers' roster captured much of the attention for clutch hits throughout that magical year, the team turned to a quiet gentleman from Virginia to deliver in a pivotal moment in Detroit's quest for the American League pennant.

John Maywood "Johnny" Grubb Jr. was born on August 4, 1948, in Richmond, Virginia, to John Grubb Sr. and Geraldine Grubb. One of three children, and the only son, Grubb gravitated to sports and baseball in particular during his childhood. "There were not a whole lot of neighbors, so I'd pretty much just watch some of the Yankee games on television and then I got a real interest in baseball," Grubb said.

As was the case with many other boys growing up in the 1950s, Grubb's favorite player—and Yankee—was Mickey Mantle. After watching Game of the Week on television, Grubb would head outside and take some cuts, imitating the players he'd watched that afternoon. "I ended up learning how to hit both right- and left-handed just from watching them on television," he said.

At Meadowbrook High School in Richmond, where his classmates included future professional golfers Lanny and Bobby Wadkins, Grubb excelled at basketball and football as well as baseball. After his sophomore season, he gave up football to focus on baseball, which, he acknowledged, was probably a smart decision. "I might have gotten hurt, as small as I was then," Grubb said.

After graduation, he enrolled at Manatee Junior College—now Manatee Community College—in Bradenton, Florida, where he played two seasons under coach Bob Wynn. After his sophomore year, Grubb was drafted for the first of four times in a two-year span. In 1969, the Boston Red Sox drafted him in the third round of the amateur draft, but Grubb chose to remain at Manatee. Later that year, the Cincinnati Reds selected him in the first round with the 14th overall pick of the amateur draft's secondary phase.

Rather than sign with the Reds, Grubb instead transferred to Florida State University in Tallahassee and starred on the 1970 squad that compiled a 49-9 record and finished as runner-up to the University of Southern California for the NCAA championship. Grubb led FSU in hitting with a .303 regular-season average. In the College World Series, he again led the Seminoles in hitting and was named to the All-Series team. Later he was named an honorable mention All-American.

The Atlanta Braves drafted Grubb in the third round of the 1970 amateur draft (secondary phase), but he opted not to sign. On January 13, 1971, the San Diego Padres selected him with the 24th pick of the first round in the secondary phase. With only two quarters remaining at FSU, he weighed his options and then signed with the Padres.

"I took pride in being a good outfielder, and thought I had a better-than-average arm," Grubb said. "And though I was not a real burner as a baserunner, I felt like I had better-than-average speed. So I felt like I had the four tools that they wanted. Especially in the National League, they want you to be able to field, run, hit, and have a good arm. And, of course, like they always said, if you can hit, they'll find a place to play you somewhere."

Grubb's professional career began in 1971 with the Class A Lodi Padres of the California League. The Padres promoted him the next season to the Double-A Alexandria (Louisiana) Aces of the Texas League. Hall of Famer Duke Snider managed the Aces, and the team's pitching coach was former Dodgers—and Tigers—left-hander Johnny Podres.

By and large, Grubb spent most of his time in the outfield in the minors but he dabbled, at the club's request, at third

DETROIT TIGERS 1984: WHAT A START! WHAT A FINISH!

base. "They were trying to get me to learn how to play a little bit of third. So I wasn't sure if they were going to have me at third or the outfield. Then they had a guy that they signed as a bonus player, Dave Roberts. They played him at third, and then they ended up moving me back to the outfield, which was fine with me. I liked the outfield."

Grubb's fast track to the major leagues continued at the end of the 1972 season, when the Padres promoted the 24-year-old outfielder to the big club in September. On September 10, he made his major-league debut as the starting center fielder in a doubleheader against the Atlanta Braves. Grubb promptly collected his first major-league hit, a seventh-inning single to right off Ron Reed. In the nightcap, Grubb got two more hits and his first major-league RBI. In seven games, Grubb batted .333 with a double and triple.

He spent the offseason playing for Obregón in the Mexican League to get more playing time and experience at the professional level. Grubb said the talent in the Mexican League was similar to that of Double-A or Triple-A clubs in the United States. His experience in Mexico apparently provided Grubb with the edge the Padres were looking for; he broke camp with the team in 1973 and his 16-year big league career was in second gear—and he'd never have to put it in reverse by returning to the minors.

In his first full major-league season, Grubb appeared in 113 games for a new manager, Don Zimmer, and played almost exclusively in center field, hitting .311 with eight home runs and 37 RBIs. He finished sixth in the National League Rookie of the Year Award voting, with the Giants' Gary Matthews winning the award running away. (Grubb did, in fact, play some third base during his rookie season. He played four innings over two games at third but never had to make a play.)

Grubb saw even more playing time in 1974—and he capitalized on it. Of all Padres who qualified for the National League batting title, he led in several offensive categories, including a .286 batting average, a .355 on-base percentage and a .758 on-base plus slugging (OPS) percentage. That year New York Mets manager Yogi Berra selected Grubb as an All-Star reserve—and the Padres' only representative—for the game in Pittsburgh. In his only at-bat in the All-Star Game, Grubb popped out to shortstop on a pitch from Oakland hurler (and eventual Hall of Famer) Catfish Hunter in the seventh inning.

"I was real happy to be on an All-Star team," Grubb said. "It was a little unusual that it was only my second year in the league. But I was just happy to be there."

Grubb played two more seasons in San Diego, hitting .269 and .284, respectively. After the 1976 season, he was traded with catcher Fred Kendall and infielder Hector Torres to the Cleveland Indians for outfielder George Hendrick. Grubb said he was looking forward to playing for Indians manager Frank Robinson, who had tapped him as an everyday player in 1977. But a hand injury just 34 games into the season made Grubb's first year in Cleveland one to forget.

"I did it on a checked swing," he said. "I tried a checked swing on one of Gaylord [Perry]'s nasty pitches. Some people call it a spitter, but it could have been a forkball, I don't know. But I tried to check my swing and I guess the knob of the bat came across my hamate bone. And it's a strange way to do it, but it broke it off and I ended up having to go in" for surgery.

In 1978, Grubb played for his fourth manager in his five major-league seasons: Jeff Torborg, who replaced Robinson during Grubb's injury-shortened the 1977 season. It turned out that 1978 was also the season in which he could fully immerse himself in studying the American League brand of baseball, and hitting in particular.

"As an athlete, you have to be able to adjust. And I didn't know much about the American League, and the National League took pride in being real aggressive on the basepaths and playing for one run, not trying to go for the big inning all the time," he said.

"In the American League, the first thing I noticed was that they kind of pitched a little backwards. In the National League, if they were behind in the count ... if the pitcher was behind in the count, you could pretty much bet on a fastball," Grubb said. "In the American League, you couldn't count on that. They could throw you a changeup, a curveball with the bases loaded and two strikes on you. They just kind of pitched a little backwards because of the smaller ballparks. And actually, I thought the pitching was better in the American League because they weren't as predictable. Like I said, you couldn't count on a fastball in fastball situations. So it took a while to get used to that. But if you watch and study the pitchers, you start learning how they pitch guys in certain situations."

Grubb also had to get used to a role he never played in the National League: that of the designated hitter. "That took a little bit of getting used to as well because you have an at-bat and then you go sit. So I had to find a way to keep myself ready," he said. "And you could either go down in the bullpen area or go up in the clubhouse and swing the bat or go down wherever you could find a place to stay loose and try to keep yourself in the game instead of just sitting there waiting around for your next at-bat.

"So you just learn to try to find out what works for you and make sure you're ready for your next at-bat. But I'm sure it prolonged my career because I played almost until I was 40," he said. "And I don't know if I'd have played that long had I been in the National League."

With his contract expiring at the end of the 1978 season, Grubb sensed the Indians were not going to re-sign him and, as the trading deadline approached, expected a trade. On August 31, 1978, he was traded to the Texas Rangers for two players to be named later. (The two turned out to be pitcher Bobby Cuellar and minor-league outfielder Dave Rivera.)

When Grubb joined Billy Hunter's Rangers for a weekend series against the Milwaukee Brewers, Texas was 65-65 and in third place in the American League West, just 4½ games behind the first-place Kansas City Royals. In his first game as a Ranger, on September 3, Grubb went 1-for-4 with a single off Ed Farmer. In 21 games with Texas to close out the '78 season, he hit .394 with a homer and six RBIs in 33 at-bats.

DETROIT TIGERS 1984: WHAT A START! WHAT A FINISH!

The Rangers finished the year in second place with an 87-75 record, five games behind the Royals.

Over the next four seasons, from 1979 to '82, Grubb hit .272 for Texas and still saw most of his playing time in the outfield. In the spring of 1983, he could sense that a change was coming in Arlington. "I hadn't had much playing time in spring training, so I knew something was going to happen," he said. "Either they were going to just release me or make a trade. And I didn't think they would just release me because I felt like I could still play."

On March 24, he got the answer. "[Rangers manager] Doug Rader called me into his office and he told me that they had made a trade. He said, 'Grubsteaks, you're going to like where you're going.' I said, 'Where's that?' And he said 'Detroit.' And, of course, I looked at him and kind of said 'Yup. That would be a good team to go to.' We knew they were strong and getting better each year and right on the verge of being a real, real good ballclub. So I was happy to go there."

In his first season with the Tigers, 1983, Grubb, wearing number 30, played in 57 games, mostly in right field and as the designated hitter; he batted .254 with four home runs and 22 RBIs. That season the Tigers were in the hunt for the American League East lead most of the summer. In fact, Detroit flirted with first place as late as August 26, when the club was just one game behind the eventual World Series champion Batimore Orioles. The Tigers wound up finishing second with a 92-70 record, but the groundwork was set for 1984.

Though he was now 35, Grubb's playing time increased in 1984, up to 86 games and 276 at-bats as an outfielder, DH, and—a more common occurrence—pinch-hitter. Now the seasoned veteran on a team featuring twentysomethings Alan Trammell, Lou Whitaker, and Lance Parrish, among others, Grubb settled into his role and enjoyed the ride. "It was fun to watch those guys play and every once in a while to jump in and do something myself," he said.

"What I remember most about that year is that I never really felt like we were out of any ballgame," Grubb said. "Any lead a team could get, we felt like we could have a big inning and jump right back in the game. And we had real good pitching, so if we had the lead, we had Willie [Hernandez] and [Aurelio] Lopez coming in to shut the door on them. The pitchers did their job, and the hitters did their job. And we just felt like we could win any game." Grubb finished the '84 season with a .267 average, eight home runs, and 17 RBIs, and set his sights on the American League Championship Series matchup with the Royals. After coasting to victory in Game One of the ALCS, the Tigers found themselves in a nail-biter in Game Two.

The Tigers jumped out to a 3-0 lead but the Royals chipped away to tie the game in the eighth inning. With one out in the top of the 11th, and with Ruppert Jones on first and Darrell Evans at second, Grubb faced Dan Quisenberry, who led the American League with 44 saves that season. The left-handed-hitting Grubb was 0-for-1 against Quisenberry during the regular season and had just two hits in 12 career at-bats against him. Grubb waited as the submariner and his batterymate, John Wathan, discussed their pitching strategy. "He got two strikes on me and Wathan went out to the mound. I was watching them when they were out there talking. I thought I could read their lips and I thought I saw them saying 'fastball.' And I thought, well, I can't trust that, but I'm going to be ready for it." Hitless in his previous three at-bats in the game, Grubb was looking to change his luck and power his team to a 2-0 series lead.

As Wathan got into his crouch, Grubb dug in. On the next pitch, he ripped a two-run double to right-center to put the Tigers up 5-3 in the game and leave them one win away from the World Series. "He threw a fastball, and I'm sure [Royals center fielder] Willie Wilson was cheating-in a little bit on me with two strikes. But I happened to get a hold of one and drove it over his head. So I'm glad I came through to help out. That was my turn, I guess, to do something to help the team." The Tigers clinched the pennant two days later, defeating the Royals 1-0 in Game Three.

One could argue that for the Tigers to play the first game of the 1984 World Series in San Diego was perhaps more special for Alan Trammell and John Grubb than other members of the team. Trammell was raised in San Diego and it's where Grubb's career had begun 12 years earlier. "That was real neat to go back. When they did the introductions, I remember they gave me a nice ovation. I wasn't sure really what they might do. You're not sure if fans are going to turn on you or not. But they were really, really nice. And, of course, we had friends that still lived back there."

Grubb made his first World Series appearance in Game Two, as the designated hitter, batting seventh. He singled to left off Padres starter Ed Whitson in the first inning. It was the fifth, and last, hit off Whitson in the inning before he was replaced by Andy Hawkins with two out. Grubb also played in Games 3 and 4, as designated hitter and a pinch-hitter, but went hitless in both games, though he was hit by a Hawkins pitch in the World Series-clinching Game Five.

The final three years of Grubb's Tigers career were no different than his first two; he played sparingly in the outfield and was used primarily as Sparky Anderson's DH. His finest statistical year in Detroit came in 1986. In 81 games, he hit .333 with 13 home runs and 51 RBIs.

Detroit returned to the postseason in Grubb's final year, 1987. The Tigers fought the Toronto Blue Jays over the final 10 days of the season and clinched the AL East title on the last day. Though his regular-season numbers were the lowest in his 16 years—a .202 average, two home runs, and 13 RBIs—Grubb excelled in the ALCS against the Minnesota Twins. Appearing in four of the five games, he batted .571 on four hits in seven at-bats.

Grubb's major-league career came to a close on October 12, 1987, in Game Five of the ALCS. He collected a hit in his final at-bat, a single to left field off his former Tigers teammate, Juan Berenguer, in the eighth inning. The Tigers lost the game, 9-5, and the series, four games to one. Four days later, the Tigers released the 38-year-old Grubb.

"Coming into that season, I was close to 40, so I knew it was getting right down to the end," Grubb said. "And I knew

Sparky probably saw me as not going to have a whole lot of playing time, a guy off the bench. So I knew it was a good chance it might be my last year, but I wouldn't allow myself to think that way. And I just had a poor season, but ended up having a good playoff for us. But I wish I'd have had a better season for us. I just didn't do that well that year."

In 1,424 major-league games, Grubb collected 1,153 hits, with 99 home runs, and finished with a .278 career average.

Grubb returned in the fall of 1987 to his hometown of Richmond, where he settled with his wife, Linda. They had two sons, Chris and Corey, and four grandchildren. The year 2009, the 25th anniversary of his Tigers' World Series victory, found him coaching the varsity baseball team at his alma mater, Meadowbrook High School. One of his former players, Cla Meredith, reached the majors with the Boston Red Sox in 2005, played for San Diego for three years and another two with the Baltimore Orioles.

Although Johnny Grubb played for four major-league teams, there's no question where his affection rested: with the Detroit Tigers. He continues to be active with the Tigers organization, participating in the annual team-sponsored fantasy camps each winter in Lakeland, Florida.

"Early in the season in spring training," Grubb said, "I remember vividly one statement Sparky made. He said, 'Look, guys, if you go out there and give them your heart and soul, they'll do the same thing. But if you dog it on them one time, they won't ever forget it.' And he was right. Those fans in Detroit—that was one of my best memories, and still is the way the fans treated me and the players. You could tell they were diehard fans. It wasn't like that at the other places that I played. Detroit is a special town. They loved their sports and loved their Tigers."

References

Web Sites:

http://www.Baseball-Reference.com

http://seminoles.cstv.com/genrel/grubb_john00.html

Other sources:

McClary, Mike. Phone interview with John Grubb, March 2, 2008.

Willie Hernandez
by Gary Gillette

IN 1973, JASON Miller's angst-enabled play *That Championship Season* won both a Pulitzer Prize and a Tony Award. The drama, set in Scranton, Pennsylvania, focused on the 25th anniversary reunion of the players and the coach of a high-school basketball team that won the state championship. Full of booze, brooding, bigotry, bitterness, betrayal, and bruised feelings, neither the now-middle-aged players nor their retired coach can cope with the way their lives have played out since their collective moment of sweet triumph.

A world away from the limelight of the Big Apple, an 18-year-old Puerto Rican ballplayer signed his first professional contract on September 11, 1973, exactly one year after the first preview of *That Championship Season* had been staged by the New York Shakespeare Festival on Broadway.

Miller's masterwork was produced by Joseph Papp, a giant of the American theater. Hernandez's masterwork was produced by Sparky Anderson, a giant of the national pastime.

Willie Hernandez, an inexperienced 19-year-old pitcher, made his professional debut in April 1974 with Spartanburg, South Carolina, the Philadelphia Phillies' affiliate in the old Western Carolinas League. When Miller's Championship Season closed after 700 performances on Broadway that same month, Hernandez had just begun working on the "screenplay" for his dramatic championship season: The first scene in the first act had the hero lead his Class A loop in starts (26), complete games (13), innings (190), and strikeouts (179) against only 49 walks. His 11-11 ledger could only partially mask his dominance, which included a 2.75 earned-run average.

The young pitcher's next stop was at Double-A Reading, like Scranton, a small, declining industrial city in the interior of the Keystone State, about 100 miles south of Scranton through the hardscrabble anthracite coal belt of eastern Pennsylvania.

High-school basketball is worlds away from Major League Baseball, and snowbound Scranton will never be mistaken for sunny Puerto Rico. Still, gritty Scranton displays more than a passing resemblance to its much-larger Rust Belt cousin Detroit, where Hernandez would rise to fame and fortune. And the movie's theme has some resonance with the career of Guillermo Hernandez.

Robert Mitchum, Martin Sheen, Stacy Keach, Bruce Dern, and Paul Sorvino starred in the 1982 Cannon Films movie *That Championship Season,* written and directed by Miller. That was the year that Hernandez notched 10 saves for the first time, graduating from the obscurity of middle relief to a top-notch setup pitcher with the Chicago Cubs.

In 1983 Dern won a Silver Bear at the prestigious Berlin International Film Festival for his celluloid performance as Scranton Mayor George Sitkowski. Meanwhile, Hernandez was earning rave reviews for his mound performances with

DETROIT TIGERS 1984: WHAT A START! WHAT A FINISH!

Philadelphia. On July 3, he tied the National League relief record by fanning six consecutive batters; in the final game of the 1983 World Series, he punched out three Orioles hitters in a brilliant three-inning hitless relief performance.

Describing Hernandez's award-winning 1984 performance is easy: The left-hander became Detroit's closer and completely stifled opponents while racking up 35 saves in 36 opportunities (including the postseason). The only glitch came on the final weekend of the season after Detroit had clinched, when Hernandez was inserted into a one-run situation with a runner on third simply to get work. A sacrifice fly tied the game and registered a meaningless blown save, ending Hernandez's then-major-league record 32 consecutive saves.

Setting a major-league record normally gets harder over time, but Hernandez's record is far more impressive than that of a later titlist, Eric Gagne, who blitzed his way to 84 straight saves from 2002 to 2004. The majority of Gagne's saves were the piece-of-cake one-inning, no runners-on-base variety; the Dodgers' right-hander recorded more than three outs in only 18 percent of those appearances—only once going as much as two innings. By contrast, Hernandez pitched more than one inning in 66 percent of his save chances, going two or more frames 18 times. He also did multi-inning stints in nonsave situations, including a four-inning outing. He also hurled four innings to earn a richly deserved save.

Hernandez's statistics in '84 were truly astounding: 80 games, 68 games finished (both major league-leading totals), a 9-3 record, 140 1/3 innings, 96 hits, only six (!) home runs, 28 non-intentional walks, 112 strikeouts, a 1.92 ERA. His 140 1/3 IP turned out be the fourth highest relief workload of the 1980s.

The All-Star, AL Pitcher of the Month for July, Cy Young Award winner and Most Valuable Player, and *Sporting News* American League Pitcher of the Year became only the second Detroit hurler to win a Cy Young Award (Denny McLain in 1968 being the first, and Justin Verlander in 2011 the third). He set Tigers records for games finished and appearances by a pitcher while becoming only the second Tigers pitcher to top 30 saves (John Hiller, the first). Appropriately, Hernandez threw the final pitches of the AL East-clinching game, the American League Championship Series-winning game, and the last game of the World Series.

From the first Cy Young Award, in 1956, to 2009, only nine relief pitchers won the award. There weren't really full-time relief pitchers until after World War II; it is certain that the Philadelphia Phillies' Jim Konstanty would have copped the award in 1950 if there were one at the time. So counting Konstanty, only 10 relief pitchers have managed to rise to the heights that Willie Hernandez achieved in 1984. Three of them are in the Hall of Fame: Rollie Fingers, Dennis Eckersley, and Bruce Sutter. Detroit's relief ace became only the second bullpen hero to be honored with both the MVP and the Cy Young Awards (the third if you count Konstanty). Hernandez was also the first player from Puerto Rico to win the award and, 25 years later, remained the only Latino hurler to take home that trophy. In a 2005 poll by *La Prensa*, published for Hispanics living in the Detroit-Toledo corridor, Hernandez was voted the fourth best Latin *lansador relevista* (relief pitcher) of the 20th century.

Cy Relievers	Team	Lg	Year
Eric Gagne	LA	NL	2003
Dennis Eckersley*	OAK	AL	1992 MVP
Mark Davis	SD	NL	1989
Steve Bedrosian	PHI	NL	1987
Willie Hernandez*	DET	AL	1984 MVP
Rollie Fingers*	MIL	AL	1981 MVP
Bruce Sutter	CHN	NL	1979
Sparky Lyle*	NY	AL	1977
Mike Marshall*	LA	NL	1974
Jim Konstanty* (pre-Cy Young)	PHI	NL	1950 MVP

* won pennant (pre-1969) or division (1969-2009)

Of the nine Cy Young firemen, Hernandez's career most closely resembles that of Konstanty, an undistinguished reliever for the Phillies in the late 1940s before a good season in relief in 1949. Then, in 1950, the "Whiz Kid" Phillies streaked to a surprise National League pennant with Konstanty having his career year as closer. The right-hander earned his first and only All-Star nod on the way to becoming the first relief ace to win the MVP. Afterward, however, Konstanty slumped and had only two good seasons in relief in his remaining six years in the majors. Hernandez, likewise, made his first All-Star team in 1984. He pitched for another five seasons, turning in one very good year and a second good one before retiring.

Pitcher	SV	G	GF	W-L	IP	H	BB	SO	ERA	OPS+	Ages
Dave Righetti	106	212	181	25-21	310	263	117	265	2.53	68	25-27
Jeff Reardon	99	193	156	16-24	263.2	221	89	213	3.35	84	28-30
Lee Smith	97	200	175	25-20	289	254	109	291	3.27	83	26-28
Dan Quisenberry	93	218	197	17-19	339.2	355	52	131	2.57	79	31-33
Willie Hernandez	87	218	185	25-20	335.2	265	71	265	2.60	61	29-31
Rich Gossage	72	157	127	20-16	246	208	73	199	2.96	76	32-34
Bruce Sutter	71	145	124	14-14	229.2	217	61	145	2.90	97	31-33
Jesse Orosco	69	172	131	26-18	247	188	103	215	2.55	73	27-29
Donnie Moore	68	161	128	16-18	240	214	61	172	2.51	72	30-32
Dave Smith	65	171	121	18-16	212.2	168	59	131	2.37	70	29-31

DETROIT TIGERS 1984: WHAT A START! WHAT A FINISH!

While Hernandez experienced a peak that few other pitchers ever achieve, he was not the dominant reliever of the era. Looking at the top 10 relievers in terms of saves from 1984-86, Detroit's closer ranks only fifth—and this is counting only Hernandez's peak years. Hernandez does, however, top the list in terms of how well he shut down enemy batsmen, holding hitters to an extremely low OPS+ (slugging average plus on-base average adjusted for league and park) of 61 (39 percent below league average).

Sporting News columnist Peter Gammons wrote that the Tigers' biggest worries heading into the 1984 season were third base and relief pitching. As predicted, the hot corner proved problematic for Detroit all summer, but worrying about late-inning relief soon evaporated. In midseason, *Detroit News* scribe Jerry Green, who had covered his first major-league game a quarter-century earlier, in 1959, was surprised when voluble Tigers manager Sparky Anderson—"looking for headlines"—started talking up Hernandez as an MVP candidate. (Relief pitching was then viewed as much less important; try finding the handful of entries for saves records in the 464 pages of lists in the 1995 *Official Baseball Record Book*. Another example is the 1990 book *Baseball's Dream Teams*, which had no relief pitchers picked for the its all-decade teams through the 1980s—nor were any given honorable mention.)

In his over-the-top fashion, Anderson summarized the 1984 season after Detroit had won its world championship. "First, I thanked God. Then I thanked Hernandez." Green called Hernandez's MVP award "a Sparky Anderson production."

Most teams would consider themselves fortunate to have a pitcher who captured the Cy Young and Most Valuable Player awards in the same season. The Detroit Tigers have three: Denny McLain in 1968, Willie Hernandez in 1984, and Justin Verlander in 2011. Of the three, Hernandez is the only reliever to have earned the double honors. (National Baseball Hall of Fame Library, Cooperstown, New York)

In high school Hernandez starred while playing first base and the outfield, but he didn't try pitching until the summer of 1973—a departure from the typical developmental pattern of major-league pitchers, who very often star as both hitters and pitchers in high school. He graduated from Martin Hernandez High School in Aguada in 1973, signing his first professional contract with the Phillies shortly thereafter on September 11.

Despite his youth and lack of experience, Hernandez that summer made the Puerto Rican national team, which won a silver medal in the Intercontinental Cup and both silver and bronze medals in the Baseball World Cup (two separate competitions). Hernandez remembered hurling a shutout in his first outing on the mound, crediting himself as having "a 100-mile-per-hour fastball and an 85-mile-per-hour breaking ball."

The promising amateur was scouted and signed for a $25,000 bonus by Phillies scout Ruben Amaro Sr. in Amaro's first year as a scout. Hernandez spent three full seasons in the minors as a starting pitcher, progressing quickly to Triple A in the middle of his second season. In 1976, however, he posted a 4.53 ERA in Oklahoma City, after which Philadelphia left the 22-year-old off its 40-player winter roster. Wisely, the Cubs snatched the unprotected youngster in the 1976 Rule 5 draft.

With Chicago, Hernandez made his big-league debut in the second game of 1977, on April 9, pitching $2^1/_3$ innings in relief of Steve Renko and surrendering one hit. The rookie went 8-7 with a 3.03 ERA in 110 innings as future Hall of Famer Bruce Sutter completed his first full season as the Cubs' closer. Hernandez's sophomore campaign in 1978 was solid (8-2, 3.77, $59^2/_3$ innings), but he suffered a rocky third year in the bigs (4-4, 5.01, 79 IP) in 1979. Things got worse in 1980 (1-9, 4.40, $108^1/_3$ IP), causing a trip to Triple-A in 1981, with Hernandez both starting and relieving before being recalled in August after the midseason strike. The left-hander rebounded in 1982, going 4-6 with a 3.00 ERA in 75 innings over 75 games.

On May 22, 1983, the Phillies reacquired Hernandez, sending veteran starter Dick Ruthven and pitching prospect Bill Johnson to Chicago.

Hernandez got the win when the Phillies clinched their 1983 National League East pennant on September 28 against the Cubs. *The New Phillies Encyclopedia* said that "the Phillies could never have clinched without him." The budding star didn't see action in the NLCS, but appeared three times for the losing Phillies in the five World Series games, facing 14 hitters and allowing only two to reach, via a walk and hit batsman. In Game Five, the unheralded reliever served notice that he had come of age, pitching three perfect frames (sixth through eighth). However, Philadelphia failed to take advantage of the opportunity to stage a comeback as Baltimore prevailed, 5-0.

In the American League, Detroit's brain trust was watching and planning for 1984. The league in the mid-1980s was full of dangerous left-handed batters; six of 10 of the leading hitters in slugging and OPS in '84 were lefties. The Tigers concluded after their 1983 second-place finish that they couldn't win

DETROIT TIGERS 1984: WHAT A START! WHAT A FINISH!

without adding a top-notch southpaw to their staff. (Closer Aurelio Lopez had completely smothered righty hitters in '83, but lefties posted a .786 OPS against him.) Hernandez filled that need; his ascent to stardom was enhanced by Sparky Anderson's need to shut down enemy lefties.

While the trade that brought Hernandez to Detroit at the end of spring training in 1984 is famous among Tigers fans, it is not really an issue among Phillies partisans—not rating as one of the franchise's worst deals as enumerated in *The New Phillies Encyclopedia* in 1993. Partly that is because the deal didn't go as Philly had planned. John Wockenfuss had a decent year primarily as a backup first baseman and catcher in the City of Brotherly Love in 1984, hitting .289 with an .807 OPS in 86 games. Fading quickly at 36, Wockenfuss was released in mid-August 1985 while hitting a "buck-62" (in the parlance of the day).

Outfielder Glenn Wilson, whose "power potential" was the key for Philadelphia, played four seasons there in the prime of his career (ages 25-28). Wilson flopped badly in 1984, recovering in 1985 to drive in 102 runs and make the All-Star team for the only time. But his RBI production tailed off to 84 in 1986, and sank to 54 in 1987, ending his career at Broad and Pattison Streets in South Philly. Wilson hit only 49 homers in 2,102 at-bats for the Phillies.

Legendary Hall of Famer Christy Mathewson wrote in 1912, "There are two ways of fooling a batter. One is literally to 'mix 'em up,' and the other is to keep feeding him the same sort of a ball, but to induce him to think that something else is coming." In 1984, Willie Hernandez did both to perfection.

Like many pitchers, Hernandez learned key elements of his craft from aging veteran moundsmen. Early on, his repertoire was pretty standard: fastball, curveball, slider, change. Because he didn't throw exceptionally hard, and because his changeup wasn't that good, he had a lot of trouble with right-handed power hitters.

Former Cy Young winner Mike Cuellar taught Hernandez the screwball as an alternative off-speed offering when the two Latino lefties played in the Puerto Rican winter league in 1983. Though the new pitch gave Hernandez another arrow in his quiver, he didn't rely on it until he was with Philadelphia, where Latino catcher Bo Diaz kept calling for it. (While the screwball hadn't yet faded from pitchers' repertoires in the mid-1980s, Latino pitchers threw it much more frequently, so Diaz had experience catching it.)

While Hernandez's famous screwball was crucial to his dominance in 1984, the pitch that elevated him from a good pitcher to an MVP was the cut fastball, with which he pounded right-handed hitters inside. Surprisingly, Hernandez didn't start depending on either pitch until 1983.

Hernandez learned how to throw the cutter—which, unlike the screwball, was becoming much more popular in the 1980s—with Chicago in the spring of 1983 from another Cy Young winner, veteran Ferguson Jenkins, at the end of his Hall of Fame career. By throwing what looked like a standard fastball on the inside part of the plate, Hernandez suckered righty hitters into swinging at something they thought would be right in their wheelhouse. But breaking the cutter in on their hands, Hernandez induced a weak popups or grounders. He was also pushing righties off the plate, setting them up for a down-and-away screwball that they couldn't handle. "All of a sudden, I could pitch inside," said Hernandez when interviewed by *Sports Illustrated* in 1984.

Like many other top relievers with devastating out pitches, Hernandez used his scroogie mostly when ahead of the batter since it would often break out of the strike zone. His fastball was average in velocity, though his delivery had enough deception for his heater to earn the time-honored "sneaky fast" label. Hernandez's No. 3 pitch, a decent curveball, was employed primarily against left-handed hitters.

Hernandez was neither preordained as Detroit's closer nor immediately handed that coveted job after his first few performances with the Tigers. In April 1984, Aurelio Lopez appeared in nine games, saving two and finishing four. In May, he was called upon 11 times, finishing all 11 games while saving five. During those two months, Hernandez appeared in 22 games, finishing 18 and recording the same number of saves as Lopez.

In his first appearance of the year, on April 3, Lopez pitched a scoreless eighth inning before Hernandez followed up with a scoreless ninth. But that was with Detroit holding an 8-1 lead, so it really was just a tune-up for both relievers. In Lopez's second appearance, he pitched four innings of one-run ball against Chicago in relief of starter Dave Rozema, fanning four and picking up the win. Hernandez again followed Lopez, pitching a scoreless ninth in a nonsave situation. Lopez's third outing didn't go so well after he replaced staff ace Jack Morris in the eighth with an 8-2 lead, allowing two runs. Hernandez followed with a scoreless ninth in another nonsave situation.

The next time Lopez didn't finish a game, he entered the fray with Detroit holding a 4-0 lead over Chicago and pitched a scoreless eighth. The Tigers scored five runs in the bottom of the frame before, with a 9-0 lead, Anderson asked Hernandez to finish. On April 27, Lopez pitched 4²/₃ scoreless innings, entering with one out in the 10th to bail Hernandez out of a jam. Detroit finally fell to Cleveland in the 19th.

May was similar. At the beginning of June, here's how the "competition" between Detroit's dynamic duo stood. Try to tell them apart without a scorecard:

Category	Pitcher 1	Pitcher 2
Games	22	20
Games Finished	18	15
Wins	2	4
Losses	0	0
Saves	7	7
Innings	41	41²/₃
Strikeouts	34	31
ERA	2.63	1.73
Opponents' BA	.221	.177
Opponents' OPS	.571	.552

DETROIT TIGERS 1984: WHAT A START! WHAT A FINISH!

Pitcher No. 1: with the slightly inferior statistics overall, is Hernandez. Pitcher No. 2 (Lopez) had one blown save (Hernandez had none), but Lopez had two more wins, a lower ERA, and lower opponents' batting stats. Over the whole of 1984, 71.5 percent of Lopez's saves qualified as either "tough" or "long"; for Hernandez, it was 62.5 percent.

Hernandez didn't take the team lead in saves for good until June 8. Detroit's meteoric 35-5 start meant the Tigers were bludgeoning their hapless opposition with such regularity that save opportunities were hard to come by. Yet the fact remains that Lopez was Detroit's closer until mid-May and then became co-closer until a week into June. Only then did the veteran Mexican fireballer become the setup pitcher for the Puerto Rican sniper who would win the Cy Young and MVP. In April 2009, Hernandez acknowledged what most fans and writers had forgotten, telling Steve Kornacki of Booth Newspapers, "I shared closing with Aurelio Lopez, who was a great closer, too. But…I was real consistent and Sparky named me the stopper.… Nobody wanted to face me."

Though superseded by Hernandez, Lopez became friends with his successor. Lopez summed it up well when he said late in the 1984 season, "Everyone in baseball is fallible. The trouble is, Willie has been infallible. That's scary."

Even though the Tigers couldn't be blamed for Hernandez's treatment in the National League—where he bridled at being stuck principally behind Sutter and Lee Smith in Chicago and Al Holland in Philly—Hernandez's pride and ambition were already simmering before the '84 season finished. "If Detroit can't give me the money I want, they might as well trade me to a team that will. Heck, if I'm the M.V.P., I may be able to ask for the world," he told *Sports Illustrated* writer Jaime Diaz. "I'm hungry to make some money." Detroit gave Hernandez a generous contract extension after hard negotiations, though the pitcher's public comments probably contributed to the future fan backlash.

The problem with Hernandez's post-1984 career—trite as it seems—was that it was no longer 1984. The reigning MVP had an excellent year in 1985, but to many fans it seemed pallid by comparison to 1984. Anyone who ever bit their fingernails to the nubs with Todd Jones on the mound in the ninth inning for the Tigers in the 2000s would wish Hernandez could time-travel. But without the benefit of hindsight, 8-10 with 31 saves in 40 chances ain't 9-3 and 32 out of 33, and Hernandez's stock in Motown began to fall. The failure of Detroit to repeat in '85 was largely blamed on its bullpen, with Hernandez and Lopez the key targets.

In 1986 Hernandez went 8-7 with 24 saves in 30 chances; tellingly, however, he was nicked for almost a hit per inning, with enemy hitters batting .251 off him as opposed to .201 in 1984-85. Making things worse was the lusty booing the erstwhile hero was getting at Tiger Stadium. By the start of 1987 Anderson was talking about a "bullpen by committee."

Hernandez lost his monopoly on the closer's job in 1987 due to two stints on the DL in April and May. Anderson auditioned younger hurlers Mike Henneman and Eric King in the role. Hernandez blew five saves in 13 chances that year, allowing more hits than innings pitched for the first time since 1981. After the aging Detroit club squeaked past Toronto to win the AL East, Anderson called on the veteran lefty only once in the five-game American League Championship Series. In Game One, Hernandez entered in the eighth with the bases loaded and the game tied. The formerly invincible fireman was treated rudely by the Twins, allowing two hits and three inherited runners to score while retiring no one—getting credit for one-third of an inning pitched only because a fourth runner was thrown out at the plate. Though Sparky rang the bullpen six times in the last three games as Detroit was upset by Minnesota, he never called for Hernandez.

Perhaps smarting over his reduced role, and definitely reminiscent of the Bobby/Roberto Clemente episode a couple of decades earlier, the proud Hernandez demanded early in 1988 to be addressed henceforth as Guillermo, his birth name, rather than its Anglicized diminutive Willie. Though completely innocuous, even that reasonable request generated controversy. Adding to the unhappiness with Hernandez was his dumping a bucket of ice water on popular *Free Press* columnist Mitch Albom in spring training that year. After the incident, Hernandez stopped talking to the media until midseason. Initially a big deal, the dousing became the subject of humorous TV commercials run by the newspaper and later made its list of fun facts for its 178th birthday in 2009.

In a way, the end in Detroit for Hernandez was fitting, given that his arrival coincided with what was expected to be a dynasty. The former MVP rebounded somewhat, allowing only 50 hits in 67$^{2}/_{3}$ innings while blowing five saves in 15 opportunities in 1988. But the hero of 1984 also threw the last pitch in a game that effectively crushed the Tigers' hopes for one last hurrah before the aging club completely fell apart. Though Detroit ultimately finished only one game back of Boston in the AL East, the closeness was really due to the Red Sox' 4-9 tailspin in the final two weeks, plus the Tigers winning their last three games after being eliminated while Boston dropped its last three.

At 7:38 p.m. on September 11, 1988, the Yankees' Claudell Washington clouted a homer to right-center off Hernandez in the bottom of the 18th inning to give New York a 5-4 win in a six-hour contest that broke the Bengals' backs. Hernandez had already pitched two full innings in relief of closer Mike Henneman, who had hurled seven innings after relieving starter Doyle Alexander.

Detroit had taken the lead with a run in the top of the 18th. After walking Rickey Henderson to begin the final frame, Hernandez was victimized by Washington, who said, "I knew it was gone when I hit it." The heartbreaking loss was the 10th in 11 games and dropped Detroit into a second-place tie, 3½ games behind eventual division winner Boston. "It could break (the Tigers') backs, said Henderson about New York's four-game sweep of Detroit. After 1988 the Mayo Smith Society wrote, "Tiger fans have a love/hate relationship with Hernandez, who probably receives more abuse from the boo-birds than any other player on the team."

DETROIT TIGERS 1984: WHAT A START! WHAT A FINISH!

The final unhappy season played out as Detroit collapsed to 103 losses in 1989, punctuated by Hernandez's making two trips to the disabled list with left elbow tendinitis, although he managed to log 15 saves in 17 opportunities in only 32 appearances. Hernandez pitched his last game in the majors on August 18, coughing up a two-run homer to the Yankees at Tiger Stadium while in a nonsave situation. The proud warrior was absent from combat for the rest of the year.

After being released by the Tigers on December 22, 1989, Hernandez made several attempts to stage a comeback. The first was with Oakland in the spring of 1990; it lasted all of two days before Hernandez voluntarily left camp because of a sore arm. Athletics manager Tony La Russa complimented Hernandez, saying, "That took guts. He walked away from guaranteed money."

The second attempt came with Philadelphia, which invited the former Phillies hurler to the club's spring camp in 1991 as a nonroster player. After failing to make the cut with Philadelphia, Hernandez appeared in eight games with Triple-A Syracuse in the Blue Jays' organization. Four years later, a 40-year-old Hernandez tried out for Yankees' replacement team in the bitter spring of 1995. Saying "I'll do whatever I can to make my comeback," the veteran with the serious hardware on his trophy shelf at home took the practice field with a bunch of fringe ex-major leaguers and a gaggle of nobodies.

New York manager Buck Showalter expressed the prevailing attitude that spring, saying, "We wanted to know why" when he heard that Hernandez was interested in trying out. The retired pitcher had been seduced by Luis Arroyo, a Yankees scout, former star relief pitcher, and fellow Puerto Rican, who had contacted Hernandez about making a comeback. Showing again his defiant streak, Hernandez said when he reported, "Nobody is going to take my chance away. If I want to play baseball again, nobody is going to stop me." Hernandez even went to Triple-A Columbus in the Yankees' system after the strike was settled. But the magic of 1984 was nothing but a memory, as International League hitters pounded the former Cy Young Award winner in his 22 games in relief before Hernandez hung up his spikes for the final time.

After giving up the game he loved, Hernandez involved himself in several business ventures as well as coaching youth and semipro baseball. He also participated in the Tigers' 2009 fantasy camp in Lakeland, Florida. He raised cattle on a ranch in Santo Domingo, Dominican Republic. But the ex-pitcher suffered from various ailments, including asthma, diabetes, and several strokes. He underwent heart surgery in 2009.

In September 2009, the Westport Country Playhouse in the tony Connecticut suburbs of New York City staged a revival of Miller's play. Later that month, Guillermo Hernandez signed autographs and posed for photos with hundreds of fans on the concourse at Comerica Park in Detroit when the Tigers celebrated the 25th anniversary of their 1984 championship season. According to Guillermo Jr., his father had been "driving me crazy" because "[h]e was so excited to come back to Detroit again and see everyone."

Many aging ex-ballplayers make a point of not going to or watching ballgames to express their bitterness or disappointment in the way they were treated or in the way the game has changed. Not Hernandez, who followed the Tigers closely and returned stateside periodically, mostly to appear at Tigers, Phillies, or Cubs events.

"Even when they have a bad ballclub, I follow them, because they gave me good memories," Hernandez said in 2009. "I played for three different teams, but I want to be known as a Tiger, and I will always be a Tiger."

Unlike Jason Miller's five fictional angry men, there was not a trace of anger or angst in Hernandez when he reflected upon his championship season—nor should there be.

Guillermo Hernandez y Villanueva was born on November 14, 1954, in Aguada, Puerto Rico. Aguada, a small city on the northwest coast of the island about 90 miles west of San Juan, is one of the earliest settlements in Puerto Rico, dating its founding to 1508-10. It is sometimes called La Ciudad Del Descrubrimiento (City of Discovery), referring to the widely held belief that Christopher Columbus landed at Aguada in 1493 when he "discovered" Puerto Rico. During the Colonial Era, the busy port of Aguada was a stopover for ships of the Spanish Empire sailing between Spain and South America.

The son of Dionicio, who worked in a large local sugar cane centrale (factory), and Dominga, a domestic, Hernandez was the second youngest child in a large, poor family with eight siblings. (Sugar cane was the primary cash crop of Puerto Rico in the first half of the 20th century before the island commonwealth began to convert its economy from agriculture to manufacturing.) His parents encouraged their children to be active in athletics—and they were rewarded when their son reached the pinnacle of success in the majors.

Hernandez married the former Carmen Rivera in 1978. They had two children together, but later divorced. Guillermo Hernandez had five children and one grandson.

References

Publications

Anderson, Sparky, with Dan Ewald. *Bless You Boys: Diary of the Detroit Tigers' 1984 Season*. Chicago: Contemporary Books, Inc. 1984.

Balzer, Howard M. *Official 1979 Baseball Register*. St. Louis: The Sporting News Publishing Company. 1979.

Campbell, Dave, Denny Matthews, Brooks Robinson, and Duke Snider. *The Scouting Report: 1984*. New York: Harper & Row Publishers. 1984.

Campbell, Dave, Harmon Killebrew, Brooks Robinson, and Duke Snider. *The Scouting Report: 1985*. New York: Harper & Row Publishers. 1985.

DETROIT TIGERS 1984: WHAT A START! WHAT A FINISH!

Campbell, Dave, Harmon Killebrew, Brooks Robinson, and Duke Snider. *The Scouting Report: 1986*. New York: Harper & Row Publishers. 1986.

Carter, Craig. *Official Baseball Record Book, 1985 Edition*. St. Louis: The Sporting News Publishing Company. 1985.

Cantor, George. *Wire to Wire: Inside the 1984 Detroit Tigers Championship Season*. Chicago: Triumph Books. 2004.

Coleman, Jerry, Ernie Harwell, Ralph Kiner, Tim McCarver, Ned Martin, and Brooks Robinson. *The Scouting Report: 1983*. New York: Harper & Row Publishers. 1983.

Cox, Paul. *Tiger Tracks 1989: An In-Depth Review of the 1988 Detroit Tigers*. London, Ontario: Mayo Smith Society. 1989.

Detroit Tigers Press/TV/Radio Guide, 1985 edition. Detroit: Detroit Tigers. 1985.

Detroit Tigers Press/TV/Radio Guide, 1986 edition. Detroit: Detroit Tigers. 1986.

Detroit Tigers Press/TV/Radio Guide, 1987 edition. Detroit: Detroit Tigers. 1987.

Detroit Tigers Press/TV/Radio Guide, 1988 edition. Detroit: Detroit Tigers. 1988.

Detroit Tigers Press Guide, 1989 edition. Detroit: Detroit Tigers. 1989.

Dickson, Paul. *The Dickson Baseball Dictionary, third edition*. New York: W.W. Norton & Company. 2009.

Dierker, Larry, Jim Kaat, Harmon Killebrew, and Jim Rooker. *The Scouting Report: 1987*. New York: Perennial Library. 1987.

Dickson, Paul. *Baseball's Greatest Quotations: An Illustrated Treasury of Baseball Quotations and Historical Lore, revised edition*. New York: Collins. 2008.

Enders, Eric. *The Fall Classic: The Definitive History of the World Series*. New York: Sterling Publishing. 2007.

Gillette, Gary, and Pete Palmer. *The ESPN Baseball Encyclopedia, fifth edition*. New York: Sterling Publishing Co., Inc. 2008.

Hoppel, Joe. *Official Baseball Guide, 1984 Edition*. St. Louis: The Sporting News Publishing Company. 1984.

James, Bill, John Dewan, and Project Scoresheet. *Bill James Presents The Great American Baseball Stat Book, first edition*. New York: Ballantine Books. 1987.

James, Bill, and Rob Neyer. *The Neyer/James Guide to Pitchers*. New York: Fireside Books. 2004.

James, Bill, Don Zminda, and Project Scoresheet. *Bill James Presents The Great American Baseball Stat Book, 1988 Edition*. New York: Villard Books. 1988.

Johnson, Lloyd. *Baseball's Dream Teams*. New York: Crescent Books. 1990.

Marcin, Joe, Larry Wigge, Carl Clark, and Larry Vickrey. *Official Baseball Guide for 1978*. St. Louis: The Sporting News Publishing Company. 1978.

Mathewson, Christopher. *Pitching In a Pinch*. Mattituck, New York: Amereon House (reprint of 1912 Knickerbocker Press edition).

Pietrusza, David, Matthew Silverman, and Michael Gershman. *Baseball: The Biographical Encyclopedia*. Kingston, New York: Total/Sports Illustrated. 2000.

Porter, David L. *The Biographical Dictionary of American Sports: G-P*. Westport, Conn.: Greenwood Press. 2000.

Quigley, Martin. *The Crooked Pitch*. Chapel Hill, N.C.: Algonquin Books. 1984.

Reichler, Joseph L. *The Baseball Encyclopedia, sixth edition*. New York: Macmillan Publishing Company. 1985.

Seaver, Tom, with Rick Hummel and Bob Nightengale. *Tom Seaver's Scouting Notebook 1989*. St. Louis: The Sporting News Publishing Company. 1989.

Siegel, Barry. *Official Baseball Register, 1982 Edition*. St. Louis: The Sporting News Publishing Company. 1984.

Siegel, Barry. *Official Baseball Register, 1984 Edition*. St. Louis: The Sporting News Publishing Company. 1984.

Siegel, Barry. *Official Baseball Register, 1985 Edition*. St. Louis: The Sporting News Publishing Company. 1985.

Siegel, Barry. *Official Baseball Register, 1989 Edition*. St. Louis: The Sporting News Publishing Company. 1989.

Siwoff, Seymour, Steve Hirdt, and Peter Hirdt. *The 1985 Elias Baseball Analyst*. New York: Collier Books. 1985.

Siwoff, Seymour, Steve Hirdt, and Peter Hirdt. *The 1986 Elias Baseball Analyst*. New York: Collier Books. 1986.

Sloan, Dave. *Official Baseball Guide, 1985 Edition*. St. Louis: The Sporting News Publishing Company. 1985.

DETROIT TIGERS 1984: WHAT A START! WHAT A FINISH!

Spatz, Lyle. *The SABR Baseball List & Record Book*. New York: Scribner. 2007.

Sumner, Benjamin Barrett. *Minor League Baseball Standings*. Jefferson, N.C.: McFarland & Company, Inc. 2000.

Wescott, Rich, and Frank Bilovsky. *The New Phillies Encyclopedia*. Philadelphia: Temple University Press. 1993.

Articles

"AL Insider," *USA Today*, July 18, 1988.

"Around the Majors/Senior Arms," *Washington Post*, March 26, 1990.

Barnas, Jo-Ann, "Year of the Tiger relived," *Detroit Free Press*, September 29, 2009.

"Beloved Tigers closer 'Willie' Hernandez will return from Puerto Rico for Whitecaps event," *Grand Rapids Press*, August 27, 2009.

Bernreuter, Hugh. "Detroit Tigers 1984 hero Willie Hernandez brings memories to Dow Diamond Saturday," mlive.com, August 28, 2009.

Brussat, Frederic, and Mary Ann Brussat. "Film Review/That Championship Season," SpiritualityandPractice.com (undated).

Curry, Jack. "Yanks Sign Ex-M.V.P. but He's 40," *New York Times*, March 6, 1995.

Diaz, Jaime. "He's Giving Batters the Willies," *Sports Illustrated*, September 19, 1984.

Felber, Bill, and Gary Gillette. "The Changing Game" in *John Thorn and Pete Palmer's Total Baseball, seventh edition*. Kingston, New York: Total Sports Publishing. 2001.

Gage, Tom. "Hernandez Tigers New Bullpen Ace," *The Sporting News*, April 2, 1984, 23-24.

Gage, Tom. "Ex-Tiger Hernandez Joins Yankees as Replacement Player," *Detroit News*, March 7, 1995.

Gammons, Peter. "Hernandez Deal May Put Tigers on Top," *The Sporting News*, April 9, 1984. 14.

Gavrilovich, Peter. "178 fun facts for the Detroit Free Press' 178th birthday," *Detroit Free Press*, May 5, 2009.

Gillette, Gary. "Requiem for the Tigers," in *The 1989 Baseball Abstract*, Kirkwood, Mo.: Mad Aztec Press. April 1989. 149-151.

Henning, Lynn. "Tigers' 35-5 start in 1984 still has power to amaze," *Detroit News* online edition. May 21, 2009.

"Hernandez leaves Phils in 3-way deal," *Chicago Tribune*, March 25, 1984.

Joy, Emilia Badillo. "The Sugar Industry of Puerto Rico," PReb.com.

Julich, Raquel. "Un Poquito De Beisbol Con Sabor Bilingue/Major League Baseball: 100-plus years of Legends," LaPrensaToledo.com, 2005.

Kornacki, Steve. "Unknown by new Tigers teammates, Guillermo Hernandez lifted Detroit to 1984 world championship," mlive.com, April 5, 2009.

Kornacki, Steve. "Brotherhood of 1984 World Series champion Tigers lives on," mlive.com, September 28, 2009.

McClary, Mike. "The 1984 Hernandez/Bergman Trade Revisited," DailyFungo.com, March 28, 2008.

Meixell, Ted. "Glenn Wilson Comes Back With Desire To Be Best/Phillies: At Spring Training," *Allentown Morning Call*. April 1, 1985.

Rothstein, Mervyn. "Joseph Papp, Theater's Champion, Dies," *New York Times*, November 1, 1991.

Sexton, Joe. "Yanks Defeat Tigers in 18th," *New York Times*, September 12, 1988.

"Sports People/Phils Invite Hernandez," *New York Times*, February 22, 1991.

Stertz, Bradley A. "It's Probably Not Too Smart for Us to Publicize This Kind of Revenge," *Wall Street Journal*, March 14, 1988.

Welch, Chuck. "'84 Tigers Celebrate Series Anniversary at Fantasy Camp Game," LakelandLocal.com, January 29, 2009.

Web Sites

http://Detroit.Tigers.MLB.com

http://SABRpedia.org (Society for American Baseball Research's online encyclopedia)

http://welcome.topuertorico.org/city/aguada.shtml

http://welcome.topuertorico.org/economy.shtml

www.BaseballIndex.org

www.Baseball-Reference.com

www.ibdb.com (Internet Broadway Database)

www.imdb.com (Internet Movie Database)

www.MapQuest.com

www.WestportPlayhouse.org

Interviews & Communications

Carlton, Russell (coordinator, baseball media relations, Detroit Tigers). E-mail messages to author.

Craig, Roger. Telephone interview by author.

Green, Jerry. Telephone interview by author.

Kornacki, Steve. Telephone interview by author.

Nelson, Rod. E-mail messages to author.

Palmer, Pete. E-mail messages to author.

Shea, Stuart. E-mail messages to author.

Unpublished Sources

Society for American Baseball Research Who-Signed-Who Database.

24-7 Baseball Modern Player Register, 1975-2009.

24-7 Baseball Relief Pitcher Reports, 1984-89.

24-7 Baseball Salary Database, 1982-2008.

24-7 Baseball/ESPN Baseball Encyclopedia Disabled List-Injury Register.

Larry Herndon
by Glen Vasey

ON OCTOBER 2, 1984, in Kansas City, in Game One of the American League Championship Series, Larry Herndon led off the fourth inning with a home run off Bud Black to put the Tigers up 3-0 in a game they eventually won, 8-1.

After the game, a group of writers waited in the clubhouse to interview him. They had already spoken to Alan Trammell and Lance Parrish, who had also homered. They'd spoken with winning pitcher Jack Morris, and with Willie Hernandez, who closed out the game with two scoreless innings.

Rich Shook, who had covered Michigan sports for UPI since 1966, recounted the scene:

"All I remember is waiting, waiting for him to come back to the clubhouse so we could interview him.... [Eventually] Dan Ewald (Detroit's PR man) let me back to the shower where Herndon was staying under the showerhead as long as he could, probably in hopes that the media would get tired of waiting and go away.

"I told him people were waiting, but he said, 'Rich, you know me, I just don't want to talk. Tell them I'm sorry.' I told him I didn't care whether he talked to us or not, but that he needed to know people were waiting. He told me he didn't want to say anything. I said, 'Fine, see you tomorrow.'

"He had somebody bring him his clothes and went out the back way. I relayed the message to everybody else.

"That's the kind of person he was. He had no need of the spotlight; all he wanted to do was play."

Larry Herndon was born on November 3, 1953, in Sunflower, Mississippi. He spent most of his youth and teenage years in Memphis, Tennessee, where he graduated from Douglass High School at the age of 17.

"I'm a lucky man.... I had great sisters and brothers and was raised by my grandmother, Estella," Herndon told MLB.com's Rich Draper in February 2005. "You know how grandmas are. She taught me how to live the right way and the Golden Rule. ... I grew up in the South, but I never had racial problems. [Herndon is an African-American.] You can always find something if you dig deep enough. But if you don't argue with somebody, there's no argument.

"I'd get things thrown at me, but ignored the negativity. I didn't have the problems Jackie [Robinson] and the others had....

"I had great admiration for the brothers who came before me. I've tried to carry myself well to honor them, for they made it easy for me."

Rich Shook had a slightly different take: "He never talked about it and I never asked, but it had to be hard growing up in Mississippi when he did."

Owing largely no doubt to his shyness and avoidance of the spotlight, very little information is available to the public regarding Herndon's "great" sisters and brothers, the circumstances that led to his being raised by his grandmother, or even at what age he moved to the Douglass neighborhood in Memphis. But it is obvious that his early life could not have been easy.

Douglass was a community formed in the 19th century when William Rush-Plummer, the son of a white slaveholder

DETROIT TIGERS 1984: WHAT A START! WHAT A FINISH!

and a slave from Africa, was granted 40 acres by his father when his family was released from slavery. The neighborhood borders the towns of Hyde Park and Hollywood and is surrounded on three sides by railroad tracks. Rush-Plummer, who went on to become an ordained minister, named the neighborhood after his hero, the abolitionist Frederick Douglass.

Douglass High School, which Herndon attended, and where he won several letters for athletic achievement, was opened in 1946. It was closed in 1981 when attendance plummeted because of crosstown busing aimed at desegregating the Memphis schools. Many blacks from the Douglass neighborhood elected to attend other schools, but few white students reciprocated. It later reopened.

During his years at Douglass, Herndon played baseball well enough to catch the eye of St. Louis Cardinals scout Buddy Lewis, who caught briefly for the Cardinals and the Boston Braves. Lewis, a longtime resident of Memphis, liked what he saw well enough to persuade the Cardinals to draft Herndon in the third round of the June 1971 draft (54th overall) even though he was only 17 years old.

Herndon signed with St. Louis, which immediately assigned him to their Gulf Coast League Rookie team, where he batted .239 in 40 games in 1971.

In 1972 he played for three teams, topping out with the Cedar Rapids team in the Class A Midwest League, accruing only 162 at-bats with all three teams and batting just .241.

In neither season had he shown any power.

In 1973 Herndon finally got some serious playing time, logging 485 at-bats, batting .287 and hitting his first three professional home runs for the Cardinals' St. Petersburg team in the Florida State League, another Class A outfit. At the age of 19, he had finally hit his stride.

The following year Herndon played for Arkansas in the Double-A Texas League, batting .285 with 16 doubles, 10 triples, and two homers, finally beginning to show some power. This display earned him his first call-up to the major leagues.

At the age of 20 Herndon was a September call-up for the Cardinals, making his major-league debut on September 4. Through the end of the season he compiled a curious-looking line—12-G 1-AB 1-H 1.000-BA 0-RBI 3-R—indicating that he was used primarily as a pinch-runner and a defensive replacement in center field.

In so doing Herndon had embarked on a major-league career that wouldn't be over for another 14 years, though he was not quite done with the minor leagues yet.

He started the 1975 season with Tulsa, St Louis' Triple-A affiliate. Three-quarters of the way through the season, the Cardinals traded him, along with minor-league left-handed pitcher Luis "Tony" Gonzalez, to the San Francisco Giants for starter Ron Bryant. Finishing the season with the Giants' Phoenix team in the Pacific Coast League, Herndon compiled a season total of .264 with 11 doubles, four triples, three home runs, and an eye-popping 29 stolen bases.

In 1976 Herndon played the last 14 games of his minor-league career with Phoenix. He batted only .246 in 57 at-bats, but his speed and defense were quite attractive to a team that had recently traded center fielder Garry Maddox to the Philadelphia Phillies.

After his call-up by the Giants, Herndon appeared in 115 games, most of them in center field. He batted .288 with a .356 slugging percentage and scored 42 runs while stealing 12 bases. It was a performance sufficient to net him *The Sporting News*' Rookie of the Year Award, and to get him named to an outfield position on the annual Topps All Star Rookie team. He was 22 years old.

In 1977 Herndon was hampered by injuries, limiting him to 49 games and a .239 batting average, but he was able to bounce back strongly in 1978, batting .259 in 151 games and helping San Francisco to an 89-73 record under manager Joe Altobelli. This was also the year in which he married his wife, Faye.

It's safe to say 1979 and 1980 were nearly identical seasons for Herndon, as he batted .257 and .258, respectively, with .384 and .385 slugging percentages. One year 132 games, the next 139. In both years he played 122 games in the outfield. Such consistency would have been marvelous had the numbers been just a bit better or had the team been steadily improving during his tenure, but the numbers were not great, and the Giants were floundering, winning only 71 and 75 games those two years. To add insult to injury, Herndon suffered through an unusually embarrassing inning on September 6, 1980: he made three errors in one inning, on three separate plays. Such an event is slightly rarer than an unassisted triple play, but it's not something ballplayers brag about.

By now Herndon was 26 years old and nine years into his pro career. But rather than stall out professionally, he batted .288 in 1981 and lifted his slugging average to .415, both personal highs. He played in 96 of the Giants' 111 games during that strike-shortened season. En route Herndon impressed people enough to win the second annual Willie Mac Award, named for Giants great Willie McCovey, for spirit and leadership.

The inaugural award had gone to Jack Clark in 1980. It is unusual for such awards, even those claiming to reward intangibles, to be delivered to quiet men who do not hit for power. Perhaps the voters saw what was to come.

Unfortunately for the Giants, the front office didn't. They traded Herndon to Detroit for pitchers Mike Chris and Dan Schatzeder on December 9, 1981.

In Detroit Herndon was joining an organization that hadn't made it to the postseason since 1972. Sparky Anderson had taken over as manager during the 1979 season, and the team had played reasonably well for him, but he had been unable to bring them home any higher than fourth place in the tough American League East. While 1982 proved no different in that regard, it was a breakthrough year for Herndon.

During one two-week stretch in May, he batted .440. On May 17 he hit a home run in his final at-bat of the game. The next day, he hit home runs in each of his first three trips to the plate. On May 20 he recorded a five-hit

DETROIT TIGERS 1984: WHAT A START! WHAT A FINISH!

game, with two triples. Not surprisingly, on May 23 he was named the American League Player of the Week. Larry Herndon had arrived, finally living up to the expectations that had been put upon him.

He closed out the season with a .292 average, 23 home runs, 88 RBIs, 92 runs scored, and a .480 slugging average, all personal highs.

In 1983 Herndon came very close to duplicating those numbers, batting .302 with 20 home runs while flip-flopping his run and RBI totals. His slugging average that year was .478, and he even managed to rap out another five-hit game, on July 11, slugging two doubles and a home run, driving in three runs and scoring four.

The big change that year, however, was visible in the team's record. They had won 92 games to finish only six games behind the world champion Baltimore Orioles. Sparky Anderson had finally put together the pieces he felt he needed to take the Tigers to the next level—the promised land of the postseason—and one of those important pieces was his left fielder, Larry Herndon, who had clearly come into his own under Sparky's leadership.

In some ways 1984 must have been difficult for Herndon. At 30 he was one of the veterans on an otherwise young team. Only Dave Bergman (31), Milt Wilcox (34), and Darrell Evans (37) were older. Herndon was entering his 14th season as a professional ballplayer, and both his personal and his team's expectations were higher than they had ever been.

The Tigers got off to a great start, taking their first nine games and 35 of their first 40, but Herndon struggled.

For the season he managed to get into only 125 games, losing playing time principally to Ruppert Jones and Johnny Grubb, although Barbaro Garbey, Dave Bergman, and Rod Allen got into games in left. Herndon managed an end-of-the-season surge to push his batting average to .280, but the surge had little punch to it. His slugging average for the season dipped to .400. He hit only seven home runs, and his RBI total dropped to 43.

When the playoffs arrived, Herndon found himself in the lineup in Kansas City for Game One. Leading off the fourth inning with his team up 2-0, he hit the home run that he did not want to talk about after the game. His team took the next two games, 5-3 and 1-0, but he didn't start in either game.

The World Series started in San Diego on October 9, and Herndon was back in the lineup. In the fifth inning he came up with a runner on and his team down by a score of 2-1. He homered, giving Jack Morris and his teammates a lead they did not relinquish. One has to wonder, since the Padres won Game Two, whether the Tigers would have prevailed had the Series gone back to Detroit with them down by two games.

Herndon batted .333 for the Series in 15 at-bats, picking up another RBI along the way. He even made the highlight reel by catching Tony Gwynn's fly ball to left field for the final out of the Series in Game Five.

But Herndon's career began winding down. His batting averages for 1985 and '86 dipped to .244 and .247, respectively, and his slugging averages dropped to .384 and .385—the same numbers he had recorded playing for San Francisco in 1979 and '80. His playing time diminished, largely due to his balky knees, and at the end of the 1986 season the Tigers released him, though they re-signed him as a free agent less than a month later.

On Opening Day of 1987 Herndon hit a home run off Dennis Rasmussen of the New York Yankees that many fans talked and wrote about for years afterward.

John Rudak, a fan who was at Tiger Stadium that day, remembered it this way: "I was sitting in the upper-deck bleachers.... As the ball was soaring I was able to say, 'That ball is still coming,' as it crashed into the facing of the center field bleachers.... The next day the *Detroit Free Press* had an overhead pictorial of the blast, with a huge arrow, showing the path of the ball."

UPI's Rich Shook remembered it as "one of the very few to reach the dead center field upper deck in Tiger Stadium.... In its own way it was as impressive as any of the over-the-roof shots."

Rob Neyer of ESPN.com selected the blast from readers' submissions as one of the Top Ten Legendary Stories from SportsNation on a site promoting his *Big Book of Baseball Legends*. There, one fan described it as the hardest-hit ball he had ever witnessed, saying that it hit the façade of the upper deck in straightaway center field 440 feet away.

"If the ball was on its way down when it hit the wall," the fan wrote, "it was just barely past its apex. It was a line drive that seemed to have just leveled off when it hit the front of the section. ... I swear that ball would have gone close to 600 feet."

In response to that posting, another fan reminisced about being "about 20 rows back from the 440 sign" that day. "The weather was bitter, in the high 30s, so the ball shouldn't have carried. I remember seeing Larry smoke the longest, hardest line shot I have ever seen in 40 years of watching baseball.... I have no doubt that it was one of the longest homers EVER hit that did not exceed approximately 100 feet in height off the ground."

It was the first of nine home runs Herndon hit that year as he boosted his batting average to .324 and slugged .520 while playing 53 games in the outfield and appearing in 23 games as the team's designated hitter.

Herndon's final home run of the year, however, proved to be among the biggest hits he would ever get.

In the final week of the 1987 season the Toronto Blue Jays began frittering away what had been a seemingly safe lead in the American League East Division by losing four straight, leaving them one game ahead of the Tigers as they came to Detroit for the final three games of the season.

The Tigers managed to take the division lead by winning the first two games of the weekend—each by a single run—meaning that Toronto had to win on the final day to force a tie and a playoff. Frank Tanana took the ball for the Tigers and Jimmy Key pitched for the Jays, and both pitchers were in rare form. The only run scored all day came on Herndon's solo shot in the second inning, a homer that drifted a few rows into the lower-deck seats in left field, giving Sparky Anderson what turned out to be his last division championship.

In the 1987 postseason, Herndon collected three hits in nine at-bats, driving in two runs and scoring one, in the Tigers' five-game loss to the Minnesota Twins in the American League Championship Series.

The 1988 season was Herndon's last as a player. Having been released again only to be re-signed once more by the Tigers during the offseason, he saw his performance plummet. His batting average fell 100 points, to .224, while his slugging average dipped nearly 200 points.

After 14 years in the majors, still one month shy of his 35th birthday, Herndon's playing days were over. His career stats include a .274 batting average, a .409 slugging percentage, 107 home runs, 605 runs, and 550 RBIs.

In 1992 Sparky Anderson and the Tigers invited Herndon back as their hitting coach. This surprised Paul Carey, the Tigers longtime radio broadcaster. "I was surprised because Larry rarely spoke his mind aloud. Shyness was his hallmark," Carey said.

But Herndon made an impression on his young charges. Spencer Fordin, in an article he wrote for mlb.com in 2004, quoted one such youngster, Tony Clark:

"Larry Herndon, my first hitting coach in the big leagues, told me, 'Every day, you play like a champion. If things aren't working out where you are, the champions will come get you.'" At the time of the interview Clark was a member of the New York Yankees and was playing in the ALCS.

"Having an opportunity to be a part of this is confirmation that the guys I came up with taught me how to go about my business the right way," Clark said. "I've been rewarded with an opportunity to be part of something special."

When Herndon came back to the Tigers in 1992, some of his old teammates were still with the team, notably Alan Trammell and Lou Whitaker, but the team struggled to disappointing finishes year after year. In 1998 the Tigers fired Herndon. "I always felt he was a scapegoat," Carey remembered.

For a while Herndon owned a coin-operated laundry, but in 2005 the Tigers came calling again, offering him the position as hitting instructor for the Lakeland Flying Tigers, their affiliate in the Florida State League (Class A Advanced). He accepted the position and as of 2010 was still with the team, offering his special brand of advice to a new generation of Tigers prospects.

The announcement of Herndon's appointment was covered by Rich Draper for MLB.com. Draper got Herndon to acknowledge that "it's a great honor to be invited back." Of course, first he talked about his daughter Myia, who was graduating from Thomas Cooley Law School in Lansing, Michigan. "I'm very proud of her. It's a big, BIG day," he said. And he talked about his other three children: Larry Jr., Latasha, and Kamelah. He talked about his "four grandbabies," his wife, Faye, and his grandmother Estella who had raised him. Other than his references to his debt of gratitude to the black players who had preceded him, all of the baseball talk in the article relies on Draper himself telling us who Larry Herndon was, and what he did.

Larry Herndon wouldn't tell you about himself. That job was left to others.

In 2008 Andy Barkett was named manager of the Lakeland Flying Tigers. Andy was delighted with the hitting coach he inherited.

"Being a hitting coach is not easy," Barkett said. "Knowing how to hit is uncommon, being able to communicate that knowledge to young men is rare, getting young men to apply that knowledge is a gift."

He said that Herndon had mastered all three qualities. "Hondo's success is due to his patience, his love of the players, his work ethic, his knowledge of the game, and his knowledge of people." (Herndon got the nickname Hondo from his high-school days in Memphis, where teammates thought he played basketball like Boston Celtics great John Havlicek, who was also nicknamed Hondo.)

On July 9, 2009, Barkett blogged about a recently concluded game:

"On the way back from Dunedin tonight. We won 4-3 …situational hitting was the difference. The intensity was outstanding tonight. There seemed to be a sense of urgency to win the game. One would assume that that would be a given in professional baseball, but it's not, unfortunately. Our hitting coach, Larry Herndon, taught me a valuable lesson that I want to share. He told me that throughout his career, when he stepped on the field for either practice or a game, he treated every day like he was preparing to play the seventh game of the World Series. Playoff baseball is wonderful.… Why not approach it like that every day you play? Why not prepare to play and approach the game like it is the biggest game of your life?"

Larry Herndon took that approach, and the results speak for themselves.

"There has always been a quietness and sensitivity about Larry Herndon, a black athlete never conflicted about who or what he was, and a man who nurtured a deep love of family, friends and baseball," MLB.com's Rich Draper said.

"Now he's back in the Tiger organization. … I think that's great," broadcaster Paul Carey said. "Larry is a wonderful guy, and you can't beat his smile."

Rich Shook, who covered Herndon for UPI for the player's entire stay in Detroit, remembered him as "one of my favorite human beings…just a quiet, polite man."

"It is an honor to work with him every day," Barkett, the Lakeland manager, said. "If he is not the best in the business at what he does, I'd like to know who is."

References

Publications

Reichler, Joseph L., ed. *Macmillan Baseball Encyclopedia, seventh ed.* New York: Macmillan & Co. 1989.

DETROIT TIGERS 1984: WHAT A START! WHAT A FINISH!

Articles

Draper, Rich. "Herndon Kept Focus On Field." mlb.com, February 21, 2005.

Fordin, Spencer. "Bench Is Strength for Yankees." mlb.com, October 11, 2004.

Web Sites

www.1980toppsbaseballblogspot.com/2010/03/257-larry-herndon.html

www.1984tigers.com

www.baseball-almanac.com

www.baseball-reference.com

www.checkswing.com/profiles/blogs/game-7-mentality

www.espn.com: SportsNation "Top 10 Legendary Stories"

www.milb.com

www.mlb.com

www.motownsports.com

www.sabr.org (the SABR Encyclopedia)

www.sports-venue.info (Tiger Stadium Timeline)

www.thebaseballcube.com

www.thebaseballpage.com

www.tigers.com

www.wikipedia.com

Interviews

Vasey, Glen. Correspondence with Andy Barkett, May 2010.

Vasey, Glen. Correspondence with Paul Carey, May 2010.

Vasey, Glen. Correspondence with Rod Nelson, May 2010.

Vasey, Glen. Correspondence with Mark Pattison, May 2010.

Vasey, Glen. Correspondence with John Rudak, May 2010.

Vasey, Glen. Correspondence with Rich Shook, May 2010.

Vasey, Glen. Telephone interview with Andy Barkett, May 29, 2010.

Howard Johnson
by David Raglin

HOWARD JOHNSON was a solid major-league player for several years. He was probably best known for a combination of power and speed that made him the darling of fantasy baseball owners as that variant of the national pastime took off in the 1980s. He was a member of two World Series championship clubs, the 1984 Detroit Tigers and the 1986 New York Mets.

Howard Michael Johnson was born on November 29, 1960, in Clearwater, Florida. He was named for his grandfather, Raymond Howard Johnson, who was known by his middle name. Howard said there were advantages to his name. "Every Sunday after church, my mother would take my brother and me to the Howard Johnson's restaurant for ice cream and lunch. The restaurant people knew me, and never charged for my lunch." His parents, Bill and Sue Johnson, were active in the community. "My father and mother worked with abused children when I was growing up, so I heard about those things," Johnson said in 1989 after he donated money from a prize he won to a home for abused children.

Johnson played several positions while growing up. A natural left-hander, his father taught him how to throw righty so that he could have more positions to play; it was a skill that served him well not only on the sandlots but throughout his pro career. A graduate of Clearwater High, he was drafted by the New York Yankees in the June 1978 draft in the 23rd round as a pitcher, but he did not sign. He was drafted by the Detroit Tigers with the 12th pick of the first round of the January 1979 secondary draft as a relief pitcher, but the Tigers moved him to shortstop.

Johnson played for the Lakeland Tigers of the Class A Florida State League in 1979. After a few games at short, the Tigers moved him to third. His main offensive statistics in his rookie season were not great (.235 average and only 18 extra-base hits), but he showed fine strike-zone judgment playing in a good pitchers' league, with 69 walks in 132 games. He also made 36 errors at shortstop and third base, which led to a move to the hot corner in 1980.

Johnson spent a second season in Lakeland in 1980 and did much better, slamming a league-leading 28 doubles, hitting .285 with 39 extra-base hits, stealing 31 bases, walking just about as much as he struck out (73 walks and 75 strikeouts),

DETROIT TIGERS 1984: WHAT A START! WHAT A FINISH!

and slicing his errors to 13. He was rewarded by being named the third baseman on the Florida State League's postseason Northern Division All-Star Team. Johnson followed that up with a strong showing in the Florida Instructional League, cementing his status as a big-league prospect.

The 1981 season was a breakthrough year for Johnson. Playing for the Birmingham Barons of the Double-A Southern League, he hit 22 home runs and drove in 83 runs, with his 75 walks helping him to a .360 on-base percentage. He received notice for a two-homer game on May 25—one of them a broken-bat homer, a rare event in those days. After the season Johnson returned to the Florida Instructional League and hit .331. That fall the Tigers added him to their 40-player major-league roster.

Johnson was assigned to the Evansville Triplets of the Triple-A American Association to start the 1982 season, but he did not stay there long. On April 13, the Tigers called up Johnson and outfielder Glenn Wilson when first baseman-outfielder Rick Leach and outfielder Eddie Miller were put on the disabled list, and Johnson made his big-league debut the next day. He hit leadoff and started the game in right field before moving to third later in the game. Johnson got his first hit to lead off the ninth against Toronto starter Jim Clancy, a hit that started a four-run rally that almost tied the game (Toronto won, 5-4). Johnson hit .188 in 12 games before being returned to Evansville on May 6. He starred for the Triplets with 23 home runs and 35 steals in 98 games before being recalled by the Tigers on August 13. He hit .347 for the Tigers the rest of the season, with a 12-game hitting streak in September, part of a 32-game stretch during which he hit .367. Johnson wore number 5 for the Tigers, the last player to wear it before it was retired in 1983 in honor of Hank Greenberg. As Tigers equipment manager Jim Schmakel told him, "Look at it this way, Howard, you're the first rookie to have his number retired."

HoJo went to spring training in 1983 fighting with Tom Brookens for the regular third baseman's job. Tigers manager Sparky Anderson liked Johnson's bat but was concerned that his glove needed more work, after he fielded .901 at third base for the Tigers in 1982. (Part of the problem was that, amazingly, he was using an outfielder's glove at third base.) When the season started, the plan was to platoon Johnson and Brookens, but soon the right-handed hitting Brookens was given all of the starts against lefties while they split the starts against right-handers. Johnson was also thought to be so tense that it affected his play, a charge that would dog him during his years with the Tigers. Johnson was hitting .212 in 27 games when he was sent back down to Evansville on May 27. (Ironically, his best game of the season with the Tigers was his last, a 2-for-4 game with a home run, two RBIs, and two runs scored.) He played only three games with the Triplets before he suffered a broken finger on June 1 and then a refracture on June 24 that eventually led to season-ending surgery. After the season the Tigers signed third baseman-first baseman Darrell Evans, the club's first big free-agent deal ever, so Johnson was sent to the instructional league to work on his outfield play.

The 1984 season started with another competitor for the third-base job, outfielder Glenn Wilson, whose poor fielding ended that experiment, helping lead to one of the biggest spring-training trades in Tigers history: Wilson and catcher John Wockenfuss to the Philadelphia Phillies for reliever Willie Hernandez and first baseman Dave Bergman. That did not give Johnson the third-base job permanently, as Anderson was still enamored of Brookens' glove, and at times both Barbaro Garbey and Marty Castillo were front-runners as well. Johnson started at third on Opening Day in Minnesota, and for a while he and Brookens platooned until players like Castillo and Garbey started to get some playing time near the end of the Tigers' 35-5 start. Johnson played in 20 of those 40 games, and while he hit only .265, his 10 walks led to a .383 on-base percentage.

Though the Tigers were able to cruise to the pennant, Johnson struggled. In early June he won the everyday third-base job, starting 72 games in an 80-game stretch, but hit only .234 and started only nine of the final 35 games. There were whispers that Anderson still did not have confidence that Johnson could play under pressure. There was a story told of a late-season game in which Anderson, picking a pinch-hitter, looked down the bench, and when his eyes met Johnson's eyes, Johnson looked away. Johnson played in only one of the Tigers' eight postseason games, coming in for defense in the final game of the World Series, getting one hitless at-bat. It was clear that he was on the outs in Detroit.

However, one club was hot after the 24-year-old, and that club could help fill a hole for the Tigers. The New York Mets had been asking about Johnson for a couple of years, and their interest intensified when they were working on a deal with the Expos for Gary Carter. Part of the price in that trade would be Hubie Brooks, so they felt they needed to get a replacement infielder. The Tigers needed starting pitcher Walt Terrell after it was clear that Milt Wilcox's arm was shot, so Johnson was traded to the Mets for Terrell in December.

Unfortunately for Johnson, he was moving from one crowded third-base situation to another, as the Mets also had Ray Knight to man the hot corner. In his book *Bats*, Mets manager Davey Johnson (no relation) talked a lot about how to get both third basemen playing time without harming either player's confidence. It did not help that HoJo got off to a terrible start, his average bottoming out at .127 on May 5, or that Terrell began his Tigers career by going 5-0. Johnson started hitting a little better, but did not get his average above .200 until an epic 19-inning victory over the Braves that started on Independence Day and ended close to 4 a.m. on July 5. Johnson did not even start that game; he entered in the ninth inning as a pinch-hitter for shortstop Rafael Santana, got a single, and scored the tying run. He blasted a two-run homer in the top of the 13th and hit a single and scored the lead run in the 18th, but both times the Braves battled back to tie the score. In the Mets' five-run 19th that finally finished off Atlanta, Johnson was intentionally walked and later scored. That game and an injury to Knight got Johnson the starting job in July, but he did not hit

DETROIT TIGERS 1984: WHAT A START! WHAT A FINISH!

and Knight recovered, so the platoon arrangement returned. The Mets and the Cardinals battled all season, trading the lead back and forth, but the Cards eventually pulled in front for good, and despite a 98-64 record, the Mets were on the outside looking in when the playoffs began. During the winter, Johnson moved to the New York area, got his broker's license, and took a job on Wall Street.

The plan for 1986 was the same as for 1985—a third-base platoon for the Mets—but Knight hit six home runs in his first nine games to win the job full time. Johnson was shifted to shortstop, the first time he had played the position regularly since his first year in pro ball. He hit a pivotal pinch-hit two-run homer on April 24 off the Cardinals' Todd Worrell to tie the game in the ninth inning in the first game of a big four-game set between the Mets and St. Louis. The Mets scored a go-ahead run in the top of the 10th, and Johnson's error at short put on the tying run with nobody out, but Roger McDowell held the Cards at bay.

Johnson was hurt on June 1 when he and Lenny Dykstra collided on a fly ball; he suffered a hairline fracture of the right forearm that kept him out of action for 21 games. In his first game back he hit two home runs, and even though the Mets lost, they were 46-20 and in first place by 9½ games. Johnson did not return to short after he came off the disabled list and played in only 56 of the final 97 games, with just 29 of them starts. He hit nine home runs in 135 at-bats during that stretch but his average was only .237 (even though his frequent walks led to a respectable .331 on-base percentage).

The Mets won 108 games, finishing in first by 21½ games, and beat the Houston Astros and Boston Red Sox in two of the most exciting postseason series in baseball history. Johnson pinch-hit in two games against Houston and in the ninth inning of Game Six of the World Series. He played the entire second game of the World Series, going 0-for-4. (He was also hitless in his other games.) Johnson was involved in a controversial situation in the Houston series when he and Mets catcher Ed Hearn produced balls they claimed had been scuffed by Houston starter Mike Scott, who had a reputation for helping himself in such ways. The winter brought rumors of Johnson going to San Diego as part of a trade for slugger Kevin McReynolds, but Kevin Mitchell ended up being the biggest hitter who went west in the deal.

Knight left the Mets for the Baltimore Orioles as a free agent after winning the 1986 World Series MVP award, but that did not mean Johnson had inherited the third-base job. Rookie Dave Magadan was the new competition in 1987, but Magadan needed surgery late in spring training for swollen lymph nodes, leaving the job to Johnson. HoJo was hitting only .220 with two home runs in 18 games when Magadan returned and was given the third-base job, but Rafael Santana was the odd man out as Johnson moved to shortstop briefly. Johnson soon moved back to third, and for the first time since his rookie season in 1982, he had a really hot streak—five home runs in 17 games in May. So even though he went homerless in the next 15 games and hit .178, he stayed in the lineup. It was the first time in Johnson's career that he was able to go through a rough stretch without being yanked from the lineup, and he took advantage of the situation.

Johnson hit three home runs in April, five in May, seven in June, and a whopping 10 in July, giving him 25 home runs with two months to go in the season, which attracted a lot of attention. He wasn't the only one; home runs in the majors were up 17 percent in 1987. It was the story of the summer, and Howard Johnson was the poster boy for the home-run surge. On July 28 he became the third Met to reach the 20/20 (home runs/stolen bases) plateau. It happened in the first game of a three-game series against the Cardinals that vaulted Johnson onto the national stage, a surprise to many people in that he had stolen only 31 bases in his five previous major league seasons.

The Mets had been playing a little over .500 ball all season and entered the series in St. Louis 8½ games back, but the Mets swept the Cards to pull within 5½ games of their nemesis. In the second game of the set, HoJo went 4-for-5 with a home run, and his two-run homer in the 10th inning off Pat Darcy the following day led the Mets to the sweep.

After that home run St. Louis manager Whitey Herzog asked umpire Joe West to inspect Johnson's bat. West found nothing wrong and later said he felt the bat was OK, but he had the groundskeeper keep the bat to avoid an incident with the volatile Herzog. Later, Houston manager Hal Lanier also accused Johnson of corking his bat. HoJo denied the charges, declaring that the rival managers were "insulting my talent with those charges. I'm not the first guy accused of using cork in my bat, but it's like they think I'm not capable of doing what I'm doing. But I'm doing it, and I'm doing it fair and square."

The controversy continued. Johnson's bat was confiscated by umpire Dutch Rennert when Giants manager Roger Craig accused Johnson of using a corked bat to hit his 30th home run of the season on August 19. Craig said, "When a man hits a ball 480 feet, I have to take a precaution. I knew HoJo well when I was with Detroit. He really hit that ball, and I don't recall him hitting them that far in Detroit." The bat was X-rayed and Johnson was exonerated. Later, Montreal manager Buck Rodgers added his name to the list of skippers accusing Johnson of cheating. The allegations were never proven.

Did Johnson cork his bats? After his career was over, Johnson said, "All I've ever said is that when they X-rayed my bats, they came up clean." and "I know a few good carpenters, yeah." Davey Johnson chimed in, "If it was corked, he had a carpenter who could do just about anything with wood. Did I see the cork? No. Did he probably cork his bat? Yes."

Johnson and Mets general manager Joe McIlvaine attributed Johnson's newfound power to his opportunity to play every day. Johnson said that when the Mets let Knight go, he spent hours in the batting cage hitting right-handed to prepare himself for the full-time job. It also might have helped Johnson to know that he was secure as the team's third baseman; there was no Tom Brookens, Glenn Wilson, or Ray Knight available if he had a bad week. After all, he started taking off in May after a slump that in the past might have put him on the bench.

DETROIT TIGERS 1984: WHAT A START! WHAT A FINISH!

The sweep of the Cardinals helped jump-start the Mets and they closed to within 1½ games in early September, but they ran out of gas and ended up in second place, three games back, with a 92-70 record. It ended up being a red-letter season for Johnson, who hit 36 home runs, stole 32 bases, and drove in 99 runs. He became the eighth player in major-league history to post a 30/30 season. He broke the record for home runs by a National League switch-hitter, formerly held by Rip Collins, who hit 34 home runs for the 1934 Cardinals.

Johnson headed to camp in 1988 with a regular job sewed up for the first time, but he started off slow in spring training, with a .115 average, until some pointed comments from manager Davey Johnson woke him up. "I haven't reached my peak yet," HoJo said. This is another proving year for me. A lot of people don't think I can do it again, so I'm out to end the skepticism." Johnson got off to a slow start, not crossing the .200 mark for good until May 11, but the Mets were off to a great start, finishing the quarter-mark of the season with a 30-11 record and a 5½-game lead in the National League East.

On April 30 Johnson had played a peripheral role in one of the big stories of the season, scoring from second on an infield single by Mookie Wilson in the top of the ninth to put the Mets in the lead for good, 6-5. The play at first was close and umpire Dave Pallone called Wilson safe. In the ensuing argument, Reds manager Pete Rose shoved Pallone, earning him a 30-game suspension. On June 2 Johnson's 13th-inning home run off Frank DiPino of the Cubs led the Mets to a thrilling 2-1 victory, one of three extra-inning game-winning home runs by the Mets in a five-game span.

By the end of July the Cardinals had almost caught up to the Mets, getting to within 1½ games, but the Mets kicked it into gear, quickly lengthening the lead back to six games. In early September their lead hit double digits, and on September 8, Johnson had the first five-hit game of his career in a 13-6 win against Chicago. The Mets finished first with a 100-60 record, and Johnson had a chance to be a regular in the postseason for the first time.

However, he would be playing shortstop. In late August the Mets brought up uberprospect Gregg Jefferies. Initially, Jefferies was installed at second base, but he later saw substantial time at third base, with HoJo moving to short in place of Santana. It was a move typical of the Mets at the time to try to squeeze as much offense into the lineup at the expense of defense. In the playoffs Wally Backman was the second baseman, Jefferies the third baseman, and Johnson the shortstop.

It didn't work as the heavily favored Mets fell in seven games to the Los Angeles Dodgers. Jefferies hit .333 but between them, Backman and Jefferies drove in only three runs. It was a terrible series for Johnson, who went hitless in the first three games, leading to a benching for Game Four (he later appeared as a pinch hitter). He started Game Five and got his only hit of the series before watching Game Six from the bench. The Mets staved off elimination that day but fell 6-0 in a Game Seven that saw Johnson come off the bench to pinch-hit in the ninth and strike out. It turned out to be the last postseason appearance of his career.

It was a disappointing season for Johnson. He hit only 24 home runs, drove in only 68 runs, and hit a full-season career-low .230. That was followed by the playoff problems. He revealed after the season that part of the problem was a sore right shoulder he'd kept quiet about, and he subsequently underwent arthroscopic surgery on October 29.

There was also lots of trade talk involving Johnson over the winter, as the Mets tried to clear up the infield logjam cased by the emergence of Jefferies. A deal to send Johnson and others to Seattle for pitcher Mark Langston and others fell through when concerns about how Johnson's shoulder might heal scared off the Mariners. The Mets also talked with Atlanta about sending Johnson to the Braves.

Meanwhile, Johnson worked to put the problems of 1988 behind him, reporting a month early to Port St. Lucie to work out with several teammates. Manager Davey Johnson announced that HoJo would be the third baseman and Jefferies would have to learn how to play second. Johnson, though, was still having trouble with the shoulder and did not hit well in Florida that year. He almost did not leave the Sunshine State a Met; a blockbuster deal fell through at the last moment that would have sent Johnson and Sid Fernandez to Seattle, Mark Langston to Boston, Wade Boggs to Kansas City, and Danny Tartabull to the Mets to give New York the right-handed power hitter they craved.

It turned out to be the best deal the Mets never made, as Howard Johnson had the finest season of his career in 1989. His 36 home runs and 101 runs batted were not his career best, but his 104 runs scored led the National League and his .287 average, .369 on-base percentage, and .559 slugging percentage were all career highs.

The season started with the only really good April of Johnson's career. He had previously hit .203 in April, but in 1989 he hit .333 with four home runs. Unfortunately, the Mets continued their pattern of not playing well when Johnson did and vice versa, finishing April with a 12-10 record. That pattern continued all season. At the All-Star break Johnson had 22 home runs, his first All-Star selection, and the first long-term contract of his career (three years for $6.1 million), but the Mets were treading water in third place with a 45-39 record. Johnson celebrated his new contract by hitting two home runs in the All-Star home run contest to help the National League win the competition, 9-5.

As the season progressed, Johnson's numbers kept piling up. On August 20 he hit home run No. 30, making him only the third player to have more than one 30/30 season to that point (Willie Mays and Bobby Bonds were the others).

Johnson's 1989 season brought him many awards: the National League Player of the Week for June 19-25, the National League Player of the Month for June (a .340 batting average with 11 home runs), the third-base spot on *The Sporting News*' National League All-Star team, the Silver Slugger award at third base for the National League, and the Sport Channel/Leukemia New York Athlete of the Year award. Johnson said upon receiving the latter honor, "It's amazing. A year ago, I couldn't have been elected dog catcher in New York." After the season, he went to Tokyo to conduct hitting clinics.

However, Johnson kept his "odd season on-even season off" pattern going in 1990, hitting .244 with 23 home runs and 90 runs batted in. The season also saw him move to shortstop in early August for the rest of the season after regular shortstop Kevin Elster injured his shoulder. The Mets rebounded a bit from their 87-75 1989 campaign, but their 91-71 record in '90 left them four games behind the Pittsburgh Pirates. Manager Davey Johnson was not around to see them climb back into the race. He was fired early in the season with the club 20-22, replaced by former Met Bud Harrelson, and HoJo lost his most fervent supporter in the Mets hierarchy.

But true to the pattern, Johnson had a great season in 1991. He had career highs in home runs (38), runs batted in (117), and runs scored (108). HoJo started the season as the regular shortstop, but he was back at third by the end of April. The 1991 season was also the year that Johnson professed his Christianity publicly. He said his wife was already a strong Christian and "a lot had been eating at me. There was the sense of emptiness, that I was missing out on something. I had come up as a baseball player wanting to make a lot of money and enjoy success. I'd done it, but was bothered about where it would go from there." He vowed that he "certainly [was] not going to forsake my love of the game or my competitiveness in it." He also switched his uniform number from 20 to 44 before switching back after five games, saying that he was uncomfortable with the new number.

He was part of a bigger switch in September when the Mets, still trying to unclog their infield, asked Johnson to play right field. It did not seem to hurt his bat; he got two hits in each of his first three games in right. Johnson welcomed the switch: "This year, for the first time, I felt old at third base. I'm 30 now, and it's taken a toll on my legs and knees." Even though he played short and right, he was named the third baseman on the National League Silver Slugger team. It was not a good season for the Mets; their 77-84 record was their first losing season since 1983, and Harrelson was fired in late September.

The Mets were in disarray, and nothing showed it more than their treatment of HoJo. After playing him at short, third, and right in 1991, new manager Jeff Torborg moved Johnson to a position in 1992 where he'd never played before: center field. Johnson did the best he could, but he did not play well in center, and it affected his bat; in 83 games in center, he hit .224 with only seven home runs. After Johnson misplayed a game-winning triple off the bat of the Dodgers' Mitch Webster, Torborg moved him to yet another position, left field.

Soon after the move, in the last week of July, Johnson hurt his wrist (probably on a slide in Philadelphia), and doctors found a hairline fracture. With the wrist keeping him from playing, HoJo underwent season-ending surgery in late August on his left shoulder and both knees (he had a cartilage tear in the right knee, and a degenerated piece of tendon in his left knee was removed.)

The Mets learned from their mistakes with Johnson in 1992 and moved him back to third base in 1993, the last year of his contract. Johnson was concerned about third base wearing him out, but he vowed to work out over the winter to prepare his body for the challenge. At the age of 32 his body was beginning to betray him, however, and word was getting around the league that pitchers could sneak a fastball by him. He was clearly becoming frustrated, as he was ejected from a game for the first time and suspended for three games for bumping umpire Jerry Layne and spinning him around.

As it turned out, Johnson was sick with an "acute viral syndrome." He went on the disabled list to recover, but even after returning three weeks later, in early July, his bat was still not responding. For the second straight year his season ended with an injury to his hand/wrist area when on July 22 he slid thumb-first into second, chipping his right thumb and ending his season—and his playing career with the Mets.

With his contract completed, Johnson was a free agent, and two injury-filled unproductive seasons greatly hurt his marketability. After overtures from the Reds, he signed a one-year contract with the Colorado Rockies with a club option for 1995. The Rockies saw him as a player who could give the second-year expansion club power from both sides of the plate and offer defensive versatility. Unfortunately, Johnson got off to his typical slow start, hitting only .133 in April, and by mid-June most of his appearances were coming as a pinch-hitter. His season ended early for the third straight year, but this time it was not because of an injury; in early August of 1994 the players walked out, and the season was over.

The Rockies did not pick up Johnson's option, and after baseball resumed, he was one of many players who was out of work. Johnson joined the group of unemployed players at a camp in Homestead, Florida, organized by the Major League Baseball Players Association. The Cubs signed him, but he did not hit well (in 169 at-bats, he managed just a .195 average), and his big-league playing career was over. At least Johnson went out with a bang, going 3-for-4 in his final game, with a single off Todd Jones in his last major-league at-bat. He went to play in Venezuela that winter, but nobody picked him up for the 1996 season, and he took a minor-league coaching job with the Butte Copper Kings, a rookie-level farm club of the Tampa Bay Devil Rays, who would begin play in the major leagues in 1998.

Johnson tried to come back with the Mets in spring training in 1997. While he did not make the team, the comeback helped heal some old wounds. The fans were really behind their former hero, and it meant a lot to Johnson: "This is something I won't ever forget. I wasn't expecting it. When I was here, I was just a player everybody just liked, and being gone for a while and out of the game, I think people can relate to that. They can relate to someone taking on a challenge and trying to meet that challenge."

One overarching aspect of Johnson's career was his seeming need to be appreciated, and when that happened he performed well. Sparky Anderson clearly had little respect for Johnson, and it seemed to affect his play. Davey Johnson treated HoJo with a lot of respect, but for his first two years in New York, the manager could not play HoJo full time because he also had Ray Knight. Once Knight was gone and Johnson won the job in spring training of 1987, and kept the job even when he got off to a slow start, he could relax, and he became a star player. As his performance deteriorated and his career with the Mets ended in the early 1990s, Johnson lamented that the people who had known him during the glory years with the Mets were gone and the new people did not have confidence in him.

Johnson was hired by the Mets as a scout in October 1997, a position he held until he was named hitting coach of the brand-new Brooklyn Cyclones of the short-season A-ball New York-Penn League in late 2000. He was promoted to manager of the Cyclones for the 2002 season and managed the Mets' Florida Instructional League club that season. He progressed through the Mets' system as a hitting coach, working for the Port St. Lucie Class A club in 2003, the Double-A Binghamton Mets in 2004, and the Triple-A Norfolk Tides in 2005 and 2006. He was promoted to first-base coach for the Mets for the 2007 season, and on July 12, 2007, he was named the hitting coach for the Mets, a post he held through the 2010 season. In 2011, Johnson played two games with the Rockland Boulders of the Can-Am League, with his son Glen.

References

Publications

Detroit Tigers media guides 1981-1984.

Articles

The Sporting News issues dated June 24, 1978; January 27, 1979; February 3, 1979; September 13, 1980; December 13, 1980; June 27, 1981; November 7, 1981; December 5, 1981; April 26, 1982; May 3, 1982; August 30, 1982; September 20, 1982; November 29, 1982; March 14, 1983; May 16, 1983; November 28, 1983; March 19, 1984; March 26, 1984; May 28, 1984; February 25, 1985; March 4, 1985; March 18, 1985; July 15, 1985; February 10, 1986; May 26, 1986; October 13, 1986; October 20, 1986; November 3, 1986; January 5, 1987; February 9, 1987; March 30, 1987; April 6, 1987; June 1, 1987; July 27, 1987; August 10, 1987; August 17, 1987; August 31, 1987; September 14, 1987; September 28, 1987; October 5, 1987; October 19, 1987; February 8, 1988; April 4, 1988; May 9, 1988; June 20, 1988; July 11, 1988; September 19, 1988; October 10, 1988; October 31, 1988; February 20, 1989; February 27, 1989; March 6, 1989; March 13, 1989; March 27, 1989; April 3, 1989; April 10, 1989; April 24, 1989; May 1, 1989; June 19, 1989; July 10, 1989; July 17, 1989; July 24, 1989; July 31, 1989; August 28, 1989; September 4, 1989; October 23, 1989; November 6, 1989; November 13, 1989; November 20, 1989; January 1, 1990; July 30, 1990; August 20, 1990; May 27, 1991; September 2, 1991; September 16, 1991; December 2, 1991; December 30, 1991; February 10, 1992; March 2, 1992; August 3, 1992; August 24, 1992; September 7, 1992; November 30, 1992; January 25, 1993; May 24, 1993; June 7, 1993; August 23, 1993; November 8, 1993; November 29, 1993; April 11, 1994; July 25, 1994; August 29, 1994; October 10, 1994; January 2, 1995; April 17, 1995; November 6, 1995.

New York Times issues dated June 21, 1989; March 1, 1991; May 3, 1991; September 4, 1991; July 22, 1992; August 25, 1992; August 26, 1992; November 21, 1992; May 28, 1993; May 27, 1993; June 12, 1993; June 15, 1993; July 7, 1993; July 24, 1993; February 20, 1994; September 28, 1994; September 5, 1996; February 21, 1997; February 11, 1997; March 26, 1997; March 27, 1997; March 27, 1997; April 6, 1997; December 5, 2001; May 31, 2002; July 14, 2007.

Ruppert Jones
by Adam J. Ulrey

IF A MOVIE of Ruppert Jones' career were to be made, its title might be What Could Have Been. This gifted five-tool player was beset by injuries throughout his career. He could hit with power to all fields and run like a gazelle. Jones called homers "accidents," maintaining that he was at the plate to make contact and get base hits. He hit 147 accidents in his career. He came to Seattle from Kansas City after being the very first pick in the 1976 expansion draft. Jones was the first Mariner to be an All-Star, in 1977 and made the team again, this time for the National League, for the San Diego Padres in 1982. As a Mariner playing in front of small crowds, Jones heard the constant chants of his name: "ROOP! ROOP! ROOP!"

Born Ruppert Sanderson Jones on March 12, 1955, in Dallas, Texas. Jones was about to become a teenager in Texas when his mother and stepfather decided to move to Berkeley, California. He didn't want to leave. "In the '60s, black folks had a better chance in California than they did in Texas," he said. Still, it was hard for Jones to make friends at Berkeley High School. "I was a country boy living in the city, different than everyone else," he said. "What acceptance I got, I earned on the playing field."

In his senior year at Berkeley High, he batted .457 with seven home runs, was unanimously named to the All-Alameda County League and All-East Bay teams, and was an All-Northern California selection. In addition to his baseball skills, he was a unanimous choice for All-East Bay honors in football, as a defensive back, and basketball, as a guard. He helped lead Berkeley to two Northern California football titles and

DETROIT TIGERS 1984: WHAT A START! WHAT A FINISH!

helped lead the basketball team to the league championship and second place in the Bay Area's Tournament of Champions in his senior year, earning All-State honors in both sports. It was little wonder that he was voted the East Bay Athlete of the Year for 1972-73. He played in the same outfield at Berkeley High with future major leaguers Claudell Washington and Glenn Burke. Jones received scholarship offers to play football at Oregon State, Arizona State, and California, but focused on baseball because he was a better outfielder than wide receiver. He signed with the Kansas City Royals, who chose him in the third round of the June draft in 1973 and signed him for $22,000.

After being signed by scout Dick Hager, Jones reported to Billings of the Pioneer League, where he batted .301 with four homers and 31 RBIs in helping the Mustangs win the pennant, and was named to the league's All-Star team. It was on to Waterloo of the Midwest League in 1974. On July 11, he was promoted by Kansas City to the San Jose Bees of the California League. When he left Waterloo, he was pasting the ball for a .353 batting average on 88 hits, and was second with 13 homers and 43 RBIs. Jones was 41 points ahead of his nearest rival for the hitting title, in a ten-club circuit with only ten batters over the .300 mark. After joining the Bees he was blanked in his first four times at bat, but came back the next night and homered and doubled to drive in two runs to help San Jose beat Bakersfield, 9-8. Between the two teams he hit 21 homers and drove in 88 runs.

The next two years were spent in Triple-A playing for Omaha of the American Association. It did not come as easily as the previous two years for Jones. He hit .243 in 1975 with 13 homers and 54 RBIs. But 1976 saw Jones rebound to have a solid year. In 102 games he blasted 19 homers, drove in 73 runs, and hit .262 before being called up by the Royals late in the season. He struggled a little after the call-up, getting into 28 games but hitting just .216 with one homer. His first major-league hit, a single, came off future Hall of Famer Gaylord Perry in his very first at-bat, on August 1, 1976, as the designated hitter against the Texas Rangers; he collected a run and an RBI on a 1-for-4 day. After just 51 at-bats, though, his time with the Royals was over. The Royals' decision not to protect Jones was difficult, but they believed they needed to protect outfielder Willie Wilson and shortstop U.L. Washington, thereby leaving Jones exposed. He was made the first pick in the 1976 expansion draft by Seattle. Danny Kaye, the comic actor and part-owner of the Mariners, was summoned by Lee McPhail to make the first selection, and Kaye called out the name of Ruppert Jones.

To say that Jones was a hit in Seattle in 1977, the Mariners' first season, would be an understatement. He was so popular that he could have run for mayor. It started with the center-field fans, Roop's Troops, and spread throughout the Kingdome. Jones could do no wrong with the fans as they cheered his every move. As much as his offense was expected and talked about, it was his defense that was drawing raves from fans and management. Each time Jones stepped to the plate the Kingdome crowd would ring out with chants of "Roop, Roop, Roop." At the plate he did not disappoint in his rookie season, hitting .263 for the year even though his impatience showed at times. He played in all but two games and was second on the team in homers with 24. He also led the team in strikeouts with 120, but finished third on the team with 76 RBIs. Unfortunately, Jones experienced the ugliness of racism, being stopped four times while driving his Mercedes-Benz. Jones said troopers just couldn't understand how a young black man could afford such a vehicle.

What happened after the season was the only thing that plagued Jones' career: injuries. After the season he underwent the first of his many surgeries, having torn cartilage removed from his left knee.

The 1978 season was a step back for Jones, as he struggled to recover fully from the surgery. If that wasn't bad enough, he had an emergency appendectomy in June and lost 15 pounds and missed a month of the season. He slipped across the board from 1977, hitting just .235 with six homers and 46 RBIs. Though his offensive production fell, Roop's fielding did not suffer. He kept making remarkable catches. "In some ways," he said, "it was a good year for me. I learned something about myself, my character. I didn't give up; I didn't let my slump bother my fielding."

Jones spent some time that year as a sportscaster. He worked for a black radio station in Seattle, KYAC, which used Jones' taped interviews with ballplayers for its sports show.

Jones rebounded to have his finest season in 1979, playing in every game and establishing career highs in runs (109), RBIs (78), hits (166), triples (9), and stolen bases (33). He attributed his success to a new offseason workout regimen.

The season was so good that Jones became the hot player talked about in almost every trade scenario. One scenario wasn't fiction: He was traded to the New York Yankees on November 1, 1979, with pitcher Jim Lewis, for four players: outfielder Juan Beniquez, catcher Jerry Narron, and pitchers Jim Beattie and Rick Anderson. The Yankees needed a center fielder and loved Jones' potential and his ability to chase down the ball in the outfield with the best of them. "I had a dream the week before I was traded," Jones explained in the stadium pressroom. "I dreamed of myself in a Yankee uniform. I knew I was going to be traded. I thought I would go either to the Dodgers or the Yankees, but in my dreams I only saw myself as a Yankee." Most scouts agreed that Roop was a top-flight player who would get better in a winning environment. In three years at Seattle, his steals went from 13 to 22 to 33. He hit the first inside-the-park homer at the Kingdome, which was like running one out in a phone booth.

As excited as Jones was to become a Yankee, his dreams soon became a nightmare. He started 1980 slowly, batting .222 through May 26 with only five homers before the first of two trips to the disabled list. During the May 26 game, he had a stomachache and later that night at a barbecue at the home of Willie Randolph he continued to complain about it. Later that evening he was rushed to emergency surgery at Pascack Valley Hospital in New Jersey, for removal of an adhesion that had caused an intestinal obstruction. The adhesion was

DETROIT TIGERS 1984: WHAT A START! WHAT A FINISH!

believed to be the result of the previous year's emergency appendectomy. Jones missed six weeks of action. Then, after coming back from surgery, he separated his shoulder on August 25, running head-first into the center-field wall at the Oakland Coliseum while attempting to catch a first-inning fly ball hit by the A's Tony Armas. Jones missed the rest of the season, winding up with the lowest full-season average of his career at .223 and only nine homers.

Jones remembered standing in center field in Oakland that August evening with two runners on base in the first inning. With Tommy John pitching, Armas powered the ball toward left center, and Jones ran to make the catch.

The next thing Jones remembered, he was waking up in the hospital 24 hours later with a concussion and a separated shoulder. "People tell me what happened," Jones said, "but there's a whole night of my life I don't remember. Initially, I was just grateful I was still alive. When I woke up feeling somewhat fine and alive, I was relieved."

Jones said he was more depressed after his abdominal surgery to remove the blockage in his intestine than after his shoulder injury. "The nurses would speak to me," said Jones, "and I'd just grumble and mumble. I always had a stern look on my face and they said they were scared of me." After a few days of feeling sorry for himself, Jones, ordinarily cheerful, paid a visit to the pediatric ward. There, he saw children "screaming in pain" and others "bald from the chemotherapy."

"That really woke me up," Jones said. "Those kids had so much courage. They would never have the opportunity to do what I had done, so what was I complaining about?"

What was supposed to be the start of long career as a Yankee ended after just one year. On March 31, 1981, late in spring training, Jones was shipped out along with Tim Lollar, Chris Welsh, and Joe Lefebvre to the San Diego Padres for Jerry Mumphrey and John Pacella.

Looking to shake off 1980, Jones headed to San Diego in '81 looking to get back to the form he had with the Mariners. He did not quite bounce back as he had hoped, hitting just .249 with four homers and 39 RBIs. But the following year showed a return to Jones' early years in Seattle.

Jones made a commitment to really work on his health and train harder than ever before. He did a lot of physical conditioning and worked on his swing mechanics. Living in San Diego, he worked on baseball instead of just working out. Before, he was in Washington state and New Jersey, where it's cold and rainy for much of the offseason. He hit about 450 balls a week off a batting tee.

The work paid off in 1982, as Jones became an All-Star for the second time in his career. After playing 32 games, he was hitting .328 with five homers and 19 RBIs. A week later he had pushed up his average to .357 with 26 RBIs, and was among the league leaders in several categories. Because of his red-hot start he became a hero of the left-field bleacherites at San Diego's Jack Murphy Stadium. Ruppert brought out his old Roop's Troops slogan and it was made into T-shirts for his crew. And while the Padres center fielder enjoyed the enthusiasm of his "Troops," he wouldn't let it go to his head. He didn't believe in statistical goals, but instead kept one simple goal in mind: to be the best ballplayer he could be every day. "Dick Williams, manager of the Padres, said something to me that I've always believed," said Jones. "He said to beat your opponent any way you can; get them with your glove or baserunning if you can't get them with your bat. Coming from someone with his experience, especially from a winner, just reinforced it."

In the All-Star Game, Jones batted in the third inning, pinch-hitting for Montreal hurler Steve Rogers, and stroked a triple off the wall in right-center, later scoring. He went on to hit .283 for the year with 12 homers, 18 stolen bases, and 61 RBIs. What hurt Jones, again, was another injury, two weeks after the All-Star break. He twisted his ankle, missed almost a month, and was never the same with the Padres after that. He played just one more year with San Diego, batting .233 with 12 homers and 49 RBIs in 1983.

Granted free agency on November 7, 1983, Jones found no takers, so he headed to camp with the Pittsburgh Pirates and hit .370 during spring training, but was released on the final cut. He found no takers except for Detroit Tigers general manager Bill Lajoie, who liked the thought of Jones hitting into the right-field seats and signed him on April 10, 1984. But first he was sent to Evansville, the Tigers' Triple-A club, before getting a second chance. His chance came in early June, when he was called up. He hit a three-run homer in his second game back to beat Toronto 5-3. Jones hit five homers and batted .283 in his first 20 games back. He platooned with Larry Herndon for the remainder of year, ending the season with 12 homers, 37 RBIs, and a .284 average. Four of his home runs either won a game or put the Tigers in the lead for good. Jones hit two rooftop homers in a ten-day span. First he became the 13th player to hit one over the right-field roof at Tiger Stadium, off the third deck in right field, which prompted Tigers fans to dub him Rooftop Jones. He then hit one on top of the roof at Comiskey Park. By then Detroit fans had warmed up to Jones, chanting his name, "Roop, Roop." "I'm enjoying this, mostly because of the adverse circumstances I went through," Jones said. "It takes a lot of support to bring in a new player into a situation of this magnitude, when nobody else was willing to bring me into any situation, let alone a winning one. I'm not bitter about what I went through, however. All good things happen for a reason."

The Tigers went on to win the World Series by beating the San Diego Padres, Jones' former team. He saw limited action, getting three at-bats with no hits, but he did get a ring. At the end of the season, on November 8, he was granted free agency, and this time the California Angels signed him on January 30, 1985.

Jones rebounded in California to hit 21 homers and drive in 67 runs in 125 games. The Angels signed him once Fred Lynn left via free agency for Baltimore, and Angels manager Gene Mauch was thrilled. "Oh boy, has he helped us," said Mauch. "We got him as an insurance policy, but he's sure paid off." Jones continued to hit the long ball in 1986, smacking 17 home runs and knocking in 49 runs, though he batted just .229. He was back in double figures with 10 steals. He continued to be a very good outfielder, moving from center field to spending most of his games in right field.

Jones played in just 85 games in 1987, batting .245 and hitting eight homers. After the season, he was released. He had played his last major-league game.

Jones signed a free agent contract on February 27, 1988, with the Milwaukee Brewers, who were looking for a left-handed pinch-hitter and occasional designated hitter. He was battling Jim Adduci for the final roster spot. He batted .361, in spring training but was unable to play in the field because of a shoulder injury. The Brewers released him before the season began. In May he was picked up by the Texas Rangers and assigned to their Triple-A farm club, the Oklahoma City 89ers. He got into 50 games there, batting .253 with 7 homers and 30 RBIs. He left halfway through the year to join the Hanshin Tigers of Japan's Central League. There he played in 52 games with 8 homers, 27 RBIs, and a .254 average. He signed a minor-league contract with Texas in May 1989 for one more try to get back to the majors. It lasted 27 games at Oklahoma City before Jones called it a career after hitting just .200 with one homer in 80 at-bats. He was 34 years old and had been playing professionally for 17 years.

In his career, Jones batted .250 with 147 home runs, 579 RBIs, 643 runs, 215 doubles, 38 triples, and 143 stolen bases. Two of his biggest hits came against Hall of Famer Dennis Eckersley. On June 3, 1977, at the Kingdome in Seattle, Jones hit a home run to right field in the sixth inning to end Eckersley's streak of $22^{1}/_{3}$ consecutive hitless innings over parts of three games, two outs short of Cy Young's record. (Eckersley was with Cleveland at the time.) In the 1982 All-Star Game, he hit a triple off Eckersley, then with the Boston Red Sox. "What could have been" will be the legacy of one Ruppert Sanderson Jones.

In his 50s, Jones was selling insurance in the San Diego area and spending time with his family, playing golf, and reading fiction, especially Robert Ludlum and John Grisham. He learned to like sales. "I don't have a college education," he said, "so the satisfaction is making a success in something other than athletics."

References

Publications

Baseball Register (1977-1988).

San Diego Padres yearbooks, 1982-84.

Seattle Mariners yearbooks, 1978-80.

Naiman. Joe, and David Porter. *The San Diego Padres Encyclopedia*.

Articles

Moore, Jim. "'Roop!' still echoes in Mariners lore." *Seattle Post-Intelligencer*, July 6, 2001.

Ruppert Jones clipping file, National Baseball Hall of Fame Library.

The Sporting News: January 19, 1976, p.44; August 21, 1976, p.9; October 2, 1976, p. 33; November 20, 1976, p.34; November 27, 1976, p.48; December 18, 1976, p. 49; April 2, 1977, p.11; December 31, 1977, p.62; January 28, 1978, p.59; June 30, 1979, p.43; February 9, 1980, p.36; July 11, 1981, p.36; May 31, 1982, p.17; June 7, 1982, p.36; June 28, 1982, p.22; July 12, 1982, p.28; July 26, 1982, p.26; September 20,1982, p.43; August 16, 1982, p.37; July 9, 1984, p.28; March 16, 1987, p.33; March 14, 1988, p.37; April 11, 1988, p.31, May 16, 1988, p.22, May 1, 1989, p.52.

Websites

http:/minors.sabrwebs.com/cgi-bin/player

www.baseball-almanac.com

www.baseball-reference.com

www.1984tigers.com

www.paperofrecord.com

www.retrosheet.com

www.timesnewsweekly.com

Rusty Kuntz
by Mike McClary

ASK CASUAL BASEBALL fans which Tigers player drove in the run that clinched the 1984 World Series, and you can't blame them if they answer Kirk Gibson. After all, Gibson's blast off Goose Gossage gets replayed time and again and is perhaps the most memorable hit in Tigers history. But the game-winning RBI, an official major-league statistic in 1984, in Game Five of the Series that year came off the bat not of a superstar, but of a player who barely inched his way onto the team at the end of spring training: Rusty Kuntz.

Russell Jay Kuntz was born on February 4, 1955, in Orange, California, to Chet and Willie Kuntz. Shortly thereafter, the family moved to Wichita, Kansas, where Chet worked as a bricklayer. "We didn't have any babysitters. So my brother, Ron, and I would go to work with my dad if he was building a house or something fun," Kuntz said. "Our job was to take a little trowel and stir up the cement to keep it moist."

Chet Kuntz traveled much of the time for his job, often leaving on Sunday morning and returning on Friday night. "We'd spend Saturday playing with him," Rusty said. "And, of course, we always went in the backyard and we played baseball."

By the time Rusty reached third grade, Chet had grown tired of laying brick and, even more so, of being away from his wife and sons, so the Kuntz family moved to Paso Robles, California, about 250 miles north of Los Angeles, where Rusty's mother had been raised. "My uncle was an auto mechanic and owned Shell gas stations [in that area]. So my dad went to school to become an auto mechanic, and that's what he did from the time I was in the fourth grade all through college," Kuntz said.

Kuntz attended tiny Paso Robles High School, a school where "if you could play a sport, you played all three," he said. "My brother and I played football, basketball, and baseball. And to tell you the truth, baseball was my least favorite of all of them. I loved basketball because of the pace of the game."

After graduating in 1973, Kuntz attended Cuesta Junior College in San Luis Obispo, just south of Paso Robles. He quarterbacked the football team, played center on the hardwood, and patrolled center field for the baseball team. It was on the baseball diamond that Kuntz made his mark. In 1975, the right-handed hitter batted .442 as a sophomore, was named to the Junior College All-Star team, and caught the eye of another college coach.

"Jim Bowen, who was the head coach with [Cal State-Stanislaus], had come over to scout our catcher, John Farmer," Kuntz said. "I had a good game, and at the end of the game he talked to Farmer, but he also called me over and said, 'Hey, where are you going to go to school next year?' Well, I wanted to go to Cal Poly San Luis Obispo because it's right there close. So I asked [Cal Poly head baseball coach] Berdy Harr if I could play on his team. Cuesta, Cal Poly, and Hancock Junior College, in Santa Maria, we played three times a week against one another, so I knew exactly what Cal Poly had as far as outfielders. And Berdy looked right in my face and told me, 'Rusty, to be honest with you I don't think you can make my bench.' That was one of those wakeup calls."

Though Kuntz's desire to play close to home didn't pan out, he impressed Cal State-Stanislaus' Bowen enough to receive a scholarship to the fledgling school near Modesto. "I wanted a place where I could play, and Stanislaus was the only one that really gave me a chance," he said.

In 1976, Kuntz's first year with the Warriors, he primarily played left field before shifting to center field for his senior season. It was a remarkable year for Kuntz and a Stanislaus team that charged to the NCAA Division III World Series championship, defeating Ithaca College, 13-6. The team doubled its pleasure in 1977 and won the title again, this time beating Brandeis University, 8-5. Kuntz was named to the all-tournament team and was selected the tournament's most valuable player. (In 2000, he was a member of the first class inducted into the Cal State-Stanislaus Hall of Fame.)

The dream season continued two days later, on June 7, 1977, when the Chicago White Sox drafted Kuntz in the 11th round of the free-agent draft. The news surprised him.

"The first year I was at Cuesta, I went in there and I hit .402 my freshman year and then hit .442 my sophomore year," he said. "But they just weren't that enthused on what I could do as a baseball player, professionally anyway. So my dad pulled me aside and said, 'Listen, you can't jump and you can't shoot a basketball. So why are you playing basketball?' I said, 'Well, I don't know.' 'Okay, you're a quarterback that can't scramble, you can't run, and they're dragging you down from behind all the time. So why don't you just look for a place that you can go play baseball and see if you can make something of yourself?' Then he showed me my stats and said, 'If you do that and they don't look at you, there's some reason why.' And I thought, Okay."

While at Stanislaus, Kuntz completed scouting questionnaires for several major-league teams—"the Mets, the Phillies, the Giants, the Dodgers, everybody in the world," he said. In the end, the only club to talk with him was the one that eventually drafted him.

"I thought, 'This is going to be good, I got drafted.' I'm waiting for the lights, camera, action, as naïve as I am at that time," Kuntz said. "I get a letter in the mail that tells me you've been selected by the White Sox in the 11th round. Get your butt on an airplane and fly back to Sarasota, Florida, as quick as you can because the Gulf Coast Rookie League has already started. And I'm going, wait a minute, where are the cameras, where's the action, where's all this hoopla?"

With his $1,000 signing bonus and an airplane ticket to Sarasota, Rusty Kuntz embarked on his career as a professional baseball player. He'd yet to sign his contract when he arrived in Florida. "When I got to Sarasota, Joe Jones was my first manager," he said. "He slipped my contract under a bathroom stall and says, 'Hey, kid, sign this thing and shove it back underneath.' So there was my hoopla."

DETROIT TIGERS 1984: WHAT A START! WHAT A FINISH!

Kuntz played two months in the Gulf Coast League and spent the winter in Paso Robles preparing for the neat season. When he arrived in Sarasota for spring training in 1978, little did he know that he was about to begin a streak of good luck in the Grapefruit League.

"It's almost like a Wally Pipp story," Kuntz said. "The center fielder for the Double-A team had a migraine headache and Tony La Russa was my manager at the time. He told me to come on over. I was slated to be the A-ball center fielder. I got to play the first game with the Double-A team, and got a couple of hits and made a catch. La Russa told me to come back the next day. So the guy still has a headache, so [La Russa] says come back again. Got a couple more hits, threw a guy out or something like that. So by the third day, now all of a sudden the guy that has the headache is feeling better, and La Russa told him, 'Hey, relax and take another day off.' And he called me back over. So I got three shots in a row, and I made the Double-A team out of spring training right there."

After a year with the Double-A Knoxville (Tennessee) Sox of the Southern League, hitting .263 in 113 games, Kuntz arrived in spring training for the 1979 season set to return to Knoxville. In the offseason, the White Sox promoted La Russa to manager of the Triple-A Iowa Oaks of the American Association. Again, he brought Kuntz over for action at the higher level, and Kuntz's performance earned him a spot on the Triple-A team. He hit .294 for the Oaks with 15 home runs.

On August 3, 1979, three weeks after the Chisox "Disco Demolition Night" debacle at Comiskey Park, La Russa was promoted to replace White Sox player-manager Don Kessinger. "[Sox owner] Bill Veeck at that time loved Tony. So he called him up at the All-Star break. At the end of the '79 season, I got called up," Kuntz recalled.

Kuntz made his major-league debut on September 1, starting in left field and batting second against the Milwaukee Brewers and right-hander Lary Sorensen at Comiskey Park. In the bottom of the first, he lofted a fly ball to Milwaukee right fielder Sixto Lezcano for an out—and his first big-league at-bat was in the books. Kuntz went 0-for-3 that night, with another fly to right and a strikeout in a rain-shortened (five innings) 4-3 Chicago win.

It took Kuntz three weeks to get his first major-league hit. It came after 11 plate appearances, with six of them resulting in strikeouts. At the Seattle Kingdome on September 23, Kuntz stepped to the plate with two out in the top of ninth inning. He'd gone hitless in his previous three at-bats against Mariners starter Rick Honeycutt. "I hit a topper over the mound that just snuck through. So my first year, I was 1-11 with an .091 average," he said. Kuntz was forced out at second on the next play and the game was over: Mariners 8, White Sox 3.

With a taste of major-league experience, Kuntz headed to spring training in 1980, his future in Chicago looking bright. "I get to go to my first big-league spring training, and now I'm basically trying to do well enough to make the Triple-A team again," he said. "Well, Tony La Russa is the manager, and he put me out there every opportunity that he could. And I just kept doing okay. I kept getting a couple knocks. And I'd play left field one day, the next day I'd play center field, and maybe two days later I'd play right field just to see what I could do. I hit okay in the minor leagues, around the .290s in Double-A and Triple-A. But I was out there for my glove. There was no hiding that."

For parts of the next four years, Kuntz was an extra outfielder with the White Sox. He made the club out of spring training in 1980 and '81, and again in '83. (He spent the 1982 season at Triple-A Edmonton before a September recall.) The 1983 season was magical for the White Sox, who won 99 games and the American League West title. Approaching the All-Star break, the White Sox, after a slow start, began to build momentum for a second-half surge. On June 21, 20 days after Kuntz's last appearance on the field, general manager Roland Hemond called him into his office. "He calls me in and says, 'Look, we've got to make a roster move. I can send you back down to Triple-A and you can do whatever. Or I can trade you to Minnesota and let you play in the big leagues and get more big-league time.' And I just asked him, 'What do you think I ought to do?' He says, 'You need to play and you can go down to Triple-A and do whatever you want. But if I was you, I would want to play [in the majors].' And I said, 'OK, then I'll do that.' So he traded me to Minnesota, and I switched locker rooms." Kuntz was dealt for minor-league third baseman Mike Sodders, who never made it to the majors.

Two days later, Kuntz appeared against his former team at Comiskey Park, now as a member of the Minnesota Twins. Manager Billy Gardner put Kuntz in the leadoff spot against Chicago lefty Floyd Bannister. "I'm a fourth or fifth outfielder playing sparingly [with Chicago], and now all of a sudden I'm the starting center fielder leading off for the Minnesota Twins," Kuntz said. "So I walk up to the plate…and I look out there and Banny's got his glove over his face. And I'm trying not to smile, too, and, oh, my gosh, it's weird. And I look out there and he's looking in. Okay, so now I put my head down and dig in to the plate. Well, the first pitch he throws to me is right under my chin. I fell flat on my back. I'm like, oh, my God!

"And so as I'm laying there looking up, now I kind of get up, and I'm finding my helmet, I'm finding the bat, I'm looking around," he said. "Well, I put everything on, and I look out there and Banny is like 'Sorry,' you know, one of those it-just-got-away-from-me kind of deals. So now I'm looking around for the helmet. Well, the second pitch that he threw to me was just a fastball [belt high], nothing on it, and I hit a home run. And I hit my first home run against Floyd Bannister."

Kuntz played in just 31 games for the Sox and Twins that year and finished the 1983 season with a combined .211 average, three home runs, and six RBIs. In December he was traded to the Detroit Tigers for pitcher Larry Pashnick.

"At the end of the season I talked to Billy Gardner, and he said there's a good chance that we might trade you because we got a Double-A center fielder that we think is going to be better than you,' he said. "And I'm sitting there thinking, you know, just so naïve: 'Wait a minute, I've been in the big leagues for about four years now, and you're going to

DETROIT TIGERS 1984: WHAT A START! WHAT A FINISH!

bring a Double-A guy up that you think's better than me?' You know, that kind of pompous ass kind of stupid talk. And they said, yeah, he's pretty good, and I said, well, all right. And this is after I hit .200. How in the heck could I say anything? I'm just happy to have a job. But, a Double-A guy? Okay, I want to see this Double-A outfielder that's so hot. Of course, it was Kirby Puckett."

The Tigers assigned Kuntz to the minor-league camp in Lakeland, Florida, for spring training in 1984. Detroit had played several games before he was called over to the big-league facility for a look. When he got to the Tigers' clubhouse, he met briefly with Tigers manager Sparky Anderson. "He said, 'I'm going to play you a lot, as many games as I can, just to see what you can do.'"

As the team prepared to break camp for the 1984 season, Anderson called Kuntz to his office to meet with general manager Bill Lajoie. "They said, 'Okay, here's the deal. We'd like to offer you a big-league contract.' And I go, 'Huh?' And Sparky said, 'Yeah, but here's the deal and here's what I need you to do.' And he laid it all out."

The Tigers' skipper, Kuntz remembered, told him how he'd be used and what the manager needed from him. "Sparky said, 'If you don't want the job, I'm going to give it to [another player], but I'm giving you first choice at it. So you can say yes or you can say no. Now, first thing out of your mouth that you don't want to do it, you don't want to be that [player]? I'll have you out of here in a heartbeat.'"

Anderson told Kuntz that he was never going to start, never going to play more than two games in a row, and never be in the mix of main guys. "You're going to be basically a backup guy, defensive replacement," Kuntz remembered Anderson telling him. "So if you want it, accept your role and be ready.' That's exactly how he used me."

On April 3, 1984–Opening Day—he made his Tigers debut against the Twins as a ninth-inning defensive replacement for Kirk Gibson. On April 13 at Fenway Park in Boston, Kuntz got his first hit as a Tiger, an RBI single off Red Sox left-hander Bruce Hurst. Throughout the first half of the season, Kuntz appeared in games and situations precisely as Anderson and Lajoie had mapped out in spring training. He was batting .432 at the end of May and .311 at the end of June, having already appeared in 50 games.

In midsummer, the Tigers found themselves desperate for pitchers. The club was feeling the crunch of early-season rainouts being made up in the form of multiple doubleheaders. So they sent Kuntz down to the Tigers' Triple-A affiliate, the Evansville (Indiana) Triplets, where he'd have to stay for at least the prescribed 10-day minimum. He said he was confident that he'd be recalled by the Tigers, but understood there was no guarantee. "I had a lot of guys on the team like Dave Bergman, guys that were going, 'Okay, we're on day nine. Okay, now it's day 10. Where is he?'" Kuntz said. "So they were really good about making sure I got called back up there again. [Some players] put pressure on [Tigers management] to have me come up again. That was great to have the teammates pulling for me."

Kuntz was recalled after playing 10 games for Evansville and finished the 1984 season with a .286 average, a pair of home runs and 22 RBIs in 84 games. He had spent the past six months preparing himself for whenever Anderson would call on him. Now, with a 104-win season behind them, Kuntz and his teammates prepared for a much bigger prize.

In Game One of the American League Championship Series, Kuntz pinch-hit for left fielder Ruppert Jones in the top of ninth inning. Facing left-hander Mike Jones of the Kansas City Royals, Kuntz flied out to right field. It was his only plate appearance in the series.

Against the Padres in the World Series, Kuntz appeared in Game Two as a pinch-hitter for Johnny Grubb, and struck out against southpaw Craig Lefferts. In Game Five, with Detroit up three games to one, Kuntz again pinch-hit for Grubb— once more against Lefferts. The game was tied, 3-3, in the fifth inning, and the bases were loaded: Kirk Gibson on third, Larry Herndon on second, and Chet Lemon at first.

"The scouting reporting on Lefferts was [that] he would come in hard early and then throw that little nothing changeup away late. So when you go to the plate, look for that first one to drive," Kuntz said. "Well, I can't tell you what happened because the adrenaline is just overwhelming. When Sparky looks down and says, 'Rusty, grab a bat.' And I'm thinking to myself, 'Oh, my God, I'm actually going to play.'"

"I go up there and I can't feel from nose to toes anyway. So I get in the box and I just remember, 'Okay, now get this guy early. Don't wait around for the nothing changeup.' Okay, here we go. First pitch, is the nothing changeup. I take a full hack and hit right off the end of the bat, and it's a little dying quail going towards right field over the second baseman. Well, they had the infield in, and Alan Wiggins [was] the second baseman and Tony Gwynn was the right fielder. The only thing I remember is hitting that little quail and looking up and go, 'Oh, my God. There's my one chance to do something in my life, and I didn't even get a good pass on it, for crying out loud.' And all of a sudden I look out and I see Gwynn. He's got his hands up in the air and he's looking up and he can't find the ball. And so immediately I turned and here's Wiggins just flying after this baseball. Well, there's no place for me to go because everyone is tagging on it. So I slow up towards first base, I look over my shoulder, and I see Gibby at third base. I'm going, 'Oh, my gosh,' and here he goes. Wiggins catches it. He turns and throws something that rolls over the mound. Gibby steamrolls to the plate and he slides in. When I saw him run and score, I was like hello, baby. Now [the at-bat] turns into a sacrifice fly, and I got an RBI."

The Tigers took a 4-3 lead and never relinquished the lead. So even though Gibson's dramatic rocket shot in the eighth inning off Goose Gossage may have been more emphatic, Kuntz is credited with the game-winning RBI of a World Series-clinching game.

"We started off 35-5, and it just kept steamrolling," he said. "Then we go through the playoffs and the World Series and win a ring. It was just unbelievable. And it was just a wonderful experience to be a part of it."

Kuntz returned to the Tigers in 1985 but appeared in only five hitless games before spending the rest of the season with Detroit's new Triple-A affiliate, the Nashville Sounds. He hit only a dispirited .222 for Nashville and on October 9 he was released by the Tigers. He was 30 years old. Two months after his release, he signed as a free agent with the Oakland Athletics but never appeared in another game—major or minor league.

With his playing career over, Kuntz spent the 1986 season delivering packages for UPS in the Stanislaus area. But he wasn't out of baseball for long. In the winter of 1987, the Houston Astros hired him as their roving minor-league outfield and baserunning coach, a role in which he served again in 1988. The following season, Kuntz was hired by Seattle Mariners manager Jim Lefebvre to be the team's first-base coach. That same year, Kuntz married the former Salli Elmore. In 1990, the couple's son, Kevin, was born. Kuntz coached in Seattle until 1993, when he took a coaching position with the Florida Marlins; it's also where, in 1997, he earned a second World Series ring. Next he moved to the Pittsburgh organization, first as the Pirates' first-base coach and then as a roving outfield instructor.

Kuntz was the Kansas City Royals' first base coach in 2008 and 2009. In 2010 the Royals named him an assistant to the general manager/field instructor, a role that focuses on player instruction at the big-league and minor-league levels. But during an in-season managerial change, Kuntz was installed as the club's third base coach.

References

Web Sites

Baseball-Reference.com, http://www.baseballreference.com, Rusty Kuntz Baseball-Reference.com page: http://www.baseball-reference.com/k/kuntzru01.shtml

Cal State-Stanislaus Hall of Fame page: http://www.warriorathletics.com/sports/2007/8/28/GEN_0828074000.aspx?tab=halloffame

NCAA Division III College World Series page: http://www.ncaa.com/history/default.aspx?id=87924

1977 College World Series statistics page: http://www.odaconline.com/div3base/1977/champ1977.htm

Rusty Kuntz bio on Royals.com: http://kansascity.royals.mlb.com/team/coach_staff_bio.jsp?c_id=kc&coachorstaffid=117366

Nashville Sounds Web site—team history: http://www.nashvillesounds.com/clubhouse/history.asp

Other Sources

McClary, Mike. Interview with Rusty Kuntz, Surprise, Arizona, March 6, 2008.

Mike Laga
by David Laurila

MIKE LAGA never did live up to his promise and become a star, but the erstwhile slugger does have his niche in Detroit Tigers history. A prolific home-run hitter in the minor leagues, Laga played parts of five seasons in a Detroit uniform, including the magical summer of 1984 when he appeared in nine games. While he was little more than a footnote in the championship season, the man who would one day be dubbed "Laga Beer" by ESPN's Chris Berman delivered six hits in 11 at-bats for a team-best .545 average.

Born on June 14, 1960, in Ridgewood, New Jersey, Michael Russell Laga grew up in nearby Ramsey in a working-class family. His father was a television repairman, and his mother both a homemaker and, in the words of her only son, "transportation for me and my three sisters; I was always keeping them busy with sports, because I played baseball, soccer, and basketball, so it was constantly go, go, go."

Despite his success on the baseball diamond, Laga went undrafted out of high school and enrolled at nearby Fairleigh Dickinson University, where he played half of one season before transferring to Bergen (New Jersey) Community College. It was there that Laga's smooth left-handed stroke began catching the attention of scouts, and in the January phase of the 1980 draft the Tigers took him with their first pick.

"It wasn't until that actual phone call came from [Tigers general manager] Bill Lajoie that I realized, 'Wow, this could be kind of neat, getting paid to play baseball,'" Laga remembered. "Before that, I was just playing. I never had great dreams of becoming a professional baseball player."

Laga reported to spring training a few months later, and it didn't take long for him to begin making an impression. "My first year I got assigned to A-ball in Lakeland," he said. "I think I had been earmarked for rookie league ball, in Bristol, Virginia, but I did so well in spring training that they moved me up to the A-class."

Laga adapted quickly to professional baseball, hitting a solid .273 with 12 home runs and 74 RBIs in 407 at-bats against Florida State League pitching. His home run and RBI totals led the team, with Lakeland Tigers teammate Howard Johnson ranking a close second in each category. He also logged an impressive .391 on-base percentage, but it was his emerging power that portended a future in the big leagues. Ironically, he credited a notoriously light-hitting shortstop for his home-run stroke.

"When I signed, I was mostly a line-drive hitter," he said. "My first manager was Eddie Brinkman, and he really started working with me on getting the head of the bat out and being more aggressive at the plate. Once I got to Double-A, and Triple-A, I was hitting a lot of home runs because I had learned to do that. Eddie was also a funny man and really relaxed us. He made us enjoy the game rather than just trying to get better all the time."

Brinkman's advice about not taking things too seriously came in handy during Laga's maiden season. In what can now be remembered as a funny moment, the nervous first-year player came to work one day without an important piece of equipment.

"We drove down to Miami for a four-game series," Laga said, "and when I got there I opened up my equipment bag and realized that I had forgotten my glove. And not only was I our first baseman, I was one of the few left-handed throwers on the team. I ended up borrowing one from one of our pitchers, and got through the first inning with it, and then it rained for the next four days straight, so it turned out that I didn't even need a glove. Boy, did I luck out there."

In 1981, Laga turned his bat into a good-luck charm. With his power now in full force, he tore up the Southern League, bashing 31 home runs to go with a .289 average and 86 RBIs in 547 at-bats for Double-A Birmingham. Most impressively, his slugging average was a hefty .536. At the age of 21, Bill and Carole Laga's son had established himself as one of the top prospects in the Tigers organization.

In 1982, Laga moved up to Triple-A Evansville, where his batting average dropped to .250, but the light-tower power—his ticket to "The Show"—was still very much in evidence. In just 444 at-bats, the lefty slugger set an Evansville team record by going deep 34 times to go with a .527 slugging percentage.

When the minor-league season came to an end, Laga got the call he was waiting for, and on September 1, he made his big-league debut at Tiger Stadium, going hitless in two at-bats with a walk against the California Angels. The next day he was back in the starting lineup and rapped out the first of his 84 big-league hits, off Angels right-hander Mike Witt. And he drove in his first two runs.

"I remember that my first hit was a double," Laga said. "It was in the gap and rolling around in the outfield, and I probably could have very easily have made it to third base, but I was nervous and hyped up and just kind of stopped at second. Ironically, throughout my big-league career, I didn't have any triples, so looking back, I should have gone." A day later, Laga went deep for the first time, driving a pitch from Oakland's Rick Langford into the Tiger Stadium cheap seats. Later in the month, on the 17th, in jaw-dropping fashion, he hit one even farther, off Boston's Brian Denman.

Then, on the 29th, after a conversation with a Detroit sportswriter, Laga launched a bomb off a future Hall of Famer.

"Because he knew that I was a home-run hitter, he asked me about the short porch in right field, and about how sometimes balls would go clear over the roof and out of the stadium," Laga recalled. "I don't know if the reporter was baiting me, or what, but he asked me, 'Mike, do you think you can do that?' and I said, 'Sure, why not? It doesn't look that far.' The next day, when I went into the clubhouse, the guys were giving me a hard time about that. We were playing against the Orioles that day, and Jim Palmer was pitching, and he hung an 0-2 curveball that I hit over the roof and onto the lumber yard. They didn't say much after I went back into the dugout besides 'Congratulations,' but after the game they were like, 'OK, we'll leave you alone now.'"

Overall, Laga had 23 hits in his first taste of big-league action, including nine doubles and three home runs, in 88 at-bats for a .261 average. The future loomed bright for the young power hitter. Or so it seemed.

Laga had high hopes for the 1983 season, but instead of establishing himself as a big-league run producer, he languished in Evansville, hitting a disappointing .231 with just 16 home runs in 355 at-bats. "My expectations were that I wanted to stay with the team," Laga said. His slugging average was just .439 against International League pitching that year. "I'm sure that it affected my mindset to have broken the [Evansville] home run record one year, and gone up to the big leagues and done [all right], and then gotten sent back down. I'm sure that sometimes it was hard for me to focus. But I did understand the situation. At that point, the Tigers were a very competitive team and were trying to get where they ultimately were in 1984, which was a team with wire-to-wire great players. Darrell Evans was in front of me at first base, and he was a 40-home run guy in both leagues; he was certainly a great hitter."

Despite his disappointing performance at Evansville, Laga again received a September call-up, but this time got only 21 at-bats over 12 games. He did little to impress, producing just four singles, for a .190 average, while striking out nine times.

Laga got married after the season, but little else changed for the aspiring power hitter in 1984. Once again unable to earn a spot on what would soon prove to be baseball's best team, Laga left spring training with his ticket punched to Evansville for the third straight year. He was able to rebound with the bat, hitting .265 with 30 home runs and a .508 slugging percentage, but the logjam that had held him back in previous seasons was still there, and Laga remained in Triple-A until September. When he finally did join Sparky Anderson's club, he saw action in just nine games, and of his six hits, four came off the bench in his only at-bat of that particular contest. His pinch-single on September 7 ignited a three-run 10th-inning rally against the Blue Jays in Exhibition Stadium. For Laga, it was emblematic of both his 6-for-11 cameo performance and the Tigers' remarkable season.

"I remember Alan Trammell getting real mad at me," said Laga, who surprisingly didn't receive a World Series ring for his efforts. "He was saying, 'Hey, can we get this guy some more at-bats so we can get his batting average down?' He

DETROIT TIGERS 1984: WHAT A START! WHAT A FINISH!

knew that when everybody looked at the stats for that year they were going to see: 'Mike Laga .545.' He was kidding, of course, about not wanting to see my name above his, but it just happened that everything worked out for me with the at-bats I did get. I remember one time up, in Toronto, I got the crap jammed out of me but blooped the ball over the second baseman's head for a base hit. Of course, everything went right for the whole team that year. To start out 35 and 5, and then crush everybody in the playoffs—all the bounces went the right way and all the balls stayed fair for us; all the breaks happened in the Tigers' favor that year."

Laga was on the cusp of his 25th birthday when the 1985 season got under way, and with Darrell Evans not getting any younger, the time appeared ripe for the young slugger to earn a spot in the Detroit lineup. Once again it was not to be. The ageless Evans continued to knock home runs out of Tiger Stadium, while Laga had to settle for hitting his—20 in 430 at-bats—for Detroit's new Triple-A affiliate in Nashville. It was a situation Laga would find himself in throughout his career, as his path to the big leagues was continually blocked by All-Star performers at his first-base position. For a player who had nothing left to prove at the Triple-A level, it was a frustrating series of circumstances.

"As a younger kid hitting 30 home runs a year, I was one of those guys where it was, 'You don't want to get rid of this guy, because he might come back and hurt you,'" Laga said. "But yet, you can't exactly move guys like Evans, Jack Clark, or Will Clark, because they're All-Stars. So I kind of got stuck. Had I been with a team that was losing 100 games a year, maybe I would have played more and got better chances."

There was no September call-up for Laga in 1985, although he did get a brief opportunity earlier in the season, starting nine games between May 15 and May 26, all on the road. Despite a pair of home runs, he did little to state his case, producing just six hits in 36 at-bats.

In 1986, Laga earned a spot on the Tigers' Opening Day roster for the first time. With Evans, by this time 39 years old, getting many of his at-bats as a designated hitter, Laga received a number of starts at first base in April. He struggled early, going just one for his first 14, but then he began to heat up, stroking seven hits in his next 17 at-bats, including three home runs. One of them came on April 29 at Tiger Stadium when he homered in the seventh inning to break a 1-1 tie and give Detroit a 2-1 win against the Kansas City Royals. It was his last home run, and last RBI, in a Tigers uniform.

Laga appeared in just five more games before injuring his wrist, and then on September 2 he was announced as the player to be named later in the August 10 deal that brought Mike Heath to Detroit. Laga was now a St. Louis Cardinal.

Laga made a good first impression with his new team, going deep in just his second at-bat, but it was a ball he pulled foul, the following day, that would attract the most attention. On September 15, Laga became the only player ever to hit a ball completely out of the old Busch Stadium.

"We were playing the Mets, and going against Ron Darling," Laga remembered. "He tried to throw a fastball up and in, and I just turned on it. I hit it clear over the light tower and up and out of the stadium. Gary Carter was the catcher, and we were just standing there when this little roar started in the crowd, with people clapping and standing up. I didn't know what was going on. ... I looked at Carter and said, 'What's going on? What's all this noise about?' He said, 'You just hit the ball out of the bleeping stadium!?' [Laga actually used the word "bleeping" in recounting the tale.] About five seconds later they put up on the scoreboard that it was the first ball ever hit out of Busch Stadium, either fair or foul. It was kind of neat, and not too many months go by where somebody doesn't mention that to me."

Laga was in the Cardinals' starting lineup 11 times in September, but outside of three home runs and the loud foul ball, his bat was mostly quiet. In 46 at-bats, he had just 10 hits to go with 18 strikeouts.

In 1987, for the second consecutive season, Laga was on an Opening Day roster. Unfortunately, there was little playing time to be had behind Jack Clark, and despite homering in his first game, by the end of April he was sent down to Louisville, having come to the plate just 12 times. Back in Triple-A, Laga proved yet again what he could do when given regular at-bats: hit for power. The powerful first sacker went deep 29 times in just 418 at-bats, hitting a career-best .304 with a sizable .605 slugging percentage. In yet another September call-up that featured limited at-bats, Laga went 4-for-29 with one home run. Starting just a handful of games, he saw most of his action as a pinch-hitter or defensive replacement.

The 1988 campaign proved to be one of the most frustrating of his career. With Jack Clark having left the Cardinals via free agency, Laga came into spring training slotted to back up the newly acquired Bob Horner at first base, but once again things didn't go his way.

"In the spring of '88, I separated my shoulder and broke my collarbone," Laga said, "and I ended up being out until mid-July. It wasn't until the first week of July that they even let me start moving my arm. That's when they said, 'OK, you can start swinging the bat gently now,' and within a week they had me out of rehab and in the big leagues. They said, 'Listen, we don't care what you hit; we want you here for your defense,' and that was all I could give them, because I had no strength in my shoulder, or arm, at all."

Laga went on to start 24 games between mid-July and mid-August—the longest stretch of big-league playing time of his career—but the results were predictable. Unable to swing the bat with any authority because of the injury, he struggled through the worst power outage of his career, belting just one home run in an even 100 at-bats. He hit just .130.

Released by the Cardinals in November, Laga signed as a free agent with San Francisco in January 1989 and spent the 1989 and 1990 seasons in the Giants organization. Following his career pattern, most of his time was spent in Triple-A, as he accumulated just 47 big-league at-bats, hitting .191 with three home runs over the two seasons. As always, his minor-league power numbers were good. In 758 at-bats as a member of the Pacific Coast League's Phoenix Firebirds, Laga went deep 45 times. In what turned out to be his final season of professional baseball in the United States, he hit .298, with a .589 slugging percentage, for Phoenix in 1990. Overall, he had played 11 minor-league seasons, mostly at Triple-A, hitting .267 with 220 home runs and an eye-opening .506 slugging percentage. Laga's big-league career had spanned parts of nine seasons—five with the Tigers and two each with the Cardinals and Giants—and he finished with a .199 average and 16 home runs.

Looking for a change of scenery after being released by the Giants near the end of October, Laga spent the 1991 and 1992 seasons playing in Japan, with the Daiei Hawks. It was a unique experience, and one that he enjoyed. "It was a whole different mindset of baseball," said Laga, who hit 31 home runs for Daiei in 1991. "The ball still has to go over the plate, and you have to hit, run, and play defense, but the Japanese fans are a whole level above American fans. They have songs for each player, and when that player comes up they play the song. They have flags, there are cheers, and if it's 15-0 in a monsoon they're still there cheering their team. There are times when any player isn't going to play well, but as long as you're busting your butt, they appreciated that. I look back at that those two years in Japan as a wonderful time."

Laga returned home before the 1993 season and, still just 32 years old, signed with the Atlanta Braves, who were looking for someone to back up first baseman Sid Bream and serve as a left-handed pinch-hitter. The veteran slugger appeared to be a good fit for that role, but the up-and-coming Ryan Klesko won the job thanks to an outstanding spring training, and Laga was assigned to Triple-A. It was an assignment he was willing to accept, but the Braves changed their mind and asked him to play in Mexico, where they had a working agreement with a team in Nuevo Laredo/Laredo. Laga refused the assignment, and was subsequently suspended, which resulted in several months of inactivity while the issue was litigated. The situation was resolved by midsummer, but by then Laga had made a decision: His playing days were over, and he would go to the University of Massachusetts to finish his degree.

Residing in Western Massachusetts in 2010, Laga remained involved in the game he played professionally for more than a decade. Employed as a loan officer for Applied Mortgage, he also spent his spare time running the Mike Laga Youth Baseball Association of Northampton. He and his wife, Robyn, have a daughter, Ashley, and two sons, Kyle and Jake.

References

Web Sites

baseball-almanac.com

baseball-reference.com

retrosheet.org

thebaseballcube.com

Other Sources

Laurila, David. Interview with Mike Laga, September 2008.

Laurila, David. Interview with Mike Laga, October 2009.

Chet Lemon
by Mike McClary

BASEBALL FANS who watched Chet Lemon during his 16-year major-league career likely recall the speedy outfielder racing across the field at Comiskey Park or Tiger Stadium to track down a line drive headed for the gap. Just as likely, they can still see him diving headlong into first base or getting hit by a pitch. But fans of the Chicago White Sox and Detroit Tigers, especially those who watched him day in and day out, remember him as being hard-nosed in the field and dangerous at the plate.

Chester Earl Lemon was born in Jackson, Mississippi, on February 12, 1955. Though his roots were in the Gulf Coast, Lemon's baseball star began to rise in Southern California. He starred at Fremont High School in Los Angeles—a pipeline for big leaguers from that era including Willie Crawford, Bob Watson, Bobby Tolan, and George Hendrick. On June 6, 1972, the Oakland Athletics selected him in the first round of the amateur draft with the 22nd overall pick.

Lemon was signed by A's scout Phil Pote and at the age of 17 arrived in Oregon to join his first professional club, the short-season Coos Bay-North Bend A's. Playing third base and shortstop, Lemon appeared in 38 games and batted .286 with a pair of home runs. Later in the season he moved on to the Burlington (Iowa) Bees of the Midwest League and joined future major leaguers Dan Ford and Champ Summers for the balance of the 1972 season. Lemon hit .256 in 36 games, primarily at third base. He returned to Burlington in 1973 for his first full season in the minors and posted sterling numbers—a .309 average, 19 home runs, 88 runs batted in, and a .513 slugging percentage—while holding down third base for the Bees.

In 1974 Oakland promoted Lemon to the Double-A Birmingham A's of the Southern League, and his performance didn't disappoint—at least at the plate. He finished the year at .290, which was good for second on the A's roster, but still

DETROIT TIGERS 1984: WHAT A START! WHAT A FINISH!

71 points behind team leader and future White Sox teammate Claudell Washington. In the field, however, Lemon gave the A's an early indication that his future wasn't likely to include an infielder's glove: He made 19 errors at third and another four at shortstop—down from 36 errors the year before.

Lemon's porous defense didn't prevent the A's from promoting him to Triple-A Tucson of the Pacific Coast League for the 1975 season—nor did it nudge them toward identifying a new position for the 20-year-old. Nevertheless, Lemon continued to hit, batting .280 with the Toros. Two months into the season, on June 15, Lemon's career took an unexpected turn when he was traded to the Chicago White Sox organization for pitchers Stan Bahnsen and Skip Pitlock.

"I had first come up with the A's in 1974," Lemon said. "It was myself and Claudell Washington, who'd later come to the Sox. I wasn't able to play, though, because I was recovering from a broken ankle. I was ready to play in 1975 but had nowhere to play. I was an infielder and Oakland had guys like Sal Bando and Bert Campaneris in those positions. I had heard a lot of talk about teams being interested in me. When I found out about the deal I thought it was a great move. I was finally going to get my chance—and in a big market as well."

Roland Hemond, White Sox general manager from 1971 to 1985, made the deal for Lemon and remembered when he first heard of him. "Jim Napier was the manager of our Knoxville club and he saw Chet play in the Southern League in 1974; he thought he could be a good player for us," Hemond recalled. "Chet had good running speed and a good arm but he wasn't accurate with his throws. So we sent him to Hermosillo, Mexico, in the winter and they said, 'This kid's got an arm but he's throwing the ball all over the field.' In spring training 1976 our manager, Paul Richards, started hitting fly balls to Chet and told him, 'You're now a center fielder.'"

Lemon remembered his move to the outfield more vividly. "In late 1975 when I was with the Sox, I was at third base and a groundball was hit towards the middle. I started running and cut in front of the shortstop and actually wound up around Jorge Orta—at second base," he said. "The very next day I was on the top step of the dugout, it was early in the day since I'd always be one of the first guys to show up. Chuck Tanner, the Sox manager, came up, put his arm around my shoulder and said—and I can remember this like it was yesterday—'Son, I want you to start taking 100 fly balls a day because if you stay an infielder you're gonna kill somebody.'"

On September 9, 1975, Lemon made his major-league debut, against the California Angels' Jim Brewer, grounding out to first base in the ninth inning of a 5-4 loss at Comiskey. Ten days later he got his first big-league start at third base—batting seventh—against the Rangers in Chicago. His first major-league hit, a single to right, came in the bottom of the second inning off Steve Hargan; he scooted to second base courtesy of an error by Texas right fielder Jeff Burroughs. Lemon finished the game 1-for-4 with a run scored and was flawless in the field, notching three putouts and a pair of assists. All told, he appeared in nine games that season, batting .257 and committing one error at third base and none in the outfield.

The 1976 season was one of dramatic change for both the White Sox and Lemon. Paul Richards replaced Tanner at the helm, owner Bill Veeck unveiled a set of retro uniforms with collars and, on some occasions, short pants, and Lemon became the White Sox' new leadoff hitter and center fielder. Six weeks into season, he hit his first major-league home run. "It was off Frank Tanana of the Angels," Lemon said. "They were beating us and I took him into the upper deck. After the game I remember hearing him on the radio and he said something like, 'Well we had a big lead and I just threw the rookie a changeup.' I thought to myself, 'OK, I'm going to own you from now on.' And I did. He even came up to me one time and told me that I owned him." (Lemon's final career stats against Tanana: a .272 average with six homers and 20 RBIs in 94 plate appearances. Only Rickey Henderson, with 11, and Mark McGwire, with seven, hit more homers off Tanana than Lemon; one has to keep in mind, moreover, that Lemon and Tanana were teammates on the Detroit Tigers from June 20, 1985, through the 1990 season.) The White Sox finished sixth in the American League West that year at 64-97 but the groundwork was set for an exciting 1977 for the club—and for their center fielder.

Entering his third season in the majors, Chet Lemon found himself playing for another Lemon—Bob—and Chet saw his career trajectory soar. He had a solid year at the plate—a .273 average, 19 homers, and 67 RBIs—and was an essential part of a club that White Sox fans dubbed the South Side Hit Men. Lemon, Richie Zisk, Eric Soderholm, and Oscar Gamble powered an offense that scored 884 runs and fueled the South Siders' 26-game improvement from 1976. The club finished third with a 90-72 record—four games back of the Rangers and a dozen behind the powerhouse Kansas City Royals.

"You know, that 1977 team was a lot like the Tigers team that won it all in 1984. Those guys played the game hard, they wanted to win," Lemon said. "We were close to winning it that season, a lot closer than people thought. We believed we could win it but we came up short in the pitching department. The Sox just weren't able to get the help that we needed to put us over the top. Still that club did some extraordinary things."

Lemon's 509 putouts in center field in 1977 set a major-league record that still stood in 2013. This factoid remains Lemon's greatest accomplishment and says a lot about his incredible talent and will forever be his legacy. It's one reason he was known as Chet the Jet; while not the greatest of baserunners, his speed in the field enabled him to catch many balls that would have dropped in for hits.

Lemon took another step forward in 1978 when he was named to the American League All-Star team—he entered the game as a defensive replacement for Jim Rice in the eighth—and hit an even .300 for the first time. He returned to the All-Star Game in 1979 and saw action almost immediately. In the second inning, he replaced Fred Lynn in center field and came

DETROIT TIGERS 1984: WHAT A START! WHAT A FINISH!

Given Chet Lemon's longevity of service to the Detroit Tigers, combined with his defensive prowess and offensive skills while with the club, some consider him to be the franchise's second-best center fielder in team history, below only Hall of Famer Sam Crawford. (National Baseball Hall of Fame Library, Cooperstown, New York)

to the plate in the third against the Astros' Joaquin Andujar. Lemon was hit by Andujar's pitch and later came around to score. He finished the game 0-for-2 with a walk and the HBP.

"It was a great feeling to be recognized as one of the best players," Lemon said of his All-Star selections. "What also was nice was getting to know the other guys. You realize that they are all just like you. I think you appreciate the [All-Star] game more as a young player and as an older player. When you're young it's a real thrill being there. When you're older you appreciate how much the game means to you. It's during that 'middle' period when you seem to lose focus. That's when you hear guys gripe that they should be there but aren't and act like they don't care."

Getting hit by Andujar's pitch in the All-Star tilt was nothing new for Lemon, particularly in 1979, when he led the league with 13 HBPs. He was hit 11 times in 1980, though it wasn't enough to lead the American League. But from 1981 through '83 he led the league in the category with an average of 16 bruising passes to first base. The reason Lemon was plunked with such regularity was his batting stance, which put him right on top of the plate. "I don't think I realized that I was that close to the plate," he said. "You know, I actually didn't mind being pitched inside, I wanted to be pitched inside. I felt I could always turn on pitches. If you look at my hits, like all those doubles, I think you'll find that I went down the left-field line in most of them. Larry Doby taught me a lot about hitting. He was my manager with the Sox for a while. He'd always say that I had one of the quickest bats through the strike zone he ever saw, so I didn't need to try to do too much."

The 1979 campaign turned out to be Lemon's finest all-around offensive season. In addition to leading the American League with 44 doubles, he set career highs in average (.318) and RBIs (86) and hit 17 home runs—more than his career average of 13 per season. In 1980 he crafted another sturdy year: .292 with 11 homers. His average broke the .300 mark again in the strike-shortened 1981 season, when he hit .302 with nine home runs and 50 RBIs. After that season, Lemon's time in Chicago came to an end. Just after Thanksgiving 1981, he was traded to the Tigers for outfielder Steve Kemp.

"In spring training 1981 I had verbally agreed to a five-year contract that would have made me the highest-paid player on the team. It was a great negotiation. [New White Sox owners] Eddie Einhorn, Jerry Reinsdorf, Roland Hemond, my agent and I all sat around a table one day and worked everything out, including some deferred compensation," Lemon said. "For some reason I hadn't gotten around to actually signing the document, though. A few weeks later they signed Carlton Fisk and his [salary] numbers came out. When I saw those I told my agent, 'Maybe we need to renegotiate.' Everything that I did in five years, I did in Chicago and now I wasn't going to be the highest-paid player anymore. I know it was childish on my part but that's the way I felt at the time."

Hemond described the trade as simply talent-for-talent. "Chet was going to be a free agent and we knew we wouldn't be able to afford the amount of money he'd command," Hemond said, "so we traded him to Detroit for Steve Kemp, who had a great year for us in 1982, driving in more than 90 runs [actually 98]."

It was clear the Tigers saw the deal as talent-for-talent as well, even though both players had prickly contract negotiations with their original clubs. Tigers General Manager Jim Campbell saw Lemon as a big piece of the Detroit lineup in 1982. "Lemon is a player we've had our eyes on for a long time," Campbell said. "He hits for power and average and is one of the better defensive outfielders in our league."

When Lemon arrived in Lakeland, Florida, for his first spring training as a member of the Tigers, manager Sparky Anderson had him penciled in as the Tigers' leadoff hitter and right fielder, shifting from center to accommodate up-and-comer Kirk Gibson. Pulled rib-cage muscles shelved Lemon for the final two weeks of Grapefruit League action, delaying his regular-season Tigers debut until the sixth game of the year, against the Toronto Blue Jays at Exhibition Stadium in Toronto. In the ninth inning, the Tigers were down 4-0 and Lemon was called on to pinch-hit for Richie Hebner. He promptly stroked a single to center, driving in two runs, as Detroit battled back to tie the game, though they eventually lost 5-4. The next day Lemon played in his first opening day at Tiger Stadium in a Detroit uniform and led off the bottom

DETROIT TIGERS 1984: WHAT A START! WHAT A FINISH!

of the first with a single. In his second at-bat, naturally, Lemon was hit by a Dave Stieb pitch. He remained almost exclusively the Tigers' leadoff hitter through late June, when he began bouncing from second in the order to seventh, and all points in between. He finished his first year in Detroit with a .266 average, 19 home runs, and 52 RBIs. Defensively, Lemon played 96 games in right field and 27 in center—the position he'd soon call home for good.

In 1983 Lemon played all but two games in center field and cemented himself as the Tigers' fifth-place hitter. On July 24 he made a game-saving catch that ranks as one of the finest of his time in Detroit. The Tigers and Angels played a nail-biter in Anaheim and Detroit took a 4-3 lead in the top of the 12th on a home run by Lance Parrish. In the bottom of the inning, with the tying run at first and two out, Angels first basemen Rod Carew launched an Aurelio Lopez pitch to the deepest part of Angels Stadium. Lemon turned, tracked the ball, and with impeccable precision leaped to take away a game-winning home run with a beyond-the-wall catch, securing the win and keeping Detroit a half-game behind the Baltimore Orioles. The Tigers finished 1983 six games back of Baltimore, and were confident of what the emerging club could accomplish in 1984. For the first time in his career, Lemon eclipsed the 20-homer mark, finishing the '83 season with 24 round-trippers to go along with a .255 average and 69 RBIs.

Now in the prime of his career, Chet Lemon was an indispensable component of Sparky Anderson's lineup and the Tigers' strength-up-the-middle core of catcher Parrish, shortstop Alan Trammell, second baseman Lou Whitaker, and Lemon. "Chet Lemon is the best center fielder in the game in either league today," Anderson said in 1984. "He isn't the fastest, but he's the best at it because he works harder at it than anyone else." Baseball fans agreed and voted him to his third All-Star appearance, where he joined Parrish and Whitaker in the starting lineup. (Teammates Trammell, Jack Morris, and Willie Hernandez were selected as reserves by the American League manager, the Orioles' Joe Altobelli.)

As the Tigers marched through the regular-season schedule toward the playoffs, Lemon was carving out his finest season in Detroit, hitting .287 with 34 doubles, 20 home runs, and 76 RBIs. "After watching Chester the last several years, I have to say without a doubt, he's the best center fielder I've seen in my 31 years in the game," Anderson said. "Chester is a Pete Rose type. He never complains. He's always there and he plays each game as if it were the seventh game of the World Series. Chester doesn't know any other way to play and that's his greatest asset. Combine all that with his little-boy desire to want to play every day and it is no wonder Chester has all those fans who sit in the bleachers in the palm of his hand."

In the three-game American League Championship Series against the Kansas City Royals, Lemon went hitless but scored the lone run in the Game Three as the Tigers clinched the franchise's first pennant since 1968. In the World Series, he showed the rest of the country what Tigers fans had grown accustomed to. In Game Three, an otherwise ugly game, Lemon dazzled.

With two out in the top of the eighth inning of a 5-2 game with Detroit in the lead and the Padres' Steve Garvey on third base, Sparky Anderson summoned lefty reliever Willie Hernandez to face the left-handed-hitting Terry Kennedy, the Padres' catcher. Kennedy laced a full-count pitch to center and sent Lemon scurrying deeper and deeper into Tiger Stadium's vast center field. As Tom Gage of the *Detroit News* described it, Lemon "backpedaled, turned, twisted, and made a fine catch."

"When the ball was hit I went back as far as I could," Lemon said. "I had been playing shallow because we watched (Kennedy) in San Diego and with two strikes he'd just be trying to make contact. After I got back on it, I just looked up, reached up, and it was there. The rest is history." The Padres were left shaking their heads. "We still had a chance if Lemon doesn't make that catch," Steve Garvey said. At the plate, Lemon stroked two singles and scored on Marty Castillo's two-run homer in the third. But in a game mired by 14 men left on base by the Tigers and 11 walks by three Padres pitchers, "(Lemon's catch) was the only tingle of the night," wrote Joe Falls of the *News*. Lemon batted .294 in the Tigers' four-games-to-one World Series victory.

He maintained his sturdy and reliable play for Detroit over the next three seasons, averaging 139 games in the field and 17 home runs at the plate. In 1987 the Tigers made a late-season charge into the playoffs by sweeping the Toronto Blue Jays on the final weekend of the season to capture the American League East title. Though the Tigers lost in five games to an overachieving Minnesota Twins club, Lemon had his best postseason, batting .274 with a pair of home runs in the American League Championship Series.

The next season, 1988, he found himself moving back to right field, making way for newly acquired center fielder Gary Pettis. It was also Lemon's last season as an offensive threat for the Tigers; he hit .264 with 17 home runs. Though he was still a regular in the lineup in 1989 and '90, he was watching his career draw to a close. On April 5, 1991, at the end of spring training, the Tigers gave the 35-year-old Lemon his unconditional release.

It was during that final spring in Lakeland that Lemon noticed a change in his health. "I had noticed that it was taking me longer to heal from injuries. I remember saying to myself, 'Am I getting old?' because I always took care of myself," he remembered. "In spring training 1991 the Tigers discovered that I had too many red blood cells in my body. The Tigers thought the numbers they got were wrong. My stomach was always hurting. I thought maybe I had an ulcer or it was just stress. The doctors couldn't find out what was causing it. They finally did an ultrasound and discovered that I had tiny little blood clots in my portal veins. My illness is usually found in older men of Jewish decent, it's practically never found in African-American men, especially in the shape that I was in. About 30 minutes after they discovered that, I was rushed to intensive care, hooked up to machines and given blood thinners. Not only did I have blood clots but I had too much blood and it was too thick, like a slush. The doctors were fearful that if one of those clots became loose… well, you know what happens when that takes place."

Lemon nearly died from his blood disorder, polycythemia vera. He spent nearly three months in the hospital in the spring of 1991. "I was in incredible pain. Just trying to turn over in bed was agonizing. I was being fed intravenously. I did not want to eat, I couldn't eat. I lost about 60 or 70 pounds and was down to about 130 pounds," he said. "I remember seeing ESPN do my eulogy. There was no way to have any type of major surgery done because I was on blood thinners to prevent clots. If they tried to operate I'd bleed to death. My (religious) faith [Lemon is a Jehovah's Witness] prohibits me from receiving blood transfusions so I'd never make it through. If they took me off the blood thinners my blood would thicken up again and I could die because of a clot."

After intensive treatment, Lemon rebounded from his illness and began coaching high-school baseball in the Central Florida area. In 1993 he started the Chet Lemon School of Baseball, and became the president of the Amateur Athletic Union district near Orlando.

His on-field performance over his 16 seasons—1,988 games played, .273 average, 215 home runs, and 884 RBIs—illustrate best what Roland Hemond, the man who acquired Lemon in 1975, said about him: "Chet was a tough kid. Great attitude, great player."

Lemon and his wife, the former Valerie Jones, have four children, Geneva, Chester, Jr., David, and Marcus. Marcus Lemon spent six seasons as a shortstop, second baseman and left fielder in the Texas and Atlanta systems before joining the Detroit organization in 2012.

References

Publications

Anderson, Sparky. *Bless You Boys: Diary of the Detroit Tigers' 1984 Season*. Chicago: Contemporary Books. 1984.

Detroit Tigers. *Detroit Tigers 1984 Media Guide*. Detroit: Detroit Tigers. 1984.

Detroit Tigers. *Detroit Tigers 1987 Media Guide*. Detroit: Detroit Tigers. 1987.

Articles

Associated Press. "Chet Lemon Is Placed On Waivers by Tigers." *New York Times*, April 6, 1991.

Associated Press. "Kemp Traded for Lemon." *Toledo Blade*, November 28, 1981.

Falls, Joe. "51,970 found guilty of impersonating Tiger fans." *Detroit News*, October. 13, 1984.

Henning, Lynn. "Lemon's catch a-Mays-ing as he thwarts comeback." *Detroit News*, October 13, 1983.

Web Sites

Chet Lemon's Baseball-Reference.com page: http://www.baseball-reference.com/players/l/lemonch01.shtml.

White Sox Interactive interview with Chet Lemon: http://www.whitesoxinteractive.com/rwas/index.php?category=11&id=2719.

www.baseball-reference.com.

Other Sources

McClary, Mike. Telephone interview with Roland Hemond, November 13, 2009.

Aurelio Lopez
by Gary Gillette

TWO WORDS: Señor Smoke. Hernandez/Lopez. Things Change. Take your pick of the trio of descriptions that defined Aurelio Lopez's baseball career.

Things change. That's a truism that, in its pithy wisdom, fails to reveal that perceptions of the past—even the recent past—can vary so widely from those of contemporary observers.

Ask any Tigers fan today who the team's biggest pitching stars were in that glorious summer of 1984. The first two answers will surely be Jack Morris and Willie Hernandez. Many also will remember Dan Petry, and maybe even a couple will mention Milt Wilcox. Those few who remember Aurelio Lopez, stalwart reliever and mainstay of the 1984 championship club's bullpen, will usually accompany their recollection with a smile while blurting out Lopez's nickname, Señor Smoke.

For cultural reasons, Señor Smoke connotes something very different north of the U.S.-Mexico border than south of it. Among Tigers fans of a certain age scattered throughout the States, Señor Smoke is a sobriquet for a Latino relief pitcher who threw hard and pitched well. However, while affectionately used, it is not a term of the highest respect like

DETROIT TIGERS 1984: WHAT A START! WHAT A FINISH!

Hammerin' Hank (applied to the dominant slugger Hank Greenberg) or Prince Hal (applied to two-time American League Most Valuable Player Hal Newhouser).

Of course, both Greenberg and Newhouser were truly great players who became Hall of Famers, while Lopez was not. But Aurelio Lopez was substantially better than most U.S. fans now remember, and the hard-throwing hurler remains a legend in his native land. Lopez was so much more than just another hard-throwing relief pitcher with a terrific nickname.

Beat writer Tom Gage has covered the Tigers for the *Detroit News* for the past quarter-century. Back when *The Sporting News* was still called the Bible of Baseball, Gage wrote the Detroit season-in-review essays for its authoritative annual *Guide*.

In the 1984 edition of *The Sporting News Guide*, Gage wrote the following in his essay entitled "Tigers Shed 'Mediocre' Label": "Aurelio Lopez was one of the league's more dominant relief pitchers with 16 saves and seven victories through August 1 before slumping in the final two months."

A year later, in the 1985 *Guide*, Gage's review was labeled, "Tigers Enjoy a Dream Season." Here is what he wrote about Lopez: "[P]itching had a lot to do with Detroit's success. The Tigers led all American League clubs with a 3.49 earned-run average and 51 saves. The bullpen duo of Hernandez and Aurelio Lopez was, perhaps, the most consistently effective segment of that pitching staff."

Between them, Hernandez and Lopez were 19-4 with 46 saves and a 2.43 ERA in 1984. Hernandez alone (1.92 ERA) had 32 saves in 33 save situations as he broke the team record for pitching appearances with 80.

Voluble Detroit manager Sparky Anderson nailed it in fewer words. "I can tell you the difference between Detroit and Toronto in two words," Anderson said just before the Tigers clinched the American League East title. "Hernandez and Lopez."

Without taking anything away from Hernandez and his great season, these remarks show just how important Lopez was to the 1984 world champion Tigers.

Aurelio Lopez is one of the greatest—and certainly the most underrated—relief pitchers in the history of the Detroit Tigers. Despite its standing as one of the American League's charter franchises, the Tigers don't exactly have a history of strong relievers. Take a look at the most basic measure, career saves. You don't have to go too far down the list (stats through 2012) to reach undistinguished territory.

Rank	Pitcher	SV (w/Detroit)	IP (w/Detroit)
1.	Todd Jones	235	479^1/$_3$
2.	Mike Henneman	154	669^2/$_3$
3.	John Hiller	125	1,242
4.	Willie Hernandez	120	483^2/$_3$
5.	Jose Valverde	110	204^1/$_3$
6.	Aurelio Lopez	85	713
7.	Fernando Rodney	70	330
8.	Terry Fox	55	344^1/$_3$
9.	Al Benton	45	1,218^2/$_3$
10.	Hooks Dauss	40	3,390^2/$_3$

The aforementioned raw save totals don't really tell the story. Jones benefited from being a closer in the Dennis Eckersley-Mariano Rivera mode; he generally was called upon to pitch the final inning and typically entered the game with no runners on base. In his seven-plus seasons in Detroit, Jones averaged almost exactly an inning per appearance while racking up his 235 saves despite allowing almost 1.5 baserunners per nine innings. Jones led the league in saves only once and was picked as an All-Star only once. He received a vote for the Cy Young Award only one time in his career—the same as Lopez. (Jones got three votes in 2000; Lopez received one vote in 1979.)

In the postseason, Lopez went 2-0 in October for the Tigers, pitching six scoreless innings, allowing five hits and two walks while striking out six. Jones pitched seven innings in eight games in the postseason for Detroit, allowing eight hits and two walks, and hitting one batter. He fanned four and was charged with one unearned run from a fielding error he committed.

When comparing Lopez to Jones, the distinguishing mark of Jones' career is mainly longevity. He was rarely brilliant and would probably have been a disaster if asked to carry the kind of workload that Lopez shouldered—whereas Lopez would probably have excelled in the cosseted milieu of the contemporary closer.

Mike Henneman took over from Guillermo Hernandez as the Tigers' closer in 1988, bridging the heydays of Bruce Sutter and Goose Gossage with Dennis Eckersley and Mariano Rivera. Henneman hurled 669^2/$_3$ innings in 491 games in his nine seasons in Detroit. While consistent, the right-hander was rarely brilliant, never leading the league in any pitching category of note, receiving only one American League All-Star nod, no Cy Young recognition, and only a solitary vote for Rookie of the Year. Henneman was at his best in his first five seasons in the majors, when he won 49 and lost only 21 while averaging more than 1^1/$_3$ innings per appearance and posting an ERA+ of 139. (ERA+ is a comparison of the pitcher's ERA to the league ERA, adjusted for ballpark; 100 is average.) In October Henneman won one game after blowing the save opportunity in three appearances in the 1987 ALCS, allowing six hits and six runs in five frames.

Hiller's career was something like Hernandez's in that it featured a brilliant peak of two consecutive seasons, with a couple of other good years. Pete Palmer, in the *ESPN Baseball Encyclopedia*, adjusts his ratings for closers to reflect the extra value of their innings. Despite his gaudy save totals, Jones managed only 4.9 Pitcher Wins while with Detroit, while Lopez totaled 7.7. Hernandez posted 9.3, Henneman (reflecting his longevity) 12.3, and Hiller 21.0. That rating better reflects Lopez's place in Detroit bullpen history.

Aurelio Alejandro Lopez y Rios was born on September 21, 1948, in the village of Tecamachalco in Puebla state, Mexico. On May 16, 1971, Lopez married Maria Celia Corral de Lopez. The couple had two children, Aurelio in 1972 and Kachia Guadalupe in 1976.

DETROIT TIGERS 1984: WHAT A START! WHAT A FINISH!

Many Tigers fans still remember Lopez fondly. The Detroit rock band Electric Six named its second album *Señor Smoke* in his honor. The album was released in 2005 in the United Kingdom by Rushmore Records, a division of Warner Bros. Records. Metropolis Records released the album a year later in the United States.

Lopez made his professional debut at the age of 19 in the minor-league Mexican Southeast League in 1967. The young pitcher showed a distinct lack of control but also a lot of talent, catching the eye of scout Ramon "Chita" Garcia of the Mexico City *Diablos Rojos* (Red Devils). Signed by Garcia, Lopez pitched for Las Choapas, a newly organized farm club of the Red Devils in the Mexican Southeast League, a minor league rated as Class A by Organized Baseball.

One year later, at 20, Lopez was pitching for the powerful Red Devils in the Mexican League; he was used mostly as a starter in his first four seasons. The prestigious Mexican League was at that time, and remains today, the pinnacle of pro baseball in that country. Starting in 1967, the Mexican League was rated by Organized Baseball as a Triple-A league.

The callow young pitcher was farmed out in 1969 by Mexico City to Minatitlan of the Mexican Southeast League, where the Las Choapas club had relocated. There he appeared in 16 games before returning to the parent club for good. While with the junior *Diablos Rojos*, Lopez hurled a perfect game against Ciudad del Carmen, winning 1-0.

In 1973, Lopez's manager, Wilfredo Calvino, converted the young righty into a full-time relief pitcher. It was a prescient move on Calvino's part, and from 1974 to '77, Lopez worked exclusively out of the bullpen (aside from two starts). Lopez led the loop in appearances and saves for four consecutive seasons (1974 through 1977), and his name is scattered today throughout the Mexican League single-season and career pitching leaders.

In 1975, Lopez set a Mexican League record by pitching in 71 games. Two years later, he broke his own record by appearing in 73 games. His 30 saves in 1977 shattered the previous Mexican League record of 24 (set in 1973); Lopez's save record stood for 14 years. He also set a record in '77 with 19 wins in relief.

Overall, Lopez pitched for 10 seasons in Mexico, all with Red Devils, who won four championships in that span, while losing in the championship series in three other years. The strong-armed right-hander compiled a 97-83 record with a 3.18 ERA in 472 games (108 starts). He also notched at least 99 saves (saves were not recorded in Mexico before 1973). In his final year in the Mexican League, Lopez went 19-8 with a 2.01 ERA and 30 saves in 73 games, winning the loop's 1977 *Jugador Mas Valioso* (MVP) Award.

Never one to shirk extra work, Lopez also pitched in the Mexican Pacific League, a winter league, winning the loop's Most Valuable Player awards for the 1973-74 and 1976-77 seasons when he was with Mazatlan and Guasave, respectively.

After his death in 1992, Lopez was honored by being inducted into the *Salon de la Fama del Beisbol Profesional de Mexico* (Mexican Professional Baseball Hall of Fame) on June 19, 1993. Lopez's biography on the *Salon de la Fama* Web site says that he was considered the fastest pitcher in the history of Mexican baseball. In his native country, Señor Smoke was also known as *El Lanzallama*—the flamethrower.

Lopez made his major-league debut in 1974 at the age of 25 after being purchased by Kansas City on August 29 from Mexico City. He appeared in eight games in September that season, allowing 21 hits and 10 walks in 16 innings while striking out only five hitters. Obviously, the young Mexican hurler wasn't ready for the big leagues yet, and the Royals sold him back to the Mexico City club the following spring.

Four years later, after dominating in the Mexican League, a more experienced Lopez returned to the major leagues with St. Louis after being purchased by the Cardinals from Mexico City on October 26, 1977. St. Louis first farmed him out to Triple-A Springfield of the American Association, where Lopez appeared in 34 games in relief in 1978, posting a 6-6 record with a 3.55 ERA. More importantly, he fanned 81 hitters in 76 innings, showing the first inkling of the kind of explosive stuff he would soon bring to Detroit. Promoted to the Cardinals in mid-July, Lopez pitched decently for St. Louis for the rest of the season, appearing in 25 games while making four starts.

Detroit acquired Lopez as part of a four-player trade with St. Louis on December 4, 1978. The Tigers sent two young left-handed pitchers, Bob Sykes and Jack Murphy, to the Cardinals, receiving veteran outfielder Jerry Morales and Lopez in return. Lopez wasn't exactly a throw-in, but at the time he was probably regarded as the least important of the four players in the swap.

Veteran Detroit baseball writer Jim Hawkins, in his analysis of the trade, described Lopez merely as a "hard-throwing right-handed reliever" who was "4-2 mainly in long relief with the Cardinals." Yet Lopez had by far the best career after the trade of any of the quartet involved, starting in the middle of the 1979 season.

Morales was a complete bust in Motown and was sent packing after one season (.211 average, .624 OPS in 129 games) splitting time in right field with lefty swinger Champ Summers. Sykes, after missing all of 1977 due to an arm problem, went 4-0 in four starts at Triple-A Evansville in 1978, posting a 1.41 ERA before being called up to Detroit. With the Tigers, he had posted a 6-6 record with a 3.94 ERA in 93 2/3 innings. After the trade, however, Sykes struggled with the Cardinals, managing only a 12-13 record and a 5.08 ERA in 62 games in 1979-81 before closing out his career in the minors in 1982. Murphy spent two disappointing years in the Cards' system and one year in the Montreal Expos' organization before finishing his career in 1981, never having risen above Double-A.

Which leaves only the unheralded Lopez. The 1980 Detroit Tigers media guide said Lopez was the "surprise player of the year [1979] for the Tigers." Further, it noted that Lopez was "rarely used until Sparky Anderson became manager." Indeed, Lopez appeared in only 13 games during Les Moss' 53 games in charge; all but one of those appearances came in Detroit losses. Even worse, Lopez was rusting away, having

DETROIT TIGERS 1984: WHAT A START! WHAT A FINISH!

pitched only one inning in the last two weeks of Moss' tenure and in Dick Tracewski's brief interregnum.

Sparky Anderson, however, saw potential in Lopez, making the Mexican hurler the club's closer in early July. The hard-throwing righty inherited the mantle of 36-year-old lefty change-up artist John Hiller, who was nearing the end of his fine career. In all, the Tigers' new manager called on Lopez 48 times in his 106 games as skipper in 1979. Lopez responded beautifully to the greater workload and greater responsibility, going 10-4 with 21 saves and a 1.87 ERA while becoming Detroit's closer of the future. To cap off his breakout year, Lopez was invited to tour Japan with an American League all-star squad during the 1979-80 offseason.

At that time, Lopez had an outstanding fastball plus a slider and a screwball, a repertoire he continued to employ till the end of his career. Like a lot of Latin pitchers, he varied his angle of delivery, sometimes dropping from three-quarters down to sidearm against right-handed hitters. His herky-jerky motion gave him good deception, and, in his prime, he could locate his fastball well or simply throw it by most hitters.

As he aged, however, Lopez—like many major leaguers in their 30s—put on too much weight, ultimately being listed as high as carrying 230 pounds on his 6-foot frame. (He was listed as weighing only 200 when he debuted in the majors.) While he continued to throw hard till the end of his career, scouts reported that his fastball lacked movement in the mid-1980s, which meant that good hitters could pound it a long way if they caught up to it—which they did frequently in his two worst years, 1982 and 1985, when he allowed 1.8 and 1.6 home runs per nine innings, respectively.

Many Latino pitchers of that era—as well as a few American pitchers—still employed the screwball, which faded into disuse in the 1990s. In Lopez's case, he would use the scroogie on the outside part of the plate to left-handed hitters, with the elusive pitch diving down and away. Lopez used the slider in a similar way to frustrate right-handed hitters, though his blazing heater was always his No. 1 offering. As he struggled to stay in the majors the last two years, Lopez reportedly experimented with several other pitches, including a splitter that he learned while pitching under Roger Craig.

From 1979 to 1984, the stalwart right-hander appeared in 304 games for the Tigers, compiling a superb 50-23, .685 record with a 3.22 ERA, 25 percent better than the league average. In 626$^{2/3}$ innings of work, he allowed only 527 hits while walking 220 hitters non-intentionally and fanning 466. He saved only 80 games (and blew 22 save opportunities for a 78.4 save percentage) during those six seasons, though he led the Detroit staff with 21 saves in both 1979 and 1980 and with 18 in 1983. Though 21 saves seems almost negligible by today's standards for a closer, Lopez's 21 saves tied for third in the American League in '79 and placed seventh in 1980. In 1983 the Detroit closer's 18 saves were good for eighth in the junior circuit; in '84, he finished 10th.

In 1982 the usually durable reliever spent 38 days on the disabled list in Detroit, his only such term in the big leagues. Placed on the Detroit disabled list in spring training with a sore shoulder, he was activated in mid-May by the Tigers. After returning, he struggled until early July, when he was demoted to Triple-A to work out his problems with Evansville. He was 4-0 (1.76 ERA) with the Evansville Triplets and was recalled by Detroit in September, pitching well for the last month of the season.

The following year, Lopez was selected for the 1983 American League All-Star team while enjoying a stupendous first half of the season: 5-3 with a 1.83 ERA and 11 saves in 30 games. He held hitters to a .176 batting average, allowing only 39 hits in 64 innings while striking out 60. The Tigers' closer did not appear in that Midsummer Classic, however, which the American League won 13-3 in a walk, breaking a streak of 11 consecutive National League victories. It turned out to be his only All-Star nod.

Then, of course, came that championship season of 1984. Despite faulty recollections and revisionist histories to the contrary, Lopez started the '84 season as Detroit's closer, the same role in which he had ended '83. Manager Sparky Anderson wrote in his diary about the Tigers' game against the future American League West champion Royals on May 9, when Lopez punched out four of the eight hitters he faced, allowing only a harmless walk: "I brought in Aurelio Lopez and I never saw him throw harder.... He struck out four and no one had a chance to hit off him. Lopey never seems to be scared. When he's on top of his game, he's better than Clay Carroll used to be for me. And Carroll was some kind of pitcher."

Needless to say, Sparky wasn't talking about Lopez as his No. 2 man. George Cantor, who covered the Tigers as a columnist in '84, identified Hernandez's breakthrough as occurring on May 4, but the record shows that Anderson didn't assign Lopez solely to setup work until June.

While Lopez spent the balance of that victorious summer in Motown as the No. 2 pitcher in Sparky Anderson's bullpen pecking order, it's not as if he was getting cuffed around while Hernandez was cruising toward his postseason accolades. In June, July, and August, Lopez went 6-0 with five saves in 39 appearances, holding enemy batsmen to a .224 average while whiffing 55 in 79 innings and posting a 3.08 ERA. September, however, was not so good—a harbinger of things to come.

In 1980, the Tigers' media guide said that Lopez "prefers heavy work load to stay sharp." And years later, Detroit pitching coach Roger Craig said that Lopez had really surprised him: "He told me that he could pitch three days in a row, and he'd be throwing harder on the third day than the first. I didn't believe him till I saw it for myself." The evidence strongly suggests that Lopez's eagerness to pitch, when combined with the quick hooks of starting pitchers that manager Sparky Anderson was famous for, led to Lopez's sudden decline.

In September 1984 Lopez's redoubtable right arm plainly wore out. In 12 games (17 innings), he allowed 21 hits and 10 earned runs while striking out only eight, saving two games but also being charged with his only loss of the season. He finished the year 10-1. The following season brought more of the same, as Lopez was hit hard for the rest of the year (.849

DETROIT TIGERS 1984: WHAT A START! WHAT A FINISH!

opponents' OPS, 5.92 ERA) after pitching decently in April and May. By midseason 1985, Anderson no longer entrusted a save situation to Lopez; by September, the bullpen phone rang for Lopez only when Detroit was trailing; by the end of the year, the veteran reliever's days wearing the jersey with the proud Old English *D* were over.

Because of the brilliant bullpen work of Lopez and Hernandez, the Tigers were the only club in the majors to win all 87 games that they led at the start of the ninth inning or later. (Note, however, that the American League average in that category was 95 percent.) The *1985 Elias Baseball Analyst* called the Detroit relief duo "the most effective one-two relief combination in baseball." As a perfect example of how quickly things change, one year later the 1986 edition of the Elias book placed much of the blame for the Tigers' disappointing '85 season on "the failure of Lopez to provide the same service…as a year earlier."

Because of Detroit's dominance in the 1984 postseason, Lopez was used sparingly. He appeared in only one game in the AL Championship Series, pitching three scoreless innings in Game Two and getting the win when the Tigers rallied in the 11th inning to defeat the Royals. In the World Series Lopez worked three scoreless innings overall, earning the win in the Game Five clincher when he fanned four Padres batters in $2^{1}/_{3}$ innings of relief. (He also appeared in the 1986 National League Championship Series with the Houston Astros, entering the climactic Game Six in the 14th inning and taking the loss after allowing two runs to the victorious Mets in the 16th.)

Detroit released Lopez after the 1985 season, when the 36-year-old veteran slumped to 3-7, 4.80 in 51 games while allowing almost a hit per inning—a sign of his declining stuff. He signed with Houston in midseason 1986, finishing his career with the Astros, who released the 39-year-old veteran in midseason 1987. Before the end, however, Lopez had one more moment in the sun, going 3-3 with seven saves and a 3.46 ERA in 45 games, helping the Astros win the National League West Division in '86.

Lopez was one of the last of the old breed of closers—guys who would take the ball anytime starting in the seventh inning or later and expect to finish the game. To truly appreciate his effectiveness, one cannot simply look at his save totals; one must look also at his won-lost record, his earned run average, and the number of innings he pitched.

At the end of 1984 Lopez's good name was included on four of the five lists of lifetime relief pitching leaders in Macmillan's *Baseball Encyclopedia*, including placing second in relief winning percentage with his career mark of .685.

Although his biography from the Mexican Baseball Hall of Fame says that Lopez was known as the Vulture of Tecamachalco, he was most definitely not a "vulture" by baseball standards during his Detroit days, even though he has erroneously been called so by some writers whose hindsight is not 20-20. Paul Dickson's estimable dictionary of the national pastime defines vulture as a "relief pitcher, typically a middle relief pitcher, who receives credit for a win to which another pitcher was more entitled; e.g., a relief pitcher whose ineffective pitching prevents an earlier pitcher from receiving the win, as when the relief pitcher blows a lead, only to wind up winning when his teammates retake the lead."

Take a look at Lopez's 1984 stat line and game logs and find out exactly where he "vultured" wins from more deserving teammates. Lopez blew only two saves all year, one of which earned him a win and one a loss. Of his nine other wins, he entered with the game tied four times, allowing no runs in any of those games. Twice he relieved a struggling starter in the fifth inning when the high-scoring Tigers held the lead and was credited with the win—a situation in which the official scorer could have awarded the *W* to another relief pitcher if he believed someone else had pitched more effectively than Lopez. The final three times Lopez came into the game with Detroit trailing and was helped by the Tigers' bats, but so what? In two of those games, he neither allowed an inherited run nor was scored upon himself. In the final instance, Lopez got the win after pitching a scoreless eighth inning against the Yankees before the Tigers took the lead in the bottom of the eighth. In the ninth Lopez was touched for two unearned runs, both scoring after Hernandez had relieved him.

There is no justification for calling Lopez a "vulture" in 1984. His gaudy won-lost record and relatively low number of saves is not a result of taking "advantage of the Tigers' late-inning offense" (as one scribe phrased it in a 2009 retrospective on the 1984 season). If anything, it was the reverse: Detroit's potent attack took advantage when Lopez shut down the opposition to win many games that the Tigers otherwise would have lost. Detroit scored an average of 0.60 runs per inning in the first three frames in 1984, then 0.57 runs per inning during the middle three frames of the game, and only 0.54 runs per inning in the seventh, eighth, and ninth, when Lopez would typically be on the hill.

A great example of how one should not apply today's standards to 1984 is that Lopez had only three holds that season, tied with Carl Willis. The team leaders, with five, were Doug Bair and Bill Scherrer! By way of contrast, the 2009 Tigers' mound corps had five pitchers with more than five holds, with the team leader amassing 28 and the runner-up notching 15 holds. Why? Because the "hold" stat requires a pitcher to enter the game with a lead and not finish the game, and Lopez often was called upon in tie games or when the Tigers were behind. In fact, Lopez answered the bell more than half the time without a lead, whereas Hernandez took the mound almost two-thirds of the time with a Detroit lead.

After retiring from baseball following the 1987 season, Lopez returned to his native village in Mexico. He was elected as municipal president (mayor) of Tecamachalco three years later.

Lopez died in a car crash in Matehuala, San Luis Potosi, on September 22, 1992. He was 44 at the time of his death, which occurred, according to *The Sporting News*, after he was ejected from his "chauffeur-driven car and crushed when it rolled over him." He was the first player from the 1984 world champions to expire.

DETROIT TIGERS 1984: WHAT A START! WHAT A FINISH!

Perhaps because of his unexpected demise, the late pitcher was immortalized in Mexico the following year, though it's safe to say that Lopez was headed for the *Salon de la Fama* regardless.

Aurelio Lopez's obituary in *The Sporting News* mistakenly states that "Lopez became a hero in his native land primarily because of the seven seasons he spent pitching for the Detroit Tigers." That is demonstrably not true, as the evidence clearly shows. Despite that mistake, the final paragraph in the *TSN* obit rings true to Lopez's character and to his life story.

"'It really wasn't my idea,'" Lopez told the *Detroit Free Press* last year [about his election as mayor of Tecamachalco]. "'But the people asked me to do it, and I couldn't say no. This is my home. You can never forget where you come from.'"

A fitting epitaph for a standup player and a hell of a pitcher in his prime—in two countries.

References

Publications

Anderson, Sparky, with Dan Ewald. *Bless You Boys: Diary of the Detroit Tigers' 1984 Season*. Chicago: Contemporary Books, Inc. 1984.

Anderson, William M. *The Detroit Tigers: A Pictorial Celebration of the Greatest Players and Moments in Tigers' History*. Updated edition. Detroit: Wayne State University Press. 1999.

Balzer, Howard M. *Official 1979 Baseball Register*. St. Louis: The Sporting News Publishing Company. 1979.

Campbell, Dave, Harmon Killebrew, Brooks Robinson, and Duke Snider. *The Scouting Report: 1985*. New York: Harper & Row Publishers. 1985.

Campbell, Dave, Harmon Killebrew, Brooks Robinson, and Duke Snider. *The Scouting Report: 1986*. New York: Harper & Row Publishers. 1986.

Campbell, Dave, Denny Matthews, Brooks Robinson, and Duke Snider. *The Scouting Report: 1984*. New York: Harper & Row Publishers. 1984.

Cantor, George. *Wire to Wire: Inside the 1984 Detroit Tigers Championship Season*. Chicago: Triumph Books. 2004.

Cisneros, Pedro Treto. *Enciclopedia del Beisbol Mexicano*. Mexico: Eighth edition. Revistas Deportivas, S.A. de C.V. 2005.

Coleman, Jerry, Ernie Harwell, Ralph Kiner, Tim McCarver, Ned Martin, and Brooks Robinson. *The Scouting Report: 1983*. New York: Harper & Row Publishers. 1983.

Detroit Tigers. *Detroit Tigers Press/TV/Radio Guide, 1978 ed*. Detroit: Detroit Tigers. 1978.

Detroit Tigers. *Detroit Tigers Press/TV/Radio Guide, 1979 ed*. Detroit: Detroit Tigers. 1979.

Detroit Tigers. Detroit Tigers Press/TV/Radio Guide, 1980 ed. Detroit: Detroit Tigers. 1980.

Detroit Tigers. Detroit Tigers Press/TV/Radio Guide, 1981 ed. Detroit: Detroit Tigers. 1981.

Detroit Tigers. Detroit Tigers Press/TV/Radio Guide, 1982 ed. Detroit: Detroit Tigers. 1982.

Detroit Tigers. Detroit Tigers Press/TV/Radio Guide, 1983 ed. Detroit: Detroit Tigers. 1983.

Detroit Tigers. Detroit Tigers Press/TV/Radio Guide, 1984 ed. Detroit: Detroit Tigers. 1984.

Detroit Tigers. Detroit Tigers Press/TV/Radio Guide, 1985 ed. Detroit: Detroit Tigers. 1985.

Dickson, Paul. *The Dickson Baseball Dictionary, third ed*. New York: W.W. Norton & Company. 2009.

Dierker, Larry, Jim Kaat, Harmon Killebrew, and Jim Rooker. *The Scouting Report: 1987*. New York: Perennial Library. 1987.

Gillette, Gary, and Pete Palmer. *The ESPN Baseball Encyclopedia, fifth ed*. New York: Sterling Publishing Co., Inc. 2008.

Hoppel, Joe. *Official Baseball Guide, 1984 ed*. St. Louis: The Sporting News Publishing Company. 1984.

James, Bill, and Rob Neyer. *The Neyer/James Guide to Pitchers*. New York: Fireside Books. 2004.

Marcin, Joe, and Larry Wigge, Carl Clark, and Larry Vickrey. *Official Baseball Guide for 1978*. St. Louis: The Sporting News Publishing Company. 1978.

Pietrusza, David, Matthew Silverman, and Michael Gershman. *Baseball: The Biographical Encyclopedia*. Kingston, New York: Total/Sports Illustrated. 2000.

Reichler, Joseph L. *The Baseball Encyclopedia, sixth ed*. New York: Macmillan Publishing Company. 1985.

Reichler, Joseph L. *The Baseball Trade Register*. New York: Collier Books. 1984.

DETROIT TIGERS 1984: WHAT A START! WHAT A FINISH!

Siegel, Barry. *Official Baseball Register, 1984 ed.* St. Louis: The Sporting News Publishing Company. 1984.

Siegel, Barry. *Official Baseball Register, 1985 ed.* St. Louis: The Sporting News Publishing Company. 1985.

Siwoff, Seymour, Steve Hirdt, and Peter Hirdt. *The 1985 Elias Baseball Analyst.* New York: Collier Books. 1985.

Siwoff, Seymour, Steve Hirdt, and Peter Hirdt. *The 1986 Elias Baseball Analyst.* New York: Collier Books. 1986.

Sloan, Dave. *Official Baseball Guide, 1985 ed.* St. Louis: The Sporting News Publishing Company. 1985.

Sumner, Benjamin Barrett. *Minor League Baseball Standings.* Jefferson, North Carolina: McFarland & Company, Inc. 2000.

Articles

Chass, Murray. "Morris Boosted Nearly a Million." *The Sporting News,* p. 40, February 23, 1987. Accessed via www.PaperOfRecord.com.

Felber, Bill, and Gary Gillette. "The Changing Game." In Thorn, John, and Pete Palmer, *Total Baseball, seventh edition.* Kingston, New York: Total Sports Publishing. 2001.

Gage, Tom. "Evans Named Tiger of the Year." *The Sporting News,*, p. 48, November 18, 1985. Accessed via www.PaperOfRecord.com.

Gage, Tom. "Hernandez Tigers New Bullpen Ace." *The Sporting News,* pp. 23-24, April 2, 1984. Accessed via www.PaperOfRecord.com.

Gage, Tom. "Lopez' Old Fastball Gives Tigers Relief." *The Sporting News,*, p. 20, July 11, 1983. Accessed via www.PaperOfRecord.com.

Gammons, Peter. "Hernandez Deal May Put Tigers on Top." *The Sporting News,*, p. 14, April 9, 1984. Accessed via www.PaperOfRecord.com.

Hawkins, Jim. "Tigers Count on More Tallies With Morales." *The Sporting News,*, p. 51, December 23, 1978. Accessed via www.PaperOfRecord.com.

Hawkins, Jim. "Tigers May Trip Over Own Mound." *The Sporting News,*, p. 28, March 3, 1979. Accessed via www.PaperOfRecord.com.

Henning, Lynn. "Tigers' 35-5 start in 1984 still has power to amaze." *Detroit News*, May 21, 2009. Accessed via www.detnews.com.

"N.L. West," in *The Sporting News,*, p. 16, June 9, 1986. Accessed via www.PaperOfRecord.com.

"Remembering Señor Smoke," *The Sporting News,*, p. 4, October 5, 1992. Accessed via www.PaperOfRecord.com.

Russo, Neal. "Redbirds Try to Right Ship With 3 Unproven Lefties." *The Sporting News,*, p. 45, December 23, 1978. Accessed via www.PaperOfRecord.com.

"We Will Miss…" *The Sporting News,*, p. S-23, January 4, 1993. Accessed via www.PaperOfRecord.com.

Web Sites

www.BaseballIndex.org

www.Baseball-Almanac.com

www.Baseball-Reference.com

www.Baseball-Reference.com/bullpen

www.BlogCritics.org

http://Detroit.Tigers.MLB.com

http://SABRpedia.org (Society for American Baseball Research's online encyclopedia)

www.SalondelaFama.com.mx (Mexican Baseball Hall of Fame)

www.Wikipedia.org

Interviews & Communications

Craig, Roger. Telephone interview by author.

Nelson, Rod. E-mail messages to author.

Shea, Stuart. E-mail messages to author.

Other Sources

24-7 Baseball Relief Pitcher reports, 1979-85 (unpublished).

24-7 Baseball/ESPN Baseball Encyclopedia Disabled List-Injury Register (unpublished).

Dwight Lowry
by Brian Borawski

DWIGHT LOWRY spent the bulk of his four-year major-league career as a backup catcher for the Detroit Tigers between 1984 and 1987, including an extended stay with the 1984 Tigers during their championship run. Aside from his early tragic death after a heart attack, he is best known as one of the relatively few American Indians to have played major-league baseball. Only 50 had donned a major-league uniform through the 2009 season, and Lowry was just the second player to come from the Lumbee tribe. Gene Locklear, who played in 292 games for the Reds, Padres, and Yankees (1973-1977), was the first.

The Lumbee tribe, from North Carolina, is the ninth largest Native American tribe in the United States and the largest east of the Mississippi River. It takes its name from the Lumbee River in Robeson County, North Carolina. The tribe's economic, cultural, and political center is in Pembroke, North Carolina.

Lowry was born on October 23, 1957, to Marvin and Berniece Lowry, in Lumberton, North Carolina, one of six children. James Locklear, editor of the tribe's newspaper, the *Robeson Journal*, wrote that baseball was no stranger to the Lowry household. Dwight's father, Marvin, played football and basketball at the University of North Carolina at Pembroke, and later played semipro baseball. Dwight got his start as a batboy for his father's sandlot team. Following in his father's footsteps as an athlete, Dwight was Pembroke High School's starting quarterback in football, a starting forward for the basketball team, and the baseball team's best hitter and starting catcher. He earned Three River All-Conference team honors in all three sports and in his senior year batted .480 as he helped lead Pembroke to a 21-3 record in baseball. Pembroke lost to the defending state champions in the state semifinals in 1976.

Lowry turned down a football scholarship from Clemson University to play baseball at the University of North Carolina. He played baseball for four years there and earned a degree in industrial relations. During his senior season, 1980, Lowry earned first-team All-Atlantic Coast Conference honors, and the Tar Heels came within one win of taking the ACC championship.

In June 1980, Lowry was drafted in the 11th round of the amateur draft by the Detroit Tigers. The Tigers' first-round draft pick that year was Glenn Wilson, and while Wilson went on to play in 1,201 major-league games and was an All-Star outfielder, he's mostly known as one of the players Detroit traded to acquire Willie Hernandez just before the 1984 season. Lowry was one of six Tigers draftees in 1980 to reach the major leagues.

Lowry struggled in his first season in the Tigers' minor-league system. After being drafted, he reported to the Lakeland Tigers of the Florida State League. Under manager Eddie Brinkman, Lakeland finished in last place in the North Division of the Class A league. Lowry hit just .197, with 28 hits, 21 walks, and 22 strikeouts in 142 at-bats.

Lowry started 1981 with the Class A Macon Peaches (South Atlantic League), managed by Tom Kotchman, just three years older than himself. While he didn't struggle as much as he had the year before, he also hadn't found his power stroke yet. He hit .251 with two home runs in 231 at-bats and was eventually promoted to the Double-A Birmingham Barons, where he hit just .154 in 19 games to finish up the season.

In 1982 and 1983, Lowry began to show major-league promise. In '82, he was back at Lakeland and spent the entire season there. He also had the advantage of playing for manager Bruce Kimm, who had been a major-league catcher. Lowry had his best season yet. He finished with a .277 batting average in 93 games. He hit seven home runs and led Florida State League catchers with eight double plays.

For Lowry, 1983 set the stage for his eventual rise to the major leagues. He played in 90 games for the Birmingham Barons, who finished with a 91-54 record and won the Southern League championship. Lowry batted .267 with a career-best nine home runs in 288 at-bats, driving in 44 runs and scoring 42. Future major-league catcher Bob Melvin was his platoon partner. Teammates Nelson Simmons, Roger Mason, and Carl Willis all made their debuts in 1984 for the Tigers, as did Lowry.

In the February 27, 1984, issue of *The Sporting News*, writer Tom Gage mentioned Dwight Lowry and Melvin as long shots to make the Tigers that season. He noted that the Tigers already had three catchers on the roster, perennial All-Star Lance Parrish, veteran John Wockenfuss, and Marty Castillo. But during spring training Wockenfuss was traded with Wilson in the deal that brought Willie Hernandez and Dave Bergman to Detroit. Although Castillo made the team, he spent most of the first two months of the season backing up Tom Brookens at third base. Bob Melvin's time didn't come until 1985, leaving the backup catching duties to Lowry.

The 6-foot-3, 210-pound catcher made his major-league debut on Opening Day, April 3, at Minnesota. With the Tigers safely up, 8-1, over the Minnesota Twins, he replaced Parrish behind the plate for the final three innings. He didn't get an at-bat that game, nor did he get to hit in his next two games as a defensive replacement. On April 13 he got his first big-league plate appearance. After replacing Parrish again, Lowry grounded out to second base.

Lowry made his first start on April 22, at home against the Chicago White Sox, but his first hit still eluded him, as he went hitless in three at-bats. On the 24th, in the first game of a doubleheader against the Twins at Tiger Stadium, Lowry singled in his first at-bat. In the fifth inning, he drew a walk and later scored on a single by Alan Trammell. The next month turned out to be both a high point and a low point for Lowry. On May 20, he belted his first major-league home run, in the second inning of a 4-3 win over Lary Sorensen and the Oakland Athletics. The blast helped the Tigers to extend their record-breaking start to 32-5.

But the homer was Lowry's last hit for Detroit until September. On June 8 the Tigers sent him to their Triple-A

DETROIT TIGERS 1984: WHAT A START! WHAT A FINISH!

affiliate, the Evansville (Indiana) Triplets, and called up his Barons teammate from the year before, Carl Willis.

The three summer months were a disappointment for Lowry. In 61 games for Evansville, he hit just .220 and his 51 strikeouts in 177 at-bats were the highest strikeouts-per-at-bats rate of any of his minor-league stints. But he was called back up in September. His two-run home run on September 29 helped the Tigers rout the New York Yankees 11-3 for their 104th victory, a franchise record. Lowry wasn't on the postseason roster, but his father said being with the 1984 Tigers was one of the biggest thrills of Dwight's life.

If 1984 was a high point of Lowry's career, 1985 was probably one of the lows. Marty Castillo started the season as the Tigers' backup catcher. This move gave Sparky Anderson some versatility because Castillo could also play third base, where he had spent almost half his time for the Tigers in 1984. Lowry spent the season with the Nashville Sounds of the American Association. In late May the Tigers brought up a catcher, but it was Bob Melvin, Lowry's Nashville teammate.

Lowry, meanwhile, had the worst season of his career. In 74 games and 203 at-bats, he hit just .182 with two home runs and 13 RBIs as Nashville finished in second place in the East Division of the American Association with a 71-70 record.

But Lowry's 1986 season put him back on the Tigers' map. He was called up from Nashville in May to back up Lance Parrish, then when Parrish went on the disabled list with a back injury, Lowry became the primary catcher. He was eventually backed up by Mike Heath, acquired by the Tigers on August 10. In Lowry's first chance as a big-league starter, he finished the season with a .307 batting average in 150 at-bats. He also set himself up as a potential starter for the 1987 season after Parrish signed with the Philadelphia Phillies in the offseason. Unfortunately for Lowry, three things kept that from happening.

The first was the emergence of Matt Nokes, who had hit well in each of his seasons in the Tigers organization. Nokes hit .285 and drove in 71 runs for Nashville in 1986 and impressed management enough for them to carry three catchers to start the 1987 season. Also hurting Lowry was the presence of Mike Heath, an above-average defensive catcher who also gave the Tigers a veteran presence at the position.

The final straw was Lowry's bad start; in eight games in April, he went 4-for-22 (.182) with one RBI. He became the odd man out when Sparky Anderson decided to keep just two catchers. Lowry was sent to the Tigers' new Triple-A affiliate, the Toledo Mud Hens. There he was a backup too, and hit just .194 although he found his way back to Detroit as a September call-up. He got into five games as a pinch-hitter or defensive replacement and in his final game singled in his only at-bat in a 10-9 loss to the Toronto Blue Jays on September 26. It was Lowry's last major-league hit.

In the same week that the Tigers lost their American League Championship Series to the Minnesota Twins, they released Lowry. A week after being released, Lowry was signed by the Twins.

Lowry started the season with Minnesota, but he was mostly used as a defensive replacement or pinch-hitter, starting just one game in April, then was sent to the Twins' Triple-A team, the Portland (Oregon) Beavers. Portland finished in second place in the Pacific Coast League's Northwest Division that year as Lowry mostly backed up Tom Nieto and filled in at first base. He finished the year with a .258 batting average with 33 runs and 32 RBIs in 244 at-bats. As with 1987, though, Lowry found himself on a team without a need for him and was cut shortly after the season ended. He was 30 years old.

In 1989, no major-league team was interested in Lowry, and he went overseas to play in the Italian professional league. During the winter, he played in the short-lived Senior Professional Baseball Association in Florida. Then he caught on with the Indianapolis Indians, the Triple-A affiliate of the Montreal Expos. Lowry had 11 hits in his first 25 at-bats and finishing the season with a .310 batting average in 30 games. After the season, Lowry, 32, decided to retire as a player. He returned to the Tigers' organization as a coach for the South Atlantic League's Fayetteville (North Carolina) Generals, Detroit's low-A affiliate. Under manager Gerry Groninger, the 1991 team finished near the bottom of the standings. But Fayetteville was less than an hour's commute from his family in Lumberton.

In 1992, Lowry returned to Fayetteville. One of the Tigers' top prospects, pitcher Justin Thompson, spent the season with the Generals and the team finished with a 74-67 record, good for fifth place in the South Atlantic League. In 1993 former Tigers shortstop Mark Wagner managed the Generals, who made the playoffs for the first time with Lowry as a coach; they lost in the semifinals.

In 1994 Lowry was named the manager of the Bristol (Virginia) Tigers, a short-season Rookie-level team in the Detroit organization. But before the season started, Fayetteville manager Wagner was promoted to manage the Lakeland Tigers, and Lowry was named to replace him at Fayetteville. The team struggled with a 62-75 record.

The next season, the Generals had a league-best 86-55 record, but didn't make the playoffs because they didn't win either half of the split season. Lowry followed that up with a 76-63 record in 1996 and because of an expanded playoff system (the league expanded from two to three divisions) and with the help of top prospect Gabe Kapler, the Generals made the playoffs but lost in the first round to the Delmarva Shorebirds. Lowry was named the Tigers minor-league manager of the year.

In the offseason the Tigers changed their affiliation at low Class A level to the West Michigan Whitecaps of the Midwest League. Lowry became the Tigers' roving minor-league catching instructor to start the 1997 season, then managed the Jamestown (New York) Jammers, the Tigers' short-season A-ball affiliate in the New York-Penn League.

Less than a month into the Jammers' season, tragedy struck. Early in the morning of July 10, 1997, Lowry collapsed and died of a heart attack. He was 39.

Later that season, the Tigers named their Player Development Man of the Year Award after Lowry. In 1998, he was inducted into the South Atlantic League Hall of Fame.

Lowry was survived by his wife, Pam; his son Zachary; and two daughters, Sesilie and Amanda. He is buried in the Bear Swamp Baptist Church Cemetery in Littleton, about a mile from his home.

References

Publications

Gillette, Gary, and Pete Palmer, eds. *The ESPN Baseball Encyclopedia, 5th ed.* New York: Sterling. 2008.

Johnson. Lloyd, and Miles Wolff, eds. *Encyclopedia of Minor League Baseball.* Durham, North Carolina: Baseball America. 1997.

The Sporting News Official Baseball Register 1988. St. Louis: The Sporting News. 1988.

Articles

Locklear, James. "Dwight Lowry's Story." *Robeson Journal*, 2007.

"Pembroke Ends Season, Loses to Tigers 5-3." *Robesonian*, June 6, 1976.

Pembroke, Williamston Meet in Semis Tonight." *Robesonian*, June 3, 1976.

"Three Rivers Honors All Conference Team." *Robesonian*, May 20, 1976.

Williams, Don. "Lowry Was a True Man of the Game." *Lubbock Avalanche-Journal*, July 14, 1997.

Web Sites

http://www.baseball-almanac.com

http://www.baseball-reference.com

http://www.lumbeetribe.com

http://www.retrosheet.org

http://www.thebaseballcube.com

Roger Mason
by Nick Edson

ROGER MASON had no idea that his first appearance as a Detroit Tigers pitcher would be a record-setting performance.

Mason, in fact, had no reason to believe that he would even pitch in the major leagues, let alone in 1984 for the eventual World Series champions, or that he would go on to pitch in parts of nine seasons for seven major-league teams.

After all, it had been only four years earlier, in late August 1980, that Mason, then a 22-year-old pitcher from Bellaire, a town of 800 residents in northern Michigan, went to nearby Traverse City for what he determined would be his final tryout camp.

"I had been to several tryout camps before and I told myself that if I didn't attract any interest this time, I would move on with my life," he said. "But a month after I got home from the tryout, I got a call from a Tigers scout."

Four years later—on September 4, 1984—he found himself on the mound after suiting up as a Tiger for the first time that day. He was a late-season call-up from the Tigers' Triple-A affiliate in Evansville, Indiana, where he had compiled a 9-7 record with a 3.80 earned-run average as a starting pitcher for the Triplets.

It was just the latest in a series of big steps that the right-hander made in crossing over from the west side of Michigan to the east side—with a goodly number of crisscrossing hops in between and afterward.

Roger Leroy Mason was born on September 18, 1957—not 1958 as some sources report—at the Meadowbrook Care Facility in Bellaire, Michigan. He was the second of seven children born to Dorr and Betty Mason. Dorr was a mechanic and Betty was a stay-at-home mother. In high school, Roger was an all-state player not only in baseball but in basketball and football as well, playing wide receiver on the gridiron, forward in hoops, and, of course, pitching on Bellaire High School's baseball team. By the time he graduated, he had grown to his pro height of 6-feet-6.

Mason carried on the three-sport excellence in college, becoming the first three-sport letterman in the history of Saginaw Valley State College. He lettered all four years in basketball and two years in football, but just one year in baseball. How could this be? Saginaw Valley didn't offer baseball as a varsity sport when he enrolled. Baseball was just a club sport then. But college officials made it a varsity sport before he graduated; Mason was a pitcher on that first varsity team.

DETROIT TIGERS 1984: WHAT A START! WHAT A FINISH!

Mason hardly expected to toe the slab the evening of his big-league debut. Dave Rozema got the start that night for the Tigers. Three of the first four batters reached base against him. Manager Sparky Anderson, as usual, had little patience that evening, pulling Rozema after Cal Ripken's sacrifice fly and Eddie Murray's RBI single left the Tigers down 2-0. Lefty Bill Scherrer got out of the inning by retiring the next two batters, but then walked leadoff batter Wayne Gross in the top of the second inning.

"They told me to start warming up in the first inning, but I thought they were pulling a rookie joke," Mason said. "Earlier, before the game started, Sparky had called down to the bullpen and kidded with Marty Castillo about his favorite college football team. So I didn't know if it was a joke or not."

It wasn't. After Scherrer's walk to open the second inning, the Tigers manager strode quickly to the mound, took the ball from the lanky lefty and motioned to the bullpen for Mason.

"I wanted to see what (Mason) could do," Anderson said after the game. "I figured since he had been a starter in Evansville, this was a good spot for him."

Mason, for his part, wasn't quite sure how to act when he was signaled into the game.

"It started when I walked onto the field before the game," he said. "Some writers were asking me if I was nervous, since I grew up in a small northern Michigan town rooting for the Tigers, then here I was in the middle of a pennant-winning season. I told them I wasn't nervous, but I was hoping they wouldn't see my legs shaking."

He was still nervous when Anderson patted his right arm to bring him into the game.

"Seriously, I didn't know whether to walk or jog or what the protocol was because I had been a starter my entire minor-league career," he said with a laugh. "I decided I better not hold the game up. I ended up jogging to the mound."

He remembered only two things about the game after that. The first thing was his first pitch in the majors. Baltimore's Rich Dauer grounded into a double play. The second was a two-run home run by Rick Dempsey in the top of the fifth inning.

He said he didn't remember striking out Ripken, the reigning American League Most Valuable Player, twice.

In all, Mason pitched eight innings in relief, giving up two runs in a 4-1 Tigers loss. His eight-inning relief performance set a Tigers record for a nine-inning game, a mark that, through 2012, still stood.

Mason went on to win a game—almost the clinching game—and record a save for the Tigers as they marched toward postseason glory.

The game he won, against Milwaukee two weeks later, on September 17, would have been the clincher had Boston held on to beat Toronto later that night. But the Blue Jays rallied, and Mason's win was good enough to clinch a tie for the AL East flag. The celebration was postponed for just one night; Randy O'Neal, another September call-up, got the victory. The pennant and the partying that followed, though, served as a mighty nice early 27th birthday present for Mason.

He earned his save in Yankee Stadium during the final series of the regular season. "I remember standing on the mound that night in Yankee Stadium"—actually, it was a day game—"rubbing up the baseball and thinking how far I had come from Bellaire to Yankee Stadium," he said. "I thought about my dad and how we used to listen to Ernie Harwell and George Kell call the games on radio and TV. I guess outside of making the Tigers that year, my next biggest thrill was being interviewed by Ernie."

Mason recalled great memories and only one regret about being part of the 1984 team.

"The excitement in Detroit was everywhere that year," he said. "I loved coming to the ballpark. One of the things I remember most is how well [equipment manager] Jim Schmakel treated everyone, even us rookies. The whole experience of being a Tiger, even for a month, was unforgettable."

Mason said he wished he had a World Series ring to make it even more memorable.

"The players vote on postseason shares [money] and they gave it to the six of us who were called up in September," he said. "Management decided who got World Series rings and the six of us didn't get one. That's the one thing I wished I had gotten out of that experience; it would have been a nice memento." The unlucky six were Mason, Scott Earl, Mike Laga, Randy O'Neal, Nelson Simmons, and Dwight Lowry, who had gotten a call-up earlier that season.

But Mason wasn't complaining. He realized how far he had come to be part of the 1984 Detroit Tigers.

He recalled the circumstances of living with a wife and child while pitching in the Double-A Southern League for Detroit's affiliate in Birmingham, Alabama. "It was a struggle getting by. I made $422 a month and that went for rent and our car," Mason said. "My wife, Terry, and I had a young son [Jeff] and we made it because Terry waited tables at a Cracker Barrel and her sister came down to live with us. When one of them was working, the other was watching Jeff." There weren't any performance bonuses in the bushes, or else Mason might have had a thicker wallet for leading the league in ERA at the all-star break.

Mason got his payday down the road, signing for $500,000 in 1994 for the Philadelphia Phillies. But the strike cut into that number, and he didn't even spend most of the shortened season with the Phillies, who sold him that April 29 to the New York Mets.

Between 1984 and 1994, Mason bounced around. He was traded by the Tigers to the San Francisco Giants for outfielder Alejandro Sanchez before the start of the 1985 season. He won five games in three years for the Giants from 1985 to 1987, spending much of that time in the minors.

Mason was granted free agency by the Giants after the 1988 season, during which he made no appearances with the parent club, and signed with Houston on February 16, 1989, appearing in only two games with the Astros that year, and going through the entire 1990 season with no major-league action. He didn't hit his major-league stride until he got to the

Pittsburgh Pirates in 1991. He was a key part of the Pirates' bullpen for two years.

That's where he got to know Barry Bonds. Sort of. Mason had surrendered Bonds' eighth career home run on July 25, 1986, at Three Rivers Stadium in Pittsburgh. Five years later, they were battling together to help Jim Leyland's team win a National League East Division title.

"I was Barry's teammate for two years with Pittsburgh," Mason said with a smile. "But I don't think he knew who I was."

Mason pitched in five National League Championship Series games for the Pirates in 1991 and 1992, allowing no runs in 7⅔ innings of relief. He earned a save in Game Five of the 1991 NLCS. He relieved starter Zane Smith with two outs in the eighth inning and Atlanta's Terry Pendleton on third base, with Pittsburgh leading the Braves 1-0. Mason got Ron Gant to pop up, and then went on to retire the Braves in the ninth, despite giving up two singles, and preserving the 1-0 victory.

After being released by Pittsburgh following the 1992 season, Mason was signed by the Mets on December 2, 1992. Fifteen days later, on December 17, he was traded to San Diego with minor leaguer Mike Freitas for pitcher Mike Maddux. After going 0-7 with a 3.24 ERA for the Padres, he was traded again, on July 3, 1993, this time to Philadelphia for pitcher Tim Mauser. He went 5-5 for the Phillies and was a standout in the postseason that year.

Mason made two appearances in the NLCS, pitching three scoreless innings. In the 1993 World Series, he pitched in four games, limiting the Toronto Blue Jays to one earned run in 7⅔ innings. He was in line to be the winning pitcher in two of those World Series games before the Phillies' bullpen fell apart, climaxed by Joe Carter's Series-clinching home run off Mitch Williams.

"Pitching in the 1993 World Series was a great experience," Mason said. "I felt a calmness out there on the mound. I think that was reflected in my numbers."

He started the 1994 season with the Phillies and was 1-1 with a 5.19 earned run average before being sold to the Mets. That's where he finished his career, going 2-4 with a 3.51 ERA.

That came 10 years after his debut with the World Series champion Tigers.

"I look back at how far I came from my final tryout camp to what I accomplished and I have to say I feel very fortunate," Mason said.

"I think back to that very first spring I spent in Tigertown with all the other minor-league players. We were assigned to dorm rooms and every floor on the dorm had bulletin boards. That's where they posted which players had made it and which had been released or reassigned. I kept checking to see if I was let go, but luckily my name never made that list. I survived."

Mason's final major-league totals are those of a survivor. He played for seven teams in nine big-league seasons over 11 years, posting a 22-35 record and a 4.02 ERA, pitching 416⅓ innings in 232 games and earning 13 saves along the way.

Mason was a teammate of Hall of Famers Tony Gwynn and Steve Carlton. He pitched for a World Series winner. He was a standout in the 1993 World Series, though for the losing team. He also experienced the humbling side of the game.

He gave up three home runs to start a game, a major-league record, surrendering four-baggers to San Diego's Marvell Wynne, Tony Gwynn, and John Kruk in the bottom of the first inning of an April 13, 1987, contest while pitching for the Giants. On a windy day in Wrigley Field two weeks later, on April 29, he lined what would have a sharp single to right field—had he not been thrown out at first base.

"Stick around long enough and the game will humble you," Mason said. "You just have to keep believing in yourself."

The tiny town of Bellaire still does. The Masons retired to Roger's home town. He established the Northern Michigan Hour of Prayer Bible study group with Terry, a nurse, in 2005. Their two children, Jeff and Amy, are grown.

"As it turns out, Detroit was only my first stop in the big leagues," Mason said. "I would have been satisfied if 1984 had been my only year. I consider myself lucky to play for my home team in my home state in one of the best years in Tigers history. It doesn't get any better than that."

Sid Monge
by Tracy J.R. Collins

Monge doesn't need a rest;
That's why he's among the best.
He is one who earns his pay
Pitching almost every day.
    –Dan Coughlin, April 24, 1979

HOW MANY baseball players, good—even great—baseball players have never played in a World Series? Moreover, how many players can say that they played for both of the teams competing in the World Series? Since the first modern World Series was played, in 1903, only one man can make these claims, Sid Monge. He will tell you that it was luck. He will even tell you about Father Time, or about the power of a positive attitude, but upon seeing a list of his accomplishments and learning of his championships at every level, two facts emerge. Sid Monge was not only a gifted athlete and pitcher, and a talented coach, but he was also a hard worker. As Dan Coughlin noted in 1979, Monge was known as the man willing to pitch every day if that was what it took to get the job done.

DETROIT TIGERS 1984: WHAT A START! WHAT A FINISH!

Isidro "Sid" Pedroza Monge was born on April 11, 1951, in Agua Prieta in Sonora state in northwestern Mexico. He was the second oldest of six children born to Consuelo and Pedroza Cardenas. He described his childhood "as not your typical childhood," adding: "It was adverse and unconventional. I don't recommend it to anyone." Monge's parents divorced when he was 8 years old. Two sisters and a brother went to live with his mother, and two other sisters and Sid went to live with his father. Monge's father, the head mechanic for a trucking fleet, went to the United States, and for the next 18 months, Monge was shuttled among aunts and uncles at the border until he could join his father in the Los Angeles area. As a 9-year-old, Monge found himself in a foreign country, learning a second language, and starting the fifth grade in Rancho Cucamonga, California. It was a tough start for anyone trying to make a life for himself, let alone someone who would grow up to be a successful major-league baseball player. Then came "Uncle Frank." Frank Pedroza, an uncle on his mother's side, was seven years older than Monge and gave him his first glove. "I looked up to him," Sid said. "He loved baseball. If he had been an outlaw, I probably would have followed that. He gave me my first glove, a right-hander's glove. I just wore it on the wrong hand." Frank made a difference in Monge's life. So did the chance to play baseball. "Baseball saved me," Sid told Bob Sudyk in May 1979. "It helped me deal with life. It totally occupied me. I was too busy playing ball to feel sorry for myself or be tempted to break the law. I was poor all my life until I signed (a professional contract)."

Monge lived with his siblings, father and stepmother in Rancho Cucamonga until his last two years of high school. But more turbulence crept into his life. Recalling the time in 2010, he said, "I'm an outsider, I'm not related to her, so I was treated like a stepchild, God rest her soul, she was kind of on the mean side to me, that's what led me to leave the house. I had had enough. I had to tell my dad that I just could not live with his new wife." So, at 16 Monge moved out. He moved to Brawley, California, near the Mexican border, rented a room and began to support himself. Monge told Cleveland sports reporter Dan Coughlin in 1979, "I was always short of cash. I was in the poorhouse. I wouldn't ask my father for anything. I was too proud. I'd earn it some way." That desire and work ethic helped him through the next few years. Unlike his high-school teammates, Monge was working 40 hours a week to pay for rent and groceries, working on his grades, and playing sports. He was on the honor roll in his last two years of Brawley High School. He also was involved in every sport imaginable. When asked what he liked to do as a kid, he quickly replied, "Sports, sports, and more sports." He played football, basketball, and baseball, and ran cross-country and track. During one season he played baseball and ran cross-country at the same time. He also outlined plans for his life. "My priority was school and preparing myself for my future. I was going to go to college and become a high-school teacher. I was going to double-major in Spanish and physical education. I had all of these ideas and plans already laid out. My dad always told me, 'Make your mind and body work—don't be a mechanic or work in the fields.'"

In June 1970, Monge graduated from high school, and on June 4, 1970, he was drafted as a pitcher by the California Angels in the 24th round of the amateur draft. He signed his first pro contract for $3,000. The Angels were interested in him because, according to Ray Herbat in *The Sporting News* in 1979, "An Angels scout saw Sid in a three-hit victory for the league championship in Imperial Valley and the California organization became interested in him." He was sent to California's Rookie League team in Idaho Falls, Idaho.

It was an anxious, exciting, and energetic time not only for Monge personally but also for the country. Other young men were getting drafted, not into major-league baseball, but into the military to fight in Vietnam. Monge's manager in Idaho, Bob Clear, who saw potential in him, was also an officer in the National Guard, encouraged Monge to join the California National Guard. By doing so, Monge could fulfill his military commitment while at the same time staying in the United States and playing baseball. Always the hard worker, Monge found that baseball and being in the military weren't enough to keep him busy. That summer he also took correspondence courses through California State University at Los Angeles. Monge completed his basic training at Fort Knox, Kentucky, and then moved back west. He learned to survive in the minor-league baseball system; he also learned how to drive a tank. For the next six years, Monge played baseball wherever he was and returned one weekend a month and two weeks during the summer to Brawley to train with the National Guard. Success followed Monge wherever he went. As happened with the Imperial Valley championship that got him noticed, Idaho Falls won the championship of the Pioneer League in his year with them.

After a 5-1 record at Idaho Falls, Monge was promoted to the Quad Cities team in Davenport, Iowa, of the Midwest League. Once again, his team won the championship, this time when he beat future Hall of Famer Goose Gossage, 3-2. Earlier in the season, on May 4, Monge pitched a no-hitter—the only one of his career—against the Cedar Rapids Cardinals, winning 6-0. He told *The Sporting News*, "This is my first no-hitter. I came close two or three times in high school, but never had one before." Including the no-hitter, he threw five shutouts for the Midwest League champions that summer. The no-hitter almost never happened. A Cedar Rapids batter hit an apparent double, but an observant Quad Cities player, Terry Tuley, noticed from the dugout that the batter had missed first base and appealed to the umpire. The umpire upheld the appeal, ruled the batter out, and Monge's no-hitter was saved.

In 1972 Monge pitched for Shreveport of the Texas League, where he slumped. He finished the season with a 5-10 record. Even so, as one of the organization's top southpaws, he was invited to spring training by the Angels. Of that summer, Monge told writer Ray Herbat in 1975, "I thought I did well and I figured even if I didn't stick with the big club I would at least go to [the Triple-A minor-league team in] Salt Lake

City. But then they sent me back to Double-A (Shreveport). I was very disappointed." During the 1973 and 1974 seasons Monge pitched in El Paso of the Texas League, which had become the Angels' Double-A affiliate. In 1973 he finished the season with a record of 7-11 and was still hoping for his chance to move up. "They said they had too many pitchers coming off the big club and they had to pitch in Triple-A. I was very depressed. I lost my first two starts and began to realize that I wasn't concentrating on the mound." That is when he met Sylvia Chavez. According to The Sporting News' Herbat, Monge believed she helped his pitching: "I met Sylvia on a blind date. Her brother-in-law introduced us. Sylvia and I talked about baseball much, and she learned how to keep charts on my pitches. I began to concentrate again and wound up with a nine-game winning streak. I'm pitching more with my head now." Monge married Sylvia in June 1974, pitched in the Texas League's All-Star Game, and finished the season at 14-5. "I finally got my head together," he said.

In 1975, he was finally given a chance in Triple-A with the Salt Lake City Gulls of the Pacific Coast League. He finished the season with a 14-9 record and a 4.63 ERA, and pitched in the playoffs. After the playoffs he was called up by the Angels.

On September 12, 1975, Monge made his major-league debut. He pitched in relief for the Angels against the Kansas City Royals. It was not a memorable debut. He threw $4\frac{1}{3}$ innings, gave up six hits and three runs, and struck out two batters. He did not figure in the decision. Yet Monge was with the big team to stay. The 1976 season was his first full year with the Angels, and although his role as a starter was not one of baseball legend, he was involved in some historic moments. On July 6 Monge gave up future Hall of Famer Frank Robinson's final home run. On September 12 the first anniversary of his arrival in the big leagues, Monge threw a fastball to 53-year-old Minnie Minoso, who was making a one-game "comeback" with the Chicago White Sox. Minoso singled and became the oldest player to get a hit in the major leagues. Monge pitched $117\frac{2}{3}$ innings and ended the season with a 6-7 record and a 3.37 ERA in 32 games. Still, it was frustrating to find himself working only four games and pitching $12\frac{1}{3}$ innings for the Angels in the 1977 season's first month. Thus, it was a relief when he was traded on May 11 to the Cleveland Indians. The Indians sent a pair of left-handed pitchers, Dave LaRoche and Dave Schuler, to the Angels for Monge, outfielder Bruce Bochte, and $250,000 cash.

For Monge the cold shores of Lake Erie were certainly a world away from sunny California and his warm Mexican homeland, but maybe it was just the change he needed, for his years with the Indians helped Monge develop as a major-league pitcher. Speaking of the trade, Monge said, "I'm pleased—real pleased—for a lot of reasons. Mr. [Phil] Seghi [Indians general manager] has promised me the opportunity to pitch and prove myself, and that's all I ever wanted."

Cleveland indeed proved to be good for the hard-working Monge. It offered his best memory in baseball as a player. On May 17, 1978, Monge pitched $6\frac{1}{3}$ scoreless innings in relief against the New York Yankees, giving up just one hit.

He savored the experience: "It was almost a perfect game. Thurman Munson blooped a single. I remember that day. I didn't sleep for days. Before 1977 it took me a few years to get established. That game turned my career around." Following his first four games for Cleveland after the trade, his manager, Frank Robinson, said, "He throws harder than I thought." Monge pitched in three of Cleveland's first four games after his arrival and was glad to be working again. He told sportswriter Russell Schneider in a Sporting News article that June: "I believe in myself and I think I can help any team, as either a starter or reliever. I prefer to start, though I can relieve if that's what they want because I've got the kind of arm that can pitch every day if necessary." It was in fact Monge's ability to keep on working that garnered him attention at the beginning of the 1979 season, his finest.

On April 24, 1979, Dan Coughlin, writing in the Cleveland Plain Dealer, described Monge as having "a good arm and a rubber arm. He can pitch almost every day. He thrives on work." He wrote that Indians manager Jeff Torborg, the bullpen coach when Monge was acquired, said of Monge: "I've been in his corner since he got here. The more we used him, the better he got. Each time out he has more confidence."

Monge had spent the winter of 1978 pitching in Culican, Mexico, for Tomatores de Culiacan. He appeared in 45 of the Tomatores' 72 games, going 5-4 with 21 saves and a 1.05 ERA. The following April, thought his arm might be burned out. Monge told Coughlin about the ability of his arm to work day after day: "In one stretch [this winter] I pitched eight days in a row. I pitched three innings one day and the next day we had a morning-afternoon doubleheader. I pitched one inning in the morning game and two-thirds of an inning in the afternoon game. I wanted to see how much my arm could take. It was amazing. My arm bounced back very effectively every day, even though it was a very hectic schedule. I'm living proof that you can do it."

Monge worked more innings in 1979 than in any other season in his career. It was his best year. He was named American League Pitcher of the Month for July. In $29\frac{1}{3}$ innings pitched during the month, Monge allowed only 17 hits and struck out 17. The Indians won 11 of the 12 games he pitched in. When Monge was asked if he had found a niche in relief instead of as a starter, he replied, "I enjoy pitching. Being the late man in the bullpen keeps you on your toes. It has changed my life in pitching because I'm concentrating on one particular thing—relief. And you know you'll be back in there the next day. I'm ready each day and when I'm brought in, I'm ready for anything." He was one of three relievers named to the 1979 American League All-Star Team (which also included Nolan Ryan and Tommy John) and the first Mexican-born pitcher to make a major-league All-Star Team. Monge posted career bests that season: a 12-10 record, 19 saves, 76 appearances, and 131 innings pitched. He won the Cleveland sportswriters' Good Guy Award for his accessibility and sense of humor. Monge was arguably the best relief pitcher in baseball that summer.

DETROIT TIGERS 1984: WHAT A START! WHAT A FINISH!

Monge pitched two more seasons for the Indians but couldn't duplicate his strong 1979 season. Life has a way of getting in the way of baseball sometimes. He and his wife, Sylvia, went through a messy divorce during the 1980 season. Monge told *Cleveland Plain Dealer* writer Burt Graeff, "The whole thing should be over within the next three weeks. The judge in Cleveland read newspaper accounts of how this had been affecting me and has tried to get it resolved as soon as possible. I guess he's an Indians fan." With his usual sunny disposition, Monge declared he was on the upswing and ready to get back to work. However, Monge's numbers never fully recovered. He finished the 1980 season with a 3-5 record, 14 saves and a 3.53 ERA, and he ended 1981 with a 3-5 record and a 4.34 ERA. According to Terry Pluto of the *Cleveland Plain Dealer*, "Monge is an enigma. In 1979 he was elected to the All-Star Team. In the last two years, he has tossed 21 home-run pitches in 147 innings. That is one gopherball for every seven innings, which is a frighteningly poor ratio." Because of his waning statistics, Monge was granted free agency on November 13, 1981, but two months later on January 21, 1982, the Indians re-signed him. Then, less than three weeks later, on February 16, he was dealt to the Philadelphia Phillies for outfielder Bake McBride.

Marvin Miller, executive director of the Major League Baseball Players Association, challenged the legality of the trade. *The Sporting News* wrote, "Miller was unhappy over a report that the Indians insisted on Monge waiving a no-trade clause before becoming a free agent." Miller accused the Indians and 10 other clubs of collusion. In *The Sporting News* on March 6, Bill Conlin wrote that Monge and McBride were both happy with their new teams and that Marvin Miller, "a man near the hot core of the malignant tumor of bilateral greed eating away at all pro sports, immediately hollered foul." But Monge said, "I couldn't be happier about this deal. I'm going to a class organization and a top contender. Add to that the fact that I'll be reunited with my catcher, Bo Diaz [who had caught Monge in Cleveland]. The trade is a real plus for me." In the end, the trade went through, and Monge started off the 1982 season as a member of the Phillies.

Perhaps a happier Monge meant more effective throwing from the bullpen. On August 30, 1982, Hal Bodley reported in *The Sporting News* that since that summer's All Star Game, "Monge has been the Phils' most consistent southpaw reliever." Once again, it was Monge's need to work and work every day that seemed to make him stronger. "It has taken time for me to get used to the hitters in this league," he said. "In the beginning it was tough. I was not getting enough work. For me to be effective, I have to pitch frequently." He became a part of history again that season. On July 19 future Hall of Fame outfielder Tony Gwynn got his first hit, a double, off Monge. Sid finished the 1982 season in fine form again with a 7-1 record. The next season began equally well.

By the middle of May 1983, Monge had won three games, all in relief, without a loss. Then on May 22, he was traded to the San Diego Padres for outfielder Joe Lefebvre. For Monge it was a welcome change if for no other reason than that he was to be reunited with Dick Williams and Norm Sherry, two of his former coaches with the Angels. It was Sherry who had told Monge he could be a baseball player. "He made me believe I could be a major-league player. He made me a baseball player," Monge said, further declaring, "I want to work. I'll do anything but dishes and windows." He was 7-3 with the Padres.

In June of 1984 Monge, with a 2-1 record for the Padres in 13 games pitched, was sold to the Tigers. With 100 regular-season games left, Monge found himself in Detroit with a team that was red-hot. In a 2008 interview, he said, "When you're traded, you're puzzled, but Sparky [Anderson, Detroit's manager] told me he was going to try and get me into as many games as possible. They didn't really need anybody like me. They were magnificent. It was like a family. They were deep in the bullpen and Willie [Hernandez] was having a good year."

It was a good year for the Tigers, but they did need Monge, and he pitched in 32 games that year. His favorite moment from that memorable season, he said it occurred on July 21, the day he got his first victory for the Tigers. He won the game in relief of Glenn Abbott, pitching four innings and allowing the Texas Rangers just one unearned run. "I didn't quite feel like a part of (the team) until the day I won my first game for them. Then I really felt like I had contributed to the season." After all, it was unlike Monge to have success happening around him without his making a big contribution to achieve it. Even though that was the only game Monge won for the Tigers, in 19 appearances, it was a fabulous season, for him and the team. After the Tigers won the World Series, he exclaimed, "I was walking on a cloud! It seemed like I didn't sleep for 16 days!"

After the celebrating was over, Monge was granted free agency for the final time on October 25, 11 days after the World Series ended. "At 36, 37 (he was actually only 33), my fastball was leaving me, so I decided to go into coaching," he said. "Father Time tells you when it is time to go." He had pitched his last game as a major-league pitcher on September 30, 1984. But despite Father Time, Monge was not quite through pitching; in 1985 he appeared in 45 games, 34 for Detroit's Nashville farm club and 11 for the Hawaii Islanders, a Pittsburgh farm team in the Pacific Coast League.

Monge loved everything about baseball, and he found a natural home waiting for him as a pitching coach. He said, "I am a true throwback, an absolute baseball junkie." He coached for the Rockford Expos (Midwest League) in 1990, the Fayetteville Generals (Carolina League, Tigers) in 1992, the Peoria Chiefs (Midwest League, Cardinals) in 2000, the Potomac Cannons (Carolina League, Cardinals) in 2001, the New Jersey Cardinals (New York-Penn League) in 2003-05, for the State College Spikes (New York-Penn League, Cardinals) in 2006, and the Johnson City Cardinals (Appalachian League) in 2007. In 2010 he was the pitching coach for the Sultanes de Monterrey in the Mexican League. Monge said he cannot help but notice that things have changed. Stardom and notoriety are greater than ever, but there is a price to pay in loss of personal privacy and security. "The glamour, the exposure, it's quite a thing nowadays. You need 17 IDs to get into the clubhouse now. The money is out of control and players do not seem as dedicated to their careers in baseball as they used to be."

Monge's own dedication, hard work, championship pitching and personality were honored in June 2004 when he was one of four men inducted into the *Salon de la Fama*, the Mexican Baseball Hall of Fame. Being honored was especially important to Monge because during his playing days he was involved with 10 different teams in Mexico in winter ball. He played with five—Culiacan, Guaymas, Navojoa, Mexicali, and Mazatlan—and also coached for five—Mexicali, Obregon, Mazatlan, Monterrey, and Guasave. He was part of six Caribbean World Series title-winning teams, three coaching and three playing from 1972 to 1990.

Perhaps a more interesting testimony to Monge's reputation not only as a player but for his personality is represented in the Sid Monge Fan Club, an active group that meets once a year at his various minor-league games. It is also a true testament to his generosity during his playing days. The club has an extensive Web site (http://www.geocities.com/sidmongefc/). Monge has four children. His oldest son, Michael, 33, graduated from San Diego State University, and was the regional distribution center manager for Frazee Paint in San Diego. His daughter, Mandy, 28, graduated in 2010 from the University of Arizona. His 22-year-old son, John, was attending trade school in Boston, and his youngest son, Andy, 10, lived with him and his current wife, Lorena, in Mexico, and was learning to throw a baseball..

References

Articles

"Angels' Monge Granted Reprieve in No-Hitter." *The Sporting News*, May 22, 1971. 43.

Bodley, Hal. "Addition of Monge Crowds Bullpen." *The Sporting News*, March 6, 1982. 28.

Bodley, Hal "Monge Regains Bullpen Form." *The Sporting News*, August 30, 1982. 41.

Coughlin, Dan. "Monge Bringing Belief to Indians." *Cleveland Plain Dealer*, April 24, 1979. C1, C3.

Conlin, Bill. "Monge, McBride Happy; Miller Isn't." *The Sporting News* March 6, 1982. 31.

Graeff, Burt. "The Real El Sid Finally Stands Up." *Cleveland Plain Dealer*, no date listed. C1

Herbat, Ray. "Salt Lake's Monge Enjoys Raindrops with Victories." *The Sporting News*, May 10, 1979. 35.

Nold, Bob. "Monge Impressive by Any Measurement." *Akron Beacon Journal*, June 3, 1979. D4.

Pluto, Terry. "Monge Signs with Tribe for $1 Million." *Cleveland Plain Dealer*, January 21, 1982. D1.

Sanchez, Jesse "Talking Beisbol: HOF Mexico Style" Baseball Perspectives page, www.mlb.com. June 17, 2004.

Schneider, Russell. "Ex-Angels Take Quickly to Indian Blankets." *The Sporting News*, June 4, 1977. 13.

"Sid Monge." Baseball-Reference.com, 30 April 2008. http://www.baseball-reference.com/m/mongesi01.shtml.

"Sid Monge Fan Club." June 15, 2008. http://www.geocities.com/sidmongefc/.

Sudyk, Bob. "Monge Travels Far on Hard Road As a Youth." *The Sporting News*, May 12, 1979, 7.

Utnick, Dave. "A Man for All Seasons." Publication and date not given.

Other Sources

Collins, Tracy. E-mail interview with Amanda Monge. August 5 and 12, 2008.

Collins, Tracy. Personal interviews with Sid Monge. June 19, 2008, and August 1, 2008.

Jack Morris
by Stew Thornley

WITH A COMPETITIVE, sometimes combative, spirit and a devastating split-fingered fastball, Jack Morris became the pitcher of the 1980s and continued his dominance into the early 1990s. His 162 victories in the 1980s were 22 more than those of runner-up Dave Stieb of Toronto.

Four times Morris was a member of a world championship team, including a one-year stint in his home state, pitching a 10-inning shutout in the final game of the 1991 World Series for the Minnesota Twins. He finished his career with 254 wins.

John Scott Morris was born on May 16, 1955, in St. Paul, Minnesota, and grew up watching the Minnesota Twins at Metropolitan Stadium in suburban Bloomington. He also remembered a television being wheeled into his grade-school classroom so they could watch the 1965 World Series, which the Twins lost in seven games to the Los Angeles Dodgers.

Morris' father, Arvid, was an electronics technician for Minnesota Mining and Manufacturing (which became 3M), and his mother, Dona, was a housewife. Arvid and Dona moved to Grand Rapids, in northern Minnesota, after their son helped Arvid retire early from 3M "thanks to baseball." Jack was the second of three children, with an older sister, Marsha, and a younger brother, Tom, a left-handed pitcher who was a college teammate for one year and later spent two seasons in the minor leagues. (Tom was drafted by the Twins in 1978 but did not sign; he then pitched two years, for Quad Cities in the Cubs organization.)

The family lived in several Twin Cities suburbs before settling into the Highland Park neighborhood of St. Paul. In addition to baseball, Morris was a ski jumper for the St. Paul Ski Club when he was in junior high school and played on the varsity basketball team for Highland Park High School. On the diamond, Morris was a third baseman and shortstop. With better control than his older brother, Tom was the top pitcher at Highland Park, and Jack's appearances on the mound in high school and on his American Legion team were relatively rare.

"He could throw hard enough to knock down the backstop in high school," Highland Park baseball coach Bill Lorenz said of Jack. "He just couldn't hit the backstop."

However, because of his strong arm, Morris was recruited by coach Glen Tuckett and given a scholarship to pitch for Brigham Young University in Provo, Utah. Until his senior year, Morris had hoped to pitch for the Minnesota Gophers under longtime coach Dick Siebert. "All through high school [Minnesota was] where I wanted to play," he said. However, the Gophers did not recruit Morris. In addition, Morris took a closer look at the Gophers' yearly schedules and realized how short they were. The Gophers at that time were making one Southern trip a year, and, before the Hubert H. Humphrey Metrodome in Minneapolis was built, the team could not start its home schedule until April, leaving barely two months to play.

"I wanted to play for a baseball school where they played in good weather and good teams," Morris said. He applied and was accepted at Arizona, Arizona State, and Florida State, but he would have been a walk-on. Then BYU offered a scholarship. The Cougars would play a schedule featuring Arizona, Arizona State, Cal State Fullerton, Hawaii. "The schedule was phenomenal," Morris said. "I knew I would get exposure. That's why I went there."

Morris lettered with the Cougars in 1975 and 1976. His Brigham Young teammates included his brother (who, unlike Jack, made the team as a freshman) for two years; Cam Killebrew, son of future Hall of Famer Harmon Killebrew; and Vance Law, who went on to the major leagues and later came back to Brigham Young as its head baseball coach. Law's father, Vernon Law, a 16-year major-league veteran who won the Cy Young Award in 1960 and worked with the Brigham Young pitchers in the 1970s. Law helped transform Morris from a youngster with a strong but erratic arm into an accomplished pitcher who was drafted after his junior season in 1976 in the fifth round by the Detroit Tigers.

Morris was assigned to the Tigers' Double-A farm team in Montgomery in the Southern League, where he struggled with his control. Morris walked a batter an inning and had a 6.25 earned run average in 36 innings pitched in 1976. Nevertheless, he was promoted to the Triple-A level in 1977.

Pitching for Evansville in the American Association, Morris lowered his walks and upped his strikeouts (both on a per-inning basis) in 20 starts with the Triplets. Morris got the call to the big leagues when the Tigers put Mark Fidrych, who had won 19 games as a rookie in 1976 but had knee and arm problems in 1977, on the disabled list.

Morris made his major-league debut in Chicago on July 26, 1977, relieving Dave Roberts in the fourth inning with the Tigers behind, 6-2. He inherited a runner at first base with no outs but got out of the inning without the runner scoring. Morris pitched four innings and allowed two runs as the Tigers lost, 8-3. Five days later, he got his first start, pitching against Bert Blyleven in Texas. Morris allowed two runs in the first inning but gave up only three hits and no runs after that as he pitched nine innings, walking five batters and striking out 11. Both he and Blyleven went nine innings, and neither got a decision as the Rangers won in 10 innings.

Morris stayed in the starting rotation, winning one and losing one over the next month. However, he also had some arm problems. The Tigers, after the situation with Fidrych, had become protective of their young pitchers and, at the end of August, shut Morris down for the season. "He's too good a prospect to fool with," said Tigers manager Ralph Houk.

Morris was back in 1978, but he was again limited by arm problems and finished the year with a won-lost record of 3-5. In 1979, he didn't even make the team out of spring training and was sent back to Evansville. However, he wasn't expected to stay long in the minors. "You better get a good look at him

DETROIT TIGERS 1984: WHAT A START! WHAT A FINISH!

now," said Evansville manager Jim Leyland, "because he won't be here in a month."

Leyland's prediction was accurate because Morris was back in Detroit, this time for good, making his first start for the Tigers on May 13. Despite the delayed arrival with the Tigers, Morris won 17 games and had an ERA of 3.28, fifth best in the American League.

To this point, Morris had relied on a standard repertoire of a fastball, slider, and changeup. In the early 1980s, he began having some problems with his slider and was on the lookout for a new pitch. "My slider started flattening out. I couldn't get the big break anymore," he said. "I was having some inconsistency with my slider, hanging a few too many. I was looking for that 'out' pitch. My fastball was still good, changeup was still good, but I was looking for that 'strike three' pitch."

It was about that time that Morris discovered the forkball, or split-fingered fastball. Although his pitching coach with the Tigers, Roger Craig, is often credited with teaching him the splitter, Morris said the credit belonged to his Tigers teammate, Milt Wilcox. In the Chicago Cubs organization in the mid-1970s, Wilcox had crossed paths with Bruce Sutter, who would make a Hall of Fame career out of the splitter. "He watched Sutter throw it," Morris said of Wilcox. "(Wilcox) couldn't throw it himself because his fingers were too short." One day Morris was throwing in the bullpen when Wilcox asked if he'd like to try the forkball. "I threw about eight or nine pitches and nothing happened," Morris related. He was ready to give up, but Wilcox suggested some adjustments with the grip and release. "I threw one and the bottom dropped out. I thought, 'I gotta work on this thing because this is ridiculously nasty.' And I threw about six more in a row that all worked the same way.... I saw what this thing could do, and I said, 'I've got to master this thing.'"

Morris said he started working on the pitch at the end of the 1982 season and started throwing it regularly in 1983, the first year he won 20 games. "In 1983 and 1984, I pretty much had it to myself in the American League," he said. "It was a total gift. It was like nobody knew it was coming. It was awesome. It was so much fun. And then everyone else started trying to learn how to pitch and then hitters started to adjust to it. My forkball was above average. I could almost tell guys it was coming, and they still couldn't hit it.... When I threw it right, nobody hit it."

Led by Morris, the Tigers got off to a great start in 1984, winning their first nine games and 16 of their first 17. Morris had four of the team's wins in that opening run. He pitched the season opener in Minnesota, where he had never lost a game in the majors, and won, 8-1.

Four days later, on a cold and wet day in Chicago, Morris was unhittable. After eight innings, the Tigers had a 4-0 lead, and Morris hadn't allowed a hit. As he sat in the dugout in the top of the ninth, his teammates stayed away from him, following the superstitious tradition of not mentioning that a no-hitter was in progress. However, Morris broke the silence and declared, "I'm going to do it." On his way back to the mound, he turned toward a couple of hecklers and said, "Just watch."

He retired the first two White Sox batters and went to a 3-2 count on Greg Luzinski. The next pitch was close, but plate umpire Durwood Merrill called it a ball. Even many of the partisan Chicago fans, hoping to see a no-hitter, howled in protest. But Morris got ahead of the next batter, Ron Kittle, then came in with a splitter. The pitch was low, but Kittle bit, trying to hold up but going too far with his swing. Morris had his no-hitter, the first for the Tigers since Jim Bunning no-hit the Boston Red Sox in 1958.

Morris won 10 of his first 11 decisions in 1984, and for a time all was well. However, he missed two starts in June with a sore elbow. He won his first game back but then lost three in a row, dropping his season record to 12-6.

Morris battled with umpires, sometimes blaming them for his problems. He resigned as the team's player representative and quit talking to the press, which had already dubbed him "Mount Morris" for his sometimes explosive temper. Roger Craig publicly said Morris should "quit acting like a baby," and relations with his fellow players weren't much better.

However, as Morris regained his form on the mound, he began talking with the press again and healed other rifts as the Tigers cruised to the American League East title and on to win the World Series. Morris went the distance and won both his starts in the World Series as the Tigers beat the San Diego Padres, four games to one.

In 1985, Morris went 16-9 with a 3.33 ERA, placing ninth in the AL in wins and ERA, third with 191 strikeouts, sixth with 257 innings pitched, and fourth with 13 complete games (two of them shutouts). He also led the league for the third year in a row in wild pitches, and gave up 110 bases on balls, second in the loop. In 1986, Morris posted a 21-8 won-lost record with a 3.27 ERA in 267 innings. His 21 wins were second in the American League, behind Roger Clemens, and he led the league with six shutouts while finishing fifth in the voting for the Cy Young Award. Morris' contract with the Tigers was up after the season, making him one of the top free agents on the market.

Fans in Morris' home state were excited about the possibility of seeing him pitch for the Twins as he came to Minnesota in late 1986 to talk with the team's owner, Carl Pohlad, and new general manager Andy MacPhail. However, Morris left without the parties reaching an agreement on a contract.

Morris and his agent, Dick Moss, had presented four proposals, including one for a two-year contract in which the salary would be determined by an arbitrator. MacPhail later decried the take-it-or-leave-it approach of Moss and Morris, who had also drawn some criticism for his opulent attire that day—a full-length fur coat. In reality, however, it was unlikely the Twins would have signed Morris, since major-league teams, operating in concert for the purpose of keeping salaries down, had adopted a hands-off policy with regard to signing free agents from other teams.. (Arbitrators later determined that teams had conspired against free agents over the course of three offseasons, and the owners had to agree to establish a $280 million fund to distribute to the players affected by the collusion.)

"No, there was no chance of signing," Morris said of his negotiations with the Twins and the role of collusion. He said he had once been asked if he would ever write a book about his career and added, "If I ever did, it would be about the collusion years in baseball. Nobody has talked about it, it has been pushed under the table. I led the charge in that whole thing, and I understood it better than anyone else. I was the premier pitcher in baseball, and I couldn't get a nickel, couldn't get a penny.

"I had actually almost agreed to terms with Mr. Pohlad when Andy MacPhail stepped out of the room. My agent and I had a few minutes to talk alone with Carl, and Carl pretty much agreed to a contract. Andy came back and excused us and told Carl there was no way he could sign me. That in itself defines what was going on. Andy was on the phone with somebody, and somebody told him, 'Nobody gets signed.' And that's the end of that story."

Morris re-signed with Detroit for the 1987 season and, with a record of 18-11, helped the Tigers win the East Division title with a record of 98-64. However, the Tigers lost in the playoffs to the Minnesota Twins. Morris lost his only start in the series, which was also the first time he had lost in Minnesota as a member of the Tigers. (Morris had been the losing pitcher for the American League in the 1985 All-Star Game at the Metrodome in Minneapolis.)

In the meantime, he went through a couple of losing seasons. His 1989 season included elbow surgery for a stress fracture, and he finished with a record of 6-14. Despite four straight wins at the end of the year, he finished the 1990 season with a record of 15-18. However, he was second in the American League in innings pitched (and tied for second in the majors) and demonstrated that he could still be counted on as a workhorse.

Morris was a free agent again after the 1990 season. With collusion by this time a thing of the past, Morris finally signed with the Twins for 1991. He had turned down a three-year contract worth more than $9 million from the Tigers to sign for a guaranteed salary of $3 million a year with the Twins and the chance to earn more based on incentives. The contract he signed also allowed him the option to become a free agent after the end of each season.

Morris was emotional as he talked about how much it meant to sign with his hometown team. He even shed a few tears, an act that would be held against him by many local fans within a year.

For the 1991 season, Morris was outstanding, posting an 18-12 won-lost record while leading the team with $246^{2}/_{3}$ innings pitched. The Twins, after having finished in last place in 1990, won the AL West title. Morris got the call for the opening game of the league playoffs. He won that game, as well as Game Four, and the Twins defeated the Toronto Blue Jays, four games to one, to advance to the World Series. Their opponents were the Atlanta Braves, another team that had finished last the season before.

Morris won the series opener against the Braves, and did not get a decision in Game Four, which the Twins lost. The series went to a decisive seventh game, and Morris was on the mound again with John Smoltz pitching for Atlanta.

The aces matched shutout innings. Morris found himself in a jam in the fifth as the Braves put runners at first and third with one out. But Morris used his split-fingered fastball to get Terry Pendleton to pop out and then went to a full count on Ron Gant. Morris placed a fastball right where he wanted it, on the low outside corner, freezing Gant with a called third strike to end the inning.

The game remained scoreless into the eighth, when the Braves mounted an even greater threat, putting runners at second and third with no outs.

While Twins fans were sweating, Morris later said he was still calm. "I never had a negative thought," he maintained. "I'm such a positive thinker, I never really felt like I was in trouble. It was my will that carried me through the game."

Morris needed every bit of his will, as well as his nasty splitter, as Gant stepped to the plate. Gant had stranded a pair of runners in each of his previous two at-bats, although this time, with no outs, even an out could bring in a run. Minnesota responded by pulling in its infield. Gant popped the first pitch foul, then went after a splitter on the outside part of the plate, resulting in a feeble grounder down the first-base line. First baseman Kent Hrbek fielded it and kept his eyes on Lonnie Smith, making sure he held at third, as he tagged Gant for the first out.

Getting Gant was the key to the inning as it now allowed the Twins to walk the dangerous David Justice to load the bases, set up a double-play, and bring Sid Bream to the plate. Bream pulled a 1-and-2 pitch down to Hrbek, who fired home to start an inning-ending first-to-home-to-first double play.

Past the jam, Morris appeared stronger, putting down the Braves in order on eight pitches in the ninth. Twins manager Tom Kelly planned to send reliever Rick Aguilera out for the 10th inning, figuring Morris, with 118 pitches to that point, had had enough. But Morris told Kelly, "I'm not going anywhere. This is my game."

Morris later said that, after getting out of the eighth inning, "I was getting stronger. I just felt like I could have gone another six, seven, eight more innings. I was getting stronger as the game went on."

Morris again retired the Braves on eight pitches in the 10th inning. In the bottom of the inning, the Twins finally scored to win the game, 1-0, and the World Series.

"I probably had the best mindset in that game that I've had in any game in my whole career, and that's because I didn't allow negative thoughts into my game," Morris said. "Even when I was in trouble, I didn't acknowledge trouble. I just said, 'Well, I'll get this next guy. We're going to win this game.' If I could bottle that, I'd be the richest man in the world. If I could bottle it and sell it to athletes or sell it to businessmen or whatever, it would be a phenomenal thing. I can't hardly even describe it, but I can tell you it was something I had never experienced before and really never experienced again."

Minnesota fans celebrated their second world championship in five seasons, but the man largely responsible for the title did not stick with the Twins. He exercised his option to become a free agent after the season and signed with the Toronto Blue Jays. Reaction from Minnesota media members and fans was sharp, and his tearful press conference when he had signed with the Twins less than a year before was held against him by many.

Morris said the difference in contract offers by the Twins to retain him and the Blue Jays to acquire him "wasn't close." Morris said owner Carl Pohlad made it clear to him that the team was looking ahead to re-signing the team's star, Kirby Puckett, after the 1992 season and was conserving money for that purpose.

"I never wanted to leave here," Morris said. "I never wanted to leave Detroit [after the 1990 season]. Had Detroit taken care of me the way I felt I should have been taken care of in Detroit, I never would have left Detroit."

In Toronto, Morris played on two more world championship teams. He was 21-6 in 1992, but arm troubles hampered his 1993 season (7-12, 6.19 ERA). He didn't pitch in the World Series that year, and the Blue Jays released him at the end of the season. Morris signed with the Cleveland Indians for 1994 and had a 10-6 record and was released a few days before a players' strike ended the season.

Morris tried but failed to catch on with the Cincinnati Reds in 1995. Confident he could still pitch, Morris made a comeback in 1996 with the St. Paul Saints, an independent minor-league team. "The Twins needed pitching bad, and I wanted to come back and maybe finish my career right here again," said Morris. "But they didn't come across the street to even look at me. I guess they were still mad that I left. I don't know what happened there."

One of Morris' teammates on the Saints was another player looking to make it back to the majors: Darryl Strawberry, who ended up being signed off the St. Paul roster by the New York Yankees. "I had a chance to go to New York with Strawberry, and at the time I didn't want to play for the Yankees," Morris said. "I regret that today. If I had one thing to go back and do again, I would have signed with the Yankees and probably put two or three more [championship] rings on my finger."

Morris eventually returned to the Twins as an analyst on the team's radio broadcasts. He and his wife, Jennifer, have a son, Miles. Morris also has two grown sons, Austin and Erik, from a previous marriage.

"Life is good," he said. "I'm a very lucky person. I have my health, I have a very loving family and an organization I'm very happy to be working for. If there was any animosity between us [Morris and the Twins] for leaving … all those bridges have been mended, and I'm very happy to be here, and I think they're very happy to have me here, and I think it's a good relationship."

References

Publications

The Baseball Encyclopedia, 10th edition. New York: Macmillan. 1996.

Baseball Register (various years). St. Louis: Sporting News. Various years.

Thorn, John, Pete Palmer, Michael Gershman, and David Pietrusza, eds., with Matthew Silverman and Sean Lahman. *Total Baseball, sixth ed.* Kingston, New York: Total Sports. 1999.

Articles

Brackin, Dennis. "Morris Good Pitcher, Better Competitor," *Minneapolis Star and Tribune*, May 24, 1987, p. 1C.

Brackin, Dennis. "Comin' at Ya: Winning Is Everything for Ultra-Competitive Morris," *Minneapolis Star and Tribune*, February 6, 1991, 1C.

Brown, Curt. "Dream Becomes Reality for Morris: Being Home Like Rebirth for New Twin," *Minneapolis Star and Tribune*, February 7, 1991, 1C.

Gage, Tom. "Ejection Ends Morris' Streak," *The Sporting News*, September 19, 1983, 14.

Gage, Tom. "Morris Finally Unbuttons Lip," *The Sporting News*, September 17, 1984, 12.

Gage, Tom. "Morris' Masterpiece Silences White Sox," *The Sporting News*, April 16, 1984, 25.

Gage, Tom. "Sour Morris Buttons Lip," *The Sporting News*, August 6, 1984, 14.

Gage, Tom. "Tigers' Ace? Try Morris," *The Sporting News*, February 9, 1980, 39.

"Momentary Morris," *The Sporting News*, May 12, 1979, 37.

Ray, Ralph. "Women Writers Win Access to Yank Clubhouse," *The Sporting News*, October 14, 1978, 36.

Roe, Jon. "Money Talks, Morris Walks: Toronto's $10 Million Offer Lands Righthander," *Minneapolis Star and Tribune*, December 19, 1991, 1C.

Roe, Jon, Sid Hartman. "Morris, Twins Make It Official: Pitcher Gets Incentive-laden Contract, Role of Staff's No. 1 Starter," *Minneapolis Star and Tribune*, February 6, 1991, 1C.

"Twins Reject All Contract Proposals from Jack Morris," *Minneapolis Star and Tribune*, December 17, 1986, 3D.

"Women Not Welcome," *Sports Illustrated*, August 20, 1990, 15.

Web Sites

http://retrosheet.org

http://www.law.umkc.edu/faculty/projects/ftrials/communications/ludtke.html

Other Sources

Brigham Young University Athletic Communications Department, Provo, Utah.

MacPhail, Andy. Speech to the St. Paul Old Timers' Hot Stove League Banquet, January 28, 1987.

Thornley, Stew. E-mail correspondence with Jennifer Frey, May 2007.

Thornley, Stew. Interview with Jack Morris, July 11, 2002, in Milwaukee following Major League Baseball's press conference to name the most memorable moments in history of the game.

Thornley, Stew. Interviews with Jack Morris May 27, 2007, and June 10, 2007, in Minneapolis.

Randy O'Neal
by Charles Faber and Paul Geisler

AS THE TALL young right-hander strode to the mound that Tuesday night in September 1984 to make his first major-league start, he was not nervous. Excited, yes; determined, yes; but nervous, no. Even though it was an important game, one in which the Detroit Tigers could clinch the American League East championship, the young man kept his composure. Listening to a Detroit radio station before the game, he had heard the doubts expressed on the air. Who is this guy? Why is he pitching tonight? Why is manager Sparky Anderson starting an unknown rookie in such a game? The questions only made Randy O'Neal more determined to show that he was not a nonentity, but a capable major-league pitcher.

The game against the Milwaukee Brewers was at Tiger Stadium on September 18. Randy struck out future Hall of Famer Robin Yount, the leadoff batter, on a pitch out of the zone. His confidence surged. "I can get these guys out," he thought. "I can do this!" For seven innings O'Neal shut out the Brewers, giving up only four hits, walking one, and striking out six. Anderson brought in Willie Hernandez to pitch the eighth and ninth, preserving the shutout and the win. Willie had not blown a save all season. "The instant I came out, I knew I had a win," Randy said. "With Willie coming in, I knew there was no doubt." In remembering the game 25 years later, O'Neal said, "I could feel then something special was coming. I had dreamed of that moment all my life. It was such a special feeling. I'm very proud of that to this day. I loved my time in Detroit, and that certainly was a great night." He had the team autograph the lineup card. He still has it and cherishes it.

Randall Jeffrey O'Neal was born in Ashland, Kentucky, on August 30, 1960, the son of Gaynelle and Ralph O'Neal. As a child he moved with his parents to Florida. He attended John I. Leonard High School at Greenacres, in the central part of Palm Beach County. From his accomplishments in high school and amateur ball, he gained enough renown to be drafted four times by major-league teams in 1979 and 1980, but did not sign, preferring to pursue the sport at Palm Beach Community College for two years and at the University of Florida in 1981, when he helped the Gators win their first Southeastern Conference championship. He was one of three pitchers named to the all-tournament team.

O'Neal was selected by the Montreal Expos in the fourth round in January 1979; by the Minnesota Twins in the second round of the June 1979 secondary draft; by the Milwaukee Brewers in the third round of the January 1980 secondary; and by the Cincinnati Reds in the third round of the June 1980 secondary. Four times drafted, each time in a fourth or higher round, and four times he refused to sign. Why? Two reasons: O'Neal did not feel ready for professional baseball, and the money was not attractive enough to lure him from continuing his education. Then, on June 8, 1981, he was selected in the first round of the secondary draft (15th overall) by the Detroit Tigers. His $35,000 signing bonus was typical for first-round draftees in the early 1980s, and this time he signed and started his professional career with the Lakeland Tigers in the Florida State League.

On August 23 O'Neal pitched a seven-inning no-hitter in a 4-0 win over Winter Haven. He said he "quickly learned to compete with men, not boys." He advanced in the Tigers' system, going to Double-A Birmingham and Triple-A Evansville before joining the big club in 1984. In 1982 he won 11 games for the Birmingham Barons in the Southern League, the only time in his professional career that he won more than 10 games in a season. In 1983 and 1984 he pitched for the Evansville Triplets in the American Association, posting

DETROIT TIGERS 1984: WHAT A START! WHAT A FINISH!

a losing record each year. However, his nine wins, ten losses, and 3.57 earned-run average in 1984 showed enough promise to earn him a big-league trial late in the season.

O'Neal made his major-league debut on September 12, 1984, in Baltimore against the Orioles with three strong innings of one-hit relief. The first two hitters he faced were eventual Hall of Famers Cal Ripken Jr. and Eddie Murray. Ripken greeted O'Neal with a single, but O'Neal retired baseball's reigning iron man his second time up.

Knowing he was about to make his first start for the Tigers in the potential pennant-clincher, O'Neal spent three hours pacing in a local mall, hoping to settle his nerves. He listened to the radio that day, too, and heard people wondering who he was and why he was starting such an important game. He remembered, "Jack Morris and Dan Petry were lobbying [manager Sparky Anderson] pretty hard to let them pitch, but Sparky had faith in me and stuck with me. It was scheduled to be my first start, and he let me keep it. I'm eternally grateful for that." Randy sensed the gravity of the game before it was over: "In about the seventh inning they brought the horses and the extra security out. I could feel then something special was coming."

O'Neal remembered that night as "a fantasy to have the opportunity to pitch that game for my first start, ahead of some of the great pitchers we had. To win it was an even bigger dream that came true."

The crowd remembered his name the next day at the ballpark. "You do your wind sprints to the foul poles with the pitchers, and my second time over I hear the crowd chanting my name, 'O-Neal, O-Neal.' Had to be 20,000 there for batting practice! I'll never forget it because it would echo in that stadium."

O'Neal got his second start and second win on September 25 with five shutout innings, again versus the Brewers. In his first three big-league outings he had accrued two wins in 15 consecutive shutout innings, allowing only seven hits, two walks, and 11 strikeouts. He pitched once more in that magic 1984 season, on the final day against the New York Yankees. That outing brought him back down to earth a bit; he gave up seven earned runs in $3^{2/3}$ innings. He finished the year 2-1 with a 3.38 ERA.

O'Neal was not on the playoff roster and did not pitch in either the American League Championship Series or the World Series. He had made his contribution the night of his first major-league start. O'Neal split the 1985 and 1986 seasons between Detroit and Triple-A, relocated from Evansville to Nashville. In 1985, he appeared in 28 games for the Tigers (starting 12 of these), going 5-5 with a 3.24 ERA. And in 1986, he appeared in 37 games (starting 11), going 3-7 with a 4.33 ERA. Over the two seasons he won eight and lost 12 for the Tigers; he won six and lost six for the Sounds.

O'Neal pitched at a time when bullpen roles were evolving. The newfound prominence of closers highlighted the need for set-up men and other relief specialists. By 1986, Randy had begun the shift from his previous role of starting pitcher to becoming a middle-relief specialist.

In January 1987, the Tigers traded O'Neal, with pitcher Chuck Cary, to the Atlanta Braves for minor-leaguer Freddy Tiburcio—who never did make it to the bigs—and outfielder-designated hitter Terry Harper. O'Neal had four wins and two losses for the Braves and one loss for their International League affiliate in Richmond. The Braves sent him to the St. Louis Cardinals that July for relief pitcher Joe Boever, who made his way to Detroit in 1993. O'Neal got minimal work with the Cardinals, pitching in one game, a start, with no decision and a 1.80 ERA in 1987, and going 2-3 with a 4.75 ERA in 10 games (eight starts) in 1988. The Cardinals more often kept O'Neal in Louisville, where he was 3-1 for the Redbirds in 1987 and 3-5 in 1988. In October he was granted free agency, and he signed with the Philadelphia Phillies in December. After he appeared in 20 games (starting only one of these) with Philadelphia, going 0-1 with a 6.23 ERA, the Phils sent him to Triple-A Scranton/Wilkes-Barre, and he was 4-4 with the Red Barons in 1989. Despite an improved 2.53 ERA, the best of his career, the Phillies released him at the end of the season.

Again a free agent, O'Neal signed in January 1990 with the San Francisco Giants, where he was reunited with Roger Craig, his pitching coach in Detroit during that pennant-winning season of 1984, and now the manager of the Giants. Craig had managed the Giants into the World Series in 1989, and remembered what O'Neal could do on the hill. This time, though, Randy appeared solely in a relief role for Craig, going 1-0 with a 3.83 ERA and no saves in 26 games spanning 47 innings. The reunion did not last the entire season. O'Neal also spent time in the Giants' farm system. He pitched three innings for High-A San Jose in his only appearance there, and got into seven games with Triple-A Phoenix. Despite five wins and no losses and a 2.97 earned run average for the Firebirds, he was released at the end of the season.

Along the way O'Neal tore his labrum and his rotator cuff and had surgery. Then he reinjured his shoulder. He continued to "play for the love of the game and the chance to compete and get back to the big leagues." He pitched in the Kansas City Royals' system for the Double-A Memphis Chicks in 1991, his last year in organized baseball, with only one win against four losses.

In 1994 O'Neal attempted a comeback with Corpus Christi in the independent Texas-Louisiana League. In two years he won seven games and lost eight for the Barracudas. After the 1995 season, Randy retired as a professional baseball player. From 1984 through 1995 he had pitched for five major-league clubs and 11 minor-league aggregations. In the majors he had compiled 17 wins and 19 losses and a 4.35 ERA; in the minors he had 61 wins and 61 losses (his ERA was 3.64). All in all, he had won 78 professional contests, none more noteworthy than his first major-league victory on September 18, 1984.

After his playing days were over, O'Neal completed his degree in business/finance from the University of Central Florida, but he retained a keen interest in baseball. He designed some interesting bats to help pitchers have a keepsake in addition to the game ball from special games. One design, which he patented, had a baseball-size hole through the barrel that was burned with a torch to symbolize a ball thrown so hard that it burned through the wood. In 1995 O'Neal and three friends purchased the Kissimmee Sticks, a wood-bat manufacturing company. They changed the name to Stix Baseball and installed Randy as president. In 1999 Randy sold the company to Easton Sports, the giant manufacturer of aluminum bats.

In 2010 he owned the Heaters Bat Company. However, his principal profession was that of educator. He was a reading teacher and baseball coach at Olympia High School in Orlando, Florida. His Titans compiled a school record 21-5 mark in 2009. Baseball remained a big part of the life of Randy O'Neal. He said he loves "coaching and teaching the game to be played the right way. I want to give back to the players and try to make a difference in their lives."

Randy lives with his family in the Orlando area. He and his wife, Kathy, married 17 years as of 2013, have a son, Blake, 16, and a daughter, Taylor, 13.

Looking back on his time in the major leagues, O'Neal said he felt "lucky to have played with so many great players and friends, in such great baseball cities and with wonderful fans."

References

Articles

Associated Press.

Dow, Bill. "Tigers Clinched the AL East 25 Years Ago Today." http://blog.detroitathletic.com/2009/09/18/tigers-clinched-the-al-east-25-years-ago-today/

"Easton Steps up to Plate, Buys Bat Biz." www.accessmylibrary.com.

"Kissimmee Stix Bio." www.boombats.com.

Lambie, J. Ellett, "Happy Anniversary Randy O'Neal—25 Years Since the Tigers Clinched." http://eyeofthetigers.com/2009/09/18/happy-aniversary-randy-oneal.

"Olympia Titans Baseball," http://www.eteamsz.com/olympiatitansbaseball.

"Randy O'Neal." http://www.baseball-reference.com/players.

"Randy O'Neal," http://www.baseball-refernce.com/minors/player.

The Sporting News.

United Press International.

Other Sources

Geisler, Paul. E-mail interview with Charles F. Faber, February 17, 2010.

O'Neal, Randy. Personal correspondence with Charles F. Faber, February 1, 2010.

Lance Parrish
by Mike Lassman

A POTENTIAL CHAMPIONSHIP baseball team should possess both a strong cleanup hitter and catcher to provide stability for the long season. One player left his mark on the 1984 Detroit Tigers by demonstrating to the blue-collar Detroit faithful that he had the strength and versatility to put on the so-called tools of ignorance and swing a powerful bat. It was appropriate that in a city with a history of making fine automobiles, Lance Parrish was nicknamed Big Wheel for keeping the team going on a daily basis during the long summers in Detroit.

Parrish's prowess on the baseball field earned him appearances in eight All-Star Games. Several questions about Parrish were often raised for most of his 1,988-game major-league career. Baseball officials and managers—including his own, Sparky Anderson—were skeptical of players who frequently did weightlifting, fearing it might hurt their flexibility. Other issues that seemed to be raised, especially in the middle of Parrish's career were about his salary, major-league baseball collusion, and his back. Could the Big Wheel's back withstand the everyday pounding that a catcher has to endure? Parrish answered many of these questions as he caught for seven teams during his 19-season career.

Parrish's hitting and fielding skills earned him three Gold Glove awards and six Silver Slugger awards. Many fans remember the spectacular long-term keystone combination of Alan Trammell and Lou Whitaker and the flair for the dramatic of Kirk Gibson. But Parrish had the steady hand that may have flown under the radar at times.

In the fifth game of the 1984 World Series, Gibson's thrilling three-run homer in the dramatic eighth inning off the San Diego Padres' Rich "Goose" Gossage will never be forgotten. In the inning before, crafty lefty Craig Lefferts had struck out Gibson. The Tigers were nursing a one-run lead, and Padres manager Dick Williams replaced Lefferts with the future Hall of Famer Gossage to face Parrish. The Big Wheel hit a solo, laser-like homer into the left-field seats to give the Tigers and their bullpen some breathing room with a brief two-run lead. Even though Gibson's was the signature home

DETROIT TIGERS 1984: WHAT A START! WHAT A FINISH!

run of the series, Parrish helped the Tigers prevail over the Padres with his critical blast.

Former Tigers catcher and Seattle Mariners and current Oakland A's manager Bob Melvin was impressed by Parrish as he developed in the Detroit system. "I learned a lot from him coming up," Melvin said. "Lance was supposedly an offensive guy, but they called him the Big Wheel because he drove that train. He was very in tune with the pitchers and was very serious about what he did behind the plate. He was as good an all-around catcher as anyone that I have been around."

Lance Michael Parrish was born on June 15, 1956, in Clairton, Pennsylvania. His father was a deputy sheriff. The family moved to California from the western Pennsylvania coal country when Lance was 6. As a child, Lance was a fan of Roberto Clemente and Johnny Bench. He attended Walnut High school in Diamond Bar, California, and had the distinction of briefly being a bodyguard for pop-music icon Tina Turner.

Around the time Parrish was in high school, many of the veteran Tigers who had led Detroit to success in 1968 and 1972 were retiring or moving on to other teams. General Manager Jim Campbell decided the Tigers should devote more effort to scouting and drafting young players. He promoted Bill Lajoie to the position of scouting director. Lajoie was responsible for the 1974 draft, and drafted three future Tigers, including Parrish. The Tigers needed a catcher to replace Bill Freehan, and they were disappointed that they had missed out on Gary Carter in a previous draft. Jack Deutsch, a Tigers scout, had spotted Parrish in high school playing third base because he had injured his finger during his senior year.

Parrish had a scholarship offer to play football at UCLA. He demonstrated his baseball skills to the San Diego Padres, the Philadelphia Phillies, the Cincinnati Reds, and the California Angels. The Angels had put Parrish through a workout that tested his offensive and defensive abilities. On draft day in June 1974 Parrish anticipated that he was going to be picked by his hometown Angels as the 10th overall pick. He was surprised when his high school coach informed him that he had been drafted by the Tigers in the first round; the Angels had passed on him and taken shortstop Mike Miley. Detroit was foreign to his Southern California upbringing. Parrish was disappointed and confused about playing for a team and a manager, Ralph Houk, he knew nothing about.

The Tigers introduced Parrish to professional baseball at Bristol (Virginia) in the Rookie-level Appalachian League as a third baseman and outfielder. The Bristol Tigers finished 52-17, good for first in the circuit's North Division. Parrish hit .213 with 11 homers in 68 games and made 20 errors. His manager was Joe Lewis, and he played alongside future Tigers Mark Fidrych, Bob Sykes, and Tim Corcoran. In 1975 Parrish returned to catching at Lakeland in the Florida State League (Class A). The Tigers tried to convert him into a switch-hitter during this season. The experiment did not work and was dropped at the end of the year. Parrish hit .220 with five homers and 15 doubles.

In 1976 Parrish was promoted to Montgomery in the Double-A Southern League. Les Moss was the skipper, and Parrish had the opportunity to play with future Tigers Alan Trammell, Steve Kemp, Tom Brookens, Jack Morris, and Dave Rozema. The Rebels won the West Division and defeated Orlando for the Southern League championship, three games to one. This was the second of three straight Southern League championships for Montgomery. Parrish's batting average was still low (.221), but he increased his home run output to 14.

The Tigers promoted the 21-year-old Parrish to Triple-A Evansville, his third consecutive step up. It was the second year that Parrish played under Moss. Parrish improved as he led the team with 25 homers and 90 RBIs. He achieved his best average in the minors with a .279 mark. Moss touted Parrish as the next Johnny Bench. For his part, Parrish insisted that the comparisons with Bench did not bother him. "I modeled my catching after him as a teenager," he said. As Bench did, Parrish caught the ball with one hand, keeping his throwing hand behind his right leg.

Parrish's play at Evansville earned him a promotion to the Tigers in the traditional September call-up. On September 5, 1977, he made his major-league debut. There were 22,062 on hand to see the Tigers for the second game of a doubleheader. They faced Rudy May and the Baltimore Orioles at Tiger Stadium, and Parrish started at catcher, batting fifth. Parrish's first plate appearance ended with a groundout to second base. Batting fifth in the lineup, he had four plate appearances and showed some patience as he walked twice. Two days later, Parrish made his second appearance, in another doubleheader against the Orioles—and made it a game to remember with his first big-league single, double, and home run. He singled in the third inning off Ross Grimsley, hit a bases-loaded double off Earl Stephenson in the fourth and homered in the sixth inning off Stephenson, finishing with four RBIs. On September 9, Parrish started the second game of a doubleheader against the Red Sox. This game featured the debut of Lou Whitaker and Alan Trammell, who continued to play with Parrish through 1986. Parrish finished his season by going 9-for-46 (.196) with three homers and seven RBIs.

Before the 1978 season Parrish toured Michigan with Ron LeFlore, Mark Fidrych, Jason Thompson, Dave Rozema, Steve Kemp, and Milt Wilcox in the annual late-January press tour to promote interest in the Tigers. In spring training the Tigers anticipated that he would back up Milt May at catcher, but Ralph Houk made a critical decision to platoon the catching spot during the season. Parrish appeared in 85 games and had 304 plate appearances, hitting .219 with 14 home runs and 41 RBIs. He was disappointed in his season and indicated that it was the first time he had platooned in his career. "I felt good in spring training. I had a lot of confidence going into the season," he said. "Then, all of a sudden, I lost it. When you're in and out all the time, it makes it hard to get any momentum going."

But Lance's personal life had a positive change as he married Arlyne Nolan after the 1978 season. They were married while Parrish Lance played winter ball for Mayaguez

DETROIT TIGERS 1984: WHAT A START! WHAT A FINISH!

in Puerto Rico. His bride was a former Miss Diamond Bar, Miss Hollywood, and Miss Southern California, and first runner-up Miss California. She met Lance while rooming at his home during her senior year in high school. "It was nice to find out the best-looking girl in school was going to stay at your house," said Parrish, who is 21 months her junior. Their wedding banquet included hamburgers at a Dairy Queen in the Virgin Islands.

Houk retired from managing (at least for the time being) and was replaced by Les Moss after the 1978 season. Parrish was "going to be the next superstar in the American League," Moss said. "He will be one of the best in the business. He has tremendous power and throws as good as anybody. When I had him at Evansville, he was the best player in the league. I think he's ready to be an outstanding player."

In 1979 Milt May was sent to the Chicago White Sox during the Memorial Day weekend to clear the way for Parrish. May said he had all but demanded that the Tigers trade him as far back as spring training when Moss, speaking candidly, told him that Parrish would be the No. 1 catcher that year. Parrish must have gained some confidence immediately after the trade; he won the American League Player of the Week honor after he hit .591 (14-for-27) with an on-base percentage of .567 and slugging percentage of .852. (Through May 30 he had hit .320.) After Les Moss had managed the Tigers to a 27-26 record, the Tigers made a bold move by firing him on June 12 and hiring Sparky Anderson, who had won two World Series with the Cincinnati Reds. Parrish received some positive news the next day, though, as his first son, David Michael Parrish, was born on June 13. (David played baseball for the University of Michigan and was drafted as a catcher by the New York Yankees.)

Parrish ended his 1979 season with a .276 batting average and contributed to the Tigers' offense by launching 19 homers and knocking in 65 runs. He did, however, have the dubious distinction of leading the American League in passed balls with 21. This became a perpetual problem; he holds the modern-era career record with 192 passed balls. "I divide the season in two, I was satisfied at the plate, but disappointed defensively," Parrish said after the '79 season. "I did too many things wrong, too many passed balls. There's a lot I've got to work on." Parrish did rank second in the league in catcher assists. "I'm not worried about Lance," Anderson said. "He learns quickly and will be our leader on this team for a long time. He's one of our undiscussables." After the season, Major League Baseball placed Parrish on the American League roster to tour Japan and play nine games. He hit two home runs in Japan. "The Japanese pitchers drove me wild," Parrish said. "They're all side-armers over there."

Anderson decided at spring training in 1980 that he wanted to get Parrish some playing time in the outfield and at first base to give him some rest at catcher and add longevity. But Parrish was injured in spring training during a collision at first base with former Tiger Ron LeFlore, then with the Montreal Expos. Once the season started the team slumped, but Parrish maintained a .300 batting average for a while and showed more confidence. "It shows in the dugout," said Anderson. "Lance is talking it up with the pitchers more. You can see that he is handling them with more authority." Relief pitcher John Hiller said, "The pitchers aren't shaking him off as much as they used to, he calls an excellent game now." Parrish did show off a bit of a temper in a game in Oakland on May 3, as he broke a water cooler pipe after the A's stole some bases against Morris and him.

Parrish made his first appearance in an All-Star Game on July 8, 1980, at Dodger Stadium in Los Angeles. Parrish struck out against Bruce Sutter as the National League prevailed, 4-2. The Tigers' season was frustrating as they finished in fourth place. Parrish missed the final week after suffering a fractured right wrist when he was hit by a pitch. Parrish finished the season with a .286 batting average, 24 home runs and 82 RBIs. He won his first Silver Slugger award, given to the best offensive player at each position.

In the strike-shortened season of 1981 Parrish struggled and hit .244 with 10 home runs and 46 RBIs. In May, pitching coach Roger Craig started calling pitches. In 1982 Anderson said, "Lance will never be a leader with his mouth, and the sooner people realize it, the better off we'll be. He is not one to pop off. He gets things done in his own way and I kind of envy him." For his part, Parrish said, "I'm enthusiastic, but I have to do things my own way. People think I'm lazy. I hear that all the time. I'm not. It's just that I can't be something I'm not, and what I'm not is a catcher who is always jumping up and down and gets excited. I get just as fired up as the next guy, but I don't have to get crazy to show it."

Parrish had a tough start in 1982, straining ligaments in his left hand on a checked swing in the second game of the season, against Kansas City. But on April 27, in his first game back in the lineup, Parrish hit a home run. He hit safely in 18 of 21 games and raised his batting average to .309. Anderson suggested that Parrish would hit better if he stayed away from weightlifting. "Look at him, he's a lot looser now and he'll get even more so the longer he stays away from the weights.…Lance can become anything he wants in this game," Anderson said. Parrish played in the 1982 All-Star Game, held in Montreal. Taking over from Carlton Fisk in the fifth inning, he set an All-Star game record by throwing out three runners, Steve Sax, Ozzie Smith, and Al Oliver, trying to steal second base. Parrish went 1-for-2 as he doubled off Cincinnati's Mario Soto.

After the All-Star Game Parrish homered in three consecutive games. The 1982 season became even more special as the Parrishes had a second son, Matthew Thomas Parrish, born on August 25. (Matthew played as an outfielder in the Tigers' minor-league system.) The Tigers, who had built up a record of 35-19 by June 12, struggled and went 16-32 afterward to send them back to .500; they finished 83-79, fourth in the American League East. Parrish, the highest-paid Tiger at $550,000, expressed displeasure with the team management. "We're always a couple players short because the team is looking for ways to save money," he said. "What we're going through gets old after a while. The people who

DETROIT TIGERS 1984: WHAT A START! WHAT A FINISH!

get ripped off are the fans." Aside from that, the season was notable for him as he set a record for home runs in a season by an American League catcher. His 32 homers, 87 RBIs, and .284 batting average earned him another Silver Slugger award. He was named Tiger of the Year by the Detroit chapter of the Baseball Writers Association of America.

The 1983 season was disappointing for the Tigers as they fell short of the Orioles in the pennant push. Parrish, however, became the first Tigers catcher in 45 years to drive in more than 100 runs. (It was the only time he had 100 or more RBIs in a season.) He finished with 27 homers and 114 RBIs. Parrish, Trammell, and Whitaker were awarded Gold Gloves. This was the first time in the history of the award that there were three winners on the same team.

Detroit got off to a sizzling start in 1984, and the fourth game, on April 7, was a harbinger of a special season. Jack Morris walked six batters, but more importantly allowed no hits by the White Sox at Comiskey Park. After the game, one of the clubhouse kids approached Parrish in the locker room: Jim Campbell had placed a call to the clubhouse. After Campbell spoke glowingly to Parrish awhile, Campbell suggested that there would be a bonus coming his way. But when Campbell realized he was talking to Parrish and not to Morris, Campbell told Parrish to get off the phone—and that there would be no bonus.

Parrish continued to show leadership with the team and especially with Morris. On May 8 Morris lost his composure in a game. "Nobody likes to play behind you when you act this way," Parrish told him. The ace was crushed. "Lance saved me," said Morris. "I try, but sometimes I can't control myself. I needed something. Lance has so much more class than I have. I'm not going to cross Lance. He's like a big brother to me and he knows just what to say to me." Baseball fans selected Parrish to start for the American League in the All-Star Game. "I feel like I've come a long way," he said. "This puts me over the hump. People are realizing and appreciating my ability."

Despite a much lower batting average that season (.237), Parrish had 33 homers and 98 RBIs to cap a wonderful Tigers season, and he won the Silver Slugger and Gold Glove awards. Lance played in his first and only World Series, against San Diego.

"I'm sure no one is going to accept the fact we are as good as we are unless we win it all and that's what everyone on this team intends to do," Parrish said. "I don't know what else you can ask of this club but all you hear about is the fact we got off to that 35-5 start. It seems to me we played the rest of the way pretty well too." He hit a homer in the American League Championship Series against the Kansas City Royals and the one off Gossage in the World Series. The 1984 season was also special for Lance as his wife gave birth to a daughter, Ashley, on October 4.

Parrish had a unique moment in 1985 as he received a kiss from Morganna the Kissing Bandit during the NBC telecast of the Tigers-Angels game on June 1. Parrish was concerned about the incident because after she kissed Fred Lynn, the Orioles' outfielder went 3-for-40 at the plate. After a good start to the season, the Tigers lost 24 of 45 games. Parrish did not catch from July 10 to July 29 due to a strained lower back. The Tigers and Parrish's agent, Tom Reich, were close to a long-term deal, but there concerns about the back injuries. Still, Parrish won another Gold Glove.

In 1986 Jim Campbell, by this time the team president, said player contracts should last no more than three years—or maybe even just one year. Parrish said he was disappointed by Campbell's new philosophy. "I'd like to play in Detroit my entire career," he said. "I haven't had any problems with the Tigers in the past about contracts. I really don't anticipate any now. When the time comes, I think we can work something out, at least I hope we can." Anderson had a goal of having Parrish, despite his creaky back, catch 120 games in 1986 with the remaining games at first or as designated hitter. Still, Parrish caught 39 of the first 41 games at catcher and hit his 200th career home run. He had 21 homers and 59 RBIs at the All-Star break. Then he went on the disabled list with a sore back. Despite the long-term injury, Parrish won his fifth Silver Slugger award. After the season, Parrish took part in a rigorous therapy program.

For 1987 the Tigers, wary of Parrish's back problems, offered him $850,000, the same salary as the previous season. Parrish declined arbitration and became a free agent. He did not like the way he was treated by the Tigers and Campbell, and decided not to sign a contract with the only major-league team that he had known. On March 13, 1987, he signed with the Philadelphia Phillies, though the negotiating process became tedious. Phillies President Bill Giles insisted that Parrish accept a provision that he could not sue Major League Baseball or file a grievance over collusion allegations. The contract provided Parrish with additional money if he was able to stay off the disabled list due to a back ailment. It helped that one of Parrish's best friends from their Tigers days, outfielder Glenn Wilson, played for the Phils. Lance was also good friends with the Phillies' perennial All-Star third baseman, Mike Schmidt "I'm very happy it's over," Parrish said of the contract talks. "I'll miss my teammates at Detroit, but I had to do what was best for Lance Parrish. I realize there are those concerned about my back condition. But I never felt better. I'm going to prove them wrong."

But Parrish struggled through much of the 1987 season. Opposing baserunners stole 13 straight bases against him early in the season. At the 29-game mark, he had a batting average of .187 with four homers and 14 RBIs. The Tigers had moved on with catchers Matt Nokes and Mike Heath. Parrish blamed Sparky Anderson for his hitting problems with the Phillies. He said he believed that Anderson had advised National League managers how to pitch to him. "Tell Sparky he did a good job," said Parrish, who in early July was hitting .224 with seven home runs and 34 runs batted in. In August he hit .290 with five homers and 15 RBIs despite being booed by Veterans Stadium fans. Parrish concluded his disappointing season by hitting .245 with 17 home runs and 67 RBIs.

Parrish had the opportunity to be a free agent again, but re-signed with the Phillies on a one-year deal. He made the National League All-Star team, but his batting average dipped still further, to .215. The Phillies did not perform as the pundits had expected. "There was not a winning attitude," Parrish said. "It always seemed that we were in a tight game and we just didn't do the right thing to win. I think everybody should accept some of the blame."

Parrish left Philadelphia on October 3, 1988, when he was traded to the California Angels for a minor leaguer, David Holdridge. He waived his right to free agency based on arbitrator George Nicolau's ruling that major-league baseball colluded to keep salaries down and to make it difficult for free agents to leave their teams. Former teammate Kirk Gibson had elected to leave the Tigers prior to 1988 and play for the Los Angeles Dodgers. The decision turned out well for Gibson. He was the National League's Most Valuable Player in 1988 and led the Dodgers to the World Series championship over the Oakland Athletics. Parrish had the choice of returning to Detroit or going to the Angels. Returning to the Tigers "would've meant again packing up my family (already settled in Yorba Linda, a suburb of Anaheim). It was just so much easier this way. Collusion was a very convenient excuse for the teams. It started with the Tigers making an issue out of the back to hold down my salary."

Parrish replaced Bob Boone, the longtime Angels catcher, in Anaheim and received much credit for handling the starting pitchers. He was thought to have contributed significantly to the Angels' pitching staff having a 2.69 ERA into June. Kirk McCaskill, Chuck Finley, Bert Blyleven, Jim Abbott, and Mike Witt formed the Angels' rotation. Parrish had a spark in his offense as he started using a 36-inch, 36-ounce bat, bigger than the one he had used for the earlier part of his career. The injury bug bit Parrish as he hurt his ribs in a collision with Milwaukee's Glenn Bragg. Still, he caught in 122 games, had a good season, and signed a three-year deal with the Angels.

Parrish had some happy years back home in California. On April 12, 1990, he backstopped a no-hitter shared by Mark Langston and Witt, and he won a sixth Silver Slugger award. Only Mike Schmidt and Parrish had six Silver Slugger awards at that point. At the age of 34, he had a .268 batting average with 24 homers and 70 RBIs in 1990. In 1992 he became the eighth catcher to reach 1,000 games with 1,000 RBIs. Six of the eight are in the Hall of Fame, with Parrish and Ted Simmons being the exceptions.

Parrish concluded his career with short stints in Seattle, Cleveland, Pittsburgh, and Toronto from 1992 to 1995. He played briefly with Albuquerque in the Dodgers' system and with the Toledo Mud Hens in 1994 in an attempt to play again with the Tigers. His last major-league game was with the Toronto Blue Jays on September 23, 1995. Parrish was struck out by Joe Hudson in the ninth inning against the Boston Red Sox in Fenway Park.

After his playing career ended, Parrish was a minor-league catching instructor for the Kansas City Royals in 1996. He coached the San Antonio Missions in 1997 and 1998, taking over as manager during 1998. From 1999 to 2001 he was a coach for the Tigers, then a television color analyst for the Tigers in 2002, then a Tigers coach again through 2005. In 2006, Parrish was manager of the Ogden Raptors of the Pioneer League and was named inaugural manager of the 2007 Great Lakes Loons of the Midwest League. The Loons went 57-82 and Parrish was fired after one season. Afterward, he and Arlyne moved from California to Nashville, Tennessee, although in 2010 he expressed his desire to get back into the game.

Parrish's playing career concluded with 324 homers, three Gold Gloves, six Silver Slugger awards, and eight All-Star team selections. Even though he played with other teams, Lance Parrish will always be known for helping the Tigers by using his catching and hitting prowess so that the Tigers could achieve one of their four world championships in 1984.

References

Publications

Zaret, Eli. *'84: The Last of the Great Tigers*. South Boardman, Mich.: Crofton Creek Press. 2004.

Articles

The Sporting News

Baseball Digest

Sports Illustrated

Web Sites

www.baseball-almanac.com

www.baseball-reference.com

www.minorleaguebaseball.com

www.retrosheet.org

Dan Petry
by Don Peterson

DAN PETRY WAS never a showman. He never sought attention. He never won 20 games. But he won between 10 and 19 games the Detroit Tigers for six consecutive seasons, and there is no denying that he was a solid player—or that he was critical to the 1984 Detroit Tigers. He was more than the No. 2 pitcher with 18 wins. His dogged work ethic and persistence epitomized the 1984 Tigers. While others were getting press and magazine articles and huge contracts, Petry simply did his job.

Much has been published about players like Jack Morris, Kirk Gibson, and Alan Trammell, but there's relatively little about Daniel Joseph Petry. Perhaps when one considers his career, personality, and demeanor in comparison with those of the others, it's not surprising.

He was serious about his craft and worked hard, and he continued doing his job until his arm gave out, at which time he went back and devoted himself to raising a family, including a son who captained the hockey team at Michigan State University and was a second-round draft choice of the Edmonton Oilers.

Petry's demeanor was consistent with how he viewed what it took to be a big-league pitcher. In his opinion, that required more than simply having an outstanding, durable arm. Sure, that was important, but it was just as important for a pitcher to know how to pitch and to prepare for each batter. He thought that becoming a successful major-league baseball pitcher was 50 percent arm and 50 percent brain. He felt that a pitcher couldn't be successful without thoughtful consideration of his craft.

Given his emphasis on the mental aspects of pitching, as opposed to merely throwing fastballs, it is not surprising to learn that Petry was born in the academic mecca of Palo Alto, California, at Stanford Hospital, which is a part of Stanford University. Born on November 13, 1958, he was the eldest child of Ron and Aleene Petry.

It was not until his family left Palo Alto when Petry was young and moved to the Anaheim area in Southern California that he began playing various sports in earnest. His athleticism immediately emerged, and he became proficient at all sports. Indeed, he loved playing virtually any sport, including baseball. He would pick up anything he could fit in his hand and throw it at make-believe targets, trees, or his garage door. This would drive his parents, Ron, a chemist with BASF, and Aleene, a phone operator, crazy.

Petry's earliest memory of playing baseball was of walking to his elementary school and playing baseball all day long. He and his friends would play almost every day. Dan was not a pitcher at this time. He played every position in the field as needed. As is often the case, the kids didn't always have complete teams on each side, but they would improvise the rules so they could continue playing. They would stop playing only when it got too dark to see the ball.

Petry's "official" baseball career began when he was 8 years old. For the first time he had a coach, and he played in a "coach-pitch" league. This meant that he got to hit against his own coach. The next year, at the age of 9, he graduated to a league in which the opposing team supplied the pitcher. This, of course, was quite a bit different from batting against his own coach. But he thrived nonetheless.

Though Petry showed outstanding all-around skills at this young age, he didn't really display any evidence that his future would include winning 125 games as a major-league pitcher for 13 years with four different teams. As a 9-year-old he pitched only once. At 10, he pitched twice. But by the time he reached the age of 11, his coaches began to notice his outstanding arm, and he began pitching more frequently.

Before he began high school, Petry continued playing several positions, including shortstop and center field, as well as pitching. Throughout his youth, he had always dreamed of playing big-league baseball, but he didn't really care what position he played as long as he was playing it in the major leagues. Nearly every week, he would watch NBC's Game of the Week on TV, and then he and his friends would go outside and play baseball, pretending to be one of the teams. Though he lived just 10 miles from the California Angels' home stadium, Petry developed a fondness for the Detroit Tigers. He had watched the Tigers win the 1968 World Series and had learned all their batting stances and pitching motions.

Petry continued playing baseball at El Dorado High School, where he graduated in a class of 200 students. El Dorado subsequently became much larger and its graduates include major leaguers Bret Boone, Phil Nevin, and Brett Tomko. But Petry was the first of the many El Dorado graduates who went on to fame as professional athletes, Olympic athletes, or actors.

El Dorado baseball coach Tim Terrell had Petry focus more on pitching; instead of playing a variety of positions, he only pitched and played shortstop. And he began to notice that he was better than most other players, and certainly most other pitchers. He could throw harder and had better control, and he became more and more dedicated to pitching.

Petry's dedication led to outstanding results, and he made his mark as a high-school pitcher. In what may seem surprising to many who saw him as a calm, collected big-league pitcher, Petry was known for his bad temper while he was a high-school pitcher. Interestingly enough, Tigers scout Dick Wiencek, who was following his high-school career and rated him more highly than other scouts did, thought that his temper was a good thing and was evidence that he was a fiery competitor.

While he was a senior in high school, Petry's athletic future was pretty much determined; Wiencek advised him to concentrate on pitching. The scout had an outstanding eye for spotting major-league talent, and was responsible for signing 72 players who reached the major leagues, including Alan Trammell, Jack Morris, Mark McGwire, Jim Kaat, Bert Blyleven, Frank Tanana, Steve Kemp, and Jason Thompson. And Wiencek proved to be spot-on about Petry. Dan pitched

DETROIT TIGERS 1984: WHAT A START! WHAT A FINISH!

his high-school team to the state championship, and he was selected to the all-state team.

Based on the advice of Wiencek, the Tigers' scouting coordinator in California, Detroit selected Petry in the fourth round of the June 1976 draft, the one that many have argued led to their 1984 World Series championship. In the first round the Tigers drafted Pat Underwood, who was gone from the team before 1984, but in subsequent rounds they took Trammell, Petry, and Morris.

Petry was not yet 18 years old, and he had a big decision to make. He had been offered a full scholarship by California State University, and his father, the BASF chemist, was not entirely supportive of Petry's desire to forgo college and pursue a future in professional baseball. This was a problem, at least at the outset. Petry was not old enough to sign a contract, and he could not sign the Detroit contract without his father's permission.

His father eventually decided it was best for Petry to follow his dreams, and gave him permission to sign. Petry inked the contract and began his professional baseball career by playing, along with Alan Trammell, for manager Joe Lewis with the Tigers' affiliate in Bristol, Virginia, in the Rookie-level Appalachian League. Petry, who was still just 17 years old, went 2-3 in 14 starts.

After receiving his professional indoctrination with the Bristol Tigers, Petry began the fast track to Detroit. Over the next three years, before arriving at Detroit, he played at each level in the Tigers' minor-league system, and he was able to play for managers whom he subsequently viewed as outstanding. In an interview in 2008, Petry looked back on these days with much appreciation. He said he was fortunate to play for "great" managers. He was able to learn how to play the game before he was required to do so in the major leagues.

In 1977, after Bristol, Petry moved on to play for the Lakeland Tigers in the Florida State League, Detroit's A-ball team. Headed by manager Jim Leyland, the team went 85-53 and Petry was 10-11 as an 18-year-old. Lakeland won the league championship. This was Petry's first experience with Leyland, who he said had the most influence on his development as a pitcher and as a baseball player.

The following year, 1978, Petry, who had acquired the moniker Peaches, moved to Montgomery, Alabama, where he and teammate Tom Brookens played for the Montgomery Rebels of the Southern League, the Tigers' Double-A team. Eddie Brinkman, Detroit's gifted shortstop earlier in the decade, managed the club. After Petry went 6-7 with a superb 2.45 ERA in 14 starts, the Tigers promoted him to their Triple-A affiliate, the Evansville Triplets of the American Association. In Evansville, and though still just 19, Petry had a 4-3 record in 13 starts. The Triplets, managed by Les Moss, had a good team, finishing with a 78-58 record. Petry played after the season in the Instructional League, where the Tigers sent their top prospects.

In 1979, Petry was glad to be reunited with Leyland in Evansville. He was 4-3 in 15 starts. Recognizing his ability, the Tigers called him up in midseason, and he got his first taste of major-league ball. Petry was only 20 years old, but he certainly believed that he belonged in the big leagues. And he pitched that way as well. He made his major-league debut on July 8, 1979, losing to the Milwaukee Brewers, 3-1. But he ended the year getting 98 innings of big-league work under his belt and going 6-5 with a 3.95 ERA for the Tigers.

Entering spring training in 1980, Petry fully expected to make the Tigers and head north with the team. But much to his chagrin, he was sent to Evansville. Determined to show that the Tigers should have kept him, he started the season strong, going 2-0 with a 2.70 ERA during the first two weeks.

The Tigers decided that Petry was ready for the big club, and they called him up. Petry pitched well, finishing his rookie year with a 10-9 record and a 3.94 ERA. Except for brief rehabilitation assignments in 1986 and 1988, he never played in the minors again.

The year after Petry made the big leagues, in 1981, a players' strike shut baseball down for about one-third of the season. During the strike, Petry worked hard to improve his pitching. He was frustrated, though, because he was not seeing the improvement that he expected, and had no live games in which to participate. Finally, though, it suddenly clicked for him. Both manager Sparky Anderson and general manager Bill Lajoie encouraged him to relax and use the strike time to become re-acquainted with his wife. He did so. When he returned after the strike, he was refreshed and ready to pitch. Despite the strike, he still got in 141 innings and posted another 10-9 record, with a much-improved 3.00 ERA.

In 1982, Petry finished ninth in voting for the American League Cy Young Award as a 23-year-old after compiling a 15-9 record and a 3.22 ERA in 35 games, all of which he started. He had eight complete games, one of them a shutout, and pitched 246 innings. He seemed to have a long career ahead of him.

Petry was 19-11 and led American League pitchers with 38 starts in 1983. Baltimore topped Detroit for the American League East crown, but after the season Petry thought the Tigers had a good chance of winning the pennant in 1984. Although Detroit's won-lost record belied it, they had a great spring training. Still, despite his optimism, Petry was surprised by the team's 35-5 start. He almost got a no-hitter at the beginning of the season—a 6-1 victory over the Cleveland Indians in which he didn't give up a hit until there was one out in the eighth inning.

Petry's 18-8 mark (with a 3.24 ERA) in 1984 was good for the third-best winning percentage (.692) in the American League, and he was the No. 2 starter for the world champion Detroit Tigers. Petry lost Game Two of the World Series to the Padres (Detroit's only loss in the Series), and was the starter in the deciding Game Five, but got no decision. He finished fifth in voting that year for the American League Cy Young Award.

In 1985 Petry was 15-13. He pitched more than 230 innings for the fourth straight season. He was selected to the All-Star team. But though he was only 26 years old, all the innings and the constant wear and tear on Petry's arm were beginning to have an effect on him.

In 1986, for the first time in Petry's career, he went on the disabled list. He missed more than two months after having arthroscopic surgery on his elbow to remove bone chips. His career as a front-line starter was effectively over. He never fully recovered from this operation, and his productivity never reached its former level.

Petry's ERA ballooned to 5.61 in 1987, and he was traded to California for outfielder Gary Pettis after the season. In 1988 for the Angels, he spent two more months on the disabled list, and he won only three games in his 22 starts. In 1989 he pitched only 51 innings for the Angels and won three games.

A free agent after the 1989 season, Petry returned to the Tigers for 1990, taking a slight cut in pay. He enjoyed a mini-renaissance, going 10-9 in 23 starts. But in June of 1991, the Tigers traded him to the Atlanta Braves for Victor Rosario, an infielder. Less than two months later the Braves sent him to the Boston Red Sox for Mickey Pina, a minor league outfielder, and Petry retired after the season ended. He went to spring training the following year with Pittsburgh, which was managed by his old mentor, Jim Leyland. But he just didn't have it anymore.

Petry was a consistent, durable starter for his 13-year career. He pitched for the Tigers for nearly a decade, and showed flashes of brilliance. Of the six straight seasons in which he won 10 or more games for the Tigers, he had at least 15 victories in four of those years. For his full 13-year career, he was 125-104 in 370 games with a 3.95 ERA. He had 11 shutouts and more than 1,000 strikeouts. In 2009 a baseball researcher called him the fourth-best fielding pitcher in major-league baseball from 1900 to 2008.

Though he had opportunities to coach or manage at the minor-league level, Petry didn't stay in baseball after he retired. Instead, he wanted to devote more time to his family. He worked in sales for International Paper for 16 years, and in 2010 was at work for the NFL's Detroit Lions, selling luxury boxes at the Lions' new stadium, Ford Field. Petry married his wife, Christine, in 1982. Their son Jeff was a second-round pick of the NHL's Edmonton Oilers. Jeff was named USA Hockey Junior Player of the Year for the 2006-07 season while playing with the Des Moines Buccaneers. As a junior, Jeff was a captain for the Michigan State University hockey team in 2009-2010 before signing with Edmonton.

References

Publications

Anderson, Sparky. *Bless You Boys: Diary of the Detroit Tigers' 1984 Season*. Chicago: Contemporary Books. 1984.

Craig, Roger, and Vern Plagenhoef. *Inside Pitch: Roger Craig's '84 Tiger Journal*. Grand Rapids, Mich.: Eerdmans Publishing Co. 1984.

David, Kurt A. *From Glory Days: Successful Transitions of Professional Detroit Athletes*. Baltimore: Publish America. 2007.

Detroit News. *The 1984 Detroit Tigers: The Magic Season*. Indianapolis: News Books International. 1984.

Kell, George, and Dan Ewald. *Hello Everybody, I'm George Kell*. Chicago: Sports Publishing. 1998.

Articles

Knox, John A. "The 100 Top-Fielding MLB Pitchers, Circa 1900-2008." In *The Baseball Research Journal*, Vol. 38, No. 1 (Summer 2009). Cleveland: Society for American Baseball Research.

Web Sites

www.BaseballLibrary.com

www.Baseball-Reference.com

www.Wikipedia.com

Other Sources

Peterson, Don. Interview with Dan Petry. August 2008.

Dave Rozema
by Chip Greene

A YEAR AFTER a Detroit Tigers rookie named Mark "The Bird" Fidrych won 19 games and the American League Rookie of the Year award in 1976, Detroit found another rookie phenom in Dave "The Rose" Rozema, giving them two right-handed starters who were, as the press wrote prior to Opening Day, "pitchers you can build a staff on." Oh, to think what might have been.

Rozema ("It's ROSE-MUH," wrote the press), was tall and slender, 6-feet-4 and 190 pounds, and had outstanding control. Indeed, during spring training in 1977 manager Ralph Houk proclaimed: "He's got the best control of any young pitcher I've ever seen." That control was crucial, because Rozema's fastball rarely exceeded 85 mph on the radar gun. Instead, he relied on a devastating changeup to get hitters out, and an "uncanny ability to make enemy batters swing at the wrong pitch."

"Because I'm big and tall," Rozema said, "people think I should gun the ball. But I don't. That's not my style... basically, I throw a lot of changeups and rely on groundballs." And he employed that strategy to great success, leading the 1977 Tigers' pitching staff with 15 wins. No other pitcher won more than eight.

As the year progressed, Rozema drew praise from around the league. "He's a hell of a pitcher," offered Cleveland manager Frank Robinson, who said Rozema could be "a 30-game winner." "He throws the ball down," Robinson said, "he gets his breaking ball over the plate. He changes speeds good." Likewise, Lyman Bostock of the Minnesota Twins said, "He has a good changeup and he moves it around well and with good control. Even if you hit it, the ball doesn't go anywhere. I thought he was impressive." Milwaukee Brewers outfielder Von Joshua commented simply, "He throws slow, slower, and slowest."

For his part, Rozema was pragmatic about his talent. "I really don't care what they say about my fastball," he said. "I've got what I've got.... I've got some other pitches [he also threw a very effective slider]. If I really heated it up and threw harder, I'd sacrifice control.... I don't think I am [slow]. I used to blow 'em down in Grand Rapids, Michigan. Fourteen K's a game."

Grand Rapids is where David Scott Rozema was born, on August 5, 1956. It's also where he was raised and first came to the notice of major-league scouts. At Central High School, Rozema was an All-City selection in his junior and senior years, and when he graduated in 1974, he was drafted and offered a contract by the San Francisco Giants. When the Giants wouldn't offer him a bonus, Rozema declined their offer. He was, after all, a 22nd-round draft choice.

"It was the weirdest thing I ever saw," Rozema said. "The Giants drafted me, and their scout, Herm Hannah, came over to my house. I thought I had a pretty good high-school record—there was one game when I struck out 20 batters in a seven-inning game after I threw out the first man on a bunt. I guess there were six no-hitters in the ninth grade—and I was expecting a nice offer.... But the way he explained it to me, it didn't sound like any fun at all. It almost sounded like they didn't want me to sign. He didn't seem very interested in me.... He didn't offer me any money at all. Not a dime. So I said, 'See ya later.' I felt I deserved to get something."

Instead, Rozema enrolled in Grand Rapids Junior College. There, "I took a whole semester of college," Rozema told *The Sporting News* in 1978. "I took American history, English, speed reading, bowling, football theory, and sports officiation.... But I didn't like school at all. I hardly ever went. The only reason I went to college was because I wanted to play baseball. And the following January, the Tigers drafted me."

Selected in the fourth round, Rozema signed with Detroit on January 21, 1975, and this time he received a bonus, $2,500. Then he was instructed to report in March to the Tigers' Lakeland, Florida, rookie camp for assignment.

Rozema began his professional career in the Class A Midwest League, playing for the Tigers' affiliate in Clinton, Iowa. Beginning the season as a reliever, the right-hander quickly established himself as one of the best in the league. On May 14, 1975, the *Cedar Rapids Gazette* reported on an 8-7 come-from-behind victory by the Cedar Rapids Giants over the division-leading Clinton Pilots. Scoring three runs in the bottom of the seventh inning, the Giants "victimize(d) ace Clinton relief pitcher Dave Rozema, who had a flashy 1.12 ERA and 2-0 record entering the game." Later in the season Rozema moved into the starting rotation, and on July 27 he defeated the Waterloo Royals, 11-1, allowing only five hits, although he had a one-hitter through the sixth inning. By season's end, Rozema had produced a 14-5 record and impressive 2.09 earned-run average while making 19 starts in 27 games.

He had also learned to throw what became his signature pitch. Interviewed during his rookie year, Rozema said, "I've always had a good fastball and slider, but I think I became a pitcher in my first year in the minors. John Grodzicki, the Tigers minor-league pitching instructor, taught me how to throw a changeup. Now it's one of my favorite pitches." It soon made him one of the best rookies in the major leagues.

Based on his success in the Midwest League, in 1976 the Tigers invited Rozema to spring training as a nonroster player. On March 31 he was one of eight players cut from Detroit's spring training squad, and shortly thereafter was ordered once again to report to the minor-league camp for reassignment.

This time, he faced tougher competition. The Tigers' entry in the Double-A Southern League was the Montgomery (Alabama) Rebels, and there Rozema was outstanding. In 19 games, all but one as a starter, he compiled a 12-4 record and posted a dazzling ERA of 1.57. On Opening Night, Rozema threw a two-hitter to shut out the Orlando Twins, 8-0, and never looked back. Of the 19-year-old right-hander, Montgomery manager Les Moss proclaimed, "That kid has all the tools. If he keeps pitching like that, he won't be around here long. He's an outstanding prospect." By season's end, Tigers manager Ralph Houk declared that "Rozema is farther along at this point than Mark Fidrych was last year."

And then came 1977. Again, Rozema was invited to spring training as a nonroster player, and this time he made sure that Houk couldn't send him back to the minors. Almost immediately, comparisons to Fidrych abounded as Rozema allowed just five earned runs in 25 innings during the spring, a 1.80 ERA. Rozema was confident from the outset, telling the press, "I think I'm as good a pitcher as [Fidrych] is. Of course, I'm sure every pitcher thinks he's the best.... I'm going to go for it. I think if I have a decent spring training, if I show them I can throw the ball over the plate and I'm not scared, I've got a real good chance of making the club.... I think I'm ready. I really think I can handle it."

When Fidrych went down on March 20 with a knee injury, Rozema was virtually assured of a spot in the starting rotation. Indeed, wrote a sportswriter, "that injury leaves Rozema as the indispensable rookie, just as Fidrych was a season ago."

DETROIT TIGERS 1984: WHAT A START! WHAT A FINISH!

Yet the 20-year-old Rozema remained nonchalant and focused, unfazed by any suggestions of pressure. "There's no pressure on me. I don't even think about pressure," he said. "All I'm thinking about is doing my job, pitching."

As expected, Rozema made the rotation. As well as the rookie had pitched, however, Houk declined to name "The Rose" his starter on Opening Day, scheduled for April 7 in Detroit against Kansas City.

"I would never put that kind of pressure on a kid," reasoned Houk. "If Kansas City kicked the ____ out of him in front of all those people, he might never be the same again. And I think he's going to be a good pitcher." (For the record, the newspaper that printed the quote did not disclose the word Houk said.)

Four days later, on April 11, in Toronto, against the expansion Blue Jays, Rozema finally made his debut. He pitched well, too, although he left the game without a decision. "Tiger Rookie Looks Good…" ran the headline the next day in the Record-Eagle in Traverse City, Michigan, about two hours from Rozema's birthplace, "but Jays Win." After breezing through the first six innings with a 3-1 lead, Rozema had allowed only seven hits and one run when, with a runner on third base, he committed a balk. "I was just holding the ball nice and loose, and I just hit my leg and the ball fell out," he said—and allowed the runner to score. Houk immediately relieved the rookie, who the manager said had "pitched real good up to that point," and the Tigers eventually lost, 5-3. Nonetheless, it had been a promising appearance by the righty, and he didn't have long to wait for his first major-league victory.

It came on April 21, in historic Fenway Park. Displaying a sinking fastball that forced Boston to hit 17 groundballs, Rozema threw a complete-game four-hit shutout against the Red Sox, winning 8-0. Interviewed after the game, Boston manager Don Zimmer was duly impressed, lamenting that "we could have been out there three days against him and not score a run, the way he was pitching." Future Hall of Famer Carl Yastrzemski went hitless against the rookie in four at-bats, and declared after the game that Rozema "has a good sinking change and fastball and has good location. He can throw it where he wants it hit."

It was an impressive first victory for Rozema, and one he would never forget. Twenty-three years later, long after he had left the game, he was interviewed by a writer for *Sports Collectors Digest* and referred to the win as "the biggest feat in my career—and not a bad start."

Indeed it wasn't. Rozema went on to win 14 more games for the Tigers in his rookie season while losing only seven, and posted the seventh-best ERA in the league, 3.09. In 28 starts he totaled 218 innings and completed 16 games, and walked only 34 batters the entire season. During one stretch, from July 16 to August 19, he won seven consecutive games.

Rozema was particularly effective against the Milwaukee Brewers; in four starts, he won four times and threw four complete games. After the rookie's final victory over Milwaukee, in August, Brewers first baseman Cecil Cooper summed up Rozema's performance this way: "He throws junk. But it's hard to hit because you don't see that kind of junk very often. He threw me one pitch tonight that I couldn't even tell what it was. I couldn't even tell if it had rotation. I think he just grabs the ball with five fingers and throws it. … He gets you to swing at what he wants you to swing at. He's tantalizing." There were a lot of equally tantalized American League batters that summer when Dave Rozema pitched.

For all that the right-hander accomplished, however, there was also one ominous sign: Injuries soon took their toll on Rozema's shoulder. In July, he suffered a three-week bout of tendinitis that caused him to miss several starts, and when the soreness returned early in September, he sat out the final three weeks of the season.

Still, Rozema received numerous postseason awards: The Sporting News named him the top rookie pitcher in the American League; Topps named him to its All-Rookie team; he was named Tigers rookie of the year by the Detroit Sports Broadcasters Association, finished eighth in league Cy Young Award balloting, and finished fourth in balloting by the Baseball Writers Association of America for Rookie of the Year, won by Baltimore's Eddie Murray. Most importantly, before the year was ended Rozema signed a three-year contract "for slightly less than Fidrych signed for a year ago."

Unfortunately, though, Rozema had peaked and injuries were primarily to blame. After defeating Texas 6-2 in his first start of 1978, a complete-game four hitter, the stiffness in his pitching shoulder returned, and he was forced to miss a start on May 18. Then, three days later, he left a game after only four innings, again complaining of similar discomfort. Finally, after missing three weeks, he had a cortisone injection in June, and finished the season a 9-12 record. But apart from the win-loss mark and injury, his stats closely matched the year prior: 209 innings pitched, a 3.14 ERA, 28 starts, almost identical WHIP (walks plus hits per inning pitched, 1.173 and 1.175)—and a lot fewer home runs (17, down from 25) allowed.

In 1979, Rozema's injuries worsened. Despite two brilliant performances, a complete-game three-hitter versus Toronto at Tiger Stadium on April 22, in which Rozema threw just 88 pitches and took a no-hitter into the sixth; and a five-hit, 2-0 shutout in Oakland on June 3, the right-hander was sidelined for nearly three months with a recurrence of his shoulder pain. In all, he appeared in just 16 games, all starts, and totaled only 97 innings for the season, posting a 4-4 record and 3.51 ERA. After the season he went to the Florida Instructional League and, for the first time, worked on a weight program in an effort to improve his arm strength.

All of this impressed new Tigers manager Sparky Anderson. As spring training got under way in 1980, Anderson, who had replaced the fired Les Moss the previous June, said: "(Rozema) got hurt the first day I was manager. He could have come back for the last two months. I could have pitched him…. But we weren't going anywhere, so why take the chance." Anderson told the press that Rozema's injury the previous season had been "only a strained muscle." This spring, he appeared to be stronger.

DETROIT TIGERS 1984: WHAT A START! WHAT A FINISH!

Yet Rozema didn't immediately endear himself to the skipper. In the fall, Anderson had set maximum weight limits for all his players; for each pound above their limit, they were fined $100. Rozema came to camp three pounds over his limit, so Anderson fined him $300. But that wasn't Rozema's last mistake.

Over the course of his career Rozema would gain a reputation for some notable off-the-field incidents. One of those took place in March 1980. With two spring training games scheduled to be played in Puerto Rico, the Tigers boarded a plane for the flight to San Juan—but Rozema wasn't on the plane. As it turned out, the pitcher had stayed out late the night before judging a wet T-shirt contest and overslept. After catching the next plane, Rozema was installed that night as the starter against the St. Louis Cardinals. In four innings, he allowed seven hits and six runs, and the Tigers lost, 11-0.

"I've got to be more serious," the 24-year-old said. "That's all Sparky is asking."

Despite the pounding in Puerto Rico, at the conclusion of spring training Anderson named Rozema a starter for the regular season. It was a short-lived assignment. For the first three weeks Rozema was the team's most consistent pitcher, with a 2-2 record in six starts. Then, in his next two starts, he lasted just $4^{1}/_{3}$ innings. Suddenly, after 78 starts in four seasons, Rozema became a relief pitcher.

Needless to say, he was astonished. "I couldn't believe it when they told me to get up and throw," Rozema said. "It was a strange feeling."

Save for a few more starts, he remained in the bullpen the rest of the year. On June 11, though, in his first start since being demoted, he faced Minnesota in Detroit and was shelled, allowing seven hits in a 9-5 loss. When he left the game in the fifth inning, the crowd booed him. After the game, catcher Lance Parrish told reporters that Rozema had "lost his changeup." "For Rozema to be as effective as he once was," Parrish said, "he has to come up with the changeup that he once had. When he was a rookie he had one of the best changes in baseball. But now it just hangs there." With a final record of 6-9, an ERA of 3.92, and only 13 starts in 42 games, Rozema's days as a front-line pitcher appeared over.

In the spring of 1981, Rozema battled for a spot on Anderson's 10-man pitching squad. The 24-year-old "has[n't] much chance of getting back into the rotation," wrote the *Ironwood Daily Globe*, but Rozema said he'd accept a bullpen role. "I don't feel like my career is on the line," he said. "As long as I can help win these games, I feel like I have a purpose. I don't want to feel left out. You can have a good life this way, too." In a total of 28 games he did make nine starts, and one was quite memorable. In an outing that Rozema afterward called "the best game of my career," he pitched a complete game two-hitter in Seattle to break Detroit's 10-game losing streak, allowing only three Mariners to reach base and retiring the last 14 batters he faced. At season's end he had split 10 decisions and posted an ERA of 3.63 in 104 innings pitched.

So he went to spring training in 1982 hopeful of resurrecting his career. He had a great reason to be optimistic:

During the offseason, Rozema had received a three-year contract for $510,000. Again, though, his spring began inauspiciously. Training camp had just got started when Rozema and teammate Kirk Gibson went out one night to a local saloon. The next morning it was reported that Rozema had required 11 stitches in his right buttock after Gibson had kicked a chair from beneath Rozema as "The Rose" tried to sit down: When he landed, a bottle of medicine he kept in his hip pocket shattered and cut him in four places. Then, on April 6, the evening before his first start, Rozema playfully shoved teammate Alan Trammell when the two visited a local nightclub. As Trammell ducked to avoid the shove, the shortstop struck his face on the rim of a beer mug and required some 40 stitches to close a gash in his forehead.

Those turned out to be mild accidents, though, in comparison to what happened on May 14. On the mound, Rozema was off to his best start in several years; in eight games, including two starts, he had compiled a 3-0 record and a 1.63 ERA. Then, in Detroit, he prematurely ended his season. In the 11th inning of an eventual 4-2 Tigers victory, a brawl broke out while Detroit was at bat. Rozema, who was the Tigers' pitcher of record at the time, wanting to "be out there protecting my guys," ran from the third-base dugout and entered the brawl feet-first. When he came down near the mound his left knee buckled, and he had to be carried off the field on a stretcher. At the hospital it was determined that he had suffered damage to all but one ligament in his knee, as well as severe cartilage damage and a broken kneecap. The next day surgeons spent five hours repairing the damage, and Rozema was placed on the 60-day disabled list.

"I just wanted to knock somebody down and get in a fight," Rozema told the press a week later. "I'll be back, though. I'm too much of an airhead to stay out of baseball."

In fact, he still had a few good seasons left. In 1983 Rozema made a solid recovery, appearing in 29 games and tossing 105 innings, including 16 starts. Beyond his record of 8-3 and ERA of 3.43, he had the most strikeouts (63) since his rookie season, and walked only 29. The next season, when the Tigers won the World Series, his numbers were almost identical: 29 games, 16 starts, 101 innings pitched and 48 strikeouts, with a meager 18 walks allowed, although his record fell to 7-6. By July of 1984, as a result of his 1982 knee surgery, Rozema was, wrote the press, "a 27-year old sore-legged pitcher without overpowering speed or stuff." With a 7-1 record on July 24, he finished the season 0-5, and during the World Series failed to make an appearance.

That turned out to be his final season in Detroit. After eight seasons as a Tiger, a record of 57-46, and an ERA of 3.38, on November 8, 1984, Dave Rozema became a free agent. Two weeks later he signed a two-year deal with the Texas Rangers that with incentives would be worth $710,000. "Going free agent was because I didn't really have a job in Detroit," he said. "I really didn't know where they were going to put me....Texas signed me to a nice contract and they're going to pitch me a lot."

Yet it never really worked out for Rozema in Arlington. Fifteen years later he reminisced for a reporter that "Texas was a 'nightmare.' We just didn't have the caliber of team needed to compete. We had a decent team on paper, but we couldn't win. It was like we always just found a way to lose games. It just wasn't happening for us." In 1985, he pitched in 34 games, all but four in relief, and posted a 3-7 record and 4.19 ERA in 88 innings; and in 1986, six days after being ejected from a game against Cleveland for arguing with the umpire, Rozema was released by Texas after appearing in six games and pitching 10 innings. And just like that, after 248 major-league games, 60 wins and 53 losses, his major-league career was over.

On May 20, 1986, Rozema was signed by the Chicago White Sox. He never pitched at the major-league level, however; in 13 games, he made 11 starts for Chicago's Triple-A affiliate, the Buffalo Bisons, and split eight decisions in 68 innings. In 1987, he appeared in seven games (five starts) for the Maine Guides, the Philadelphia Phillies' International League entry, and was 3-0 with a 2.92 ERA. Finally, in spring training of 1988 Rozema made several relief appearances for the Phillies, but was sent to their minor-league complex on March 18, and didn't pitch again for a major-league affiliate.

He had one last competitive trip to the mound, however: In 1990, Rozema pitched three games for the St. Petersburg Pelicans of the Senior Professional Baseball Association and compiled a record of 2-0 before the league folded.

And then his career was truly over.

With his playing days ended, Rozema returned to Detroit to live and work. Just before Christmas of 1985, he had married Sandy Sklarski in a double ceremony with onetime teammate and still best friend Kirk Gibson, who married Sandy's sister JoAnn. Eventually, Rozema took a position as a salesman with Diagnostic Imaging, a medical X-ray company. "We've got a lot of different products that we sell," he told *Sports Collectors Digest* in 2000. "I enjoy it." In his spare time he also enjoyed golf and fishing. Though he never played golf during his playing days, he became very good at the game, eventually playing to a seven handicap and often playing golf with his wife.

Rozema maintained his ties to baseball, too. He remained very active with the Tigers organization, and could occasionally be heard on TV and radio. He also frequented the ballpark.

He had come a long way since Central High School in Grand Rapids. Just how far was acknowledged in 2001, when Rozema was inducted into the Grand Rapids Sports Hall of Fame, along with more than 100 athletes, owners, and coaches from West Michigan who have achieved prominence in their sports on a local, state, or national level. In addition to Rozema, Jim Kaat, Mickey Stanley, and Wally Pipp are among other baseball players previously inducted. For the tall, slender rookie known as "The Rose" that's rather select company.

References

Publications

Cedar Rapids (Iowa) *Gazette*

Daily Intelligencer (Doylestown, Pennsylvania)

Daily Press (Escanaba, Michigan)

Daily Telegram (Adrian, Michigan)

Galveston (Texas) *Daily News*

Herald-Palladium (Benton Harbor, Michigan)

Ironwood (Michigan) *Daily Globe*

Ludington (Michigan) *Daily News*

Paris (Texas) *News*

Record-Eagle (Traverse City, Michigan)

The Sporting News

Sports Collectors Digest

USA Today (April 9, 1984)

Valley Independent (Monessen, Pennsylvania)

Waterloo (Iowa) *Courier*

Wisconsin Rapids (Wisconsin) *Daily Tribune*

Web Sites

baseball-reference.com/bullpen/Dave_Rozema

http://armchairgm.wikia.com/Dave_Rozema

http://minors.sabrwebs.com

http:/www.grshof.com/about.htm

http://www.spotstarters.com/?p=1284

Other Sources

National Baseball Hall of Fame and Museum

Acknowledgments

My thanks to Chuck Ailsworth, Society for American Baseball Research, for some minor-league statistical data.

Bill Scherrer
by Jeffrey Shand-Lubbers

ALWAYS APPRECIATIVE of being able to play baseball for a living, late in his career Bill Scherrer admitted, "There's nothing like being in the ballpark. I've seen the real world and you can keep it. I'd rather stay in the bubble."

Scherrer's bubble eventually included countless minor-league stops and appearances in a variety of countries. Born William Joseph Scherrer in Tonawanda, New York, on January 20, 1958, Scherrer graduated from Cardinal O'Hara High School in 1976, earning a *Parade* magazine All-American selection in baseball. In June of that year, he was drafted in the sixth round of the amateur draft by the Cleveland Indians, but did not sign. Because he did not sign, he became eligible for the secondary phase of the amateur draft, held in January 1977. He was taken by the Cincinnati Reds with the first overall pick and spent the entire season with the Shelby Reds in the Class A Western Carolinas League, where he won nine games and lost nine. He was stingy with hits (132 in 158 innings), but was wild (105 walks).

From 1978 to 1981, Scherrer bounced around between four minor-league teams from low-A to Double-A. His minor-league high point was in 1979, when, pitching for the Tampa Tarpons in the Class A Florida State League, he went 12-3 with a 1.81 earned-run average in 25 games and tossed 10 complete games, four of them shutouts. He struck out 140 while walking only 65 and didn't give up a home run all season. Still, in 1982, he found himself back in Tampa, a minor leaguer for the fifth straight year. He was later promoted to the Double-A Waterbury Reds of the Eastern League. His third minor-league team that season, the Triple-A Indianapolis Indians, won the American Association championship.

Called up to the Reds after the American Association Season, Scherrer made his major-league debut on September 7, 1982, pitching two perfect innings in Cincinnati against the Los Angeles Dodgers. He pitched in five games with the Reds that September (and got in a sixth game as a pinch-runner). His final two appearances were as a starter. Those two starts turned out to be the only nonrelief appearances of Scherrer's major-league career. In his first three games he threw two scoreless innings of relief each time, allowing one hit and no walks and striking out two. In all after his call-up, he pitched 17⅓ innings, allowing 17 hits and no walks, and fanning seven while posting a 2.60 ERA.

Scherrer spent the entire 1983 campaign with Cincinnati, one of two seasons he spent entirely in the major leagues, and set a Reds rookie record by appearing in 73 games. He notched a 2-3 record with 10 saves and a 2.74 ERA. His first major-league win came on May 20 at Wrigley Field when he retired the only two Cubs batters he faced in the seventh inning. The Reds scored five runs in the eighth and went on to win 9-5. Scherrer's first major-league save came in his next appearance, three days later, when he threw three hitless innings in Cincinnati against the St. Louis Cardinals after entering the game as a pinch-runner for Dan Driessen. And on September 17, Scherrer was on the mound for an inning with Johnny Bench behind the plate; Scherrer was thus the last pitcher Bench caught in his career.

Scherrer again started the 1984 season with the Reds. After two straight seasons finishing in the basement of the six-team National League West, the Reds started the season with a promising record of 19-14, but they stumbled over the next two months and arrived at the All-Star break with a 39-48 record. Scherrer did not quite match the effectiveness he showed in the 1983 season.

On July 11, Cincinnati demoted Scherrer to the Triple-A Wichita Aeros as part of a 10-player shakeup in response to what was viewed as disappointing play by a promising team. Scherrer was one of multiple Reds players who did not hesitate to express his displeasure for the moves, saying, "I won't put on a Reds uniform again. I told them I want to be traded. I will never play in this city again." At the time of his demotion Scherrer had an ERA of 4.99 with 35 strikeouts in 52⅓ innings pitched.

On August 27, the Detroit Tigers, who were leading their division by 12 games, acquired Scherrer from the Reds for a player to be named. Five days later, right-handed pitcher Carl Willis, who had appeared in 10 games for the Tigers that season, was Cincy-bound.

Speaking of the turnaround in his 1984 season, Scherrer said, "I was finished in baseball. But I got a break, and when you get one break, you've got to take advantage of it, because that might be all you get." Of his luck to be traded to a contending team, he said: "I could have gone to any other team and I go to the Detroit Tigers."

Scherrer made his first appearance with the Tigers the day after he was traded. Detroit was down 4-1 in Seattle, and Scherrer replaced starter Juan Berenguer in the bottom of the seventh inning with two outs and runners on second and third. Scherrer got left-handed Alvin Davis, the eventual American League Rookie of the Year, to ground out to first. Detroit scored three runs to tie; then Willie Hernandez relieved Scherrer in the bottom of the eighth inning and got the win as the Tigers scored another run in the top of the ninth to win 5-4.

Perhaps the more memorable story from the game is the one Scherrer told in the book *'84: Last of the Great Tigers*. Before the game, manager Sparky Anderson asked Dave Bergman to stand at the plate as a left-handed batting frame of reference as Scherrer threw warm-up pitches. Scherrer threw a pitch that tailed straight into Bergman's back, and the first baseman pulled a muscle trying to get out of the way. He played that night but missed the team's next eight games.

Scherrer earned his only 1984 win with the Tigers on September 8 during an important series with Toronto. Earlier in the week, the Tigers' lead over the Blue Jays had dwindled to 7½ games. Scherrer relieved Jack Morris, who was suffering from stiffness in his shoulder, in the fifth inning of a tie game and retired five of the six batters he faced, three of them on strikeouts. Detroit went on to win the game 10-4, giving

DETROIT TIGERS 1984: WHAT A START! WHAT A FINISH!

them a double-digit lead in the standings that they did not relinquish the rest of the season. Scherrer pitched in all three games of that series, throwing three scoreless innings and giving up only one walk, no runs, and no hits. In the book *Bless You Boys*, a diary of the 1984 season, Sparky Anderson said after the series, "The Blue Jays have a great team. The only difference between them and us is our bullpen."

Despite the Tigers never being seriously challenged for the division title after their remarkable 35-5 start, the series in Toronto was probably the most important one for the team all season long. In his book *Inside Pitch*, Tigers pitching coach Roger Craig said, "Our championship, in my opinion, had been a foregone conclusion since we swept the Blue Jays in Toronto earlier this month."

Craig also said after Scherrer's only win, "As much as I liked Carl Willis, Scherrer is the one we need now—he's more advanced as a pitcher and there is a shortage of left-handers in our system." Alluding to Scherrer's luck in going from Triple-A to the Tigers, Craig remarked, "He must be a collector of rabbit's feet and four-leaf clovers; he toiled for six years in the minor-league system of the Cincinnati Reds and couldn't find a spot on a team going nowhere. Now he's on the best team Baseball '84 has to offer."

On September 23, Scherrer pitched a hitless inning at home against the New York Yankees in Detroit's 100th win of the season. In that game, he bridged the gap between starter Jack Morris, who earned his 19th and final win of the season, and MVP and Cy Young Award winner Willie Hernandez, who earned his 32nd and final save of the campaign. With the win, Sparky Anderson became the first manager to win 100 games in both the American League and National League.

Scherrer did not pitch in the American League Championship Series against the Kansas City Royals, which the Tigers won in a three-game sweep under the best-of-five format then in effect. He made three appearances in the World Series. His first was in Game Two, the Tigers' only loss in the World Series, when he faced five batters, allowing two hits and no runs. The first batter he faced was the left-handed future Hall of Famer Tony Gwynn, who pushed a bunt toward first baseman Darrell Evans. Evans fielded the ball cleanly but was unable to make the out at first base as Scherrer did not cover the bag in time. Scherrer made up for his mental miscue by picking off Gwynn, who was then called out trying to steal second (pitcher to first baseman to shortstop).

His second appearance came in Game Three, in relief of starter Milt Wilcox to start the seventh inning. Scherrer gave up two hits and an earned run in two-thirds of an inning as the Tigers won the game, 5-2.

Scherrer's final career postseason appearance came in the deciding Game Five. By the fourth inning, Tigers starter Dan Petry had already given up six hits and two walks. After Petry surrendered a double, a sacrifice fly, and a single to successive batters, Anderson called on Scherrer to face Gwynn with runners on second and third. (Petry's outing of $3^2/_3$ innings was the shortest outing by the starting pitcher of the winning team in a World Series clincher since the Yankees'

Ralph Terry hurled a paltry $2^1/_3$ innings against the Reds in 1961.) Against Gwynn, Scherrer induced a fly ball that preserved a 3-3 tie. He retired two of the three batters he faced in the fifth inning before being replaced by Aurelio Lopez. The Tigers took the lead in the bottom of the fifth inning and went on to win the game, 8-4, clinching the club's first World Series title in 16 years.

Despite his solid pitching performance in the World Series, Scherrer may be best remembered for his World Series ring. The next season, Scherrer was at dinner with teammates Kirk Gibson and Milt Wilcox in Anaheim, California. A woman at the restaurant was raving over the beauty of the World Series rings of Gibson and Wilcox before asking Scherrer why his was different, which he had not noticed before. During the team's next series, in Seattle, writer Vern Plagenhoef of the *Grand Rapids Press* volunteered to pay for an appraisal of Scherrer's ring. Scherrer was told that the stone in his ring was actually made of glass and that the true value was somewhere between $90 and $250, compared with the highest quality rings, valued at about $3,000.

Upon realizing this, Kirk Gibson mailed his ring back to the Tigers in protest of Scherrer's receiving one of lesser value. Tigers president Jim Campbell defended Scherrer's ring, saying that it merely reflected the value of the postseason bonus the team had voted to give to Scherrer, who was with the club for only one month of the regular season. He had been allotted a one-third share of the bonus and the least expensive of the three different types of rings that had been given. Said Campbell, "If the players wanted him to get a full share, they should have voted him a full share."

Of the one-third share he did receive, Scherrer said, "To have my teammates vote me a one-third share was very generous. They could have given me a fifth share and I would have been happy."

Similar to the dropoff in production he experienced with the Reds in 1984, Scherrer was not quite able to match his brief but effective 1984 performance with Detroit in 1985. He finished with a 4.36 ERA in 66 innings with a 3-2 record in 48 games pitched for a Tigers team that many thought going into the season was as good as if not better than the 1984 World Series team but finished a middling third, 15 games behind Toronto.

Scherrer began the 1986 season with the Nashville Sounds, the Tigers' Triple-A affiliate. A bit more than a month later, he was back with the Tigers but lasted only a month and a half before being sent back to Nashville. In his final game as a Tiger, on June 29, he pitched an inning and a third against the Milwaukee Brewers. He finished the season with a 7.29 ERA in 21 innings and 13 games pitched with Detroit. He became a free agent after the season.

Despite his proclamation that he would never return to Cincinnati after being demoted by the Reds in 1984, Scherrer accepted the Reds' invitation to spring training in 1987. He did not make the team out of spring training but was recalled from Nashville (which in 1987 went from the Tigers' affiliate to the Reds' affiliate) in June. Of his first appearance with

DETROIT TIGERS 1984: WHAT A START! WHAT A FINISH!

Cincinnati in three years, he said, "It felt a little weird. But I'm happy to be back." In his first six games, from June 10 to July 1, Scherrer gave up eight earned runs in seven innings for an ERA of 10.29. He reduced his ERA fairly steadily until the end of July, but August was a nightmare. After a stretch in which he posted a 6.14 ERA in five appearances (five earned runs in 7 1/3 innings) between August 1 and August 14, Scherrer was sent back to Nashville. He was recalled again on September 5 but threw only 1 1/3 innings in three appearances the rest of the season and was given his release on October 27. For the season he finished with a 1-1 record and a 4.36 ERA in 33 innings pitched in 23 games. He was 4-1 with Nashville.

In January he signed a contract with the Triple-A Rochester Red Wings, the Baltimore Orioles' top farm club. He started the 1988 season with Rochester but was recalled in late April by the Orioles, who at the time were in the midst of their record-setting season-opening 21-game losing streak. In his brief time with the club, Scherrer was saddled with loss No. 20. With the Orioles tied with the Minnesota Twins, 4-4, on April 27, Scherrer, making his second appearance for the Orioles, entered the game in the bottom of the eighth inning and gave up consecutive home runs to Kent Hrbek and Tim Laudner, a walk to John Moses, and a balk, sending Moses to second, before being replaced by Doug Sisk, whose error sent Moses home. The Orioles scored two runs in the top of the ninth but lost by 7-6. Leaving the southpaw Scherrer in to face the right-handed Laudner prompted manager Frank Robinson to apologize after the game to what at that point had become a national media following of the league's worst team. Scherrer's outing also prompted this remark from Thomas Boswell of the *Washington Post*: "What do you do after you give up a homer, a homer, a walk, and a balk? Take a cold Scherrer." Scherrer made two more appearances with the team but was released a week after being recalled from Rochester.

He signed with the Philadelphia Phillies on June 25 and made eight appearances with the team before being released on August 1. For the following few months he continued to bounce around and signed minor-league contracts with the Chicago Cubs, Pittsburgh Pirates, and Texas Rangers without making appearances with any of the parent clubs. Besides the Orioles and Phillies, he pitched that season for four Triple-A teams.

In early 1990, Scherrer won the Caribbean championship with Escogido of the Dominican Republic, a team that featured current and future major-league players including Nelson Liriano, Jose Vizcaino, Luis de los Santos, Marquis Grissom, and Junior Felix. Scherrer said of his time with the team: "It's even wilder, more vocal down there. They get real crazy." He then reported to spring training with the New York Mets, although he did not break camp with the team. Scherrer then signed with an Italian team but stayed for only of two weeks. Of that experience, he said: "I didn't know what I was thinking of—other than, get money and play ball."

In late July 1990, Scherrer, who at this point had an infant son at home, signed with the Kitchener (Ontario) Panthers of the semipro Intercounty Baseball League. Once or twice a week he made the 100-mile drive from his home in Tonawanda, near the Canadian border, to Ontario, where he would proudly say, "I'll brag about winning here as I would winning in Indianapolis or winning the World Series." Regarding the money he was making, Scherrer acknowledged, "I'm not getting rich doing this—I can't even say it's a living."

But Scherrer's passion for the game was still evident. He was envious of Canadian baseball's teaching of fundamentals. Regarding his teammates, some of whom were at least ten years younger than he, and their passion, Scherrer said, "I am impressed with our players. Canadians go full-bore, they work on things."

Once his playing career finally ended, Scherrer became a scout, first with the Florida Marlins, for whom he covered western Pennsylvania, Ontario, Quebec, and New York, looking at both college and high-school players. He became part of another World Series-winning franchise as a scout with the Marlins in 1997.

In 1994, the *Toronto Sun* awarded Scherrer its annual Scout of the Year award for going above and beyond the call of duty. As he pitched batting practice to a prospect in Cortland, New York, in the rain while wearing white dress shoes, the batter lined a pitch back at Scherrer that knocked him to the muddy ground. Walking off the field to a standing ovation from the other scouts in attendance Scherrer remarked, "Reminded me of the old days. I'd come in the game, guys in the other dugout would stand and cheer."

After scouting for the Marlins, Scherrer again returned to the Reds, this time as a scout in 1998, and worked for the team until 2002. He won his third World Series title in 2005, as a scout with the Chicago White Sox, for whom in 2009 he was a special assistant to general manager Ken Williams.

Twenty years after discovering the value of his 1984 World Series ring, Scherrer raved about the ring he got from the White Sox. It was valued at about $20,000. Scherrer praised White Sox owner Jerry Reinsdorf, who presented 432 identical rings made of 14-karat gold with the White Sox logo in diamonds. Perhaps alluding to the tiered system of awards the Tigers implemented after their 1984 Series victory, Scherrer said of the 2005 White Sox ring, "It shows you what a class guy Jerry Reinsdorf is. He had the same style of ring for everyone."

Scherrer always stayed true to his New York roots, both during and after his professional playing days. While waiting out the riots that surrounded Tiger Stadium after Detroit's 1984 World Series victory over San Diego, Scherrer approached journalist Erik Brady, who had covered him in high school, and beamed, "Didja hear? The Bills beat Seattle." Brady looked at him and said, "Billy, you just won the World Series." Scherrer laughed and responded, "I know, but I've only been a Tiger since August. And I've been a Bills fan all my life." In addition to his scouting duties, Scherrer in 1993 began working as an instructor at the Rick Lancelloti Buffalo School of Baseball. And in 2006 he was elected to the Greater Buffalo Sports Hall of Fame.

Scherrer finished his major-league playing career with a record of 8-10 and an ERA of 4.08 in 228 appearances. To date, only two other retired players who pitched in 200 or more games, Kelly Wunsch and Scott Stewart, had fewer career decisions than Scherrer. He proved to be an effective left-handed specialist. Over the course of his career, left-handed batters hit .210 in 404 at-bats against him, with only six home runs, and a minuscule .292 slugging percentage.

References

Publications

Anderson, Sparky. *Bless You Boys: Diary of the Detroit Tigers' 1984 Season*. Chicago: Contemporary Books, Inc. 1984.

Craig, Roger. *Inside Pitch: Roger Craig's '84 Tiger Journal*. Grand Rapids, Mich.: William B. Eerdmans Publishing Co. 1984.

Detroit Tigers. *Detroit Tigers 1985 Yearbook*. Detroit: Detroit Tigers. 1985.

Detroit Tigers. *Detroit Tigers 1986 Yearbook*. Detroit: Detroit Tigers. 1986.

Zaret, Eli. *'84, The Last of the Great Tigers*. South Boardman, Mich.: Crofton Creek Press. 2004.

Articles

Boswell, Thomas. "Hey, This Isn't Funny!" *Washington Post*, April 28, 1988.

Brady, Erik. "Don't Be Buffaloed: Bills' Faithful No. 1." *USA Today*, January 15, 1992.

"Deals, Baseball." *Seattle Times*, October 10, 1998. Retrieved from http://community.seattletimes.nwsource.com/archive/?date=19981010&slug=2776749

Elliott, Bob. "Elliott on Baseball." *Toronto Sun*, June 5, 1994.

Elliott, Bob. "Elliott on Baseball." *Slam! Sports*, May 14, 2006. Retrieved from: http://slam.canoe.ca/Slam/Columnists/Elliott/2006/05/14/1579442.html

Elliott, Bob. "Twins Scout Is Our No. 1." *Toronto Sun*, June 9, 2007.

Elliott, Bob. "Where Are They Now?" *Toronto Sun*, January 14, 2005.

Frayne, Trent. "Pair of Waves Collide in Centre." *The Globe and Mail* (Toronto), October 11, 1984.

Kaplan, Jim. "Inside Pitch (Statistics Through July 15)." *Sports Illustrated*, July 23, 1984. Retrieved from http://vault.sportsillustrated.cnn.com/vault/article/magazine/MAG1122344/index.htm.

Loewen, Gary. "Pitcher of Dreams Dazzled By Diamonds." *The Globe and Mail* (Toronto), September 6, 1990.

Myers, Jim. "'Beisbol' Captivates Caribbean." *USA Today*, February 5, 1990.

"Vikes, Giants Swap Veterans." *Pittsburgh Post-Gazette*, July 13, 1984.

Rosenberg, Michael. "Like '07, Tigers of '85 Also Had Tough Act to Follow." *Detroit Free Press*, September 28, 2007.

Schoenfeld, Bruce. "Monge Contents Himself With World Series Aura." *San Diego Union-Tribune*, October 12, 1984.

Schoenfeld, Bruce. "Tigers' Middle Relievers Did Their Job on Padres." *San Diego Union-Tribune*, October 15, 1984.

"Sports People: Red Shuffle." *New York Times*, July 12, 1984.

"Tigers Win 100th Game, 4-1." *Washington Post*, September 24, 1984.

"Tigers Get Reliever Scherrer." *San Diego Union-Tribune*, August 28, 1984.

Zwolinski, Mark. "Baseball Institute Plans to Expand." *Toronto Star*, July 31, 1990.

Web Sites

http://www.baseball-reference.com/players/s/scherbi01.shtml

http://www.niagarafallsreporter.com/niagarabaseballhof.html

http://www.thebaseballcube.com/players/S/Bill-Scherrer.shtml

Nelson Simmons
by Malcolm Allen

OUTFIELDER NELSON Simmons parlayed a passion for pumping iron into a barrel chest, watermelon-sized biceps, and the ability to wallop baseballs a long way from home plate. In 1985, at the age of 22, the switch-hitter became the first Detroit Tigers player to hit a home run from each side of the plate in the same game. But too much work in the weight room and off-field problems combined to derail his promising major-league career less than two years later.

Nelson Bernard Simmons was born on Thursday, June 27, 1963, in Washington, D.C. That day at Metropolitan Stadium in Minneapolis, the ninth-place Tigers suffered their fourth consecutive loss. Detroit's slugging first baseman, Norm Cash, tied a record by playing the entire contest at first base without a single fielding chance. In some strange way, perhaps it was an omen for the dearth of opportunity awaiting Simmons when he grew up to be a big leaguer.

The story started well. After moving to San Diego, Simmons had such an outstanding baseball career at Madison High School that the Tigers made him their second-round pick in the June 1981 free-agent draft, on assistant general manager Bill Lajoie's recommendation. Through 2012, Kansas City Royals pitcher Al Fitzmorris remaiins the school's only other alumnus to reach the majors. Simmons declined scholarship offers from Arizona State and Hawaii, did an about face on his plan to join the Army, and turned pro to help out his mother financially.

Simmons signed quickly and joined the rookie-level Bristol (Virginia) Tigers in plenty of time to lead the Appalachian League in at-bats. In 69 games, the 6-foot-1 185-pounder—he would put on more pounds as he matured—batted .296 with 14 doubles, 10 home runs, and 45 runs batted in. When Detroit manager Sparky Anderson visited the Tigers' minor-league complex in Lakeland, Florida, the following spring, he noticed the 18-year-old Simmons and announced, "I guarantee you that kid is a big leaguer if I've ever seen one."

"It's the most important thing that happened to me," Simmons said. "From that point on, I wanted to make all his comments come true." He earned Florida State League All-Star honors in 1982, batting .293 for Lakeland and ranking third in the circuit in total bases. After an eight-game taste of Double-A ball with the Birmingham Barons late in the season, he returned to the Barons a year later to help them win a Southern League championship.

Baseball America rated Simmons' throwing arm the strongest among Southern League outfielders in 1983, but his .272 batting average and .401 slugging percentage were his worst figures since turning pro. "He went backward," Anderson said later. "Plus, he had a sour way about him." Sparky speculated that his own high praise for the teenage Simmons might have done more harm than good. "I think he got confused. No sooner did he have a good spring than some agent got his head turned around."

Simmons rebounded to lead the Tigers' Florida Instructional League club in RBIs that fall, but his star had dimmed enough that Detroit shopped him around in trade talks for pitching. No acceptable offers came in, though, and by the summer of 1984, the Tigers were awfully glad about that.

Moved up to the Triple-A Evansville Triplets in 1984, Simmons went through a slump in May that caused his manager to doubt whether Simmons could handle Triple-A. But Simmons got so hot in the second half that skipper Gordon MacKenzie called him "the most improved player in the American Association." Simmons earned player-of-the-week honors for the week of July 16-22 by mashing 15 hits in eight games, nine of them for extra bases. He finished with a league-leading 41 doubles, complementing a .307 batting average with 22 home runs and 83 RBIs. "He made a believer out of me," MacKenzie said. "He's a young Ken Singleton." (Singleton at the time was winding down a major-league career in which he hit 246 home runs and drove in 1,065 runs.)

Simmons made his major-league debut at Tiger Stadium on September 4, going 1-for-4 and driving in Detroit's only run against the American League's only 20-game winner of 1984, Mike Boddicker of the Baltimore Orioles. Simmons spent the next two weeks on the bench, watching the Tigers wrap up the AL East race they had seized control of early with a 35-5 start. "We won the championship at Double-A last year, but I got to tell you, it was nothing like this," Simmons said in the midst of the division-clinching celebration. "These people know how to party."

Simmons got into eight of Detroit's final 11 regular season games after the September 18 clincher, starting six, and notching a pair of three-hit games against the Milwaukee Brewers. In 30 at-bats overall, he batted .433 to solidify his reclaimed status as a top Tigers prospect. Though ineligible to participate in the playoffs, he got an up-close view from the dugout as the Tigers romped through the postseason, winning their first World Series in 16 years by beating Simmons' hometown San Diego Padres.

Simmons wore a different championship Tigers uniform after that, leading the Dominican Winter League in both RBIs and runs scored in helping the Tigres del Licey go all the way. He had nothing left to prove heading into spring training, but had no clear place on a Detroit team coming off 104 regular-season victories.

Anderson made it clear that he'd prefer to send Simmons back to Triple-A unless he could guarantee him at least 250 at-bats in the majors. Once Simmons got off to a hot start in Grapefruit League action, Detroit's skipper gushed that he might just give the 21-year-old 600 trips to the plate as the Tigers' everyday designated hitter. Before the ink was dry on Sparky's quotes in the *Detroit News*, however, Simmons was stuck in a 1-for-25 rut that nearly cost him his place on the Opening Day roster. Then he blasted homers in four straight

DETROIT TIGERS 1984: WHAT A START! WHAT A FINISH!

exhibition contests to lock up a spot on the team, and finished spring training with more than twice as many RBIs as any of his teammates.

But adversity found him on Opening Day before the umpire had a chance to holler "Play ball!" "I was making throws from the outfield before the game when I felt something stretch and pop in my left side," Simmons said. "I threw the ball, but when I went to make the next throw, I could hardly lift my arm." He spent the afternoon with an ice pack on a pulled rib-cage muscle, needed help getting dressed to go home, and spent the first month of the season on the disabled list. "It can't get worse than this," Simmons said at the time. "Getting hurt before the first game.... I can't believe it."

Detroit had seven outfielders on the roster when Simmons returned on April 30. He hit his first big-league homer off the Chicago White Sox' Gene Nelson in a pinch-hitting role on May 4 and spent most of the next seven weeks as the left-handed half of a DH platoon with Alejandro Sanchez. After getting into 30 games with a .240 average and three homers, Simmons was demoted to Triple-A Nashville just before his 22nd birthday.

He batted just .245 in 49 games with the Sounds, but nine home runs in 188 at-bats got him back to the Tigers in mid-August. "I screwed up last time," Simmons said. "I tried to hit everything out of the park to impress Sparky and give him enough reasons to keep me around. I forgot about just being myself."

Given a second chance, Simmons drove in 11 runs in his first half-dozen games, and belted four home runs. With Detroit already trailing the division-leading Toronto Blue Jays by double digits, Anderson vowed that Simmons would get every opportunity to sink or swim. "I'm going to let him play every game the rest of the year unless he gets hurt," said Sparky. "What he does against the really good pitchers we face will tell me a lot. That's when you judge."

Despite a 2-for-30 slump at the end of the year that dropped his batting average to .239, Simmons' 10 homers in 75 games earned him Tigers Rookie of the Year honors. On September 16 against Baltimore at Tiger Stadium, he became the first player in Tigers history to homer from both sides of the plate in the same game. One of his blasts made him the first Detroit player since 1973 to clear the 440-foot barrier in straightaway center field.

But the same barrel chest and huge biceps that allowed Simmons to hit baseballs a long way got him into his manager's doghouse. Despite getting perennial all-star production out of devoted weightlifter Lance Parrish, Anderson believed too much iron-pumping was bad for baseball players, and told Simmons so after confronting him about his training habits.

"I feel so much better when I'm lifting," Simmons explained. "He [Anderson] did help me because he got me to stop bench-pressing, but when I'm strong I'm more confident. Look at all the guys who lift weights: Lance Parrish, Fred Lynn, a lot of guys."

Simmons hit the weights all winter and reported to camp even bigger in 1986. He hit .308 with three home runs in spring training, but Anderson was convinced that the added bulk was cutting into Simmons' already negligible speed. Coupled with the fact that Simmons was not a threat to win a Gold Glove, when the final roster cuts came, that got Simmons sent back to Triple-A for being too one-dimensional. A bitter Simmons told reporters, "It's obvious to me Sparky doesn't want me around," and announced his intention to request a trade.

Three weeks and a day after Detroit opened the season without him, Tigers fans were stunned to learn that Simmons had been released. General manager Bill Lajoie had taken a trip to Nashville, and come away unimpressed with the slumping slugger, who was off to a .200 start without a homer through 14 games. "I hadn't been satisfied with his effort since the third week of spring training," Lajoie said. "We don't think he has a chance of making our club in the near future, and this gives him a chance to go somewhere else."

Sparky was even more blunt. "I don't think anybody felt he could play in the big leagues," said the skipper who once called Simmons "a big leaguer if I've ever seen one." "There's no sense wasting time if someone can't play." When Sparky's apparent change of heart was pointed out to him, he explained, "I never said I thought he might become a good player. I said he might become a good hitter, but then his body got bigger than the moon."

The Baltimore Orioles signed Simmons five days later, and the non-baseball reasons for the stunning release of Detroit's 1985 Rookie of the Year started to trickle out. What we know is this: In the early-morning hours of April 29, police were summoned twice to Simmons' hotel room at the Executive Inn in Nashville for a disturbance involving a female friend and, later, the overnight desk clerk. One source said the incident involved a spray-paint duel, but no police report was filed at the time and subsequent assault charges by the woman against Simmons were eventually dropped.

If Tigers fans were left scratching their heads by the events, so was Simmons. "I think it took half a season to get over it, and my stats reflected it," he said later. "I know in my heart I didn't do anything wrong. I think Sparky disliked my weightlifting so much; he was looking for an excuse to let me go. When I had some personal problems, that was the excuse he needed."

In 89 games with the Rochester Red Wings, Baltimore's Triple-A affiliate, Simmons hit .273, but with only 8 home runs and 37 RBIs. The next spring however, he was back in the mix for a big-league job, and Orioles skipper Cal Ripken Sr. explained why: "When you watch him hit ball after ball over the fence from both sides of the plate, you tend to notice."

With Baltimore outfielder Mike Young missing time early in the year with a torn thumb ligament, Simmons found himself back in the majors. He batted .265 with one home run in 16 games, but was sent back to Rochester when Young returned in the second week of May. There, Simmons hit .271 with just three homers in 64 games before being traded to the Seattle Mariners for pitcher Mike Brown on August 11. Simmons hit .306 with 17 home runs and 86

RBIs in 145 games over the next year and a half for Seattle's Triple-A Calgary Cannons, but never got the call to return to the big leagues.

In Mexican winter ball in 1988-89, Simmons won a batting title playing for Mazatlan and ranked in the top three in both homers and RBIs to earn an invitation to spring training from the St. Louis Cardinals. He survived until the final cut, but he went back to his hotel and smoked marijuana when he learned he'd been demoted to Triple-A Louisville. That came back to cost him when—after getting off to a .316 start five games into the season—he flunked a drug test and was released for violating the organization's substance-abuse policy.

Simmons spent 1990 and 1991 in the Oakland Athletics organization, batting .256 with 15 homers at Double-A Huntsville in '90, then .272 with eight homers at Triple-A Tacoma a year later. He played only 24 games with American professional clubs in the two years that followed, spending most of his time with Jalisco in the Mexican League, where he hit .382 with 34 home runs and 95 RBIs in 1993. That performance included another batting title.

"I've done a lot of things I'm not proud of, and I did test positive once for marijuana," Simmons admitted months later. "But I know guys who have crack in their back pocket and they're out there making millions. All I need is for someone to give me a chance." In 1994, the California Angels invited him to his first major-league spring training in five years, but Simmons didn't make the team.

With major leaguers still out on strike out the outset of 1995, Simmons joined his eighth organization, this time as a Pittsburgh Pirates replacement player. That was a largely forgettable chapter in baseball history, but Simmons' contribution deserves to be remembered. He hit .418 with seven homers and 28 RBIs that spring before the real Pirates came back, and, in the words of Pittsburgh baseball writer Joe Rutter, "also became the first replacement player to cop a big-league attitude by briefly refusing to talk to reporters."

"I almost wish I could change my name and go play baseball where nobody knows me," Simmons once said. "People have long memories in this game and, unfortunately, they still remember the bad things about me."

Simmons faded out of organized ball after hitting .281 with nine homers and 58 RBIs in 107 games for Triple-A Calgary in 1995, playing for three clubs in the now-defunct Western Baseball League in ensuing seasons before wrapping up his career with a brief stint in Mexico in 2000. Simmons played in the San Diego Adult Baseball League well into his 40s, and coached at West Hills High School for a spell. In 2012, he joined the San Diego Baseball Academy as a hitting instructor."

His son Goldy, a 6-foot-5 right-handed pitcher who throws in the 90s, was drafted by the Oakland Athletics in 2006 and the Atlanta Braves in 2007, but didn't sign with either team. He spent 2008 pitching at San Diego City College and 2009 at San Diego State University, and was drafted by the Chicago White Sox in the 23rd round in 2009. Goldy spent two summers pitching Rookie-level ball in the Chisox system before being released.

References

Articles

Gage, Tom. "Fade Out For Tigers Fair-Haired Boy." *The Sporting News*, May 12, 1986: 58.

Gage, Tom. "Simmons Could Be Tigers' Regular DH." *The Sporting News*, April 1, 1985: 37.

Gage, Tom. "Simmons Might Not Find Any Room At The Top." *Detroit News*, March 1, 1985: 1C.

Gage, Tom. "Simmons Returns With A Bang—Or 3." *The Sporting News*, September 2, 1985: 30.

Gage, Tom. "Simmons Sidelined For 15 Days." *Detroit News*, April 9, 1985: 3D.

Gage, Tom, and Lynn Henning. "Simmons Released." *Detroit News*, April 30, 1986.

Henning, Lynn. "Hotel Scuffle Helped Finish Simmons." *Detroit News*, May 6, 1986: D1.

Justice, Richard. "Simmons' Bat and Glove Complicate Orioles' Outfield: Ex-Tiger May Be Ahead of Lacy, Sheets, Traber, Young." *Washington Post*, March 19, 1987: B3.

Nightengale, Bob. "Trying Again." *The Sporting News*, March 14, 1994: 18.

Ritter, Jon. "Major Replacements." *Pittsburgh Tribune-Review*, March 6, 2005.

Web Sites

http://www.baseball-reference.com

http://www.retrosheet.org

http://www.thebaseballcube.com

Acknowledgements

Mike Micheli of the San Diego Adult Baseball League.

Alan Trammell
by John Milner

ON A CRISP mid-October day in 1984, Alan Trammell played a key role in putting the Detroit Tigers on the verge of the World Series championship their fans and city had been waiting for since the "Sock It to 'Em Tigers" team of 1968 upended the St. Louis Cardinals. The Tigers led their National League opponent, the San Diego Padres, two games to one as the teams prepared for Game Four at Tiger Stadium. The teams had split the first two games in San Diego, and the Tigers pulled ahead by winning Game Three. Game Four proved to be a pivotal point in the Series. As happened often during the Tigers' magical season, they pulled ahead in the first inning when Lou Whitaker reached on an error and Trammell smacked a home run into the left-field seats. In the third inning, Whitaker reached again, on a single, and as more than 52,000 fans in the historic ballpark roared, Trammell again stepped to the plate attempting to add his name to the list of Tigers legends. Trammell was up to the task and hit a home run into the upper deck—a hit that all but cemented the Series for the Tigers. Jack Morris held on for the win, and the next day Kirk Gibson put the finishing touches on the Tigers' first championship in 16 years. Based on his consistency and heroics, "Tram" was named the Series' Most Valuable Player, a well-deserved honor.

Alan Stuart Trammell was born on February 21, 1958, in Garden Grove, California, near Anaheim and a stone's throw from Disneyland, to Forrest and Anne Trammell. He grew up as a fan of the Padres and as a teenager worked as a vendor at San Diego Chargers football games and professional soccer matches at San Diego Stadium (the name of which was changed in 1980 to Jack Murphy Stadium). Trammell and his friends often sneaked into Padres games by getting there early and just "hanging out" until game time. From a young age, Trammell was involved in sports. At Kearney High School, he focused on basketball and baseball, with basketball being his first choice. He received basketball scholarship offers from some colleges to play point guard. Although talented, he was humble about his abilities, much as he would be with the Tigers. Brad Griffith, a coach at Kearney High, said, "He was a great athlete, but was always humble, didn't go around projecting himself as the big man on campus." Trammell was named to the California Interscholastic Team in both basketball and baseball. Jack Taylor, his high school baseball coach, remembered Trammell's work ethic: Most scouts who saw him wondered if he would ever be able to hit well enough, but Trammell worked hard at improving his skills at the plate. From scores in the 42-48 range given initially by scouts for the Major League Scouting Bureau (the bureau scores prospects on a 20-80 scale with a score of 55 indicating major-league ability) his scores improved to as high as 58.6.

Two Tigers scouts, Rick Ferrell and Dick Wiencek, liked Trammell, and Detroit selected him in the second round of the 1976 amateur draft. He had offers to play college baseball at UCLA and Arizona State, but signed with the Tigers for $35,000. "Once signed, I was committed. I wasn't going to be stopped, nothing could stop me in my mind," Trammell said. "I was going to work and do whatever it took." (Wiencek was responsible for signing Trammell, as well as five other future major leaguers that year: Jack Morris, Dan Petry, Steve Kemp, Dave Stegman, and nondrafted free agent Steve Baker.)

After playing in the state all-star baseball game, Trammell began his professional career two days later, as a shortstop with the Bristol (Virginia) Tigers in the Rookie-level Appalachian League, where he hit .271 in 41 games and played in the league all-star game. Toward the end of the season, he bypassed Class A altogether and was moved up to the Double-A Montgomery Rebels in the Southern League, where the 18-year-old hit only .179 in 21 games. Despite his low batting average, the Tigers saw his potential. Defensively, he was quite advanced, and as he developed physically, Detroit figured his batting would improve. That fall, he was sent to the Instructional League in Florida and met Lou Whitaker for the first time. They were roommates at the Edgewater Hotel in St. Petersburg and became, if not inseparable, then joined at the keystone sack. "The very first day, we clicked," said Trammell. In 1977, he began the season at Montgomery, where he played shortstop and Whitaker second base—the start of a long-standing double-play combination. Trammell hit .291 in 134 games with 50 RBIs and 19 triples, which broke the league record set by Reggie Jackson 10 years earlier. (Oddly, he had only 9 doubles.) He was named the league's Most Valuable Player. Montgomery won the league championship over Jacksonville; the day after the clincher, Trammell was called up to the Tigers.

Trammell and Whitaker made their major-league debuts on September 9; at a little over 19½ years old, Trammell was the youngest player in the league. Whitaker was 20 years and 4 months old. Whitaker batted second and Trammell ninth as both collected their first big-league hits off veteran Boston right-hander Reggie Cleveland. Trammell singled to center field in the third inning, and added another single in the sixth inning off Rick Wise. Trammell scored his first big-league run in the contest, and handled two chances in the field flawlessly.

On February 21, 1978, his 20th birthday, Alan married Barbara Leverett. They had met during his sophomore year in high school, but didn't begin dating until he was a senior. They would eventually have three children, Lance (named after Lance Parrish), Kyle, and Jade Lynn. When the 1978 season started, Detroit manager Ralph Houk gave Trammell and Whitaker the opportunity to start for the Tigers, and they responded with good seasons. Houk spoke highly of his young duo: "Those two kids, they just play good every day. They're the best I've ever seen for their age. On the double plays, knowing where the ball is going to be, that's something you can't teach." Whitaker won the American League Rookie of the Year award, while Trammell finished fourth in the voting. Trammell finished with a batting average of .268 with 2 home runs, 34 RBIs, and 49 runs scored. On July 7, against the Texas Rangers at Arlington, he went 5-for-6, with a double, two RBIs, and two runs scored. Trammell and Whitaker led

DETROIT TIGERS 1984: WHAT A START! WHAT A FINISH!

the league in double plays at their position. Each took part in 95 twin killings—although they weren't always involved in the same 95.

Trammell attributed his consistency on defense to observing two former major-league shortstops, Mark Belanger of the Baltimore Orioles and Eddie Brinkman, who had played with Detroit and was an instructor with the Tigers early in Trammell's career. Trammell commented, "They both got in front of every ball. They tried to throw accurately. They were consistent."

Over the next few years after his debut season, Trammell worked to maintain his stellar fielding and increase his prowess at the plate. He worked at being able to hit the ball to all parts of the field and to become stronger, eventually filling out to 175 pounds on his 6-foot frame. Along with adding strength, Trammell was able to maintain his quickness, which could be seen by his steal of home against the Oakland Athletics on June 12, 1979, at Tiger Stadium off right-hander Dave Heaverlo—the first steal of home for a Tiger since 38-year-old Al Kaline did it in 1973. In 1980, Trammell had his breakout year. He batted .300 with 168 hits, 9 home runs, 65 RBIs, and 107 runs scored. He earned the first of his six trips to the All-Star Game. Fielding at a .980 pace and making only 13 errors, he received his first Gold Glove, the first for a Tiger since Aurelio Rodriguez in 1976 and the first for a Detroit shortstop since Brinkman in 1972. After the season, Trammell signed a seven-year, $2.8 million contract, paving the way for a long-term stay in Detroit.

In both 1981 and '82, Trammell's average fell to .258, but in the strike-shortened '81 season, he won another Gold Glove by committing only nine errors for a .983 fielding percentage.

In 1983, he bounced back to have his best year yet, batting .319 with 14 homers and 66 RBIs. His average was good enough for fourth in the American League, one point behind his keystone partner Whitaker. He also won a Gold Glove again with a .979 fielding average and only 13 errors, and won *The Sporting News*' American League Comeback Player of the Year Award. It was the first of two consecutive seasons in which Trammell and Whitaker won Gold Gloves at the same time; only eight other shortstop-second base

For many Tigers fans, Alan Trammell embodied the 1984 team. He stayed a fan favorite throughout his 20-year playing career, all with Detroit. He later became a coach for the team, as well as Tigers manager 2003-05. Although his managerial tenure ended badly, he was cheered lustily a year later when he shared the mound with Sparky Anderson before Game Two of the 2006 World Series, the Tigers' first appearance in the Fall Classic since 1984. (National Baseball Hall of Fame Library, Cooperstown, New York)

DETROIT TIGERS 1984: WHAT A START! WHAT A FINISH!

combinations have won the award in the same year. Trammell, along with Whitaker, made his acting debut, so to speak, during the offseason as well. The television show *Magnum, P.I.*, starring native Detroiter Tom Selleck, filmed an episode showcasing Selleck's love of the Tigers in which his character makes a trip to Detroit. It was actually filmed in Hawaii and featured Trammell and Whitaker in a scene.

As Trammell had been developing over the previous few years, the Tigers had been maturing as well. Beginning with the 1978 season under Houk, the Tigers put together an 11-year string of winning seasons. Houk retired after 1978, and Sparky Anderson, who had won two World Series titles with Cincinnati's Big Red Machine ballclubs during the 1970s, took over for Les Moss midway through the 1979 season. Anderson, along with a group of talented players, took the Tigers to the next level. They flirted with the playoffs in the strike-shortened 1981 season and finished second behind the Baltimore Orioles in 1983, but 1984 definitively became the Year of the Tiger.

Trammell suffered an embarrassing injury after the 1983 season. He and his wife attended a Halloween party and Trammell was wearing extra-tall Frankenstein boots to go with his costume and fell into some bushes. At the time, he wasn't sure if he'd hurt himself, but during offseason workouts in San Diego, his knee didn't feel right. He ended up having arthroscopic surgery on his left knee in November. He worked hard at his rehabilitation and was ready to go for the start of spring training in 1984.

Detroit jumped out to a 35-5 record to start the 1984 season, winning its first nine games and 16 of its first 17. During the Tigers' hot start, Trammell was at the front of the pack with a .403 batting average in April from his No. 2 spot in the batting order. Trammell had become accustomed to the more closed stance that hitting coach Gates Brown had been working with him to develop since the previous year. With Whitaker leading off and Trammell behind him, the Tigers jumped out to many early leads and prompted Sparky Anderson to say, "Whitaker and Trammell—they're the key to our ballclub." The Tigers captured the American League East title with 104 wins. Trammell finished the season with a .314 batting average, 14 home runs, 85 runs scored, and 69 RBIs. He won his fourth Gold Glove in five years and was selected to the American League All-Star Team, although he didn't get into the game in San Francisco.

The Tigers swept the Kansas City Royals in three games in the American League Championship Series. Trammel hit .364, with a homer in Game One. In the World Series, Detroit faced Trammell's boyhood team, the San Diego Padres. After splitting the first two games in San Diego, the Tigers returned home to Detroit and took the next three games to win the Series four games to one and become world champions for the first time since 1968. Trammell won the World Series Most Valuable Player Award. He batted .450, with nine hits and six RBIs in the five games. He hit two home runs in Game Four. After the Series, Trammell had surgery on the knee he injured the previous Halloween, and on his shoulder, which had bothered him more as the season wore on. The World Series triumph made rehabilitation a little easier to take during the offseason.

The next couple of seasons saw the Tigers continue winning, but unable to break into the postseason. Trammell's average dropped to .258 in 1985, but he was selected for the All-Star Game in Minnesota. He got his first All-Star at-bat, but failed to get a hit. In 1986, his average rose to .277 and he hit 21 home runs. Third baseman Darnell Coles said he thought Trammell was the most important player on the team. "That's because of his consistency," said Coles. "He's always out there, he always knows what's going on, he's always talking. He keeps everybody going." Trammell became only the second Tiger to have at least 20 homers and 20 stolen bases in the same season, and he repeated the feat in 1987. Kirk Gibson had been the first Tiger to accomplish the feat, doing so four years in a row (1984-87), and Curtis Granderson has since accomplished it as well.

In 1987, Sparky Anderson asked Trammell to bat cleanup. He responded with the best season of his career and carried the Tigers to the division title as they swept the season-ending three-game series at home over the Toronto Blue Jays and won the division title over Toronto by two games. Trammell had 205 hits for a .343 average with 28 home runs, 105 RBIs, 21 stolen bases, and 109 runs scored. He became the first Tiger to collect 200 hits and 100 RBIs since Al Kaline in 1955; and his RBI mark was also a record for Tigers shortstops. He made his fourth All-Star team (slated to start in 1984, he had sat out the game due to injury), reaching safely on an error in his only at-bat. Trammell won his first *Sporting News* Silver Slugger award, given to the best hitter at each position. He was nosed out by George Bell of Toronto for the MVP award in one of the most controversial votes in history. Bell had slumped at the worst time possible—two showdown series in the season's final two weekends against Detroit, with each game decided by one run—while Trammell had carried the Tigers to the title by hitting .416 with 6 homers and 17 RBIs in September. Despite this, Bell got 332 points to 311 for Trammell. His teammate Lou Whitaker had taken second base up after the last game and wrote, "To Alan Trammell, 1987 AL MVP. From Lou Whitaker," as an indication of his sentiments. The Tigers were eliminated by the upstart Minnesota Twins in five games in the ALCS. Trammell hit just .200.

In 1988, Trammell batted .311 with 15 home runs and 69 RBIs as the Tigers finished one game behind the Boston Red Sox for the AL East Division title. He was selected as the starting shortstop for the All-Star team, but did not appear because of an elbow injury. He earned his second consecutive Silver Slugger award.

The 1989 season saw Trammell battle injuries and bat just .243. Detroit also fell to last place in the division, 30 games behind Toronto. That broke an 11-year streak of winning seasons for the Tigers.

In 1990, Trammell rebounded, finishing fourth in the league batting race. He hit .304 with 14 homers and 89 RBIs. He was selected for what turned out to be his final

DETROIT TIGERS 1984: WHAT A START! WHAT A FINISH!

All-Star Game. He failed to get a hit in one at-bat at the game played at Chicago's Wrigley Field. He won his third Silver Slugger award.

Beginning in 1991, his 15th major-league season, Trammell's playing time gradually began to drop off. Hobbled by knee and ankle injuries, he played in only 101 games that year and batted just .248. He collected his 2,000th major-league hit during the season, however. In 1992, he dealt with a nagging elbow injury and broke his ankle early in the season. He played in only 29 games and batted .275.

The 1993 season saw Trammell play four positions—shortstop, third base, left field, and center field—as well as perform designated-hitter duty in five games. He played in 112 games altogether and batted .329 with 12 home runs, 72 runs scored, and 60 RBIs. The Cleveland Indians expressed interest in signing him as a free agent after the season, but Trammell didn't want to leave Detroit. "I wanted to be with one club my whole career, and it's happened," he said. "I'm not going to go anywhere else. It means something to me to be with one club."

In 1994 and 1995, both abbreviated because of the players' strike, Trammell played 76 and 74 games, respectively, mostly at shortstop, and batted .267 and .269. On September 13, 1995, Trammell and Whitaker played in their 1,918th game together to surpass the American League record held by George Brett and Frank White of the Kansas City Royals. That season was Whitaker's last; Trammell played one more year, 1996 (66 games, .233 BA). He played primarily shortstop, but also played second and third base and even an inning in left field. Perhaps in preparation for the future, she served as a player-coach for many of the younger, inexperienced Tigers. On June 25, Trammell reached a milestone by becoming the 10th Tiger to reach 1,000 RBIs in his career with an infield single against Oakland. After the season, Trammell retired as a player; he ended his playing career with a single up the middle in his last at-bat, just as he had in his first big-league at-bat.

Trammell's statistics stack up nicely against those of other Tigers greats. He, Ty Cobb and Al Kaline are the only Tigers to have played 20 seasons with the organization. (Only Cobb, Kaline, Whitaker, and Charlie Gehringer played in more games for the Tigers.) For his career, Trammell batted .285 with 185 home runs and 1,003 RBIs. He ranks in the top 10 in Tigers history in games played (2,293), hits (2,365), runs (1,231), doubles (412), and stolen bases (236). He was voted Tiger of the Year three times, was selected for the All-Star team six times, won three Silver Slugger Awards and four Gold Gloves. He had four consecutive-game hitting streaks of more than 20 games. Trammell hit at least .300 seven times, putting him in the company of Hall of Fame caliber shortstops. He finished with a fielding average of .976—.977 over 2,139 games at his primary position of shortstop. His uniform number 3 (he did wear 42 briefly in 1977) was not used until 2007 and 2008 when Gary Sheffield, with Trammell's permission, wore it. At some point, Trammell's number may be retired. Trammell and Whitaker were honored during a spring training game in 1997 and in Detroit on June 7 that season for their contributions during their careers.

Retired as a player, Trammell stayed with the Tigers. In 1997 and 1998, he worked as an assistant to general manager Randy Smith, helping in scouting and player instruction. He also worked as a pregame analyst for a CBS Radio program, *Inside Pitch*. In 1999, Trammell returned to uniform as a coach for manager Larry Parrish, working as hitting coach and instructing the Tigers' outfielders and baserunners. Before the 2000 season, the Tigers hired Phil Garner as their new manager, but failed to inform Trammell that he would not be asked back as a coach. Trammell found out through the media, souring the relationship between him and the organization. He moved on to a position as a first-base coach with his hometown Padres, whom he began following as an 11-year-old in 1969 in their first season as an expansion team.

In 2002, Trammell appeared on the Hall of Fame ballot for the first time. The results were disappointing to many; he received only 15.7 percent of the vote, with 75 percent being needed to gain entry. In the seven subsequent years, he never received more than 18 percent of the vote. In 2001, *The New Bill James Historical Baseball Abstract* rated Trammell as the ninth best shortstop of all time, putting him ahead of 14 Hall of Fame shortstops. Upon his retirement, Trammell had more home runs and a higher fielding percentage than any shortstop then in the Hall. These statistics make it even more frustrating that Trammell has not gotten more support for the Hall of Fame. He has been inducted into the Michigan Sports Hall of Fame (2000) and the San Diego Hall of Champions' Brietbard Hall of Fame (1998), but, Cooperstown has thus far still eluded him.

On October 9, 2002, two years after he left the Tigers, he returned, hired as the 35th manager in the team's history. The Tigers entrusted him with trying to bring back the winning ways the organization had experienced during his playing days. His coaching staff included his onetime Tigers teammates Kirk Gibson as bench coach and Lance Parrish as bullpen coach. Trammell also hired Bob Cluck, a friend since he was 18—as his pitching coach. The well-respected Cluck spoke highly of Trammell, who had helped him as an instructor at his baseball school. "His teaching skills are incredible, I've watched him teach a lot of years," Cluck said. "Even though he hasn't coached very long, he's been a teacher for over 20 years. When he was playing he was able to break things down—both hitting and defense—that really made sense to kids, and we teach those same things every day." Trammell also invited his longtime keystone partner, Lou Whitaker, to be a spring-training instructor at spring training in Lakeland, Florida. Whitaker lived nearby. Sparky Anderson also made his first appearance during spring training since retiring in 1995 to contribute some of his experience to what Trammell and Tigers were trying to accomplish. Still, in his first season, 2003, the Tigers hit rock-bottom with 119 losses. The team was made up of primarily older players and some talented youngsters who probably should have been getting their experience in the minors rather than in the major leagues. On

DETROIT TIGERS 1984: WHAT A START! WHAT A FINISH!

top of the poor season in 2003, Trammell had to deal with the loss of his mother, who died of a heart attack in September. His parents had divorced when he was a teenager, and he was very close to his mother. He left the team for a few days to be with family in San Diego. In 2004, Trammell guided the Tigers to one of the biggest improvements in major-league history. They won 29 more games than the previous year, finishing at 72-90. Things seemed to be progressing on schedule for Trammell, but the 2005 season was disappointing. The Tigers finished at 71-91 as a late-season swoon dropped them out of contention. After the season, Trammell was let go as manager of his beloved Tigers. He was offered a position with the organization, but declined it.

In 2006, the Tigers, with most of their players continuing the progress Trammell and his staff had begun, reached the World Series under new manager Jim Leyland, but lost to the St. Louis Cardinals. Trammell returned home to San Diego during the season and took a year off from baseball. He came back to be honored with Sparky Anderson before Game Two of the World Series in Detroit. He received a loud ovation from the capacity crowd at Comerica Park.

In 2007, Chicago Cubs manager Lou Piniella hired Trammell to be his bench coach. The Cubs took National League Central Division titles in each of Trammell's first two years there. After four years with the Cubs, Trammell joined the Arizona Diamondbacks as their bench coach in 2011. His old teammate, Kirk Gibson, had been selected to manage the Diamondbacks and wanted Trammell to help as part of the coaching staff. In their first year in Arizona, Gibson and Trammell helped lead the team to a division title before losing in the first round of the playoffs. Currently, Trammell continues to serve as the bench coach for the Diamondbacks.

References

Books

Anderson, Sparky. *Bless You Boys: Diary of the Detroit Tigers 1984 Season*. Chicago: Contemporary Books. 1984.

Janoff, Barry. *Alan Trammell: Tiger on the Prowl*. Chicago: Children's Press. 1985.

Thorn, John, and Pete Palmer, eds. *Total Baseball: The Official Encyclopedia of Major League Baseball (4th ed.)*. New York: Viking Press/Penguin Group. 1995.

Sullivan, George, and David Cataneo. *Detroit Tigers: The Complete Record of Detroit Tigers Baseball*. New York: Macmillan. 1985.

Articles

Detroit Free Press, August 1978, October 1984, February and March 1997, September 2003.

New York Post, June 1996.

San Diego Union Tribune, January 2002.

Sports Illustrated, September 12, 1983; May 28 and October 22, 1984; August 17, 1987.

The Sporting News, July 1977, June 1979, September 1980, and May and September 1984.

USA Today, July 1991, August 1992, September 1995, October 1996 and October 1998.

Web Sites

www.baseball-almanac.com

www.baseballlibrary.com

www.baseball-reference.com

www.metrotimes.com

www.mlb.com

www.pbsfonline.com

www.thebaseballpage.com

www.wikipedia.org

Other Sources

Bill Deane, baseball research.

Detroit Tigers Baseball Club.

National Baseball Hall of Fame and Library research.

Lou Whitaker

by John Milner

FROM THE LATE 1970s to the mid-1990s, a visitor to Detroit's Tiger Stadium would hear many crowd noises. One noise in particular could confuse spectators unless they were attuned to the Tigers stars of this period. Often, after the visiting team had been retired in the top of the first inning, a distinctive "oooooooo" sound would swell from the crowd in the ballpark and project itself through the air to those outside the stadium. For the unknowing fan, there might be wonderment as to why the Tigers' leadoff hitter was being so mercilessly "booooooed," especially with the game in its infant stages, without a chance for the hitter to conduct himself in a manner to deserve the ridicule. The vast majority of the crowd, though, were Tigers fans and would know that the sound echoing from within could only mean one thing: "Sweet Lou" Whitaker was about to come to bat for the Tigers. Over his long career, the Tiger Stadium faithful would show their appreciation by serenading Whitaker with "Looooooou" each time he made an appearance and would more often than not be rewarded with a base hit or a stellar defensive play from his second-base post.

Louis Rodman Whitaker Jr. was born on May 12, 1957, in Brooklyn, New York. Lou never knew his father, Louis Sr. When he was about a year old, his mother, Marion Arlene Williams, a restaurant worker then pregnant with Lou's sister Matilda, moved with her family to Martinsville, Virginia, then a town of about 20,000. Lou was raised there by his mother and grandmother's family in a house that eventually held 16 people, including aunts, uncles, and cousins. His mother worked the 5 p.m.-to-midnight shift at a drive-in restaurant to support her family. Most nights, Lou would be up waiting for her to get home. The family was not well off, but was close and had food on the table. As a youngster, Lou's legs grew crooked, and the family couldn't afford the necessary orthopedic help. His family, primarily his uncles, would therapeutically "work" his legs every day and eventually they straightened out.

On Lou's father's side, the relationship was nonexistent. Lou Sr. was involved in illegal activities in New York, and consequently Lou has never used the "Jr." as part of his name and had no desire to establish contact. A 1979 article in *The Sporting News*, quoted Lou as saying: "He's never done anything for me. I don't hate him. I haven't got time to hate anybody. I just don't care to meet him. There's nothing emotionally happening between us." While in Virginia, Whitaker enjoyed a positive upbringing. He spent a lot of time at the Charity Christian Church and at English Field, a playground. He played his first organized baseball at the age of 10 and found that he could be successful in the sport. By the time he was 13, locals marveled at his prowess on the diamond, especially his strong arm. At Martinsville High School he excelled as a pitcher for the Bulldogs. He played infield, but also experienced success on the mound. A Tigers scout, Wayne Blackburn, filed a report on Lou during his junior season and saw potential in him.

On the way to Martinsville the next spring, Blackburn was in a car accident, so the Tigers never got a report from him during Lou's senior season. The Tigers had no choice but to go with Major League Scouting Bureau reports. One scored Lou as a 50 (on a 20-80 scale) and the other a 55. As luck would have it, the 55 was from Billy Jurges, whose opinion was greatly respected by Bill Lajoie, then the Tigers' scouting director. Jurges typically was tough when it came to scoring prospects, and when Lajoie saw a 55, he figured that Whitaker must be of good quality. Jurges had scored him high as a pitcher as well with a "major-league" curveball. After completing a stellar senior season, Lou, who had just turned 18 a few days before, was drafted by the Detroit Tigers in the fifth round (99th overall) of the June 1975 amateur draft as a third baseman. Whitaker had signed with Ferrum (Virginia) Junior College, but never played a game for them upon being drafted by the Tigers.

Lajoie drove to Martinsville to sign Whitaker, after Blackburn had failed to convince him in his initial attempts. Lajoie figured that maybe Lou didn't want to leave home to be on his own. A new suitcase and a set of clothes helped to seal the deal with Whitaker, and Lajoie drove Lou to his first assignment, at Bristol, Virginia, of the Rookie-level Appalachian League, where he played third base.

In one game Whitaker committed three errors and cried afterward, but he came back the next day ready to get back at it. The Tigers were impressed from the beginning. Whitaker played in 42 games with Bristol and batted .237, which wasn't spectacular, but he showed potential. He began making strides with a confident attitude and playing ability. Whitaker told Tigers general manager Jim Campbell when he met him in 1976 spring training, "I'm Louis Whitaker and I'll be playing for you soon." Whitaker backed up his statement by having a great year at Class A Lakeland. He played third base and in 124 games batted .297 and was named the Most Valuable Player of the Florida State League. After the season Lou met someone who became an important part of his blossoming career. Campbell had made the decision to move Lou to second base and pair him with Alan Trammell.

Trammell had been drafted in 1976 and had played at Bristol that season. During the 1976 Fall Instructional League in St. Petersburg, Florida, the pair were roommates at the team hotel. Their careers were intertwined from that time on. Whitaker initially balked at the idea of playing second base, but eventually relented. That fall they worked with Eddie Brinkman, a former major-league shortstop for the Senators and Tigers, who was an instructor for Detroit. After the Instructional League season, Brinkman and the Tigers could see they had something special in the young double-play duo. Brinkman said, "Whitaker is such a natural athlete that he took to second base right away." Campbell had promised the pair sports coats if they performed well. They didn't disappoint. Campbell recalled that he drove them to a store "they went right to the rack where they had two suits already

DETROIT TIGERS 1984: WHAT A START! WHAT A FINISH!

picked out. I had promised them a sports coat, remember, but I bought them suits."

When the 1977 season began, Trammell and Whitaker played for the Montgomery Rebels of the Double-A Southern League, and became close friends. Whitaker said, "We did everything together," and Trammell echoed that statement: "We didn't have anybody else. We comforted each other a little. If one of us had a bad night, the other one wouldn't let him stay down. We became pretty close." Whitaker played in 107 games for Montgomery and had 111 hits, four triples, three home runs, and a .280 batting average. Trammell was named the league's MVP, but Brinkman, who managed the team, said, "They could've been co-MVPs that year." Montgomery won the league championship and, after the Rebels defeated Jacksonville in the playoffs, Whitaker and Trammell were rewarded with a trip to the major leagues.

On September 9, 1977, Lou Whitaker made his major-league debut in the second game of a doubleheader in Boston, starting at second base against the Red Sox in front of nearly 35,000 fans. Although the Tigers lost, 8-6, Whitaker showed that he was capable of being successful at the big-league level. In the first inning, he ripped a single in his first at-bat against veteran right-handed pitcher Reggie Cleveland. Lou also collected his first stolen base in that inning. In his second at-bat, he drove in a run with a double to left field. Rick Wise struck Lou out in his third at-bat, but Whitaker greeted Wise with a single to center field his next time up. In his final trip to the plate, Bill Campbell, the Red Sox' tough closer, struck him out. Lou finished his debut with three hits in five at-bats with one run, one double, one stolen base, and one RBI. Trammell had success as well, collecting two hits in his debut.

As the season drew to a close, the Tigers finished in fourth place in the American League East Division. Whitaker played in 11 games and batted .250 in 32 at-bats. He was flawless at second base, handling 35 chances without an error. During the offseason, the Tigers sold second sacker Tito Fuentes, who had batted .309 in 1977 but made 26 errors, to the Montreal Expos. The Tigers also acquired Steve Dillard from Boston, so that if Whitaker was not ready they would have someone to play second base while Lou developed. Whitaker and Trammell performed so well in spring training that both went north with the club and by May, they became entrenched as the starters at second base and shortstop, replacing Dillard and Mark Wagner. Manager Ralph Houk compared the duo to the combination of Tony Kubek and Bobby Richardson that he had managed at the New York Yankees' Denver farm club. "It's the damnedest thing," said Houk. "You tell one of them something and he says, 'We can do it.' Like they're a team." Houk played a crucial role in their development by letting them play through mistakes without putting pressure on them.

When Whitaker made an Opening Day appearance in front of 52,000 fans at Tiger Stadium for the first time, the Tigers fans had already picked up the chant of "Looooooou." Whitaker could hardly believe it. "I thought they were booing me at first," he said. During the season, the 20-year-old Whitaker continued to impress the Detroit brass, as well as his teammates. Midway through the season, Houk was asked if he had ever seen a better young second baseman in his four decades in baseball. "No," he answered without hesitation. "The only one I could think of was Bobby Richardson. He was a hell of a ballplayer, but not as good as Whitaker. Those two kids [Trammell and Whitaker], they just play good every day. They're the best I've ever seen for their age. On the double plays, knowing where the ball is going to be, that's something you can't teach."

Whitaker's always-present confidence in his abilities came through when asked if anything had bothered him. "Didn't anything bother me from spring training on," he said. They stuck with us and gave us a chance and now we're playing every day. I'm playing with a lot of baseball instinct. I try not to let anything get me down." The Tigers won 86 games in 1978, 12 more than the year before and their best in six years, but still finished only fifth in their division. Houk left at the end of the campaign.

Whitaker batted .285 with 12 doubles, seven triples, and three home runs. His first homer came on July 28, a two-run shot in the bottom of the ninth off Enrique Romo to defeat the Seattle Mariners, 4-3, at Tiger Stadium. Defensively, he finished with a .978 fielding average, making 17 errors. He and his keystone partner, Trammell, led the American League with 95 double plays. Whitaker was named the American League Rookie of the Year by the Baseball Writers Association of America, winning 21 of 28 first-place votes. He was only the second American League second baseman, after Rod Carew of Minnesota in 1967 to win the award. (In *The Sporting News* ballot, which was voted on by the players, Whitaker was second to Paul Molitor of Milwaukee.) The Detroit Sports Broadcasters Association named Lou the Tigers Rookie of the Year.

The 1979 season brought changes to the Tigers that eventually led to success for the team and Whitaker. Les Moss replaced Houk as manager. Moss lasted only 53 games and was replaced by George "Sparky" Anderson, who had managed Cincinnati's Big Red Machine teams earlier in the 1970s and had won two World Series. The Tigers finished in fifth place again, 18 games behind the Baltimore Orioles. Whitaker batted .286 with 121 hits, 75 runs scored, and 20 stolen bases in 121 games. At second base, his errors fell from 17 to nine. In November Whitaker was married to Crystal McCreary at Blessed Sacrament Cathedral in Detroit.

Before the 1980 season the Tigers traded Ron LeFlore to Montreal for pitcher Dan Schatzeder, opening up the leadoff position for Whitaker. Anderson and the Tigers felt that Lou would be the ideal leadoff hitter. "He's got a great eye and he doesn't pull the ball," said Anderson. "There's no other spot better suited to him." By the beginning of June, it was obvious that the plan was failing miserably. Whitaker's batting was below .200, and on June 8 Anderson took Whitaker out of the leadoff spot. "He's got to relax," Sparky said. "Hitting somewhere else will give him a breather."

Whitaker hadn't experienced anything like this. He began to hear a scattering of boos from the crowd, but he dealt with

DETROIT TIGERS 1984: WHAT A START! WHAT A FINISH!

it in a professional manner. "I can't let it get to me, "he said. "I'm not hitting very good, but I do what I can to help. My fielding hasn't suffered. I don't throw bats or helmets. I don't use obscene language. Those things just make you look bad." Batting coach Gates Brown continued to work with Lou on being more aggressive at the plate, to avoid being too selective and putting himself into bad hitting counts. The Tigers once again finished fifth, 19 games behind the Yankees. Whitaker finished with a .233 average in 145 games, but his defense was still strong with a .985 fielding percentage.

In 1981 major leaguers went on strike on June 12 and did not resume playing for 50 days. As a consequence, the season was played in two halves. The Tigers finished fourth in the first half, but were one game behind Milwaukee entering the final weekend of the second half and could have made the playoffs by sweeping the Brewers. But the Brewers thwarted the Tigers by taking the first two games of the series. Whitaker ended the abbreviated season with a .263 batting average and five home runs. He had been hitting near .300 until a leg injury sidelined him for nearly three weeks. His fielding was again stellar at .985.

Lou really flexed his muscles during the 1982 season. Restored to the leadoff spot by Anderson in July, he responded by hitting .313 the rest of the way, pounding out 15 round-trippers and batting .286 for the season. Whitaker seemed to be maturing and developed a knack for hitting balls into the short upper-deck porch in right field at Tiger Stadium, as most left-handed hitters enjoyed doing. He made only 10 errors that season and led AL second basemen with 470 assists, 120 double plays, and a .988 fielding average. Detroit finished a disappointing fourth, 12 games behind the division-winning Brewers. After the season Whitaker signed a five-year contract for about $3.5 million.

In 1983, Whitaker and the Tigers both took another step forward. The Tigers won 92 games and finished second in the division, six games behind Baltimore, and if they had not lost five of seven games to the Orioles down the stretch, they might have overtaken them for the division crown. Whitaker played in 161 games and collected 206 hits for a .320 average, finishing third in the American League batting race (his partner Trammell finished fourth at .319). Whitaker was the first Tigers left-handed batter to collect more than 200 hits since 1943 (Dick Wakefield) and the first Tigers second basemen to collect more than 200 hits since 1937 (Charlie Gehringer). Lou whacked 12 home runs and drove in 72 runs.

Whitaker credited hitting coach Gates Brown with giving him some advice that helped him turn the corner as a hitter. "In the past, if I got two or three hits in a game, I'd kind of let up," Whitaker said. "I'd lose my concentration at the plate if we had a team beat. I went to Gates and told him this. He told me none of the great hitters give up outs. He said, 'Get all you can get.'" Milwaukee's manager, Harvey Kuenn, chose Whitaker as a reserve on the All-Star squad. It was the first of five consecutive All-Star selections for Whitaker. In the game, played in Chicago's Comiskey Park, Whitaker batted twice and had a triple and a sacrifice fly for two RBIs in the American League's 13-3 win. At the end of the season, Lou was selected as Tiger of the Year for his accomplishments, won his first Silver Slugger Award for being the best hitter at his position in the league, was chosen for his first AL Gold Glove Award, and finished eighth in the league Most Valuable Player vote.

The 1984 season began in unbelievable fashion; the Tigers won their first nine games and 35 of their first 40. Detroit never relinquished first place the entire season and finished with 104 wins, winning the East Division by 15 games. Whitaker played in 143 games and had 161 hits for a .289 average. He scored 90 runs and hit 13 home runs. Once again he won the Gold Glove award for American League second basemen and his hitting got him his second consecutive Silver Slugger Award. Lou's productivity and the Tigers' fantastic season contributed to his popularity as he was voted to start the All-Star Game at San Francisco's Candlestick Park. A nagging wrist injury and a sore back and shoulder almost kept him on the bench, but he played and contributed a single and a double in three at-bats. The National League won the game 3-1.

In the first round of the playoffs, Detroit faced the Western Division champion Kansas City Royals. Lou had three singles in 14 at-bats and scored three runs as the Tigers swept the Royals in three straight to go to the World Series against the National League champion San Diego Padres. The Tigers were making their first World Series appearance since the storied 1968 championship team that defeated the St. Louis Cardinals in seven games. The teams split the first two games, in San Diego. In Detroit, the Tigers won the next three games and took the world championship. In Game Four, which put the Tigers in command of the Series, Whitaker had two hits, including a double, and scored two runs as the Tigers won, 4-2. He led off the first inning with a double and Trammell followed with a home run. In the third, Whitaker singled and scored when Trammell hit another homer. Game Five was doubly memorable for Whitaker; Detroit clinched the Series with an 8-4 win behind two home runs by Kirk Gibson; and Lou's wife gave birth to their second daughter on the same day. Whitaker finished with a .286 average for the Series and added six runs, two doubles, and four walks to the team effort. (Whitaker and Trammell, made a television appearance on a *Magnum, P.I.* episode in '84. The series' title character, played by Tom Selleck, was a Tigers fan—as was Selleck—and visited Detroit while working on a case. He "bumped" into Whitaker and Trammell, not recognizing them, during his trip to the Motor City.)

The 1985 season began on an odd note for Lou. In spring training, Sparky Anderson was very high on a rookie, Chris Pittaro. Sparky decided that he would move Whitaker to third base to make room for Pittaro at second. He called Whitaker in to his office and asked him to try it for the good of the team. Initially Lou agreed, but after three days and an article in which Lou had mentioned not being comfortable at third, Sparky talked to him and decided that he would move Lou back to second and try Pittaro at third. The year started well

DETROIT TIGERS 1984: WHAT A START! WHAT A FINISH!

for Lou as he led the American League in mid-May with a .368 batting average (he finished at .279), but the 1984 magic wasn't there. The Tigers finished in third place, 15 games behind the Toronto Blue Jays. Whitaker had his best season so far for power numbers. He hit 21 home runs, including one that cleared the right-field roof at Tiger Stadium, the first leadoff hitter or second baseman to accomplish the feat. He contributed 73 RBIs and scored 102 runs. Lou won his third consecutive Gold Glove and Silver Slugger awards. He was selected as a starter for the All-Star Game at the Metrodome in Minnesota While traveling to the game, Whitaker left his uniform in his car at the airport in Detroit. Upon realizing his mistake, he asked that an emergency uniform be sent, but it was lost in transit. Lou purchased a replica jersey from a vendor and wrote the number 1 on the back. He borrowed a Cleveland Indians batting helmet and a glove from Cal Ripken Jr. He went 0-for-2 in the game, and the American League lost, 6-1. His "uniform" was eventually collected by the Smithsonian Institution for display purposes.

In 1986 the Tigers improved, but finished in third place, 8½ games behind Boston. Once again Lou was selected to start in the All-Star Game and he hit a two-run homer off Dwight Gooden of the New York Mets in the second inning at the Astrodome in Houston. The home run proved to be the difference in a 3-2 American League victory. He ended up at .269 for the year and had 157 hits, 95 runs, 20 homers, and 73 RBIs. He did not win the Gold Glove Award for the first time in four years as Frank White of the Kansas City Royals reclaimed the award that he had won prior to Whitaker's three-year run.

The next year, the Tigers reached the postseason. Detroit won 98 games and finished two games ahead of Toronto after sweeping them in the final weekend of the season at Tiger Stadium. They went on to face the upstart Minnesota Twins in the playoffs and were defeated by the underdog Twins, four games to one. Minnesota went on to win the World Series by defeating the St. Louis Cardinals in seven games. In Game Two, at the Metrodome, Lou hit his only career playoff home run, off Twins right-hander Bert Blyleven. Whitaker hit just .176 in the series. This was his last postseason appearance. During the season he batted .265 with 16 home runs and 59 RBIs, and scored 110 runs, which led him to regain the Silver Slugger Award. He was selected as a reserve for the All-Star Game in Oakland, but did not get into the game during the National League's 2-0 victory.

The 1988 season ended in embarrassment for Whitaker. With the Tigers in the midst of a pennant race in September, Lou tore cartilage in his knee while dancing with his wife at an anniversary party. "We were doing a fast dance and I did the splits," Whitaker said. "The first time, nothing happened. The second time I went down, I heard something pop." Lou didn't need surgery, but his absence left a hole in an already depleted Detroit lineup that had suffered other injuries. Whitaker had been one of the team's hottest hitters at the time of the injury. Lou felt bad that he couldn't contribute, and it made it worse when the Tigers finished in second place, one game behind the Red Sox. He finished with a .275 average, 12 home runs, and 55 RBIs in his abbreviated season.

The bottom fell out of the team in 1989. The Tigers finished 30 games behind Toronto, in last place in their division. Early in the season, Whitaker was put into the third spot in the order. From that position, he attempted to hit more for power, but his average dropped. He ended up hitting a career-high 28 homers and drove in 85 runs (also a personal best), but his batting average fell to .251. With all the problems the Tigers had with injuries as well as players having down years, Whitaker was a bright spot. He felt that he needed to make up for the embarrassment at the end of the previous season, and Sparky understood how important his contribution was by saying, "I hate to think of what the season would be like without him, so I won't. I know how it is to dwell on everything that's gone wrong this year. But there are always positive individual accomplishments you can focus on."

The 1990s saw the Tigers franchise steadily decline, along with its 1980s stars. Whitaker's average dropped to .237 in 1990, but he hit 18 home runs. He rebounded in 1991 by increasing his average to .279 and socking 23 homers with 78 RBIs. Detroit had a losing record while finishing third in 1990, but won 84 games and finished second in 1991. The 1992 season was a crossroads for Whitaker. He had another solid year (.278 average, 19 homers, 71 RBIs). Sparky Anderson began to rest Lou against left-handed pitchers and at the end of the season, Lou was granted free agency from the Tigers. The Tigers fell to sixth place that year, and there were opportunities for Whitaker to play elsewhere. Lou and his wife wanted to stay in Detroit to keep life stable for their daughters, but he was courted by his old Tigers associate, Bill Lajoie, who was the general manager of the Atlanta Braves. There was also interest from the Orioles and Yankees. Eventually, Lou decided to stay in Detroit and signed a three-year, $7.5 million contract. This turned out to be the last contract Lou signed with the Tigers.

His playing time steadily declined over the next three years, going from 119 games in 1993 to 92 games in 1994 and 84 games in 1995. His batting average for those three years was very good given his limited time,.290, .301, and .293, respectively. The Tigers finished fourth in 1993 with 85 wins. The 1994 season saw the American and National Leagues split into three divisions for the first time. There was also the matter of a players' strike that cut the season short. Detroit finished fifth—last—in a reconstituted AL East. They finished fourth in 1995, Sparky Anderson's last season after 16-plus years at Detroit's helm. Whitaker, his Tigers contract expired, had offers from the Tigers, as well as overtures from the Atlanta Braves, Oakland Athletics, New York Yankees, and Boston Red Sox, but he decided that he would call it a career after 19 seasons with the Tigers.

His career totals include 2,390 games, with 2,369 hits, 1,386 runs, 1,084 RBIs, 244 home runs, 143 stolen bases, a batting average of .276, and an on-base percentage of .363. He finished with an overall fielding average of .984, and despite

DETROIT TIGERS 1984: WHAT A START! WHAT A FINISH!

the hubbub of a potential switch to the hot corner in 1985, the only defensive position he ever played was second base. Upon completing his career, Lou joined Rogers Hornsby and Joe Morgan as the only second basemen to score 1,000 runs, have 1,000 RBIs, collect 2,000 hits, and launch 200 home runs, including four of the inside-the-park variety.

Along with Alan Trammell, who retired after the 1996 season, Lou was involved in a couple of other records. On September 13, 1995, they played in their 1,915th game together, which surpassed the American League record set by George Brett and Frank White of Kansas City. The double-play duo was also a member of an exclusive club of middle infielders who had won Gold Gloves in the same season—the eighth combination to accomplish the feat, doing so twice (1983-84). Also, Whitaker found himself in the top 10 in 10 career offensive categories for Detroit. This includes top-five finishes in games (third), at-bats (fourth), and runs (fourth). Defensively, he finished as the Tigers' all-time leader in double plays turned with 1,527, and was second in assists with 6,653.

Whitaker settled into retirement by keeping a low profile, moving to Lakeland, Florida, and living there with his wife and daughters. He helped his wife open an upscale boutique in the Lakeland area. "If I wanted to play, I'd have to make a decision," he said. "My wife and I are going into business. She has supported me, and I'm going to do what I can to support her." Whitaker also became heavily involved in his religion. He concentrated heavily on missionary work for the Jehovah's Witnesses. He routinely spent at least 840 hours a year on such work. In 1997, the Tigers honored Whitaker and Trammell before a spring-training game and at Tiger Stadium in Detroit before a June 7 game. In the winter of 2001, Whitaker became eligible for the Baseball Hall of Fame vote. His statistics matched up favorably with those of many Hall of Fame second basemen—especially Joe Morgan—but Whitaker was named on only 2.9 percent of the 515 votes cast and was dropped off the ballot; leaving his election to the Hall up to the Veterans Committee. In 2003, the Tigers hired Trammell as their manager and he opened the door by inviting Lou to help out during spring training. The spring coaching role lasted through 2009. Whitaker felt that with his four daughters—Asia, Angela, Jessica, and Sarah—being almost fully grown, he could devote some time to help the Tigers as an instructor. Whitaker helped his buddy Trammell in the ensuing years as well during spring training and continued to live in Lakeland and spend time with the things he loved: his religion, his family, and baseball.

References

Books

Thorn, John, and Pete Palmer, eds. *Total Baseball, 4th ed.* New York: Total Sports. 1997.

Sullivan, George, and David Cataneo. *Detroit Tigers: The Complete Record of Detroit Tigers Baseball.* New York: Collier. 1985.

Articles

Associated Press, September 1988.

"Baseball's Igniters," July 1984.

Cleveland Plain Dealer, June 1983.

Detroit Free Press, August 1978, February and March 1997, January 2001, and November 2003.

Detroit News, March 1996, January 2001, February 2003, and February 2004.

Detroit Tigers scorebook, 1979.

New York Post, June and October 1984 and April 1985.

Sports Illustrated, September 1983.

The Sporting News, September 1976, October 1977, April 1978, May 1978, August 1978, September 1978, February 1979, July, August, and November 1982, and May 1985.

USA Today, April and August 1992, September 1995, and April 2004.

Web Sites

www.baseball-almanac.com

www.baseball-reference.com

www.thebaseballpage.com

www.wikipedia.org

Other Sources

Bill Deane.

National Baseball Hall of Fame.

Milt Wilcox
by Maxwell Kates

IT IS A QUESTION many players ask themselves as they face the twilight of their baseball odyssey: Do I end my career with five more years of acceptable performance, or do I overexert myself and risk severe injury by playing my best season on a major-league diamond? One player who chose the latter option was right-handed pitcher Milt Wilcox. A model of consistency in his previous seven seasons with the Detroit Tigers despite several shoulder injuries, he pitched through pain in to win a crucial 17 games during that blessed 1984 season. Then his major-league career ended within two years of the Tigers' winning the world championship, though Wilcox made the successful transition to life after baseball.

Milton Edward Wilcox was born in Honolulu on April 20, 1950. Moving with his family to Oklahoma at the age of 2, he was raised in Del City, a suburb of Oklahoma City. After he graduated from Crooked Creek High School in 1968, the Cincinnati Reds selected him in the second round of the June draft. Wilcox signed a $20,000 bonus contract with scout Tony Rubello and began his professional career with the Reds' entry in the Rookie Gulf Coast League. Later promoted to Tampa of the Class A Florida State League, he threw two shutouts and four complete games in eight starts. Pitching again for Tampa in 1969, Wilcox went 4-1 with a 5.48 ERA in 15 appearances. In 1970, he was invited to train with the Reds, and was assigned to Indianapolis, the team's Triple-A affiliate. Early on, however, Wilcox struggled with his fastball and his curve. Consequently, after watching his young pitcher endure a three-game losing streak, Indianapolis manager Vern Rapp encouraged him to add a changeup and a slider to his repertoire. Wilcox rebounded to win seven of his next nine decisions. On July 4, he threw a seven-inning no-hitter, baffling the Evansville Triplets as he pitched 60 sliders and only 29 fastballs. As Wilcox told Indianapolis reporter Les Koelling after the game, he was "concentrating on keeping the pitches low and not hanging any...more on the last hitter in every inning."

Wilcox completed the American Association season with a record of 12-10. Fanning 110 hitters in 168 innings, he led his league with five shutouts before earning a September promotion to Cincinnati. Within five days of joining the Reds, Wilcox recorded two victories for manager Sparky Anderson. In his major-league debut against the San Diego Padres, on September 5, the admittedly anxious pitcher surrendered seven hits, including a home run to Al Ferrara, and walked four, going five innings in a starting assignment that he won, 6-2, after four innings of one-hit relief by Clay Carroll. Anderson, himself a rookie manager, offered some words of advice to calm Wilcox' nerves:

"All he had to do was pitch the same way he did at Indianapolis. There aren't any superhumans in the major leagues and I think the kid has learned that." Wilcox proved Anderson's point on September 9 when he pitched a five-hit, one-walk shutout against the Dodgers. Only Maury Wills reached as far as second base. In five September appearances, Wilcox was 3-1 with an ERA of 2.42 as the Reds steamrolled to the National League West Division crown. Wilcox won the clincher in the National League Championship Series, giving up only one hit and striking out five in three innings of relief as the Reds swept the best-of-five series against Pittsburgh. But Wilcox lost Game Two of the World Series, giving up three hits and two runs in relief while retiring only one batter. The Reds lost the Series to Baltimore in five games.

"You've got to give (Indianapolis manager) Rapp a lot of credit," reported Anderson in his evaluation of Wilcox. "He's sending us some fine pitchers." Unfortunately for Wilcox, he competed with as many as eight other starters for a spot in the 1971 rotation. Anderson viewed him as a five-inning pitcher and declared him "expendable." Wilcox started the season in Cincinnati and pitched in 14 games, but was optioned to Indianapolis. Despite the disappointment of being returned to the minor leagues, Wilcox once again pitched well. Pitching for Indianapolis, he fashioned a record of 8-5 with 62 strikeouts and 22 walks in 102 innings while limiting American Association hitters to a 2.20 ERA. Promoted to Cincinnati at season's end, he appeared in four more games and for the year he went 2-2.

As the manager of the Cleveland Indians' affiliate at Wichita, Ken Aspromonte was particularly impressed by Wilcox's performance at Indianapolis. When promoted to manage the Indians, Aspromonte insisted on acquiring him, and the Indians sent outfielder Ted Uhlaender to Cincinnati for Wilcox on December 6. Aspromonte told sportswriter Russ Schneider "how good Milt was for Indianapolis," adding that "when [general manager] Gabe [Paul] told me we had a chance to get [him], I told him not to wait a minute." Wilcox had a better chance to flourish with the rebuilding Indians, and as an added bonus, he joined his hero, Gaylord Perry, in the rotation.

"I'm a heck of a lot better off here than there. If it hasn't been for the trade, I probably would have been sent back to the minor leagues," Wilcox said at the time of the trade. While he was dominating the Tokyo Lotte Orions in Cactus League action, advance scout Dan Carnevale enthusiastically offered that "this kid can pitch. All he needs is to believe in himself. I'll bet that if he wins his first two games he'll win 20."

Three weeks into the strike-delayed 1972 season, Wilcox appeared destined for stardom. His won-lost record was 4-2, while his ERA of 0.92 was among the lowest among junior circuit starters. Despite a May 12 loss, Wilcox still had fashioned a fine 4-3 mark with a 1.24 ERA when his photo graced the cover of *The Sporting News*—and bad luck struck again. Diagnosed with strep throat, he was confined to bed rest for a week. Wilcox returned to action in late May, but his mojo apparently went on the disabled list, as he endured a seven-game losing streak from June 14 through July 7, an experience that only hurt his confidence.

"I tried to pitch too soon and hurt my shoulder. I didn't say anything about it, thinking it would go away. But it didn't. It bothered me the rest of the season," Wilcox recounted. He

DETROIT TIGERS 1984: WHAT A START! WHAT A FINISH!

had torn a shoulder muscle and was prevented from lifting his arm properly, let alone throw overhand. Pitching sidearm on a regular basis, he developed tendinitis. Wilcox ended the season with a record of 7-14, hardly fulfilling Carnevale's preseason hopes. In hindsight, he admitted that he probably tore his rotator cuff, "but that was before anyone knew what that was!"

After two more disappointing seasons (8-10 and 2-2), the Indians traded Wilcox to the Chicago Cubs for pitcher Dave LaRoche and outfielder Brock Davis on February 25, 1975. The change of scenery did not help as Wilcox posted an ERA of 5.63 in 25 relief appearances. Frustrated with the direction of his career as he was demoted to Wichita of the American Association in 1976, he considered quitting baseball.

The Detroit Tigers foresaw enough residual value in Wilcox to rescue him from the Cubs' farm system, purchasing his contract from Wichita on June 10, 1976, and sending him to their Evansville team in the American Association. There, his record of 6-5 with a 3.41 ERA earned an invitation to spring training with the Tigers in 1977. Manager Ralph Houk offered the following scouting report:

"He was scattery.... he wasn't getting his breaking ball over consistently, but he still looked pretty good. I figured then he'd be the guy we'd call up if we needed someone. We just sent him out to make sure his arm was sound." At Evansville, Wilcox blossomed under manager Les Moss. He tossed six complete games in 14 starts, striking out 69 hitters, and posted an impressive American Association ERA of 2.44.

"I can't explain it, but I think I'm throwing the ball harder now than when I first came up," Wilcox later said. "At Evansville, it seemed I got a little stronger and I got a little more confident every time I pitched." Meanwhile, Houk's rotation was struggling. With Mark Fidrych relegated to the disabled list for the second time in the season, rookie Dave Rozema was the de facto ace. Jack Morris was still a month away from earning his first promotion to the parent club. The Tigers purchased Wilcox's contract on June 22. After one relief victory, he was given a chance to start. Shuttling between the rotation and relief roles, he won his next five decisions. Ending the year at 6-2 with a 3.64 ERA, Wilcox shrugged off suggestions of being the Comeback Player of the Year: "How can I come back when I've never been anywhere before?"

As Fidrych, Rozema, and Morris were counted on to contribute greatly in starting roles in 1978, manager Houk did not intend to include Wilcox in his rotation. Wilcox moved his family, which included daughter Stacy and son Brian, to the Detroit area, where he pursued bowling as an offseason callisthenic exercise. As he told Jim Hawkins of the *Detroit Free Press*, he could no longer "afford to be just mediocre." When Fidrych and Rozema continued to struggle with arm injuries, Wilcox returned to the rotation and pitched his strongest season yet. Leading the Tigers with 16 complete games and 132 strikeouts in 215 1/3 innings, Wilcox produced 13 victories as the Tigers recorded their first winning season since 1973.

After Ralph Houk left as the Tigers' manager, Wilcox was reunited with Les Moss in 1979. Although Moss named him to start on Opening Day, unusually bad April weather—even by Detroit standards—twice postponed the assignment, which ultimately went to Rozema. Luck continued to elude Wilcox as the season unfolded, as he lost three decisions by two runs or less during Moss' brief tenure as manager. With the Tigers treading water at 27-26 on June 12, the Tigers fired Moss when given the opportunity to hire Sparky Anderson. For Wilcox, this reunion was less than congenial, as he had not enjoyed a favorable relationship with Anderson in Cincinnati. Demoted to the bullpen after two mediocre starts, Wilcox demanded a trade. But soon after the All-Star break, he returned to the starting rotation, won 12 games for the season and finished second to Jack Morris in wins, complete games, innings, and strikeouts, and led the staff in starts. Wilcox remained consistent at the dawning of the 1980s, winning 13 games in 1980, 12 in strike-shortened 1981, and another 12 in 1982. Detroit came within 1½ games of an AL East Division mini-title in the second half of 1981, and Wilcox contributed with a 3.03 ERA in 24 starts. He pitched 16 scoreless innings against the Yankees, a complete game against the Brewers without any walks, and a pair of pickoffs over the course of the season (reaching a career high of five in 1983).

Ironically, Wilcox' most famous game at this stage of his career was one he did not even pitch. Maxwell Lapides remembers the events that transpired at Comiskey Park in Chicago on July 12, 1979:

> "I was born in Detroit but living in Chicago at the time. I went to see the Tigers every time they played the White Sox. This one day I left work for the ballpark, but a cop stopped me as I entered the parking lot.
> " 'Where do you think you're going?'
> " 'I'm going to watch the ballgame.'
> 'Don't you have any idea what they're planning? Do yourself a favor and go home.'"

Lapides missed one of the most violent demonstrations ever to disgrace a baseball diamond in Disco Demolition Night. In cooperation with a Chicago radio station, the White Sox admitted 47,795 spectators for 98 cents and a disco record. The albums were collected for the purpose of destroying them between games of a doubleheader. The Tigers and Pat Underwood won the first game, 4-1. Then the ruckus began.

"I was the scheduled pitcher for the second game," Wilcox recalls. "I was actually walking to the bullpen to warm up when the records blew up on the field. Then everything went insane." Hordes charged the field to express their vitriol against the disco music and lifestyle, throwing records like Frisbees and tearing patches of grass. Despite pleas for the fans to return to their seats, the violence intensified and the nightcap was called off—and later declared to be a Chisox forfeit to Detroit.

For Wilcox, the new decade brought the return of the injury bug. In a bench-clearing donnybrook after George

DETROIT TIGERS 1984: WHAT A START! WHAT A FINISH!

Brett hit the deck twice on two Wilcox offerings on August 5, 1980, Milt reinjured his shoulder. In October 1981, he dislocated his index finger in a charity basketball game, threatening the survival of his pitching career. Although Wilcox recovered to pitch in 1982—he threw a one-hitter against the Royals on his bithday—April 20—with Jerry Martin's second-inning single the sole blemish—shoulder and back injuries sidelined him as the Tigers lost ground to the Orioles, Red Sox, and Brewers. On April 15, 1983, Wilcox pitched within one batter of a perfect game. He retired the first 26 White Sox he faced before pinch-hitter Jerry Hairston reached base on a single. Wilcox had to settle for a 6-0 victory—and American League Player of the Week honors. No sooner had he pitched his masterpiece than the impending free agent raised contractual matters with general manager Jim Campbell. Wilcox posted double digits in wins for the sixth consecutive year in 1983. Winning 11 against 10 losses, he fanned 101 and sported a 3.97 ERA. True to his word, he filed for free agency. The front office could not justify matching the San Diego Padres' offer of a two-year, $1.1 million deal to an aging right-hander with a history of arm trouble. Only when negotiations to secure Walt Terrell in a trade with the Mets failed did the Tigers match San Diego's offer. Following the direction of new general manager Bill Lajoie, the Tigers signed him on December 29.

Entering the 1984 season, the American League East had a surplus of talented clubs, including the defending world champion Baltimore Orioles, the powerful New York Yankees, and the up-and-coming Toronto Blue Jays. Even after finishing second to Baltimore in 1983 with 92 wins, the Tigers were expected to finish no higher than third—particularly after a moribund spring finish of 11-17. However, as Sparky Anderson told the Detroit Free Press, "I'm satisfied with everything about this club"—even comparing them to the juggernaut 1976 Cincinnati Reds. Anderson had every reason to feel confident about the Tigers in 1984. During the first two months of the season, they proved him correct, roaring ahead with a record of 35-5. Like the rest of the pitching staff, Milt Wilcox appeared impenetrable, even with his delicate arm.

"When we jumped off to the great start, I said, 'I'm not missing a start this year. I don't care what it does to me in the long run, I don't want us going into any losing streaks and have it be my fault.'"

Wilcox won his first start, 3-2, over the White Sox in Chicago's home opener. By mid-May, his record had improved to 6-0, including a 4-3 nailbiter over the Oakland Athletics at Tiger Stadium on May 20. He never disclosed the level of pain through which he allowed himself to pitch.

"I stayed healthy enough to never miss a start, but I had a feeling this was possibly my last year. I had seven cortisone shots that year," Wilcox said. The risk of shoulder separation proved most problematic.

"We'd inject the joint with Xylocaine, which deadens the pain, and then follow it with the cortisone to quiet the inflammation. It started in May and went through the end of the season. I'd go through withdrawal from the cortisone. I'd get hot flashes, sweat, and my heart would start beating real fast. I kept a lot of the symptoms away from the trainers because I didn't want them to refuse me from getting it anymore." Even teammates like Darrell Evans were unaware:

"There was often a question whether Milt was able to pitch on a given night, but he always went out there," said Evans. "We weren't aware of what he was going through at the time. The guy's a warrior and you have to have enough of these guys and that's why it's so hard to win."

Wilcox established a personal mark for wins with his 14th victory over Oakland on August 21, defeating Detroit native Lary Sorensen at Tiger Stadium. Meanwhile, he began alternative therapy using dimethyl sulfoxide, a wood byproduct intended for horses. Despite any evidence that the treatment was safe or effective on humans, Wilcox mixed the solution with oil, applying the ointment after he pitched.

"We had something special and we all wanted it real bad and that's why you saw guys like Milt fight through the hard times.... Milt was having a great year and he knew what he meant to that ballclub," Evans said. Wilcox victimized the Blue Jays twice in September for his 16th and 17th wins of the season. After destroying the opposition all season to win their first divisional title since 1972, the Tigers mauled the Kansas City Royals in the American League Championship Series. After outscoring the Royals 13-4 in the first two games, the Tigers sent Wilcox to start Game Three and potentially clinch the pennant. But would his shoulder cooperate?

"We were in Kansas City and I told Sparky and Roger [Craig, the pitching coach] I needed another cortisone shot. Problem was, I'd taken one just two weeks before. With cortisone, the more you use it, the less effective it becomes.... I flew from Kansas City to Chicago, rented a car and drove to a resort called Pheasant Run. [Dr. Robert] Tietge gave me a shot in my AC joint and I flew back to Kansas City and then came back to Detroit with the team so that nobody would notice."

The treatment worked and Wilcox pitched perhaps the most important game of his career. Pitching with a protracted repertoire of "slurves" and "yackadoos" to the approval of 52,168 delirious fans, he limited the Royals to two hits in a rare eight-inning appearance; Wilcox never completed a game all season, setting a record for most starts in a season (33) without a complete game, broken a year later by the Atlanta Braves' Steve Bedrosian. The Tigers scored only one run, on a groundout by Marty Castillo that allowed Chet Lemon to score from third base, but that hardly seemed to matter. The American League championship banner was flying high in Detroit. Darrell Evans remembered how effectively Wilcox baffled the opposition, both that game and the entire season:

"He was the third guy and different from the two power guys, Jack [Morris] and Dan [Petry]. Then Milt comes in and throws all his changing speeds. He knew when to walk a guy, when to challenge a guy, and then you get him in a big-game situation like that one and he pitches as good a game as has ever been pitched, probably. He went through so much for us and never complained."

DETROIT TIGERS 1984: WHAT A START! WHAT A FINISH!

After the Tigers and Padres split two games in San Diego, Wilcox returned to the mound at Tiger Stadium to pitch Game Three of the World Series. He bent but did not break, giving up one run while stranding eight Padres through his six-inning stint. It was evident that although he won, 5-2, Wilcox was in so much pain that he could barely brush his teeth after the game. Two nights later, the Tigers were world champions. As Eli Zaret described it decades later, Wilcox literally "sacrificed what remained of his right shoulder in order to get that start."

Talk of an emerging baseball dynasty in the Motor City combusted in 1985 as the world champions fell to third place, finishing 84-77. Among the greatest disappointments was Wilcox's record of 1-3. His weathered shoulder lasted only eight games and ended his season in early June. At season's end, Wilcox filed for free agency, but with five healthy starters in Detroit's rotation, including Walt Terrell, his career with the Tigers was over. Nevertheless, he went to the Dominican Winter League, where he posted a record of 7-3 with a 3.40 ERA for Aguilas. Although he lost a few miles per hour off his split-fingered fastball, he said his arm felt the best it had in five years, and his repertoire convinced the Seattle Mariners to offer him a one-year, $150,000 contract. Wilcox was expected to provide leadership to a staff featuring young hurlers Mark Langston, Matt Young, and Mike Moore. Seattle pitching coach Phil Regan remarked that "Milt still has it" and that "he'll get stronger the more he throws."

Instead, Wilcox was winless in Seattle, losing all eight of his decisions and posting a gaudy 5.50 ERA. In his final appearance, a ninth-inning relief stint on June 12, he surrendered a double to Carlton Fisk and a home run to Harold Baines in an 8-4 loss to the Chicago White Sox, although he retired the last batter he faced: Jerry Hairston, his nemesis from the 1983 would-be perfect game. The Mariners released him two days later. On the comeback trail, he joined a Detroit senior league in 1987 before receiving a tryout with the Giants the following year. Despite posting credible numbers with the St. Petersburg Pelicans of the Senior League in 1989—15-4 with a 3.44 ERA over two seasons—he never returned to the major leagues.

After retiring with a record of 119-113, Wilcox returned to Detroit, where he worked as a baseball instructor for children and a broadcaster, and made public appearances. He began to participate in the Tigers' fantasy camp. As he told Joanne Gerstner of the *Detroit News*, "It's a thrill…to put on the uniform again and be part of the game we all love."

In 2003, he briefly returned to professional baseball as a broadcaster for the West Michigan Whitecaps . The same year, he established Ultimate Air Dogs, a carnival attraction in which trained dogs enter aquatic long-jump competitions. An accomplished chinchilla breeder as a player, Wilcox stages up to 35 events each year 90. After many years in Michigan, Milt relocated to Jacksonville, Florida, where he recently married his wife, Cathi. Though his baseball career is long over, Milt Wilcox never lost his drive to compete.

"I've been in front of 50,000 people with 50 million watching on television," he told Joe Lemire of *Sports Illustrated*. "The thrill I get from dog jumping is the same as when I was playing ball."

References

Publications

Middlesworth, Hal, ed. *Detroit Tigers 1978 Yearbook*. Detroit: The Detroit Baseball Club, 1978.

Middlesworth, Hal, and Dan Ewald, eds. *Detroit Tigers 1979 Yearbook*. Detroit: The Detroit Baseball Club, 1979.

Middlesworth, Hal, ed. *Detroit Tigers 1980 Yearbook*. Detroit: The Detroit Baseball Club, 1980.

Middlesworth, Hal, ed. *Detroit Tigers 1982 Yearbook*. Detroit: The Detroit Baseball Club, 1982.

Paladino, Larry, ed. *Detroit Tigers 1983 Yearbook*. Warren, Mich.: Paladino Publications, 1983.

Paladino, Larry, ed. *Detroit Tigers 1984 Yearbook*. Warren, Mich.: Paladino Publications, 1984.

Paladino, Larry, ed. *Detroit Tigers 1985 Yearbook*. Warren, Mich.: Paladino Publications, 1985.

Shine, Neal, and Bill McGraw. *The Roar of '84*. Detroit: The Free Press, 1984.

Smith, Fred T. *Tiger S.T.A.T.S.* Ann Arbor, Mich.: Momentum Books Ltd., 1991.

Zaret, Eli. *'84: The Last of the Great Tigers—Untold Stories From an Amazing Season*. South Boardman, Mich.: Crofton Creek Press, 2004.

Articles

Eisenstadt, David. "Season to Remember: Baseball Dreams Become Reality at Tigers Fantasy Camp," *Toronto Sun*, May 29, 2005. Available from http://www.tcgpr.com/baseballcamp.html. (accessed December 8, 2007).

Falls, Joe. "Baseball Is All Business," *The Sporting News*, May 2, 1983.

Gage, Tom. "Finger Dislocation Worries Wilcox," *The Sporting News*, November 21, 1981.

Gerstner, Joanne. "Adults Become Kids Again: Fans Cherish Their Time With Heroes," *Detroit News*, February 7, 2000. Available from www.mel.org. (Accessed December 17, 2007. par 19).

Hawkins, Jim. "Chinchillas Now Part of Wilcox Tiger Act," *The Sporting News*, July 29, 1978.

Hawkins, Jim. "Outspoken Milt Gets Tiger Attention," *The Sporting News*, September 1, 1979.

Hawkins, Jim. "Tigers Discover a Winner—Dead-Armed Wilcox," *The Sporting News*, August 6, 1977.

Hawkins, Jim. "Wilcox Sets Sights on 30 Wins—as Career Total," *The Sporting News*, November 12, 1977.

Koelling, Les. "Sliders From Milt, A Starvation Diet, Triplets Discover," *The Sporting News*, July 18, 1970.

Lawson, Earl. "83 Percent Red Turnover in Three-Year Howsam Reign," *The Sporting News*, January 24, 1970.

Lawson, Earl. "Wilcox Gives Pitcher-Rich Reds More Reason to Strut," *The Sporting News*, September 26, 1970.

Lemire, Joe. "Lost & Found: Milt Wilcox" *Sports Illustrated*, July 2, 2007.

Macnow, Glen. "Elder Statesman Role for Wilcox?" *The Sporting News*, February 10, 1986.

Schneider, Russell. "Milt Wilcox: What an Injun Bargain!" *The Sporting News*, May 27, 1972.

Schneider, Russell. "Tribe Dumps Three Dissidents, Sees Wilcox as Key '72 Hurler," *The Sporting News*, December 25, 1971.

Schneider, Russell. "Wilcox a Wonder as Tribe Fireman," *The Sporting News*, May 25, 1974.

Schneider, Russell. "Wilcox Kicks Up His Heels as Shoulder Heals," *The Sporting News*, May 26, 1973.

Stone, Larry. "The Mariners' 10 Worst Free Agent Signings," *Seattle Times*, June 27, 2007. Available from http://seattletimes.nwsource.com/html/sports/2003751195.marimoney17.html. Accessed December 8, 2007.

Twentyman, Tim. "Baseball Keeps Manager Young: As a Player and Now as a Coach, Corte Has Been a Stalwart on Jet Box Senior Team Since 1969," *Detroit News*, May 12, 2007. Available from www.mel.org. Accessed December 17, 2007.

Vanochten, Brian. "Wilcox Eager for Television Chance: Former Tiger Joins Broadcasting Team," *Grand Rapids Press*, June 7, 2003. Available from www.mel.org. Accessed December 16, 2007.

Web Sites

www.baseball-reference.com

www.retrosheet.org

Acknowledgments

Charlie Bevis, Ken Breen, Clifford Blau, Matthew Bohn, Bill Gilbert, Maxwell Lapides, Alain Usereau, Milt Wilcox, Bill Young.

Carl Willis
by Mike McClary

BY THE TIME the 1984 Detroit Tigers reached the postseason, rookie right-hander Carl Willis was getting to know his new club, the Cincinnati Reds. Although his time in Detroit was short, Willis stepped in for that championship club at crucial points of the season when the Tigers were thin on pitching. Seven years later, he became an integral part of another World Series team—and that time, he stuck around for the fun.

Carl Blake Willis was born on December 28, 1960, in Danville, Virginia, to Ola and Mack Willis. He was raised 15 miles south in Yanceyville, North Carolina, where he began playing baseball at the age of 9. Willis graduated from the now-defunct Piedmont Academy in Providence, Virginia, and attended the University of North Carolina-Wilmington, where he was a standout pitcher for head coach Bill Brooks.

In 1979 the team had finished with a record of 21-16. In 1980, Willis' first year on campus, the club plummeted to 8-24. During his sophomore year, the team rebounded to a 32-15 mark. Meanwhile, Willis was emerging as a reliable, durable, and versatile pitcher. In 1982 he led the Seahawks with 15 appearances, eight wins, and a pair of saves. And by this time, major-league scouts were taking notice of him. After his junior year, he was selected by the San Francisco Giants in the 31st round of the 1982 amateur draft, but opted to return to school for his senior year.

In his senior season, 1983, Willis led the team with seven wins, a 2.79 earned-run average, and three saves. He won 20 games during his career at UNC Wilmington, at a time when most colleges played fewer games than they do in the 21st century.

Six weeks after Willis closed the book on his college career, he opened another volume, this one as a professional. On June 6, 1983, the Detroit Tigers selected him in the 23rd round (581st overall) of the amateur draft. Three days later Willis embarked on his professional career as Detroit assigned him to its Bristol (Virginia) Tigers affiliate in the Rookie-level Appalachian League—but he wasn't there long.

After just $2^{2/3}$ innings of work in Bristol, and one loss, Willis was on the fast track as the Tigers moved him up to the Single-A Lakeland Tigers of the Florida State League. There, Willis notched three wins in four relief appearances and tossed $9^{2/3}$ scoreless innings. His next stop, still in his first season, was Double-A Birmingham (Alabama) of the Southern League. In 14 games for the Barons, Willis went 3-1 with a 3.98 ERA. "He has a good arm and a fine future ahead of him," said Bill Lee, Birmingham's assistant general manager. "He has a good fastball and slider and excellent control. Keeps the ball down and throws strikes."

"He's a quiet kid," Lee noted. "He's a real professional. He doesn't say much. He just goes out and gets the job done. He's very cool and calm on the mound." In less than three months in professional baseball, Willis finished the abbreviated 1983 season with a record of 6-2 and a 2.76 ERA.

That winter his career trajectory elevated rapidly when he caught the eye of Tigers pitching coach—and fellow North Carolinian—Roger Craig during the Instructional League in St. Petersburg, Florida. "He kept all his pitches low in the strike zone," Craig wrote in his diary of the 1984 season, *Inside Pitch: Roger Craig's '84 Tiger Journal*. And that was enough to convince him that Willis deserved a nonroster invitation to spring training in 1984.

That season the Tigers bullpen was all but set with veteran right-handed relievers Doug Bair and Aurelio Lopez as well as swingmen Juan Berenguer and Dave Rozema. Nevertheless, Willis impressed throughout the spring and was among manager Sparky Anderson's final roster cuts—despite being tabbed by Anderson as the next Rollie Fingers. Similar comments by Sparky of other Detroit prospects often served as the kiss of death to their big-league careers. But such was not yet in evidence for Willis.

As the Tigers prepared for the season opener in Minneapolis, Willis was assigned to the club's Triple-A Evansville (Indiana) Triplets of the American Association. Willis excelled for manager Gordie Mackenzie and by early June he had posted a 4-0 record, a 2.67 ERA, and 10 saves.

On June 7 the Tigers promoted Willis and he joined the team in Baltimore for a series against the defending World Series champs. "I didn't expect anything like this to happen so soon," Willis said. "I was just happy for the opportunity to play when I first signed. I wouldn't have believed it if I had been at Double-A right now. So this is just unbelievable."

"The Tigers told me I was brought up here to pitch, not to sit," he said. "Sparky told me I would be used primarily in long relief. But he also said I may be used in short relief if he felt Lopez and Hernandez were being overworked. He also told me I would probably become their late-inning right-hander in a couple of years." Two days later, on June 9—exactly one year after he began his professional career in Bristol—Willis made his major-league debut.

With two out in the sixth inning and the Tigers losing 4-0, Willis relieved Lopez and coaxed Orioles catcher Rick Dempsey into a groundout to third to end the inning. Willis threw $2^{1/3}$ stellar innings, allowing just a double to Eddie Murray and an intentional walk to John Lowenstein.

"Carl is going to be outstanding; he doesn't pitch scared," Roger Craig wrote on the day Willis was promoted. "I'll never forget what he told me in spring training after he first threw batting practice. When I asked him how he felt, he said he was nervous. I shrugged that off and offered reassurance by telling him he had thrown strikes. 'Aw, I can always throw strikes,' he responded. That impressed me. The kid doesn't have one year of pro ball under his belt, but he did have some swagger."

Willis appeared primarily in relief but made his first start on June 19 at Tiger Stadium, against the New York Yankees. He yielded nine hits (including a two-run homer by Don Mattingly) and four runs, all earned, while striking out three in the Tigers' 7-6 victory—but did not factor in the decision. His first came on June 27 when he took the loss in one inning of relief against New York at Yankee Stadium.

On July 2 Willis was sent down to Evansville to make room on the roster for shortstop Doug Baker, brought up to fill in for the injured Alan Trammell. On August 5, Willis was recalled to help the Tigers weather a storm of three straight doubleheaders. It didn't turn out well. In the middle pair of twin bills, against the Red Sox in Boston, he started the nightcap and didn't make it out of the first inning, surrendering five hits and four earned runs in just a third of an inning. His ERA was now 8.36. Willis atoned for that effort the following day, pitching two shutout innings in the first game of the final doubleheader. It was his final appearance with Detroit.

On August 27 the Tigers bolstered their relief corps by acquiring lefty Bill Scherrer from the Cincinnati Reds for a player to be named later. On September 1 the Tigers sent Willis to Cincinnati to complete the trade. "Trades are a part of baseball," Willis said. "It's a good move for me."

"I don't think I would have been given much of a chance with the Tigers because they have Lopez and Hernandez in the bullpen." he added.

Willis said he wasn't completely stunned by the trade. Tigers general manager Bill Lajoie told him that the Reds had tried to acquire him in June. "At least I know that I wasn't a throw-in in the trade," Willis said. "The Reds were really interested; so I'm excited. I really couldn't have asked for a better break."

In his two brief stretches with the Tigers, Willis was 0-2 and surrendered 25 hits and 13 earned runs in 16 innings.

At the time of the trade, the Reds were mired in last place in the National League West and had the major leagues' worst record. "The Reds are looking for a dependable man to come out of the bullpen," Willis said. "I know that I didn't get a chance to pitch in a role that I was used to with the Tigers. I have pitched in short relief from almost the time I left UNCW last year. So I think my days as a starter are over. I feel comfortable as a short reliever."

Willis was right; he did not start another game over the final eight years of his career.

On September 1 Willis made his Reds debut, at home against Pittsburgh. He gave up just one hit and one walk in three innings of middle relief, pitching the third through fifth innings of a game the Reds won 7-5. coming from behind in the bottom of the 11th. Four days later he pitched again, in San Diego against the Padres. In one-third of an inning, he surrendered two runs, both earned, on two hits. He earned his first big-league save on September 22 against the Astros, pitching the bottom of the 13th inning in the Astrodome to hold a 2-1 Reds lead. Three days later, Willis made his final appearance of the 1984 season, taking the loss in the Reds' 4-2 defeat against the Braves. His final line for his first season in the majors: 0-3 and a 5.96 ERA.

Over the next two seasons, Willis shuttled between Cincinnati and its Denver Triple-A club, the Zephyrs. In 40 games for the Reds, he picked up a pair of wins and one save while being tagged for three losses in 66 innings. On December 10, it looked as if Willis' Reds career was over.

Left off the Reds' 40-man roster, he was available in that winter's Rule 5 draft and was selected by the California Angels. As he had been two years earlier, Willis was a final spring-training cut by the Angels and, as dictated by Rule 5, he was returned to the Reds.

He again split time between Cincinnati and Denver in 1986 and finished with a 1-3 major-league record and a 4.47 ERA in Cincinnati, and 1-3 and 4.68 in Denver. Willis spent the entire 1987 season with the Reds' new Triple-A affiliate, the Nashville Sounds of the American Association, going 6-4 with a 3.33 ERA. "I'm just on the wrong club," he said. "There is no sense in me playing Triple-A for Cincinnati next year. I don't want to hold anyone else back. It doesn't seem like Cincinnati has any plans for me. I hope they are going to try and trade me over the winter." On January 19, 1988, the Reds granted his wish when they dealt him to the Chicago White Sox for minor leaguer Darrell Pruitt.

Willis spent most of the 1988 season (4-4, 4.22) at the White Sox' Vancouver affiliate in the Triple-A Pacific Coast League. He appeared in six games for the White Sox in '88 with an 8.25 ERA and no decisions in 12 innings of work. In the offseason he was on the move again—and to a familiar club: the Angels, who selected him in the minor-league draft. In 1989 Willis was back in the PCL, this time for the Angels' top farm club in Edmonton, finishing 5-7 with a 3.69 ERA. A free agent after that season, Willis signed with the Cleveland Indians, who assigned him to their Pacific Coast League club in Colorado Springs, where any enjoyment over his 5-3 record was tempered by an ERA of 6.39.

After the 1990 campaign Willis' career finally gained traction when he signed in December with the Minnesota Twins. He quickly became an indispensable piece of the team's bullpen in the early 1990s. Though he started the season at Triple-A Portland, it was a brief stay (1-1, 1.64 in 11 innings spread over three games). In 40 big-league games that year, Willis posted an 8-3 record with a 2.73 ERA—his best statistical season—for a Twins club that won 95 games in a stunning worst-to-first reversal from the year before.

In the 1991 American League Championship Series against the Toronto Blue Jays, Willis appeared in three games, allowing just two hits in $5^{1}/_{3}$ scoreless innings. After eliminating the Blue Jays in five games, the Twins moved on to face another worst-to-first team, the Atlanta Braves, in the World Series.

In Game Three at Atlanta's Fulton County Stadium, Willis tossed scoreless eighth and ninth innings in relief of Steve Bedrosian; the Braves won, 5-4, in 12. The next night Willis relieved a fellow former Tiger, Jack Morris, in the seventh inning with Twins clinging to a 2-1 lead. After two quick outs, Braves left fielder Lonnie Smith took Willis deep to tie the game at 2-2. It was the only hit off Willis in his inning and a third of work. The Braves won the game 3-2.

He appeared in Game Five and allowed three earned runs on four hits, including a home run by Brian Hunter, as the Braves rolled over the Twins, 14-5. Two days later, in Game Six, Willis redeemed himself in his fourth World Series appearance throwing $2^{2}/_{3}$ innings of scoreless relief in the Twins' stirring 4-3, 11-inning victory that forced a seventh game. None of the Twins relievers saw duty in that decisive game; Morris pitched a legendary 10-inning shutout as the Twins sealed their second World Series title in five seasons.

In essence, Willis duplicated his fine 1991 season in 1992. His 7-3 slate and 2.72 ERA virtually matched his basic numbers from the year before. He finished 21 games (as opposed to nine in 1991) despite pitching almost ten fewer innings over 19 more games. In retrospect, the 1993 season, although showing just a slight slippage in Willis' numbers (3-0, 3.10 ERA), foreshadowed some difficulty in that he still finished 21 games but appeared in six fewer games and pitched $21^{1}/_{3}$ fewer innings. He did a two-game stint in Portland, making two appearances and surrendering two runs (one earned) in four innings—not bad until one notes that he gave up six hits and a walk. The situation came crashing down in 1994, as Willis struggled through $59^{1}/_{3}$ innings ($1^{1}/_{3}$ more than in 1993), giving up 89 hits to finish 2-4 with an unsightly 5.92 ERA. That the end had arrived became painfully clear in 1995. Willis appeared in three games but only two-thirds of an inning, in which he faced 12 batters while surrendering five hits, five walks, and seven earned runs.

Not surprisingly, the Twins released Willis on May 4, 1995. Six weeks later, on June 27, he again signed with the Angels and was assigned to the club's Triple-A Vancouver Canadians in the PCL. Willis appeared in 20 games for Vancouver, posting a 2-2 record with one save and a 4.11 ERA. At the end of the 1995 season, at the age of 34, Willis' career came to an end. His final line: 267 games, a 22-16 record, 13 saves, and

DETROIT TIGERS 1984: WHAT A START! WHAT A FINISH!

a 4.25 ERA with four major-league teams.

Upon his retirement, Willis spent 13 seasons in the Cleveland Indians organization as a pitching coach, first in the minors and then seven seasons as the club's major-league pitching coach on the staff of manager Eric Wedge. In 1998 Willis was inducted as a charter member the UNC-Wilmington Athletic Hall of Fame.

In 2010 Willis joined the Seattle Mariners as a minor-league pitching coordinator, but on August 9 was promoted to be pitching coach for the parent club. In the offseason he resided in Durham, North Carolina, with his wife Rachel, daughter Ally, and sons Daniel and Bryson.

References

Publications

Craig, Roger, with Vern Plagenhoef. *Inside Pitch: Roger Craig's '84 Tiger Journal*. Grand Rapids, Mich.: Eerdmans, 1984. 86.

Detroit Tigers. *1984 Detroit Tigers Media Guide*. Detroit: Detroit Tigers. 1984.

University of North Carolina-Wilmington. *2010 UNC Wilmington Media Guide*. Available at http://www.uncwsports.com

Seattle Mariners. *2010 Seattle Mariners Information Guide*. Available at http://www.mariners.com

Articles

Atkins, Lissa D. "Divided loyalty is part of the game back home: Atlanta is their team; Twins' pitcher is their hero." *Greensboro News-Record*, October 24, 1991. C1.

Carree, Chuck. "Tigers deal ex-Seahawk ace Willis." *Wilmington Morning Star,* September 1, 1984. 1D.

Carree, Chuck. "Willis' future isn't with Reds." *Wilmington Morning Star,* August 31, 1987. 1B.

Carree, Chuck. "Willis makes majors in exactly one year." *Wilmington Morning Star*, June 13, 1984. 1D.

Web Sites

Carl Willis Baseball-Reference.com page: http://www.baseball-reference.com/players/w/willica01.shtml

1983 Bristol Tigers Baseball-Reference.com page: http://www.baseball-reference.com/minors/team.cgi?id=13031

1983 Birmingham Barons Baseball-Reference.com page: http://www.baseball-reference.com/minors/team.cgi?id=12330

1983 Lakeland Tigers Baseball-Reference.com page: http://www.baseball-reference.com/minors/team.cgi?id=22375

The Brass
Tom Monaghan
by Gary Gillette

TOM MONAGHAN has accomplished a great many things in his yet-unfinished life. The billionaire entrepreneur? Certainly. Successful businessman? Sure. Collector? Formerly, but not in any defining sense. Conservative Catholic leader? Definitely. Visionary? Maybe. Twenty-first- century evangelist and savior of Western civilization? Possibly, if you talk to him.

However you label the owner of the Detroit Tigers from 1983 to 1992, or whatever you choose to say about him—and he really doesn't care, either way—Monaghan is a true believer. Believing his story to be a real-life Horatio Alger tale, Monaghan marches with a determined step well to the right of, and far behind, the materialistic march of modern, secular society.

The life of this unlikely public figure continues to serve as both inspiration to many deeply religious Catholics as well as an object lesson to others regarding the corrupting influence of money and ego. F. Scott Fitzgerald's 1925 classic American novel *The Great Gatsby* and Tom Wolfe's *The Bonfire of the Vanities*—a late-century cultural touchstone of greed, power, and arrogance in New York City—bear more than a passing resemblance to the arc of Tom Monaghan's life. Yet the tragic central figures of Fitzgerald's and Wolfe's works—primarily motivated by greed and power—are not nearly so complex or as interesting as Monaghan, whose life can hardly be viewed as tragic.

It would be facile to simply call Monaghan a "Master of the Universe," yet Wolfe's vivid description of the self-anointed potentates of Wall Street rings more than a little true. In his religious fervor, Tom Monaghan really does seem to want to play the role of such a master. The difference is that Monaghan the younger wanted to be a master in both the real and the spiritual realms: In effect, he dared attempt to defy the lesson of Matthew 6:24 by serving both God and mammon. In his retirement, Monaghan has mostly limited himself to trying to serve God.

If one had any doubts about Monaghan's ambitious goals, a 2008 *DBusiness* magazine profile of Monaghan, entitled "Earning His Wings," would dispel them. As a publication covering the business community of Southeastern Michigan, DBusiness is not known for its hard-hitting journalism, and its publisher knows and admires Monaghan. So the profile was definitely friendly, which makes it especially revealing. "The devout Catholic patriarch of Ave Maria University now spends his days toiling in the Florida sunshine, making sure that he and his disciples are on the right path to heaven."

Tom Monaghan became a billionaire because he had an idea that almost anyone else could have had. When one thinks about it, it's almost as if Monaghan had a flash of genius and then plucked a billion bucks out of the air.

The dust jacket of Monaghan's 1986 autobiography, *Pizza Tiger*, summarized his philosophy quite nicely: "Tom Monaghan built Domino's Pizza around a single concept: Pizza should be delivered hot to the customer in thirty minutes or less. His commitment to the customer, his attention to the details of production, and his dedication to quality have revolutionized the pizza industry and made Domino's Pizza a household name in America."

Note that quality came third in the priority list (not a criticism). "Quality control" was primarily process and quantity control—which is nothing to dismiss. Portion control was rigorous, for good reason. Countless restaurants have failed because the owner didn't understand the value of portion and inventory control, or because employees took too many five-finger discounts or slipped their friends too many freebies.

While Monaghan's flash of genius was critical, it didn't void the need for endless hours of monastic devotion that included years of hands-on experience, experimentation, and learning different skills on the job. But the foundation of the billion-dollar pizza delivery franchise business was there: Locate takeout-only stores with very limited menus near dormitories or student ghettos in college towns full of young men who don't plan and can't or won't cook, but who have discretionary income. Then deliver reliably hot and consistent pizza to drunk, stoned, and sleep-deprived college students in a half-hour or less. (Military bases were also excellent locations.)

Monaghan's desire for complete control served him well when he was building his empire. After he became emperor of all he surveyed, however, his lust for control sometimes got him into trouble. Monaghan could be seen as a modern-day King Lear, but with a lust for control in the name of doing God's work.

Thomas Stephen Monaghan was born in Ann Arbor, Michigan, in 1937 to Francis Monaghan, a truck driver, and Anna Monaghan, an aspiring nurse. Tom had one brother, James, two years younger. Francis Monaghan died of peritonitis on Christmas Eve 1941.

Struggling to bring up two boys after her husband's death, Anna felt she had to place her sons in foster homes so that she could complete nursing school. The boys were placed in a succession of foster homes, then endured six years in a Catholic orphanage in Jackson, Michigan, run by Felician nuns from Poland. There Sister Mary Berarda became young Tom's mentor as well as a mother figure. Monaghan has spoken fondly of Sister Berarda in many interviews, crediting her with giving him the will to succeed while instilling a moral compass that would guide him the rest of his life. Despite this encouragement and visits from his mother, life in the orphanage was hard, and Tom did not thrive.

After becoming a nurse and taking the boys back home when Tom was in the sixth grade, Anna (now living in Traverse City, Michigan) ended up fighting incessantly with her rebellious older son. Tom was again placed in foster care, including living with a farm family in rural northern Michigan, which he liked. Through all his travails, young Tom dreamed of baseball, architecture, and his idol Frank Lloyd Wright.

A parish priest served as a father figure to the lost boy. Tom applied to and was admitted to St. Joseph's, a minor seminary in Grand Rapids, Michigan. Tom's religious training in the 10th grade lasted less than a year before he was expelled for disciplinary reasons, crushing his dream of becoming a priest. Back home again, Tom's already tenuous relationship with his mother deteriorated further, and he would spend half a year in a state facility for juvenile delinquents. Rescued from his purgatory there, Tom was taken in by an aunt and uncle in Ann Arbor while he finished high school. Tom graduated from St. Thomas High School in 1955, ranked last in his class of 44.

Unable to get into the University of Michigan, Monaghan attended Ferris State College in rural Big Rapids, Michigan. After getting good grades in his freshman year, Monaghan wanted to apply to Michigan. Lacking money for tuition, however, Monaghan enlisted in the Marines—while intending to join the Army! He served honorably from 1956 to 1959. After being discharged, the gullible (by his own description) veteran was duped by someone he met while hitchhiking and swindled of all the money he had diligently saved out of his meager military pay.

After returning to Ann Arbor, Monaghan intended to work his way through the University of Michigan while studying architecture. But he proved far better at business than academics, dropping out twice during his first year there before giving up on college.

Monaghan's relationships with his nuclear family are as complex as his business dealings. When he first became famous, Monaghan told the hard-knocks story of his youth, the orphanage, and Sister Berarda over and over, letting people erroneously believe that he had grown up as an orphan. When the media learned that Anna was still alive, it was quite a surprise to the fourth estate and an embarrassment to her estranged child.

Anna died in 1988, reportedly after reconciliation, and Monaghan's tone toward her became much softer—if still not overly affectionate. "She did the best she could," he told *People* magazine in 1989, while also saying that his mother "couldn't stand" him. Based on Tom's many negative comments about his mother in his autobiography, the feeling was mutual.

Tom Monaghan married Marjorie Zybach, a Lutheran, in 1962 after meeting her while delivering pizza to a dormitory at Central Michigan University in Mount Pleasant. The couple had four daughters in the next decade: Mary, Susan, Margaret, and Barbara.

Though she has reportedly attended Mass every Sunday with her husband for almost five decades, Marjorie remained a faithful Lutheran. Unlike the spouses of many famous people, "Margie" neither sought out nor was victimized by the media spotlight, remaining virtually unseen and unheard by the public as her husband became a globetrotting businessman. She was heavily involved in her husband's pizza business, serving as bookkeeper, financial adviser, company payroll supervisor, and corporate director over the years.

That doesn't mean that Mrs. Monaghan didn't have a life or mind of her own, as she first demonstrated when she ignored her mother's strong dislike of her beau. In 1989 the National Organization for Women organized a boycott of Domino's because of its owner's outspoken pro-life stance and his funding of anti-abortion causes. Yet later that year, in the *People* piece about her husband, Marjorie pointedly commented, "If men had babies, there would be no laws against abortion."

An obsession with control has defined Tom Monaghan's life. When he did not have control, the confident rebel refused to follow the rules. When he did have control, he reached for more while consistently refusing to follow the rules.

Monaghan was driven by his sense of morality, which reinforced his unwillingness to compromise. He expected nonnegotiable loyalty from his employees and punished those he deemed disloyal—even otherwise excellent employees who lacked his defining zeal for making pizza.

Measured by his own words as well as those of outside observers, Tom Monaghan was stubborn, hypercompetitive, and a micromanager. News about Monaghan and quotes by him—especially in *Pizza Tiger*—also suggest he was obsessed with his reputation and status and exhibited emotional instability. This was especially true in his youth, when he was quite willing to resort to fisticuffs to solve problems. But his well-chronicled spending sprees on more than 200 cars plus Frank Lloyd Wright houses and objects—including $8 million for a handmade Bugatti and $1.6 million for a Wright dining room set—showed that he did not outgrow those characteristics after making a fortune.

Nevertheless, those same traits can drive success in some business contexts. Founders are often in love with their own ideas, behaving like missionaries trying to convert others to their product or service. A person with that level of passion is well suited to handle the risks and intense downturns often associated with a startup business. Monaghan was able to overcome failures time and again with Domino's, partly due to his unwillingness to accept the realities of his situation. Ultimately, Monaghan overcame his control-freak tendencies enough to allow management experts to help shape Domino's direction during its long, uneven, and very complicated expansion.

Monaghan wanted others to succeed while they admired him for what a good person he was as he strove to be the best or the greatest in whatever he did. Franchising turned out to be a good business model for Monaghan's personality.

In 1960 Monaghan found his vocation as well as his salvation in the unlikely form of a pizza parlor—though it certainly wasn't clear at the time. He and his brother bought a shuttered, nondescript pizzeria named DomiNick's in Ypsilanti near Eastern Michigan University. The purchase price of less than $1,000 was secured with a down payment of less than $100 cash. Within a year, Tom traded a used Volkswagen Beetle to his sibling (who had a day job with the Postal Service) and became the sole owner.

DETROIT TIGERS 1984: WHAT A START! WHAT A FINISH!

Though the beginning was modest, Monaghan was ambitious and quickly moved to expand his operation. He was fast-talked into taking on a wastrel partner, then opened a second store in Mount Pleasant in 1961. The partnership soon owned more pizzerias, including one in Ann Arbor serving the lucrative University of Michigan market. With the original pizzeria providing most of the cash flow and with Monaghan doing most of the work, the partnership collapsed and was dissolved, with Monaghan fully liable for the partnership's mountain of debt.

In 1965, Monaghan incorporated and renamed his growing enterprise Domino's Pizza after his rights to the DomiNick's name were withdrawn by the original owner. Living a spartan lifestyle and working almost 24/7, Monaghan kept things afloat and paid off the debt created by his ex-partner. Two years later, the pizza business was going well enough that Monaghan licensed his first franchise—also located in Ypsilanti. He spent the rest of the 1960s building his franchising business, assiduously refining his pizza production methods, and surviving calamities like the fire that destroyed his underinsured headquarters and commissary in 1968.

An ill-advised deviation from his sound, student- and military-based business plan (an expansion into serving residential neighborhoods) caused a major crisis in 1970. Though Domino's narrowly avoided bankruptcy, Monaghan was forced to give up control of the company for a year and was sued by his franchisees. Continuing his maniacal devotion to his work, the single-minded pizza entrepreneur started expanding his chain again, opening his 100th store in 1975 and his 200th in 1978. In between, he survived another franchisee insurrection plus a bitter trademark-infringement lawsuit by Amstar (maker of Domino Sugar) that was tried in federal court in Atlanta. That litigation cost Monaghan a lot of money, time, and energy in the late 1970s as Domino's lost at the trial level, then won upon appeal in 1980.

Battle-scarred but definitely unbowed, with an unswerving devotion to customer service and an unshakeable faith in his ultimate success, Monaghan forged ahead. Aided by a nationwide popularity in fast-food franchising, he rapidly expanded his business in the 1980s. By 1983, it had all come together for the energetic pizza baron. In that momentous year, Domino's opened its 1,000th store as well as its first franchise outside the United States. Riding high, Monaghan also purchased the Detroit Tigers for $53 million—the most money ever paid for a sports franchise at the time. If that weren't enough, he founded the Ave Maria Foundation. (Though no longer affiliated with Domino's or the Tigers, Monaghan remained in 2013 as chair of the foundation.)

The Detroit Tigers were owned by a John Fetzer, a colorless—but very well-respected—broadcasting tycoon who had made his fortune as a pioneer in the early days of radio in the 1920s and 1930s. Fetzer had turned away many inquires about selling the club in the three decades that he had owned the Tigers. Yet team president Jim Campbell handpicked Monaghan as a potential buyer, looking toward the inevitable day that Fetzer decided to sell.

New owner Tom Monaghan was living a fantasy life as his Tigers steamrolled all competition in 1984, winning a World Series championship and making an estimated $10 million or more in profits on his investment in the first year.

Helicoptering from Domino's headquarters in nearby Ann Arbor to Tigers games, landing on the roof of a taxicab company across the street, Monaghan was both extremely visible and very likable. He was treated favorably by the media for his accessibility and wide-eyed enthusiasm for the game; for decades, the Detroit press had rarely had access to the former owner. Things couldn't have gone better.

As it turned out, lots of things could go wrong, and not just on the field. And they did. Keeping Fetzer as chair of the board after the sale, Monaghan also retained the Tigers' management team—who looked like geniuses in 1984. Yet their hidebound resistance to change and Domino's unforeseen troubles would ruin the club before the end of the decade.

Although Fetzer had made his fortune in broadcasting, the conservative Tigers were not nearly so innovative in televising their games under his ownership, showing only 52 games in 1983 (including only seven home games). Under Monaghan, the Tigers made a deal to broadcast an additional 80 games on pay cable via PASS (Pro Am Sports System) in 1984, catching up with other clubs in large markets that had taken advantage of cable TV's huge potential.

Watching their hometown heroes on TV in the mid-1980s was sweet for Detroit fans, who had only to flip the channel to see how chic their blue-collar team had become. In 1983 Roy Scheider starred as a fading ballplayer in the upbeat Disney television movie *Tiger Town*, filmed at Tiger Stadium with cooperation of the team. On the CBS hit show *Magnum, P.I.*, hunky Tom Selleck—jauntily sporting an ever-present Tigers cap—saved damsels in distress while solving crimes as he raced around Hawaii in his Ferrari.

After 1984 the Tigers were proclaimed to be a budding dynasty, though that dynasty proved to exist only in the high hopes of the fans and in the palavering of the pundits. The Tigers finished third in both 1985 and 1986 (behind Toronto and Boston, respectively) as Sparky Anderson's charges struggled. The American League East was a tough division, though it certainly wasn't home to any great teams in the mid-1980s. Yet the Tigers won only one more division title, edging Toronto on the final day of 1987 in a barn-burning finish to one of the greatest pennant races of all time. They followed that triumph by being abruptly upset by the underdog Minnesota Twins in the 1987 American League Championship Series.

By the end of the '87 season, it was clear that something was wrong in Tigertown, as fan support for the club had waned since 1984. Monaghan wondered openly about the relatively small weeknight crowds at Tiger Stadium during the last few days of the season when the Tigers were struggling to catch Toronto, and Detroit failed to sell out its home ALCS games.

Two years later the Tigers hit rock bottom, winning just 59 games. In response, Monaghan—acting more like a sports groupie than an experienced, clear-eyed business executive—

made the mistake of tapping his friend Bo Schembechler to turn the Tigers around. Schembechler, the autocratic former University of Michigan football coach and athletic director, had zero experience in professional sports. His attempt to impose a football-style mentality on a radically different sport ended in disaster; meanwhile, business troubles caused Monaghan to drain the club of the cash needed for rebuilding so he could service Domino's hefty debt (estimated at one point at a half-billion dollars).

Schembechler came aboard the foundering Detroit ship on January 8, 1990, as president and chief operating officer, with Jim Campbell becoming chairman of the board and CEO. Campbell, general manager or president of the Tigers since 1962, was Major League Baseball's longest-tenured executive. Bill Lajoie initially remained as general manager in the new regime, a post he had held since October 1983. This administrative overlap demonstrated Monaghan's inability to grasp how truly desperate the situation was.

Moving into this ossified management group, Schembechler tried to shake things up by emphasizing athleticism when scouting and drafting prospects (in direct contrast to the Tigers themselves, who were anything but athletic). A year later Schembechler hired Joe McDonald as senior vice president of player procurement and development, allowing Schembechler to take over some of the GM duties. In September 1991 Jerry Walker was hired as senior vice president of major league personnel, filling essentially a general manager's role. McDonald served under Walker before being canned in 1992.

For three stormy years Schembechler ran the sinking ship despite being completely out of his element. In one of his worst miscalculations, he forced legendary broadcaster Ernie Harwell to retire after the 1991 season. Whole forests of pulpwood trees in Quebec were leveled to provide the newsprint needed for the abuse heaped upon the Tigers by the media and by outraged fans. Even worse, Schembechler and the Tigers witlessly allowed the embarrassing soap opera to drag on for a full year as Harwell milked every moment of his farewell season at WJR's microphone.

Nine years after he had fulfilled a boyhood dream in buying the Tigers, after reports that the club had to borrow money from the American League to make its payroll, Monaghan sold the Tigers. That was painful enough. What made it worse, because no other qualified buyer could be found, was that Monaghan had to sell out to his longtime rival, Detroit Red Wings owner and fellow Michigan pizza mogul Mike Ilitch (co-founder and co-owner with his wife, Marian, of the Little Caesars Pizza chain).

Schembechler and Campbell were fired in August 1992 as Ilitch prepared to assume control. Claiming he had a guarantee for 10 years, Schembechler sued Monaghan in what became a bitter dispute over his compensation package—sketched out on a restaurant napkin! The suit was settled out of court two years later.

Detroit fans were pleased when Ilitch demonstrated a commitment to revitalizing the team that was sorely lacking from the cash-strapped Monaghan, whose enthusiasm for his underperforming baseball club had waned long before the end. Another positive was that Ilitch quickly spent millions of dollars sprucing up the corner of Michigan and Trumbull. That contrasted starkly with Monaghan, who had tried to persuade the virtually bankrupt city of Detroit to subsidize a new ballpark after 1987 when he decided that Tiger Stadium was no longer viable.

Monaghan said in a 2008 interview with the *Ann Arbor Business Review* that when he purchased the team, "I thought the stadium was a shrine." He wanted to restore it: "[I]t had a lot of historical significance and it meant a lot to me." Yet within four years, the pizza tiger was reportedly looking for sites for a new ballpark, expressing disappointment with attendance at Tiger Stadium.

"Probably the biggest mistake I ever made was buying the Tigers," Monaghan told *DBusiness* 16 years after he sold the team, adding that he had lost focus on Domino's when he had opportunities to make changes during the pizza-delivery wars of the mid-1980s. Monaghan's leadership approach could be effective during the founding stage of an organization or when an organization was ethically challenged, but he faced a "new territory" challenge in an existing industry in baseball.

As the new owner of the Detroit Tigers in 1983, he would probably have been better served by reaching outside of his comfort zone, especially by seeking out the best practices of the most effective team owners. That would have built an internal team better equipped to compete in the contemporary environment. Ideally, Monaghan should have surrounded himself with executives and advisers who thought differently than he so that they could establish a solid and innovative business plan for the future.

That was not Tom Monaghan, however. The narcissistic, self-made "Pizza Tiger" was in many ways an extension of his mentor John Fetzer, whom he viewed as "far and away the greatest owner in the history of baseball." That same great man had personally blessed Monaghan as the holder of Detroit's legacy and traditions; those orthodox ties hurt the Tigers' long-term success. Monaghan took the helm of a well-established aristocratic organization in need of a rejuvenation and, for the most part, magnified the weaknesses of the aristocracy.

The hoopla and happiness of 1984 started to unravel later that decade as Monaghan enjoyed his fame and fortune while neglecting his core business. In 1985 Domino's opened almost a thousand new outlets, finishing with more than 2,800 stores. In 1989 the fast-growing international chain celebrated the debut of its 5,000th store.

According to Monaghan, he dramatically reordered his priorities after reading C.S. Lewis' *Mere Christianity*. The book's chapter on pride struck a nerve with the wealthy exec, who concluded that he was "probably the biggest sinner in the world." Taking a self-styled and self-defined vow of poverty, Monaghan sold many of his expensive possessions.

After his soul-searching, the wealthy executive devoted himself again to his foundering pizza business. The divestiture of many of the ancillary assets acquired along the way was no doubt also made necessary by Domino's problems—not the least of which was servicing its crippling debt.

One of those extraneous assets was an executive retreat and gold resort called Domino's Lodge on Drummond Island, east of Michigan's Upper Peninsula in chilly northern Lake Huron. The island was the scene of one of Monaghan's weirdest adventures: a lavish, Gatsby-like party staged in November 1987 for about 70 friends, VIPs, and Tigers players. Monaghan said he planned the party to celebrate Detroit's presumed World Series victory before Detroit was upset in the ALCS. Guests were flown in and out on nine private planes. Limousines, yachts, and a helicopter provided local transportation. A jet was reportedly sent back to Detroit for the sole purpose of picking up a forgotten tuxedo. Columnists and commentators clucked about Monaghan's profligacy, one calling it "wretched excess."

The over-the-top party included the making of an ersatz movie starring the guests, with local citizens hired to line the red carpet and scream like groupies at a gala Hollywood premiere. Fake money imprinted with the images of Tom and Marjorie was distributed; the scrip could be redeemed by guests for luxury gifts. Estimates of the extravaganza's cost ranged from $300,000 to a cool $1 million.

It's hard to tell whether the self-confident and headstrong Monaghan simply ignored the remote location's limitations when planning his retreat/resort—or simply was ignorant of them. The compound was six hours from Detroit by car and almost two hours east of the Mackinac Bridge, and can have frost in July and August. In either case, Monaghan took a bath, recouping only $3 million of the $28 million he reportedly had poured into the ill-fated investment.

The early 1990s saw more troubles for Monaghan. After losing or settling several multimillion-dollar, high-profile lawsuits by people injured by Domino's drivers in auto accidents, the company withdrew its famous 30-minute-or-free guarantee. Monaghan sought a buyer for the company, asking a billion dollars to no avail for several years.

After almost four decades in the pizza business, Monaghan in 1998 turned over management of the company that made him rich and famous and had financed his dreams and his ideals. He sold 93 percent of Domino's to Bain Capital for what was reported to be a billion dollars, staying on the board of directors and retaining the title of chairman emeritus. It was only after Monaghan sold the company that female employees were allowed to wear slacks instead of skirts at the company's headquarters.

Monaghan's primary tangible legacy in Ann Arbor is the enormous, spectacular Domino's Farms office park, its centerpiece a half-mile-long building paralleling heavily traveled U.S. 23 at its intersection with busy M-14 east of the city in Ann Arbor Township. The Frank Lloyd Wright-inspired, copper-cladded, green-neon-accented modernist structure contains nearly one million square feet of space. Monaghan spent $2 million on his custom-built personal office there.

Due to its grand scale and attendant financing issues, Domino's Farms' signature building took 15 years to complete.

Meanwhile, Monaghan's dream of building a leaning, 30-story "Golden Beacon" tower—modeled on a larger Wright design that was never built and quickly dubbed the "Leaning Tower of Pizza"—had to be shelved.

In 1987, Monaghan founded Legatus, an effort to meld business and religion. The organization's website describes its founding with religious imagery: "Just hours after meeting Pope John Paul II in May 1987, the inspiration for Legatus hit Tom Monaghan like a 'lightning bolt.'" Monaghan himself has described the moment as "divine inspiration."

According to the organization, "Like Tom, Legatus members are business leaders—men and women with varying interests and diverse talents who all share one overriding goal: to become better Catholics and, in turn, positively impact their business and personal lives."

Only Catholic CEOs of major companies were eligible through the original criteria for membership in Legatus. Though broadened somewhat since then, the organization remains limited in most cases to owners, managing partners, and top executives in companies worth $10 million or more.

In a 1999 profile in the *New York Times*, Monaghan talked frankly about his devotion to doing God's work via Legatus. "I listen to every idea, and if I don't agree I give a decisive but sensitive response. That's what I did with the franchisees my whole career. Legatus is a volunteer group. If people don't like what I'm doing, they can go form their own organization."

Carrying out his self-imposed duty as an American Catholic business missionary, Monaghan founded Ave Maria Institute in 1998, which became a small Catholic school called Ave Maria College in Ypsilanti. (*Ave Maria* is Latin for Hail Mary.) Trying to simultaneously speed up and assure accreditation for the school, Monaghan made a deal in 2000 to take control of St. Mary's College in the Detroit suburb of Orchard Lake, a foundering century-old historically Polish Catholic college with a geographically unrestricted charter from the State of Michigan.

The quasi-merger of the two Catholic schools experienced many problems and was dissolved three years later when Monaghan's administrators—who obviously hadn't done proper due diligence—figured out that the St. Mary's charter couldn't be used to get Ave Maria College accredited. The shotgun marriage, though, did produce a memorable quote from St. Mary's president, Dr. Thaddeus Radzilowski, who noted that Monaghan "wanted a school that produced three-hundred-pound tackles who were also theology majors." (Among Monaghan's dreams was starting a Division I football program at the 400-student college.)

The much more ambitious Ave Maria Law School opened in Ann Arbor in 2000. The brainchild of Catholic legal scholar and University of Detroit Mercy law professor Steve Safranek, the new law school was designed as a bastion of conservative Catholic legal studies, turning out morally upright lawyers who would infuse the body politic with their conservative Catholic values.

The triumphal start for the law school quickly melted down, however. When Monaghan tried to move Ave Maria College and

DETROIT TIGERS 1984: WHAT A START! WHAT A FINISH!

Ave Maria Law School to his planned new campus at Domino's Farms, the Ann Arbor Township Planning Commission refused to change the zoning. As a result, in 2003, Monaghan announced the founding of Ave Maria University in Naples, Florida, with rumors flying that the college and law school of the same name would soon relocate there. Though the Ave Maria Law School administration denied any plans to move, the announcement of the long-expected move came immediately after the law school received full accreditation in 2005.

Confusion, controversy, and contention followed the decision. Some faculty and staff members openly criticized the pending move; some of the dissenters were fired. Lawsuits followed, including one by founding faculty member Safranek, who was fired after being censured, suspended, and having his tenure revoked.

Many existing law school students transferred out, and the quality of incoming students deteriorated markedly. The school fell from a top-five ranking to the lowest tier in the prestigious *U.S. News & World Report* ratings of American law schools by 2008, remaining in the *U.S. News* basement in 2010, and joining the ranks of the unranked in 2012. In 2009 Ave Maria was the only law school to flunk the US Department of Education fiscal stability test.

While Ave Maria Law School garnered headlines, bereft St. Mary's College was absorbed by Madonna University of Livonia, Michigan, losing its independence along with half of its faculty as it became merely a branch campus. Ave Maria College closed in 2007 after buying out its handful of remaining students in Michigan.

Controversy ensued in Florida as well. Jesuit Father Joseph Fessio, a friend and a former student of Cardinal Joseph Ratzinger (later to become Pope Benedict XVI) was fired from his position as provost at Ave Maria University, then rehired without any administrative responsibilities the next day after an outpouring of support from hundreds of students and some faculty members. The only explanation ever given by the university for the sudden firing of the conservative priest—labeled "orthodoxy's ultimate champion" by a biographer of Ratzinger—was "irreconcilable difference over administrative policies and practices." Fessio continues to live at and support the university.

Probably the fairest and most insightful profile of Monaghan in recent years came in a very unlikely wrapper: the racy men's magazine *GQ*. The writer, a Catholic named James O'Brien, mused: "The boldness of its very existence pulls me in and pushes me away. I feel my own faith pale by comparison. I think about how I honor some of what it honors, but at the same time I am the thing from which it is running."

Monaghan's move to the Sun Belt was more than a change of venue from a crowded Rust Belt metropolis to wide-open space on the edge of Southwest Florida's Everglades. It was also an attempt to free himself and his grand visions from the constraints of what he viewed as unfriendly liberals in government and their stifling regulation. The contrast between the governmental cultures of Michigan and Florida is obvious, and uncounted thousands of other citizens and business owners have made that same choice.

The move also gave Monaghan complete control of his planned Catholic utopia—or so he thought. His 2006 comments about banning contraception and pornography from Ave Maria brought threats from the American Civil Liberties Union of a lawsuit if he tried to impose his personal morality on the town government.

While Monaghan backed away from his absolutist stance, subsequent remarks make it clear he expected and would try to ensure that Ave Maria residents and businesses will make the "right" choice. Misguided initiatives at Ave Maria University like a planned dress code (quickly rescinded) that would have mandated jackets and ties or suits for male employees and would have banned slacks for female employees during work hours reinforced the divide between Monaghan's acolytes and critics.

Monaghan's ambition for Ave Maria town and university are as lofty as the controversial 100-foot-tall oratory (based on his design sketches) that dominates the town and faces the campus. Though drastically scaled back from his original plans, Monaghan's oratory cost between $24 million and $40 million, part of the pizza baron's investment of more than $200 million of his own money. Unlike in Michigan, where he reportedly micromanaged his academic holdings through surrogates, Monaghan appointed himself chancellor of Ave Maria University despite his lack of any academic credentials. After several years holding classes in temporary quarters in Naples, the university moved to its gleaming new permanent campus adjacent to the eponymous town in 2007. The law school relocated to Naples that same year.

Unfortunately, the slumping real estate market and 2008 financial meltdown delayed the development substantially, and reports of slow home sales and other financial problems with the development have surfaced afterward.

In the penultimate paragraph of the *DBusiness* profile, the indefatigable entrepreneur spoke about his core values. "I realize what I'm doing is setting myself up for criticism. The most important thing to me is to get to heaven. I feel the most important thing I can do for my fellow man is [to help] him get there."

References

Publications

Anderson, Sparky, with Dan Ewald. *They Call Me Sparky*. Chelsea, Mich.: Sleeping Bear Press. 1998.

Anderson, William M. *The Detroit Tigers: A Pictorial Celebration of the Greatest Players and Moments in Tigers History. Updated Edition*. Detroit: Wayne State University Press. 1999.

Detroit Tigers. *Detroit Tigers Press/TV/Radio Guide*, 1984 edition. Detroit: Detroit Tigers. 1984.

Detroit Tigers. *Detroit Tigers Press, TV & Radio Guide, 1987 edition*. Detroit: Detroit Tigers. 1987.

Dupuy, R. Ernest, and Trevor N. Dupuy. *The Encyclopedia of Military History from 3500 B.C. to the Present*, rev. ed. New York: Harper & Row, Publishers. 1977.

Monaghan, Tom, with Robert Anderson. *Pizza Tiger*. New York: Random House. 1986.

Ewald, Dan. *On a Handshake: The Times and Triumphs of a Tiger Owner*. Champaign, Ill.: Sagamore Publishing. 1997.

Articles

"ACLU Opposes Creation of 'Catholic Town,'" *Catholic News Agency*, February 23, 2006.

Allen-Mills, Tony. "'Pizza Pope' Builds a Catholic Heaven." [London] *Sunday Times*, February 26, 2006.

Alson, Peter, and Julie Greenwalt. "Tom Monaghan." *People*, September 25, 1989.

Adamy, Janet. "Will a Twist on an Old Vow Deliver for Domino's Pizza?" *Wall Street Journal*, December 17, 2007.

"Around the Majors." *Washington Post*, February 22, 1991.

"Ave Maria/An Amazing Achievement." *Naples Daily News*, August 25, 2007.

Blake, Marsh. "Pie in the Sky: What Happened When a Billionaire Pizza Mogul Tried to Build an Elite Catholic Law School." *Washington Monthly*, September 1, 2009.

"Best Law Schools [2010]." *U.S. News & World Report*.

Bishop, Katy. "No Pants: Ave Maria University's New Employee Dress Code Requires Women to Wear Skirts, Dresses." *Naples Daily News*, March 9, 2010.

Bishop, Katy. "Whatever Happened To? Ave Maria Law School Move to Collier County." *Naples Daily News*, January 2, 2010.

Boyer, Peter. "The Deliverer: A Pizza Mogul Funds a Moral Crusade." *New Yorker*. February 19, 2007.

Brickey, Homer. "The Party's Over—Except for the Criticism." *Toledo Blade*, November 8, 1987.

Brown, Ben. "Some Pizza Party: Lobster, Caviar, Wine." *USA Today*, November 3, 1987.

Brzozowski, Carol. "Earning His Wings." *DBusiness*, May 2008.

Cox, Jennifer. "In the Beginning: Michigan Town Feels 'Duped' by College." *Naples Daily News*, August 20, 2007.

Dillon, Liam. "Ave Maria Graduates First Class at New Collier Campus." *Naples Daily News*, May 10, 2008.

Dillon, Liam. "Ave Maria Oratory: Baptism of a Church." *Naples Daily News*, March 30, 2008.

Dillon, Liam. "High-Profile Priest on Inside and Outside of Life at Ave Maria." *Naples Daily News*, April 12, 2008.

"Domino's Founder to Retire, Sell Stake." *Los Angeles Times*, September 26, 1998.

"Drummond Islanders Resist Conquest by Pizza King." *Chicago Tribune*, April 30, 1989.

Elliott, Marci. "Ave Maria Founder Tom Monaghan Is a Man of Faith, Plans and Action." *Naples Daily News*, April 13, 2003.

Goddard, Jacqui. "The City of God That Was Built on Pizza." *The* [London] *Times*, July 21, 2007.

Gordon, Deborah L. "Settlement of Safranek, Lyons & Pucillo vs. Thomas Monaghan, Ave Maria School of Law, Bernard Dobranski and Ave Maria Foundation." Press release, October 18, 2007.

Haire, John. "The Haire Net." *Cass City* (Michigan) *Chronicle*, November 11, 1987.

Wood, Kieron. "Keeping the Faith." Sunday Business Post on *The Post.IE* (Ireland), October 5, 2003.

Hansen, Susan. "Our Lady of Discord." *New York Times*, July 30, 2006.

Huber, Jeff, and Jerry Soucy. "Tom Monaghan's Pizza Pilgrimage." EpluribusMedia.org, March 11, 2006.

"Madonna University Takes Over St. Mary's College" *Orchard Lake Good News*, undated.

Marklein, Mary Beth. "Birth of Clean Town: Ave Maria." *USA Today*, July 23, 2007.

"Naples, Florida: The Market Difference." Scripps Southwest Florida Group, 2007.

O'Brien, James. "Hail Mary, U.S.A." *GQ*, June 2007.

"Profile of Tom Monaghan, Archconservative." *Progressive Christian Guide to Public Policy* blog, October 15, 2007.

Prud'homme, Alex. "Taking the Gospel to the Rich." *New York Times*, February 14, 1999.

Rigg, Sarah A. "From Pizza to Philanthropy: A Conversation with Tom Monaghan at Domino's Farms" *Ann Arbor Business Review*, December 11, 2008.

Riley, Naomi Schaefer. "Domino's Illuminatio Mea/ Tom Monaghan Goes from Pizza Delivery to Educational Deliverance." *Wall Street Journal*, August 19, 2006.

Shapiro, Bill, and Vince Bielski. "Domino's Pizza." *Mother Jones*, March-April 1994.

Sloane, Julie. "Tom Monaghan/Domino's Pizza." *Fortune Small Business*, September 1, 2003.

St. John, Paige, "Pizza King's 'Yes' to Michigan Isle." *Chicago Tribune*, June 18, 1989.

Taylor, Bill. "On a Mission from God." *Toronto Star*, March 2, 2006.

"Top Ave Maria Official Dismissed." *Naples Daily News*, March 21, 2007.

Turley, Jonathan. "Ave Maria Law School Invokes Status as Religious Institution and 'Ecclesiastical Abstention' to Dismiss Law Professors' Lawsuit." *Res Ipsa Loquitur* blog, July 5, 2009.

Vlasic, Bill. "Monaghan Finds Drummond Buyer." *Detroit News*, April 5, 1992.

Vlasic, Bill. "New Domino's Lodge Owners Plan Few Changes." *Detroit News*, April 7, 1992.

Williams, Roger. "The Great Tom Monaghan." *Florida Weekly*, April 19, 2007.

Interviews

Lou Beer, Esq.

Tom Linn, Esq.

Dave Mesry

Dr. Ted Radzilowski

Rocque Lipford, Esq.

Web Sites

Amazon.com

AODonline.org [Archdiocese of Detroit]

AveHerald.com

AveMaria.com

AveMaria.edu

AveMariaDistrict.com

AveMariaLaw.edu

AveWatch.org

BarnesandNoble.com

BarronCollier.com

BibleGateway.com

Buildings.com

CollierGov.net

DeborahGordonLaw.com

DioceseofVenice.org

DominosBiz.com

DrummondIsland.com

Encyclopedia.Jrank.org

FreeRepublic.com

FundingUniverse.com

Latin-Dictionary.org

Legatus.org

Madonna.edu

Mapquest.com

NNDB.com

Pulte.com

Snopes.com

YPO.org [Young Presidents' Organization]

E-mail Communications

Steve Weingarden, Ph.D., organizational psychologist.

Bill Lajoie
by Richard L. Shook

A LOT OF PEOPLE had a hand in making the Detroit Tigers the World Series champions in 1984, but by far the biggest hand belonged to Bill Lajoie, extraordinary scout and general manager.

Lajoie always found the best part of his job to be finding talent. He considered himself a scout at heart, first and foremost. It's one of the reasons he quit being the Tigers' general manager in 1991 and one of the reasons he remained in baseball even as he aged into his 70s in the first decade of the 21st century.

Lajoie directed the drafts that landed the Tigers the bulk of their homegrown teams of the 1980s and his free-agent and trade acquisitions kept the franchise viable for several seasons after he left.

Mainstays of the '84 team were Jack Morris, Alan Trammell, Lou Whitaker, Lance Parrish, Dan Petry, Kirk Gibson, Tom Brookens, and Howard Johnson, all of whom were drafted either by Lajoie or under his direction. Morris, Trammell, Petry, and Steve Kemp were all taken in Lajoie's 1976 draft (Kemp in January, the others in June), still regarded as one of the best in baseball history.

Way down on that list was a shortstop named Ozzie Smith, whom the Tigers did not sign. His earlier draft choices included Mark "The Bird" Fidrych and Jason Thompson.

Lajoie stole Gibson from the National Football League, which would have certainly made him a first-round draft choice had Detroit not signed him in 1978 following his junior year at Michigan State; and his coup of getting left-handed reliever Willie Hernandez and first baseman Dave Bergman from Philadelphia for outfielder Glenn Wilson and utility man John Wockenfuss on March 24, 1984, was the deal that catapulted the Tigers to the top of the baseball world that year.

Lajoie was a master at finding pieces of the puzzle that were missing. Time and again he brought in key players or role performers who could do things to help the Tigers.

"I'm not interested in what they can't do," he would often say. "I'm interested in what they can do."

It's a philosophy that works well for getting those one or two final pieces to the championship puzzle.

You have to give up to get, though, and sometimes what you give up turns out to be something very good indeed.

Lajoie got roasted a lot for trading an obscure right-handed minor-league pitcher to Atlanta to get crafty veteran right-hander Doyle Alexander, a move designed to get Detroit to the 1987 postseason. The obscure right-hander Lajoie traded on August 12 wasn't obscure very long, though, and John Smoltz went on to be a very good pitcher for the Braves for a very long time.

There was no carping about the move while the crafty Alexander was going 9-0 down the stretch with a 1.53 ERA in 88$^{1/3}$ innings to help Detroit sneak past Toronto for the American League East title. The shine came off that feat, though, when Minnesota roughed Alexander up twice in the playoffs, knocking out a heavily favored Detroit team. Alexander started out decently in 1988 but had an up-and-down 14-11 season and sputtered through 1989, going 6-18 in the Tigers' horrible 53-109 season. Lajoie didn't care; his objective was getting Detroit into the playoffs, and that objective was met.

Although he wasn't named general manager until after the 1983 season, Lajoie said he "had been making the trades and such for a couple of years."

His first move as the announced general manager was the signing of free agent corner infielder Darrell Evans on December 17, 1983. It was the Tigers' first significant free-agent acquisition, designed to fill a hole—a power void at first base.

It was also a signal that Detroit, previously not a significant player in the free-agent market, was now serious about obtaining players who might put them into the playoffs.

Later in his tenure, Lajoie signed free agents like infielder Bill Madlock, who also played an important role in getting Detroit the American League East championship in 1987. After the disastrous 1989 season, he signed utility man Tony Phillips, center fielder Lloyd Moseby, and first baseman Cecil Fielder to bring the Tigers back to respectability. Among his trade acquisitions were right-hander Walt Terrell before the 1985 season, left-hander Frank Tanana in June 1985, and catcher-infielder Mike Heath in August 1986.

The deal that made the difference in 1984 was the late spring-training swap that brought Hernandez and Bergman over from Philadelphia, a trade that had its seeds during the 1983 postseason when manager Sparky Anderson, doing radio commentary, eyeballed the left-handed workhorse reliever pitching the Phillies into the World Series.

"You get that guy," Anderson told Lajoie after the Series, and we'll win it next year."

Lajoie succeeded Jim Campbell as general manager in 1983. Up to then Campbell had worn both the president's and GM's hats. "I only took the job because of Mr. Fetzer [John E., then owner of the franchise]," Lajoie said. "Jim didn't want to give up anything but Mr. Fetzer sold him on making the change."

Fetzer was looking down the road because he had been looking for a buyer for the Tigers before he died and wanted to hand over a stable organization. He wound up selling the franchise to Domino's Pizza magnate Tom Monaghan in time for the 1984 season.

But the farm system began drying up, and Lajoie was forced to patch and fill on the open market. The loss via free agency of Lance Parrish after 1986, Gibson (in the "second look" collusion case) after 1987, and Morris after 1990 also hurt. Gibson became the National League's Most Valuable Player in 1988, led the Dodgers to the World Series, and hit one of the most dramatic World Series home runs of all time. Morris won 18 games to lead the Twins into the Series in 1991, and left them after the season to win 21 for the Blue Jays and help them to their first World Series title.

"After we won we had a couple of pretty good years, but then it started going downhill," Lajoie said. "I stayed in the job. I wasn't crazy about it to start with. I felt my strength was

DETROIT TIGERS 1984: WHAT A START! WHAT A FINISH!

in scouting and the farm department."

Monaghan had brought in retired University of Michigan football coach Bo Schembechler to be president of the team and bring some football-style organization to a franchise that had slipped behind the times.

Campbell frequently sat in on Lajoie's conversations with other general managers, scouts, and agents, which wasn't a major hassle but was a little off-center.

When veteran baseball man Joe McDonald was brought in to run the farm system, Lajoie quietly asked to switch jobs.

"I didn't spend 15 years training you to be a general manager just to give you your old job back," Campbell told Lajoie.

On top of that, Monaghan was running into money problems himself. He had a fortune tied up in property, but didn't have a quarter to buy a cup of coffee. That spilled over onto the baseball side and he too began looking for someone to take the baseball team off his hands.

He wasn't overjoyed about that person being a pizza business rival, but since Mike Ilitch (Little Caesars) was the only one stepping up to the plate, Monaghan eventually sold the club to him in August 1993.

Before then, though, Lajoie decided the job just wasn't fun anymore.

"My children were out of college. My wife had died. I couldn't see taking that any more. I didn't need anything."

Schembechler offered to double his salary, but it never transpired. At the same time the clumsy firing of legendary Hall of Fame broadcaster Ernie Harwell in late 1990—to take place after the 1991 season—was burning up newspapers and airwaves.

"I stayed until January [of 1991] but I had handed in my resignation in October. I engineered the Mickey Tettleton trade [that January 11 for right-handed pitcher Jeff Robinson] before I left."

When Ilitch brought the club, he fired Campbell and Schembechler the day the deal was completed, and went looking for the best baseball guy he could find to reinvigorate the franchise. That guy was Bill Lajoie.

"I almost came back," Lajoie said. "I agreed to terms with Mike. They always kept an apartment so I had them send the rental agreement over and I signed it."

Ilitch, though, was tired of holding press conferences and got Lajoie to agree to return in a couple of weeks for the announcement. Lajoie said he would handle everything by himself but agreed to fly home to Florida and return later.

"I got on the flight but it stopped in Memphis," Lajoie said. "I got off the plane to stretch my legs and asked myself, 'What the heck are you doing? You're stepping right back in the crap you just left.' So I called the next day and told them I didn't want the job. I told them, 'You've got Jerry Walker and Jerry will do a good job.' I just didn't want to do it anymore."

Lajoie's retirement capped a streak of 35 years connected in some way with professional baseball. His affinity for spotting talent kept him in pro ball after he had failed to make the majors as a player.

"I was a 165-pound center fielder that didn't have power," he said. "And there were only 16 teams then."

Lajoie played on perhaps the best and certainly the most successful Western Michigan University baseball team ever, the 1955 squad that lost in the NCAA championship game, 7-6, to Wake Forest.

The Broncos were 22-5 with a 9-0 record in the Mid-American Conference. They took their battle in the final game down to the eighth inning before it was decided. Lajoie had two hits, including a double, and scored two runs in the championship game.

Those days were before the draft, so Lajoie took his bachelor's degree and All-America playing status and signed with the Baltimore Orioles.

"I was on a major-league contract five times," Lajoie said. "In fact, when I signed, I signed a major-league contract; that was 1955. I wanted to get my options out of the way so they just couldn't keep sending me down. Later on it became a popular thing with players. I just came up with that myself; that's what I wanted. [Orioles GM and manager] Paul Richards made the deal. He was not averse to creative thinking."

On March 15, 1960, he was traded with slick-fielding but light-hitting shortstop Willy Miranda by Baltimore to the Los Angeles Dodgers to complete a deal in which the Orioles obtained slugging first baseman Jim Gentile.

"I broke my leg playing in Omaha, a Dodgers farm club," he said. "I broke my leg jumping into the fence. I was hitting .320 or better, having a really good season. It happened in August and during the winter Kansas City traded for me. [Lajoie was traded to the Athletics on October 11, 1961, with Gordie Windhorn for Jay Ward, Bobby Prescott, and Stan Johnson].

"But not having therapy and the stuff they do today, I still didn't run very well."

He had ankle complications, and "then it became a survival thing. It was a case of hit as much as you can so you can have a job next year.

"It just went downhill from there. It became more of a job. I had a family. I tore a triceps in the spring but I was able to survive that. Finally I just started teaching school [at Detroit Northern High School]. The guy I was working with was a part-time scout for the Cincinnati Reds. He was the baseball coach, too. I started going to ballgames; started watching players for him. This was 1964, I believe." Lajoie's minor-league career had ended in 1964. He gave me 10 bucks for gas after I had watched 30 days of baseball. I said, 'You pot-licker. I drive around for a month and all you give me is 10 dollars for gas?' So I took the reports and sent them to Cincinnati myself. I knew the scouting director [Herk Robinson] because he had signed me when I was with Baltimore. He gave me the [part-time] job the next year.

"In 1965 I was able to get the first pick in the draft [16th overall] and sign the guy—Bernie Carbo, he was Rookie of the Year in some publications. So I was on my way. They gave me hell because they took [Johnny] Bench and Hal McRae after Carbo, but I said, 'Hey, you got all three, so quit complaining.'"

Lajoie switched to the Detroit organization after the Tigers' 1968 world championship season, managing the system's

DETROIT TIGERS 1984: WHAT A START! WHAT A FINISH!

Bristol (Virginia) Tigers in the Rookie-level Appalachian League in 1969 before returning to the talent-search side of the business in 1970.

The native of Wyandotte, Michigan, was named scouting director in 1974 and the following season was elevated to director of player procurement, a title he held until he ascended to vice president and assistant general manager to Jim Campbell in 1979.

Even though Lajoie had professed to have had enough when he quit the Tigers, he worked as first a scout and later special assistant to Atlanta general manager John Schuerholz through the 2000 season. In 2001 and 2002 he was senior adviser of baseball operations for the Milwaukee Brewers.

Lajoie worked for the Boston Red Sox as special adviser to the general manager in scouting from 2002 to 2005, which included the team's World Series championship in 2004. In 2006 he switched to the Los Angeles Dodgers as senior adviser to general manager Ned Colletti. His duties included professional scouting, consulting on trades, player acquisitions, and roster moves. He joined the Pittsburgh Pirates in 2009 as a senior adviser to the general manager.

Lajoie died of cancer December 28, 2010, at his home in Osprey, Florida. He was survived by and his second wife, Mary.

References

Publications

Macmillan Baseball Encyclopedia. New York: Simon & Schuster. 1996.

Other Sources

Shook, Richard L. Telephone interview with Bill Lajoie, July 3, 2008.

Lajoie trade box (deals during his time as GM of the Tigers):

DATE	TEAM	POS	ACQUIRED	POS	LOST
12/17/83	SF	1B	Darrell Evans (Free Agent)		
3/24/84	PHI	LHP	Willie Hernandez	RF	Glenn Wilson
		1B	Dave Bergman	C-1B	John Wockenfuss
4/10/84	SD	CF	Ruppert Jones (Free Agent)		
12/7/84	NYM	RHP	Walt Terrell	3B	Howard Johnson
1/30/85	CAL			CF	Ruppert Jones (Free Agent)
6/20/85	TEX	LHP	Frank Tanana	RHP	Duane James
10/7/85	SF	LHP	Dave LaPoint	RHP	Juan Berenguer
		RHP	Eric King	C	Bob Melvin
		C	Matt Nokes	RHP	Scott Medvin
11/13/85	OAK	LF	Dave Collins	1B	Barbaro Garbey
12/12/85	SEA	3B	Darnell Coles	RHP	Rich Monteleone
7/9/86	SD	LHP	Mark Thurmond	LHP	Dave LaPoint
8/10/86	STL	C	Mike Heath	RHP	Ken Hill
				1B	Mike Laga
8/10/86	Release			1B	Dave Engle
3/13/87	PHI			C	Lance Parrish (Free Agent)
6/4/87	LAD	3B	Bill Madlock (Free Agent)		
8/12/87	ATL	RHP	Doyle Alexander	RHP	John Smoltz
12/5/87	CAL	CF	Gary Pettis	RHP	Dan Petry
12/7/87	LAD	RHP	John Wetteland (Rule 5 Draft)		
2/27/88	BAL	3B	Ray Knight	LHP	Mark Thurmond
3/29/88	LAD			RHP	John Wetteland (Rule 5 Draft Return)
8/31/88	BAL	CF	Fred Lynn	C	Chris Hoiles
		RHP	Cesar Mejia		
		RHP	Robinson Garces		
10/28/88	SD	1B	Keith Moreland	RHP	Walt Terrell
		3B	Chris Brown		
3/23/89	CWS	RF	Kenny Williams	RHP	Eric King
3/23/89	SD	UT	Mike Brumley	UT	Luis Salazar
12/5/89	OAK	UT	Tony Phillips (Free Agent)		
12/7/89	TOR	CF	Lloyd Moseby (Free Agent)		
1/15/90	Japan	1B	Cecil Fielder (Free Agent)		
6/4/90	NYY	RHP	Lance McCullers	C	Matt Nokes
		RHP	Clay Parker		

Sparky Anderson
by Cindy Thomson

GEORGE LEE "Sparky" Anderson is one of the great baseball men of all time in terms of success, integrity, and personality. He led the Cincinnati Reds to back-to-back championships in 1975 and 1976, and the Detroit Tigers to a World Series title in 1984, becoming the first manager to win the World Series in both leagues. Four times in his career, teams he managed won more than 100 games, and in six other seasons his teams won at least 90 games. In his 26 years managing in the majors Anderson amassed 2,194 victories, five pennants, and three World Series championships.

Born in Bridgewater, South Dakota, on February 22, 1934, to LeRoy and Shirley Anderson, George relocated with his family in 1942 to Southern California, where his father and grandparents found wartime work in the shipyards. LeRoy played some semipro baseball and passed his love of the game on his son. Young George became a batboy for the University of Southern California's Trojans baseball team, coached by Raoul "Rod" Dedeaux, an early influence in Anderson's baseball life.

During his childhood Anderson played a lot of sandlot ball. In 1951 his American Legion team won a national championship at Briggs Stadium in Detroit (later renamed Tiger Stadium), the place where Anderson later managed the Tigers. His Dorsey High School team won 42 consecutive games, and Anderson was named an all-city player in his junior and senior years. Despite passing up a school closer to home and having to take two buses to get to Dorsey, Anderson chose it for its baseball program.

While still in high school, Anderson worked a summer job loading lumber on boxcars. In the evenings he played with a semipro team. He graduated from Dorsey High in 1953 and Dedeaux offered him a partial baseball scholarship to USC. Anderson never went to college, though, because a Brooklyn Dodgers scout he had met years earlier on the sandlots, Lefty Phillips, offered him $250 a month to play for the Dodgers' Santa Barbara team in the Class C California League. Anderson's parents knew and trusted Lefty, who by the time Anderson graduated from high school had moved up from sandlot scouting to scouting for the Dodgers. Anderson called Lefty "the sharpest baseball man I ever met."

Phillips knew Anderson's limitations and told him that to make it in baseball he would have to work very hard. Anderson was only 5-feet-9 and weighed just 170 pounds, but his determination and will to win gave him an edge. Anderson's boyhood friend Billy Consolo signed his first major-league contract that same year, with the Boston Red Sox. Consolo was one of baseball's bonus babies, with the rule at the time requiring the team providing the bonus to keep him on its major-league roster for two seasons. Anderson's signing gave him a steady income, even if it wasn't as a bonus baby, and he bought an engagement ring for his childhood sweetheart, Carol Valle. The two had known each other since the fifth grade and began dating in high school. They married in October 1953, at the end of Anderson's first minor-league season as shortstop for the Santa Barbara Dodgers. He played in 141 games and hit for a .263 average.

The playing manager at Santa Barbara was George Scherger, a man Anderson would later invite to coach for him in Cincinnati. Anderson described Scherger as a man who wanted to win badly. Whenever the team lost, there would be extra practice the next day. This drive influenced Anderson, who adopted it when he became a manager himself.

Anderson moved around in the Brooklyn minor-league system, playing in Pueblo, Colorado, Fort Worth, Los Angeles in the Pacific Coast League, and Montreal in the International League. In Pueblo he hit .296 in 1954. In 1955 he moved up to Double A with the Texas League's Fort Worth Cats. Tommy Holmes was the manager. (The team produced several future big-league managers. Anderson; Dick Williams, who was Anderson's opposing manager in the 1972 and 1984 World Series, managed in the majors for 21 seasons, and joined Anderson in the Hall of Fame in 2008; Danny Ozark, who managed the Philadelphia Phillies and San Francisco Giants; Norm Sherry, who managed the California Angels and coached on several major-league teams; and Maury Wills, who managed two years in Seattle.)

Anderson received his nickname in Fort Worth. A radio announcer dubbed him Sparky because of his feistiness. It was a trait that sometimes got him into trouble. He wanted to win so badly that he could not tolerate anything that got in the way.

In 1958 the Dodgers put Anderson on their 40-man roster. He later remembered, "I had no right to think I could break in with a club that had [Gil] Hodges, [Charlie] Neal, Don Zimmer, Junior Gilliam, Dick Gray, [Carl] Furillo, Duke Snider, Gino Cimoli, Norm Larker, and Johnny Roseboro— and with a pitching staff built around Sandy Koufax, Don Drysdale, and Johnny Podres. I simply didn't belong in that kind of company." Sparky was sent back down to Montreal. Dodgers Manager Walter Alston broke the news of his demotion to him at a time when most managers left this duty to the traveling secretary. This impressed Sparky, who as a manager followed that example. He was told that the Philadelphia Phillies had expressed an interest in him, and since they had an International League farm team in Miami, they would be able to get a look at him.

Sparky played reasonably well in Montreal, batting .269 and stealing 21 bases for the Royals. He even hit two home runs. ("That's what's so good about not hitting many. You remember them all," he said.) He was named the club's most valuable player and finished second in the running for the league MVP. He did indeed catch the eye of the Phillies, who traded for him and made him their starting second baseman.

Sparky's first day in the big leagues came on Opening Day of 1959 against Cincinnati at Philadelphia's Connie Mack Stadium. In the eighth inning, he singled home what became the winning run in a 2-1 game. He received his first media barrage afterward. In his autobiography *The Main Spark*, he

DETROIT TIGERS 1984: WHAT A START! WHAT A FINISH!

wrote that there was no more media attention for him until August that year. He played in 152 games, but batted only .218 and drove in only 34 runs. It was to be the only year he played in the big leagues.

That year he noticed a difference in the routine compared with the Dodgers' big-league spring camp. The Dodgers operated on a set schedule, discipline that Sparky would come to value. In Philadelphia no one kept track of when players rolled in for practice, and often there would be no coaches around, according to Sparky's account. The Phillies that year were a last-place team, as they had been the year before. Sparky said he would never forget the thunderous boos the hometown crowd greeted the Phillies with as they took the field on Opening Day. There was definitely not an attitude of winning in Philadelphia, and Sparky had been raised in an organization with the opposite outlook.

Sparky later said, "I realized you can't be in a game as a professional unless winning and losing are everything, your whole life."

During 1960's spring training, when he didn't make it into many games, Sparky knew he would not stay with the team. He had hoped he would be traded to another major-league team, but instead was sold to Toronto. With one child and another on the way, Sparky was about to quit. Toronto's owner, Jack Kent Cooke, offered him $10,000 to play, $2,000 more than he had made in Philadelphia. Because he had bills to pay, he accepted. Cooke told him he planned to sell him to a major-league club, but Sparky did not believe it would happen. He called the 1960 season a turning point in his career. He decided to start observing baseball strategies with the idea of one day becoming a manager. After four more years in the minors, all with the Maple Leafs, he landed his first managerial job, in Toronto in 1964. He uttered what would be the beginning of many boasts that he would later regret by saying, "If I can't win with this club, I ought to be fired."

Anderson's temper made him a prophet. He was fired at the end of the season and soon realized that jobs for managers who could not control their emotions during the games were few. By his own admission, he was lucky to get his next job, with the St. Louis Cardinals' farm club in Rock Hill, South Carolina, in 1965 because the Cardinals were desperate to find a manager just before spring training. Bob Howsam was the Cardinals' general manager; the association proved to be advantageous a few years later. In 1968, when Howsam was the GM of the Cincinnati Reds, Sparky was hired to manage the Reds' minor-league club in Asheville, North Carolina.

Anderson could not make ends meet during his minor-league managing career, so he took various odd jobs, including a factory job, a stocking job at Sears, and some offseason gigs selling used cars.

Then, after five years as a minor-league manager, Anderson landed a major-league coaching job with the San Diego Padres in 1969. At the end of the season he resigned to accept a job coaching with the California Angels under his old mentor Lefty Phillips. But he never took that job.

While the ink was still drying on Anderson's contact with the Angels, California general manager Dick Walsh received a phone call from Bob Howsam, the Reds' GM, requesting permission to speak with Sparky about managing in Cincinnati. It was Walsh who broke the news to Sparky.

Sparky's hiring prompted Cincinnati newspapers to declare: "Sparky Who?" He was only 35 years old and unknown to the public.

One of Anderson's first moves as Reds manager was to make Pete Rose the team's captain. Because Willie Mays was so well received in San Francisco as the Giants' captain, Anderson thought Rose could serve the same role in Cincinnati. Rose was very popular, a hometown boy, and the top player on the team. With Rose delivering the lineup to the umpire before the game, perhaps people would not focus on "Sparky Who?"

Anderson inherited a talented team and remarked to his coach, George Scherger, that it would win the division by 10 games. These types of statements were often seen as exaggerations, and Sparky himself admitted that he was overconfident, but the fact remained that the 1970 Reds were an excellent team. Catcher Johnny Bench was on the verge of a breakout career season. Tommy Helms, Lee May, Tony Perez, Bernie Carbo, and Bobby Tolan joined Rose on that team. The Reds had finished in third place in 1969, winning 89 games, and they were primed to be winners. The 1970 team brought in rookie shortstop Dave Concepcion and pitchers Don Gullett and Pedro Borbon. In July of that year the team moved from aging Crosley Field into the new Riverfront Stadium and began to play on artificial turf.

Sparky Anderson accomplished his share of firsts as a big-league manager: first to win 100 games in a season for teams in each major league, first to win a World Series in each league, first to win 800 games for teams in both league. But the secret to accomplishing such feats, Anderson once averred, "you've got to be fired by the other league." (National Baseball Hall of Fame Library, Cooperstown, New York)

DETROIT TIGERS 1984: WHAT A START! WHAT A FINISH!

The Reds won 102 games in Anderson's major-league managerial debut season, a record that gave them the National League West Division championship over the Los Angeles Dodgers by 14½ games. The Reds swept the Pittsburgh Pirates in the best-of-five National League Championship Series to take the pennant and meet the Baltimore Orioles in the World Series. The Reds fell to the Orioles in five games, but it was a stunning first year for Anderson.

Anderson brought his work ethic with him to Cincinnati, and some players called his spring training a "slave camp." GM Howsam insisted on a clean-cut look for the team: no facial hair, no long hair, and suit jackets for traveling, which Anderson supported and enforced. He believed that mannerisms and dress carried over into a kind of self-discipline that helped his players work together as a team.

But probably more central to Sparky's success as a manager was the way he cared about his players. He allowed them to question him, and even encouraged it. He said, "I know there are managers who would never allow themselves to be put on this level with their own ballplayers, but as far as I'm concerned, it's a form of communication."

The following season was not a good one; the Reds finished below .500 and in fifth place. The following offseason brought the "Big Deal." The Reds traded Lee May, Tommy Helms, and utility man Jimmy Stewart to the Houston Astros for Joe Morgan, Denis Menke, Jack Billingham, Cesar Geronimo, and Ed Armbrister. Cincinnati made the trade to gain speed at first and third base, essential for playing on Astroturf.

Besides being known as Sparky, Anderson was called Captain Hook because he never hesitated to pull a pitcher out of the game. The Big Red Machine was not blessed with superior starting pitching, and in an age when complete games were still common, Anderson's tendency to replace pitchers during a game drew notice. He said, however, that he could always sense when a pitcher was just about to lose his effectiveness. His players realized that while he cared for players as individuals, he would not cater to one man. Second baseman Joe Morgan said, "In his passion for winning, he will not ever put the feelings of any individual above the team."

The Reds returned as pennant winners in 1972 and faced the Pirates again. This time the NLCS went five games with the Reds coming out on top. The finish was so exciting that before the World Series against the Oakland A's, Anderson made a statement he later regretted. He told the press that the two best teams in baseball had already played a series (Cincinnati and Pittsburgh) and that the World Series would be anticlimactic. Although he said what he really thought, the statement fired up the Oakland team. After the Reds lost the first two games, Anderson realized how much he had underestimated his opponents. The Reds lost to Oakland in seven games, but the Big Red Machine was building momentum.

In 1973 the Reds again won their division, but lost to the New York Mets in the League Championship Series, three games to two. In 1974, the Reds finished second behind the Los Angeles Dodgers, despite winning 98 games.

The Reds teams of 1975 and '76 secured the label of dynasty and have been considered two of the best of all time. In 1975 they took first place early in June and never relinquished it. Pitcher Don Gullett was on his way to a remarkable season when he fractured his thumb. Without their star pitcher, the rest of the staff had to pick up the slack. Because the Reds' bullpen was strong, the Captain Hook strategy was key. And with hitters like Morgan, Rose, George Foster, and Ken Griffey Sr. batting over .300 and Bench and Perez driving in more than 100 runs, the Big Red Machine usually outscored their opponents anyway. The Reds finished the season 20 games ahead of the second-place Dodgers with 108 wins, and swept Pittsburgh in the NLCS.

The 1975 World Series has gone down as one of the greatest ever. As the Series opened, Sparky began feeling the pressure. He was more cautious this time about feeling overconfident. The Boston Red Sox were the American League champs after sweeping the Oakland A's in the ALCS. The opening game was an eye-opener for the Big Red Machine when they faced the pitching mastery of Luis Tiant and lost 6-0. After winning the next game in a tight match, the Reds won Game Three in extra innings. Tiant pitched the Red Sox to another victory in Game Four, but the Reds came back to win Game Five. When the Series returned to Boston, rain delayed play for 72 hours. Game Six, however, proved to be worth waiting for—the game that many, including Sparky himself, say was the single best game in World Series history.

Captain Hook pulled pitcher Gary Nolan after two innings, trailing 3-0. The Reds got to Tiant this time and evened the score in the fifth. By the eighth inning, leading 6-3, the Reds were thinking the championship was in the bag. After Pedro Borbon put two runners on, he got the hook and was replaced by Rawly Eastwick, who got two batters out. Then Bernie Carbo, a former Red, came in to pinch-hit. Carbo had already had a pinch homer in the Series, and Sparky didn't figure he had another in him. But on a 2-2 count, Carbo drove the ball over the center-field wall to tie the game. After the Reds were retired in order in the ninth, the Red Sox loaded the bases with nobody out—but were unable to score. In the 10th inning, Red Sox outfielder Dwight Evans made a spectacular catch on a line drive by Morgan, robbing him of a possible home run and then doubling up Griffey off first base. The Reds threatened in the 12th, but didn't score. In the bottom of the 12th, Pat Darcy, the Reds' eighth pitcher in the game, came in to face catcher Carlton Fisk, who hit a high fly ball to deep left field. As Fisk ran to first base, he—and everyone else in the park—wondered if the ball would stay fair. Fisk jumped up and down waving his arms toward fair territory in what has become an iconic image. It was a homer, barely, hitting the foul pole. The Red Sox won, sending the Series to a deciding Game Seven. Sparky later said, "How can a manager of a losing team call it the greatest game ever played? Well, winning or losing, a man can't lie to himself."

Game Seven was a come-from-behind affair with the Reds finally coming out on top, 4-3, and winning their first world championship under Anderson. Sparky was unprepared for

DETROIT TIGERS 1984: WHAT A START! WHAT A FINISH!

the media blitz that continued to follow him into the next season and the expectation of winning another championship, but he soon learned to make the media his friend and to encourage his players to do so also. Pete Rose said, "He didn't make an enemy out of the press. He used it. And he taught us how to use it." Later, Lance Parrish echoed this sentiment in Detroit: "Sparky let us know it wasn't fair to treat the media any differently that we would treat anyone else. They had a job to do."

Pete Rose and Joe Morgan led the league in several offensive categories in 1976, and while the Reds had no big winning pitchers, they did have seven pitchers who won at least 11 games each. After their 102-win regular season, the Reds did not lose a postseason game, sweeping the Philadelphia Phillies and then the New York Yankees in the World Series.

During that World Series, a reporter asked Anderson to compare his catcher to Yankees backstop Thurman Munson. Sparky said, "Don't ever embarrass nobody by comparing him to Johnny Bench." Sparky meant it as a general statement. When he returned home to California, he wrote Munson a letter of apology.

In 1977 the Reds finished second behind the Dodgers, and although 1978 was a better year, they finished second again. The Big Red Machine was being dismantled. Bob Howsam retired after the season. Winning was expected in Cincinnati, and Anderson was fired late that year. He was upset about how it happened. The Reds had just finished a tour in Japan, and management did not want to fire Sparky before that had been completed. But it was late, and most major-league clubs had already chosen their managers for the coming season. The firing was unpopular with the fans in Cincinnati and with the players. Joe Morgan said, "Sparky's firing was wrong and to this day, I don't understand it." It was a blow that Sparky didn't see coming.

Anderson was about to sign a long-term contract to manage the Chicago Cubs in 1979 when Detroit Tigers general manager Jim Campbell got wind of the deal. He contacted Sparky, who realized that the team was filled with young players. He had enjoyed mentoring young players in his minor-league days.

At the press conference announcing his hiring, Anderson made another of his infamous predictions, saying the team would win a world championship in five years.

With talent like Alan Trammell, Lou Whitaker, Kirk Gibson, Lance Parrish, Jack Morris, and Dan Petry, Sparky was confident. He also realized that discipline and conduct as a professional would have to be taught. Kirk Gibson later said, "He wanted me to learn the game of baseball and learn how to treat people right. It took four to five years to get through to me."

As he did in Cincinnati, Anderson kept an open-door policy. Players were encouraged to speak their minds, but Sparky had the final say. He called the team "rougher than a three-day beard." He started with fundamentals, drilling the players until their skills became routine. He insisted on coats and ties for traveling, saying, "If you carry yourself proudly, you look like a pro."

In 1981 the Tigers surprised the American League by making an East Division pennant run during the second half of the strike-split season. In 1983 the team began to show its potential by winning 92 games. The next season was magical.

The 1984 Tigers led their division wire to wire, starting off by winning nine straight games, and then going an unbelievable 35-5 to leave their opponents in the dust in what became a 104-win season. What Sparky had in Detroit, which he had never had in Cincinnati, was two superior starting pitchers to lead his rotation, Jack Morris, who pitched a no-hitter in April, and Dan Petry. Reliever Guillermo Hernandez, acquired in a trade in March, was an All-Star while winning the American League Cy Young and Most Valuable Player Awards.

But pitching was not the team's only strength. Trammell led the team in batting with a .314 average. Parrish was an All-Star that year, won the second of three straight Gold Gloves, and hit 33 home runs.

When the team clinched the division championship, Anderson felt vindicated. He remembered thinking, "No one will ever question me again." No matter what happened in the postseason, the best team, he said, was the one that had won 104 games in the regular season and wore a big "D" on its uniforms.

The Tigers swept the Kansas City Royals in the AL Championship Series. Sparky took a team to the World Series for the fifth time in his career, this time against a National League club, the San Diego Padres. The first game was close, with Detroit winning, 3-2. After the game, Lou Whitaker complimented his manager: "When Sparky came to us from Cincinnati, he brought us back to fundamentals. We had a lot to learn and it's paying off." The Tigers lost Game Two, but that was the only game they would lose, and they became world champions before the hometown crowd.

After the Series, Sparky's wife wanted him to quit. He thought about it. It had been a tough year. He was proud of the team and happy for the city of Detroit, but for five years he had struggled with trying to prove Cincinnati wrong for firing him, and with the success of Detroit that year, the pressure he put on himself became almost unbearable. He had to get back to the business of baseball and to enjoying the game again. He couldn't do that if he quit.

There would be no back-to-back championships for Anderson in Detroit. In 1985 and again in 1986 the team finished third. The 1987 Tigers were not expected to do much better and early in May were in last place. Anderson chose that time to make another prediction, saying his team would be in the race by the end of the season. The Tigers started putting together some win streaks. Before a season-ending series in Detroit against the Toronto Blue Jays, the Tigers were one game behind Toronto. Detroit finished with a flourish, winning three straight one-run games to clinch the AL East title, although the Tigers lost to Minnesota in five games in a best-of-seven ALCS.

DETROIT TIGERS 1984: WHAT A START! WHAT A FINISH!

The team that year had no outstanding talent save for Alan Trammell, who finished second in the voting for Most Valuable Player. Anderson said, "We had no business running with the big boys. It was pure determination." Pitcher Jack Morris said, "In 1984, we probably had the best club I ever played on in Detroit. In '87 we were less talented but typical overachievers. We didn't realize we weren't that good."

Sparky's efforts with the team that year won him the American League Manager of the Year award. He said, "When I look back on that year, I still feel a high. The guys on that team can be proud of themselves for the rest of their lives."

In 1988 the team finished second behind the Red Sox, but 1989 saw the Tigers lose 103 games. For a man who wanted to win more than anything else, it was a horrible year. Anderson was also experiencing personal problems as his daughter was undergoing a painful divorce in California and he felt guilty about his own absence from the family.

Anderson, who believed that because baseball had blessed him he had a responsibility to give back to the community, was always participating in charity events. In May of that year he attended an event at Children's Hospital and afterward grew so fatigued that Tigers president Jim Campbell sent him home to California to rest. When Sparky left Detroit, he believed he wouldn't manage again. He blamed himself for Detroit's terrible year, but with the team he had and the injuries they suffered, even Sparky Anderson could not coax a winner. He was finally able to give up his obsession for winning after spending 17 days away from the team. He said, "My greatest gift today is knowing I have a tomorrow."

Anderson continued to manage mediocre teams in Detroit through 1995. That season, during spring training, he drew a lot of attention for refusing to manage replacement players during a player strike. But he said later that that was not the whole story. He knew that management would never open the season with replacement players; it was a ruse. "I managed 25 years at that time in the major leagues, and I was no joke. I wasn't going to be part of a joke. That was the biggest travesty I have ever seen in my career."

Sparky was granted a leave of absence and returned to manage that year when, as he predicted, the strike was settled and replacement players were dismissed. While rumor said he was forced out of the game, Anderson had been considering retiring for some time. He left as one of baseball's winningest managers, fifth all-time as of 2010. He was the first manager to win the World Series in both leagues. In 1984 and 1987 he won the American League Manager of the Year award. He was inducted into the National Baseball Hall of Fame in 2000. Anderson died at age 76 of dementia November 26, 2010, in Thousand Oaks, California.

References

Publications

Anderson, Sparky, with Dan Ewald. *They Call Me Sparky*. Sleeping Bear Press. 1998.

Anderson, Sparky. *Bless You Boys: Diary of the Detroit Tigers' 1984 Season*. Contemporary Books. 1984.

Anderson, Sparky, and Si Burick. *The Main Spark: Sparky Anderson and the Cincinnati Reds*. Doubleday & Company, Inc. 1978.

Articles

Pattison, Mark. "Excerpts From CNS Newsmaker Interview with Sparky Anderson" Catholic News Service, August 29, 1996.

http://en.wikipedia.org/wiki/1984_Detroit_Tigers_season

Yuhasz, Dennis. "Sparky Anderson Biography," baseball-almanac.com.

Gates Brown
by Dave Gagnon

ASK ANY SERIOUS Tigers fan over the age of 50 and they'll tell you that the sound of Tiger Stadium was always a little bit louder than normal when Gates Brown was announced as a pinch-hitter. And why not? After 13 seasons in Detroit, not only did the "Gator" retire as the American League's all-time pinch-hitting king, but so many of his hits were of the clutch variety, either tying the game or putting the team ahead. One would think that in order to have enjoyed that kind of success off the bench, Gates would've had to have been ready to hit at all times. You would think he studied pitchers like a hawk for nine innings—trying to gain any advantage he could for when he took the plate. But, surprisingly, that wasn't always the case for Gates.

Once in 1968, Mayo Smith decided to put in his pinch-hitting specialist far earlier in the game than normal. Gates, who usually didn't come off the bench until a tight spot near the end of the game, was caught off-guard. "I was sitting at the end of the dugout, eating a couple of hot dogs," Gates recalled. "It was only the fifth inning (and) I never expected Mayo to call on me to pinch hit that early." Since he didn't want Smith—who often harped on Gates to lose a few pounds—to see him eating during the game, Gates quickly shoved the

DETROIT TIGERS 1984: WHAT A START! WHAT A FINISH!

dogs down his shirt before heading to the plate. "That's the only time I ever wished I'd strike out," said Gates. But being the clutch hitter he was, Gates didn't get his wish. Instead, he cracked a double and ended up having to slide head-first into second. While Tigers fans roared and cheered, Gates realized he had made quite a mess of himself. "I had mustard and squashed meat all over me," Gates laughed, recalling that all his teammates were bent over laughing.

So despite his success as one of the greatest hitters off the bench in major league history, Gates Brown wasn't a pinch-hitting robot after all. He was simply one of the guys. He played poker with teammates. He snored. He played catch with relievers during games. He was a press favorite. But most importantly, he always supported his teammates—so much so that his first big league manager, Charlie Dressen, often referred to him as "Governor Brown." But that was Gates Brown in a nutshell—a team player who always said and did the right things to help his team win.

William James "Gates" Brown was born in Crestline, Ohio, May 2, 1939 (the same day that Lou Gehrig's consecutive games streak came to an end). He was nicknamed "Gates" by his mother when he was just a toddler—although, to this day, he has never figured out why his mother chose it. "My mother started calling me Gates when I was small," Gates said. "I still don't know where she got it. But the name stuck."

Crestline, like much of northern Ohio in the 1940s and '50s, wasn't the greatest area to grow up in. Poor, flat, and desolate, most kids from the area got in trouble with the law at some point. A sociologist would say it wasn't their fault the kids turned to a life of crime; but a result of where they grew up.

Brown didn't make it out Crestline with a clean record. Even though he was a standout football star at Crestline High School, Gates got into more than his fair share of trouble growing up. When he turned 18, he was arrested for breaking and entering and was sent to the Mansfield State Reformatory in nearby Mansfield, Ohio. The same prison used in the film *The Shawshank Redemption*.

Even though he had played some baseball in high school, it was in the Mansfield prison where Brown's true talents as a ballplayer were developed. At 5-foot-11 and 200-plus pounds of pure muscle, a prison guard who coached the pen's baseball team encouraged Brown to try out at catcher. In awe of his raw ability with the bat—and encouraged that baseball might lead Brown out of a life of crime—the coach wrote letters to several major league teams, including the Detroit Tigers.

In fall 1959, Detroit sent scouts to the prison to see Brown. Impressed, one of them called onetime Tiger Pat Mullin, now the team's top scout. Mullin made the trek from Detroit to see for himself. After Brown belted a daunting home run in Mullin's presence, the Tigers decided to help him get paroled a year early. Gates was signed to a $7,000 bonus pact almost immediately upon his release.

Brown mentions that other clubs, including the Cleveland Indians and Chicago White Sox, were interested in springing him. But he stuck with Detroit because "they didn't have any Negroes at that time and I figured they'd have to have some soon." In fact, Ozzie Virgil, a Dominican, had joined the Tigers in 1958—becoming the Motor City's first black ballplayer. But Gates was right in that the Tigers obviously lacked the integration of most other big league clubs in the late-1950s.

Prior to his first professional season in 1960, Mullin advised Brown to give up catching and switch to the outfield. The switch was fine with Gates, who was more concerned about staying out of trouble than he was about a position-change.

Brown—on legal probation from Mansfield during his first season—joined the Tigers' organization in Duluth that year. Gates shone almost immediately—especially for someone only a few months out of prison. In 121 games, Gates hit .293 with 10 homers. He also led the Northern League with 13 triples and was second in both stolen bases (30) and runs scored (104). But his real character test wouldn't come until later.

The following year he headed south to Durham of the Carolina League. It was here that Brown found out firsthand that being black and an ex-con was fuel for the fire for Southern crowds. "It was tough just being a Negro down there," Gates said. "They still used the N-word down there, you know?"

Being an ex-con didn't help as Southern newspapers printed stories about his criminal history, leading to more quips and threats from the crowds. "They called me all the names, 'Con,' 'Jailbird,' the whole thing. They were pretty vicious," Brown recalled. But Gates had to learn to ignore the jeers and to use the negativity as motivation to improve. "Some of the guys wanted to go up into the stands after those people, but I told them to just let it lay. It made me do better. It made me try harder. I decided that they could beat me physically, but no way were they going to beat me mentally," he recalled. "And do you know something, I hit the ball hard that season and led the league in hitting," topping the circuit in 1961 with a .324 mark. His outstanding play actually began to win over the same Durham fans who had heckled him earlier in the season. "By the end of the year, they were all on my side," Brown said, laughing.

After showing continued success at the minor league level—including another .300 campaign for Denver in 1962—it was clear that Brown was on the fast track to join the big club. And with the Tigers' lack of early-season success in 1963, Brown was called up from Triple-A Syracuse June 17—one day before Dressen was named the team's new manager. It would be Dressen who would call on Gates to take his first major league hacks.

Brown officially debuted for the Tigers against the Boston Red Sox on June 19 at Fenway Park. With Boston up 4-1 in the fifth inning, Brown entered the game as—what else?—a pinch-hitter for pitcher Don Mossi.

With Dressen getting his first look at the young outfielder, the situation was much like when Pat Mullin came to see Brown play at Mansfield for the first time. Ironically, Mullin was in attendance that day in Fenway—having been hired by Dressen to serve as the first-base coach. Again, as he had during his Mansfield tryout, Gates would not disappoint his

DETROIT TIGERS 1984: WHAT A START! WHAT A FINISH!

onlookers. He hit a booming 400-foot home run well into the Boston sky, becoming only the third Tiger in history to homer in their first at-bat.

Brown remained with the club for the rest of the season, primarily as a pinch-hitter. Detroit rebounded with him on the team and had a winning record for the rest of the year. Overall, Brown hit .268 with two home runs in his rookie season. He stuck on the parent club for 1964. He was used primarily as the starting leftfielder for Dressen. Playing alongside Al Kaline in right field and a troika (Bill Bruton, George Thomas, and Don Demeter) in center, Brown hit .272 with 15 home runs and was second on the team with 11 stolen bases.

Despite his solid 1964 season however, Brown lost his starting job in the outfield in 1965 to a young power hitter named Willie Horton. And even though he was disappointed in returning to his role as a pinch hitter and reserve outfielder, Gates would never let his personal frustration get in the way of the team. He slugged 10 home runs that season in barely half the at-bats he had in 1964. And despite his stocky 225-pound frame, Brown also managed to steal another six bases and was regarded unofficially as the fastest Tiger on the team. He didn't know it then, but Brown was on his way to becoming the most successful pinch-hitter in American League history.

Despite Brown's clutch contributions, his reserve status—and a budding mix of young outfielders—made it difficult for him to get raises from his bosses in Detroit. In fact, prior to the 1965 season, Brown had to pass up winter ball for the first time. With a wife and one child—plus a second on the way—Brown took a second job as a furniture salesman in the offseason.

Brown pressed on, however, and returned in 1966 and had similar success in the same role—hitting .325 as a pinch hitter. Overall he hit .266 with seven home runs in only 169 at-bats. Although he remained quietly disappointed with his role, it was clear that Brown was the Tigers' best offensive option off the bench.

Tragedy befell Brown and the Tigers that season, however. Charlie Dressen, the Tigers skipper whose arrived less than 24 hours after Gates was called up, died August 10. Dressen had been suffering from heart and kidney problems for most of the season.

Brown struggled with injuries in 1967 before finally being shelved with a dislocated wrist. Even when he played, he never could find his swing under new manager Mayo Smith. As a pinch-hitter, he hit only .154 (4 for 26). However, that Tigers team nearly made the World Series before they were beat out by the "Impossible Dream" Red Sox on the final day of the season. Mayo Smith and the rest of the Tigers vowed to return to the 1968 season with a vengeance. But the greatest turnaround of all would come from Gates Brown.

Discouraged by his poor season in 1967, Brown came to spring training on a mission in 1968. He was no longer upset about a lack of playing time, he just wanted to contribute. The Tigers, however, weary of Brown's poor and injury-filled campaign in 1967, decided to bring back Eddie Mathews as the team's primary left-handed pinch-hitter. General manager Jim Campbell and Smith even said that they thought about trading Brown, but couldn't come close to pulling a trade because Gates had packed on a few pounds while waiting for his wrist to heal, a turnoff for prospective trading partners.

Brown got his chance to prove them wrong, however, on the second day of the season; when Smith, having already used Mathews earlier in the game, called on Brown to pinch-hit in the ninth inning in a tie game. Brown grabbed a bat and hit a game-winning home run off John Wyatt. It was the how the 1968 Tigers won their first game of the season. "We took off from there," said Brown.

Brown did everything he could to tarnish the image of what would be known as the Year of the Pitcher. He hammered six hits in his first 10 pinch-hit at-bats on his way to an AL-record 18 pinch hits that season. Tigers fans soon became accustomed to watching the Gator come off the bench and deliver over and over in key situations. But none was more key than during a Sunday doubleheader August 11 against the defending American League champs, the Boston Red Sox.

In the lid-lifter that day, the Tigers were in an extra-inning struggle with the Bosox until Mayo Smith finally found a time for Brown to get in the game in the bottom of the 14th inning. Tiger Stadium erupted when he was announced. But their cheers were nothing compared to when Brown smacked the game-winning home run a minute later.

Then in the second game, Brown strode to the plate in a tie game in the bottom of the ninth. With Mickey Stanley creeping off of third, Gates singled to right to drive in the winning run, giving him an unheard-of two game-ending hits in the same day. Even 16-year vet Kaline admitted he had never heard the Tiger Stadium crowd cheer like they did for Brown that day.

In fact, Brown hit so unbelievably well in 1968 that Smith even started him in 16 games. Not bad for a guy who was trade bait when the season began. In the end, Brown hit an astounding .370 in 1968—more than over 100 points higher than his career average, 135 better than the team average, and 140 better than the American League's collective average. He was the only full-season Tiger to hit above .300 that season. He also averaged an extra-base hit every six at-bats—a remarkable stat when you consider that the mighty Alex Rodriguez only averaged one every 7.2 at-bats in his MVP season of 2007.

Brown was not only clutch with the bat in 1968, he was also clutch as a teammate. One night during the season, he interrupted a melee between Denny McLain and Jim Northrup and made them understand the importance of what the team was trying to accomplish as a whole. During a road trip in the middle of the 1968 season, Brown was playing poker with a bunch of other players, including Northrup and McLain. Halfway through a hand, Northrup caught McLain cheating. Enraged, he flew across the bed and grabbed McLain by the throat. John Hiller, who was seated next to Brown, recalls Northrup screaming, "I'm gonna kill you, you bastard! I'm gonna kill you!" Red-faced and exasperated, Northrup continued to wring McLain's neck in anger. But he was eventually pulled off from behind by Gates. A shocked

DETROIT TIGERS 1984: WHAT A START! WHAT A FINISH!

Hiller remembers Brown looking Northrup dead in the eye and saying, "You're not gonna touch him until after we win the pennant. Then he's all yours."

Brown also remained popular with the Detroit writers that season. When asked about his remarkable success in the clutch, Gates developed a common response to give to reporters: "I'm square as an ice cube, and I'm twice as cool," he always told them. Detroit media couldn't get enough of Gates.

Neither could Tigers fans. When the World Series rolled around and the Tigers lost Game 1 to St. Louis' Bob Gibson—who also struck out 17—Mayo Smith was bombarded by letters to put Brown into the starting line-up. One Tigers fan even wrote Smith asking him to start Brown at shortstop and bat leadoff during the series. "That guy must be nuts," reacted Gates when told of the letter.

In fact, Brown only had one appearance during the World Series: a pinch-hit fly out to left off Gibson in Game 1. But for anyone who remembers how untouchable Gibson was that October day, it's a miracle any man could come off the bench and even touch the ball. But Gates did. In fact, he just missed the sweet spot.

Throughout the rest of his career, Brown enjoyed continued success as a pinch-hitter—including a .346 pinch-hitting campaign in 1971—but nothing quite like the 1968 season.—although Gates did enjoy more time in the baseball spotlight by becoming Detroit's first ever designated hitter in 1973, a position tailor-made for the game's Gates Browns.

Moreover, Brown became so beloved that some sportswriters who were adamantly against the DH when it was first implemented later said it didn't bother them as much as they thought it would. One of the reasons: it was great for Tigers fans to see Brown at the plate every day.

The whole country got a chance to see Brown a year later when Joe Garagiola, host of NBC's pregame show, *Baseball World of Joe Garagiola*, did an unusual two-part story on Gates. Garagiola rarely devoted his weekly show to anyone for two separate shows, but did so for Brown. The shows, which aired July 8 and 15, 1974, featured Brown and Garagiola back in Gates' old stomping grounds at the Ohio State Reformatory in Mansfield. The program consisted of an interview in Brown's former prison cell; as well as several rap sessions with current inmates.

Brown said he agreed to the interview inside the prison itself in hopes to that it might prevent "even more youngsters" from making the mistake of a lifetime. But he also mentioned that even if you did make the mistake of breaking the law, incarceration didn't mean the end. "It's what you do when you get out that counts," Gates told the inmates. The two-part program received wide acclaim.

After suffering through a 102-loss season in 1975, Brown decided to hang up his cleats at age 36. However, Gates loved the game too much to give it up completely. So he became a scout for the club less than three weeks after the season ended. Almost immediately, Brown went from sitting in a major league dugout to scouting teams in Florida; assisting in the free agent draft; instructing the Tigers' rookie league team; and visiting various colleges nationwide to find new talent.

Brown continued his work as a scout until 1978, when he returned to the Tigers to become the new hitting coach under manager Ralph Houk. The Tigers' team batting average rose from eighth in the American League in 1977 to second overall in Gates' first season. That year the Tigers also enjoyed their first winning season in five years.

When Sparky Anderson arrived in Detroit in 1979, he kept Brown on. Gates helped bring along the hitting talents of Kirk Gibson, Alan Trammell and Lou Whitaker. Brown remained with the Tigers through their world championship in 1984. Gates wanted to continue coaching the Tigers beyond 1984, but couldn't agree on a contract extension with the front office. He quit November 14, 1984—almost 25 years since he signed his first professional contract fresh out of Mansfield.

Things weren't always rosy for Brown in his years since the 1984 championship. In 1991 he was part of a business group that purchased Ben G Industries, a plastics molding company that was relocated from the Detroit suburb of Mount Clemens, Michigan, to Detroit after its purchase. The company was doomed almost from the start. First it was alleged that the previous owners had stolen $458,000 from Ben G before it was sold to Brown's group. Then the Internal Revenue Service got involved and found that as the company's president, Brown had failed to oversee the payment of taxes during his first two years of ownership. A civil suit was served to Brown by the IRS seeking more than $61,000. However, Gates never faced criminal charges.

Brown also had to settle another IRS allegation a few months before the trial with Ben G began. This time it was at the personal level. Brown and his wife, Norma, were accused of shorting income on their personal taxes and ordered to pay more than $36,000 in back taxes and penalties dating from 1992 to 1997.

Brown was not forgotten from the baseball world, however. He was inducted into the Michigan Sports Hall of Fame in 2002. Beside Gates during his acceptance speech was his former hitting pupil, Lance Parrish, and former big-league pitcher and Zeeland, Michigan, native, Jim Kaat. Many of the voters admitted that Gates' amazing story was a huge reason why they chose him.

Brown has always liked to revisit and reflect upon that magical season of '68. He had reached the pinnacle of his profession. He was a World Series champion. His climb from a prison cell to shaking hands with the likes of Bob Hope and Ed Sullivan is truly a great comeback story. But if you asked Gates, his contribution to the 1968 season was for his parents.

"I can never make up for all the grief I gave them in my life. I can never make up for all the humiliation they suffered, all the torture, when I spent time in (Mansfield)," Brown said. "But I promised them, when I got out of there I would never go back. If I didn't make it in life, it would not be because I didn't try. You know, you can do bad things in a big city and nobody ever knows about them. But do something wrong in small town [Crestline's population was only 6,000] and everybody knows. That's why I was so happy we won it all. I could finally give them something else to talk about."

In his 13 years as a player with Detroit, Brown was a part of nine winning ball clubs. He also was a part of seven more as a coach. Most Tigers fans will tell you that, despite his reserve role, Brown was a huge part of the successful era in Motown. His ability to come through in the clutch has not been matched by any in the annals of AL history. His .370 average in '68 was the eighth-best season ever for a pinch-hitter. He had 107 pinch hits in his career, the most ever in the American League. He also still holds the AL record for pinch-hit at-bats (414) and home runs (16).

But it wasn't just with his bat, but with his attitude, in which Brown became so successful on the diamond. He was everyone's favorite teammate. He was a huge crowd favorite. He was Gates Brown, the underdog who went from prisoner to champion.

References

Brown's quotes about being hounded by Southern fans while in the minors: Joe Falls article, *The Sporting News,* March 22, 1975, and Rich Koster article, *St. Louis Globe-Democrat,* October 19, 1968.

Brown's troubles with the IRS: David Shepardson article, *The Detroit News,* date unknown, and Anthony Neely article on the Summa-Harrison scandal, April 1993.

Hot dog story and quotes: Detroit Tigers press release, August 18, 1978.

Joe Garagiola interview info. and quotes: Detroit Tigers press release, July 1, 1974

Poker story with McLain and Northrup and quotes: *Detroit Tigers Encyclopedia,* p. 99.

Reference to Mayo Smith receiving letters to start Gates at shortstop during the World Series: Rich Koster article, *St. Louis Globe Democrat,* October, 19, 1968.

Billy Consolo
by Joanne Hulbert

WILLIAM ANGELO Consolo was born in Cleveland, Ohio, on August 18, 1934, the same day as Roberto Clemente. His family moved to Los Angeles when he was a child, and at the age of 8, he began playing baseball alongside his brother Horace, who preferred third base. While on the local playgrounds he met George Anderson—later known as Sparky. They signed up at the local park, where it cost 50 cents to play baseball, and a lifelong friendship began. The Twentieth Century movie studio was just around the corner and some of the games they played were against the Our Gang actors and other child stars. Billy began to attract attention from some West Coast scouts while playing on the sandlots. He first attracted notice at the Rancho Cienega Playground; his slingshot arm, base-running speed, and hitting power for a kid his age were bound to generate talk among the scouts spying the amateur ballfields around Los Angeles.

At the age of 12 Consolo donned his first uniform, with the Douglas Post American Legion. Scouts characterized him as that little scampering runt, playing with boys four and five years older and holding his own quite handily. At 13, Consolo began playing semipro baseball in the California winter league, and crossed paths with future big leaguers Johnny Lindell, Paul Pettit, and Erv Palica. There was plenty of playing time during the long Southern California season. As a proficient cleanup hitter on the Dorsey High School team that won 42 consecutive games and the city championship, Billy advanced to the Crenshaw Legion Post 715 team that won the Junior American Legion National Championship at Detroit's Briggs Stadium in 1951.

The scouts who paid attention to Consolo's progress considered him a prize for any team that won the race to sign him. He was called the best prospect Los Angeles had to offer, and everyone waited for him to finish high school in January 1953. Teams courted him in many ways. On a visit to Cleveland with his father in the summer of 1952, the Indians invited Consolo to work out with the team. The club's director of scouting, Laddy Placek, called him the greatest prospect he'd ever seen, and General Manager Hank Greenberg told Billy, "Don't do anything until you hear from me." Greenberg was later blamed for hesitating and losing out on a player who might have solved the Indians' infield problems.

The Brooklyn Dodgers, a team that signed many of Consolo's Legion teammates, also courted him, but Billy ultimately favored the Boston Red Sox. Joe Gordon, representing the Detroit Tigers, was willing to go as high as $100,000, the Consolo family reported, and handling all the offers quickly became unmanageable. The team representatives waving money were all given two hours to promote their offers.

DETROIT TIGERS 1984: WHAT A START! WHAT A FINISH!

"Boy, I never want to go through that again," Consolo said. "You really got worries when you're signing away your future like that. Fellows kept calling me up beforehand and wanting to act as my agent. They didn't care about me. All they talked about was the money I could get. I decided on the Red Sox because their offer was good and I like the people. They came right out and named a figure and some of these other clubs you couldn't pin down."

Ted McGrew, a scout for the Boston Red Sox, arrived with an offer of $60,000—some reports say $65,000—in hand for a bonus contract, and Consolo signed on February 2, 1953, the day he graduated from Dorsey High. The Red Sox hoped they had found a second baseman to make plays that hadn't been seen since the days of Bobby Doerr.

Five players from the Crenshaw Legion team moved on to major-league baseball including Paul Schulte, a right-handed pitcher in the Red Sox farm system, and his sandlot pal, Sparky Anderson, to the Dodgers' system. Consolo soon followed. He had never experienced the game as a bench warmer, but he would soon. (Amateurs getting bonuses of more than $4,000 were required to stay on major-league rosters for two years.)

The exact terms of the contract were not made public, but it was generally thought Billy got about $15,000 immediately and would receive the balance of $45,000 in three annual installments. The first thing he did was put the bulk of the money in bonds and buy a pair of $25 featherweight baseball shoes that ended up not breaking in as he had expected. He gave the shoes away, bought a new pair, and continued using an old glove he'd had for five years. Lou Boudreau, Boston's manager, talked him into trying a lighter 33-ounce bat. All this, he hoped, would prepare him for his first experience, just a few weeks from high-school graduation, for life in the big leagues.

Before Consolo made his first major-league hit, a front-office executive for one of the losing teams in the bidding frenzy commented to a sportswriter, "He is a sweet ballplayer. We knew he was a great prospect, too, but with the new bonus rule we wondered how smart it would be to bid big money for him and then stick him on the bench for two years. Now he comes in to pinch-run and maybe he pulls a rock like he did against the Yankees and he goes back to the bench and broods about it for a week, instead of playing and forgetting it. Pretty soon you may have a guy who is so used to sitting on the bench he never makes it as a regular. It's happened before in this league."

Boudreau admitted the bench was not the best place for Billy. "Consolo should be out playing every day," he said. "No sense kidding about it. Billy would be much better off with two years in the minors. He'd come back as a great player. He's going to be one just the same, but his development may be slower. He certainly has improved a lot from the day he first showed up for spring training in Sarasota."

Consolo also knew that the minor-league experience would have been to his advantage. "I know it, but I couldn't afford to pass up the bonus," he said. "I've never sat on the bench in Legion ball or in high school. But I haven't been wasting my time. I've learned a lot by watching."

Once spring training was finished, Consolo experienced only fleeting moments of an occasional private lesson from the coaches and a few of the regular players. He was stymied by the major-league curveballs that jumped around unlike anything he had experienced back on the Los Angeles playgrounds. Since he was a Red Sox bench warmer he was restricted to a half-hour of batting practice before games, and he rarely got more than his quota of six cuts. He'd ask one of the catchers for a few fastballs and a pitcher for breaking balls in order to become more familiar with big-league curves. When a pitching prospect came by for a tryout, Billy volunteered to stand in at bat.

One day, while the Red Sox were in Washington for a series against the Senators, a cluster of reporters asked Senators manager Bucky Harris—who knew the Boston scene well—for his take on the Boston players.

"Oh, they have got some pretty good boys," Harris said. "Two or three of them have got a chance to become good ballplayers. But to me they've only got one potential star, and he's not playing."

The reporters thought he was referring to Jim Piersall, Tom Umphlett, Milt Bolling, or Dick Gernert, but they were surprised at his explanation. "Oh, I guess they are all right, but the kid who takes my eye isn't playing. It's that Consolo kid. I can't explain it, but I spend all my time watching him when the Red Sox are here."

"Have you ever seen him really play in a game?" asked the reporter.

"No, I haven't," said Bucky, "but I'm looking forward to it."

The next day, May 30, in the first game of a doubleheader, Consolo got into the game—it was his first major-league start—and rewarded Harris for his patience. He came to bat in the fifth inning and smashed a drive against Griffith Stadium's distant wall in left center, a hit that traveled more than 400 feet and put the Sox ahead 2-1 in a game they won 4-3. The hit impressed Harris no end.

"Even though I wasn't playing much, when I walked out on the field at age 18 or 19, I said, 'Here I am playing second base for the Red Sox. I'm one of the best 16 second basemen in baseball.' I kept that attitude, even though down deep I probably knew I couldn't do it. But that's what I felt when I walked out on the field," Billy said.

During his first year with the Red Sox, Consolo appeared in 47 games and was at bat 65 times, mostly as a pinch-hitter or a fill-in for an injured or ailing everyday player. He made his debut in the second game of an April 20 doubleheader against Washington in Fenway Park, pinch-running for Mickey McDermott in the Red Sox' seven-run seventh. He grounded out in his first at-bat in the same inning, replaced George Kell at third, and recorded his first major-league assist and error. That he didn't get into the lineup every day confounded him, despite his understanding about his bonus-baby status. It was several weeks into the season before he gave up the daily habit of checking the starting lineup that Boudreau posted on the clubhouse bulletin board. He waited for his name to appear, and when it did not, he would walk away, shaking his head in astonishment.

The Red Sox finished 1953 in fourth place, an improvement over the sixth-place team of 1952. Ted Williams was back from flying a fighter in Korea and reported for spring training in Sarasota, Florida, in March 1954, and 15 minutes into the first day fell and broke his left collarbone. The team roster needed immediate shuffling while Ted recuperated. The first exhibition game, against the Philadelphia Phillies, found Consolo on second base, where he put on a sensational performance with five assists, four putouts, and two base hits, and earned a bold headline in the *Boston Herald*: "Consolo Standout As Sox Win, 2-1."

Lou Boudreau gave Billy a heap of credit for his performance, saying, "He sure handled himself nicely going right or left and belted that ball in the eighth."

George Kell was impressed, too: "He can run, hit, and field. What more do you need, except probably a little experience?"

Bill Cunningham of the Boston Herald took a special interest in the young players. He frequently stopped by the room shared by Harry Agganis and Consolo in Sarasota and found it had become a gathering place for the younger players. He often found them stretched out on their beds with three or four others occupying the chairs, sitting on suitcases or on the floor. They talked of nothing but baseball, sometimes engaging in arguments over the rule book or trying to call up a newspaperman like Cunningham to settle how to rule a play if there were such dilemmas as "two outs, three men on base, the count three-two on the batter." He commended them for their devotion to the game and for not spending nights out "studying the nocturnal scenery on Longboat Key, a very pretty diversion, incidentally."

Reporters who were keeping tabs on the progress of the team encouraged speculation that Consolo would find himself in the starting lineup on Opening Day. If and when Consolo did go to second base for anything like an extended assignment, they wrote, he might stay there as long as Bobby Doerr did, or longer. Even Boudreau, they offered, said Consolo looked about ready. Bill Cunningham offered a warning to second baseman Billy Goodman about the hazard of a star-quality rookie breathing down his neck. The Yankees had Wally Pipp, a stalwart first baseman, conscientious and hard-working. One day he had a headache and chose to sit out a game, and a rookie subbed for him. That rookie was Lou Gehrig. Billy Goodman beware, they warned.

But the Boston front office did not heed their suggestions. The team stayed with its fixtures at second, third, and shortstop, gave first base to Agganis, and Consolo went back to the bench for the second year of his confinement.

Red Sox announcer Curt Gowdy promoted a campaign, "Fill Fenway Park on Opening Day," but with the absence of Ted Williams in the lineup, the debut of Agganis—nicknamed the Golden Greek and the new hope for 1954—had to suffice. Billy Goodman would have started at second on Opening Day, but manager Boudreau used a mix of Goodman, Hoot Evers, Charlie Maxwell, and Karl Olson to fill in for Williams. Even so, Consolo started only four games when Goodman was in left during Williams' injury. Consolo's sporadic appearances defined his 1954 season. An occasional sensational performance caught the attention of the fans and the reporters, but bench-warming continued to be his primary occupation.

With Consolo's two-year forced conscription on the Red Sox' big-league roster over, did the Boston brain trust send him to the minors for playing time, seasoning, experience? Nope. Instead, for year after year, Billy continued to languish on the Red Sox bench.

1955: Age 20. The Red Sox, relieved of the bonus-rule restriction, sent Consolo to Oakland, where he played in 159 games, almost all at second base, and batted .276. In Boston, he played in eight games—only four at second—with 18 at-bats. Billy Goodman played 143 games at second, Eddie Joost 19, and Owen Friend and Grady Hatton one each.

1956: Age 21. Goodman again ruled the roost, getting 95 starts at the keystone sack. Ted Lepcio vaulted above Consolo on the depth chart, with 52 starts. Even September acquisition Gene Mauch got six starts in his one month with the Red Sox. Billy got all of two starts at second and played $58^{2}/_{3}$ innings total there over 25 games.

1957: Age 22. Despite Goodman's having been exiled to pinch-hit duty, Consolo became the fourth-stringer at second. Lepcio took a plurality (61) of starts at second base. Gene Mauch had 56, and Ken Aspromonte started 23 games to Consolo's 14. However, Billy saw more action at shortstop (42 games, 38 starts, $350^{2}/_{3}$ innings total) than at second, and even put in a couple of games at third base.

1958: Age 23. Consolo was the third option at second, having gotten more playing time than Aspromonte at least, but well behind new second sacker Pete Runnels and the demoted Lepcio. He was also the third choice at shortstop behind new would-be infield sensation Don Buddin and Billy Klaus. Consolo was the second-stringer at third base, but he got in just one inning of work behind 1958 iron man Frank Malzone. Consolo hit a dreadful .125 in 72 at-bats.

1959: Age 24. Consolo was not only out of the picture at third base—Malzone played every inning of the season—but also, surprisingly, at second base. Runnels, Pumpsie Green, Herb Plews, and Lepcio saw action there, as did in-season acquisition Bobby Avila. Consolo started a pair of games at shortstop and was confined to pinch-hitting or pinch-running duty otherwise. Soon, he would be out of the picture altogether for Boston.

On June 10, 1959, in the last game Consolo played in a Red Sox uniform, he committed an error that led to an unearned run that put the game out of reach for Boston despite a furious comeback which left the Red Sox one run short in a 10-9 loss to the Detroit Tigers. On June 11, four days before the trading deadline, the Red Sox made a two-for-two swap, sending right-handed pitcher Murray Wall and Consolo to the Washington Senators for infielder Herb Plews and pitcher Dick Hyde.

Immediately there was trouble with the trade when Hyde revealed that he had a sore arm and would be unlikely to pitch for some time. Hyde and Wall were "reverse traded" while Consolo stayed with the Senators and Plews with the Red Sox. Consolo finally received his chance to spend less time on a bench and more time out on the field, appearing in 79 games, nearly all at shortstop, In 1959 Consolo had 216 at-bats, his most since 1954 (the last season he played under Lou Boudreau), when he had 242. He finished the season in Washington with a .213 average.

Cookie Lavagetto, Washington's manager for 1960, anticipated a dilemma at second base in 1960 and found no easy solution. Although he had converted Consolo to shortstop, he had shortstop Zoilo Versalles, whom he had given a late-season tryout at short in 1959, looking ready to take on the position full time. He was willing to give Billy the first crack at second, saying, "Consolo at second could step up our double-play production. He has more range than any of the other candidates, and when he teams up with Versalles, it could be a pleasure to watch."

But as it turned out, Versalles appeared in just 15 regular-season games, from September 13 to October 2, at shortstop, while Consolo appeared there in 100 games as well as a handful at second and third. Although his fielding was commendable, his bat still betrayed him. His average was a dismal .207. He was released at the end of the season.

Despite his release, the Minnesota Twins, newly relocated from Washington, signed Consolo in 1961 to a look-see deal. He made the team out of spring training, but appeared in just 11 games with only five at-bats, appearing in his last game on May 28, at second base. Jose Valdivielso, another former Senator, despite an equally anemic batting average of .195, edged Consolo out as Lavagetto's utility infielder. On June 1, in order to improve their pinch-hitting strength—pinch-hitters had gone 9-for-61, a .147 average—the Twins traded Consolo to the Milwaukee Braves for infielder Billy Martin, and the Braves immediately sent Consolo to Milwaukee's Triple-A team, the Vancouver Mounties.

Consolo gave serious thought to retiring from baseball when he was traded to the Braves, but by mid-July he was adjusting to the minor-league environment and started hitting doubles and triples again, scoring 63 runs and tallying 40 RBIs with a .283 average in 99 games, showing some of the stuff that had once attracted the attention of scouts and managers. To retain him on their roster, the Braves brought Consolo up just before the October 17 deadline. Although he never played a major-league game for the Braves, he was kept as future trade material.

During the Rule 5 major-league draft in November 1961, the Phillies picked Consolo. Still branded in the press as the Red Sox bonus player, Consolo was expected to handle second or third base capably.

Consolo's career in a Phillies uniform was brief, as he appeared in just 13 games in 1962, only once in the field, and on May 8 he was sold to his hometown Los Angeles Angels. General Manager Fred Haney picked up Consolo as insurance for the infield because Billy Moran had been sidelined in September 1961 with a back injury. Although Moran was holding his own so far, Haney didn't want to be caught without a utility player if Moran's back gave out again.

Soon enough it was apparent that Moran's back was going to hold up just fine, as he appeared in 160 games for the Angels. Consolo got into 28 games as a backup infielder, pinch-hitter and pinch-runner. On June 26 the Angels put him on waivers and the Kansas City Athletics picked him up. Consolo appeared at shortstop with the Athletics that day. He replaced Dick Howser, who was sidelined for seven weeks after he fractured his left hand putting a tag on Luis Aparicio against the White Sox two days before.

Kansas City afforded Consolo more playing time than he'd seen in years. He appeared in 54 games—48 at shortstop, with 42 of those starts—and got 154 at-bats. His average of .240 was his best in five years. None of that mattered. Kansas City tried to send him to the minors, thinking he had only four years of major-league experience and that he was much older than his reported 28 years. Billy requested his unconditional release, pointing out that he met the requirement of eight years of major-league experience, and that meant the trip to the minors was without his consent. He got his release on November 2, and in 1963 he was signed by the Cleveland Indians and offered a trial at their spring-training camp and a minor-league contract with the Jacksonville Suns of the International League. When it came to returning him to Jacksonville, Consolo gave serious consideration to leaving baseball. Billy informed Indians personnel director Hoot Evers, an old teammate from Boston, "I'm going back home to Los Angeles to think it over." Evers said he would have been surprised if Billy returned.

With his decision made, Billy retired from baseball, having appeared in 603 big-league games over 10 years for six teams, with 1,178 at-bats, 260 hits, 158 runs, and a lifetime average of .221. He turned to his offseason career as a barber, an occupation he inherited from his father, and ran a 12-chair shop at the Los Angeles Statler Hilton Hotel, little realizing at the time that the job would prepare him for his next career in baseball. The haircut may have cost a buck or two, but the baseball talk came at no extra charge. His boyhood friend Sparky Anderson, not having made it as far as a player as Billy had, was making a name for himself as a major-league manager in Cincinnati, having guided the Reds to World Series wins in 1975 and 1976. During the 1979 season, he became the manager of the Detroit Tigers and asked Consolo if he'd be interested in returning to baseball.

"There was no decision to make. It was like being rejuvenated. Sparky asked me how long I needed to make a decision and I told him about three seconds."

Sparky vowed to go all the way to the World Series, but the 1979 Detroit team he inherited required more work than he anticipated. While some of the coaches carried out Anderson's directives and assisted with the player pushing, Billy Consolo's job was twofold. He was known for his ability to lighten up the mood of the clubhouse, his way of taking pressure off with his humor and supply of tall tales. Any player who thought the worst had happened to him could count on Billy to come

DETROIT TIGERS 1984: WHAT A START! WHAT A FINISH!

up with something even worse. He could talk about anything: the price of haircuts, what they used to talk about at King Arthur's Round Table, or the height of the fence in center field at Fenway Park. "Billy was a beautiful storyteller," wrote Dan Ewald, a former sportswriter and Tigers executive. "He could spin a story you might think was 100 percent true. It might have been. Sometimes, when he would tell one of them again, you'd get a new piece. That made it worth listening to the old stories."

Consolo's second role required him to provide a sane environment for his lifelong friend. Sparky Anderson's volatile moods were a hazard to his players as well as his own well-being. Billy served Sparky well on his staff, and was always close at hand to keep him grounded. When Sparky, mentally and physically exhausted from the relentless grind of managing a club that tried its best but came up short in 1989, was sent home to California to recuperate, Billy Consolo, his friend since they dominated the sandlots of Los Angeles and who lived with him during the season, accompanied Sparky on the way home. Billy stayed with Sparky until 1992. Ten years (two of them consisting of fewer than a dozen games) playing major-league baseball, and 14 years on the coaching staff, left Billy Consolo with no regrets about his baseball career. He died on March 27, 2008.

Looking back on his best of times, he once said: "I never felt like anybody the Red Sox ever brought up was better than I was. But when they played every day, you could tell that somebody saw something in them. Baseball players, when you know they can play, you see it early. Not that you're going to quit or anything like that, but they have something. I think any baseball player, when he gets beat out of a position or a job, it's nothing against the guy. They just see something better in the other guy. They are there for a reason."

References

Publications

Anderson, Sparky, with Dan Ewald. *Bless You Boys. Diary of the Detroit Tigers' 1984 Season*. Chicago: Contemporary Books. 1984.

Anderson, Sparky, with Dan Ewald. *Sparky!* New York: Prentice Hall. 1990.

Light, Jonathan Fraser. *The Cultural Encyclopedia of Baseball, Second Edition*. Jefferson, N.C.: McFarland & Co. 2005.

Kelley, Brent. *Baseball's Bonus Babies*. Jefferson, N.C.: McFarland & Co. 2006.

Snyder, John. *Red Sox Journal*. Cincinnati: Emmis Books. 2006.

Articles

Ballew, Bill. "Tigers' Coach Billy Consolo Back With Sparky Again." *Sports Collectors Digest*, June 2, 1995. 160-162.

Birtwell, Roger. "Rookie's Father Says Other Clubs Wanted to 'Fiddle Around' Too Much." *Boston Globe*, April 30, 1953. 21.

Boudreau, Lou, "Managing a Young Team." *Atlantic Monthly*, August 1953. Boston. 76-79.

Carmichael, John P. "Veeck Had Scheme to Sign Consolo." *Boston Globe*, March 16, 1954. 6.

"Consolo To Be Inducted Into National Guard." *Cumberland (Md.) Evening Times*, July 25, 1957. 31.

Costello, Ed. "Consolo Standout As Sox Win, 2-1." *Boston Herald*, March 9, 1954. 11-12.

Cunningham, Bill. "Consolo, Agganis Real Competitors." *Boston Herald* March 10, 1954. 29.

Cunningham, Bill. "Boudreau Rates Sox Dark Horse." *Boston Herald*, March 14, 1955. 9.

Dyer, Braven. "Slick DP Combo Throws Lifeline to Angel Hurlers." *The Sporting News*, May 23, 1962. 32.

"Goodman In LF As Bosox Make Infield Shift." *Troy (N.Y.) Record*, April 29, 1954. 34.

Hirshberg, Al. "Bosox Lidlifter Lineup About Set as Drilling Starts." *The Sporting News*, February 25, 1953. 14.

Hurwitz, Hy. "Red Sox' Latest Bonus Baby Wishes He Could Be Shipped to Minors." *The Sporting News*, March 11, 1953. 11.

Hurwitz, Hy. "Yawkey High on Consolo as Kid Prospect." *The Sporting News*, May 20, 1953. 4.

Hurwitz, Hy. "Red Hot Job Battles Seen at Four Spots in Camp of Red Sox." *The Sporting News*, February 26, 1958. 19.

Hurwitz, Hy. "Red Sox Land Hyde in 4-Man Deal With Nats." *The Sporting News*, June 17, 1959. 18.

Hurwitz, Hy. "Consolo Reached Red Sox in One Hop." *The Sporting News*, July 15, 1953. 4.

Hurwitz, Hy. "Some Bosox Bonus Talent in Final Test." *The Sporting News* November 26, 1958. 30.

Kahan, Oscar. "Total of 35 Choices biggest Grab-Bag Haul in 47 Years." *The Sporting News*, December 6, 1961. 9.

King, Joe. "Amalfitano Rated Prize Bonus Boy." *Boston Globe*, February 26, 1954. 21.

King, Joe. "Few Prize Pay-Offs In Bonus Plunges. Five Standouts, Many Flops in Five Years." *The Sporting News*, November 20, 1957. 1-2.

Lebovitz, Hal. "Consolo May Call It Quits After Failing With Indians." *The Sporting News*, April 6, 1963.

Lewis, Allen. "Phils See Roy as Big Hypo to Flimsy Attack." *The Sporting News*, December 6, 1961. 30.

Lewis, Allen. "Mauch Paints Phils' Future in Rosy Color." *The Sporting News*, February 7, 1962. 24.

Lewis, Allen. "Carey's Loss Sparks Talk of Phil Swap." *The Sporting News*, March 7, 1962. 21.

Lowe, John. "Westlake Resident Remembered as 'Beautiful Storyteller.'" *Detroit Free Press*, April 3, 2008.

"Major Flashes." *The Sporting News*, March 25, 1959. 26.

Mehl, Ernest. "Howser Injury Deals Kaycee Rugged Blow." *The Sporting News*, July 7, 1962. 42.

Montville, Leigh, "Not So Easy Riding on the Red Sox Bus." *Boston Globe*, March 25, 1981. 1.

Newcombe, Jack. "$60,000 Bench Warmer." *Sport Magazine*, September, 1953. 22-59.

Povich, Shirley. "Nats Hoping Killebrew Shadow Will Spur Yost." *The Sporting News*, January 8, 1958. 4.

Povich, Shirley. "Consolo Top Banana Among Bunch of Six on Nat Keystone List." *The Sporting News*, February 24, 1960. 16.

Sampson, Arthur. "Only White, Kell, Goodman Set—Boudreau." *Boston Herald*, January 27, 1953. 17.

Sampson, Arthur. "Consolo Has Right Attitude to Become a Star." *Boston Sunday Herald*, March 7, 1954. 44.

Sampson, Arthur. "Sox Situation Not Hopeless—Yawkey." *Boston Herald*, June 2, 1959. 25.

Siegel. Arthur. "Ex-Sox Bonus Player Consolo Quits Baseball." *Boston Globe*, March 27, 1963. 49.

Other Sources

Nowlin, Bill. "Consolo on Runnels and Williams, and More." Interview. February 2000.

Roger Craig
by Richard L. Shook

ROGER CRAIG AND "split-finger fastball" will forever be linked in baseball history. It was Craig's work teaching first Jack Morris and then Mike Scott how to throw the pitch that gave the former right-handed pitcher lasting fame. "People think I invented that," Craig said. "I did not. Bruce Sutter did. I just found a way to teach it and it worked out."

A split-finger fastball is cousin to the forkball, the difference being that the latter is set way back in the hands near the webbing while the former is closer to the fingertips. "The forkball is deeper and you can't throw it as hard," Craig said. "The key to it is you throw it like a fastball. You don't try to turn it over or cut it." The pitcher uses the same motion, arm slot, and arm speed as he does for his fastball, but the ball dips as it nears the plate. The pitcher has to figure out what release point works for him, but its effectiveness comes because the batter's brain says a fastball is coming and by the time he figures out that it isn't, it's too late. The ball dives under the bat.

"The first guy I really worked on was Milt Wilcox," Craig said. "He was a gutty pitcher." Wilcox came to the majors with an overpowering fastball, but a sore shoulder prompted him to go into the trickery business. He got by with a sharp slider, but Craig wanted to tinker. "Let's try something else," he told Wilcox. "You have to have pretty good hands, and he did not, but it became a good pitch for him.

"But with Jack [Morris], it became a great pitch. Any pitching coach would be glad to have him. He was kind of tough to handle at times," Craig said. "Jack used a blooper pitch, but he telegraphed it. He had big fingers so we worked on it between starts. He had a good one but he didn't want to throw it during a game. He said, 'Naw, I like my changeup.' But I asked him, 'For one game, let's just try it.' So the first six innings he had about eight strikeouts and he ended up having one of the best around."

Craig said Randy O'Neal, who pitched in the majors from 1984 to 1990, "had one of best I ever saw. It was so good he could hardly get it over the plate. Juan Berenguer [whose big-league career stretched from 1978 to 1992] had a good one, so did Aurelio Lopez [1974-87]. I taught Mike Scott [of Houston], and a lot of my pitchers for San Francisco threw it."

DETROIT TIGERS 1984: WHAT A START! WHAT A FINISH!

That secured Craig's reputation as a pitching guru. He went on to manage the San Francisco Giants for seven seasons, taking over in September 1985.

Craig enjoyed a successful career as a pitcher, helping the Brooklyn Dodgers to their first World Series win, in 1955, and also pitching for the 1959 World Series champion Dodgers—the franchise having relocated to Los Angeles—and being traded to St. Louis in time to help the Cardinals win the World Series in 1964.

Oh, and along the way Craig also gained a measure of notoriety for losing 20 games in consecutive seasons for the 1962-63 New York Mets.

"I played and coached and managed in the World Series. That's quite a feat. Not many guys have done that," Craig said.

He came to the Tigers after two years of managing the San Diego Padres, 1978-79. "Sparky [Anderson, Detroit manager] called me. He wanted me to come up and be his coach. So I did," Craig recalled.

After the Tigers fell just short in 1983, when most of the team felt it was a better outfit than the league champion Baltimore Orioles, general manager Bill Lajoie made a late spring-training trade that solidified the Tigers, acquiring left-handed reliever Willie Hernandez from the Philadelphia Phillies to take over from Aurelio Lopez as Detroit's closer.

"I had a really good feeling in spring training. I started doing a diary. I did notes every day. Vern [Plagenhoef, who covered the Tigers for Booth Newspapers at the time] saw me doing it and said, 'You ought to write a book.' So I did." The book, *Inside Pitch: Roger Craig's '84 Tiger Journal*, was snapped up by Detroit fans hungry for anything that celebrated their world championship team.

"We got off to such a great start," Craig said of the Tigers' renowned 35-5 record out of the gate in '84. "We had a balanced team. At every position we had maybe not a superstar, but a good ballplayer. Lance [Parrish] was a great catcher and leader. We had a pretty good pitching staff. Berenguer and Rozey [Dave Rozema] could start and relieve. But Willie was the key. And Sparky did a great job. I've been around a lot of them and he probably was one of the greatest. But it wasn't an easy year for him. He worried. Every time we lost a couple of games he'd say, 'Toronto is going to catch us.' But he was right on top of everything. He was married to baseball, 24/7. He'd stay up all night watching games. He was easy to work for, though. He'd give you a job to do and let you do it."

The magic ended after the World Series win in 1984, though. Craig asked for a raise, didn't get it, and decided his time in Detroit had come to an end. In his book, Craig said he decided to retire. But baseball had other ideas.

"In the middle of the [1985] season, Al Rosen called me," Craig said. "He asked if I was interested in becoming his manager. Bob Lillis was the manager with Houston then and I told Al I wouldn't take his job. Al told me, 'You won't be taking his job, I'm moving to the San Francisco Giants and they're about to lose 100 games.'"

In San Francisco in 1985 Craig made Will Clark his first baseman and Robby Thompson his second baseman even though neither player had any Triple-A experience. The infusion of young talent and energy bumped San Francisco from 100 losses to a brief visit to first place before fading to third at the end of the season. Under Craig, who made "humm baby" a baseball catchphrase during this era, San Francisco won its division in 1987, then won the 1989 pennant, getting swept in the so-called Earthquake Series by Oakland. "I spent seven years there," Craig said. "It was a great city and a lot of fun. I enjoyed managing there." Craig retired after the 1992 season, giving his advice when asked.

"I helped Bob Brenly when he managed the Arizona Diamondbacks," Craig said. "I did it for three years and he ended up giving me a World Series ring—paid for it out of his own pocket, I found out later. He said, 'You trained me to become a major-league manager.' It's nice to know people don't forget you. I helped Tram [Alan Trammell, who managed Detroit from 2003 to 2005] a little bit in spring training, too. Since then, I've been retired. I've played a lot of golf."

Craig returned to Detroit on September 27, 2009, to help the Tigers celebrate the 25th anniversary of the 1984 season despite learning "the day before I have prostate cancer. I'm 79 and they told me I might die of something else before I die of cancer. If I went today I'm one of the luckiest guys who ever lived. I played, coached, and managed baseball. I'd have done it for nothing, but it kept my family going."

Family was always big for Craig, one of 10 children raised by John Thompson and Mamie Irene Craig in Durham, North Carolina.

"My dad was a shoe salesman; he was on the road a lot," Craig said. "Raising 10 kids, I don't think he made more than $50 a week in his life. I was number eight. My mom worked at Watts Hospital in Durham. She was like the housemother at a nursing home. My parents never really had a lot. It's still amazing they raised 10 kids with the little money they made. But we never felt we were poor. We never complained about it."

That's where Craig got his rock-solid roots. He said his parents were the biggest influences on his life.

Craig's road to the mound started at shortstop. Although he was 6-feet-4, big for a shortstop even now and huge by the standards of the 1940s and '50s, Craig was slender and was only the No. 2 pitcher on his high-school team.

"We had an outstanding pitcher, Julius Moore. We ended up being the two best in the state [North Carolina]. He signed with the Yankees but broke his wrist in a car accident and never pitched much higher than B ball [there was Class A, B, C and D in those days, as well as Double-A and Triple-A]. But he had a major-league arm in high school. He'd strike out 17, 18 a game. He had better control than I did."

Craig was followed in high school by what is still known as a bird dog, a person who gets paid sort of on a free-lance basis to scout amateur prospects. His bird dog reported to Frank Rickey, the brother of the boss of the Brooklyn Dodgers, Branch Rickey. It was Frank Rickey who signed Craig for the Dodgers out of high school.

In 1950 Craig was sent to Class D Valdosta of the Georgia-Florida League. He pitched 23 games for Valdosta, turning in a 14-7 slate and a 3.13 earned-run average, which got him promoted to Newport News of the Class B Piedmont League, where he pitched six more games, losing once and being tattooed for a 7.11 ERA.

Craig spent all of the 1951 season with Newport News. He went 14-11 with a 3.67 ERA in 38 games, 28 of them starts. Then he was drafted, serving his obligatory two years in the Army.

"I was lucky," he said. "I was pretty good in basketball and I played both baseball and basketball at the Fort Jackson [South Carolina] post. I was a little disappointed. All my buddies went to Korea, but in those days you did what they told you. I wanted to go."

Future major leaguers Ed Bailey (Cincinnati), Frank House (Detroit), and Heywood Sullivan (Boston) caught Craig in those years and kept telling him his stuff was good enough to get him to the majors.

"Then in 1954 I broke my left elbow. I tripped," Craig said. "I talked the doctor into not putting a cast on it and went to spring training the next day."

Al Campanis, the Dodgers' scouting director, saw Craig doing one-handed push-ups and came over to yank on his left arm. Nice move, Al; it put Craig out of action until midseason.

Even with his truncated season, he wound up splitting time with three teams in 1954, working 20 games back at Newport News (8-3, 2.50) before moving up to Class A Pueblo of the Western League, where he pitched in six games (1-1, 9.64), and then working two innings in three games for Elmira of the Class A Eastern League, giving up six runs, two of them earned.

Craig opened 1955 with Triple-A Montreal of the International League and was 10-2 with a 3.54 ERA before being summoned to help the Brooklyn Dodgers win the pennant and then their first World Series.

"I was 10-2 in July when they called me up," he said. "I beat the Yankees in the fifth game of the World Series that year."

Craig pitched 21 times in 1955, starting 10 games and going 5-3 with a 2.77 ERA and the following season he was a regular member of the rotation.

"I hurt my arm in the last game the Brooklyn Dodgers ever played. It was raining and sleeting in Philadelphia when I pitched. Today I know it was a rotator cuff, but this was 1957. I had to learn how to pitch all over again.

"One of best things that ever happened to me came in 1958," Craig said, although the good fortune came in a most roundabout way.

"My arm was hurting so bad in spring training they sent me to St. Paul," he said. "The manager, Max Macon, pitched me every fourth day to see if I could build up arm strength." Craig struggled through 28 games for St. Paul of the Triple-A American Association in 1958, going through a 5-17 season with a 3.91 ERA. On top of that, he was still having arm problems, so near the end of the season Macon gave Craig shock treatment.

"He told me, 'We got a chance to win this thing so you'd be better off to go back home to get your education. You're never going to pitch in the big leagues again.'" Craig said. That lit a fire under Craig, who tossed a couple of complete games down the stretch.

Craig pitched in 14 games (6-7, 3.19, six complete games, and a shutout) for Spokane of the Pacific Coast League in 1959 but was brought up to what had become the Los Angeles Dodgers, where he posted a 2.06 ERA, missing the ERA title because he was $1^{1}/_{3}$ innings short of the 154 needed to qualify for the title (one inning pitched per game the team played); the Giants' Sam Jones led with a 2.83 mark. Craig showed his effectiveness by winding up in a seven-player tie (Johnny Antonelli, Bob Buhl, Lew Burdette, teammate Don Drysdale, Sam Jones, and Warren Spahn) for the league lead with four shutouts. He clearly held his own in excellent company.

"They had all those great players," Craig said. "I saw Jackie Robinson, Duke Snider, Pee Wee Reese, Roy Campanella, Don Newcombe, Jim Gilliam. ... It was like an All-Star team and I said, 'I don't really belong here.'

"It was very special, a great experience. I was just fortunate enough to be on the only world championship they won [in Brooklyn]. The Los Angeles Dodgers, that was a different club," he said. "We still had Gil Hodges and Snider, but Pee Wee was a coach. Maury Wills came up and was an outstanding player. We had Gilliam and Wally Moon, who was famous for what they called 'Moon shots,' home runs over the left-field fence in the Los Angeles Coliseum. We had Don Drysdale and Sandy Koufax, Stan Williams, and Clem Labine. We beat the Chicago White Sox in the World Series [in 1959]."

Craig was used more and more out of the bullpen in 1960 and '61, then was allowed to be taken by the New York Mets in the 1962 expansion draft. He gained a certain amount of fame for going 10-24 and 5-22, losing 18 straight decisions over the 1962 and '63 seasons.

"I lost a lot of ballgames," he said, "but I had 27 complete games in those two years. I started the first game the New York Mets ever played."

The St. Louis Cardinals traded for Craig after the 1963 season. Although he was only 7-9 in 39 games, 19 of them starts, he posted a 3.25 ERA and helped the team come from seventh place in late July to gain a berth in the World Series, where the team defeated the last great New York Yankees team of that era; Craig won Game Four in a relief effort.

Craig worked long relief for Cincinnati in 1965 and pitched a handful of games for Philadelphia the following season before his arm gave out. He also returned to the minors, working six games for Seattle of the Pacific Coast League in 1966.

The Dodgers hired Craig to scout in 1967 and in 1968 made him the manager of their Albuquerque farm club in the Double-A Texas League, where he also pitched his last pro game.

After terms as a major-league pitching coach for San Diego and Houston, Craig was hired by the Padres to manage their team in 1978. He guided San Diego to its first over-.500 finish in the franchise's history, at 84-78, but a slip back in 1979 to 68-93 cost him his job.

That was when Anderson rescued him to teach Detroit's young pitchers.

References

Publications

Craig, Roger, and Vern Plagenhoef. *Inside Pitch: Roger Craig's '84 Tiger Journal*. Grand Rapids, Mich.: Eerdmans Publishing Co. 1984.

Articles

Treder, Steve. "Humm Baby!" *Baseball Analysts*, January 11, 2007. http://baseballanalysts.com/archives/2007/01/humm_baby_1.php. Accessed October 30, 2009.

Web Sites

Lee Sinins' Complete Baseball Encyclopedia; http://www.baseball-encyclopedia.com/. Accessed October 30, 2009.

Other Sources

Shook, Richard L. Telephone interviews with Roger Craig, October 5, 2009; July 15, 2010.

Alex Grammas
by Maxwell Kates

THERE WAS NEVER an Alex Grammas question on *Family Feud*. However, if Richard Dawson were to have asked a hundred of his contemporaries how they remembered Grammas, the survey would invariably point to three answers: flawless fielding, excellence as a third base coach, and his Hellenic heritage. As a National League utility infielder for ten years, Grammas drew favorable comparisons to a young Phil Rizzuto. After retiring, he was a third-base coach for a quarter-century, mainly for teams managed by Sparky Anderson. Forever proud of his ancestry, Grammas in 1976 became the first Greek-American ever to manage a major-league team for a full season.

Peter Grammatikakis was a Greek immigrant to the United States who left his home in Agios Dimitrios for Birmingham, Alabama, early in the 20th century. Attracted by the reputation of the southern metropolis as a "Magic City," he truncated his name to Grammas and established himself in the wholesale candy trade. Peter married Angeline, the American-born daughter of Greek immigrants from Geraki. Their son Alexander Peter was born in Birmingham on April 3, 1926. Both Alex and his brother, Cameron, loved baseball, and seized any opportunity to pursue their national pastime between grammar school and Greek school. Both brothers served in World War II before playing college baseball at Mississippi State University. Alex maintained that Cameron was the better player:

"He has played A-ball at Colorado Springs and hit about .335.... They were going to send him back out to Colorado Springs the following year. [He] just didn't want to do it, so he quit. I wish he hadn't because he would have made it—no question about it," Grammas recalled in a 1998 book on Greeks in the game.

Once he graduated with a bachelor's degree in business in 1949, Alex was signed to his first professional contract by Doug Minor of the Chicago White Sox. After batting .327 with Muskegon in the Class A Central League, he was promoted in 1950 to Memphis, where he led Southern Association shortstops in fielding. Before that season, on January 29, 1950, Alex married the former Tula Triantos. Traded to the Cincinnati Reds' organization in 1951, he continued to impress with his quick fielding and timely hitting. On loan to Kansas City one year, he led American Association shortstops in putouts and assists. The Pittsburgh Pirates valued Alex and his defensive abilities enough to look into acquiring him in a proposed six-player trade in 1952 with Ralph Kiner as the headliner in the swap. Although the Pittsburgh deal fell through, the Reds offered Alex in another trade the following winter. On December 2, 1953, he was dealt to the St. Louis Cardinals for pitcher Jack Crimian and $100,000.

Measuring 6 feet and weighing 175 pounds, Alex could not have been more excited than to make his major-league debut as a Cardinal: "I was hoping [they] would get me. I can't think of anything better than playing next to Red Schoendienst. He's the best there is in the majors," Grammas said. Finishing tied for third in the National League with a record of 83-71 in 1953, the Cardinals under new owner August A. Busch viewed Grammas as "the missing piece" to transform the team into bona-fide contenders. Unfortunately, Grammas' enthusiasm proved costly in his first spring training with St. Louis. On February 21, 1954, he injured his right arm during a sliding drill. Although X-rays proved negative and Alex made the varsity squad, he spent his rookie year trying to regain confidence after suffering the painful injury. A year after batting .304 in the minor leagues, he hit only .264 with 57 runs and 29 RBIs playing for the Cardinals. Grammas scored three runs (once after reaching on an error and twice after walking) before collecting his first big-league hit, a single off Cincinnati's Harry Petkowski on April 19, 1954, in a 6-3 Cards win at home. And he did not hit his first home run until September 3, when he parked a Paul Minner pitch in a losing effort to the Chicago Cubs. (Grammas had gone 0-for-4 against Minner in his big-league debut, a 13-4 Opening Day loss to the Cubs at Busch Stadium in St. Louis on April 13, 1954.) As for the Cardinals, they finished the season in sixth place with a record of 72-82, 25 games behind the New York Giants.

Although Alex led the senior circuit in fielding average in 1955, he batted only .240. Early in the 1956 season, on May 16, he was traded back to the Reds along with outfielder Joe Frazier for infielder-outfielder Chuck Harmon. After years of obscurity, the Reds found themselves in a pennant race with the Brooklyn Dodgers and the Milwaukee Braves. Manager Birdie Tebbetts credited Alex as "a big difference in our ballclub ... since we've been using him"; Cincy finished third, two games behind Brooklyn and one behind Milwaukee. His confidence improved in 1957, particularly on the heels of a triple play executed against the New York Yankees in a spring training contest. Gil McDougald was in scoring position at second base with Mickey Mantle on first when Yogi Berra hit a line drive to the Cincinnati shortstop. Alex forced McDougald out at second before catching Mantle in a rundown. During the 1957 season, Grammas, playing behind All Stars Johnny Temple, Roy McMillan, and Don Hoak, had only 99 at-bats. He hit .303, second on the Reds only to Frank Robinson's .322

The Reds traded Alex back to the Cardinals in a six-player deal on October 3, 1958. During his second tour of duty in St. Louis, he earned the reputation of carrying "a sharper bat, a better arm, surer hands, and can handle three positions well." Batting .269 in 1959, Alex, by now 32 years old, spent time teaching younger players the value of maintaining a proper attitude as a team player. Tim McCarver remembered:

"I was 17 years old when I first came up with the Cardinals, just up from high school. My first night on the bench [a September 1959 game], Henry Aaron was up with a couple of guys [on]. I liked Henry Aaron a lot growing up. I let out with one of those 'Come on, Henry!' or something to that effect. Everyone naturally looked at me and Alex Grammas came over and said, 'You know, up here in the big leagues, we tend to cheer for our players, not the opposition.'"

Traded again on June 5, 1962, this time to the Cubs, Alex completed his playing career in Chicago a year later. His lifetime statistics in ten National League seasons included 236 runs, 90 doubles, 10 triples, 12 home runs, 163 RBIs, and a .247 batting average. By now, the Grammas family had expanded to include daughters Lynn and Mary Ann, along with twin sons Peter and Alexis. The patriarch needed to plan for his family's future.

During the offseasons, Alex worked in the produce business with his uncles. The experience was valuable preparation for a supermarket venture he entered into with his friend Harry Walker. The business partnership proved to be an important strategic alliance when Walker was hired to manage the Pirates in 1965. After managing the Cubs' Texas League affiliate at Fort Worth in 1964, Alex began the first of 25 seasons as a major-league third-base coach. He remained a Pittsburgh coach for five years before resigning at the end of the 1969 season, having managed the last five contests the Bucs played that year. General manager Joe L. Brown offered a glowing recommendation of Alex, both as a coach and as a man. When the obscure 35-year-old George Lee Anderson was hired to manage the Cincinnati Reds in 1970, Grammas was his choice as first lieutenant:

"I coached third base myself for Preston Gomez the year before. On my one season on that job, I watched all the other third base coaches in the league. I thought Grammas was the best and Eddie Yost of the Mets, next best," Anderson told Si Burick of the *Dayton Daily News*. "I told [general manager Bob] Howsam I needed a real professional at third base, and I'd like to offer the job to Grammas. I called Alex and told him I was hoping for a relationship like [Al Lopez] with the White Sox coaches." For 19 of the next 22 years, Alex remained a valuable member of Sparky Anderson's coaching staffs.

As the Reds prepared to open their new Riverfront Stadium, a dynasty was dawning in Cincinnati. Nobody dared to ask "Sparky Who?" after the Reds opened the 1970 season with a torrid .700 winning percentage in their first 100 games before tapering off, as it were, to 102-60 and an NL West Division title and a sweep of the Pirates in the National League Championship Series before a World Series loss to Baltimore. After the Reds disappointed in 1971, tumbling to a fourth-place tie with Houston, they pulled off a blockbuster deal with the Houston Astros, bringing, among others, All-Star and eventual Hall of Fame second baseman Joe Morgan to the Queen City. Grammas helped Morgan improve his defensive abilities and later successfully converted outfielder Pete Rose to a third baseman. However, if you ask Alex today, he will reserve his highest praise for his prize pupil, a young shortstop from Venezuela named Dave Concepcion:

"You're talking about a guy I love. He's probably the finest infielder I ever had the pleasure to work with. If not the most talented, he's near the top. He even named his son after me, David Alejandro," Grammas said in a 2009 interview. As Sparky Anderson later told sports reporter Dan Ewald, "Concepcion had the tools but he needed a lot of polish. Alex Grammas spent hour after hour teaching him the tricks. Grammas and David sweat and bled from all the work they put in together. Grammas hit David more ground balls than Donald Trump has dollar bills ... and Grammas taught him to concentrate on situations. It wasn't good enough to field the ball. He had to learn what to do after he got it."

The Reds won their division easily in 1972 before facing a challenging Pittsburgh Pirates team in the NLCS. The Reds and Pirates split the first four contests, forcing a deciding Game Five before a packed house in Cincinnati. Pittsburgh was leading, 3-2, as the game entered the bottom of the ninth inning. As

DETROIT TIGERS 1984: WHAT A START! WHAT A FINISH!

Pirates reliever Dave Giusti waited to deliver the first pitch to Johnny Bench, a commotion ensued at home plate. Alex remembers "standing at third base and I didn't know what was going on." He was later told that Bench's mother wandered down to the railing to offer words of encouragement, advising, "Johnny, this is it. Let's go. Do something." Bench, the National League's Most Valuable Player in 1972, listened to his mother and tied the game with a leadoff home run. A pair of singles by Tony Perez and Denis Menke brought Bob Moose in from the Pittsburgh bullpen. George Foster, at second base as a pinch-runner for Perez, made it to third on Cesar Geronimo's fly ball. With two outs after a Darrel Chaney popup, the entire stadium seemed to be on its feet as Moose uncorked a wild pitch to Hal McRae, sending pinch-runner Foster home for a 3-2 victory. For the second time in three years, Cincinnati was going to the World Series (which they lost to Oakland in seven games). For Alex, it was "the most spine-tingling game I was ever connected with."

The Big Red Machine won their division again in 1973, although losing to the New York Mets in the NLCS, before going all the way in 1975, defeating the Boston Red Sox in a sterling seven-game World Series. Game Seven was Alex's last in a Cincinnati uniform before he was hired to manage the Milwaukee Brewers. Even as a player, he was deemed the most likely of his teammates to succeed as a manager. He had already piloted the Pirates on an interim basis in 1969, leading the Bucs to a 4-1 record. Now he would be challenged to manage a struggling franchise that had never in its brief history won more than 76 games per season. Not even the presence of Hank Aaron could prevent a late-season meltdown in 1975, as the Brewers lost 59 of their last 84 games to finish at 68-94. Despite the financial security of a three-year contract, Alex had his work cut out for him:

"When you take a ballclub that ended up the way the Brewers did last year, you've really got to be happy if you can wind up playing .500 ball. That means winning 13 games more. That's more realistic than to think we can win the pennant," he said. Leading the Brewers both on the field and by example was, once again, Hank Aaron. Alex admitted years later to Larry Stone of the *Seattle Times* that he "was proud to have Hank on [his] team." describing the home-run king as "the kind of guy everybody liked." Aaron was the first to admit that by 1976, his skills were deteriorating. Facing California's Dick Drago at County Stadium on July 20, Aaron hit his 755th career home run without any accompanying media fanfare. Nobody would have known it would be his last in a major-league uniform—and the highlight of an otherwise disappointing season for the Brewers.

An omen to the 1976 campaign presented itself early in the schedule on April 10. The Brewers trailed the visiting New York Yankees 9-6 in the bottom of the ninth inning when third baseman Don Money hit a walk-off grand slam. Or did he? Before delivering the pitch to Money, Dave Pagan did not notice umpire and fellow Canadian Jim McKean call time out as requested by the Yankees' Chris Chambliss. Never one to shy away from a protest, Yankees manager Billy Martin insisted that the home run should be nullified. McKean upheld Martin's protest, and Money subsequently flied out. The Brew Crew's rally was stymied as the Yanks topped Milwaukee, 9-7.

Despite the promise of success with a Sparky Anderson protégé at the helm, the Brewers ended the 1976 season in the American League East cellar; posting a record of 66-95, they finished 32 games behind the Yankees. Grammas took the disappointment in stride, offering that "it's a little difficult to adjust to…but you have to be realistic. If not, you drive yourself crazy and I have no intention of driving myself crazy."

Clearly a roster overhaul was in order for the Brewers in 1977. Power-hitting George Scott was traded to the Red Sox for slugging 1st baseman Cecil Cooper after calling the Brewers "the laughingstock of baseball." After a weak season at the plate, catcher Darrell Porter was packaged with pitcher Jim Colborn to the Kansas City Royals for a trio of young players, Jim Wohlford, Bob McClure, and Jamie Quirk. Another player acquired via the free-agent route was third baseman Sal Bando. With Don Money moving to second base and Robin Yount emerging as one of the brightest young shortstops in baseball, the Brewers opened the 1977 season with a formidable infield. If only infielders could pitch. Jerry Augustine led the squad with 18 losses (and 12 wins) for a team that went 67-95. Only the haplessness of the expansion Toronto Blue Jays prevented a second consecutive last-place finish for the Brewers.

Despite enjoying popularity among the fans in Milwaukee, Alex lacked the support of all his players. The alienation began when he imported the dress code from Cincinnati that prohibited players from sporting facial hair. A significant minority of the Milwaukee roster in 1975 sported Fu Manchu mustaches. Along with Colborn, Porter, Scott, and Yount, Brewers players Gorman Thomas, Kurt Bevacqua, and Pete Broberg were all depicted on their 1976 Topps cards wearing their Fu Manchus. Under the stewardship of Grammas, the free-spirited players were required to shave their whiskers against their will by Opening Day 1976. Discontent with the manager continued in 1977 to the point that utility player Mike Hegan told reporter Lou Fitzgerald that "Alex Grammas is a nice guy, but as a manager he makes a good third-base coach."

Hegan's immediate release proved to be a pyrrhic victory for Alex. The manager was not given the opportunity to complete his three-year contract as he became one of the casualties in the front-office upheaval known as the Saturday Night Massacre. Again sardonic in his outlook, Grammas allowed that "I'm sure the Brewers are going to be a much better team." He was right; they went 93-69 for George Bamberger in 1978.

When one door closed in Milwaukee, another, in Cincinnati, was reopened as Grammas returned to the Reds in 1978. Sparky Anderson was ecstatic that "Grammas is back with us.… He will coach again at third base. I have said 'Greek' is the best at that job, so there is where he will be stationed." It was a brief homecoming for Alex as the Reds finished in second place. Under new general manager Dick

DETROIT TIGERS 1984: WHAT A START! WHAT A FINISH!

Wagner, second place was no longer good enough, and Anderson was fired. While Sparky began the 1979 season in exile, Alex had accepted the Atlanta Braves' offer to coach third base. However, when Anderson was hired to manage the Detroit Tigers on June 12, Alex seemed to be a natural fit to the coaching staff:

"With Grammas, I had such a good rapport from the bench to the third-base coach's box that, after a while, we didn't even have a regular sign. In the early days, I found myself giving him the wrong sign at times, but he realized it and would change it to the right thing. Once in a while, he'd even change the right sign, like a quarterback checking off the coach's play at the line of scrimmage because the defensive alignment wasn't right for the strategy. Alex would hear a whistle on the other side and realize they anticipated what we intended to do, so he did something else."

Alex followed Sparky to Detroit in 1980, and had the opportunity to coach two more bright infield pupils, Alan Trammell and Lou Whitaker. Although experts scoffed at the manager's prediction of a world championship within five years, the Tigers produced precisely that. After winning 35 of their first 40 games in 1984, the Tigers spent the entire season in first place before dispatching the Kansas City Royals in the AL Championship Series, then defeating the San Diego Padres in the World Series.

With Detroit struggling in its quest to defend its title in 1985, a left-handed starter was on general manager Bill Lajoie's shopping list. Meanwhile, the Texas Rangers had a southpaw they were eager to trade. Remembering him as "the best pitcher—not only in the American League," Grammas recommended the pitcher in a trade. On June 20, 1985, the Tigers welcomed native Detroiter Frank Tanana back home. The crafty southpaw lent stability to the Tigers' rotation for eight years, and was the winning pitcher in the decisive final game of the 1987 season, pitching a 1-0 shutout over the Blue Jays to win the division over second place Toronto.

Although the Tigers contended yet again in 1988, success would be short-lived as Detroit in 1989 posted the worst record in baseball of 59-103. Veterans who had contributed to the 1984 success were ineffective, retired, or playing elsewhere. (Jack Morris would join them as an ex-Tiger in 1991.) They were replaced by a new batch of players, younger and cheaper and uncomfortable with an older coaching staff; these players were not afraid to voice their concerns to the front office. Consequently, despite winning 84 games in 1991, the Tigers released three of their coaches, among them Alex Grammas. At 65 years old, he decided it was time to retire.

His baseball career behind him, Alex returned to Birmingham to pursue his favorite hobbies, fishing and golf. In 1992, he reaped the dividends of the eight years he spent at Greek school as a child when he traveled to Greece for the first time.

"All my life, my father was telling me good things about Greece," Grammas recalled. "When he was talking, I was laughing, but when I saw with my own eyes, I realized he hadn't said enough about Greece. I love Greece very much.... When I walked up to the Acropolis and saw the Parthenon, the hairs on my head were standing straight up. I couldn't believe it." He has since returned to Greece several times, and a later recent trip was the most special for him:

"I decided to take the entire family to Greece—all 21 of them. I thought it was important for my grandchildren to learn about their heritage and see where their ancestors came from," Grammas said in 2009. "We visited Athens, took a cruise of the [Greek] islands, and stayed overnight at the house where my father was born. I'll tell you—the day we arrived, they announced Athens was getting the Olympics. The entire city went mad. You've never seen anything like it."

Alex Grammas devoted more than a half-century of his life to baseball as a player, coach, and manager. He played ten years in the major leagues, coached an additional 25, and earned three World Series rings. He gained the respect and admiration of students and peers and delighted in watching his pupils become stars. Dave Concepcion became one of the most successful shortstops in Cincinnati before teaching the trade to another budding superstar, Barry Larkin. Grammas continued to live in Birmingham in retirement and, at age 82, said he enjoyed good health. His philosophy on life advised that "nothing can be stopped except time, so please enjoy every minute."

The survey says that Alex Grammas has listened to his own advice.

References

Books

Aaron, Hank, and Lonnie Wheeler. *I Had a Hammer: The Hank Aaron Story*. New York: Harper Collins Publishers. 1991.

Anderson, Sparky, and Si Burick. *The Main Spark: Sparky Anderson and the Cincinnati Reds*. Garden City, N.Y.: Doubleday & Company Inc. 1978.

Berger, Jack H., ed. *Pittsburgh Pirates 1969 Media Guide*. Pittsburgh: The Pittsburgh Pirates. 1969.

Dewey, Donald, and Nicholas Acocella. *Total Ballclubs: The Ultimate Book of Baseball Teams*. Toronto: Sport Media Publishing Inc. 2005.

Eisenath, Mike. *The Cardinals Encyclopedia*. Philadelphia: Temple University Press. 1999.

Fehler, Gene. *Tales From Baseball's Golden Age*. Champaign, Ill.: Sports Publishing. 2000.

Finoli, David, and Bill Ranier. *The Pittsburgh Pirates Encyclopedia*. Champaign, Ill.: Sports Publishing. 2003.

Honoré, Aaron J. *Beards: On Men, On Women, On Gods and More—How Facial Hair Serves as Both a Means to An End and An End of Communication.* New York: Fordham University. 2005.

Johnson, Lloyd, and Miles Wolff. *The Encyclopedia of Minor League Baseball, 2nd ed.* Durham, N.C.: Baseball America. 1997.

Mishler, Todd. *Baseball in Beertown.* Neenah, Wis.: Big Earth Publishing. 2005.

Preston, Joseph G. *Major League Baseball in the 1970s: A Modern Game Emerges.* Jefferson, N.C.: McFarland, 2004.

Swirsky, Seth. *Every Pitcher Tells a Story: Letters Gathered by a Devoted Baseball Fan.* New York: Crown Publishing Group. 1999.

Thorn, John, Phil Birnbaum, and Bill Deane. *Total Baseball: The Ultimate Baseball Encyclopedia, 8th ed.* Toronto: Sport Media Publishing Inc. 2004.

Zervos, Diamantis. *Baseball's Golden Greeks: The First Forty Years, 1934-1974.* Canton, Mass.: Aegean Books International. 1998.

Articles

Halofan, Rev. "The 100 Greatest Angels: Frank Tanana" on Halos Heaven (February 13, 2006). http://www.halosheaven.com/story/2006/2/14/23549/1427. Internet. Accessed February 21, 2009.

Stone, Larry. "Little Fanfare Surrounds Aaron's HR No. 755," *Seattle Times*, July 22, 2007. http://seattletimes.nwsource.com/html/mariners/2003800294_hank22.html. Accessed February 21, 2009.

Web Sites

www.retrosheet.org

http://en.wikipedia.org/wiki/Memphis_Chicks

Acknowledgments

Matt Bohn, George Demetriou, Alex Grammas, Tula Grammas, Merle Harmon (1926-2009), Aaron Honoré, Thomas Karn, Randy Messel, Larry Moffi, and Al Yellon.

Dick Tracewski
by Peter M. Levine

RICHARD JOSEPH "Trixie" Tracewski was an average-hitting, good-fielding shortstop whose career in baseball spanned both the National and American Leagues, four World Series rings, and a Detroit Tigers record span as both a base and bench coach. Also known as "Dick Tracy" by many fans in Los Angeles during his four years with the Dodgers (1962-1965), he played shortstop, second base and third base in his eight years as a player, retiring with a fielding percentage of .961. In a career distinguished by professionalism and respect from virtually everyone he encountered from umpires to managers, Tracewski was a witness to and participant in baseball history.

Tracewski was not only multitalented as a player, but after being promoted from the minors to his first coaching position with the Tigers in 1972, took on a range of coaching roles under multiple managers and general managers. Beloved and remembered by fans in Detroit for his ever-steady presence at both the first- and third-base coaching boxes, he found his career extended and expanded under Hall of Fame manager Sparky Anderson, who invited him to remain with the team in 1980 and gave him additional responsibilities. This included mentoring a new generation of ballplayers such as Alan Trammell and Lou Whitaker, as well as two brief stints as Detroit manager in 1979 and 1989, the latter occurring when Anderson took a leave of absence.

A member of two Dodgers championship teams, 1963 (his rookie year) and 1965, as well as part of the Tigers' 1968 World Series winner, Tracewski played or worked for three of baseball's leading minds in Walter Alston, Billy Martin, and Anderson. Although perhaps better known for his coaching career, as a rookie he scored the eventual winning run in the opener of the Dodgers-Yankees World Series. Tigers manager Mayo Smith also credited him for helping to turn around the 1968 season with a game winning three-run home run against Cleveland June 23 that spurred a winning streak.

Tracewski was born February 3, 1935, in Eynon, Pennsylvania, a small town in the northeastern part of the state, as the youngest of four children. He was always an excellent athlete and baseball player, in some ways following in the footsteps of his older brother, a minor leaguer in the Philadelphia Athletics system who also played professional football. Tracewski's parents were Polish immigrants who instilled in him a work ethic that was reflected in his baseball career—his father having arrived in the United States at age 16 and then returning to Europe at 18 to fight for his newly adopted country in World War I.

Tracewski established himself a rising star during his teen years and in high school, playing for Archibald High and leading teams in the highly popular and competitive sandlot games that took place on Sundays, as well as with American Legion teams. He attracted the attention of major league scouts, including Ray Welsh of the Pittsburgh Pirates, who advised Tracewski, then a high school sophomore, to focus on shortstop. As he approached age 17 and awaited signing offers from the many scouts he had come to know, Tracewski was surprised to find that no offers were forthcoming. This was particularly true of the Cleveland Indians, who had previously indicated a serious interest in the young infielder.

As Tracewski related in a 2007 interview, this was when fortune smiled upon him. Brooklyn Dodgers scout Phil Weinnert got lost on the way back from Binghamton, New York, to his Philadelphia home. He came across a local baseball game in Jessup, Pennsylvania, which featured the Peckville VFW team and wound up watching the entire game. As was frequently the case, Tracewski stood out, and after the game Weinnert approached him to ask when he might see another game. After several failed efforts, Weinnert returned personally and invited Tracewski to come with his father to Brooklyn for a workout. He thus found himself, at 17, at Ebbets Field, spending four days hitting and fielding with Jackie Robinson, Pee Wee Reese, Duke Snider, and Gil Hodges.

Shortly thereafter, the Dodgers signed him as an amateur free agent in 1953 and he launched what was to be a long career, along with a signing bonus of several hundred dollars. He was quickly sent to Dodgertown in Vero Beach, Florida, where he began a six-year career in the minors which saw him crisscross the country, playing at every level in the team's farm system. Tracewski also performed two years' military service during this period, posted with other baseball players at Fort McPherson, Georgia, outside Atlanta. It was during this period where he had his greatest regret as a pro ballplayer. Given the option to develop skills as a switch-hitter, he chose not to. When he finally arrived in the major leagues he realized what a mistake this was as "I had to face pitchers like Bob Gibson and Juan Marichal who were so nasty against right-handers."

Tracewski was called up to the Dodgers from their AAA Omaha farm team in 1962, beginning his 42-year big league career with a debut as a pinch-runner in the final game of the first ever series at the new Dodger Stadium. Although he was never to experience a losing season as a player, Tracewski still remembers that first year painfully, as the Dodgers lost a two-game lead at the end of the season courtesy of three straight defeats to St. Louis. This was followed by a playoff loss to the San Francisco Giants in only the fourth-ever such series in major league history. That Dodgers team grew stronger from the experience, however, and behind the pitching of Tracewski's friend, Sandy Koufax, would win the first of two World Series with Trixie as a utility infielder.

It was in the 1963 World Series that Tracewski would experience what he considers his greatest moment as a professional baseball player. In his first-ever postseason at bat, Tracewski singled off future Hall of Famer Whitey Ford and scored what proved to be the winning run on a John Roseboro home run. With Koufax pitching a 2-1 victory, the Dodgers proceeded to sweep the Yankees. Although many still remember him for a key diving stop in Game 4 of the Series, Tracewski still remembers that first World Series hit with fondness and emotion. He was also on the field during the notorious moment in the August 22, 1965, game when Roseboro was struck in the head with a bat swung by Juan Marichal, a strong memory for him even today. It was as a Dodger that Tracewski was nicknamed Trixie, a sobriquet that sticks to this day. During summer pool parties hosted by reliever Ron Perranoski, Tracewski could frequently be found performing back flips, front flips and other tricks and was thus dubbed Trixie by his teammates.

Tracewski played in three of Koufax's four no-hitters (going 3 for 7 at the plate) and also was part of the 1965 world champion team before being traded to the Tigers for pitcher Phil Regan on December 15, 1965. This proved to be the start of a new phase of his career—one which initially frustrated him, as his playing time was already dwindling and he could see the end approaching. Tracewski even went so far as to approach Tigers general manager Jim Campbell shortly after arriving in Detroit with a request to be traded. He argued that since he'd arrived it was clear his playing time would be limited and asked that Campbell move him where he'd have a chance to extend his career. After considering the request briefly, Campbell refused, asking Tracewski to be patient. Although he indeed became more of a spot player for the team, Tracewski quickly established himself as an important part of the Tigers with his fielding skills, ability to cover multiple positions, work ethic, and knack for clutch hitting. During 1968 he played in 90 games for the Tigers, hitting four home runs, including the three-run shot against Cleveland in the nightcap of a June 23 doubleheader, the opening salvo in a 4-1 Detroit win that Mayo Smith credited with spurring on the team in its pennant run.

It was shortly after the 1969 season that Campbell offered Tracewski a coaching position with the Tigers, which Trixie enthusiastically accepted as a golden opportunity to extend his professional career. He quickly established himself as an excellent coach and mentor to young athletes, leading second-year Tigers manager Billy Martin to promote him from the minors and make him first-base coach. Success followed Tracewski to his new coaching position, as the 1972 team won the American League East. Martin, however, would only last another season, canned after famously ordering his pitchers to throw spitballs. It was during Martin's tenure that Tracewski, generally known as among the nicest men in the game, experienced his only ejection, an incident Martin found highly amusing. The ejection aside, Tracewski established a strong rapport with umpires throughout the major leagues, a relationship of mutual respect and even friendship. This was perhaps strengthened by the fact that Hall of Fame umpire Nestor Chylak was a longtime neighbor of his in Peckville, Pennsylvania.

Tracewski's baseball knowledge and teaching abilities would play a significant role in the Tigers' restructuring efforts, which began with the hiring of Ralph Houk for the

DETROIT TIGERS 1984: WHAT A START! WHAT A FINISH!

1974 season. Although the next few years saw many losses, they also witnessed the signing of a new generation of Detroit heroes, a group that began to pay dividends in 1978 when the team finished 86-76. In one year alone, the team added Alan Trammell, Lou Whitaker, Jack Morris, and Dan Petry—all instrumental parts of the Tigers' future success. Tracewski remains particularly proud of his work with Trammell, the shortstop he worked with closely as a young ballplayer and watched grow into one of the game's best. Even more than a decade after Trammell's retirement as a player, Tracewski believed strongly that Trammell should be in the Hall of Fame. Tracewski expressed his frustration at the lack of recognition for his student, stating, "There is no justice in baseball" when Ozzie Smith—a great player in his own right whose career paralleled Trammell's—receives more than 300 votes for the Hall while Trammell collected barely 70.

He was named manager for two games in 1979—winning both—pending the arrival of Sparky Anderson, the man Tracewski worked with for virtually the rest of his career. He continued as base coach and mentor for the Tigers, a perennial AL power for much of the 1980s. He also served as bench coach and right-hand man to Anderson, whom he considers among the greatest managers of all time. Tracewski credits Anderson for reinforcing the importance of always giving 100 percent—from spring training to the final out—and also cites his ability to understand and communicate with modern-day players. Working closely, Anderson established plans for every aspect of the game and every player, communicating on a daily basis with those like David Wells, who thrived under such a method—and never with others who were best left alone. Although Anderson was known by some as Captain Hook, Tracewski points out that he only lived up to that moniker when he had a strong bullpen.

Tracewski managed the Tigers again for three weeks during 1989 while Anderson recovered from exhaustion. This was a bittersweet time as he watched his close friend approach the end of his managing career—and the Tigers go from league power to a team that lost more than 100 games. He retired after the 1995 season. He returned to northeastern Pennsylvania, having moved his family there after being traded to the Tigers from the Dodgers three decades earlier.

During a career spanning several decades of baseball history, Tracewski played in virtually every major league ballpark and watched the game change in myriad ways. When Tracewski entered the majors he received a base salary of $7,200, an amount he quickly doubled through a then-record payout of $14,500 to members of the world champion Dodgers. As he recalls it, the manager's authority was unquestioned during that period and players used spring training to get fit for the regular season. Players during his coaching years were more independent and generally arrived fit for spring games. They also enjoyed considerably more job security and were able to focus almost entirely on baseball. Like most of his counterparts, Tracewski always worked during the offseason; the added job security, he asserted, became one of the biggest changes he witnessed in the game. A close second would be the fact that players are now bigger, stronger, and faster. As Tracewski posited, those who reminisce about the good old days perhaps do not realize how much the game has changed. Among other things, Tracewski also believes modern equipment has degraded, noting in particular the low quality of wood used in bats which now shatter with a frequency unheard of during his playing days.

Indicative of the strong friendships and relationships he had in the game, as well as his unique perspective, Tracewski cited the top five players he saw:

1) Sandy Koufax—Tracewski's friend to this day and roommate with the Dodgers who performed "feats which will never be duplicated."

2) Maury Wills—a man who changed the game, bringing back the days of Ty Cobb with his 100 steals a season.

3) Al Kaline—the best all-around field player he'd ever seen and a precursor to today's five-tool player.

4) Dick McAuliffe—his Tigers teammate and a three-time All-Star at second base during the 1960s.

5) Alan Trammell and Lou Whitaker—the shortstop-second base combination that epitomized Tigers teams of the 1980s.

Tracewski considers himself lucky in many ways to have played or worked for some of the greatest baseball minds around. This includes the late Walter Alston who managed him with the Dodgers and was a close second to Sparky Anderson, as the manager Tracewski respected most. He fondly remembers breaking in as a coach under Billy Martin, whose innovations and fire led the younger Tracewski to believe Martin had invented the game. Tracewski also feels blessed to have worked with Ralph Houk on the successful rebuilding project that GM Jim Campbell oversaw with the mid-1970s Tigers.

In retirement, Tracewski has participated regularly in Tigers fantasy camps, gone to spring training, and maintained contact with current and former Tigers like Alan Trammell. Since retiring from baseball in 1995, Tracewski has continued to be active, playing golf with his friends Sandy Koufax, and at least one trip a year to Detroit. He recently had the opportunity to tour old Tiger Stadium, marveling at the shape of the grass field as his grandson ran the bases on what he considers one of the great ballparks in which to play or watch a game. Tracewski also had one last trip to Vero Beach planned, as the Dodgers prepare to close down Dodgertown and move to Arizona after the 2008 exhibition season, as Tracewski longed for another chance to walk the fields and basepaths where his remarkable four-decade pro career began.

References

Articles

"No. 43—Dick Tracewski—Eynon." *The Times-Tribune* (Scranton, Pa.), November 15, 2004.

McAuliffe, Josh, "Son of immigrant coal miner finds himself on the field with Jackie Robinson," March 11, 2007.

McAuliffe, Josh, "Lion in Winter: A League of His Own, Richard 'Dick' Tracewski" March 11, 2007

Web Sites

www.baseball-reference.com (Dick Tracewski entry)

www.wikipedia.com (Dick Tracewski entry)

Other Sources

Levine, Peter M. Richard Tracewski telephone interview, June 1, 2007

The Broadcasters

Paul Carey

by Matt Bohn

FOR 19 SEASONS, Detroit Tigers baseball on the radio meant "Ernie and Paul." From 1973 to 1991, Paul Carey and Ernie Harwell formed one of the most fondly remembered broadcast duos in Tigers broadcast history. One of their successors as the Tigers radio voices, Dan Dickerson, remembered "a real comfort level of turning on Ernie and Paul. I mean it was just 'Ernie and Paul.' How many broadcasters are known by their first names only?" Carey's deep, resonant voice (Red Sox broadcaster Joe Castiglione called him "Mr. Pipes"), was compared by one newspaper columnist to that of Vaughn Monroe, the Big Band Era bandleader and baritone vocalist. Another columnist referred to Carey as the "Voice of God." Carey's broadcast partner, Ernie Harwell, commented, "Paul has got a fantastic voice, the best voice I've ever heard on anybody. He makes anyone who works with him sound like a soprano." For those 19 seasons, that deep voice brought the middle three innings of each Tigers game to the radio listeners.

Paul Carey was born in 1928 in Mount Pleasant, Michigan, to Joseph P. and Ida (Brugge) Carey. His father was a professor of geography at Central Michigan University in Mount Pleasant and later was chair of the geography department. Paul's interest in Tigers baseball dates back to the Mickey Cochrane era. "In 1934, I was just a little too young," he recalled in 2008. "I was 6 years old—too young to appreciate baseball, I think. In 1935 ... that's when I started listening to the Tigers and started becoming a Tiger fan." Carey finally witnessed his first Tigers game at Navin Field. New York Yankees pitcher Red Ruffing beat Tigers hurler Tommy Bridges in that contest. "I think I may have cried all the way home that day," he remembered. (It was likely a 7-4 win by the Bronx Bombers on August 29, 1937.)

Growing up listening to Tigers broadcaster Harry Heilmann describing the games on radio, Carey knew at an early age that he wanted to be a sportscaster. "It probably started out about in the sixth grade," he recalled. "I would hang a little bicycle horn from the ceiling on a string and it looked like it was like a microphone. And I had football and baseball games with spinners, or dice, and I'd play them and I'd announce them as we went along." As a teen during World War II, Carey hitchhiked to Detroit with a friend and watched Heilmann do a re-creation of a Tigers road game. Standing on the sidewalk, Carey watched Heilmann describe the play-by-play from ticker-tape reports as he sat in a booth in front of the Telenews Theater on Woodward Avenue.

Graduating from Mount Pleasant High School in 1946, Carey placed among the top ten in his class. He enrolled first at Central Michigan University in his home town, and transferred to Michigan State University two years later. "Central, at that time, didn't have any radio facilities at all and Michigan State had a longstanding radio station," Carey said. "So I transferred to Michigan State."

While still a student at Michigan State, Carey landed his first job in radio at WCEN, a start-up station in Mount Pleasant. There he had his first experience with baseball play-by-play. "The very first baseball play-by-play I did was my first week in radio," Carey recalled. "We went on the air on August 8, 1949, and in that first week, we tried to do a lot of things to get the people listening to us, and one of the things we did at the end of that first week was a Sunday afternoon game at Island Park in Mount Pleasant." Setting up a microphone on a card table at ground level behind the backstop, Carey broadcast a game between the Mount Pleasant town team and a team from a nearby town. "So that was my first taste of doing baseball. But I didn't do any baseball again, frankly, until I started doing the Tigers," he said.

Carey also covered the football and basketball games of Mount Pleasant High School and Central Michigan University on WCEN. Because the station stayed on the air only during daytime hours, Carey had to record Friday night games and air the recording on Saturday. Transportation to his job at WCEN was also a challenge. "I was hitchhiking back and forth from Michigan State my senior year at college to work weekends in Mount Pleasant," Carey recalled. "Going back and forth and relying on the kindness of people to pick

DETROIT TIGERS 1984: WHAT A START! WHAT A FINISH!

you up to take you 70 miles north to Mount Pleasant.... it's amazing that we were able to do that."

After graduating from Michigan State in 1950, Carey continued to work at WCEN until he was drafted during the Korean War. After serving in the infantry with the Army for two years, he returned to Mount Pleasant and went right back to work at WCEN, providing play-by-play for high-school and college football games just days after returning from the service.

In the spring of 1953, Carey moved to WKNX radio and WKNX-TV in Saginaw, Michigan, where he gained some experience in television. Carey remembered, "I wound up being the afternoon disc jockey at WKNX for three years and three months. And I was program director of the radio station for two years. And I did a lot of commercial work on television and it got so that I got the feel of it." Working at WKNX, Carey did little sports play-by-play, though he did cover the Thanksgiving Day games between Saginaw High and Arthur Hill High School in Saginaw.

Hired as a staff announcer by Detroit AM radio powerhouse WJR in June 1956, Carey began a scoreboard show on the station that fall. His experience doing that show led to his being assigned to handle the Tigers' pregame shows from Briggs Stadium on the handful of home night games that WJR covered in 1958. Carey recalled being nervous about the assignment: "I was kind of out of my depth. I'm nervous and never enjoyed interviewing anyway." He credited Mel Ott, the Hall of Famer who was then a member of the Tigers' broadcast crew, with helping him get through the season. "One of the finest people I have ever known in my life," Carey said of Ott. "I think he sensed that I was nervous and needed help. And Mel went on with me three or four times by himself. Or he would help me find somebody. He was just the biggest help to me and just a wonderful person." Carey continued doing the pregame shows through the 1959 season. When the format changed in 1960, Ernie Harwell took over Carey's pregame show. "I was just as happy not to do it," he said.

In 1964, Carey became the producer of the Tigers' radio network. When broadcaster Ray Lane announced that he was leaving the Tigers radio crew in 1973 to focus more on TV work, a friend persuaded Carey to send in an audition tape and apply for Lane's job. "And I didn't have any tape," he recalled. "I had never done a game. So I didn't have anything to call on. So I manufactured a game. I kind of wrote a script and I got a crowd noise record and I may even have had a wind noise record. I made a mock broadcast of a game from Arlington Stadium between the Texas Rangers and the Tigers." Figuring he would not have a chance to get the job, Carey was surprised and thrilled when he beat out 150 other applicants to be hired as Ernie Harwell's partner on radio. Summing up why he believed he got the job, Carey said, "I think without question the fact that I did the Tiger network for eight years…but more importantly, I had been working at WJR since 1956 and WJR owned the rights to the Tiger games and I was one of their sportscasters. I think that was the thing that got me the job more than anything else—not my ability to do baseball because I hadn't done it." Not to that point, anyway.

Working alongside Harwell, Carey was part of a broadcast team that was remembered fondly—particularly by the Tigers broadcasters who followed them. Tigers radio voice Dan Dickerson first listened to the duo while in his teens and he recalled, "There was such a smooth transition from Ernie to Paul: different styles, different voices but both were just so good. I don't think there's any question that's why I became such a loyal radio listener. I listened through thick and thin, I'm telling you. They lost 19 straight in '75, I'd listen to most games just because I liked it. I don't think there's any question those two helped me get hooked on baseball."

Television broadcaster Mario Impemba echoed Dickerson's feelings. "Growing up in Detroit, the Ernie Harwell-Paul Carey team greatly influenced the way I broadcast a game today," Impemba said. "No one could really match Paul's thunderous pipes, but his style is what caught my attention as a young listener. Paul was outstanding at letting the ballpark sounds fill a broadcast. His style was straightforward and easy on the ears. I think he had a tremendous respect for the game. The story was always the game and not the announcer. Too many announcers today try to become the show and overshadow the game. Paul knew his job was to report what was happening on the field, nothing more, nothing less. He let the game breathe which allowed his listeners to use their imagination."

Carey also provided play-by-play for Detroit Pistons basketball in three different stints (1969-73, 1975-76, and 1981-82). Carey found basketball an easier sport to do than baseball. "I always figured basketball was probably the sport I could do better than anything," he said. He found baseball more difficult because of the slower pace of the game. "You have periods of time where there is very little going on. That's when someone like Ernie would excel because he had these stories and memories, and that's how Harry Heilmann excelled. He had these wonderful stories of his days in baseball and the people he knew. I didn't have that background. So I had to scrounge and do a lot of research and a lot of study."

In 1975, WJR, seeking to save money, told Carey that he would have to take on added duties; not only would he have to provide play-by-play, but he would have to be the engineer for the baseball broadcasts. "I was faced that winter with the proposition of no longer being a Tiger announcer or taking on the engineering job as well as being an announcer. And I wanted to continue to be a Tiger announcer," he recalled. "I was told in 1975 that it was the coming thing—that others would be following suit shortly. Well, to this date, 2008, there's no major-league announcer who has also been his own engineer. I'm the only one who's ever done it." For 16 seasons, Carey handled engineer duties as well as providing play-by-play. "After a while I got very accustomed to it but I never did really like it," he said of his dual role.

Having broadcast many subpar Tigers teams for several years, Carey had a different feeling about the team coming into the 1984 season. During spring training in Lakeland, Florida, a reporter from the Lakeland Ledger asked him to predict where the Tigers would finish. Carey remembered, "I was a pessimist anyway, and I picked them to finish third." When he walked into the Tigers' clubhouse the day his prediction hit the paper, "Kirk Gibson and Lance Parrish just jumped all over my case because I picked them to finish third. 'Don't you know better, Carey?! We're going to win it all!' And they knew then they were going to win it all. There was no question."

When the Tigers did make it to the World Series in 1984, Carey's joy for his team's success was overshadowed by the illness of Patti, his wife of 23 years. Ernie Harwell recalled in his book Tuned to Baseball, "To me, the gutsiest performance of the World Series didn't happen on the diamond. It happened in our radio booth. It was the performance of Paul Carey who worked under tension and pressure which would have been unbearable for a lesser man. He broadcast most of the Series knowing that his wife, Patti, had been stricken with a malignant brain tumor." Carey learned just before Game Three of the World Series that his wife's condition was terminal. "Here he was in the happiest time for the Tigers," Harwell wrote. "But for Paul, it was the saddest time of his life." Carey remembered the prognosis: "Optimistically they gave me nine to fifteen months. She lasted five. That was a very tough time in my life."

Though busy with covering the Tigers and with studio work, Carey still found the time to help a young broadcaster looking for advice. Tigers announcer Dan Dickerson recalled that in 1984 he was working at a radio station in Grand Rapids, Michigan, and was struggling with scant success to gain some notice in the Detroit market. He contacted Carey. "I just asked if I could come in and see how he did his job and kind of shadow him for a Sunday afternoon. He said 'Sure.' So I went down to [the station] ... and he sat with me and told me what he did and how he did it. I was just trying to pick his brain a little bit but he spent hours with me on a Sunday afternoon, which obviously are busy days in the fall.... But I'll never forget that he gave me the time of day when nobody else did."

By 1990, Carey was ready to retire. He was thinking about retiring after the 1990 season, but reconsidered when he learned that he would no longer have to do engineer duties in 1991. "I wanted to experience being just an announcer again," he said. Telling WJR station manager Jim Long in November 1990 of his intention to retire, Carey was shocked when he learned just a few weeks later that Harwell had been fired. Remembering the 1991 season as "bittersweet," he said, "I was not looking forward to not doing the games. But I was looking forward to traveling and having the time from mid-February until October on my own. I was ready to retire." After an emotional goodbye to Ernie and the fans, Carey retired at the end of the year.

Carey married the former Nancy Wackerly in 1987. They began to spend their winters in the Pensacola, Florida, area, and in Rochester, Michigan, the rest of the year. He was still keeping up with baseball every day, though he didn't go to many games at Comerica Park. In the spring of 2008, Carey underwent surgery to remove a blockage in his right carotid artery. The day before the surgery, he got a phone call from a close friend: Ernie Harwell. "The day before, he prayed with me on the telephone. I think that's really special."

References

Publications

Castiglione, Joe, and Douglas B. Lyons. *Broadcast Rites and Sites: I Saw It on the Radio With the Boston Red Sox*. Lanham, Md.: Taylor Trade Publishing, 2004.

Eichorn, George B. *Detroit's Sports Broadcasters on the Air*. Charleston, S.C.: Arcadia Publishing, 2003.

Harwell, Ernie. *Tuned to Baseball*. South Bend, Ind.: Diamond Communications, 1985.

Keegan, Tom. Ernie Harwell: *My Sixty Years in Baseball*. Chicago: Triumph Books, 2002.

Articles

Associated Press. "Carey Joins Harwell On Tiger Radio." *Saginaw News*, February 2, 1973. B6.

Atkins, Harry. "Ernie wanted to continue beyond 1991, but told 'no.'" *Saginaw News*, December 20, 1990. D1, D5.

Crowe, Steve. "Carey leaving on own, gets 'misty' over Ernie." *Detroit Free Press*, December 20, 1990. 6G.

Crowe, Steve. "Ernie, Paul finally at loss for words." *Detroit Free Press*, October 5, 1991. 1B.

"Departing." *Saginaw News*, June 23, 1956, TV & Radio Section. 2.

Dow, Bill. "Seasons of George Blaha, 30." *Detroit Free Press*, January, 18, 2006. 1E.

Hardy, Dick. "Ernie added color to game." *Bay City Times*, October 6, 1991. 8F.

Harwell, Ernie. "Catching up with the Tiger family" *Detroit Free Press*, June 23, 2008. 2B.

"High School Graduation Activities for 86 Seniors Is Underway This Week." *Isabella County Times-News*, May 30, 1946. 1, 4.

"Joseph P. Carey, Outstanding M.P. Citizen, Dies." *Mount Pleasant Daily Times*, August 30, 1968. 1.

Kornacki, Steve. "Harwell's streak ends." *Detroit Free Press*, April 25, 1989. 5D.

DETROIT TIGERS 1984: WHAT A START! WHAT A FINISH!

Mariotti, Jay. "A minor adjustment: Tiger broadcasters get a taste of the farm life." *Detroit News*, June 22, 1981. 4D.

Rubin, Neal. "The Tigers' Utility Voice: Second banana Paul Carey, glad to skip the fame game, gets top marks on his own." *Detroit Free Press*, June 24, 1990. 1G, 3G.

"Obituaries: Ida M. Carey." *Mount Pleasant Morning Sun*, November 9, 1979. 2.

Tuschak, Beth. "Harwell, Carey turn work to play." *Detroit News*, April 8, 1989. 6C.

Vincent, Charlie. "Strictly Professional: Ernie and Paul—cool and calm in broadcast clincher." *Detroit Free Press*, September 19, 1984. 3D.

White, Sue. "Thanks for the memories: WKNX-AM, a pioneer of radio's golden age, bids its final farewell to mid-Michigan." *Saginaw News*, August 1, 2004. C1, C4.

Other Sources

Bohn, Matt. Phone interview with Paul Carey, June 25, 2008.

Bohn, Matt. Phone interview with Dan Dickerson, June 29, 2008.

Impemba, Mario. E-mail messages to the author.

Bill Freehan
by Trey Strecker

WIDELY REGARDED AS one of the game's best defensive catchers and the best catcher in the American League during his prime, Bill Freehan was a fierce competitor and a committed leader on the diamond. Described by sportswriter Arnold Hano as "a thinking man's catcher" and "an elemental ballplayer," the 6-foot, 2-inch, 205-pound Freehan displayed "an unusual blend of brawn and brains." Freehan is in select company with Charlie Bennett, Mickey Cochrane, Lance Parrish, and Ivan Rodriguez as one of the most popular and talented backstops in Detroit baseball history.

The eldest son of Ashley Freehan, a sales representative for a seat insulation company, William Ashley Freehan was born on November 29, 1941, in Detroit. Growing up in suburban Royal Oak with his three siblings, the young Freehan began catching on the Detroit sandlots one day when his Little League team's catcher didn't show up and he moved from shortstop behind the plate. During one Little League All-Star game, Freehan was bowled over in a collision at home plate by future teammate Willie Horton. When Bill was 14, his father bought a mobile-home development, and his family moved to St. Petersburg, Florida, where Freehan attended Bishop Barry High School, playing baseball, basketball, and football. During the summers, Freehan returned to Detroit to play sandlot baseball, where, only 15, he captured the eye of Tigers scout Louis D'Annunzio, who called Freehan "the best sandlot catcher he'd seen."

After graduating from high school in 1959, Freehan hoped to attend the University of Notre Dame, but the school required that he choose football or baseball, so he accepted an athletic scholarship to the University of Michigan, catching on the baseball team and playing end and linebacker on the football squad. At Michigan, Freehan once caught all three games of a tripleheader between Michigan and Michigan State, then, according to his mother, "he went out dancing until one in the morning." Always strong defensively, the sophomore catcher pounded Big Ten pitching, batting .585 in 1961 and drawing the attention of major league scouts. Although he entertained offers from several teams, the 19-year-old Freehan signed with his hometown Tigers for a $125,000 bonus in 1961. But, even as he was breaking into the big leagues, the Tigers' bonus baby continued attending school part-time over the offseason, completing his bachelor's degree in history with a 3.1 grade point average from Michigan in 1966. Freehan explained, "My deal with my dad was, I didn't see a dime of my bonus until I got my degree."

For the 1961 season, the Tigers farmed him out to Duluth-Superior in the Class C Northern League, where Freehan hit .343 with seven home runs and 26 RBIs in 30 games for manager Bill Swift before he was promptly promoted to Knoxville in the Sally League. There, he batted .289 in 47 games before a late-September call-up to Detroit, where Freehan managed four singles in ten at bats. In 1962, Freehan played the entire season for Denver's American Association entry, playing stellar defense behind the plate and batting .283 with nine home runs and 58 RBIs. Called up to Detroit after the season, he saw no action. On February 23, 1963, Freehan married Patricia O'Brien, his high-school sweetheart from St. Petersburg and the sister of St. Louis Cardinals pitcher Dan O'Brien (1978-79).

Brought up to the Tigers again in 1963, Freehan got on base nine straight times, managing three home runs, one triple, three doubles, two singles, and three walks in fifteen plate appearances. Over the remainder of his rookie season, the twenty-one-year-old receiver committed only two errors in 73 games behind the plate, although he hit only .243. "I wanted to hit well," Freehan said. "I just never put that ahead of my primary responsibility. The catcher has to be the captain of the field. I felt if I did my job behind the plate, I was contributing to the team in the best way I could." Always a perfectionist, one Tigers front-office man said, "Bill's biggest trouble is that he thinks he never should have a bad day."

The next year marked Freehan's arrival as the dominant catcher in the American League. A right-handed hitter who crowded the plate, Freehan became the first Detroit catcher to hit .300 since Mickey Cochrane batted .319 in 1935. At the time of his first All-Star selection in 1964, Freehan had caught fewer than 200 major league games, but over the course of the season, the Detroit backstop demonstrated that he deserved to be an All-Star. Freehan committed only seven errors in 141 games—catching the final 56 games of the season and logging a stretch of 517 consecutive innings behind the plate—with a .993 fielding percentage, and he belted 18 home runs with 80 RBIs. More importantly, during the 1964 campaign, Freehan became the team's spiritual leader," according to writer Jim Sargent. Manager Charlie Dressen noted that even a veteran pitcher like Dave Wickersham was willing to let the young catcher call the game. "He suddenly grew up," Dressen remarked, "and his pitchers have confidence in him now. So do the other players. Quick-like, the Tigers had a leader." Arnold Hano noted that Freehan "leads the way sergeants lead, not second lieutenants. He leads by example." General manager Jim Campbell said, "We put the full load on Freehan's shoulders and he didn't stumble."

Although Freehan caught 129 games in 1965, he was frequently dinged up by injuries. In spring training, Freehan suffered a severe muscle spasm in his lower back while rounding second base, the injury putting him on the bench for three weeks. On May 29, a foul tip off the bat of Cleveland's Max Alvis injured his throwing hand and, on June 25, a pitch deflected off Minnesota rookie Sandy Valdespino struck Freehan's bare hand in the exact spot as the foul tip. While he avoided the disabled list, Freehan only hit a meager .234 in both 1965 and 1966. Still primarily known for his defensive prowess and his game-calling skills, Freehan won the first of five consecutive Gold Gloves in 1965 and, on June 15, 1965, he set a record by making 19 putouts in a single game—thanks in large part to Denny McLain's 15 strikeouts in 6.2 innings of relief work.

At the beginning of the 1967 season, Freehan experimented with moving closer to the plate on the advice of new manager Mayo Smith and batting coach Wally Moses, and his hitting improved. Although he was hit by pitches twenty times that year, he hit .282 with 20 home runs and 74 RBIs. It was an exceptional season, as Freehan caught 138 games with only six passed balls and eight errors, and he played in 155 games; no other catcher in the majors led his team in games played. Moreover, much to the consternation of Smith and the Tigers, Freehan caught all fifteen innings of the 1967 All-Star Game in Anaheim. On September 10, Freehan was hit by a pitch in the third inning of the first game of a doubleheader, spoiling Joel Horlen's otherwise-perfect game. At the end of the season, on September 26, Freehan was ejected from a game for the first time in his career, slamming his mask into the dirt after the Yankees' Horace Clarke stole second base. "I wasn't arguing about the stolen base," Freehan explained later. "The pitch was a strike.... [Umpire Hank] Soar called it a ball. I couldn't believe it." His next ejection would occur nearly eight years later, on August 12, 1975, when he argued over a ball-four call to the Texas Rangers' Mike Hargrove. Although Detroit finished one game behind Boston's "Impossible Dream" team for the AL flag, Freehan had an outstanding season, and he was voted the 1967 Tiger of the Year by the local chapter of the Baseball Writers Association of America.

During the Tigers' 1968 championship season, Freehan caught 155 regular-season games and all seven World Series games. In the regular season, he set career-high marks with 25 home runs, 73 runs scored, and 84 RBIs, and he was hit by pitches 24 times. Bothered that he was hitless in the first five games of the World Series, Freehan shrugged, "You've got to understand that you're facing Bob Gibson in three of those games. That's not a joy for anybody." In the first five games of the World Series, the Cardinals tested Freehan's arm, stealing 11 bases in 16 attempts, but he managed to corral the running game in Games 6 and 7.

Freehan's role in one of the most controversial plays in World Series history is familiar to most Tigers fans. The Cardinals led 3-2 when speedster Lou Brock tried to score from second on Julian Javier's single to left field. Freehan caught Willie Horton's perfect one-hop throw and blocked the plate, and Brock, who decided not to slide, was tagged out. "I've got to thank [University of Michigan football coach] Bump Elliott if I block the plate well," Freehan said. Writing about the play, the *Los Angeles Herald*'s Milton Richman said, "What makes [Freehan] so extraordinary is that he plants his two big feet firmly in the ground, doesn't bother giving the base runner barreling down on his from third base so much as a sidelong glance and plain refuses to budge even when said base runner hits him at midship like a torpedo. For that he has the respect of ballplayers everywhere. They know they don't make catchers like Freehan anymore." White Sox manager Eddie Stanky added, "On any close play at the plate, it's like running into a freight train."

Freehan also caught Tim McCarver's foul popup near the first-base dugout to secure the final out in Game 7. The sight of Mickey Lolich leaping into Freehan's arms will always be an iconic image in Detroit baseball lore. "When Lolich jumps on you, well, he's not a small man," Freehan said. "But it was a great feeling!" Finishing the World Series 2-for-24 with a double, Freehan observed, "I know I wasn't very successful in hitting, but I've got the same World Series ring as everybody else." Remarkably, Freehan was the only AL player to finish among the top three in MVP voting in both 1967 and 1968.

In 1969, the Tigers finished in second place, a distant 19 games behind Baltimore, and Freehan batted a respectable .262 with 16 home runs in 143 games. Throughout the 1969 season, the catcher kept a ballplayer's clubhouse diary, which would be published the next year as *Behind the Mask: An Inside Baseball Diary*. Published a decade after Jim Brosnan's

DETROIT TIGERS 1984: WHAT A START! WHAT A FINISH!

The Long Season and the same year as Jim Bouton's *Ball Four*, Freehan's *Behind the Mask* did not display the literary insights of Brosnan's book or the scandalous revelations of Bouton's. For the most part, the book was, as Freehan explained, "a story about a ballclub. A catcher, a manager, and the pitcher." Unfortunately, as the 1970 season opened, pitcher Denny McLain was in the headlines again, serving a suspension related to a gambling investigation, so when *Sports Illustrated* published excerpts from Freehan's diary, it was no surprise to anyone that the McLain passages were featured in the magazine. At the center of the controversy was Freehan's accusation that McLain was often allowed to break club rules and that the coaching staff was powerless to stop him. McLain is "the best pitcher in the American League," Freehan wrote, "but it's an individual thing vs. a team thing." Ironically, after these excerpts were published, the same Tigers who resented McLain's special treatment felt Freehan had violated the sanctity of the clubhouse. "My book is about what it's like to be a catcher and go through a season," Freehan explained, "but what appeared in the magazine was not an accurate representation." Sportswriter Joe Falls speculated that some of the vitriol surrounding Freehan's book was due to poor timing: "If they had won the pennant last year, what Freehan had to say about McLain might have come out as being rather humorous: Look at that Denny, will you? Isn't he a rascal?"

Thus, 1970 was a rough year for Freehan. While his defense behind the plate was still impeccable, his batting average dropped to .241, and the team fell to fourth place. Still bothered by the 1965 spring training base-running injury, Freehan consented to spinal surgery to prolong his career as an everyday catcher. "Some days were good and some days were bad," Freehan recalled. "It got so my legs would be numb on certain days when I stepped out of my car at the ball park." On September 2, 1970, Freehan had bone graft surgery on the fifth vertebra of his lower back. As always, the durable catcher recovered quickly, and three months later, he was hiking on a deer-hunting weekend with Al Kaline, Mickey Stanley, and other players.

Although fans booed Freehan after the publication of *Behind the Mask*, all was forgotten when the catcher made a strong comeback from the surgery in 1971. Under Billy Martin, the Tigers bounced back into second place, and Freehan topped AL catchers with a .277 batting average, 21 home runs, and 71 RBIs, while he caught 144 games, more than anyone else in the league. Freehan had the opportunity to start the All-Star game at Tiger Stadium in place of the injured Ray Fosse, and had a three-homer game in a 12-11 loss to Boston that August 9.

With a healthy back and the acquisition of new backup catcher Tom Haller, Freehan anticipated another good season behind the plate in 1972. Freehan caught 105 games that season, batting .262, hitting 10 home runs and driving in 56 RBIs, but he fractured his right thumb late in the season when tagging out Boston's Carl Yastrzemski on a play at the plate. The Tigers finished first in American League East, but they were defeated by Oakland in the American League Championship Series. Freehan hit better in this postseason than he did in 1968, securing a .250 average and a home run in Detroit's Game 3 victory, but the Athletics stole seven bases thanks in part to Freehan's bum thumb.

"Defense…isn't just talent," Freehan believed, "that's concentration and work. I always called my games. Sure, I always had eye contact with my manager, but I was the one calling the pitches." The next year, when Billy Martin platooned him at catcher and questioned his game-calling skills, the proud Freehan resented his manager. Feeling that he was not given sufficient opportunity to prove himself, Freehan struggled with a lowly .234 average and 29 RBIs, playing in only 110 games (his lowest total in ten years). "I was never platooned before, not even part-time. I wouldn't have minded if the figures showed I couldn't hit right-handers. But they don't. I wouldn't mind losing my job if I was doing a lousy job." What bothered Freehan more than his poor performance at the plate was that Martin also second-guessed the pitches Freehan called, even publicly questioning some pitches that were ordered from the bench.

Freehan returned in 1974 prepared to prove himself, splitting time at catcher and first base under new manager Ralph Houk. With his poor showing the previous season and with the rise of Thurman Munson and Carlton Fisk as the league's premier catchers, Freehan felt he had to reestablish himself, but only two months into the season, the American League's All-Star catcher for the past ten years was shifted to first base. In the Tigers' biggest offensive bonanza of the year, Freehan belted a grand slam and drove in seven runs against the Yankees on September 8, 1974. Although his offensive production improved from the previous year—he hit .297 with 18 home runs and 60 RBIs in 1974—Freehan was the cornerstone of a December deal that would have sent him with Mickey Stanley—"remains of a bygone era," according to Detroit sportswriter Jim Hawkins—to the Philadelphia Phillies for catcher Bob Boone. As Freehan was preparing his family for the move to Philadelphia, the deal was nixed by the Phillies at the last minute.

Nevertheless, after the trade failed, Freehan could see the writing on the wall. Going into spring training in 1975, Houk tabbed Freehan as the Tigers' starting catcher, unless "one of these other guys proves he's better than Bill is." At age 34, Freehan caught 113 games, hitting .246 with 14 home runs and 47 RBIs, and he returned to the All-Star game for the eleventh time. But over the winter, the Tigers traded for Milt May, putting Freehan in a reserve role for the first time in his career. May caught only six games before being sidelined for the season with a broken ankle. Freehan, as part of a backstop triumvirate, caught 61 games in 1976 as did Bruce Kimm (John Wockenfuss was behind the plate in 59 contests), and on December 12, 1976, the Tigers gave Freehan his unconditional release. Although he still believed he could contribute on the diamond, he realized how fortunate he was to have played on his hometown team for his entire 15-year major league career. Still, when the Tigers offered Freehan a job managing Montgomery in the Class AA Southern League, he declined, explaining that "I can't feed my family on a minor league manager's salary."

In retirement, Freehan still felt the pull of the game, particularly when he saw the opportunity to teach. "You can't take the baseball out of the boy," he said. After he retired from major league baseball, Freehan served as the president of Freehan-Bocci & Company, an automobile manufacturer's representative agency he founded in suburban Detroit in 1974, where he worked with former teammate Jim Northrup. Freehan succeeded his 1960s Tigers teammates Norm Cash and Hank Aguirre in the broadcast booth to handle color commentary for Tigers games on cable television in 1984—their first world championship season since 1968—and 1985. In 1989, disturbed by an NCAA investigation that revealed illegal payments to players, Freehan called University of Michigan athletic director Bo Schembechler to ask about the once-successful baseball program. Two weeks later, he put his business career on hold and took over as the Wolverines' head baseball coach. Weathering two years' probation, Freehan coached Michigan baseball until 1995, reestablishing the integrity of the program and finishing with a 166-167-1 record. He left coaching to devote more attention to his business interests, although he was lured back to serve as Detroit's organizational catching instructor from 2002 to 2005. Today, Freehan lives in the Detroit suburb of Bloomfield Hills with his wife Pat. The Freehans have three daughters: Corey Sue, Kelley, and Cathy.

A driven leader and the best catcher in the American League for almost a decade, Freehan was an intelligent and durable backstop who caught more than 100 games for nine consecutive seasons. He won five Gold Gloves, was selected for 11 All-Star teams and played in eight All-Star games, retiring with a .262 lifetime batting average, 758 RBIs, and 200 home runs (100 at home and 100 on the road). When he retired, Freehan held the major league career records for most chances (10,714) and putouts (9,941), and highest fielding average for a catcher (.993). Bill James ranks Freehan as the twelfth best catcher of all time. Freehan was inducted into the Michigan Sports Hall of Fame in 1982, and Tigers fans voted him as catcher in 1999 for the All-Time Tiger Team.

References

Books

Cantor, George. *The Tigers of '68: Baseball's Last Real Champions*. Dallas: Taylor. 1997.

Freehan, Bill (Steve Gelman and Dick Schaap, eds.). *Behind the Mask: An Inside Baseball Diary*. New York: World. 1970.

Hawkins, Jim, and Dan Ewald. *The Detroit Tigers Encyclopedia*. Champaign, Ill.: Sports Publishing. 2003.

James, Bill. *The New Bill James Historical Baseball Abstract*. New York: Free Press. 2001.

Articles

Hano, Arnold. "Bill Freehan: Tough Leader of the Tigers." *Sport*, August 1968, 57-62.

Sargent, Jim. "Bill Freehan: A Key Member of the 1968 Champion Tigers." *Baseball Digest*, June 2000, 58-65.

Web Sites

"Bill Freehan." Baseball-Reference.com.

Other Sources

Bill Freehan clipping file, National Baseball Hall of Fame Library.

Ernie Harwell
by Matt Bohn

FOR FIFTY-FIVE seasons, baseball fans were able to get a greater enjoyment out of baseball because of the play-by-play descriptions of Ernie Harwell. In his easygoing laidback Southern drawl, he would exclaim that a home run was "long gone," that a batter on a called third strike "stood there like the house by the side of the road." Ernie might announce that a foul ball in Tiger Stadium might be snatched by a fan from Saginaw or St. Clair Shores. Modest about his own contributions to baseball, Harwell said in a 2005 interview about baseball broadcasting, "The game has got to be paramount. People are going to listen to the game no matter who's announcing it, they want to find out who's winning and what the score is and everything else is pretty much secondary."

Ernie Harwell was born in Washington, Georgia, on January 25, 1918. His father and uncle ran a furniture store that also served as a funeral parlor. As a child, Ernie loved baseball, playing the game as much as possible and listening to it on radio. The local druggist, knowing of young Ernie's

DETROIT TIGERS 1984: WHAT A START! WHAT A FINISH!

enthusiasm for the sport, encouraged him to broadcast an imaginary Atlanta Crackers game for patrons of the drugstore. Harwell's attempts at play-by-play were greeted with gentle gales of laughter by drugstore patrons as young Ernie had a speech impediment that hindered his attempts to pronounce the letter "s." His parents eventually paid for him to take elocution lessons.

In 1934, the 16-year-old Harwell saw his first major league game while visiting a relative in Chicago. That same year, he also gained a job. Dissatisfied with the amount of space devoted to Atlanta baseball in *The Sporting News*, Harwell wrote the paper a letter offering to serve as their Atlanta correspondent. Hoping to seem older than his 16 years, Harwell signed his name "W. Earnest Harwell." Impressed with samples of Harwell's writing, the paper invited him to write regularly.

Through his high school and college years, Harwell also worked part time for the Atlanta Constitution sports department. In 1940, during his senior year at Emory University, he made his radio debut, landing a job as sports director at radio station WSB. Hosting a twice-nightly fifteen-minute sports program, Ernie was able to interview some of the biggest names in sports at the time including Ty Cobb, Ted Williams, Connie Mack and heavyweight boxer Jack Dempsey.

A year after graduating from Emory University in 1940, Harwell married Lulu Tankersley. Ernie and Lulu's union would be a lasting one. In August, the Harwells celebrated 68 years of married life. They raised four children together.

In 1942, with World War II raging, Harwell enlisted with the Marines. During his time in the service, he was a correspondent for the Marine newspaper *Leatherneck*. He got his first taste of baseball play-by-play in 1943, while still serving in the Marines. Atlanta Crackers owner Earl Mann asked Ernie to do the Crackers broadcasts and he agreed, provided that he could donate his pay to the Red Cross. His stint as a Crackers announcer quickly came to a halt, though. Some civilian listeners felt it was wrong for a serviceman to broadcast baseball games. The Marines told Ernie he could no longer work Crackers games. Mann, however, impressed with Harwell's style, told him that when he was discharged from the service, the Crackers' announcing job was his.

Discharged from the Marines in early 1946, Harwell approached Mann about the Crackers job. At this time, station WATL had obtained the rights to Crackers broadcasts. The station wanted to hire its sports director, Stan Raymond, as the Crackers' voice. Mann, true to his word, insisted that Ernie be the Crackers' radio voice. Pushing for Ernie's hiring, Mann finally won out on the day before the 1946 season opener.

After losing out on an opportunity to broadcast for the New York Giants in 1947 because of a sponsor conflict, Harwell got the chance to broadcast the Brooklyn Dodgers' games the following year. Regular play-by-play man Red Barber was scheduled to cover the Olympics for CBS that summer. The Dodgers asked Harwell to fill in; then, when Barber was stricken with an ulcer that July, the Dodgers needed another announcer immediately. Crackers' president Mann was willing to let Ernie go to Brooklyn, but for a price. So, in the only deal of its kind, Harwell was traded to the Brooklyn Dodgers in exchange for catcher Cliff Dapper. Harwell became a member of the Dodgers' broadcast crew August 4, 1948. Lead announcer Red Barber, still recovering from the effects of a bleeding ulcer, rejoined the team a month later. Ernie said in a 2005 interview, "He [Red] was still weak and he couldn't do a whole lot, so Connie [Desmond] and I did pretty much the bulk of the work the rest of the season. The first game he came back to was when Rex Barney pitched a no-hitter at the Polo Grounds. And that was the first game I ever worked with Red."

In 1949, Ernie added television to his duties as a Dodgers announcer. Barber, Desmond and Harwell took turns handling the television portion of the home broadcasts that year—one man on TV, the other two on the radio. Harwell realized right away that television dictated a different approach to play-by-play than radio. "I thought that came pretty much automatic," he said. "I realized that you had to keep your mouth shut a lot more on TV than you did on radio and it wasn't too difficult for me to move back and forth from one medium to another." Only home games were broadcast on television at the time. On road trips, only two of the three broadcasters would make the trip with the team: "We sort of usually had two guys rather than three in the booth at a time. One guy just sort of took off and didn't do that particular game."

Offered a better opportunity with the Giants in 1950, Ernie moved from Ebbets Field to the Polo Grounds, where he was teamed with announcer Russ Hodges. His second year with the Giants turned out to be what he called in his memoir, *Tuned to Baseball*, "the most thrilling season of my broadcasting career." That season, the Giants and Dodgers tied for the pennant, leading to a three-game playoff series before the World Series. The coaxial cable having just been laid, the series was the first sporting event to be broadcast live from coast to coast. On the day of the third and deciding game, Ernie was assigned to cover the game nationally over NBC-TV. In *Tuned To Baseball*, he recalled "I would be on NBC-TV coast-to-coast on the biggest game in baseball history. Hodges, my partner, would have to settle for radio." Ernie felt fortunate—there would be four radio announcers from various outlets that day, but he would be the only television announcer covering the game.

As it turned out, Russ Hodges' description of the famous game-winning Bobby Thomson home run ("The Giants win the pennant!") became one of the most famous play-by-play moments in sports history. Ernie's contribution to the "shot heard 'round the world" was largely forgotten. In those days, few games were recorded for future play. When accepting the Ford Frick Award in 1981 at the Hall of Fame induction ceremony, he said, "Television had no instant replay, no recording in those days. Only Mrs. Harwell knows that I did the telecast of Bobby Thomson's home run."

Dropped by the Giants after the 1953 season, Harwell moved to Baltimore, becoming the first broadcaster for the new American League Orioles. Working in Baltimore, Ernie covered subpar baseball teams (the Orioles, formerly the St. Louis Browns, went 54-100 their first season) but had the opportunity to work with other great baseball voices, including Chuck Thompson and Herb Carneal. In 1957, Orioles (and former Tigers) third baseman George Kell spent some time with Harwell in the broadcast booth while recovering from a beaning. At Harwell's invitation, Kell broadcast some innings of play by play. Kell's broadcasting was well received and eventually led to his becoming a full-time baseball announcer with the Detroit Tigers.

Kell later returned the favor. In 1959, while he was doing Tigers radio and TV with Van Patrick, the sponsorship of the Tigers broadcasts changed from the Goebel brewery to Stroh's, the new sponsor decided to replace Patrick with a voice not identified with Goebel. Kell recommended Harwell for the job and told him of the opening. Though he had a strong position in Baltimore, Ernie always liked Detroit and decided to make the move, signing with the Tigers during the 1959 World Series

Kell and Harwell teamed up on Tigers radio and television, splitting play-by-play duties equally from 1960 to 1963. Ernie told *Detroit News* reporter Lynn Henning in 2002, "I'd do the first four-and-a-half innings on TV, and George would do the same thing on radio. Then we'd swap." After Kell left radio in 1963, Harwell was teamed with former Tiger manager Bob Scheffing for a year before being assigned to radio only beginning in 1965.

Ernie, an avid baseball historian, was known for his generosity to his broadcast colleagues. Ray Lane told of an example of Ernie's willingness to help a colleague when he became Harwell's broadcast partner in 1967. Forty years later, Lane remembered how Harwell called him and kindly offered him the use of his vast personal collection of baseball books and records. Lane recalls Harwell saying, "Listen—I have all these things from past history. I have record books…down in my basement. Anything that you ever need concerning baseball—it's yours to use. I'll make the offer one time and any time you want to take a look at any of this stuff, you're welcome to it." Ernie's collection of baseball books and memorabilia was later donated to the Detroit Public Library. Lane, appreciative of Harwell's kindness to a fledgling broadcaster, called him "the true Southern gentleman."

Harwell and Lane first worked together during 1967, a season marked by riots in Detroit and a near-miss of the AL flag for the Tigers. When the Tigers won the American League pennant the following season, Ernie covered the World Series on NBC Radio with Pee Wee Reese. He was also asked to select the national anthem singers for the games played at Tiger Stadium. For one of the games, Harwell asked singer Jose Feliciano to sing the anthem. Feliciano's nontraditional rendition was met with angry public reaction and even some calls for Harwell to lose his job. But Ernie stood by his selection of Feliciano and weathered the controversy.

Though Harwell felt fortunate to work alongside a number of good broadcast partners in Detroit, his longest professional association began in 1973 when he was teamed with Paul Carey. Ernie and Paul worked together for nineteen seasons. In sharp contrast to later Tiger broadcasters, there was very little on-air banter between the two. Harwell worked the first three and last three innings and rarely commented during Carey's middle three innings of play-by-play. Harwell explained this in an April 5, 1987, *Detroit Free Press* article, saying, "I talk enough during six innings. That's the way I feel about it. With Paul I don't want to interrupt the flow of his game. There are so many times guys come in just to be coming in and we just try to avoid that." Reflecting on their approach in a 2005 interview, Ernie said, "I guess our philosophy was we were there for each other, but we didn't do a lot of chit-chat. If there was a pitching change and Paul was on the air, I'd probably come in and give some other scores or make some comments—or vice versa. I think if anything really significant happened that we felt like needed discussion, we would discuss it. But we didn't talk about stuff after every pitch like some of the guys do now. We concentrated on the game."

Though the two had little on-air conversation, they were known for having a good working relationship. Carey told *Detroit Free Press* sportswriter Joe Lapointe in 1987, "Basically what it comes down to is we have very different personalities. And I think that's why it works well. I'm a fretter and a worrier. I like the responsibility of the small details. I think Ernie does not. Ernie would like to come in and enjoy the overall atmosphere of the ballpark. Ernie feels that everything is going to come out all right." Carey said in all their years together, they had never had an argument. "I've never had a harsh word between us. I don't think anybody ever has arguments with Ernie Harwell. I have a temper. People might get mad at me. But I don't think anybody could ever get mad at Ernie Harwell."

While still covering the Tigers every day during the regular season, Harwell was no stranger to network baseball audiences at All-Star or postseason time. Ernie broadcast the 1958 and 1961 All-Star games for NBC Radio. He covered many American League Championship Series on CBS Radio from the mid-1970s to the late 1980s as well as providing play by play for NBC Radio during the 1963 and 1968 World Series.

Harwell was also a football voice as well, working Baltimore Colts games during the 1950s. After his arrival in Detroit, Harwell covered football for one more year (1963) as a voice of the Michigan State Spartans. Asked by Lynn Henning in 2002 if he felt his style was better suited to baseball than football, Harwell said, "I probably fit it [baseball] better than I did with football. There were some people in my early days who thought I was a better football than baseball broadcaster. I think, in football, it moves along, and if you have an authoritative voice, and don't correct yourself and can call the play quickly, and beat the crowd noise, you can be a great football announcer. Nowadays they have a lot more advantages. They can look at videos, at replays. I enjoyed football, but baseball is a better game for radio than any other sport."

On August 2, 1981, Harwell was presented with the Ford Frick Award by the National Baseball Hall of Fame. Ernie

DETROIT TIGERS 1984: WHAT A START! WHAT A FINISH!

was only the fifth broadcaster to receive the honor, and the first living broadcaster—let alone active broadcaster—to be selected. In his acceptance speech, Harwell was modest about his accomplishments, saying "I know that this is an award that is supposed to be for my contribution to baseball. But let me say this: I have given a lot less to baseball than it's given to me. And the greatest gift that I've received from baseball is the way that the people in the game have responded to me with their warmth and their friendship."

After the 1990 season, the 72-year-old Harwell tried to negotiate for three more seasons as a Tigers broadcaster. However, he was flatly told by Tigers president Bo Schembechler that radio station WJR and the Tigers wanted Harwell to broadcast for just one more year and then announce his retirement. The Tigers and WJR refused to allow Harwell to go on broadcasting beyond 1991.

Announcing his firing at a December 19, 1990, press conference, Harwell said, "I wanted to go on longer, but they decided they didn't want me to go on longer. Bo was very forthright. He told me, 'We don't want you to come back.' I have no bitterness. I was surprised when the one-year deal came up. My health is fine." Harwell was quoted as saying in the *Detroit News*, "I was told they wanted to go in a different direction. I would have preferred to have the decision on my shoulders rather than have somebody tell me."

Schembechler countered that Harwell was asked to retire because the team and the radio station were afraid he would retire suddenly and they would be left scrambling to find a replacement. The December 20, 1990, edition of the *Detroit News* quoted Schembechler as saying, "It's our judgment that he's coming down close to the end of his career. We didn't want to have to go out and search." However, Schembechler's explanation rang hollow with fans. Reaction from the public was swift and negative—shock and anger. Former Tigers pitcher Denny McLain called the move "classless and gutless." A volunteer at a Grosse Pointe hospital told *The Sporting News* that when the nuns working there heard of the Harwell firing "they said some words I didn't think they knew." It was a public relations disaster for the team and the radio station.

Harwell while hurt by the firing, harbored no bitterness about it. A deeply spiritual man, he preferred to forgive and move on. After an emotional farewell to Tigers fans at the end of the 1991 season (as well as to radio partner Paul Carey, who had announced his retirement that year), Harwell found work elsewhere in 1992. Broadcasting 14 games on radio for the California Angels as well as CBS Radio's Game of the Week, he found he missed covering one team day after day. He told *Detroit News* reporter Dave Dye in 1993, "Working for CBS was great. I think it gave me an added dimension. But I don't think there's anything an announcer enjoys more than being with one team. You do a much better job when you're there every day. As a national announcer, you don't have the familiarity or the feeling for a team as a guy that is there all the time."

After Michael Ilitch bought the Tigers in 1992, he asked Harwell to come back for one more season as a radio voice of the team. Working with Rick Rizzs and Bob Rathbun, Ernie provided play by play for the third, fourth and fifth innings of Tigers broadcasts during the 1993 season. Originally planning to retire after that season, Harwell was persuaded to come back the following year on TV. Joining 1968 Tigers alumni Jim Price and Jim Northrup, Harwell became a member of the Tigers' cable broadcasting crew on PASS (Pro Am Sports System, a pay-cable channel) in 1994. That season, he appeared in 25 PASS telecasts providing play by play for the first three and last three innings.

Harwell continued covering Tigers games for PASS (and eventually for over-the-air station WKBD) through the 1998 season. He returned to WJR-AM for the final season at Tiger Stadium in 1999 and provided continuity in the narration of Tiger games as the team moved to Comerica Park. In 2002, at age 84, Harwell announced he was retiring. The season became one long goodbye. In each city that the Tigers visited Harwell was honored. In most visiting stadiums, he was asked to throw out the ceremonial first pitch. In Cleveland, the visitors' broadcast booth was renamed in his honor. Comerica Park's press box was renamed the Ernie Harwell Media Center. The respect and appreciation shown to Harwell by the fans and the teams were reminiscent of the outpouring from the fans when it seemed that 1991 would be the final year of his career. The only difference was that this time Ernie was leaving of his own accord.

When the Tigers played their last game, in Toronto, that season, Ernie signed off saying, "I have just finished my baseball broadcasting career. And it's time to say goodbye, but I think goodbyes are sad and I'd much rather say hello. Hello to a new adventure. I'm not leaving, folks. I'll still be with you, living my life in Michigan—my home state—surrounded by family and friends. And rather than goodbye, please allow me to say thank you. Thank you for letting me be part of your family. Thank you for taking me with you to that cottage up north, to the beach, the picnic, your work place and your back yard. Thank you for sneaking your transistor under the pillow as you grew up loving the Tigers. Now I might have been a small part of your life. But you've been a very large part of mine. And it's my privilege and honor to share with you the greatest game of all."

After his retirement , Harwell returned to the booth on a few special occasions. During the 2006 AL Division Series between the Tigers and the Yankees, he provided a few innings of play-by-play over the Tigers radio network and ESPN. "I'm going to drop in for a bit," he said. "I'm so honored. Anything they want me to do suits me fine. It's nice to be thought of again." In May 2007, Harwell joined Mario Impemba for a few Tigers games on Fox Sports Net Detroit. Outside of baseball, he still kept busy as a spokesman for Blue Cross/Blue Shield of Michigan. Harwell said in 2006, "I'm fine and I'm working hard. I've got a ten-year contract with Blue Cross/Blue Shield with a ten-year option, so I've got to live to be one hundred and six." He laughed, "I'm going to do that or die trying."

Sadly, Harwell could not fulfill the terms of that deal. He was diagnosed in September 2009 with inoperable bile duct cancer. He informed both his commercial audiences for Blue Cross and—in a special midgame message during a Detroit-Kansas City contest at Comerica Park later that month—Tigers fans that he was nearing the end of his earthly journey. He did so with the humility and dignity that was the hallmark of his work behind the microphone. Close to eight months after he made public his diagnosis, on May 4, 2010, Ernie Harwell died at his suburban Detroit home.

References

Publications

Carneal, Herb and Stew Thornley. *Hi Everybody!* Minneapolis: Nodin Press. 1996.

Harwell, Ernie. *Life After Baseball*. Detroit: Detroit Free Press. 2004.

Harwell, Ernie. *Tuned to Baseball*. South Bend, Ind.: Diamond Communications. 1985.

Keegan, Tom. *Ernie Harwell: My Sixty Years in Baseball*. Chicago: Triumph Books. 2002.

Kell, George and Dan Ewald. *Hello Everybody, I'm George Kell*. Champaign, Ill: Sports Publishing. 1998.

Patterson, Ted. *The Golden Voices of Football*. Champaign, Ill.: Sports Publishing. 2004.

Articles

Crowe, Steve. "Harwell succeeds Kell as Tigers' TV Voice." *Detroit Free Press*, March 8, 1997. 1A.

Dye, Dave. "Say It Isn't So, Bo: Tigers did Harwell wrong." *The Sporting News*, December 31, 1990. 3.

Dye, Dave and Bill Halls. "Harwell joins Price, Northrup on PASS." *Detroit News*, April 19, 1994. 4C.

Green, Jerry. "Tigers, Ernie Harwell call it quits." *Detroit News*, December 19, 1990. 1A and 4A.

"Harwell back in a familiar chair." *Detroit News*, March 4, 1993. 1C and 6C.

"Harwell to call two games." *Grand Rapids Press*, May 22, 2007. D1.

Henning, Lynn. "Ernie Harwell Signs Off, Detroit will miss man, voice. Retiring Tigers announcer regards fans, city fondly." *Detroit News*, September 26, 2002. 1F.

"Insiders Say." *The Sporting News*, December 31, 1990. 3.

Lapointe, Joe. "Ernie and Paul: Together 15 years and still in tune." *Detroit Free Press*, April 15, 1987. 9E and 11E.

Parker, Rob. "Harwell leaves booth with class." *Detroit News*, September 30, 2002. 1D.

Reidenbaugh, Lowell. "Reichler, Richman Saluted as Winners of Spink Award." *The Sporting News*, August 15, 1981. 30.

Spadafore, Jim. "Harwell makes return in visitors' radio booth." *Detroit News*, May 5, 1992. 5C.

Spoelstra, Watson. "Harwell-Kell Combo Will Air Tiger Tilts." *The Sporting News*, October 21, 1959. 18.

Spoelstra, Watson. "Kell Will Return to Motor City Mike." *The Sporting News*, February 13, 1965. 9.

VanOchten, Brian. "Sound familiar? Ernie's back at mike tonight. Harwell will join ESPN, radio announcing teams for guest appearance." *Grand Rapids Press*, October 6, 2006. E2.

Other Sources

Bohn, Matt. Phone interview with Ernie Harwell, June 29, 2005.

Bohn, Matt. Phone interview with Ray Lane, June 28, 2007.

Al Kaline
by Nick Waddell

ALBERT WILLIAM Kaline was born December 19, 1934, to Nicholas and Naomi Kaline in Baltimore. His father, a broom maker by trade, was a semipro baseball player, and began working with young Al to develop a pitcher's arm. Nicholas would squat down, while his son threw a variety of pitches. By the time he was 9, Al had learned a fastball, curveball, and changeup, and the work paid off. Kaline, while pitching for Westport Grammar School, won ten straight games. The legendary arm strength and accuracy that would make Kaline one of the most complete ballplayers of his time was evident early on. During a picnic festival, Kaline threw a ball 173½ feet. The disbelieving judges ordered him to throw again, believing that the measurement was off. Kaline threw again, this time 175 feet. While developing his arm, Kaline also learned to overcome osteomyelitis, a chronic bone disease that forced the removal of diseased bone from his left foot. To combat the physical impairment left behind, Al taught himself to run on the side of his foot. The determination to overcome injury became a trademark of Kaline's career.

A freshman at Southern High School in Baltimore 1949-1950, he tried out for the football and basketball teams. He quit football midway through the season when he broke his cheekbone, but in basketball, he led all scorers as a freshman. When spring came, Al tried out for baseball. Coach Bill Anderson immediately noticed Al's pitching, but because there was no place for Kaline as a pitcher, Anderson began teaching him to play center field, with the idea that Kaline would play one year of junior varsity ball and move up to varsity as a sophomore. That idea was short-lived, however, as Anderson placed Kaline on the varsity after watching his defensive prowess and offensive skills during a practice game. Position changes would follow Kaline to the majors as well.

Scouts from every major league team followed Kaline's every move. They watched as he hit .333 as a freshman and .418 as a sophomore, improving his defense as the year went on. After his sophomore year, Kaline was chosen in 1951 to play in an annual game sponsored by the Hearst newspapers, played at the Polo Grounds in New York. This game became a proving ground for Kaline, who hit two singles and a home run, and was named most valuable player. The next day, Kaline traveled to Yankee Stadium to watch his first-ever major league game, as the Yankees took on the St. Louis Browns.

Despite two great seasons in high school ball, the best for young Kaline was yet to come. He hit .469 as a junior and .488 as a senior to go along with his stellar defense. The combination earned Kaline more attention from the major leagues, specifically the Brooklyn Dodgers, St. Louis Cardinals, Philadelphia Phillies, and Detroit Tigers.

Tigers scout Ed Katalinas had followed Kaline's high school career, and was determined to make him the next Tigers great. When asked about Kaline's ability, Katalinas said, "To me he was the prospect that a scout creates in his mind and then prays that someone will come along to fit the pattern." Katalinas watched as Kaline played in seemingly every recreational ball league Baltimore had to offer during the summer, even hitting .609 one year in American Legion ball. The Tigers had finished the previous season last for the first time in franchise history, and were determined not to repeat that performance. Katalinas tried desperately to persuade Tigers president John McHale Sr. to sign Kaline, but McHale was more interested in pitcher Tom Qualters. After Philadelphia signed Qualters, the door was open for the Tigers to sign Kaline. Katalinas wrote McHale asking that he fly to Baltimore to watch Kaline play in person. McHale did, and was so impressed by Kaline's abilities that he immediately flew back to Detroit to get permission from Tigers president Spike Briggs to sign Kaline to a bonus contract. Briggs agreed, and Katalinas was given the task of signing Kaline.

Players could not be contacted by major league clubs until after high school graduation. The day after Kaline's graduation, Katalinas descended upon the Kaline residence with a contract in his pocket. Katalinas was greeted by Nicholas and Al, but was quickly left alone with the young player. Katalinas offered $15,000 in bonus money and $20,000 in salary over three years. Kaline discussed the offer with his parents, and agreed to the contract. He later said the bonus money helped pay off his parents' mortgage and his mother's eye surgery. Al signed the contract and turned it over to his father, who was also required to sign. Before Nicholas could sign, Al said he had promised to play in an Amateur Day game in a few days, and asked if he could still play. Katalinas realized then that he had a special talent in the young Kaline—not only with baseball, but with life. He knew Kaline would never break a promise, and agreed to let Al play. Nicholas then signed the contract, and Al Kaline became a Detroit Tiger. Since the bonus was more than $6,000, Kaline was assured he would be with the big league club for at least two years.

On June 25, 1953, Katalinas drove 18-year-old Kaline to his first game at Shibe Park in Philadelphia, where he new team was playing against the A's. The idea was to have Kaline play sparingly for two years with the major league club, and then be farmed out to a minor league team for two or three years for seasoning. Kaline quickly saw action that day, though. Wearing number 25, Kaline was told to play right field in the bottom of the eighth. Kaline had never played right field, but ran out with his glove and took the position. No ball was hit anywhere close to him, and he jogged back to the dugout with relief, until he realized he would lead off the top of the ninth. Kaline stepped in against Harry Byrd for his first big league at bat. Kaline dug in and drove a belt-high fastball to center field for an out. Kaline got his first hit, a single, July 8, 1953, off the Chicago White Sox' Luis Aloma. He scored his first run July 21 when he pinch-ran for Walt Dropo and came home from first on a double by Don Lund against the Washington Senators. That run from first to home earned Kaline the nickname "Baltimore Greyhound."

Kaline's first brush with greatness occurred later in 1953 when manager Fred Hutchinson introduced the budding star to Ted Williams. Williams spent ten minutes with Kaline, giving him tips on how to hit low balls, and on offseason workouts like swinging a heavier bat and squeezing a baseball. Williams' advice became a trademark of Kaline's game, especially his offseason. The hitting advice Williams gave Kaline was on display September 16 when Kaline started his first game, this time in center field. He rapped out three singles and drove in his first run in an 8-3 Tigers victory over the Boston Red Sox. Kaline continued to show flashes of brilliance, even getting a hit off the great Satchel Paige in a game against the St Louis Browns. Kaline's first home run came during a ninth-inning pinch-hitting appearance at Cleveland. Although Kaline played in only 30 games, he had done enough to impress Hutchinson. According to a 1953 *Sporting News* article, the Tigers worked with Kaline at second base and shortstop, but eventually kept him in the outfield.

After the 1953 season, Kaline returned to Baltimore to work during the offseason in a sporting goods store, allowing him to take Williams' advice and squeeze a baseball during the day. While on breaks, Kaline would take a bat in the backroom and swing until his arms got tired. He also continued dating his high school sweetheart, Madge Louise Hamilton. Al was attracted to her not only because of her beauty, but also because she could talk baseball. Just before Kaline left for spring training, he proposed to Louise, who accepted. They were married after the 1954 season.

While playing winter ball in Cuba, everyday outfielder Steve Souchock broke his wrist, allowing Kaline to get valuable spring training time in right. It was assumed that Souchock would be the starter in right when his wrist healed and Kaline would return to the bench. But Souchock's wrist didn't heal, and the 19-year-old Kaline became the starting right fielder in 1954. Kaline impressed everyone that season with his defense, and his offense soon became adequate; he hit around .250 for most of the season before the All-Star break. After the break, Kaline went on a tear and increased his average to .283 by the end of August. About a month later, in a home game, Kaline suffered his first major injury. A fly ball hit toward right at Briggs Stadium had Kaline racing toward some box seats that poked out into foul territory. Kaline ran into the wall protecting the seats, and was knocked out. He also twisted his knee and was hospitalized for five days. After the incident, Tigers president Spike Briggs ordered the seats removed lest Kaline be injured again. Kaline finished up his first full season with a .276 average. His lack of power, though, was a concern. Kaline had only 25 extra-base hits, including four home runs, and only 43 runs batted in.

Kaline went into the offseason knowing he had to improve his prowess at the plate. He didn't disappoint the fans or new manager Bucky Harris that year, even earning comparisons to Joe DiMaggio. On April 17, he blasted three home runs, including two in the sixth inning. By the end of April, Kaline had a 14-game hitting streak to go with a .453 batting average. He was voted by the fans as the American League's starting right fielder for the All Star Game. After the break, Kaline continued to hit. By the end of July, Kaline was leading the league in batting average, runs, runs batted in, hits, and home runs. The hot hitting continued until the beginning of September, when Kaline fell into a slump. To help himself out of it, Kaline focused on the fact that he was only a few hits away from 200 for the season, and that if he achieved that plateau, he would be the first Tigers outfielder in 12 years to have 200 hits. Kaline broke out of the slump, and ended the season with exactly 200 hits. He won the American League batting championship with a .340 average. Kaline, at the age of 20, was one day younger than Ty Cobb when Cobb won the batting title in 1907, making Kaline the youngest batting champion ever, a mark that has endured for more than a half-century. The comparisons to DiMaggio that had followed Kaline all season were summed up in the October 5 issue of *The Sporting News*, which outlined how Kaline was more similar to DiMaggio than Cobb.

Before the 1956 season, Kaline bulked up—perhaps due to being on the "banquet circuit." In an effort to become more comfortable with reports and the public, Kaline made as many appearances as possible. Early in the season, Kaline seemed to be uncomfortable at the plate because, according to manager Bucky Harris, he was reaching too much for pitches and being too impatient. Kaline had put extra pressure on himself to follow up his amazing 1955 season. Despite his slow start, Kaline was voted to start the All-Star Game for the second straight year. During the festivities, Kaline sought out Ted Williams, who reaffirmed what Harris had already told him: He was pressing, and needed to be more disciplined at the plate. After that, Kaline went on a tear, and raised his average from .276 to finish at .314. During the offseason, the estate of Spike Briggs' father sold the Tigers to an 11-man syndicate headed by radio station owners Fred Knorr and John Fetzer. Briggs stayed on as general manager.

Before the 1957 season, Al Kaline met businessman Frank Carlin, who offered Kaline and Detroit Red Wings forward Gordie Howe positions in a new business venture. Howe and Kaline were to be salesman gaining subcontracts for automotive parts design. Kaline was reluctant, but Louise was certain it was a good venture, which is all Al needed to hear. Kaline, Howe, and Carlin formed Michigan Automotive Products Corporation (Mapco). Kaline was vice president, and found the business easier than he had originally believed. The business was so successful, the trio also formed Howe-Kaline-Carlin Corporation.

The offseason was not without controversy, though. Kaline believed he deserved a raise, as did Briggs, but Briggs did not offer a figure near what Al wanted. Briggs sent Kaline a contract, which was reportedly sent back unsigned, without a note. Briggs was insulted, and declared in a speech that Kaline thought he was as good as Mickey Mantle, and wanted to be paid as such. Briggs said he was offended by the returned unsigned contract, which he said included a $3,000 bonus, and Kaline returned it without an explanation, and without a holiday greeting. responded, and was criticized in the press. Kaline eventually got his contract, but the price he had to pay was larger. Many fans viewed Kaline as an

DETROIT TIGERS 1984: WHAT A START! WHAT A FINISH!

ego-driven player, and many reporters implied as such with pointed, sometimes hostile questions. Kaline became so upset that he began to ignore the press, becoming more introverted than he already was.

The 1957 season was successful for Kaline. As in 1956, he started slowly, but was still chosen to start in the All-Star Game. Again, as in 1956, after the All Star break, Kaline began to hit, and raised his batting average to .300 near the end of August. His success was coupled with the birth of his first son, Mark Albert, on August 21. Kaline's strong hitting and stellar defense helped the Tigers finish fourth, and gave Kaline his first of 10 Gold Gloves. Kaline repeated his strong hitting and stellar defense in 1958, as he hit .313 and earned a second straight Gold Glove as the Tigers still finished fifth.

The 1959 season was one of change and of improvement for Kaline. He was shifted to center field after regular Harvey Kuenn was hit on the arm. Kaline preferred right field, but played well in center. When Kuenn returned from his injury, new manager Jimmy Dykes kept Kaline in center and moved Kuenn to right. Kaline thrived in the new position, and began to show signs of being a gritty and tough leader. After being hit in the cheek by an errant throw, Kaline sat out five games. He began to get restless on the bench, demanding that Dykes play him. When Dykes expressed concern because the cheek was still swollen, Kaline replied "I don't bat or throw with my cheek." Kaline was selected to start in the All-Star Game, this time over fellow center fielder Mickey Mantle. Kaline also got his 1,000th career hit off Billy Pierce of the White Sox. The Tigers finished in fourth place, while Kaline finished second in the batting race with .327 to Kuenn's .353. Kaline also picked up his third Gold Glove.

Before the 1960 season Bill DeWitt was hired as president and general manager of the Tigers. DeWitt immediately shook up the team by trading for Norm Cash, then sending batting champion Kuenn to Cleveland for home run leader Rocky Colavito. By May, the Tigers and Kaline had both had their ups and downs. Kaline was hitting only .250, which many people figured was due to off-field distractions. In an effort to reduce taxes, Frank Carlin, Kaline's partner with Howe, persuaded Kaline and Howe to purchase racehorses because the expenses were tax-deductible for three years. Horse racing was considered taboo for ballplayers, and the story became a focal point. Kaline quickly sold his interest in the HKC stable, distancing himself from racing and betting. The season grew to be more frustrating for the Tigers and for Kaline. Normally mild-mannered, Kaline was ejected for arguing a strike call with an umpire, but true to his form, Kaline approached the umpire after the game and apologized. He admitted he knew he was wrong as he walked back to the dugout. The prolonged slump cost Kaline a chance at starting another All-Star Game, although he was chosen as a reserve, making his sixth straight appearance. After DeWitt made history by trading a hitting champion for a home run leader, he made history again by trading manager Dykes for Cleveland manager Joe Gordon. The turmoil of the season took its toll on Kaline, as he finished with a .278 average, his lowest since 1954. (Gordon resigned after the season.)

In 1961, the Tigers hired Bob Scheffing as their new manager. Scheffing immediately turned to Kaline to become more of a leader, and the star responded. Kaline was not vocal but led by example, stepping up when needed. Kaline flourished all season, and was chosen to his seventh All Star Game. He ended the year second in the batting race with a .324 average, and was voted AL Comeback Player of the Year.

In 1962, Kaline began the season by expressing the desire not only to play in the World Series, but to have a twenty-year career. He also decided to be more aggressive at the plate, citing his low number of strikeouts from the previous season as the reason. Kaline shot out to .358 by May 21, but that good fortune ended five days later in Yankee Stadium. In the bottom of the ninth with two out and the Tigers leading 2-1, Elston Howard hit a fly to shallow right. Second baseman Jake Wood and first baseman Norm Cash could not reach it. The only hope was for Kaline to make the grab. He dove for the sinking ball, landing on his right shoulder. Kaline made the catch but broke his collarbone. It was predicted that he would miss at least two months. Before the game, Scheffing told reporters, "We're where we are because of Kaline. Where we go from here depends on him." Scheffing did not realize how right he was. During the 57 days that Kaline missed, the Tigers lost 7.5 games in the race for the pennant, falling to 10.5 games back. The layoff was not all bad for Kaline, though, as Louise gave birth to their second son, Michael Keith. Kaline was also chosen to start the first of the two All-Star Games that season—his eighth straight start—but could not play because of the injury. By the time the season was over, Kaline hit .304 and 29 home runs, two more than his previous best, all while missing 54 games. The Tigers finished 10.5 games behind the first-place Yankees, but Kaline earned his fifth Gold Glove, and finished sixth in the AL MVP voting.

As the 1963 season began, Kaline again changed his approach, deciding to get on base more, and let the slugging duo of Cash and Colavito drive in the runs. The team started slowly, but Kaline's approach kept him hitting well enough to be chosen for another All-Star Game. Kaline battled a knee injury all season, which eventually cost him a batting title to Carl Yastrzemski when he was forced to miss a few games. He finished second with a .312 average to Yaz's .321, hit 27 home runs, drove in 101 runs, placed second in MVP voting, and earned his sixth Gold Glove.

Kaline experienced more injuries in 1964. He injured his left foot, the same foot on which he had had surgery as a child, while running in a spring training game. Kaline hid the injury from manager Charlie Dressen at first, believing he could overcome it. By the end of April, however, the injury became too painful, and Kaline was forced to sit out a few games. Still, he was chosen to the All-Star Game for the tenth straight year, but withdrew due to injury, saying the rest would do his foot some good. The Tigers finished in fourth place that season, and Kaline finished with a respectable .293 average and his seventh Gold Glove.

DETROIT TIGERS 1984: WHAT A START! WHAT A FINISH!

Kaline's average dropped to .281 in 1965 while he was wearing a special shoe to protect his foot. He did earn his eighth Gold Glove splitting his time between center field and right field. During the offseason, Kaline had surgery on the foot. It helped him hit better in 1966, which became a tough year for the Tigers on and off the field. Dressen, who missed time the previous season after a heart attack, fell ill again on May 16. He was replaced by coach Bob Swift, who himself was diagnosed with cancer that season. Dressen and Swift both died later in the year. Frank Skaff finished the season as manager. Despite the distractions, Kaline was chosen for his 12th straight All-Star Game, and helped the Tigers finish third, while hitting .288 with 29 home runs. He also earned his ninth Gold Glove.

The Tigers had high hopes for 1967 under new manager Mayo Smith. Smith moved Kaline back to right field. Kaline was chosen to the AL All-Star team for the 13th year in a row, but a freak injury kept him out for 26 games. After a strikeout in a frustrating loss to Cleveland, Kaline slammed his bat into the bat rack and broke his hand. Unlike 1962, the Tigers stayed in contention without Kaline, going 15-11. The Tigers battled all year, but finished tied for second behind the Red Sox. Kaline hit .308 with 25 home runs (including his 300th) and 78 runs batted in, despite missing 31 games. Kaline won his tenth and final Gold Glove. The Red Sox lost to the St Louis Cardinals in the 1967 World Series. It would be that same Cardinals teams against which Kaline would live out his dream.

Nineteen sixty-eight was a season of new endeavors. During the offseason, Kaline, now 33, withdrew from Mapco to focus on baseball. He played in his 2,000th game April 18 in a 5-0 victory over the Indians. Kaline hit his 307th home run on May 19, passing Hank Greenberg as the Tigers' career homer leader. The success was short-lived; Kaline's arm was broken by a Lew Krausse pitch just six days later, and he did not return until July 1. In Kaline's absence, Jim Northrup took over right field and played well. When Kaline returned, he was used mostly as a pinch hitter, and filled in at first base. Despite the reduced role, Kaline figured prominently in the pennant run. He scored the tying run in Denny McLain's 30th victory on September 14. On September 17, Kaline pinch-hit for Norm Cash, and ended up scoring the run that won the Tigers the pennant. After the game, Kaline told Smith he did not deserve to play in the World Series because other players had stepped up in his absence. Smith, knowing what Kaline meant to the Detroit organization, had other ideas. To get his star in, Smith put center fielder Mickey Stanley at shortstop, Jim Northrup in center, and Al Kaline in right. The move proved successful as the Tigers rebounded from a three-games-to-one deficit to win three straight games, including Game 7 over Bob Gibson. The Tigers had won the World Series behind Kaline's .379 batting average and two home runs.

Kaline had reached one of his goals, to play in the World Series. Now it was time to fulfill his goal of a twenty-year career. As Kaline marched toward that mark, he continued to hit, and gain accolades. In 1969, he was voted to the Greatest Tiger Team of All Time. August 2, 1970, was Al Kaline Day, upon which the city renamed Cherry Street behind the stadium Kaline Drive. In 1971, Kaline was selected to play in his seventeenth All-Star Game, held that year in Detroit. He went 1-for-2 and scored on a Harmon Killebrew home run in the bottom of the sixth. On July 1, 1972, Kaline hit his 369th home run, tying Ralph Kiner for 18th place all-time. He also helped the Tigers to the playoffs, in which they lost to the eventual champion Oakland Athletics. It was also Kaline's twentieth season in the big leagues. The 1974 season was Kaline's last, and his first as a full-time designated hitter. He was named to his 15th and final All-Star team. He rapped his 3,000th hit September 24, a double off Dave McNally, in his home town of Baltimore.

Kaline finished his career with 3,007 hits, 498 doubles, 75 triples, 399 home runs, 1,622 runs scored, and 1,583 run batted in, while batting .297. What makes his numbers even more impressive is the fact that he missed 594 games in his career, the vast majority due to injury—the equivalent of two-and-a-half seasons. With a career .987 fielding percentage, he was also one of the best fielders of his time, with ten Gold Gloves to prove it. In a 2001 Sporting News article, both Ernie Harwell and Yogi Berra declared that Kaline had the best arm in the outfield ever.

In 1976, Kaline began a second career as a color commentator on Tigers television broadcasts. In 1980, Al Kaline was elected to the Baseball Hall of Fame alongside Duke Snider, Chuck Klein, and Tom Yawkey. Kaline thanked his family for their support, then said:

"If there is one accomplishment of which I am particularly proud, it is that I have always served baseball to the best of my ability, never have I deliberately done anything to discredit the game, the Tigers, or my family. By far, being inducted into the Hall of Fame is the proudest moment of my life."

Kaline spent more time as a broadcaster—25 years—than as a Tigers player. He also participated as a spring training instructor, even teaching a young Kirk Gibson about playing the outfield. In 2001, Kaline left the broadcast booth to become a special adviser to Tigers owner Mike Ilitch. In 2003, new general manager David Dombrowski named Kaline and his former teammate Willie Horton as special assistants to the general manager. Because of the broadcasting and special assignments, Al Kaline has been associated with the Tigers for 60 years. For that, some people know him as Mr. Tiger. Others still refer to him simply as Number Six.

References

Books

Butler, Hal. *Al Kaline and the Detroit Tigers*. Chicago: Henry Regnery Co. 1973.

Cantor, George. *The Tigers of '68: Baseball's Last Real Champions*. Dallas: Taylor. 1997.

Harrigan, Patrick J. *The Detroit Tigers: Club and Community 1945-1995*. Toronto: University of Toronto Press. 1997.

Hirshberg, Albert. *The Al Kaline Story*. New York: Julian Messner. 1964.

Whitt, Alan. *They Earned Their Stripes: The Detroit Tigers All-Time Team*. Champaign, Illinois: Sports Publishing, Inc. 2000.

Articles

Berra, Yogi and Ernie Harwell. "The Best I Ever Saw." *The Sporting News*, July 9, 2001.

Falls, Joe. "Summer Without Baseball: Kaline Making Adjustments." *The Sporting News*, February 1, 1975.

Salsinger, H.G. "Kaline More Like DiMaggio Than Cobb." *The Sporting News*, October 5, 1955.

Web Sites

www.baseball-almanac.com

www.baseballhalloffame.org

www.baseball-reference.com

www.detroittigers.com

www.retrosheet.org

George Kell
by Matt Bohn

IN A CAREER THAT spanned fifteen seasons, George Kell batted .306 in 1,795 career games. Narrowly beating out Ted Williams for the batting title in 1949, he hit over .300 in nine seasons. A ten-time All Star, Kell was finally inducted into the Baseball Hall of Fame in 1983. When his playing career was over, he turned to the microphone and was a Tigers broadcaster for 37 seasons. Kell's Arkansas twang endeared him to Detroit fans with such "Kell-isms" as "It's a bright, sunshiny day," "It's a bunt, and a dandy," and "I don't think you can hit a ball any harder than that."

The son of Clyde and Alma Kell, George Clyde Kell was born August 23, 1922, in Swifton, Arkansas. George's father a barber, had been a pitcher on the Swifton town team. Clyde, a native of Imboden, Arkansas, was such a great pitcher that the Swifton Town Team offered to buy him a barber shop if he moved to Swifton and pitched for the team all of the time. Clyde accepted the offer.

George, the oldest of three boys (brother Everett "Skeeter" Kell played for the Philadelphia Athletics in 1952), loved baseball from an early age. "I was a [St. Louis] Cardinal fan as a kid," Kell told the Associated Press in 1950. "We used to make the trip up to St. Louis a couple of times a season. I worshipped the old Gas House Gang—Dizzy Dean, Pepper Martin, Joe Medwick, Leo Durocher." In his autobiography *Hello Everybody, I'm George Kell*, he recalled, "There was never a time in my life when I didn't think about playing baseball. I loved the game. I loved every part about it."

Graduating from high school at 16, Kell enrolled at Arkansas State University at Jonesboro in the fall of 1939. Since the university did not have a baseball team, Kell played on the intramural softball team and then for the Swifton town team in the spring of 1940. It was also in the spring of 1940 that Kell got his first chance to play baseball professionally.

The Brooklyn Dodgers had an affiliate in Newport of the Class D Northeast Arkansas League. The Swifton postmaster, Clyde Mitts, often traveled to watch the team play. One day, after Newport team lost a doubleheader, Mitts told the team's general manager about the baseball playing ability of George Kell. The GM was interested. After discussing it with his father (who would have preferred that young George stay in college), he agreed to join the Newport team the next day. In the 1940 season, Kell played in 48 games and batted a puny .160. During the 1941 season, Kell fared better—this time batting .310 in 118 games. Following the 1941 season, Kell's contract was sold to the Durham Bulls of the Class B Piedmont League.

After a brief stint with Durham, Kell was signed by Lancaster of the Class B Interstate League, then affiliated with the Philadelphia Athletics. Leading all of professional baseball with a .396 average in 1943, Kell attracted the attention of Athletics owner-manager Connie Mack, who offered him the opportunity to play for the A's after Lancaster was finished with the playoffs. Mack wanted Kell to play just one game with Philadelphia. In his debut with the A's on September 28, 1943, Kell hit a triple in his first at bat. "I tried to act very calmly like it was just another time at bat for me," Kell wrote in his autobiography. "But I was dying to pinch myself to make sure this was all really happening."

Kell then returned to Arkansas to teach at a junior high school. Kell remembered, "Because of the war, they were using anyone who had at least some college experience. I also coached the basketball team and studied as hard as the kids so that I wouldn't get shown up in class."

DETROIT TIGERS 1984: WHAT A START! WHAT A FINISH!

Playing on a regular basis with the A's in 1944, Kell hit for a .268 average in 139 games. Nearly repeating his numbers in 1945, he batted .272 in 147 games. In early 1946, hitting .299, Kell found himself traded. On May 18, he went to the Detroit Tigers for outfielder Barney McCosky. Kell commented in the May 23, 1946, issue of *The Sporting News,* "It's the biggest break I've ever had in baseball."

Sixty years later, Kell told reporter Bill Dow, "Mr. Mack said, 'George, come up to my suite; I need to talk with you,' and that's when he told me I was traded to the Tigers for Barney McCosky, It was such a shock and felt like a rejection, but Mr. Mack told me, 'George, you're going to be a good ballplayer, and I'm sending you to a team that will pay you the kind of money that I can't.' As it turned out, it was the greatest day in my life."

Kell made his Detroit debut in the first game of a doubleheader against the league-leading Boston Red Sox in a jam-packed Briggs Stadium: "I was scared to death.... In the first inning, Johnny Pesky slashed one down third base, I made a backhand stab and threw him out, which really calmed me down. I was young, full of enthusiasm and played hard, and the Detroit fans accepted me and were so good. It was the beginning of a great romance."

With the Tigers, Kell had his greatest years—batting .better than .300 average every season from 1946 to 1951. In 1946, while batting .327, Kell struck out just twenty times. The next season, Kell made the American League All-Star team for the first time, but as he recalled in his autobiography, "I felt I had to prove myself all over again. I had to prove the previous season was not a one-year fluke." He finished 1947 with a .320 average in 152 games.

"From a personal standpoint, 1948 turned out to be the worst year of my career," Kell wrote. That season he was sidelined with two injuries. The first injury came in the second game of a May 8 doubleheader at Yankee Stadium when Kell's wrist was broken by a pitch from Vic Raschi. The injury prevented him from playing until May 31. At Yankee Stadium again on August 29, Kell's jaw was fractured by a ground ball from Joe DiMaggio. Talking to an Associated Press reporter about the injury two years later, Kell said, "I must have been out on my feet. They tell me afterwards that manager Steve O'Neill tried to take the ball away from me, and I wouldn't let them have it." This injury ended his season, leaving him with a still-impressive .304 average in just 92 games played.

If 1948 was the worst year of Kell's career, 1949 was perhaps the best. That season, he edged out Ted Williams for the batting title on the last day of the season. Fifty years later, Kell recalled the final day for *Detroit Free Press* reporter Gene Guidi: "I went into the game trailing Ted Williams by a couple of points and didn't think I had a chance because I figured Ted was good for a couple of hits that day. Bob Lemon was pitching for Cleveland against us and he was always tough, but I got a double and single my first two at-bats." Later in the game, Bob Feller came out of the bullpen to face Kell. George remembered, "He walked me in the fifth inning and then got me out in the seventh." Late in the game, it was learned that Williams had been hitless in the Red Sox game against the Yankees. Kell's 2-for-3 game would give him an average of .3429—enough to push him past Williams (.3427) for the batting title. In the ninth inning, manager Red Rolfe wanted to put in a pinch-hitter to bat for the third baseman. Kell insisted on batting. "I remembered Ted Williams not sitting out the last day of the (1941) season after he was already at .400, and I wasn't about to back into a batting title against him." As Kell stood on deck in the ninth inning, batter Eddie Lake grounded into a double play to end the game. "I celebrated by throwing my bats in the air," Kell said. "It was quite a feeling."

In 1950, a season in which the Tigers narrowly missed winning a pennant, Kell hit .340 in 157 games. His average was second only to Boston Red Sox second baseman Billy Goodman's league-leading .354. Kell had a career-high 114 runs and 101 RBIs. In addition, he led the league with 218 hits and 56 doubles, and committed only nine errors. In that season, "I was confident about every aspect of my game," he said in his autobiography.

Kell followed that season up with another great year, batting .319 in 1951 and leading the AL with 191 hits and 36 doubles. But on June 3, 1952, Kell's playing career as a Tiger ended when he was traded to the Boston Red Sox. The blockbuster deal included eight other players. Kell, pitcher Dizzy Trout, shortstop Johnny Lipon, and outfielder Hoot Evers were traded for pitcher Bill Wight, first baseman Walt Dropo, third baseman Fred Hatfield, shortstop Johnny Pesky, and outfielder Don Lenhardt. General manager Charlie Gehringer told Kell that the Tigers hadn't wanted to trade him, but they needed to do something to shake up the team, and the Red Sox wouldn't accept any deal that's didn't include Kell. "I sure didn't want to leave Detroit, but the only thing that made it better was going to Boston because that's the other great baseball town in the American League," Kell said later. He finished the 1952 season with a .311 batting average.

For five seasons, George Kell (right) and Ernie Harwell were the Tigers' play-by-play team—sort of. When the games were on both radio and TV, one took the radio mike and the other the TV mike, switching places in the middle of the fifth inning. (National Baseball Hall of Fame Library, Cooperstown, New York)

DETROIT TIGERS 1984: WHAT A START! WHAT A FINISH!

In Boston, Kell's closest teammate became his onetime rival for the batting title, Ted Williams. Kell said in 2005, "We were already close when I went to Boston; we were primarily a young ballclub and he was an elder and I was past 30, so we hit it off real good." Continuing his habit of .300-plus hitting, Kell batted .307 in 1953, with 141 hits and 73 RBIs, and a career-high twelve home runs that year. His tenure in Boston was brief, on May 23, 1954, he was traded to the Chicago White Sox for Grady Hatton and $100,000.

"It was a totally different feeling in 1954 when the Red Sox traded me to the White Sox," Kell said in his autobiography. "More than anything else, I felt like I was being used." For the first time since 1945, his average dipped below the .300 mark that year. Playing in only 97 games, Kell hit .276 in 1954. In 1955, he bounced back in 1955 and led the Chisox with a .312 average and 81 RBIs, but wasn't completely happy: "(T)hat trade took something out of me. I had lost something. That deal got me to thinking about retiring."

At the end of the 1955 season, White Sox manager Paul Richards left to pilot the Baltimore Orioles. Once with the Orioles, Richards wanted Kell to join him there and on May 21, 1956, George, along with pitchers Mike Fornieles and Connie Johnson and outfielder Bob Nieman, was traded to the O's in exchange for pitcher Jim Wilson and outfielder Dave Philley. Though he was flattered that Richards would want him as his third baseman, Kell's thoughts of retirement grew stronger. "After that season…I made up my mind I would play one more year. I really didn't even feel like doing that, but the Orioles had made quite a commitment to get me. I figured I owed it to them," Kell said.

Kell was beaned twice in 1957, his final season. On May 6, at Briggs Stadium, Kell was knocked down when he was hit above the right ear by a Steve Gromek pitch. Though Kell not seriously injured, he was sidelined for ten days. Then just five weeks later, in a June 9 game at Comiskey Park in Chicago, Kell was beaned again, this time by pitcher Dick Donovan. Though again avoiding serious injury, he again sat out for ten days.

During his period of recovery, George sat in the Orioles' radio-TV booth with Ernie Harwell. Kell was no stranger to broadcasting by this time, having worked with Harry Heilmann on a fifteen-minute radio show in Detroit in the early 1950s. In his memoir *Tuned to Baseball*, Harwell recalls joking with George, "Now you're learning the art of free-loading.… All the hot dogs you can eat and all the pop you can drink." Harwell remembered, "After a couple of games, I asked him to broadcast an inning for us. He did. He liked it and the listening audience liked him."

Kell retired after the 1957 season, saying in January 1958, "It's hard to retire, but it's a lot easier than waiting around until someone tells you you're through." He expressed a desire to spend more time with his 12-year old son and 9-year old daughter, saying, "A baseball player just doesn't get to see much of his family. I was away from them entirely for three months a year and at least half the time during the season."

Kell had planned to spend his retirement tending to his 800-acre farm in Swifton. However, CBS Television was interested in hiring a former player to host a ten minute pre-game interview during the "Game of the Week" telecasts. Paul Richards recommended Kell for the job. Kell told Neal Russo in May 1958, "I jumped at the offer. I didn't want to turn my back on baseball completely.… Besides, I'm away from home only one night a week and I never work more than two days a week."

Kell discovered that as a former player, he had an advantage as a sports interviewer. He told Fred Petrucelli in November 1958, "My connections in baseball proved to be very valuable and that's where I had an edge. After all, I was talking and working with people with whom I had played for many years." Kell was able to set up the interviews himself, citing as an example, "I was able to line up baseball personalities pretty easily myself. I called Ted Williams for a spot on the show and he agreed readily. I don't know how some of the players would have reacted if the advertising boys had signed 'em up."

When Tigers broadcaster Mel Ott was killed in an automobile accident in November 1958, Detroit business manager Harry Sisson offered Kell the job as his replacement. Kell was hesitant to give up so much time away from his family. After talking with Tigers owner John Fetzer, Kell agreed to team up on radio and TV with Van Patrick. Kell reflected in his autobiography, "Before I left that room, I had signed a five-year contract to work all one hundred fifty-four Tigers games as the No. 2 broadcaster. To this day I can only speculate as to why I changed my mind and signed that contract. I'm really not certain." He credited John Fetzer's sincerity and his own love of the Tigers for helping persuade him to take the job.

During the 1959 season, Kell provided play-by-play for the middle three innings of each Tigers game. At the end of the 1959 season, he covered the playoff games between the Los Angeles Dodgers and Milwaukee Braves for ABC Television. Originally, the plan was for Kell to work with Buddy Blattner, but when Dizzy Dean used his connections with the sponsor to block Blattner from doing the broadcast, Kell found himself providing all of the play-by-play and color commentary by himself.

After his broadcast partner, Van Patrick, was fired in 1959, Kell's old friend Ernie Harwell became his new partner. Together, they broadcast Tigers games on radio and television beginning in 1960. Wanting to spend more time with his family, Kell resigned after the 1963 season. Tigers owner Fetzer did not want Kell to leave the broadcasts, however. Kell recalls that Fetzer told him, "We are going to work this out some way so that you're still part of the team and everyone is satisfied."

Kell sat out the 1964 season and was rumored to be in line to replace Mel Allen as the voice of the New York Yankees. However, his heart was with the Tigers, and when Fetzer arranged for him to do only forty to fifty broadcasts a season rather than a full schedule of games, Kell couldn't resist coming back. He rejected an offer from ABC to do the Game of the Week. With the Tigers, he told reporter Jack Craig in

DETROIT TIGERS 1984: WHAT A START! WHAT A FINISH!

1970, "I just drive to Memphis and take a jet to wherever the Tigers are playing. And if it's a Saturday day game, I get home late the same night."

Though a Tigers fan, Kell resisted being a "homer" on the air. "I'm for the Tigers, but I'm not a cheerleader," he told writer Joe Falls. "When he [Fetzer] hired me, he told me there were some announcers who irritated him by rooting so openly for their team. He told me to report accurately and fairly. Naturally, I'm for the Tigers—you've got to be honest about this thing—but he told me I could show my allegiance by the tone of my voice, rather than going rah-rah-rah."

One of the highlights of his broadcasting career was to be able to provide play-by-play for the 1968 World Series. In *Hello Everybody, I'm George Kell*, he said, "If I have one regret from my playing career, it's the fact that I never had the opportunity to play in a World Series. Every player wants to get that chance at least once in his career. So getting into one as a broadcaster for the Tigers was very special for me." Having previously provided play-by-play for the 1962 World Series over NBC radio, George covered the World Series games from Detroit for NBC television in 1968.

Kell's achievements on the field were recognized when he was elected to the Baseball Hall of Fame in 1983. Though proud of his accomplishments as a player, Kell was overwhelmed by the honor, telling Joe Falls that July, "(W)hen I think of being there with Babe Ruth and all the rest, I'm in awe."

Aside from his baseball broadcasting duties, Kell had other business and political interests to keep him busy. Besides raising Black Angus cattle on his farm in Swifton, he had also invested in an automobile dealership in Newport, Arkansas. He accepted an appointment to a ten-year term on the Arkansas Highway Commission. Proud of his appointment to the office, Kell said "I treated that appointment very seriously. I felt as though I not only was representing the Kell name, but also all the good hard working people of the state of Arkansas."

In 1991, Kell missed twenty Tigers broadcasts to take care of his wife Charlene as she battled cancer. George and Charlene Felts had met in the fifth grade and were high-school sweethearts. Secretly married May 24, 1941, they spent fifty years together and raised two children (George Jr. and Terrie) before Charlene's death on August 20, 1991. Devastated by his wife's passing, George, a devout Methodist, relied on his deep religious faith to give him strength as he grieved the passing of his wife.

A few years after Charlene died, George met a woman named Carolyn at a local bank for which he was a director. Eventually working up the nerve to ask her to dinner, George said in his autobiography, "I suppose one thing led to another until finally I asked her if she wanted to be tied down to an older man and marry me." George and Carolyn were married May 7, 1994.

After enduring surgeries on his knee and on a broken disk in his back, Kell announced his retirement from broadcasting in January 1997.

Kell's home in Swifton was destroyed by fire in 2001. Miraculously, Kell was rescued from the burning home. Carolyn Kell told *Detroit News* sportswriter Tom Gage, "We don't like to think of what might have happened if a volunteer fireman hadn't been driving by the house at that very time. He went up the stairs and dragged George out. God was on his shoulder that night. That's what I tell George. From playing to broadcasting, all his life, God has been on his shoulder."

Kell, still an avid Tigers fan, returned to Detroit on October 14, 2006, to throw out the first pitch before Game 4 of the American League Championship Series between the Tigers and the Oakland Athletics. Greeted by a standing ovation at Comerica Park, the 84-year-old Kell threw the ball to Tigers coach Andy Van Slyke. Kell commented, "Andy said I threw it better than [Mickey] Lolich." (Lolich had thrown out the first pitch the previous night.) Kell was touched and overwhelmed by the reaction the Detroit fans had to his return to Detroit. "I'm overwhelmed," Kell said. "I didn't expect all of this. The standing ovation sounded like Joe DiMaggio was on the field. It was a little bit more than I expected."

On the morning of March 24, 2009, George Kell died in his sleep in Swifton. He was 86. His son, George Kell, Jr., had preceded him in death in 2007. Former Tiger manager Sparky Anderson summed up Kell's life, saying, "George Kell was a professional in everything he did—on the field, in the broadcast booth and the way he treated everyone he met. He led by example. Baseball will never forget him." George Kell was buried in Swifton Cemetery.

References

Books

Kell, George and Dan Ewald. *Hello Everybody, I'm George Kell*. Champaign, Ill.: Sports Publishing. 1998.

Smith, Curt. *Voices of the Game*. New York: Simon & Schuster. 1987.

Articles

Associated Press. "George Kell Never Argues With Umpires, Says Players Get Better Deal If Quiet." *Danville (Virginia) Bee*, September 13, 1950. 9.

Associated Press. "Kell Quits Baseball Without 'Pink' Slip." *Lawton Constitution* (Oklahoma), January 7, 1958. 11.

Basenfelder, Don. "Wheaton and Kell Bloom as Red Roses; A's Believed Holding Inside Track for Slugging Pair; George Tops Hitters." *The Sporting News*, September 9, 1943. 7.

"Blattner Charges Dizzy Threw Curve, Quits Duet; Tiff Over Playoff TV Job Led to Blowup." *The Sporting News* October 28, 1959. 23.

DETROIT TIGERS 1984: WHAT A START! WHAT A FINISH!

"Cadillac Agency, Golf Resort Helped Kell to Make up Mind." *The Sporting News*, August 31, 1963. 18.

Chi, Victor. "Charlene Kell, George's wife, dies of cancer." *Detroit Free Press*, August 22, 1991. 1F.

Craig, Jack. "Airing Ball Games an Honor." *The Sporting News*, July 25, 1970. 54.

Crowe, Steve, and John Lowe. "As George Kell, who retired Tuesday after 37 seasons as a Tigers broadcaster might say… 'It's all over!' Hall of Famer Announces Retirement." *Detroit Free Press*, January 29, 1997. 1E.

Crowe, Steve. "Kell came to Detroit and brought Harwell with him." *Detroit Free Press*, January 29, 1997. 3E.

Crowe, Steve. "For openers, Kell pays a visit. Retired announcer admits: 'Yeah, this really does seem strange.'" *Detroit Free Press*, April 8, 1997. 6C.

Dow, Bill. "Kell's Well. Ex-Tiger third sacker returns to Detroit for 'Baseball as America.'" *Detroit Free Press*. March 7, 2006. 1D.

Ellis, Jim. "Big Gus Unlimbers Big Guns on Return to Limping Orioles." *The Sporting News*, May 15, 1957. 15.

Ellis, Jim. "Birds Take Wing Despite Injuries to Kell, Francona." *The Sporting News*, June 1, 1957. 20.

Falls, Joe. "Another Chapter on Baseball Broadcasters." *The Sporting News*, August 28, 1965. 14.

Falls, Joe. "Fans favor jocks on TV." *The Sporting News*, May 31, 1980. 34.

Falls, Joe. "Kell realizes dream in Hall of Fame." *Detroit News*, July 31, 1983. 1D.

Gage, Tom. "Talking with…George Kell. *Detroit News*, April 30, 2001. 4F.

Gage, Tom. "Kell misses calling games, remains an avid Tiger fan. He had Hall of Fame playing career, but never lost enthusiasm for broadcasting." *Detroit News*, June 23, 2003. 4F.

"George Kell Now Cattle Raiser." *The Sporting News*, March 16, 1949. 25.

Guidi, Gene. "Tigers Corner: Kell traveled tough road to 1949 batting crown." *Detroit Free Press*, September 25, 1999. 5B.

Hammer, Dave. "Former Tiger Kell remembers career—Trip to Cooperstown helps 82-year-old forget pain from accident." *Grand Rapids Press*, August 7, 2005.

"Kell stays a fan." *Grand Rapids Press*, October 15, 2006. C1.

Lowe, John. "George Kell, Hall of Fame third baseman and voice of Tigers, dies." *Detroit Free Press*, March 25, 2009. 1C and 6C.

"NBC and CBS Saturday TV Starts April 5; Brave-Dodger, Yank-Phil Tilts First to Air." *The Sporting News*, April 2, 1958. 32.

Petrucelli, Fred. "Kell a Smash Hit First Season on TV and Happy in Role."*The Sporting News*, November 19, 1958. 15.

"Recalling Kell." *Detroit Free Press*, March 25, 2009. 6C.

Russo, Neal. "He's 'Old Pro' of Video in Rookie Season; Kell Clouting at .300 Clip as Aircaster. Ex-Hot Sack Star Making Grade on TV." *The Sporting News*, May 28, 1958. 13-14.

Silva, Chris. "Tigers great Kell a hit with first pitch." *Detroit Free Press*, October 15, 2006. 2D.

Spoelstra, Warren. "With Tigers All's Well, After Club Acquires Kell." *The Sporting News* May 23, 1946. 6.

"Tiger Kell rescued from his burning home." *Grand Rapids Press*, October 9, 2001.

Traub, Todd. "Hall of Famer Kell Dies." *Arkansas Democrat Gazette*, March 25, 2009.

"Yanks Swamp Tigers After Losing 3-2 Tilt." *Syracuse Herald Journal*, May 9, 1949. 59.

Young, Dick. "Kell Reported in Line For Yank Radio Job." *The Sporting News*, October 24, 1964. 32.

Web Sites

Retrosheet. http://www.retrosheet.com

George Kell obituary, Jackson's Funeral home website. http://www.jacksonsfh.com/ Accessed March 27, 2009.

Other Sources

McClary, Mike. Interview with George Kell, March 14, 2007. http://www.detroittigerspodcast.com/2007/03/14/the-detroit-tigers-podcast-episode-4-its-a-dandy/ Accessed June 23, 2007.

Larry Osterman
by Matt Bohn

LARRY OSTERMAN'S career as a Detroit Tigers broadcaster spanned twenty seasons over four different decades, including two world championships. A modest, hard-working sportscaster, Osterman was known and respected by his colleagues for his professionalism. George Kell, his television broadcasting partner, said of Osterman, "I learned more about broadcasting from Larry Osterman than anyone I ever worked with."

Born in the small town of Malcolm, Nebraska, in 1935, Osterman spent the summer months of his childhood searching the radio dial for baseball games. A St. Louis Cardinals fan, Larry would listen to the St. Louis games over KMOX, and would sometimes pull in the broadcasts of the Triple-A Kansas City Blues, as well as the Chicago Cubs and the Chicago White Sox. "On Sunday afternoons I would lie on the living room floor and listen to baseball games that were re-created on KOWH, Omaha," Larry recalled in a 2005 interview conducted by mail. "They had a continuous loop of crowd noise running behind the announcer. About every minute, you would hear a guy groan. A minute later, the same guy would groan. Another minute later...same guy... same groan...."

From an early age, Osterman knew what career he wanted to pursue. "Becoming a play-by-play man was the first and only thing I set for myself as a career goal," Osterman told Jack Moss in the May 12, 1974, issue of the *Kalamazoo Gazette*. The hours young Larry spent listening to sports broadcasts on the radio prepared him for his future path. "Every night I would be turning the radio dial, trying to pick up the broadcast of baseball games," Osterman recalled in 2005. "In the fall and winter, I'd do the same, checking out announcers doing football, basketball and hockey radio play-by-play." Osterman was most impressed by the styles of such broadcasters as Bill King, Chuck Thompson, Ken Coleman, and Ray Scott: "I believe they were instrumental in how I eventually worked a game. I felt they had an approach to the game that would wear well with the radio listeners. I never copied them, but their styles certainly had an influence on my broadcasts."

After graduating from Malcolm High School in the top four of his class in 1953, Osterman enrolled at the University of Nebraska. Leaving college (later earning a degree from Western Michigan University), he took a job as sports director at KCOW in Alliance, Nebraska. It was at KCOW that he broadcast baseball play-by-play for the first time. "We were to do the radio broadcast of a semipro baseball game in Minitara, Nebraska," Osterman told the Kalamazoo Gazette in 1974. "There was no press box at the field, so we drove our car up near the diamond and put a batting cage in front of it for protection and I broadcast from the front seat."

In 1959, Osterman went to Kalamazoo to serve as sports director for the John Fetzer-owned radio station, WKZO. By 1961, Osterman was assigned to cover the Detroit Tigers' spring training camp in Lakeland, Florida. "I'll never forget the first time that I covered spring training in Florida in 1961. George and his then-partner, Ernie Harwell, invited me to accompany them to Ybor City for dinner at a Spanish restaurant," Osterman remembered in 2005. "I couldn't wait to get back to Lakeland, to call my wife, and tell her that I had dinner with George Kell and Ernie Harwell!" Osterman's coverage of Tigers spring training camps gave him the opportunity to become acquainted with many of the Detroit players, but his dream of being a play-by-play announcer of a baseball team still eluded him. Whenever a position became available on the Tigers broadcast crew, Osterman made it clear to John Fetzer that he was interested in the job. Finally, in 1967, Osterman got his chance.

At the close of the 1966 season, Tigers radio broadcaster Gene Osborn was fired. When TV announcer Ray Lane moved from television to radio, Osterman was hired as Kell's partner on WJBK-TV's Tigers broadcasts. Beginning in 1967, Osterman would broadcast play-by-play for the middle three innings of each Tigers telecast.

Though he had a great deal of experience broadcasting college sports for WKZO, Osterman quickly discovered that being a major league broadcaster was a different proposition entirely. Stepping onto the field at Yankee Stadium for the first time in 1967, he thought to himself, "This is a hell of a long way from Malcolm, Nebraska!" He credited his broadcast partner with making the transition to the major leagues more smoothly. "I learned more about the game of baseball from George Kell than anyone in my entire life!" Osterman said. "George Kell took the time to introduce me to people in the major leagues. He always introduced me as his 'partner.' He provided guidance on how to become a big-leaguer, how to fend for yourself on the road. He provided a tremendous bridge between my previous career working college games to a much higher profile level of sports broadcasting."

Osterman was able to broadcast many memorable moments in his early seasons as a Tigers telecaster. In 1967, the Tigers barely missed winning the pennant for the first time since 1945. The following year, Osterman had the pleasure of describing the Tigers' championship season. "Individually, the highlight was the game in which McLain won his thirtieth," Osterman told Kalamazoo's *Encore* magazine in 1989. "That was pretty exciting stuff because it was the only time that George missed doing a game in his entire broadcasting career. His daughter was getting married that day, so I did the entire nine innings."

In 1975, the rights of the Tigers telecasts went from WJBK-TV to WWJ-TV. The new rightsholder wanted to use members of its own sports staff on Tigers telecasts as a cross-promotion. As a result, Osterman's role on the telecasts was reduced. Beginning in 1975, he went from broadcasting three innings of play-by-play on each televised game to working only as color commentator on road telecasts.

By 1977, Al Kaline had been added as a color commentator to Tigers telecasts, making the broadcast booth even more crowded. Osterman said in 2005, "I have always

DETROIT TIGERS 1984: WHAT A START! WHAT A FINISH!

been of the opinion (and still am) that three in a booth is one too many. I also was of the opinion that two Hall of Famers were ultimately going to be the main men and I was going to be the odd man out." He found himself without a place in the Tigers broadcast booth the following year.

Leaving his post at WKZO in early 1978, Osterman began hosting sports radio shows over WWJ-AM in Detroit. While Osterman was also providing coverage for University of Michigan football during this time, he quickly realized that he missed doing baseball play-by-play. Hearing about an opening on the Cincinnati Reds' TV crew, Osterman contacted the team about the job, only to be informed that they had just hired his friend, Ray Lane. "That same day I ran into Lane at the Detroit Sports Broadcasters Association luncheon. I told him of my interest in the Reds job and congratulated him on his successful application. He asked me if I had heard about the Minnesota Twins switching rights-holders and that they were looking for an announcer. I called KMSP that afternoon, sent a tape, flew to Minneapolis and joined the Twins broadcast crew within a couple of weeks."

From 1979 to 1983, Osterman paired with Bob Kurtz to cover telecasts of the Twins. On the air, he did all nine innings of play-by-play. During this time, Osterman was versatile in covering other sports as well. He provided coverage for the Detroit Red Wings, the Major Indoor Soccer League, and Michigan and Michigan State football—all on ON-TV, a pay-TV service—as well as the 1980 U.S. Olympic hockey exhibition schedule on ESPN.

Osterman also was active in producing instructional baseball videos. In the early 1980s, he produced a series of instructional baseball tapes marketed to Little League baseball players from the ages of 8 to 18. The series, "The Baseball Masters," included baseball tips from Al Kaline, George Kell and former Twins manager Frank Quilici.

In 1984, Osterman returned to broadcasting Tigers games, this time over a new cable channel, PASS (Pro-Am Sports System.) Larry remembered, "The startup of PASS was unique in that there weren't many sports broadcast companies in the entire country. In fact in our first year we were feeding cable systems throughout the U.S. One of my daughters watched our games regularly on a Florida cable system. We fed a lot of our games to NESN, a new and similar operation serving the New England area out of Boston. The timing could not have been more favorable. A 35-5 start does a lot to increase the interest in a ball club."

Teamed first with Bill Freehan and later with Jim Northrup, Osterman provided play-by-play for seventy to eighty-five Tigers games on PASS from 1984 to 1992. After being assured in December 1992 by the general manager of PASS that he would return to the booth the following year, Osterman was shocked to learn a month later that he was fired. The firing was explained as a "marketing decision" by PASS. Osterman told Steve Crowe of the *Detroit Free Press* at the time, "I'm shocked and more than a little disappointed about the whole thing for a lot of reasons. There was nothing that led up to it; nobody said they were unhappy with my work."

Osterman continued to work on other PASS programs including the Central Collegiate Hockey Association game of the week. Though Osterman continued to look for work with a major league baseball broadcast crew, he kept busy covering college basketball and the International Hockey League's Kalamazoo Wings.

In 1998, Osterman moved to Florida to become an educational television producer for the Pinellas County School district. Although the job has an educational focus, he finds it sometimes bring him back to his baseball roots. "We're doing some interesting stuff," Osterman reported in the April 9, 2001, edition of the *Kalamazoo Gazette*. "We did some more things with the Tampa Bay Devil Rays major league baseball team, using some of the players and our kids for word-usage educational messages. We spent two days in the Devil Rays' camp shooting and have gotten some great reviews on the final product." Osterman and his wife Shirley currently live in Largo, Florida. Married in 1957, they have four children.

References

Books

Kell, George and Dan Ewald. *Hello Everybody, I'm George Kell*. Champaign, Ill.: Sports Publishing, 1998.

Articles

"As a voice of the Tigers, Kalamazoo's Larry Osterman is a PASS master." *Encore* magazine (Kalamazoo, Michigan), February 1989:

Crowe, Steve. "PASS fires Osterman, teams Price, Northrup." *Detroit Free Press*. January 21, 1993:

Hawkins, Jim. "Campbell Sees Tiger Crisis as Springboard For Rise." *The Sporting News*, February 1, 1975.

Moss, Jack. "Career gamble pays off for Osterman." *Kalamazoo Gazette*, May 7, 1980.

Moss, Jack. "It's Not Easy For TV 'Pro'; But WKZO's Larry Osterman Takes a Realistic View." *Kalamazoo Gazette*, June 26, 1977.

Moss, Jack. "Larry Osterman going strong these days in Florida." *Kalamazoo Gazette*, April 9, 2001.

Moss, Jack. "Osterman a Television Big Leaguer." *Kalamazoo Gazette*, May 12, 1974.

Moss, Jack. "Osterman Gets Job in Detroit." *Kalamazoo Gazette*, February 16, 1978.

Moss, Jack. "Osterman gives the Wings a class voice." *Kalamazoo Gazette*, October 14, 1993.

DETROIT TIGERS 1984: WHAT A START! WHAT A FINISH!

"Osborn Out: Osterman New Member of Tiger Air Team." *The Sporting News*, December 31, 1966.

"Osterman on move." *Kalamazoo Gazette*, March 14, 1979.

Wagner, Bob. "From hockey to baseball; Osterman, Neal friendship leads to video productions." *Kalamazoo Gazette*, December 6, 1981:

Other Sources

Bohn, Matt. Interview with Larry Osterman conducted by mail, June 28, 2005

What a Finish!
by Brian Borawski

American League Championship Series Game One

October 2, 1984
Tigers 8, Royals 1
Tigers Lead Best-of-Five Series, 1-0

Big players produce during big moments, and two of the Tigers' breadwinners, Jack Morris and Alan Trammell, came up huge in Game One to give the Detroit Tigers a 1-0 lead in their quest for a World Series championship. The Tigers started things early. Lou Whitaker led off the first inning with a single and immediately came in on Trammell's triple. After Kirk Gibson lined out to third, a sacrifice fly by Lance Parrish put the Tigers up 2-0 before the Royals touched their bats. The Tigers added a run in fourth on a Larry Herndon home run, and another run in the fifth as Alan Trammell struck again, hitting a homer of his own. Tram wasn't done, because in the seventh he drove in Lou Whitaker on a single, his third hit of the game. In the meantime, Morris looked like his April self. He cruised through the first six innings, and it wasn't until the seventh inning that the Royals tagged him for a run, with Jorge Orta smacking a leadoff triple and coming home on a Darryl Motley groundout. In those seven innings, Morris gave up only five hits and the one run, and he struck out four while walking only one. An RBI double by Darrell Evans, followed by an RBI single by Marty Castillo driving home pinch-runner Dave Bergman in the eighth, put the Tigers up 7-1, and Willie Hernandez closed out the game by pitching two perfect innings. The Tigers added a run in the top of the ninth on a Lance Parrish home run, but this game was for all intents and purposes decided after the Tigers batted in the first inning. It was an all-around dominating performance by the Tigers. Good pitching and good hitting. Can't ask for more than that, especially in a five-game series, where anything can happen.

American League Championship Series Game Two

October 3, 1984
Tigers 5, Royals 3, 11 innings
Tigers Lead Best-of-Five Series, 2-0

While the first game was over pretty much after the first inning, this game showed why the Kansas City Royals captured the American League West title. As in Game One, the Tigers went up quickly in the first to take a 2-0 lead. Lou Whitaker reached on an error and moved to second on a long fly ball to center by Alan Trammell. Kirk Gibson drove in Whitaker with a double, and scored himself on Lance Parrish's double. The Tigers extended their lead to 3-0 when Gibson hit a solo homer in the top half of the third. The Royals began a comeback in the bottom of the fourth against starter Dan Petry. Pat Sheridan scored on a force-play grounder by Jorge Orta to cut the lead to 3-1. KC added a run in the seventh on an RBI single by pinch-hitter Dane Iorg, then tied the game off Willie Hernandez in the eighth on a pinch-double by Hal McRae that drove in pinch-hitter (and ex-Tiger) Lynn Jones. Neither team scored in the ninth or 10th inning, but in the 11th, the Tigers broke the tie. Lance Parrish led off with a single and moved to second when catcher Don Slaught fumbled Darrell Evans' bunt. After a force play at third produced the first out, John Grubb drove in both runners with a double. The Royals got two men on with two outs in the bottom of the 11th, but Aurelio Lopez pitched out of the jam to earn the win. And now the Tigers had two chances to take the series at home. In the National League Championship Series, the Chicago Cubs had cruised to a similar 2-0 lead, and it appeared that there would be a rematch of the 1945 World Series.

1984 American League Championship Series Game Three

October 5, 1984
Tigers 1, Royals 0
Tigers Win Best-of-Five Series, 3-0

Things started out innocuously enough. The Tigers drew first blood in the second. Barbaro Garbey led off with a single and was forced out at second by Chet Lemon. Darrell Evans singled, sending Lemon to third. Marty Castillo hit a grounder to shortstop that had the makings of a double play, but he beat the relay to first base and Lemon scored. And that was it. The Tigers got no more hits the rest of the game, as Charlie Leibrandt pitched the game of his life. It wasn't good enough. Milt Wilcox went eight innings, giving up only two hits and two walks while striking out eight Royals. The Royals' first hit came in the fourth, the second in the eighth. Both were singles, and no Royal made it past first base off Wilcox. In the ninth, Willie Hernandez came in to finish things, getting the only save of the ALCS. He gave up a pinch-single to Hal McRae with two out, but like Wilcox, he didn't let the runner past first base. The final out of the ALCS was a foul pop-up by Darryl Motley to third baseman Castillo. The Tigers were going to the World Series, and they did it in grand fashion. Kirk Gibson was named the series' Most Valuable Player. Things did not go as well for the Chicago Cubs. After they had taken a 2-0 lead in the NLCS, the San Diego Padres won all three of their home games, clinching the series on October 7 to earn the right to face the Tigers in the World Series.

1984 World Series Game One

October 9, 1984
Tigers 3, Padres 2
Tigers Lead Best-of-Seven Series, 1-0

For the third time in their first four postseason games, the Tigers put a run on the board in the first inning. Lou Whitaker led off with a double and Alan Trammell drove him in with a double. The lead was short-lived. Terry Kennedy drove in two runs with a double in the bottom of the first off starter Jack Morris. For the first time in the postseason, the Tigers were behind. Over the next three innings, each team got only one hit (and each came in the third). What looked like

DETROIT TIGERS 1984: WHAT A START! WHAT A FINISH!

a shootout had settled down to a pitchers' duel. Jack Morris had calmed down, and Padres starter Mark Thurmond was equally effective. Then the Tigers pounced. In the top of the fifth, Lance Parrish doubled with two out and Larry Herndon hit a two-run homer to give the Tigers a 3-2 lead that they held the rest of the way. Andy Hawkins and Dave Dravecky gave San Diego four innings of scoreless relief, but they were too late. Morris went the distance, giving up only five hits after being roughed up in the first inning. The Padres threatened in the sixth by getting their first two men on base with singles, but Morris struck out the next three batters. If anyone needed any convincing of Detroit's dominance in this game, it was when San Diego's Kurt Bevacqua doubled to right field but was cut down at third by perfect throws from right fielder Kirk Gibson and second baseman Whitaker. With the win, the Tigers had, for the time being at least, home-field advantage. Dan Petry would get the ball in Game Two, and everyone hoped he would be as effective as Morris had been.

1984 World Series Game Two

October 10, 1984
Padres 5, Tigers 3
Best-of-Seven Series Tied 1-1

One thing the Tigers did well in the fall classic was get off to an early lead and knock out the starting pitcher. This game was no exception; the Tigers got to Padres starter Ed Whitson in the first inning. Lou Whitaker led off with a single and Alan Trammell singled him to third. Kirk Gibson followed with a single to drive in Whitaker and send Trammell to third, then stole second. Lance Parrish knocked in Trammell with a sacrifice fly. Darrell Evans drove in Gibson with a single, and the Tigers were off to a 3-0 lead. Whitson got one more out before giving up another single to John Grubb and taking an early shower. But the Padres wouldn't roll over. Alan Wiggins, leading off for the Padres in the bottom of the first, reached on a bunt single and eventually scored on a sacrifice fly by Graig Nettles to make it 3-1. The Padres struck again in the fourth inning. Starter Dan Petry gave up a single to Kurt Bevacqua, leading off. Bevacqua went to third on a single by Garry Templeton and scored on a grounder by Bobby Brown to cut the lead to one run. The big blow came in the fifth. With one out, Petry gave up a walk and a single, and Bevacqua hit a three-run homer to put the Padres up, 5-3. The Padres took a page out of the Tigers' book by coming up with some great bullpen work. Andy Hawkins, who had replaced Whitson in the first inning, went 5 1/3 innings, gave up only one hit, and picked up the win. Craig Lefferts gave up only one hit in the last three innings to earn the save. The two relievers shut down the Tigers for the final 8 1/3 innings. The Tigers' pen was almost as good, Aurelio Lopez, Bill Scherrer, Doug Bair and Willie Hernandez giving up only three hits in 3 2/3 innings. The four relievers kept the Tigers in the game, but the hitters couldn't get the bats going. So they left San Diego tied at one game apiece. The Tigers let this one slip from their fingers, and hoped to wrap up the Series at home.

1984 World Series Game Three

October 12, 1984
Tigers 5, Padres 2
Tigers Lead Best-of-Seven Series, 2-1

Milt Wilcox got the nod in Game Three after pitching an incredible game a week before in the ALCS. He started this game on a decent note: He allowed three baserunners in the first two innings, but none crossed the plate. In the bottom of the second, the Tigers once again gave their starter a nice cushion. Chet Lemon got a one-out single and moved to second on a wild pitch by Tim Lollar. Darrell Evans moved Lemon to third base on a deep fly, and Marty Castillo came up big, hitting a home run to give the Tigers a 2-0 lead. The home team wasn't done. Lou Whitaker drew a walk and Alan Trammell doubled him home. A walk to Kirk Gibson and an infield single by Lance Parrish loaded the bases before Lollar was yanked. Reliever Greg Booker walked Larry Herndon to force in Trammell, but finally stopped the bleeding by getting Barbaro Garbey to fly out (he had led off the inning with a groundout). After only two innings, the Tigers had a 4-0 lead, and they had knocked out the Padres' starter. This was a trend throughout the Series. The Tigers added a run in the third when Kirk Gibson was hit by a pitch with the bases loaded (after walks to Evans, Whitaker, and Trammell) to score Detroit's final run—all without the aid of a base hit. The Padres tagged Wilcox for a run in the third. Alan Wiggins led off with a single, Tony Gwynn singled him to third, and Wiggins scored when Steve Garvey forced Gwynn at second. Wilcox pitched six innings before handing the ball to Bill Scherrer, who gave up a run in the seventh. Gwynn singled with one out. Garvey doubled him to third, and Gwynn scored on a sacrifice fly by Graig Nettles. Willie Hernandez ended any chance of the Padres coming back by throwing 2 1/3 innings of one-hit ball. With the win, the tide had once again turned in the Tigers' favor. For the second straight game, the Tigers forced the Padres to work deep into their bullpen, and Detroit's strong pitching never gave San Diego a chance to come back.

1984 World Series Game Four

October 13, 1984
Tigers 4, Padres 2
Tigers Lead Best-of-Seven Series, 3-1

Jack Morris had an outstanding first half in 1984. He had a miserable second half by comparison (7-6, 4.25 ERA versus 12-5, 3.08 in the first half), getting roughed up more often than Tigers fans cared to see. But once the playoffs started, Morris was locked in, and definitely could be mentioned as a potential World Series MVP candidate. This game was basically the Alan Trammell and Jack Morris Show. The Tigers struck quickly once again. In the bottom of the first, Lou Whitaker reached base on an error and Trammell hit a two-run homer. After only two batters, the Tigers were up 2-0. In the third, it was déjà vu, as Whitaker singled with one out and

DETROIT TIGERS 1984: WHAT A START! WHAT A FINISH!

Jack Morris could have been considered a serious candidate to win the 1984 World Series MVP award, having pitched two complete-game victories. But his clutch pitching in the Fall Classic would be noted in 1991 with the Minnesota Twins, and in 1992 with the Toronto Blue Jays. (National Baseball Hall of Fame Library, Cooperstown, New York)

Trammell hit his second two-run belt of the game to give the Tigers a 4-1 lead (the Padres' Terry Kennedy had hit a bases-empty home run in the second). Detroit threatened more in the third, getting two more baserunners on before starter Eric Show got the hook. As good as Trammell was with the bat, Jack Morris was as good on the mound. Morris went the distance, giving up only five hits and two runs (one of which didn't come until the ninth, when Garvey doubled, advanced on a groundout, and scored on a wild pitch). Morris struck out four and walked no one, carrying the Tigers to within one game of the championship.

1984 World Series Game Five

October 14, 1984
Tigers 8, Padres 4
Tigers Win World Series, 4-1

For the fourth time in the five games against San Diego, the Tigers got to the Padres in the first inning (Detroit didn't score until the second in Game Three). Lou Whitaker led off the bottom of the first with a single, but was out on a force-play grounder by Alan Trammell. Kirk Gibson followed with a home run to put the Tigers up 2-0. Lance Parrish singled and stole second, moved to third on a single by Larry Herndon, and scored on a single by Chet Lemon. Starter Mark Thurmond was pulled after only a third of an inning, during which he gave up five hits. Reliever Andy Hawkins got the Padres out of that jam. Larry Herndon was caught stealing third, and Barbaro Garbey popped out to end the inning. Starter Dan Petry had a nice three-run cushion to work with. After giving up a single in each of the first two innings, Petry faltered in the third and imploded in the fourth. Bobby Brown led off the third inning with a single, advanced to third on a pair of groundouts, and scored on Steve Garvey's single. In the fourth, Petry gave up a leadoff walk to Kurt Bevacqua, who went to third on a double by Garry Templeton and scored when Brown lined out to center field. Alan Wiggins singled to drive in Templeton, and suddenly the game was tied. Manager Sparky Anderson had seen enough, and brought in Bill Scherrer, who got Tony Gwynn to fly out to end the inning. The Tigers struck back in the bottom of the fifth. Kirk Gibson, who did it all in this game, singled and moved to second on a fly out by Lance Parrish. Herndon walked. Hawkins was replaced by Craig Lefferts, who walked Chet Lemon to load the bases. Gibson scored on Rusty Kuntz's sacrifice fly—it was actually a popup caught in shallow right field by second baseman Alan Wiggins—to put the Tigers up 4-3. In the bottom of the seventh inning, the Tigers added a run on a solo homer by Lance Parrish off Goose Gossage, who had taken over for Lefferts with one out in the inning. With two innings left to play, the Tigers had a two-run cushion, but it was shaved to one as the Padres' Bevacqua hit a solo home run in the eighth. The Tigers had just one inning to score some insurance runs for reliever Willie Hernandez. And insurance he got. In the bottom of the eighth, Marty Castillo walked and Whitaker reached on a bunt. Trammell bunted them over and set up one of the most memorable at-bats in Tigers history. Kirk Gibson, the next batter, hit a massive three-run homer off Gossage to give the Tigers a comfortable four-run lead. (Gossage had talked his manager, Dick Williams, out of intentionally walking Gibson, declaring that he would strike him out.) The Padres managed a single off Hernandez in the ninth, but never really threatened. Except for Gossage (four runs in $1^{2}/_{3}$ innings), the San Diego bullpen performed well; Hawkins and Lefferts gave up only one run in six innings. Gibson finished the game 3-for-4 with three runs and five RBIs. The Tigers' relievers performed strongly again: Scherrer gave up no runs and one hit in his one inning; Aurelio Lopez gave up no runs and no hits and struck out four in his $2^{1}/_{3}$ innings and got credit for the win; and Willie Hernandez gave up one run on three hits in his two-inning stint. Hernandez earned his second save of the Series. In all, they went 4-0 in the postseason in front of their home fans. And for the first time in 16 years, the Tigers had won the World Series. Many had contributed to the Tigers' victory, but Trammell got the Most Valuable Player Award over Gibson and Morris. Any of the three would have been an excellent choice.

The 1984 Detroit Tigers and the Baseball Hall of Fame
by Alan Reifman

GREAT TEAMS TEND to have great players. And great players—the very best of them, anyway—have a chance to end up in the Baseball Hall of Fame. The 1984 Detroit Tigers were a great team, seemingly with several great players. Yet not only have no members of that team made it to the Hall; only one player even remains remotely within striking distance. As longtime Detroit newspaper writer George Cantor points out in his book about the 1984 Tigers, *Wire to Wire*, "Aside from the 1981 Dodgers, no team that won a [World] Series prior to 1984 has failed to place at least one player in the Hall." Amplifying on Cantor's point, I have listed the Hall of Fame players from World Series championship teams of a similar era to the Tigers (Table 1). It should be noted that Sparky Anderson, who managed Detroit's '84 champions, was inducted into the Hall of Fame in 2000; the focus here, however, is on players.

Even people not connected to the Motor City have made the case for members of the 1984 Tigers squad. Rob Neyer, whose *Big Book of Baseball Lineups* seeks to determine each franchise's best historical lineups, writes: "If you study the issue with any sort of sophistication, it's pretty clear that [shortstop Alan] Trammell, like...[third-base teammate Darrell] Evans, ranks among the all-time greats at his position."

Tigers in the Hall of Fame Voting

Players become eligible for election to the Baseball Hall of Fame after they have been retired for five years. Voting is done by the Baseball Writers Association of America. Because most of the '84 Tigers' top players remained active in the major leagues for at least a decade beyond the World Series championship season, it was not until the decade of the 2000s that they even began to be considered for the Hall. For members of the '84 Tigers who did receive such consideration, Table 2 shows their final year of play, the first year in which they started receiving Hall of Fame votes, and the percentage of voters who cast ballots for them each year they were eligible. A player must attain a threshold of at least 5 percent in a year's voting to remain on the ballot in future years, and must receive the support of 75 percent of the voters in a given year's balloting to be elected to the Hall. As long as a player keeps receiving at least 5 percent of the vote, he may remain on the ballot for up to 15 years.

As seen in Table 2, Morris started out in the early 2000s garnering vote percentages in the lower 20s. He then made steady gains until reaching a plateau in the low-mid 40s, as the decade of the 2000s reached a close. In 2010, for the first time, Morris burst over the 50 percent threshold (52.3 percent). Trammell, who began to appear on the ballot a couple of years after Morris, has easily exceeded the 5 percent level every year, but had yet to crack the high teens in his vote percentage until 2010, when he reached 22.4 percent. Six other members of the 1984 Tigers (Evans, Kirk Gibson, Guillermo Hernandez, Howard Johnson, Lance Parrish, and Lou Whitaker) were "one and done," each obtaining less than 5 percent support in his first time on the ballot and thus being eliminated immediately from further consideration.

How Strong is the Case for Tigers Players?

Two forms of Internet communication—e-mail-based "list serve" discussion forums and pages on the Web—have facilitated the rapid exchange of baseball analysis, stemming from the vast amounts of player performance data available online. In particular, these two venues have provided for robust discussion of players' worthiness for the Hall of Fame. SABR, the Society for American Baseball Research, operates a list serve e-mail exchange (SABR-L) in which members can send in comments for distribution to all other members. In January 2008, around the time of that year's Hall voting, a number of contributors to SABR-L marshaled and distributed their arguments about various contending pitchers' deservingness for the Hall. One hurler included in the discussions was Morris, providing me with a number of valuable leads. Though Morris probably generates more Hall of Fame discussion than any other member of the '84 Tigers, he is not alone. Accordingly, the remaining sections examine in greater depth the cases for and against the election of Morris, Trammell, and Evans, drawing from these analyses.

Jack Morris

Three measures (at least) of Hall of Fame readiness, all either directly or indirectly attributable to Bill James, have been proffered over the last 15 years. The first is the Hall

Lou Whitaker was stricken from the Hall of Fame ballot after one year when he failed to be voted by the required 5 percent of electors' ballots. It's regarded by Tigers fans as one of the most egregious snubs in the history of Hall of Fame elections. (National Baseball Hall of Fame Library, Cooperstown, New York)

DETROIT TIGERS 1984: WHAT A START! WHAT A FINISH!

of Fame Monitor. The pitchers' version of this yardstick incorporates wins, winning percentage, strikeouts, earned run average, saves, no-hitters, annual league leadership in various categories, number of games pitched, World Series starts and wins, playoff wins, postseason awards, and All-Star appearances. For many of these statistics, a pitcher can earn points for both career and season-specific milestones. James characterized players' likelihood of making the Hall based on Monitor scores: "If he has 100 points or more, he is likely to get in the Hall of Fame. Above 130, he is almost certain to be in the Hall of Fame." Morris' value is 122.5.

Next out of James' laboratory was the concept of Win Shares. As the name implies, the statistic attempts to apportion "shares" of teams' wins to particular players. Several documents are available on the Internet that explain—and in some cases critique—Win Shares. A virtually universal reaction has been that the formulas used in computing Win Shares are quite complex. Be that as it may, Win Shares have also been introduced into Hall of Fame discussions. SABR member and Hall of Fame eligibility analyst Bill Gilbert concisely summarizes the situation:

> "Many systems exist for evaluating player performance. One such system, the Win Shares method, developed by Bill James in 2002, is a complex method for evaluating players which includes all aspects of performance—offense, defense, and pitching. James has stated, 'Historically, 400 Win Shares means absolute enshrinement in the Hall of Fame. 300 Win Shares makes a player more likely than not to be a Hall of Famer. However, future standards may be different. Players with 300-350 Win Shares in the past have generally gone into the Hall of Fame. In the future, they more often will not.'"

On this marker, Morris clocks in at 225.

Finally, Michael Hoban has developed a variation on Win Shares, called Non-traditional Evaluative Win Shares, or NEWS. The NEWS method totals a player's Win Shares from his 10 best seasons, and then adds a lesser weighted component for the player's seasons beyond his best 10. Noting that Morris has a NEWS score of 185 and that "235 is considered to represent obvious HOF numbers for a starting pitcher," Hoban declares Morris' credentials "not even close."

For fans who prefer their statistics traditional, rather than sabermetric, Morris' greatest career difficulties appear to have been with his earned-run average numbers. Figure 1 plots, for each year of Morris' career (1977-1994), his ERA, the American League leader's ERA (whoever that may have been in a given year), and the league average ERA. As can be seen, Morris (solid black line) consistently recorded higher ERA figures than the yearly leader (dashed lines). Further, there was only one stretch (1983-1987) in which Morris' ERA was consistently better than the league average (gray line).

Alan Trammell

As seen in Table 2, shortstop Trammell has always received a lower share of the Hall of Fame vote than has Morris in the years they have both been eligible, and Trammell continues to fall further behind. Yet, on the Monitor (118.5, with 100 considered "likely" Hall material) and Win Shares measures, Trammell's numbers appear to make him Hall-worthy. Says Gilbert: "The 2006 class of Hall of Fame candidates is not strong. It consists of 15 holdovers and 14 players eligible for the first time. No one on the list has even 350 Win Shares. Four holdovers have over 300 Win Shares, Andre Dawson with 340, Bert Blyleven, 339, Dave Parker, 331 and Alan Trammell with 318. Will Clark heads the list of newcomers with 331 Win Shares. None of the other newcomers on the ballot have 250."

Gilbert is not alone in touting Trammell's candidacy, as seen in Rob Neyer's comment in the second paragraph above, to the effect that Trammell was one of "the all-time greats at his position." Even casual observers would likely have noted Trammell's excellence both defensively, with four Gold Glove awards (1980, 1981, 1983, 1984), and offensively, with three Silver Sluggers (top offensive performer at one's position, 1987, 1988, 1990). Among the theories for Trammell's failure to do better in the official voting, one involves a possible shift in offensive standards for judging shortstops (and, in the case of Trammell's double-play mate, Lou Whitaker, second basemen). Neyer notes that Trammell and Whitaker "had the great misfortune to retire approximately five years before middle infielders started hitting forty-plus homers in a season with alarming regularity. What looked like Hall of Fame numbers in the 1980s don't look all that great now, early in the twenty-first century."

Darrell Evans

Even more so than Trammell's, third baseman Evans' strengths as a Hall of Fame candidate are a well-kept secret; in '84, he actually played more games each at designated hitter and first base than at third. In fact, it seems that only hard-core sabermetricians like Rob Neyer and Mike Hoban still carry the torch for Evans. Writes Neyer: "Nobody knows how good Evans was because a great deal of his value came from all

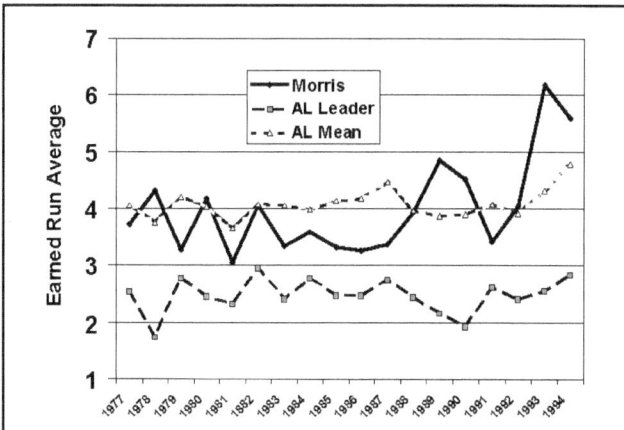

Figure 1. ERA Comparisons: Jack Morris vs. League Leader vs. League Average, 1977-1994.

the walks, and it's just now that baseball writers are beginning to understand that the base on balls isn't something that just 'happens' to the batter."

Hoban characterized a 280 NEWS score as "clear HOF numbers." Evans just exceeds this value, with a 281.

Evans' career statistics, however, do not make an overwhelming case for his induction, in my view. Even accepting that Evans' best attributes—his ability to get on base and his power—should be given considerable weight, his performances relative to other players in his league (National from 1969 to 1983 plus 1989; American from 1984 to 1988, coinciding with his Detroit tenure) did not appear to dramatically set him apart. On OPS (on-base-average plus slugging percentage), his best within-league rankings were third (1973), fourth (1983), and eighth (1985); being among the league leaders only three times in a roughly 20-year career does not seem to convey dominance. On Bill James' Win Shares scale, Evans' total of 363 is not enough in Gilbert's eyes to convince Hall of Fame electors. Further, on Bill James' older Hall of Fame Monitor system, Evans' value is 42, well short of the 100 considered to place one in the "likely" Hall category.

Conclusion

In a sardonic tone, Rob Neyer begins the concluding section of his chapter on the Tigers with the following advice for a young person aspiring to make baseball's Hall of Fame: "Don't hang around with Pete Rose, and don't grow up to become a Detroit Tiger." The experiences of the 1984 squad's top players may reinforce Neyer's sentiment in many observers' minds. However, the cases for Morris, Trammell, and Evans each have some areas of weakness, relative to the high standards of the Hall of Fame.

Should neither Morris nor Trammell receive the required 75 percent of the votes from the baseball writers before the players' respective 15-year windows expire, there is also a theoretical possibility that they (or any other former player) can be elected by the Veterans Committee several years down the road; consideration by the Veterans Committee requires a player to have been retired for at least 21 years. It is also possible that, if any members of the '84 Tigers do receive consideration by the Veterans Committee, the lens through which players are judged at a later date will be different from today's. Perhaps statistics such as OPS will be given greater weight. Perhaps the "steroid era" of recent times will lead voters to discount high home-run totals and appreciate other forms of offensive contribution. And then again, maybe not. Former Pittsburgh second baseman Bill Mazeroski exemplifies someone who made the Hall of Fame thanks to evaluators' evolving perceptions over many years regarding his accomplishments. During Mazeroski's final appearance on the writers' ballot (1992), he received only 42.3 percent of the vote. As the years went by, however, Mazeroski's defensive contributions and their potential Hall-worthiness began to garner greater attention, culminating in his 2001 Hall of Fame election by the Veterans Committee.

References

Books

Cantor, George. *Wire to Wire: Inside the 1984 Detroit Tigers Championship Season.* Chicago: Triumph. 2004.

James, Bill. *Whatever Happened to the Hall of Fame?* New York: Fireside. 1995.

James, Bill, and Jim Henzler. *Win Shares.* Morton Grove, Ill.: STATS, Inc. 2002.

Neyer, Rob. *Rob Neyer's Big Book of Baseball Lineups.* New York: Fireside. 2003.

Articles

Curry, Jack. "Anderson Saunters In as Doors to Hall Open." *New York Times* (http://www.nytimes.com/2000/03/01/sports/baseball-anderson-saunters-in-as-doors-to-hall-open.html). Accessed February 22, 2010).

Gilbert, Bill. "Rating 2006 Hall Candidates by Win Shares." The Birdhouse (http://stlcardinals.scout.com/2/482944.html). Accessed December 28, 200).

Hoban, Michael "Chapter Two: The NEWS Hall of Fame Monitor." *The Seamheads Sentinel: Sunrise Edition* (http://seamheads.com/blog/chapter-two-the-news-hall-of-fame-monitor/). Accessed October 16, 2007)

Hoban, Michael. "2008 BBWAA Hall of Fame Ballot" (http://seamheads.com/blog/2007/12/03/2008-bbwaa-hall-of-fame-ballot/). Accessed December 3, 2007.

Hoban, Michael. "The Best Players NOT in the Hall of Fame." (http://seamheads.com/blog/2007/11/26/the-best-players-not-in-the-hall-of-fame/). Accessed November 26, 2007.

National Baseball Hall of Fame. "BBWAA Elects 'Hawk' to the Hall of Fame" [explains balloting procedures]. (http://community.baseballhall.org/Page.aspx?pid=569). Accessed February 19, 2010.

Web Sites

http://www.baseball-reference.com/e/evansda01.shtml (Darrell Evans statistics).

http://www.baseball-reference.com/m/morrija02.shtml (Jack Morris statistics).

http://www.baseball-reference.com/t/trammal01.shtml (Alan Trammell statistics).

DETROIT TIGERS 1984: WHAT A START! WHAT A FINISH!

http://web.baseballhalloffame.org/hofers/rules.jsp (Hall of Fame election rules).

http://en.wikipedia.org/wiki/Baseball_Hall_of_Fame_balloting%2C_2008 (2008 balloting, with links to see balloting from previous years).

Table 1: World Champions From 1975-1997 And Their Hall of Fame Players

Year	Team	Hall of Fame Players
1975	Cincinnati	Johnny Bench, Joe Morgan, Tony Perez
1976	Cincinnati	Bench, Morgan, Perez
1977	New York (AL)	Catfish Hunter, Reggie Jackson
1978	New York (AL)	Goose Gossage, Hunter, Jackson
1979	Pittsburgh	Willie Stargell, Bert Blyleven
1980	Philadelphia	Steve Carlton, Mike Schmidt
1981	Los Angeles (NL)	none
1982	St. Louis	Ozzie Smith, Bruce Sutter
1983	Baltimore	Eddie Murray, Jim Palmer, Cal Ripken Jr.
1984	Detroit	none
1985	Kansas City	George Brett
1986	New York (NL)	Gary Carter
1987	Minnesota	Blyleven, Carlton*, Kirby Puckett
1988	Los Angeles (NL)	Don Sutton* (released in August)
1989	Oakland	Dennis Eckersley, Rickey Henderson
1990	Cincinnati	Barry Larkin
1991	Minnesota	Puckett
1992	Toronto	Roberto Alomar, Dave Winfield
1993	Toronto	Alomar, Paul Molitor
1994	Canceled/strike	
1995	Atlanta	**
1996	New York (AL)	Wade Boggs
1997	Florida	**

* Not on postseason roster.
** Team had HOF-eligible players retired less than five years.

Table 2: Hall of Fame Votes (Percentage of Voters) for Selected Tiger Players (75% Required for Election)

Player	Last Played	1995	1996	1997	1998	1999	2000
Evans	1989	1.7*					
Hernandez	1989	0.4*					

Player	Last Played	2000	2001	2002	2003	2004	2005	2006	2007	2008
Gibson	1995	N/A	2.5*							
Johnson	1995	N/A	0.0*							
Morris	1994	22.2	19.6	20.6	22.8	26.3	33.3	41.2	37.1	42.9
Parrish	1995	N/A	1.75*							
Trammell	1996	N/A	N/A	15.7	14.1	13.8	11.0	17.7	13.4	18.2
Whitaker	1995	N/A	2.9*							

		2009	2010	2011	2012
Morris (cont.)		44.0	52.3	53.5	66.6
Trammell (cont.)		17.4	22.4	24.3	36.8

*Removed from future balloting due to low support (5% threshold to stay on ballot).

Tiger Stadium
By Dan Scott

TIGER STADIUM. That's the name this venerable ballpark has known since 1961, after John Fetzer, originally part of an 11-man syndicate, took sole ownership of the Detroit Tigers.

Tiger Stadium. That was the name of the ballpark when the world championship was brought home to Detroit as Mayo Smith's proud group led by Al Kaline, Denny McLain, Mickey Lolich, Bill Freehan, and Willie Horton stormed back from a three-games-to-one deficit to shock the St. Louis Cardinals in 1968.

Tiger Stadium. The name of the park where Sparky Anderson's crew led wire-to-wire in 1984 with an outstanding crew led by Alan Trammell, Lou Whitaker, Jack Morris, Willie Hernandez, and Kirk Gibson.

Tiger Stadium. The only All-Star Game held under this name in 1971—and only one of three held at "The Corner" (of Michigan and Trumbull, that is)—where Reggie Jackson hit his famous light-tower shot.

Tiger Stadium. The proud name of the park where the Tigers played in the American League Championship Series in 1972 and 1987, but could not advance to the fall classic.

Tiger Stadium. Probably the only ballpark, professional or amateur, that posted a sign at the door of the visitors' clubhouse decreeing, "Visitor's Clubhouse: No Visitors Allowed."

Tiger Stadium. The name on the park when Detroit closer Todd Jones threw one final strike for the last out of the last major-league game played there, on September 27, 1999.

Tiger Stadium. The outline of the name on the decaying wall of a proud but willfully ignored ballpark, as the wrecking ball started tearing down the physical manifestation of more than 100 years of Detroit baseball on June 30, 2008.

This celebrated park bore witness to its first championship team as Tiger Stadium in 1968. After that well-recorded comeback over the Cardinals, the ballpark hosted some pretty good Tigers teams, really good Tigers players, and significant moments in baseball history. The stadium and its confines, however, also saw their share of negativity and controversy.

Tiger Stadium hosted the All-Star Game in 1971 (as well as in 1941 and 1951 as Briggs Stadium). During the 1976 season the ballpark hosted sellout crowds electrified by the performance of rookie Mark "The Bird" Fidrych. The Corner saw some talented teams in 1972 and 1987 and a really, really good team in 1984. While the players have been transient, the revered baseball cathedral endured, and saw its own share of drama; and not always during one of the 6,783 games played at the corner of Michigan and Trumbull. Tiger Stadium saw some internal damage (the press box was gutted by a fire in 1977), endured attempts at facelifts (in 1978 and 1992), was sold to the city of Detroit for $1 (in 1978 by Fetzer), was called an unflattering name (by then-team president Bo Schembechler), stopped being used as a football field (the Detroit Lions moved to suburban Pontiac in 1975), limited access to seats (bleacher closures in 1980 and 1985), was no longer used as a primary stage for baseball (October 1999), and even starred in an HBO movie (*61** in 2000).

A group known as the Old Tiger Stadium Conservancy, led by Hall of Fame broadcaster Ernie Harwell, tried to raise enough money to preserve part of the old ballpark before the wrecking ball completely leveled it. The Conservancy was but one of many organizations sharing the same goal: to preserve at least part of The Corner so that more than 100 years of baseball memories could tangibly be passed on to future generations. The effort, like the others that preceded it, ultimately proved unsuccessful.

In the 1971 All-Star Game, every run scored during the American League's victory was a result of a home run. Out of the six that were hit, none was more memorable than the 540-foot blast delivered by the Oakland A's Reggie Jackson. That baseball hit a light transformer on the right-center-field roof section. That turned out to be the last All-Star Game at Tiger Stadium. From then until the beginning of the 1972 season (the Tigers were the American League East Division winners), John Fetzer, who owned the team from 1960 to 1983, worked closely with the city to build a domed facility right along the Detroit riverfront. This attempt failed for a variety of reasons, including voter rejection of a bond issue and alleged funding malfeasance brought out in lawsuits. The land proposed for the ballpark facility ended up becoming Joe Louis Arena.

The year 1977 was busy for both the team and the stadium. Not only did Tigers fans begin what was to become a 1,918-game partnership between Alan Trammell and Lou Whitaker in September (it ran through 1995), a three-year, $15 million renovation began, soon after the press-box fire. Tigers general manager Jim Campbell deadpanned that it probably would have been better if the press box caught fire while it was full of reporters. The press-box replacement was completed in time for the start of the '77 season. After the sale of the stadium to the City of Detroit, the city qualified for public monies to fund additional renovations.

This upgrade gave the interior of the park a new look—no longer were the wooden seats and surrounding areas green. The interior was painted in what became a familiar and welcoming blue; the wooden green seats were replaced with blue and orange plastic ones. A new scoreboard was also part of the upgrade.

Campbell, whose contract dealings with players were often heavy-handed, showed the same kind of determination when it came to the fans. In 1980, and again in 1985, Tiger Stadium's "Bleacher Creatures" showed themselves to be worthy (in a limited sense of the word) descendants of Navin Field's outfield denizens during the climactic game of the 1934 World Series. Fans in 1980 pelted the Milwaukee Brewers outfielders with debris as they tried to play the game, just as fans in '34 had hurled whatever they could get their hands on following a harsh slide into Tigers third baseman Marv Owen by St. Louis Cardinals left fielder Joe "Ducky" Medwick. In 1985, the bleacherites annoyed fellow spectators by chanting

DETROIT TIGERS 1984: WHAT A START! WHAT A FINISH!

a profane variant of the Miller Lite "Less Filling, Tastes Great" catchphrase. In both 1980 and 1985, it was decided that the offenders were fueled not by what happened on the field but by robust beer sales. As a result, sections of the bleachers were closed off for two weeks in 1980 and a month in 1985. The two-week closure in 1980 resulted in tighter security and restrictions on beer sales. The one-month closing in 1985 again brought limits on beer sales.

Talks for a new ballpark resurfaced in the late 1980s. Fetzer's sale of the team to Domino's Pizza owner Tom Monaghan in 1983, a world championship in 1984, and an AL East flag in 1987 had prevented discussions from becoming more serious. As fans' interest in the Tigers became heavily linked to the ballpark itself, and as they sensed that talks on a new stadium were potentially gaining traction, a group called the Tiger Stadium Fan Club twice organized what was referred to as "The Big Hug." Each human chain around Tiger Stadium lasted about 15 minutes and made the point that any attempt to build a new ballpark and move its primary tenant would be met with stiff resistance.

The pressure for a new stadium ratcheted up in the early 1990s. With the appointment of legendary University of Michigan football coach Glenn "Bo" Schembechler to the Tigers' presidency, the ability to make unpopular decisions and comments remained firmly entrenched—if not enhanced—in that office. Not only was Schembechler held accountable for the infamous Ernie Harwell firing in 1991, he also made a bold demand to the Economic Club of Detroit. In a speech on June 21, 1991, Schembechler commented that the Tigers needed a new facility, as the Lions, Red Wings, and Pistons had gotten over the previous two decades, in order to win. Schembechler declared that "it was unfair" being denied a new park. "You cannot shackle us to a rusted girder in Tiger Stadium … and expect us to win," he said—words that drew the ire and fire of many a Tigers fan. Schembechler declared that financing to build a new facility had to be in place by that August 1. It was not to be.

A year later, in 1992, Monaghan sold the team to a pizza competitor. Mike Ilitch, owner of the Little Caesars pizza chain and the NHL's Red Wings. Ilitch launched an upgrade of Tiger Stadium in 1993. The players' parking lot was converted into what became known as Tiger Plaza. Inside the ballpark, the Tigers Den was created. This area, on the lower deck between first base and third base, was upgraded to padded seats and came with waiter service.

These upgrades weren't enough to build a winning team. Off the field, voters twice rejected bond issues that would have financed a new ballpark. On the field, the Tigers started a string of losing seasons that started in 1994 and didn't end until 2006, their seventh year in their current home, Comerica Park. Tiger Stadium's last season, 1999, was sub-.500 at 69-92. Tigers ownership felt that a new ballpark would revive the team, the fans, and the city. After city voters finally voted for stadium financing, ground was broken for Comerica Park in October 1997. Under the financial agreement the voters approved, the city paid for less than 40 percent of the $300 million price tag to build the new park.

In 1999 the Tigers drew more than 2 million fans for the first time in more than a decade. Marketing was based on nostalgia instead of a competitive team. The money the Ilitch family was putting into facilities at Tiger Stadium and Comerica Park didn't translate to better play. Fans from all over the country paid one last trip to Tiger Stadium. Ernie Harwell recalled, "We've had a lot of people from all over the country come in. I've had people tell me, 'I'm from West Virginia' or, 'I'm from Arkansas' or, 'I'm from Georgia' or, 'I'm from Oklahoma' and 'I wanted to see the ball park for the last time.'"

With Comerica Park open, fans, Tigers ownership, and the city of Detroit were now faced with a conundrum. The Tigers played in the newest ballpark in the majors, but still left Tiger Stadium standing. Part of the deal with the move to Comerica Park resulted in seven years of payments to Ilitch, ranging from $200,000 to $400,000 per year, to maintain Tiger Stadium and keep it secure. Several options were offered to keep it as a viable facility. Entrepreneurs presented plans to the city that ranged from building shops and apartments to making renovations to moving in a minor-league ballclub. Instead, Tiger Stadium was used only sporadically, and its condition declined.

Tiger Stadium got one last big—and relevant—starting role in baseball when comedian Billy Crystal decided to do a movie based on the 1961 American League home-run race between Yankees teammates Roger Maris and Mickey Mantle. In 2000, Crystal converted what he could in Tiger Stadium to make it look like Yankee Stadium, and then digitally enhanced the rest of it in post-production. After filming was done, Crystal had all the green paint that was used to cover up the blue and orange power-washed off. As the credits rolled at the end of the movie, the role of Yankee Stadium was shown as portrayed by Tiger Stadium!

Even with Tiger Stadium an emptied shell, it's not as if Tigers fans took to its successor. Comerica Park's initial season, 2000, drew fans out of curiosity, just as 1999 had drawn fans to The Corner out of nostalgia. The losing ways, including a truly awful 43-119 season in 2003, depressed attendance throughout the first half of the new decade. The Tigers had a breakout year in 2006 that resulted in a World Series appearance, and more than 3 million fans paid their way into the new stadium in 2007 as Detroit defended its American League crown. That eclipsed the team's previous attendance record of more than 2.7 million, at Tiger Stadium in 1984, their last previous World Series season.

As the city moved closer to taking the wrecking ball to Tiger Stadium, the Detroit Economic Growth Corporation contracted with Scheider Industries of St. Louis to auction off parts of Tiger Stadium as a way or raising revenue. One could bid on Al Kaline's locker, purchase coverings for the on-deck circles, buy one of the World Series banners that hung off the upper deck façade in right field—or even one of the clubhouse urinals. Seats, sold in pairs, could be purchased

DETROIT TIGERS 1984: WHAT A START! WHAT A FINISH!

without going through an auction. A pair of regular blue seats could be purchased for $279; a pair of Tigers Den seats could be purchased for $399.

In July 2007, the Detroit City Council voted to demolish the ballpark. The ballpark was to be down by September 2008. Demolition began on June 30, 2008; as it proceeded, the city agreed to keep the dugout-to-dugout portions of the ballpark intact if the Old Tiger Stadium Conservancy could raise almost $400,000 by August 1. Then demolition was halted, and the Conservancy was given a March 2009 deadline to raise $15 million to build a museum and preserve part of the stadium. But Detroit's Depression-level economy, coupled with the quick turnaround time demanded by the city, doomed the effort.

Today, Tiger Stadium lives on only in the memories of baseball fans everywhere.

> "You know what I'd like to see whenever we get a new stadium? They tear down this Tiger Stadium, the stands, and keep the field. Build new stands like the old Navin Field... and keep the field. It could be a park and kids could play baseball there and say, 'That's the same second base where Charlie Gehringer played, the same right field where Al Kaline played, the same first base where Hank Greenberg played, the same field where Ty Cobb played.' Preserve the field. It's the field. The field of dreams."
>
> –Tigers president Bo Schembechler, 1991

References

Books

Pattison, Mark, and David Raglin. *Detroit Tigers Lists and More: Runs, Hits, and Eras*. Detroit: Wayne State University Press. 2002.

Articles

Lapointe, Joe. "Backtalk; Farewell, Old Friend of Summers Past." *New York Times*, September 26, 1999.

Montville, Leigh. "Tiger Tales." *Sports Illustrated*, July 12, 1999.

"Selling Tiger Stadium: One Piece at a Time." *Sports Collectors Daily*. http://www.sportscollectorsdaily.com/latest/selling-tiger-stadium-one-piece-at-a-time.html. Accessed August 12, 2008.

Sidlow, Edward I., and Beth M. Henschen. "Major League Baseball and Public Policy, or Take Me Out to the Ballgame, Wherever the Game May Be." *Policy Studies Review*, vol. 15, no. 1, spring 1998. 65-88.

Wright, Dave. "Tiger Stadium / Detroit Tigers / 1912-1999." *Ballpark Digest*. http://www.ballparkdigest.com/stadiums/past/tiger_stadium.htm. Accessed August 12, 2008.

Web Sites

http://forums.nyyfans.com/showthread.php?t=1609.

http://schneiderind.com/tigerstadiumsale/. Accessed August 12, 2008.

http://www.baseball-reference.com/teams/DET/1999.shtml. Accessed August 12, 2008.

"Tiger Stadium." Ballparks of Baseball—The Fields of Major League Baseball. http://www.ballparksofbaseball.com/past/TigerStadium.htm. Accessed August 12, 2008.

"Tiger Stadium (Detroit)." http://www.nationmaster.com/encyclopedia/Tiger-Stadium-(Detroit). Accessed August 12, 2008.

"Tiger Stadium (Detroit)." http://en.wikipedia.org/wiki/Tiger_Stadium_%28Detroit%29#cite_note-7. Accessed August 12, 2008.

http://www.savetigerstadium.org/the_plan.pdf.

Contributors

Chuck Ailsworth (Scott Earl) has a BS and MS from Michigan State University. He is a SABR member and a third-generation and lifelong Tigers fan. He lives with his wife of 18 years and his two children in Southeast Michigan.

Kent Ailsworth (Scott Earl) and his wife Ann are both registered nurses in Traverse City, Michigan. He's a third-generation Tigers fan. Long ago, a profound Grandma A. switched allegiance from Ruth and Gehrig to the Old English D. Dad and family continued the Bengal tradition/addiction. Unfortunately, Ann still loves pinstripes.

Blessed to be born in Baltimore, Maryland, to a mother who still keeps score and roots for the Orioles, **Malcolm Allen** (Nelson Simmons) now resides in Brooklyn, New York, with his wife Sara and daughters Ruth (named for The Babe) and Martina. The former Memorial Stadium usher's book about Joaquin Andujar is almost complete.

Bill Bishop (Kirk Gibson) is a graduate of the University of Michigan public health program and works as a safety and health engineer. His two daughters, who are his pride and joy, were raised to be ardent Tigers fans.

A native of Hemlock, Michigan, **Matt Bohn** (Paul Carey, Ernie Harwell, George Kell, Larry Osterman) has been a Detroit Tigers fan since childhood. His interests include writing, genealogy, theatre and the history of baseball broadcasting.

A graduate of Michigan State University, **Brian Borawski** (Dwight Lowry, 1984 season recap) is a CPA with his own tax and accounting practice. A lifelong Tigers fan, Brian writes about his favorite team at Tigerblog (www.tigerblog.net) and he also writes a weekly "Business of Baseball" report at *The Hardball Times* (www.hardballtimes.com).

Tracy J.R. Collins (Sid Monge) teaches English Literature at Central Michigan University. She is grateful for the opportunity to write about this team because she saw her first professional game in Detroit during the summer of 1984. Thanks to that experience, she either wanted to marry Kirk Gibson or be Alan Trammell.

Now into his 59th season as a Tigers fan, **Cliff Corn** (Glenn Abbott) has attended at least one regular season game in each of the 30 current stadiums plus 14 others either not in use or torn down. Cliff, originally from Kansas, resides in Salem, Oregon, and is a retired high school mathematics teacher.

Nick Edson (Roger Mason) was the longtime sports editor of the *Traverse City Record-Eagle*. He covered the 1984 Detroit Tigers in spring training, AL playoffs and the World Series. He is a member of the Michigan Basketball Coaches Hall of Honor and has written a book called *Beyond the Games*, a collection of his 50 favorite columns in 30 years of sportswriting.

Charles Faber (Randy O'Neal) is a retired university professor and administrator currently living in Lexington, KY. In addition to college textbooks and numerous journal and encyclopedia articles, he has written books on the American presidency. His baseball publications include three editions of *Baseball Ratings*, *Baseball Pioneers*, and *Spitballers*, all published by McFarland.

A retired English professor, **Jan Finkel** (proofreader and fact-checker) lives with his wife on Deep Creek Lake in western Maryland. Besides great books and baseball, which he sometimes confuses, he enjoys country music and jazz. His son and daughter and their spouses are wonderful people—and, coincidentally, live in Nashville and New Orleans.

David Fleitz (Darrell Evans), a SABR member from Bowling Green, Ohio, is a systems analyst by day and a baseball writer at night. He has written six books, including biographies of Shoeless Joe Jackson, Louis Sockalexis, and Cap Anson, his latest effort being a volume about the Irish and early baseball.

Dave Gagnon (Gates Brown) splits his time between running a small accounting firm and being a baseball fanatic. While completing 1040 returns, he's got a headset on listening to the Tigers in his office. He had to cut short one client consultation to watch Tigers play the Yankees in the 2006 American League Division Series.

Paul Geisler Jr. (Randy O'Neal) grew up in San Antonio, Texas, and has been a Lutheran pastor for over thirty years. He lives in Lake Jackson, Texas, with his wife Susan and their three children: Sarah, Brydon, and Johanna. He loves anything baseball—playing, watching, coaching, researching, and writing.

Gary Gillette (Willie Hernandez, Aurelio Lopez, Tom Monaghan, Building the Team) is the co-editor of the *ESPN Baseball Encyclopedia* as well as the executive editor of the *ESPN Pro Football Encyclopedia*. His most recent book is *Big League Ballparks*, a complete history of major league parks, co-authored with Stuart Shea, Matt Silverman, and Eric Enders. Gillette is a member of the SABR board of directors and is co-chair of SABR's Ballparks Committee. He is also a board member of the Tiger Stadium Conservancy. Gillette lives in Detroit's historic Indian Village with his wife Vicki and their children, Karolina and Kamil.

When not reading and writing about baseball, **Chip Greene** (Dave Rozema) is a full time management consultant. His grandfather, Nelson Greene, pitched parts of the 1924 and '25 seasons for the Brooklyn Dodgers. Chip has contributed to several upcoming SABR book projects, as well as *Yankees Annual* magazine and the SABR Biography Project.

A fourth-grade teacher, **Douglas Hill** (Barbaro Garbey) also has a passion for sports writing. A former newspaper journalist, Hill's a regular contributor to the Detroit Tigers blog www.dailyfungo.com and is a co-founder of Detroit-centric hoops web site www.detroitpslbasketball.com. He's also working on his first book, *Hardwood Legends: Stars of the Detroit Public School League*.

The phone rang during the "clinch-the-'84 pennant" party at the house of **Larry Hilliard** (Tom Brookens). Fellow Michigan Tech alum Pat Kilroy was calling from the corner of Michigan and Trumbull, describing Tigers fans "dancin'-in-the-streets." Kilroy planted a patch of Tiger Stadium outfield grass in Greenbelt National Park, in Maryland. It wasn't that long ago that the two saw Brooky coaching prospects in Aberdeen and Bowie, near their current Maryland domiciles.

Joanne Hulbert (Billy Consolo), citizen of Red Sox Nation and co-chair of SABR's Boston chapter, has written about several players with Boston ties for SABR publications. She also maintains an extensive file of baseball poetry as co-chair of SABR's Baseball Arts Committee. She chose to write about Consolo having previously only a vague recollection of him.

Maxwell Kates (Milt Wilcox, Alex Grammas) is a chartered accountant living in Toronto. He has lectured at the Limmud Conference at York University in 2004 and the SABR Convention in Seattle in 2006. His writing has appeared in several books and periodicals including *The Miracle Has Landed*. In 2008, he predicted the Tigers would eclipse their 35-5 start of 1984. They opened the season 0-7.

Myra Kreiman (photo editor) covered two Olympics and sports news photography during her career as a senior photo editor at *Newsweek* magazine. She fell in love with baseball as a young girl watching Mickey Mantle swing his bat in Yankee Stadium. She is currently a photo consultant in the New York area.

Mike Lassman (Lance Parrish) graduated from Eastern Michigan University and served as a sports information assistant. Mike earned a law degree from the University of Detroit and serves as labor and employment counsel for the Department of Army in Virginia, and is a proud husband and father of two sons.

David Laurila (Mike Laga) grew up in Michigan's Upper Peninsula and now writes about baseball from his home in Cambridge, Massachusetts. He authors the Prospectus Q&A series at baseballprospectus.com and is the author of *Interviews From Red Sox Nation* (Maple Street Press). He is currently writing a book about the Tigers.

Jason Lenard (Juan Berenguer) is a marketer by day, working in the great city of Detroit. He credits his grandma for getting him interested in baseball, and his wife and two sons for keeping his passion for the game alive. Jason's favorite baseball moment was catching a Wendell Magee home run ball barehanded at Comerica Park.

Len Levin's (copy editor) connection to the Tigers is through his wife, who grew up in Michigan as a Tigers fan. A New Englander, he roots for the Red Sox but always admired the way the Tigers management put teams together. His career has been as a newspaper and freelance copy editor.

An international consultant working in almost anywhere they ask, **Peter M. Levine** (Dick Tracewski) is expert in finding ways to track those beloved Detroit Tigers. He especially enjoys Latin America where beisbol is life to some and is convincing his 6-year-old son that Detroit rocks/Michigan rolls (a struggle with the maternal side).

David MacGregor (Doug Bair) is a screenwriter and playwright who teaches in the English department of Wayne State University. In the summer, he and his son tour major- and minor-league ballparks and are always pleasantly surprised at the number of free tickets they are handed by generous fellow fans.

Jeanne Mallett (Detroit in 1984), a lifelong Tiger fan, thinks her cousin, Jim Schmakel, Tiger equipment manager, has the best job in the world. With the best job taken, Jeanne wrote plays, then practiced law and now writes short stories and essays. Jeanne's first World Series game was the decisive game 5 in 1984.

Mike McClary (Johnny Grubb, Rusty Kuntz, Carl Willis, proofreader) attended his first Tigers game in 1977 and saw Jack Morris make his first career start at Tiger Stadium—and he's been beating the drum of Morris-as-Hall-of-Famer ever since. A freelance writer and native of St. Clair Shores, Michigan, Mike writes about the Tigers at DailyFungo.com and hosts the weekly Detroit Tigers Podcast. He lives in Scottsdale, Arizona.

Kevin McGraw (fact-checker) first saw the Tigers play at Briggs Stadium with his dad in 1959. A Detroiter for 27 years, he moved to Cleveland in 1981. So he now also roots for his wife Barbara's Indians—except when they play the Tigers! Kevin has been a SABR member since 1980.

John McMurray (Marty Castillo) is chair of SABR's Deadball Era Committee. He contributed to SABR's 2006 book *Deadball Stars of the American League* and is a past chair of SABR's Ritter Award subcommittee, which annually presents an award to the best book on Deadball Era baseball published during the year prior. He has contributed many interview-based player profiles to *Baseball Digest* in recent years.

DETROIT TIGERS 1984: WHAT A START! WHAT A FINISH!

John Milner (Alan Trammell, Lou Whitaker) has been involved with education as a teacher and coach for 23 years and is currently a counselor at Tivy High School in Kerrville, Texas, near San Antonio. John has been married to Yvette for 17 years and has a 14-year-old son, J.T., and an 11-year-old daughter, Olivia. John grew up in Michigan and developed a love for the Tigers from his dad and grandfathers. His first major league game attended was Mark Fidrych's first start in 1976.

Jerry Nechal (Dave Bergman) is an administrator at Wayne State University. He has previously written about "The Worst Team Ever" in the Baseball Research Journal and completed a biography of Mickey Stanley. Other interests include architecture and hiking. He continues to long for a bleacher seat in old Tiger Stadium.

Born within weeks of their 1968 championship, **Richard Newhouse** (Doug Baker) has been hopelessly attached to the cats from his native Michigan ever since. Still living in his hometown of Holland in West Michigan, he now has three women—a wife and two daughters—coming between him and those darn Tigers.

Bill Nowlin (fact-checker) is national vice president of SABR and the author of close to 20 Red Sox-related books. Bill is also co-founder of Rounder Records of Massachusetts. One of his big regrets was finding his flight to Detroit canceled for Boston's final visit to Tiger Stadium.

Mark Pattison (project manager, proofreader) earns his keep as media editor for Catholic News Service in Washington. He's secretary-treasurer of the Mayo Smith Society, editor of its *Tigers Stripes* and *E-Mayo Flash* newsletters, and a board member of the Baltimore-Washington SABR chapter. Outside baseball, he's been president of the Washington-Baltimore Newspaper Guild and of the PTA at his daughter's school, coordinator of Shepherd Park neighborhood Halloween festivities in D.C., and has improved on the banjo to the level of aggressively mediocre.

Don Petersen (Dan Petry) is a graduate of the University of Chicago and Harvard Law School. He is a professor at Cooley law school. Most impressively, he has been a Detroit Tigers season-ticket holder since 1994. He hopes to contribute to the book written about the next Tigers' World Series victory.

David Raglin (Mayo Smith, project manager, fact-checker), is the vice president of the Bob Davids Chapter of SABR in the Baltimore-Washington region, and has been the Mayo Smith Society's sabermetrician and principal writer for its *Tigers Stripes* and *E-Mayo Flash* newsletters since their respective foundings in 1984 and 2004. His Census Bureau job requires him to count America's 300 million-plus residents using both his fingers and his toes.

Alan Reifman (The 1984 Detroit Tigers and the Baseball Hall of Fame) is professor of human development and family studies at Texas Tech University and a SABR member. He received his PhD from the University of Michigan and it was during his first semester of graduate school in Ann Arbor that the '84 Tigers were completing their world championship run.

The highlight of **Dan Scott**'s (Tiger Stadium) time as a Tigers fan was getting up at 0300 every morning to watch all of the Tigers' 2006 playoff games while supporting Operation Iraqi Freedom in Camp Fallujah as an active-duty Marine. Dan's appropriately painted basement has been dubbed "Tiger Stadium—Baltimore Annex."

Jeffrey Shand-Lubbers (Bill Scherrer) is often the only fan at a baseball game under 50 years old religiously keeping score. A lifelong Tigers fan currently living in New York, he claims to have vague memories of watching the 1984 World Series despite being only 4 years old.

Carl Shinkle (Scott Earl) is a native Oregonian (at least third generation). He grew up in the shadow of Mt. Hood, in the Columbia Gorge, and has always lived in sight of the mountain (on clear days). He taught English classes for 30 years at North Salem High School, retiring in 1998.

Richard L. Shook (Bill Lajoie, The Drafting of Kirk Gibson, The Herndandez-Bergman Trade) is a longtime chronicler of the Tigers for various news organizations. He covered several playoffs and World Series for UPI in the 1980s as a columnist and analyst. He also served as an official scorer for the AL in Detroit for 20 years. He also coached high school baseball in Ann Arbor, Michigan, from 1998 to 2008.

Trey Strecker (Bill Freehan) teaches English and sport studies at Ball State University. He edited *Dead Balls and Double Curves: An Anthology of Early Baseball Fiction* (Southern Illinois University Press, 2004) and *The Collected Baseball Stories of Charles Van Loan* (McFarland, 2004), and also edits *NINE: A Journal of Baseball History & Culture*.

Cindy Thomson (Sparky Anderson) is co-author of *Three Finger: The Mordecai Brown Story*, and author of *Brigid of Ireland* and *Celtic Wisdom: Treasures From Ireland*. She is a frequent contributor to several magazines and works as a freelance writer from her home in central Ohio. Visit her online: http://www.cindyswriting.com and http://threefinger.com.

Stew Thornley (Jack Morris) is an author of books on sports history for adults and young readers. He received the SABR-Macmillan Baseball Research Award in 1988 for his first book, *On to Nicollet: The Glory and Fame of the Minneapolis Millers*.

DETROIT TIGERS 1984: WHAT A START! WHAT A FINISH!

Adam J. Ulrey (Ruppert Jones) is a lifetime Los Angeles Dodgers fan working at Sacred Heart Hospital in Eugene, Oregon. He enjoys spending time fly fishing on his creek and the lakes and rivers of Oregon. He lives in Dexter, Oregon, with wife Jhody, son Camran and his two dogs Behr and Montana.

Glen Vasey (Larry Herndon) is SABR's leading biographer of the 107 Home Run Club, having previously written about Dan Litwhiler for the book Spahn, Sain and Teddy Ballgame. He is also the author of "Everyone Comes Home in October," a personal-experience essay published in *The Miracle Has Landed*. He is wonderfully supported in these endeavors by his lovely wife Emily.

Rick Vosik (Rod Allen) lives in Omaha, Nebraska. He became a Tigers fan in 1968, when he attended his first major league baseball game at Tiger Stadium. With the Tigers' World Series championship, he was hooked for life. He is chief financial officer for an industrial company, and in his spare time coaches youth baseball.

Nick Waddell (Al Kaline) is a Wayne State University graduate in chemical engineering, but more importantly, he is a lifelong Tigers fan. Currently, he resides in Chicago attending law school, and proudly wears his Old English D whenever he can.

www.ingramcontent.com/pod-product-compliance
Lightning Source LLC
Chambersburg PA
CBHW051403070526
44584CB00023B/3267